Karl Ludwig Peter

Chronological tables of Greek history

Karl Ludwig Peter

Chronological tables of Greek history

ISBN/EAN: 9783337280185

Printed in Europe, USA, Canada, Australia, Japan

Cover: Foto ©ninafisch / pixelio.de

More available books at **www.hansebooks.com**

CHRONOLOGICAL TABLES

OF

GREEK HISTORY.

ACCOMPANIED BY A SHORT NARRATIVE OF EVENTS, WITH REFERENCES
TO THE SOURCES OF INFORMATION AND EXTRACTS FROM THE
ANCIENT AUTHORITIES,

BY

CARL PETER.

TRANSLATED FROM THE GERMAN

BY

G. CHAWNER, M.A.
FELLOW AND LECTURER OF KING'S COLLEGE, CAMBRIDGE.

EDITED FOR THE SYNDICS OF THE UNIVERSITY PRESS.

CAMBRIDGE:
AT THE UNIVERSITY PRESS.
1882

TRANSLATOR'S PREFACE.

The regulations recently issued for Section C in the second part of the Classical Tripos mark a new departure in the nature and extent of the knowledge required by the University, from Students of Ancient History. The translation of Dr Peter's work has been undertaken in the hope that it may supply a want likely to be felt by candidates, who in examination "will be expected to illustrate and support their statements by reference to the ancient authorities."

The Translator has to offer the most cordial thanks to Dr Peter for his courtesy in authorising the present translation, and to Mr Oscar Browning, Fellow and Historical Lecturer of King's College, for his kindness in promoting the issue of the book.

Cambridge,
May, 1882.

AUTHOR'S PREFACE.

THE plan and aim of my Greek and Roman Chronological Tables have been set forth in detail, partly in the prefaces to the first editions of those works (1835 and 1841), partly in my essays "Ueber den Geschichtsunterricht auf Gymnasien" (Halle, 1849) and "Zur Reform unserer Gymnasien" (Jena, 1874). I shall therefore merely repeat here, that, according to the view I there developed, a suitable foundation must first be laid in the lower forms by a general view of the whole field of history, and that in the highest form history must be taught in such a way as to afford pupils some insight into historical criticism, and at the same time, so far as is possible at this stage, to educate in them the faculty of forming an independent judgment. But, for the reasons I have adduced, this can only be effected by a study of the history of the two ancient classical races, and by a first introduction to the sources from which that history is derived. It is with this end in view that the chronological tables are designed to aid both teachers and pupils by a statement and brief estimate of the original authorities, by citation of the same for each individual fact, and by transcription of specially instructive passages.

I have only to add that the literary notices in the second and third edition were revised by Professor Corssen, my friend and former colleague, whose premature death was a severe loss to the learned world; that in the third edition I had to thank Professor G. Hertzberg, of Halle, for several additions and corrections; and that the fourth edition was brought out wholly under the supervision of my son, Professor Hermann Peter, who in this fifth edition also has given me his help, more especially in those portions which deal with the history of literature.

From the circumstance that the Chronological Tables have maintained themselves in use for upwards of forty years, and that quite recently a fifth edition of both has become necessary, I may venture to draw the pleasing conclusion that they have been productive of some good. It is my earnest hope that they may still continue in the future to promote the true aims of school teaching.

C. PETER.

JENA, May, 1877.

INTRODUCTION.

GREECE, ITS DISTRIBUTION, PHYSICAL CHARACTERISTICS, AND OLDEST INHABITANTS.

GREECE ('Ελλάς) is the southernmost part of the great eastern peninsula of Europe, which lies between the Adriatic and Black Sea to the south of the Danube, and stretches out into the Mediterranean. On the north it is bounded by the Keraunian and Kambunian mountains, on the west by the Ionian and Sicilian seas, on the south by the Myrtoan or Libyan, on the east by the Ægean. Its greatest length (between the 41st and 36th degree) is about 280 miles, its breadth (between the 21st and 26th degree) varies from 211 to 93 miles. Its area comprises about 38,600 square miles.

This region presents two natural divisions: for whilst north and central Greece constitute one uninterrupted mass, the Peloponnese is a peninsula, formed by the incursion of the sea on the east and west, and only connected with central Greece by a narrow isthmus. Further, a large number of islands situate on the east and west are included under the term Greece.

The configuration and character of north and central Greece are determined by a mountain chain, which forms a chief branch of the mountains that cover the whole of the great peninsula, being itself an offshoot of the Dalmatian Alps, from which it runs, discharging its function of watershed between the Adriatic and Ægean seas, in a south-easterly direction to the promontory of Sunium, the south-easternmost point of central Greece. At its entrance upon Grecian territory at the 40th degree of latitude, where Lakmon forms the junction of the several chains, it sends out the Keraunian and Kambunian ranges, which mark the boundaries of the country; it then continues its course under the name of Pindus as far as the 39th degree. Here a fresh junction is formed at Tymphrestus by the branching-out of two cross chains, Othrys and Œta, both of which run in a parallel direction at a short distance from one another to the Ægean sea. Southwards of Tymphrestus the main range is continued in the heights of Parnassus, Helikon, Kithæron, Parnes and Hymettus, till it comes to an end in the promontory of Sunium.

The whole district to the westward is for the most part covered with parallel chains of this main range. This part has therefore little of the regular organisation of the eastern; and as it moreover possesses but few harbours, and is removed by its position from the civilising influences which in olden times all came from the east, its share in the development of Greek culture was insignificant, and almost exclusively communicated through colonies of other more favourably situated states. As these parallel chains traverse the entire length of the western division, we can easily understand, that the longest of all the rivers of Greece is to be found here, the Achelous (Aspropotamo), which, rising on Lakmon, discharges itself into the Corinthian gulf.

viii INTRODUCTION. Greece, its Distribution, Physical Characteristics, and Oldest Inhabitants.

The development of the east is all the more rich and manifold by contrast. Here, travelling from north to south, we come first of all upon the outspreading basin of a fertile valley, which is encircled and shut in by the Kambunian range on the north, on the west by Pindus, on the south by Othrys, on the east by Pelion and Ossa (both of which chains connect Othrys with the Kambunian mountains). This basin is traversed by a broad curve of the Peneius, which takes its rise upon Lakmon, and finds its way into the sea through the narrow vale of Tempe between Olympus, the easternmost peak of the Kambunian range, 10,500 feet in height, and Ossa, about 6,500 feet in height, this being the only break in the chain. The waters, which everywhere stream down in abundance from the heights, form the two lakes, Nessonis at the foot of Ossa, and Bœbeis at the foot of Pelion.

Between Othrys and Œta there follows next in succession the narrow valley, widening only by degrees and always of limited extent, but at the same time of extraordinary fertility, which is drained by the Spercheius: this river has its source on Tymphrestus and divides the valley as far as the coast into two fairly equal halves. Œta reaches close down to the shore; at which point its precipitous cliff leaves only a narrow strip of land, known as the pass of Thermopylæ [1]. The coast-line, up to this point destitute of a single harbour, is here broken in the neighbourhood of the mouth of the Spercheius by the Malian gulf (gulf of Zeituni), and somewhat to the northwards between Othrys and Pelion by the Pagasæan gulf (gulf of Volo).

South of Œta we find another basin-shaped valley, similar in character to that of the Peneius, but of less extent. It is shut in by Œta, Parnassus, Helikon, Kithæron, Parnes, and on the east by Knemis. The Asopus finds an outlet between Parnes and Knemis, whilst the Kephissus collects in the lake Kopais, which has only a subterranean egress. Other waters form a second lake, Hylike. But besides this basin, the country south of Œta further comprises the mountain district of Parnassus and Kornx (the latter, lying to the westward runs directly south), the southern slope of Œta itself, the mountain district of Knemis, and finally a district of peninsular form, which stretches from Kithæron and Parnes to the promontory of Sunium, and is for the most part (in the east) mountainous, but contains several fertile plains. Stretching along the whole east coast south of Œta lies the mountainous island of Eubœa (Negroponte), only separated from the main land by a narrow channel, or Euripus. The south coast of this region is remarkable for its fine harbours.

The boundary between north and central Greece is formed by Œta and the gulf of Ambrakia (Arta), which cuts deep into the western coast. From the Peloponnese central Greece is divided by the Saronic and Corinthian gulfs (gulfs of Ægina and Lepanto). It is united to the Peloponnese by the isthmus of Corinth, a narrow and low ridge of hills, which at the narrowest part is not fully four miles broad. On the north the way is blocked by the Gerancia range, on the south by the Oneion range, the former shutting out central Greece, the latter the Peloponnese.

The Peloponnese itself, like the rest of Greece, is a land of mountains, but is of an essentially different conformation. The heart of the country is formed by a central region of the nature of a plateau, some 1,950 square miles in extent, in shape of a square fairly regular, and shut in by a circle of lofty skirting mountains, which are only interrupted by a short open space on the west. The course of these skirting ranges is marked by the mountains Pholoe, Lampeia, Erymanthus, Aroania, Kyllene (7,500 feet high), Artemision, Parthenion, Parnon and Lykæus. The rest of the peninsula consists, in part of the gradually subsiding slopes of the skirting ranges (so especially on the west and north), partly (in the east and south) of branch ranges; which run out from these skirting mountains and in some instances stretch far out into the sea. The most important of these branch ranges is the Taygetus, which

---

1) Described in Herodot. VII, 176.

INTRODUCTION. Greece, its Distribution, Physical Characteristics, and Oldest Inhabitants. ix

stretches from the southern extremity of the central region to Cape Tænarum, reaching an altitude of 7,910 feet. Further east, Parnon extends south as far as Cape Malea; on the west, Ægaleus runs out from the south-west corner of the skirting ranges. The fourth of the branch chains, starting from the north-east corner, continues to run eastwards till it ends in the promontory of Skyllæum. The sea forces its way between these chains and forms deep gulfs (the Argolic, Laconian and Messenian). Hence the extraordinarily rich development of Peloponnesian coast (416 miles to 8,300 square miles)[2]). The nature of the ground precluded rivers of large size: they are mostly coast rivers of short course and slender volume. The only rivers which deserve mention as of more than ordinary importance are, the Eurotas, between Taygetus and Parnon; the Pamisus, between Taygetus and Ægaleus; and the Alpheius, which, rising on Parnon at the south-east corner of the skirting ranges, winds along through the central region, and thence finds an outlet at the open space between Pholoe and Lykœus already alluded to.

On the whole, the soil of Greece is of such a nature that, leaving out of consideration the valleys, which are for the most part of insignificant extent, no great amount of produce can be won from it except at the cost of severe labour. But the climate is mild, and the deficiency of the soil is amply compensated by the facilities for navigation in which the wide extent of the coast and its wealth of harbourage invite the people to engage. A further peculiarity of Greece is seen in its great variety of climate and soil, and in the distribution of the whole country into petty districts separated from one another by lofty ranges, which proved a serious obstacle to the union of the whole population. The Peloponnese was distinguished from the rest of Greece by its internal strength and inaccessibility, and was for that reason frequently regarded as the acropolis of all Greece.

The character of the mainland is in general shared by the islands: of these, some are ranged round the west and south coast (Kerkyra, Loukas, Ithaka, Kephallenia, Zakynthus, Kythera), others cover the Ægean sea. Of these latter, a number form the group of the Cyclades, centred round Delos: the remaining islands of small size in the Ægean sea are comprised under the name Sporades. To the south, this island tract is hedged in by the two large islands of Krete and Cyprus.

The distribution of the mainland into districts is as follows:

I. Northern Greece is divided into two districts, Epirus and Thessaly, which are separated by Pindus: of these, the latter comprises, in addition to the two valleys of the Peneius and Sperchieus, Magnesia, the mountain land of Pelion and Ossa.

II. Central Greece contains eight districts: 1) Akarnania; 2) Ætolia, both on the extreme west, separated by Korax from the rest of central Greece, and from one another by the Achelous; 3) Lokris, of the district so called one-third, lying on the southern slopes of Korax, is Lokris of the Ozolæ: the two remaining parts, Epiknemidian and Opuntian Lokris, lie upon the eastern slope of Knemis and its offshoot Mykalossus; 4) Phokis, on the east and southern slopes of Parnassus and the mid course of the Kephissus; 5) Doris, on the southern slope of Œta and the upper course of the Kephissus as far as Parnassus; 6) Bœotia, a basin shut in by Œta, Parnassus, Helikon, Kithæron, Parnes and Knemis; 7) Attica, the peninsula situated to the south of Kithæron and Parnes (not quite 860 square miles in area but with a coast-line of 112 miles); 8) Megaris, in the district of the Geraneia range.

III. The Peloponnese comprises the six following districts: 1) Arcadia, the central highland; 2) Achaia, the northern slopes of the ranges skirting Arcadia; 3) Argolis, together with

---
2) Hence too the Peloponnese is shaped like a leaf, see Strab. p. 83, 326: ἔστιν ἡ Πελοπόννησος ἐοικυῖα φύλλῳ πλατάνου τὸ σχῆμα, and so frequently in the old writers.

x INTRODUCTION. Greece, its Distribution, Physical Characteristics, and Oldest Inhabitants.

Sikyon, Corinth and Phlius, the most easterly portion of the peninsula, situated partly on the slopes of Kyllene, partly on the Oneian range, partly comprising the district of those easterly chains which branch off from the ranges skirting Arcadia; 4) Laconia, the district of Parnon and Taygetus and of the river Eurotas; 5) Messenia, the country west of Taygetus, as far as the river Neda on the north-west; 6) Elis, comprising partly the slopes of Lykæus, partly flat coast land where a break occurs in the skirting ranges, partly the slopes and ramification of Pholoe and Erymanthus.

The Pelasgian race is for the most part designated as the oldest population tenanting the whole of Greece. An offshoot of the vast and wide-spread Indo-Germanic family, and coming from central Asia, it spread itself over the whole of Greece and the coasts of the neighbouring seas at a period antecedent to all historical knowledge, partly under the common name Pelasgians (of whom the Tyrrhenian Pelasgians are a special branch), partly under the name of Leleges, Kaukones, Kuretes, Kares, partly under other special names of branch tribes³).

From the earliest ages Epirus had a Pelasgic population, which it preserved to the latest times⁴): the most celebrated of the Pelasgic tribes which dwelt there are, the Greeks, Chaones, Thesprotians and Molossians. It always remained a stranger to Hellenic development⁵). The Selli on the western slope of the Tomaros range and south of the lake Pambotis (lake of Janina) are a solitary exception, inasmuch as they at a remote period exercised a not unimportant influence on the whole of Greece, partly through the oracle of Dodona, which lay in their territory, partly by their migration⁶).

Thessaly, before the immigration of the Thessalians⁷) called Hæmonia after Hæmon, the son or the father of Pelasgus⁸), was inhabited at the earliest period partly by Pelasgians⁹), partly by offshoots of Pelasgic tribes, viz. the Lapithæ, Perrhæbians, Phlegyans, Magnetes, Phthians,

---

3) The Pelasgians belong to the Indo-Germanic family, as is proved by the relationship subsisting between the Greek and the other Indo-Germanic tongues. Indeed the Greeks themselves regarded the oldest population as primitive and aboriginal, and hence styled themselves προσέληνοι and γγγενεῖς. A most important passage with reference to the spread of the Pelasgians is Strabo pp. 220 and 221 : Τοὺς δὲ Πελασγοὺς ὅτι μὲν ἀρχαῖόν τι φῦλον κατὰ τὴν Ἑλλάδα πᾶσαν ἐπενόμησε καὶ μάλιστα παρὰ τοῖς Αἰολεῦσι τοῖς κατὰ Θετταλίαν, ὁμολογοῦσιν ἅπαντες σχεδόν τι. So also Herodotus says (II, 56): Τὴν νῦν Ἑλλάδα, πρότερον δὲ Πελασγίην καλευμένην, cf. Thucyd. I, 3, and speaks of the olden time as that in which the Pelasgians were in possession of the whole of Greece. The most important passage with regard to the Tyrrhenian Pelasgians is Thuc. IV, 109 : Καί τι καὶ Χαλκιδικὸν ἔνι βραχύ, τὸ δὲ πλεῖστον Πελασγικὸν τῶν καὶ Λῆμνόν ποτε καὶ Ἀθήνας Τυρσηνῶν οἰκησάντων. Kaukon is cited Apollod. III, 8, 1 amongst the sons of Lykaon and grandsons of Pelasgus, whereby the Kaukones are brought under the common head of the Pelasgic stock. With regard to the Leleges, Kuretes, and Karians (perhaps also tho Thrakians), their affinity to the Pelasgic stock cannot be proved by the special testimony of ancient writers, but can only be inferred from the precise similarity of their position. Cf. the following notes.

4) Cf. Strab. p. 221 : πολλοὶ δὲ καὶ τὰ Ἠπειρωτικὰ ἔθνη Πελασγικὰ εἰρήκασιν, ὡς καὶ μέχρι δεῦρο ἐπαρξάντων.

5) For this reason the ancients do not generally reckon Epirus as a part of Greece, see Strab. pp. 328. 334. Dio Cassius, LIII, 12.

6) The Selli, also called Helli and Hellopes, were likewise a Pelasgic stock, cf. Strab. p. 327 and 328. The oracle at Dodona was very ancient, and formerly the only one in Greece (Herod. II, 52: τὸ γὰρ δὴ μαντήϊον τοῦτο νενόμισται ἀρχαιότατον τῶν ἐν Ἕλλησι χρηστηρίων εἶναι καὶ ἦν τὸν χρόνον τοῦτον μοῦνον); it was dedicated to Zeus, who is therefore called Hom. Il. XVI, 234 Dodonœan and Pelasgian; the Selli themselves are his ὑποφῆται, cf. id. v. 236. With regard to this oracle see especially Hesiod. fragm. 80. ed. Göttling. Herod. II, 52—57. Strab. p. 328. Pausan. I, 17, 5. VIII, 23, 4. The possession of the oldest oracle and the primitive service of Zeus show us in the land of the Selli a primeval seat of Greek culture. The high esteem in which agriculture was there held (and this, the foundation of all culture, was certainly imported by the Pelasgians) is proved by the remarkable invocation of Mother Earth, which is said to have been first used by the priestesses at Dodona: Γᾶ καρποὺς ἀνίει, διὸ κλῄζετε μάτερα γαῖαν, Pausan. X, 12, 5. With regard to the migrations of the Selli cf. p. 4. obs. 6 and 7.

7) See p. 9, obs. 27.

8) For the old name Hæmonia cf. Strab. 443. Dionys. Hal. I, 17, etc. For the relationship between Hæmon and Pelasgus (i. e. in other words, the affinity of the Hæmonians to the Pelasgic stock) cf. Eustath. on Hom. Il. II, 681. Steph. Byz. sub voc. Αἱμονία. After the spread of the Æolians the district was also called Æolis, cf. Herod. VII, 176.

9) Thessaly is everywhere designated as a chief seat of the Pelasgians; see e. g. the passage of Strabo quoted in obs. 3. Hence too, at a still later time, a part of the country was called Pelasgiotis, hence too Πελασγικὸν Ἄργος itself, see Hom. Il. II, 681, cf. Æschyl. Suppl. 250 ff.; hence finally the name Larissa for towns occurring thrice in Thessaly, see Strab. 440, which recurs everywhere, where a Pelasgic population is found, cf. id., and is commonly referred to the mother or the daughter of Pelasgus, see Pausan. II, 23, 9. Eustath. on Hom. Il. II, 681. Dionys. Hal. I, 17.

Achæans, Dolopians, and Ænianes[10]). Iolkus and Halus on the Pagasæan Gulf were held by the Minyans[11])

In central Greece the Leleges are the chief element in the old population. Their home was in Akarnania, Ætolia, the whole of Lokris, in Megaris, and Bœotia[12]). Ætolia was moreover the home of the Kuretes[13]); Bœotia of the Hektenes, Aones, Temmikes, Hyantes, Thrakians, and the Minyae of Orchomenus[14]). The population of Attica is Pelasgic[15]). Doris was in the oldest times the seat of the Pelasgic Dryopes[16]).

Bœotia and Attica, in central Greece, were the chief centres of culture in the oldest times, and consequently the chief seats of the oldest folklore. Both appear originally in close connexion[17]); Megaris in the earliest times was only a part of Attica[18]).

The Peloponnese was at a very remote age *par excellence* a Pelasgic land, and thus originally bore the name, Pelasgia[19]).

Arcadia, the heart and central land of the peninsula, was regarded[20]) as the peculiar home of the Pelasgians. Here Pelasgus was born, and from his stock there sprang in the third generation Arcas, the eponymous Hero of the land[21]); here too the population remained Pelasgic

---

10) The country was later divided into the four districts, Phthiotis on the south-east, Pelasgiotis on the north-east, Hestiæotis on the west, Thessaliotis in the centre, Strab. 430. In Phthiotis dwelt the Phthians and Achæans, who are marked as Pelasgic by the fact that Phthius and Achæus are called the brothers of Pelasgus and sons of Larissa, Dionys. Hal. I, 17: the Lapithæ in the plain of Pelasgiotis and the Perrhæbians on the mountains are comprehended under the collective name of Pelasgiots, Strab. 441. In Pelasgiotis and Gyrton lived also the Phlegyæ, Strab. 330. 442. These and the Magnetes in the mountainous district of Pelion and Ossa, and the Dolopians and Ænianes on the north slope of Œta, are likewise to be held Pelasgic, even though no express mention is made of the fact.

11) With regard to them see obs. 14 and p. 7. obs. 21.

12) The most important passage with regard to the Leleges in general and their extension as referred to above is Strab. 321 and 322: τοὺς δὲ Λέλεγάς τινες μὲν τοὺς αὐτοὺς Καρσὶν εἰκάζουσιν, οἱ δὲ συνοίκους μόνον καὶ συστρατιώτας.—ὅτι μὲν οὖν βάρβαροι ἦσαν οὗτοι, καὶ αὐτὸ τὸ κοινωνῆσαι τοῖς Καρσὶ νομίζοιτ᾽ ἂν σημεῖον· ὅτι δὲ πλάνητες καὶ μετ᾽ ἐκείνων καὶ χωρὶς καὶ ἐκ παλαιοῦ, καὶ αἱ Ἀριστοτέλους πολιτεῖαι δηλοῦσιν· ἐν μὲν γὰρ τῇ Ἀκαρνάνων φησὶ τὸ μὲν ἔχειν αὐτῆς Κουρῆτας, τὸ δὲ προσεσπέριον Λέλεγας, εἶτα Τηλεβόας· ἐν δὲ τῇ Αἰτωλῶν τοὺς νῦν Λοκροὺς Λέλεγας καλεῖ, κατασχεῖν δὲ καὶ τὴν Βοιωτίαν αὐτοὺς φησιν· ὁμοίως δὲ καὶ ἐν τῇ Ὀπουντίων καὶ Μεγαρέων· ἐν δὲ τῇ Λευκαδίων καὶ αὐτόχθονά τινα Λέλεγα ὀνομάζει, τούτου δὲ θυγατριδοῦν Τηλεβόαν, τοῦ δὲ παῖδας δύο καὶ εἴκοσι Τηλεβόας, ὧν τινας οἰκῆσαι τὴν Λευκάδα· μάλιστα δ᾽ ἄν τις Ἡσιόδῳ πιστεύσειεν οὕτως περὶ αὐτῶν εἰπόντι· ἤτοι γὰρ Λοκρὸς Λελέγων ἡγήσατο λαῶν, τούς ῥά ποτε Κρονίδης Ζεύς, ἄφθιτα μήδεα εἰδώς, λεκτοὺς ἐκ γαίης λάας πόρε Δευκαλίωνι. Leleges and Kares are according to Herod. I, 171. Strab. p. 661 the same race, and the former is only its older name.

13) See Strab. loc. cit. Their chief seat is Pleuron, Hom. Il. II, 531, from which place they engage in bloody struggles with the Ætolians at Kalydon. Pleuron and Kalydon, the scene of the legend of the Kalydonian Boar, see Hom. Il. IX, 529—600. II, 641. Apollodor. I, 8. Paus. VIII, 45, 4. cf. Ovid. Met. VIII, 260 ff.

14) See Strab. p. 401. 410. Paus. IX, 5, 1. Old names of Bœotia: Aonia, Messapia, Ogygia, Kadmeis, Steph. Byz. sub voc. Βοιωτία, cf. Strab. p. 407. Thuc. I, 12. For the Minyæ see Herod. I, 146. Strab. p. 414: Καλεῖ δὲ Μινύειον τὸν Ὀρχομενὸν ἀπὸ ἔθνους τοῦ Μινυῶν· ἐντεῦθεν δὲ ἀποικῆσαί τινας τῶν Μινυῶν εἰς Ἰωλκὸν φασιν, ὅθεν τοὺς Ἀργοναύτας Μινύας λεχθῆναι cf. p. 7. obs. 21.

15) The Athenians prided themselves on being the only race of all the Greeks which dwelt on the land where it sprang up. See Herod. VII, 161: (μοῦνοι ἐόντες οὐ μετανάσται Ἑλλήνων). Thuc. I, 2. II, 36. Plat. Menex. p. 237 n. For their Pelasgic origin see Herod. VIII, 44: Ἀθηναῖοι δὲ ἐπὶ μὲν Πελασγῶν ἐχόντων τὴν νῦν Ἑλλάδα καλεομένην ἦσαν Πελασγοὶ οὐνομαζόμενοι Κραναοί. Old names of the district, Akte or Aktæa, Atthis, Mopsopia, Ionia, Poseidonia, Strab. p. 397. Paus. I, 2, 3.

16) The Dryopes are marked as Pelasgic, inasmuch as Dryops is called the son of Arkas, see Arist. in Strab. p. 373, or the grandson of Lykaon, Tzetzes on Lykophr. 480. The district was hence called originally Dryopis. (Of Phokis no other ancient inhabitants are mentioned except the Phokians; here too, in all probability, the oldest population was akin to the Leleges.)

17) The myths of Ogygos and Kekrops are common to both districts, see Paus. IV, 5, 1. 33, 1. Strab. p. 407. For the Ogygian flood, which is said to have taken place 1020 years before the first Olympiad, see Akusilaus, Hellanikus, and Philochorus in Euseb. Præp. Evang. X, 10. p. 489. As for Attica, the legend of the contest between Poseidon and Athena for the possession of the land deserves special mention, concerning which see Herod. VIII, 55. Apollod. III, 14, 1. Paus. I, 24, 3, 5. For the shape taken by the abundant legends of both lands after Kadmus and Kekrops see p. 3. obs. 2 and 3. p. 4. obs. 8. p. 6. obs. 22. p. 8. obs. 24. In the rest of central Greece, with the exception of the legend of the Kalydonian boar, myth has nowhere found a place.

18) See Paus. I, 19, 5. 39, 4. Strab. p. 393. Plut. Thes. 25.

19) Pelasgia the name of the whole Peloponnese, Ephorus in Strab. p. 221. Another old name of the peninsula is Apia, Paus. II, 5, 5. Plin. II. N. IV, 4, 5. (Hom. Il. I, 270. III, 49?) perhaps also Argos, Apollod. II, 1, 2. Dionys. Hal. I, 17. The name Peloponnese occurs first in the Hymn to Apollo, 250. 290.

20) Ephorus in Strabo p. 221. Hence too Arcadia was called Pelasgia, Paus. VIII, 1, 2.

21) Pelasgus, son of the earth, begat Lykaon; the latter begat 22 (or 31 or 51) sons, amongst whom were Nyktimos, Kaukon, and the two first founders of Pelasgic settlements in Italy, Œnotius and Peuketius, and a daughter Kallisto: Arkas was the son of the latter and Zeus, and in his turn had three sons, Azas, Apheidas, and Elatus. See Paus. VIII, 1—4. Apollod. III, 8—9. Dionys. Hal. I, 11. Of Pelasgus we are informed by Paus. (loc. cit. I, 2): Πεποίηται δὲ καὶ Ἀσίῳ τοιάδε ἐς αὐτόν· "Ἀντίθεον δὲ Πελασγὸν ἐν ὑψικόμοισιν ὄρεσσι Γαῖα μέλαιν᾽ ἀνέδωκεν, ἵνα θνητῶν γένος εἴη." Πελασγὸς δὲ βασιλεύσας τοῦτο μὲν ποιήσασθαι καλύβας ἐπενόησεν, ὡς

xii INTRODUCTION. Greece, its Distribution, Physical Characteristics, and Oldest Inhabitants.

without admixture up till the very latest times[22]. The country, owing to its physical characteristics, was split up into a number of detached cantons, and throughout, whilst Greece was at the height of her prosperity, was cut off from her historical development and confined within its own narrow bounds[23]).

Achaia, called originally Ægialus or Æginlea[24]), in the earliest times had a twofold population, corresponding to a division of the country into two halves west and east of the promontory of Rhium. The first half was the original home of the Kaukones and Ætolian Epeians[25]), the eastern half that of the Ægialeans[26]). Issuing from this latter half, the Ionians at a later period spread themselves over the whole district, which now received the name of Ionia[27]).

In the district of Argolis, which owing to the nature of the ground is split up into a number of independent townships (under which head Sikyon, Phlius and Corinth also fall), all noteworthy accounts of the oldest population confine themselves merely to Argos, which lies on the interior of the Argolic Gulf, and appears, as well as Arcadia, as the chief seat of the Pelasgians[28]).

The original population of Laconia and Messenia, and common to both, consisted of Leleges[29]).

The oldest inhabitants of Elis were the Kaukones[30]), and later the Epeians, who spread over the land from the north, and the Pylians from the south: these two peoples confined the Kaukones to the mountains of Triphylia and the neighbourhood of Dyme[31]).

The oldest population on the islands consisted for the most part of Karians[32]).

μὴ ῥιγοῦν τε καὶ θέεσθαι τοὺς ἀνθρώπους μηδὲ ὑπὸ τοῦ καύματος ταλαιπωρεῖν· τοῦτο δὲ τοὺς χιτῶνας τοὺς ἐκ τῶν δερμάτων τῶν ὑῶν—οὕτός ἐστιν ὁ ἐξευρών, καὶ δὴ καὶ τῶν φύλλων τὰ ἔτι χλωρὰ καὶ πόας τε καὶ ῥίζας οὐδὲ ἐδωδίμους, ἀλλὰ καὶ ὀλεθρίους ἐνίας σιτουμένους τοὺς ἀνθρώπους τούτων μὲν ἔπαυσεν ὁ Πελασγός.

22) Herod. VIII, 73. Paus. V, 1, 1.

23) The distribution into small independent states, clearly pointed to by the number of Lykaon's sons, continued till the time of Epaminondas. Of these, only Tegea and Mantinea are already conspicuous in the earliest times; the rest preserved their ancient manners and customs in perfect seclusion, so that the Arcadians collectively were still about 600 B. C. styled acorn-eating men, Herod. I, 66. Paus. VIII, 1, 2.

24) Ægialos, Paus. II, 5, 5. VII, 5, 1. Strab. p. 333, 383. 386. Hom. Il. II, 574 (?); Ægiales, Apollod. II, 1, 1, 4. Tzetzes on Lykophr. 177. So called from King Ægialeus, Apollod. II, 1, 1. Paus. VII, 5, 1.

25) Hence Dyme was called Epeiis by Hekataeus, Strab. p. 341, by others Kaukonis, id. p. 342.

26) Πελασγοὶ Αἰγιαλέες, Herod. VII, 94.

27) Strab. p. 333, 383. Herod. VII, 94. For the Ionians see p. 5. obs. 12 and 13.

28) This follows from the genealogical tables of the rulers of Argos, Paus. II, 15, 5. Apollod. II, 1. which begin with Inachus or Phoroneus as founder of the race, and in which there always appear a Pelasgus, an Argos, and likewise a Larissa (name of the citadel of Argos). Hence also, "Pelasgic Argos," Strab. p. 369. In those genealogical tables also Io, daughter of Inachus, Herod. I, 1, or of Isaus, Paus. and Apollod. loc. cit., cf. Æschyl. Prometh. . 827 ff. Further Niobe, daughter of Phoroneus, for whom see Hom. Il. XXIV, 602 ff. Paus. I, 21, 5. VIII, 2, 3. Danaus appears in the same table as a descendant of Inachus in the tenth generation, cf. Syncell. pp. 62—66. Euseb. Præp. Evang. pp. 487—491. For Danaus see infr.

29) See Paus. III, 1. IV, 1. Apollod. III, 10, 3 ff. According to this Lelex is the ancestor of the rulers of Laconia; but as his eldest son Myles succeeds him as ruler in Laconia, and another son Polykaon emigrates to Messenia and there founds his rule, the inhabitants of Laconia and Messenia are hereby pointed out as of kindred race, and in each case as Leleges. The list of the descendants of Lelex in Laconia further comprises Eurotas, Lakedæmon, Amyclas, Sparte and Taygete, mere names, grounded upon localities in this district. (With regard to Messenia it is further noticeable, that Kaukones are also found there, which the legend expresses by saying that a Kaukon was born to Messene, the wife of Polykaon.)

30) Kaukon son of Lykaon, Apollod. III, 8, 1. For the Kaukones in Elis see Strab. p. 345: οἱ μὲν γὰρ καὶ ὅλην τὴν νῦν Ἠλείαν ἀπὸ τῆς Μεσσηνίας μέχρι Δύμης Καυκωνίαν λεχθῆναί φασιν, cf. Hom. Od. III, 366.

31) Strabo proceeds in the passage cited in the preceding note: 'Ἀντίμαχος γοῦν καὶ Ἐπειοὺς καὶ Καύκωνας ἅπαντας προσαγορεύει, τινὲς δὲ ὅλην μὲν μὴ κατασχεῖν αὐτούς, δίχα δὲ μεμερισμένους οἰκεῖν, τοὺς μὲν πρὸς τῇ Μεσσηνίᾳ κατὰ τὴν Τριφυλίαν, τοὺς δὲ πρὸς τῇ Δύμῃ, and we see that by these different accounts is signified the twofold character of the population, according to the distinction drawn above, cf. Strab. p. 351. For the struggles between the Epeians and Pylians see Strab. p. 351, cf. Hom. Il. XI, 670 ff. XXIII, 630 ff. The genealogy of the rulers of the Epeians is according to Paus. V, 1, 2 as follows: Aethlios, son of Zeus—Endymion—Paeon, Epeius, Ætolus—Eleius, grandson of Epeius. Ætolus, the brother of Epeius, emigrated to Ætolia, which was called by his name. Paus. V, 1, 6.

32) Kar, son of Phoroneus, Paus. I, 40, 5. With regard to the Karians as being the oldest inhabitants of the islands, the chief passages are Thuc. I, 4 and 8. On Leukas dwelt Leleges; but they according to Herodotus and Strabo were not different from the Karians, see obs. 12.

CHRONOLOGICAL TABLES.

2   FIRST PERIOD.   From the Earliest Times to the Migration of the Dorians and Herakleidæ.

FIRST PERIOD.

FROM THE EARLIEST TIMES TO THE MIGRATION OF THE DORIANS AND HERAKLEIDÆ.

X—1104 B.C.

PREHISTORIC AGE.

Pelasgian tribes, the earliest inhabitants of Greece known to us (from legend), lay amid continual migrations the first foundation of civilised life, their progress being advanced by their struggles with one another and also by the foreign influence, which they first admit, then happily overcome. The way is paved for the development of a peculiar Hellenic nationality, by several wars, undertaken more or less in concert, and by a national folk-lore, which arises chiefly from these wars and assumes artistic shape. With the establishment of the Dorians and Herakleidæ in the Peloponnese permanent settlements become general in all parts of Greece, and the first condition of a steady inner development is thus satisfied.

AUTHORITIES. Our historical knowledge of this period, so far as this is possible, is to be drawn from Hellenic legend, which lies before us, partly in the epic poems of Homer, Hesiod, and the so-called Homeric hymns, to all of which it gave birth, partly in the geographical writings of Strabo (born circ. 60 B.C. His work, Γεωγραφικά in seventeen books, was composed in the first years of the reign of the Emperor Tiberius) and of Pausanias (Ἑλλάδος περιήγησις circ. 150 A.D.), partly in the collection of Apollodorus (Βιβλιοθήκη in three books, circ. 140 B.C.), partly in later writings of various contents, e.g. in the Biographies of Plutarch (born 50 A.D.), in Diodorus Siculus (born 1 A.D.), in the 'Ονομαστικόν of Julius Pollux (circ. 180 A.D.), in Eusebius, a contemporary of Constantine the Great (παντοδαπὴ ἱστορία in two books; part of the first book is preserved in the εὐαγγελικῆς ἀποδείξεως παρασκευή of Eusebius himself, the second book in the Latin translation of

Hieronymus, and both books in an Armenian translation), in Synkellus (ἐκλογὴ χρονογραφίας circ. 800 A.D.), and in the Scholia of Eustathius and others on Homer, and of Tzetzes on Lykophron (in xlith smcl. A.D.). From these fragmentary records our history is pieced together. As for chronology, the so-called Marmor Parium yields some important materials. This is a marble table, found on the island of Paros, which was executed in the third century before Christ, and is now at Oxford: it contains a list of dates taken out of Greek history from the earliest times down to the year 264, with chronological notes: but the part preserved only goes down to 355 (it may be found printed in C. Müller's Fragm. Histor. Græc. vol. I.). Further, scattered notices are found in the fragments of the so-called logographi, Hekatæus, Pherekydes, Akusilaus, Hellanikus, and also in those of Ephorus; lastly, more numerous and of greater value, in Herodotus and Thucydides.

X—1104 B.C. PREHISTORIC AGE. 3

B. C.	(LEGENDARY) HISTORY.	GENEALOGY of the most illustrious royal families in	
		Argos.	Athens.
1533[1])	Immigration of Kekrops from Sais in Lower Egypt into Athens[2]).		Kekrops[3]).
1500	....	....	Kranaus.
1466	Immigration of Danaus from Chemmis in Upper Egypt into Argos[4]).	Danaus[5]).	Atthis.
1433	....	Hypermnestra = Lynkeus.	Erichthonius.

1) The chronology of this period is based, partly upon the genealogies of the most celebrated families, our accounts of which are in fair accordance; partly, upon the computation of the time of the Trojan war; for which latter see p. 8, obs. 25.

2) The legends of the immigrations of Kekrops, Danaus, Kadmus, and Pelops, originated at a later period, and have only so far a certain historical significance, as they exhibit the conviction of the Greeks themselves of an influence, which at a very remote period the East exercised upon the development of Greece. Of these, the legend of the immigration of Kekrops is the latest in its origin. Theopompus (in ivth saecl. B.c.) first mentioned as a colony of Ægyptians at Athens (Fr. 172 ed. Müller); the statement that Kekrops came from Sais, is found first in Eusebius and other later writers. The older legend, based on the notion that the Athenians were aboriginal and pure from admixture with foreigners (see Int. obs. 15), made Kekrops into a twin-shaped being, in its upper part human, but from the hips downwards a snake [Demosth.] Epit. p. 1398. Justin. II, 6; and related of Erechtheus (or of Erichthonius, Isocr. Panath. p. 248. d. Apollod. III, 14, 6. Paus. I, 2, 5], that he was the son of the Earth, Hom. Il. II, 546. Herod. VIII, 55. According to the Marm. Par., Kekrops commenced his reign in 1581, according to Eusebius in 1537, according to Hellanikus and Philochorus in 1507.

3) The chief passages referring to the royal houses at Athens are Apollod. III, 14, 15, 16. Paus. I, 2, 5. 5, 3. Strab. p. 397. Kekropia, the citadel of Athens, is said to have received its name from Kekrops.

This prince died without leaving a male heir; he was therefore succeeded by Kranaus (αὐτόχθων ὤν, Apoll. III, 14, 5); Atthis, daughter of Kranaus (from whom, it is asserted, the name Attica comes), married Amphiktyon, who, however, was expelled by Erichthonius. For the names of the country and people cf. Herod. VIII, 44: Ἀθηναῖοι δὲ ἐπὶ μὲν Πελασγῶν ἐχόντων τὴν νῦν Ἑλλάδα καλεομένην ἦσαν Πελασγοί ὀνομαζόμενοι Κραναοί, ἐπὶ δὲ Κέκροπος βασιλέος ἐπεκλήθησαν Κεκροπίδαι, ἐκδεξαμένου δὲ Ἐρεχθέος τὴν ἀρχὴν Ἀθηναῖοι μετονομάσθησαν, Ἴωνος δὲ τοῦ Ξούθου στρατάρχεω γενομένου Ἀθηναίοισι ἐκλήθησαν ἀπὸ τούτου Ἴωνες.

4) See Herod. II, 43, 91. Paus. II, 16, 1 and the most detailed account of all, Apollod. II, 1. According to this latter passage Danaus, like his brother Ægyptus, before whom he flies from Chemmis, is a descendant of Ino, see Int. obs. 28 (Ino—Epaphus—Libye—Belus—Egyptus, Danaus). Gelanor, on the arrival of Danaus at Argos, makes over the sovereignty to him; and this the latter then bequeaths to Lynkeus, the consort of his daughter Hypermnestra. For his 50 daughters cf. Strab. p. 371: δ (i.e. the springs at Argos) ταῖς Δαναΐσιν ἀνάτρωσιν, ὣς ἐκείνων ἐξευρουσῶν, ἀφ' οὗ καὶ τὸ ἔπος εἰπεῖν τοῦτο. "Ἄργος ἄνυδρον ἐὸν Δαναοὶ θέσαν Ἄργος ἔνυδρον," and for Danaus himself, id.: Τὴν δὲ ἀκρόπολιν τῶν Ἀργείων οἰκῆσαι λέγεται Δαναός, ὅς τοσοῦτον τοὺς πρὸ αὐτοῦ δυναστεύοντας ἐν τοῖς τόποις ὑπερβαλέσθαι δοκεῖ, ὥστε κατ' Εὐριπίδην "Πελασγιώτας ὠνομασμένους τὸ πρὶν Δαναοὺς καλεῖσθαι νόμον ἔθηκ' ἄν' Ἑλλάδα."

5) Apollod. II, 1 ff. Paus. II, 16.

4   FIRST PERIOD.   From the Earliest Times to the Migration of the Dorians and Herakleidæ.

B. C.	(LEGENDARY) HISTORY.	GENEA of the Hellenes.
1400	Flood of Deukalion[6].	Deukalion[7].
1366	Immigration of Kadmus from Phœnicia into Thebes[8].	Hellen.
1333	....	Æolus[10]), Dorus[11]), Xuthus.
1300	....	Ion, Achæus[12]).

6) The oldest home of the legend of the flood of Deukalion was the valley of Dodona (cf. Int. obs. 6), see Aristot. Meteorol. I, 14: ὁ καλούμενος ἐπὶ Δευκαλίωνος κατακλυσμός· καὶ γὰρ οὗτος περὶ τὸν Ἑλληνικὸν ἐγίνετο μάλιστα τόπον καὶ τούτου περὶ τὴν Ἑλλάδα τὴν ἀρχαίαν· αὕτη δ᾽ ἐστὶν ἡ περὶ Δωδώνην καὶ τὸν Ἀχελῷον· οὗτος γὰρ πολλαχοῦ τὸ ῥεῦμα μεταβέβληκεν· ᾤκουν γὰρ οἱ Σελλοὶ ἐνταῦθα καὶ οἱ καλούμενοι τότε μὲν Γραικοὶ, νῦν δ᾽ Ἕλληνες. With Deukalion and his descendants the legend migrated to Thessaly, Apollod. I, 7, 2 (in this case Deukalion's ark landed, according to Hellanikus, Schol. Pindar, Ol. IX, 64, on Othrys, or again, according to Apollod. loc. cit., on Parnassus upon the peak Lykoreo), and still further to Lokris, Bœotia, even to Attica, in all which countries Parnassus was regarded as the landing-place of Deukalion, Schol. Pind. loc. cit. Strab. p. 332, 425. Paus. I, 18, 7. 40, 1. X, 6, 1. Marm. Par.

7) Deukalion, the son of Prometheus (the fire-giver and consequently the author of civilisation), see Apollod. I, 7, 2. Hesiod and Hellanikus in Schol. Apollon. III, 1085. 1086, lived according to Arist. loc. cit. in Dodona, or according to Schol. Pind. loc. cit. in Opus, or in Kynos, see id. and Strab. 425, or in Lykoreia in Phokis, see Marm. Par., or in Delphi, see Plut. Quæst. Gr. p. 292; according to Dionys. Hal. I, 17 he is thought to have migrated (from Parnassus) to Thessaly, cf. Strab. p. 432. But according to the common tradition his son Hellen is said to have first founded a settlement. For him and his descendants see Hesiod in Tzetzes on Lykophr. 284 : Ἕλληνος δ᾽ ἐγένοντο θεμιστοπόλοι βασιλῆες | Δῶρός τε Ξοῦθός τε καὶ Αἴολος ἱππιοχάρμης, | Αἰολίδαι δ᾽ ἐγένοντο θεμιστοπόλοι βασιλῆες | Κρηθεύς τ᾽ ἠδ᾽ Ἀθάμας καὶ Σίσυφος αἰολομήτης | Σαλμωνεύς τ᾽ ἄδικος καὶ ὑπέρθυμος Περιήρης. Æolus generally passes for his eldest son, to whom accordingly the father's sovereignty in Thessaly descends, whilst the two other sons emigrate to seek new homes, see Strab. p. 383. Konon in Phot. p. 437. For the conception of Thucydides as to the method, in which the extension of the Hellenes took place, and their earliest ethnographical relations generally, see the locus classicus I, 3 : Πρὸ γὰρ τῶν Τρωικῶν οὐδὲν φαίνεται πρότερον κοινῇ ἐργασαμένη ἡ Ἑλλάς· δοκεῖ δέ μοι, οὐδὲ τοὔνομα τοῦτο ξύμπασά πω εἴχεν, ἀλλὰ τὰ μὲν πρὸ Ἕλληνος τοῦ Δευκαλίωνος καὶ πάνυ οὐδὲ εἶναι ἡ ἐπίκλησις αὕτη, κατὰ ἔθνη δὲ ἄλλα τε καὶ τὸ Πελασγικὸν ἐπὶ πλεῖστον ἀφ᾽ ἑαυτῶν τὴν ἐπωνυμίαν παρέχεσθαι, Ἕλληνος δὲ καὶ τῶν παίδων αὐτοῦ ἐν τῇ Φθιώτιδι ἰσχυσάντων καὶ ἐπαγομένων αὐτοὺς ἐπ᾽ ὠφελίᾳ ἐς τὰς ἄλλας πόλεις καθ᾽ ἑκάστους μὲν ἤδη τῇ ὁμιλίᾳ μᾶλλον καλεῖσθαι Ἕλληνας, οὐ μέντοι πολλοῦ γε χρόνου ἠδύνατο καὶ ἅπασιν ἐκνικῆσαι. τεκμήριον δὲ μάλιστα Ὅμηρος· πολλῷ γὰρ ὕστερον ἔτι καὶ τῶν Τρωικῶν γενόμενος οὐδαμοῦ τοὺς ξύμπαντας ὠνόμασεν οὐδ᾽ ἄλλους ἢ τοὺς μετ᾽ Ἀχιλλέως ἐκ τῆς Φθιώτιδος, οἵπερ καὶ πρῶτοι Ἕλληνες ἦσαν, Δαναοὺς δὲ ἐν τοῖς ἔπεσι καὶ Ἀργείους καὶ Ἀχαιούς· ἀνακαλεῖ· οὐ μὴν οὐδὲ βαρβάρους εἴρηκε διὰ τὸ μηδὲ Ἕλληνάς πω, ὡς ἐμοὶ δοκεῖ, ἀντίπαλον ἐς ἓν ὄνομα ἀποκεκρίσθαι· οἱ δ᾽ οὖν ὡς ἕκαστοι Ἕλληνες

κατὰ πόλεις τε ὅσοι ἀλλήλων ξυνίεσαν καὶ ξύμπαντες ὕστερον κληθέντες—, with which Herodotus also agrees, when he calls (VIII, 44) Ion a στρατάρχης of the Athenians. The passages in Homer are Il. II, 684. XVI, 595. Od. I, 344, XI, 495. XV, 80. For the primitive seats of the Hellenes see Strab. loc. cit. and p. 431. According to Apollodorus in Strab. p. 370 the name Hellenes, as a collective name of the Greeks, occurs first in Hesiod and Archilochus, therefore in 8th sæcl. B.C., and it is exceedingly probable, that at this very time, with the growing consciousness of a common nationality, the belief in their common descent from Hellen and Deukalion gradually grew up and established itself among the Hellenes.

8) Kadmus, son of Agenor, Eurip. Bacch. v. 171, of Tyre in Phœnicia, Herod. II, 49. Eurip. Phœn. v. 639 (but also according to others of Sidon, Eurip. Bacch. loc. cit., or even of Thebes in Egypt, Diodor. I, 23. Paus. IX, 12, 2), was sent forth by his father in search for Europa, who had been carried off by Zeus, and came by way of Krete, Rhodes (Diodor. V, 58), Thera (Herod. IV, 147), Samothrace, Lemnos, Thasos (Herod. II, 44. VI, 47), to Bœotia, where, at the instance and under the guidance of the oracle at Delphi, he founded the Kadmea, and by sowing the dragon's teeth created a new race, that of the Σπαρτοί, see Paus. IX, 12, 1. Schol. Eurip. Phœn. 638. Aristoph. Ran. 1256. Kadmus (from the Phœnician word kedem, land of the morning) is the representative of the Phœnician colonisations of the Greek islands and mainland and of the influence of the Phœnicians upon the development of the Greeks. Besides the colonies on the above-mentioned spots, which were everywhere founded with a view to commerce and mining, Cyprus and Kythera are also mentioned as seats of Phœnician settlers, see Herod. I, 105. Furthermore the service of Aphrodite Urania (= the Astarte of the Phœnicians) at Athens and Corinth (Paus. I, 14, 6. Strab. p. 379), the worship of Melikertes (= the Phœnician god Melkarth) at the latter place (Plut. Thes. 25), the sacrifice of human victims amongst the Minyæ (see infr. obs. 21), and the subjection of Attica and Megara under the rule of Krete (see infr. obs. 16 and 20), all point back to a time, in which at all these places Phœnician settlements exercised a ruling influence. As an example of their influence upon the culture of the Greeks, special prominence is usually given to the introduction of the alphabet, which is ascribed to them; see especially Herod. V, 58 : Οἱ δὲ Φοίνικες οὗτοι οἱ σὺν Κάδμῳ ἀπικόμενοι—ἐσήγαγον διδασκάλια ἐς τοὺς Ἕλληνας καὶ δὴ καὶ γράμματα, οὐκ ἐόντα πρὶν Ἕλλησιν ὡς ἐμοὶ δοκέειν, πρῶτα μὲν τοῖσι καὶ ἅπαντες χρέωνται Φοίνικες, μετὰ δὲ χρόνου προβαίνοντος ἅμα τῇ φωνῇ μετέβαλον καὶ τὸν ῥυθμὸν τῶν γραμμάτων. Περιοίκεον δέ σφεας τὰ πολλὰ τῶν χώρων τούτων τῶν χρόνων Ἑλλήνων Ἴωνες, οἳ παραλαβόντες διδαχῇ παρὰ τῶν Φοινίκων τὰ γράμματα μεταρρυθμίσαντές σφεων ὀλίγα ἐχρέωντο· χρεώμενοι δὲ ἐφάτισαν, ὥσπερ καὶ τὸ δίκαιον ἔφερε, ἐσαγαγόντων Φοινίκων ἐς τὴν Ἑλλάδα Φοινικήια κεκλῆσθαι. Cf. Diod. III, 67. Plin. II. N.

of the most illustrious royal families in

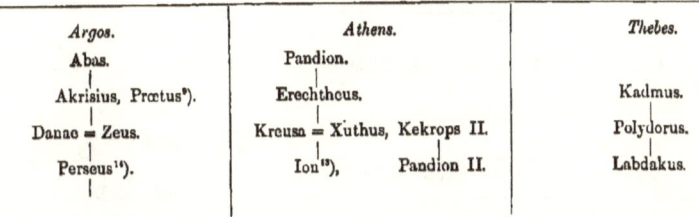

Argos.	Athens.	Thebes.
Abas.	Pandion.	
Akrisius, Prœtus⁹).	Erechtheus.	Kadmus.
Danae = Zeus.	Kreusa = Xuthus, Kekrops II.	Polydorus.
Perseus¹⁴).	Ion¹³), Pandion II.	Labdakus.

VII, 56. Hygin. Fab. 277. That the Greek alphabet is related to the Phœnician is clearly proved by the names and original forms of the Phœnician and Greek letters.

9) Akrisius and Prœtus were at war with one another: Prœtus was expelled by his brother, but established himself at Tiryns, and there asserted himself, whilst Akrisius remained at Argos, see Paus. II, 16, 2. Apollod. II, 2, 1. Strab. p. 372 and 873. Cf. Hom. Il. VI, 152—210. Of the walls, with which according to the legend the Cyclopes surrounded Tiryns, Apollod. II, 2, 2. Paus. II, 16, 2, important remains are still preserved—one of the most remarkable monuments of the so-called Cyclopean structure.

10) A most important passage with regard to the fortunes and wanderings of the three brothers is that already cited from Strabo (p. 383): φασὶ δὲ Δευκαλίωνος μὲν Ἕλληνα εἶναι, τοῦτον δὲ περὶ τὴν Φθίαν τῶν μεταξὺ Πηνειοῦ καὶ Ἀσωποῦ δυναστεύοντα τῷ πρεσβυτάτῳ τῶν παίδων παραδοῦναι τὴν ἀρχήν, τοὺς δ' ἄλλους ἔξω διαπέμψαι ζητήσοντας ἵδρυσιν ἑκάστῳ αὐτῷ· ὧν Δῶρος μὲν τοὺς περὶ Παρνασσὸν Δωριέας συνοικίσας κατέλιπεν ἐπωνύμους αὑτοῦ, Ξοῦθος δὲ τὴν Ἐρεχθέως θυγατέρα γήμας ᾤκισε τὴν Τετράπολιν τῆς Ἀττικῆς, Οἰνόην, Μαραθῶνα, Προβάλινθον καὶ Τρικόρυθον. Later, the greater part of all the Hellenes was comprehended under the name Æolians, see Strab. p. 333: πάντες γὰρ οἱ ἐκτὸς Ἰσθμοῦ πλὴν Ἀθηναίων καὶ Μεγαρέων καὶ τῶν περὶ τὸν Παρνασσὸν Δωριέων καὶ νῦν ἔτι Αἰολεῖς καλοῦνται: thus to Æolus was attributed an especial wealth of posterity. According to the passage quoted obs. 7, he had five sons, Kretheus, Athamas, Sisyphus, Salmoneus, Periores; according to Apollod. I, 7, 4 he had seven sons (in addition to those mentioned Deion and Magnes) and five daughters; according to others the number was still greater, and from these sons and daughters were derived the old ruling families in numerous towns and districts; thus from Sisyphus (for whom see Hom. Il. VI, 152 ff. Od. XI, 593 ff. Paus. II, 1, 2) the rulers of Corinth are said to be descended, from Athamas those of the Minyan Orchomenus, from Kretheus those of Iolkus, and from Kretheus again Neleus and Nestor at Pylus, etc.

11) For the Dorians see the important passage Herod. I, 56: Δωρικὸν γένος—πολυπλάνητον κάρτα· ἐπὶ μὲν γὰρ Δευκαλίωνος βασιλέος οἴκεε γῆν τὴν Φθιῶτιν· ἐπὶ δὲ Δώρου τοῦ Ἕλληνος τὴν ὑπὸ τὴν Ὄσσαν τε καὶ τὸν Οὔλυμπον χώρην, καλεομένην δὲ Ἰστιαιῆτιν· ἐκ δὲ τῆς Ἰστιαιήτιδος ὡς ἐξανέστη ὑπὸ Καδμείων, οἴκεε ἐν Πίνδῳ Μακεδνὸν καλεόμενον· ἐνθεῦτεν δὲ αὖτις ἐς τὴν Δρυοπίδα μετέβη καὶ ἐκ τῆς Δρυοπίδος οὕτως ἐς Πελοπόννησον ἐλθὸν Δωρικὸν ἐκλήθη. For the first settlements of the Dorians in Hestiæotis cf. besides Diod. IV, 37. 67, Strab. p. 437. 475. 476.

12) See the passage of Strabo (p. 383) quoted in obs. 10, which in reference to the sons of Xuthus proceeds thus: τῶν δὲ τούτου παίδων Ἀχαιὸς μὲν φόνον ἀκούσιον πράξας ἔφυγεν εἰς Λακεδαίμονα καὶ Ἀχαιοὺς τοὺς ἐκεῖ κληθῆναι παρεσκεύασεν, Ἴων δὲ τοὺς μετ' Εὐμόλπου νικήσας Ὀρφικὰς οὕτως ηὐδοκίμησεν, ὥστ' ἐπέτρεψαν αὐτῷ τὴν πολιτείαν Ἀθηναῖοι. ὁ δὲ πρῶτον μὲν εἰς τέτταρας φυλὰς διεῖλε τὸ πλῆθος, εἶτα εἰς τέτταρας βίους.—οὕτω δὲ πολυανδρῆσαι τὴν χώραν τότε συνέπεσεν, ὥστε καὶ ἀποικίαν τῶν Ἰώνων ἐστεῖλαν εἰς Πελοπόννησον Ἀθηναῖοι καὶ τὴν χώραν ἣν κατέσχον ἐπώνυμον ἑαυτῶν ἐποίησαν Ἰωνίαν ἀντ' Αἰγιάλου κληθεῖσαν, οἵ τε ἄνδρες ἀντ' Αἰγιαλέων Ἴωνες προσηγορεύθησαν εἰς δώδεκα πόλεις μερισθέντες. Cf. Paus. VII, 1, 2 (according to which passage Achæus returned to Thessaly). Herod. VII, 94. Euripid. Ion, v. 59 ff. (according to which Ion is the son of Apollo and Kreusa, but adopted by Xuthus). But Achæus at the same time passed for a Pelasgian, see Introduction obs. 10, cf. also Paus. loc. cit., which makes the sons of Achæus, Archandrus and Architeles, come from Thessaly to Argos in the time of Danaus; but even the Ionians are looked upon by Herodotus as Pelasgians, see I, 56. VII, 94. Such a proof as the genealogy, which connected the Ionians and Achæans with the Hellenic stock, had by no means found full or universal recognition.

13) Ion (who, according to Conon Narrat. 27, was also made king of Attica) is held to be the founder of the four Athenian tribes (φυλαί), see Herod. V, 66: τετραφύλους ἐόντας Ἀθηναίους δεκαφύλους (ὁ Κλεισθένης) ἐποίησε, τῶν Ἴωνος παίδων Γελέοντος καὶ Αἰγικόρεος καὶ Ἀργάδεω καὶ Ὅπλητος ἀπαλλάξας τὰς ἐπωνυμίας. Cf. Euripid. Ion v. 1579 ff. Pollux VIII, 109. Plut. Solon. 23. The names of the four tribes: Γελέοντες (other readings: Τελέοντες, Γεθέοντες), Ὅπλητες, Αἰγικορεῖς, Ἀργαδεῖς.

14) See Apollod. II, 4, 1—5. Paus. II, 16. Schol. Apollon. IV, 1091. After Perseus had escaped the machinations of his grandfather, who in consequence of an oracle apprehended death at his hands, and had performed marvellous exploits in other lands (cutting off Medusa's head, rescuing Andromeda), he returned to Argos, sought out his grandfather in Pelasgiotis, who had retired thither to avoid him, killed him unintentionally by a quoit-throw, then, returning to the Peloponnese, exchanged Argos, which had been rendered distasteful to him by his grandfather's death, for the territory of Tiryns, the heritage of Megapenthes the son of Prœtus; there he built himself a new town and citadel, Mykenæ. Important remains of both are still in existence: of the citadel, the gate with two lions represented in relief above it; of the town, besides other less important ruins, the so-called treasure-house of Atreus. On this point cf. Paus. loc. cit. § 4 and 5.

6   FIRST PERIOD.   From the Earliest Times to the Migration of the Dorians and Herakleidæ.

B. C.	(LEGENDARY) HISTORY.	of the Hellenes.	GENEA
		Dorus.	
1266	Immigration of Pelops from Asia Minor into Elis¹⁵).	....	
1233	....	Ægimius¹⁹).	
1225	Argonautic Expedition¹⁷).		
1213	Expedition of the Seven against Thebes²⁰).		
1200	....	Pamphylus, Dymas.	

15) Pelops was, according to the (later) legend, the son of Tantalus, king of Mysia, or Phrygia, or Lydia, or Paphlagonia, Paus. II, 22, 4. V, 13, 4. Diodor. IV, 74. Strab. p. 571. 580. Schol. Pind. Ol. I, 27. Expelled from his home by Ilus, the king of Troas, he comes to Pisa, conquers the king Œnomaus in a chariot race, and wins, as the prize of his victory, the king's daughter Hippodameia and his kingdom Elis, see esp. Pindar. Ol. 1, 67 ff. Paus. V, 17, 4. 10, 2. VI, 21, 9. Homer knows Tantalus Od. XI, 581, and also πλήξιππος Pelops, Il. II, 104, but knows nothing of the descent of Pelops from Tantalus or of his immigration into Greece. For the proverbial wealth and power of Pelops see Thuc. I, 9; Αἰγοσσι δὲ καὶ οἱ τὰ σαφέστατα Πελοποννησίων μνήμη παρὰ τῶν πρότερον δεδεγμένοι Πέλοπά τε πρῶτον πλήθει χρημάτων, ἃ ἦλθεν ἐκ τῆς Ἀσίας ἔχων ἐς ἀνθρώπους ἀπόρους, δύναμιν περιποιησάμενον τὴν ἐπωνυμίαν τῆς χώρας ἐπηλύτην ὄντα ὅμως σχεῖν καὶ ὕστερον τοῖς ἐκγόνοις ἔτι μείζω ξυνενεχθῆναι—. For the name Peloponnese cf. Int. obs. 10.

16) King Pandion II, according to the legend, divided his kingdom (which also comprised Eubœa and Megaris) amongst his four sons mentioned above; Ægeus, as the eldest, received Kekropia; Nisus the Isthmus and Megaris; Lykus Marathon with Eubœa; Pallas the mountainous district in the east and south of the peninsula (cf. the distribution of the country into 4 parts, Aktœa, Mesogœa, Paralia, Diakris, Pollux VIII, 109), see Sophokles in Strab. p. 392. Schol. Aristoph. Lysistr. 58. Lykus was expelled by Ægeus, Herod. I, 173; Nisus lost his life through an invasion of king Minos of Krete, Apollod. III, 15, 8, in which Megaris was also taken, and Ægeus compelled to pay a tribute (consisting of 7 youths and 7 maidens, who had to be sent every nine years to Krete, there to be sacrificed to the Minotaur), Apollod. loc. cit. Plut. Thes. 15. Paus. I, 27, 9.

17) Herakles, the son of Zeus and Alkmene, connected both by Alkmene and Amphitryon with the Perseid family, was born at Thebes, Hom. Il. XIX, 97 ff.; for Amphitryon had killed his uncle and father-in-law Elektryon, and had therefore fled from Mykenæ, see Hesiod, Scut. Herc. v. 11. 60. Hated and persecuted by Hera, he was in consequence of a rash oath of Zeus (see Hom. Il. loc. cit.) compelled to serve Eurystheus, a far paltrier man, by whose orders he performed difficult and demeaning tasks, Hom. Il. VIII, 362. Of these tasks Homer only mentions one, that he fetched up the hound of Hades from the lower world and brought it to Mykenæ, Il. V, 395. Odyss. XI, 622; further, reference is made in Homer to the murder of Iphitos, Od. XXI, 22—30, to the murder of the sons of Nestor, Il. XI, 690 ff., and to his expedition against Troy, Il. XX, 145. XXI, 442; Homer knows nothing of the later legends of his death, see Il. XVIII, 115. Od. XI, 600 ff. In Hesiod mention is found of some few other legends, e.g. that of the Nemean lion, Theog. 326—332, of the Lernæan hydra,

id. 314 ff., of the oxen of Geryones, id. 287, of the slaughter of the eagle, which devoured the liver of Prometheus, id. 530, and of Kyknus, Sc. Herc. 122 ff. All else belongs to the further development of the myth; which process was completed, partly under Phœnician influence (of Melkarth), partly in conformity with new ideas springing up amongst the Hellenes themselves; hence the twelve labours, the motive of the bondage under Eurystheus, the voluntary death by burning on Œta (Soph. Trachin.), etc. The whole myth is presented in its most perfect form in the connected arrangement of the various details by Apollodorus II, ch. 4, 5 to ch. 7. Cf. also Xen. Mem. II, 1, 21.

18) With Atreus the sovereignty of Mykenæ passed from the Perseidæ to the Pelopidæ. That is to say, Sthenelus married Nikippe, the daughter of Pelops, Apollod. II, 4, 5, and made over the sovereignty of Midas to the two sons of Pelops, Atreus and Thyestes; see id. § 6. But when Eurystheus marched to Attica against the Herakleidæ regent, then to be the successor of Eurystheus, see Thuc. I, 9. The sovereignty of Mykenæ next passed to Agamemnon, the elder son of Atreus, while the younger son through his marriage with Helena, the daughter of Tyndareus (Apollod. III, 10, 6. 7), became possessed of Sparta. For the genealogy of the Atridæ see Hom. Il. II, 105 ff.; for their power see the continuation of the passage quoted from Thucydides in obs. 15, (I, 9):—καὶ τῶν Περσειδῶν τοὺς Πελοπίδας μείζους καταστῆναι· ἅ μοι δοκεῖ Ἀγαμέμνων παραλαβὼν καὶ ναυτικῷ ἅμα ἐπὶ πλέον τῶν ἄλλων ἰσχύσας τὴν στρατιὰν οὐ χάριτι τὸ πλεῖον ἢ φόβῳ ξυναγαγὼν ποιήσασθαι· φαίνεται γὰρ ναυσί τε πλείοσιν αὐτὸς ἀφικόμενος καὶ Ἀρκάδι προσπαρασχών, ὡς Ὅμηρος τοῦτο δεδήλωκεν (Il. II, 576, 610), εἴ τῳ ἱκανὸς τεκμηριῶσαι· καὶ ἐν τοῦ σκήπτρου ἅμα τῇ παραδόσει εἴρηκεν αὐτὸν πολλῇσι νήσοισι καὶ Ἀργεῖ παντὶ ἀνάσσειν (Il. II, 108). οὐκ ἂν οὖν νήσων ἔξω τῶν περιοικίδων (αὗται δ᾽ οὐκ ἂν πολλαὶ εἴησαν) ἠπειρώτης ὢν ἐκράτει, εἰ μή τι καὶ ναυτικὸν εἶχεν.

19) Herakles assisted the Dorian Ægimius (or Æpalius, Strab. p. 427) in the struggle against the Lapithæ; in return for which Ægimius, conformably to the condition laid down by Herakles, adopted his son Hyllus and made over to him the third part of his territory and the succession to the throne, Apollod. II, 7, 7. Diod. IV, 37. Pind. Pyth. I, 62. V, 66. Hence the union of the Dorians and Herakleidæ, and hence too the division of the Dorians into the three tribes of the Υλλεῖς, Πάμφυλοι and Δυμᾶνες, see Herod. V, 68. Steph. Byz. s. v. Δυμᾶνες.

20) Theseus, son of Ægeus (or Poseidon) and Æthra the daughter of king Pittheus of Trœzen, see Apollod. III, 16, 1. Plut. Thes. 3. Paus. I, 27, 8, was brought up in Trœzen: then, on his way to Athens, he slew Periphetes, Sinis, the Krommyonian sow, Skiron, Kerkyon,

X—1104 B.C.   PREHISTORIC AGE.   7

LOGY
of the most illustrious royal families in Argos, Athens, and Thebes.

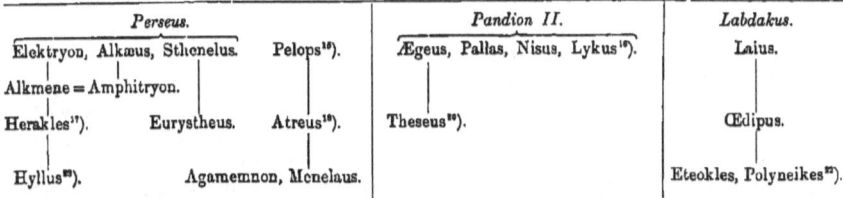

Damastes or Prokrustes, Plut. Thes. 6—11; then subdued and exterminated the Pallantidæ, the sons of Pallas (see obs. 16), Plut. 13, caught the Marathonian bull, Plut. 14. Paus. I, 27, 9, next slew the Minotaur and thereby put an end to the tribute (obs. 16), Plut. 15—22, cf. Hom. Od. XI, 321. Schol. Hom. Il. XVIII, 590; and when, after the death of Ægeus, he had himself come to the sovereignty, he made Athens the central point and seat of government for the whole country, by abolishing the deliberative assemblies in the single districts as hitherto constituted, and combining them in the Prytaneium at Athens (συνοικισμός, feast of the συνοίκια and of the πανάθηναια), Plut. 24. Thuc. II, 15; invited strangers to Athens and founded the feast of the μετοίκια, Plut. loc. cit.; divided the people into the three orders of the εὐπατρίδαι, γεωμόροι and δημιουργοί, Plut. 25, furthermore conquered the Amazons, who had invaded Attica, Plut. 26. 27. Paus. I, 2, 1. 17, 2. Æsch. Eumen. 685, reduced Megaris again to subjection, and founded the Isthmian games, Plut. 25; but was nevertheless, in spite of these heroic deeds and services (he is said also to have wished to set aside the monarchy and to introduce a democracy, Plut. 25. Thuc. II, 15), during his absence with his friend and comrade Peirithous in the attempt to carry off Kora for the latter, Plut. 31. Apollod. III, 10, 7, supplanted in the sovereignty by Muestheus, who stirred up the nobles against him; finally he died in Skyros, Plut. 30—35. For the succession of kings, see p. 12, obs. 9.

21) In the legend of the voyage of the Argonauts the scene is laid at Iolkus and Halus on the Pagasæan Gulf, which in consequence of their favourable situation (see Int.) had probably at a very early time raised themselves, like Corinth, to great prosperity by commerce and sea-traffic, and attained great wealth; and for this very reason necessarily recommended themselves to the Phœnicians as places to settle at. In Halus (Herod. VII, 197. Strab. p. 433, or perhaps in Orchomenus, Paus. IX, 34, 5) dwelt Athamas, king of the Minyæ, son of Æolus (Hesiod in Tzetzes ad Lykophr. 284. Apollod. 1, 7, 3), who by Nephele begot Phrixus and Helle, and afterwards Learchus and Melikertes by Ino (cf. obs. 8). After his death he was succeeded by his brother Kretheus, of whose 5 sons, Pelias, Neleus, Æson, Pheres, Amythaon (Hom. Od. XI, 254, ff.), the first mentioned made Iolkus the seat of his rule, and from hence despatched Jason, son of Æson, whom he had robbed of his share in the sovereignty, to fetch back the golden fleece of Phrixus. This is the outline or framework, in which the Argonaut legend is set; and for it see Hom. Il. VII, 467. Od. XII, 69—72. Hesiod Theog. 955—962. 991—1003. Fragm. 65. 86. 111. 114. 145. 183. Pindar. Pyth. IV. Herod. 1, 2. IV, 179. VII, 197. Apollod. I, 9. Paus. IX, 34, 4. I, 44, 11. By degrees all celebrated heroes of the time were claimed by the legend as participators in the voyage: besides Argus, the builder of the ship Argo, Herakles, Orpheus, Kastor and Polydeukes, Theseus, Peleus, Telamon, Idas and Lynkeus, Zetes and Kalais, Meleagrus etc., see Apoll. I, 9, 16. The goal of the expedition, at first conceived only as at an indefinite distance, becomes

fixed, in proportion as the east (after the VIIIth century) becomes better known, and so the route is described with increasing exactness with the chief stations Lemnos, Lampsakus, Kyzikus, Heraklcia, Sinope. But at the same time all that the Greeks knew of legendary sea-voyages and sea-adventures, was gradually incorporated in the legend, so especially by Apollonius (circ. 200 B.C.) in his epic poem, the Argonautica. The connexion of the Argonautic legend with Phœnician influence, besides the name Melikertes and the adoration paid to Melikertes as to a god, is still further attested by the intended sacrifice of Phrixus and Helle, by the common belief at Halus, which, as the sequel of the meditated crime, was still retained in the fifth century, that if the head of the house of the Athamantidæ allowed himself to be seen in the Prytaneium there, he must be sacrificed to Zeus Laphystius (i. e. the devourer), Herod. VII, 197, and by the close connexion of the legend with Lemnos, a chief centre of Phœnician settlements, etc.

22) The genealogy of the house of Kadmus, see Herod. V, 59—61. Apollod. III, 4, 2. 5, 5 ff. Paus. IX, 3. The Œdipus legend—for the earlier and simpler form of which, differing in several points from the later, see Hom. Od. XI, 271—280. Il. XXIII, 680. Paus. IX, 5, 5. Pind. Ol. II, 43—45—was afterwards expanded and recast by the tragic poets in the form in which it appears, notably in the 'Seven against Thebes' of Æschylus, in the 'Œdipus Rex' and the 'Œdipus at Kolonus' of Sophokles, and in the 'Phœnissæ' of Euripides; also in the compilation of Apollodorus, III, 5, 7—9. For the expedition of the Seven, with regard to which there are found, even in Homer, several details chiefly concerned with Tydeus, Il. IV, 376. V, 802. X, 285, see the collection of the various legends, Apollod. III, 6. The names of the Seven: Adrastus (for whom see Herod. V, 67. Pind. Nem. IX, 25—65, grandson of Bias), Amphiaraus (who was enticed by his wife Eriphyle to take part in the war, Hom. Od. XI, 327, great-grandson of Melampus; but Bias and Melampus, grandsons of Kretheus, the son of Æolus, were by Prœtus placed in possession, each of a third, of the kingdom of Argos, Herod. IX, 34. Apollod. II, 2, 2. Paus. II, 18, 4. Diod. IV, 86), Kapaneus (the descendant of Prœtus in the fourth generation), Hippomedon, Parthenopæus, Tydeus, Polyneikes, see Apollod. III, 6, 3. On the way to Thebes the Nemean games were founded, Apollod. id. § 4.

23) Herakles had entrusted his children to Keyx, the sovereign of Trachis. But at the demand of Eurystheus he sent them away to Theseus, with whom they found shelter and protection. In consequence of this, Eurystheus invaded Attica, but was defeated in a battle on the field of Marathon, and killed, see Apollod. II, 8, 1. Paus. I, 32, 5. 44, 14. Herod. IX, 27. Thuc. I, 9. Cf. Strab. p. 377. Diod. IV, 57. Hyllus, after waiting in compliance with the oracle for the third harvest, thereupon marched towards the Peloponnese, to subdue his heritage, the kingdom of the Perseidæ, but was slain at the Isthmus in a duel with Echemus of Tegea, see Herod. IX, 26. Apollod. II, 8, 2. Paus. I, 41, 3. 44, 14. VIII, 5, 1. 45, 2. Diod. IV, 58.

8   FIRST PERIOD.   From the Earliest Times to the Migration of the Dorians and Herakleidæ.

B. C.	(LEGENDARY) HISTORY.
1200	
1198	Expedition of the Epigoni against Thebes[24]).
1193—1184[25])	Trojan War[26]).
1166	
1183	
1124	Invasion of the Thessalians into what is now called Thessaly; the Bœotians expelled from Arne in Thessaly[27]).
1104	The Dorians under the conduct of the Herakleidæ, Temenus, Aristodemus, and Kresphontes in the Peloponnese; the Ætolians under Oxylus in Elis[28]).

24) According to Apollodor. III, 7, 2 the expedition of the Epigoni was ten years later than that of the Seven; yet on account of Hom. Il. VI, 222, we must suppose an interval of at least 15 years. Those taking part in the expedition are the sons of the Seven (hence Epigoni), viz. Ægialeus, son of Adrastus, Diomedes, son of Tydeus, Sthenelus, son of Kapaneus, Promachus of Parthenopæus, Thersandrus of Polyneikes, Alkmæon of Amphiaraus. The last named is the leader of the expedition; and Thebes is taken after the flight of Laodamas, son of Eteokles. Thersandrus is made king of Thebes. See Herod. V, 61. Apollod. III, 7, 2—4. Paus. IX, 5, 7. 8, 3. Cf. Hom. Il. IV, 406. Pindar Pyth. VIII, 41 ff.

25) The date as determined above rests upon the testimony of Eratosthenes (in the second half of the third century B. C.) and Apollodorus, see Clem. Alex. Strom. I, 21, p. 402: Ἐρατοσθένης τοὺς χρόνους ὦδε ἀναγράφει· Ἀπὸ μὲν Τροίας ἁλώσεως ἐπὶ Ἡρακλειδῶν κάθοδον ἔτη ὀγδοήκοντα, ἐντεῦθεν δὲ ἐπὶ τῆς Ἰωνίας κτίσιν ἔτη ἐξήκοντα, τὰ δὲ τούτοις ἑξῆς ἐπὶ μὲν τὴν ἐπιτροπίαν τὴν Λυκούργου ἔτη ἑκατὸν πεντήκοντα ἐννέα, ἐπὶ δὲ προηγούμενον ἔτος τῶν πρώτων Ὀλυμπίων ἔτη ἑκατὸν ὀκτώ, accordingly 776 + 108 + 150 + 60 + 80 = 1183; Diodor. I, 5: Ἀπὸ δὲ τῶν Τρωϊκῶν ἀκολούθως Ἀπολλοδώρῳ τῷ Ἀθηναίῳ τίθεμεν ὀγδοήκοντα ἔτη πρὸς τὴν κάθοδον τῶν Ἡρακλειδῶν, ἀπὸ δὲ ταύτης ἐπὶ τὴν πρώτην Ὀλυμπιάδα δυσὶ λείποντα τῶν τριακοσίων καὶ τράκοντα, συλλογιζόμενοι τοὺς χρόνους ἀπὸ τῶν ἐν Λακεδαίμονι βασιλευσάντων, consequently 776 + 328 + 80 = 1184, so too id. XIV, 2, 3. XIX, 1. Dionys. Hal. I, 74. One of these numbers we find also in Thuc. I, 12, and thus the date of the Trojan war adopted above appears to have been the foundation, or at least an essential part, of a widely extended chronological system for the history of the earliest period. Yet many different accounts are found. Thus 1217—1208, Marm. Par., about 1280, Herod. II, 145, cf. II, 13, etc. (The discrepancy Thuc. V, 112 is only apparent, reference there being only made to round numbers.) Starting from another basis, the dates given for the Trojan war and likewise the succeeding events would be brought down about one hundred years later, see p. 14, obs. a.

26) For the oath, which Tyndareus exacted from the suitors for the hand of his daughter Helena, as occasion of the Trojan war, see Apollod. III, 10, 7—9, cf. Thuc. I, 9: Ἀγαμέμνων τέ μοι δοκεῖ τῶν τότε δυνάμει προύχων καὶ οὐ τοσοῦτον τοῖς Τυνδάρεω ὅρκοις κατειλημμένους τοὺς Ἑλένης μνηστῆρας ἄγων τὸν στόλον ἀγεῖραι. The chief heroes of the war on the side of the Greeks (who are comprehended in Homer under the collective names of Δαναοί, Ἀργεῖοι, Ἀχαιοί, see Thuc. I, 3) are, besides Agamemnon and Menelaus, Achilles, son of Peleus, the sovereign of Phthia, Nestor of Pylus, Odysseus of Ithaka, Ajax, Telamon's son, from the island of Salamis, Diomedes, son of Tydeus, Sthenelus, son of Kapaneus, Ajax, son of Oileus, Idomeneus, from the island of Krete, etc. Priam was the king of the Trojans, and his family was descended from Dardanus (Dardanus—Erichthonius—Iros—Ilus—Laomedon—Priam). On their side only Hektor and Æneas stand prominently forward as heroes, the former a son of Priam, the latter of Anchises (Tros—Assarakus—Kapys—Anchises). The Trojans were moreover assisted by Phrygians, Lykians, Mæonians, Thrakians, and even by Pæonians from the banks of the Axius. On the strength of the Greek forces Thucydides makes the following observation, I, 10: νομίζειν δὲ (εἰκὸς) τὴν στρατιὰν ἐκείνην μεγίστην μὲν γενέσθαι τῶν πρὸ αὐτῆς, λειπομένην δὲ τῶν νῦν, τῇ Ὁμήρου αὖ ποιήσει εἴ τι χρὴ κἀνταῦθα πιστεύειν, ἣν εἰκὸς ἐπὶ τὸ μεῖζον μὲν ποιητὴν ὄντα κοσμῆσαι, ὅμως δὲ φαίνεται καὶ οὕτως ἐνδεεστέρα· πεποίηκε γὰρ χιλίων καὶ διακοσίων νεῶν (more exactly 1186), τὰς μὲν Βοιωτῶν εἴκοσι καὶ ἑκατὸν ἀνδρῶν (II, II, 510), τὰς δὲ Φιλοκτήτου πεντήκοντα (id. 719), δηλῶν ὡς ἐμοὶ δοκεῖ τὰς μεγίστας καὶ ἐλαχίστας, according to which the number of the combatants amounted to some 100,000 men; to this, according to Hom. Il. II, 123 ff., the number of the Trojans was in the proportion of 1 to 10. The political relations of the Greeks appear in Homer such as we find them later in the monarchical period in the Hellenic states in general, and in that of Sparta in particular; only that in Homer they are nowhere circumscribed, and nowhere rest on laws or other settled principles, but everywhere come under divine ordinance. A king stands everywhere at the head (οὐκ ἀγαθὸν πολυκοιρανίη, εἷς κοίρανος ἔστω, Il. II, 204), of divine descent (διογενεῖς βασιλῆες), to whom, as such, there belonged by way of provision a public estate (τέμενος), and to whom men brought complimentary presents and portions of the spoil (γέρατα, δωτίναι, δῶρα, θέμιστες); near, but subordinate to him, were the nobles forming his council (γέροντες, μέδοντες, ἡγήτορες, ἄριστοι, βασιλῆες, ἄνακτες); lastly the people, which was assembled, yet not by any settled rule, and only to hear the resolution of the king and his council; besides these classes of perfectly free persons, there were still the θῆτες and δμῶες, the latter either taken as spoil in war or bought of pirates. Very noticeably, mention is made of Phratries and Phylæ in the following passage: κρῖν' ἄνδρας κατὰ φῦλα, κατὰ φρήτρας, Ἀγάμεμνον, ὡς φρήτρη φρήτρηφιν ἀρήγῃ, φῦλα δὲ φύλοις, Il. II, 362.

27) For the determination of the date see obs. 25. For the event see Thuc. I, 12: καὶ μετὰ τὰ Τρωϊκὰ ἡ Ἑλλὰς ἔτι μετανίστατό τε καὶ κατῳκίζετο ὥστε μὴ ἡσυχάσασα αὐξηθῆναι· ἥ τε γὰρ ἀναχώρησις τῶν Ἑλλήνων ἐξ

X—1104 B.C. PREHISTORIC AGE.

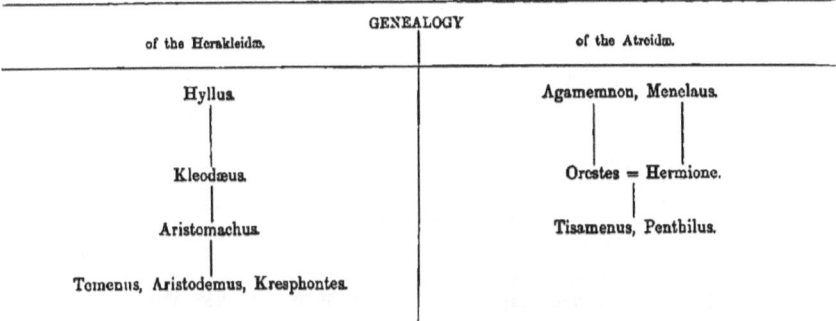

GENEALOGY of the Herakleidæ. | GENEALOGY of the Atreidæ.

Hyllus — Agamemnon, Menelaus.

Kleodæus — Orestes = Hermione.

Aristomachus — Tisamenus, Penthilus.

Temenus, Aristodemus, Kresphontes.

Ἰλίου χρονία γενομένη πολλὰ ἐνεόχμωσε καὶ στάσεις ἐν ταῖς πόλεσιν ὧν ἐπὶ πολὺ ἐγίγνοντο, ἀφ᾽ ὧν ἐκπίπτοντες τὰς πόλεις ἔκτιζον. Βοιωτοί τε γὰρ οἱ νῦν ἐξηκοστῷ ἔτει μετὰ Ἰλίου ἅλωσιν ἐξ Ἄρνης ἀναστάντες ὑπὸ Θεσσαλῶν τὴν νῦν Βοιωτίαν, πρότερον δὲ Καδμηΐδα γῆν καλουμένην ᾤκισαν, ἦν δὲ αὐτῶν καὶ ἀποδασμὸς πρότερον ἐν τῇ γῇ ταύτῃ, ἀφ᾽ ὧν καὶ ἐς Ἴλιον ἐστράτευσαν. The Thessalians, coming from Thesprotia (Herod. VII, 176; Θεσσαλοὶ ἦλθον ἐκ Θεσπρωτῶν οἰκήσοντες γῆν τὴν Αἰολίδα, τήνπερ νῦν ἐκτέαται), established themselves in the country, which now first received from them the name Thessaly, see id., and expelled the Arnæans from the valley of the Sperchelus, the latter throwing themselves into Bœotia and taking possession of it, see Thuc. loc. cit. Diod. IV, 67. Paus. X, 8, 3. Strab. p. 401; they further expelled the Dorians dwelling on Pindus, who in their turn expel the Dryopes dwelling on the southern slope of Œta, and found here the so called Doric tetrapolis, see Herod. I, 56. VIII, 78. Paus. IV, 34, 6.

28) Aristomachus, the grandson of Hyllus, in the third fruit of the oracle (see obs. 23) more correctly discerning the third generation, renewed the expedition against the Peloponnese, but, mistaking the direction of the oracle, that he should pass into the land "by way of the sea-strait," took his way over the Isthmus, and was in consequence defeated and slain. His son Temenus with his brothers and the Dorians now marched to the promontory of Antirrhium, there built ships (hence Naupaktus, see Ephorus in Strab. p. 426), and crossed over to the Peloponnese, conducted by the "three-eyed guide," the Ætolian Oxylus (Ephor. in Strab. p. 357). There Tisamenus was defeated in a great battle; whereupon Temenus took possession of Argos, Aristodemus of Sparta, Kresphontes of Messenia, see Thuc. I, 12. Herod. I, 56. VI, 52. Isocr. Archidam. p. 119. Ephor. in Strab. p. 357. Apollod. II, 8. Paus. II, 18, 6. V, 3, 5. Oxylus with the consent of the Herakleidæ took possession of the land of the Epeians, after the Ætolian Pyrrechmes had there defeated the Epeian Degmenus in a duel, see Ephor. loc. cit. Paus. V, 4. Tisamenus with the Achæans turned to the land now called Achaia, and overthrew the Ionians: whereupon the Achæans established themselves in the country, Paus. II, 18, 7. VII, 1, 3. Herod. I, 145. VIII, 73. Polyb. II, 41, 4. Strab. p. 383.

int
SECOND PERIOD.

1104—500 B. C.

THE AGE OF THE INNER DEVELOPMENT OF THE HELLENES.

When the Dorians had permanently established themselves and their empire in the Peloponnese, the movement, which had hitherto continued almost uninterruptedly, subsided in the rest of Greece also. In consequence, an impulse makes way in the several states, leading men to develope and determine their internal organisation. In most states monarchy is speedily abolished. Its place is taken by an aristocratic constitution: this, as a rule, degenerates and is overthrown. Then, after a short interruption of the natural development by tyranny, the tendency to democracy begins to assert itself in a large number of instances. At the same time the consciousness of unity, the feeling of nationality, gradually grows up in all the Greek states. This result is chiefly due to two causes: firstly, to the extension and growing importance of the Hellenic Dorians; and, secondly, to the influence of the national games and Delphic oracle. Colonies spread the influence and commercial dealings of Greece beyond the boundaries of the country, and draw the surrounding coasts of the Mediterranean into the circle of Hellenic life.

During this period Greek literature, following in its peculiar development the laws of an inherent necessity, takes its commencement with epic and lyric poetry: whilst art cannot as yet free itself from the fetters of the traditional and symbolic, and so its advances are at first confined to mere technical acquirement.

Obs. The authorities are in general the same as in the former period. The most important information for this period is to be found above all in Herodotus; but still—with the exception of Plutarch, whose biographies of Lykurgus and Solon belong to this age—we have little to go upon except scattered notices. For the Greek colonies these notices are to be looked for, besides Herodotus and Strabo, chiefly in the Περιήγησις of the so called Skymnus of Chios (ed. Meineke), and in an excerpt from the geographical lexicon ('Εθνικά) of Stephanus of Byzantium (Vth saecl. A. D.); for the national games and questions connected with them Pindar and the Scholiasts on that author yield plenty of material; for the constitutional history the Politika of Aristotle are the most important and instructive authority.—We have only very scanty information about the three centuries, which lie between the migration of the Dorians and the first Olympiad, and to a certain extent form the boundary line between mythical and historical Greece.

FIRST SECTION.

1104—776 B.C.

FROM THE DORIAN MIGRATION TO THE FIRST OLYMPIAD. DEVELOPMENT OF THE CONSEQUENCES OF THE DORIAN MIGRATION.

B.C.	(LEGENDARY) HISTORY.
1104	Temenus, king of Argos[1]), Aristodemus, king of Sparta[2]), Kresphontes, king of Messenia[3]). Aristodemus dies, and leaves the sovereignty to his twin-sons Eurysthenes and Prokles, the forefathers of the two royal houses of Sparta[4]).

1) According to Apollod. II, 8, 4. Paus. IV, 3, 3, the possession of the three countries Argolis, Messenia, and Laconia, was decided by lot between Temenus, Kresphontes, and the sons of Aristodemus (see obs. 2), cf. Eurip. in Strab. p. 366. Polyæn. I, 6. Schol. Soph. Aj. 1271. Still the countries did not by any means come at once into the full and unqualified possession of the conquerors. In Argolis Temenus fortified Temenium in the neighbourhood of Argos; and from this place he carried on the war against Tisamenus and the Achæans, and so gained Argos, see Paus. II, 38, 1. cf. Strab. p. 368. Polyæn. II, 12. As for the further history of Argos we may now observe, that Temenus was murdered by his sons, Apollod. II, 8, 5. Paus. II, 19, 2, and that of his successors upon the throne we have the following mentioned (besides Pheidon, for whom see obs. 28): Keisus, Medon,.....Lakides,..... Meltas, with whom the kingship at Argos (probably not before the fifth century B.C., see Herod. VII, 149) ended, see Paus. II, 19, 2. Cf. id.: Ἀργείοι δὲ ἅτε ἰσηγορίαν καὶ τὸ αὐτόνομον ἀγαπῶντες ἐκ παλαιοτάτου τὰ τῆν ἐξουσίαν τῶν βασιλέων ἐς ἐλάχιστον προήγαγον, ὡς Μηδωνι τῷ Κείσου καὶ τοῖς ἀπογόνοις τὸ ὄνομα λειφθῆναι τῆς βασιλείας μόνον. Μέλταν δὲ τὸν Λακίδου τὸν ἀπόγονον Μήδωνος τὸ παράπαν ἔπαυσεν ἀρχῆς καταγνοὺς ὁ δῆμος. According to Herod. I, 82, the whole east coast of Lakonia (therefore Kynuria also) belonged originally to the territory of Argos, which for several centuries stood at the head of the Dorian states of the peninsula.

2) This according to Hesiod, VI, 52 was the view adopted by the Spartans themselves, whilst "the poets" (and after them most of the later authors, see Xen. Ages. VIII, 7. Apollod. II, 8, 2. Strab. p. 364. Paus. III, 1, 5. IV, 3, 3, etc.) made Aristodemus die before this, and only the sons enter upon the occupation of Sparta. According to Ephor. in Strab. p. 364, 365, Lakonia to begin with was distributed into six parts, and the former inhabitants were allowed to remain in possession of their homes with the same privileges as the conquerors, but were afterwards reduced to subjection under Agis the son of Eurysthenes. According to Paus. III, 2, 6 Ægys was first made subject under Archelaus; Amyklæ, Pharis, Geranthræ under Teleklus; and Helos, according to § 7 id., not till the reign of Alkamenes.

3) Kresphontes gained Messenia by a stipulation with the former inhabitants, who recognised his sovereignty (with the exception of the Neleidæ of Pylus, who emigrated to Athens, see obs. 9), and to whom in return he ceded equal privileges with the Dorians; he made Stenyklarus his capital, where accordingly the Dorians chiefly resided. See Ephor. in Strab. p. 361. Paus. IV, 3, 3. He was afterwards killed, together with the whole of his family, by the discontented Dorians; only one of his sons Œpytus was saved, and he succeeded his father on the throne, Paus. loc. cit. § 5. Apollod. II, 8, 5. The succeeding kings up to the first Messenian war are Glaukus, Isthmius, Dotadas, Sybotas, Phintas, Antiochus and Androkles, Euphaes, Paus. IV, 3, 5. 6. 4, 1. 3. 5, 2. For the nature of the country as compared with Lakonia see Eurip. in Strab. 366: τὴν Λακωνικὴν φησιν ἔχειν "πολὺν μὲν ἄροτον, ἐκπονεῖν δ᾽ οὐ ῥᾴδιον, κοίλη γὰρ, ὄρεσι περίδρομος, τραχεῖά τε δυσείσβολός τε πολεμίοις," τὴν δὲ Μεσσηνιακὴν "καλλίκαρπον κατάρρυτον τε μυρίοισι ῥέμασι καὶ βουσὶ καὶ ποίμναισι εὐβοτωτάτην οὖτ᾽ ἐν πνοαῖσι χείματος δυσχείμερον οὔτ᾽ αὖ τεθρίπποις ἡλίου θερμὴν ἄγαν."

4) For the reason why both twins (who were only born in this year) were made kings, so that in consequence the kingship, for the future also, remained divided between the descendants of both, see Herod. VI, 52; still the house of Eurysthenes was the more important and ranked higher, see id. 51. Yet neither of the royal houses was named after these progenitors, but one after Agis, the son of Eurysthenes, the other after Eurypon, the grandson of Prokles (Agidæ or Agiadæ and Eurypontidæ), see Paus. III, 2, 1. 7, 1. Plut. Lyc. 2. They were placed during their minority under the guardianship of their uncle, Theras, and, when they had grown up, were continually disagreeing amongst themselves, Herod. VI, 52. Paus. III, 1, 6, and so too their descendants, Herod. loc. cit. Arist. Pol. II, 6. The succession of kings here recorded (which is of some value and interest as one of the chief points on which the chronology is based) is chiefly founded upon Pausan. III, 2—10. Herod. VII, 204. VIII, 131, and, as regards the duration of their reigns, upon Eusebius Chron. Arm. ed. A. Mai I, 166, ed Schöne II, p. 58 ff. (following Apollodorus, Müller, fragm. histor. Græc. I, p. 443 f.).

SECOND PERIOD. 1104—500 B.C.

B. C.	DORIANS.	ATHENS.	COLONIES.
			1) *Doric:*
1074	Corinth made subject by Aletes to Dorian rule[5]). From Argos, directly or indirectly, Sikyon, Trœzen, Epidaurus, and Ægina are dorised.		Thera[7]).
1066	Megara Dorian[6]).	Death of Kodrus, abolition of the monarchy, institution of archons holding office for life and chosen from the family of the Neleidæ[9]).	Melos[10]), Kos with Kalydnus and Nisyrus, Knidus, Halikarnassus, Rhodes, several towns in Krete[11]).

5) Aletes was the son of Hippotes, who derived his descent from Antiochus, the son of Herakles (Herakles—Antiochus—Phylas—Hippotes—Aletes), see Paus. II, 4, 3. Diod. in Syncell. p. 176. C. According to Didymus in Schol. Pind. Olymp. XIII, 17 the establishment of Doric rule in Corinth took place in the thirtieth year after the immigration of the Dorians. Hippotes had accompanied the expedition of the Dorians, but having killed the seer Karnus at Naupaktus had in consequence become a fugitive, see Conon. 26. Apollod. II, 8, 3. Paus. III, 13, 3. Aletes (so named from the flight and wandering of his father) conquered Corinth by entrenching himself, like Temenus at Temenium, upon the hill Solygeius near the town, and from here making war upon the city, see Thuc. IV, 42. The admission of the Dorians took place by way of compromise, and so the former inhabitants remained in their homes (they formed five tribes by the side of and subordinate to the three Dorian tribes, Suid. s. v. πάντα δενώ), see Paus. loc. cit. Here ten kings after Aletes held rule (the fifth of the number being Bakchis), and after this Prytanes, changing annually, till the time of Kypselus, see Paus. loc. cit. §. 4. Diod. loc. cit.

6) Sikyon by Phalkes, a son of Temenus, see Paus. II, 6, 4; Trœzen, as may be inferred from Ephor. in Strab. p. 389, by Agræus, another son of Temenus, see Paus. II, 30, 9: Epidaurus by Deiphontes, the son-in-law of Temenus, see Paus. II, 29, 5 cf 26, 3. From Epidaurus Ægina was then dorised, see Herod. VIII, 40, cf. V, 83. Paus. II, 29, 5 (by Triakon, Schol. Pind. Nem. III, 1. Tzetzes on Lyk. 176.). That these towns were at an earlier period in a manner dependencies of Argos, is proved by several relics of this relation preserved to a later time, see Herod. VI, 92. Thuc. V, 53.

7) The colony was led forth by Theras, a descendant of Kadmus and Œdipus, who, as uncle of the kings Eurysthenes and Prokles, filled the office of regent at Sparta, see obs. 4, and, after his occupation had come to an end, could not endure the thought of living there as a subject; the Minyæ, who had sought refuge in Sparta, attached themselves to him. The most important passage is Herod. IV, 145—149. cf. Callim. Hymn. in Ap. 74. Strab. p. 347. 484. Paus. III, 15, 4. VII, 2, 1. 2.

8) Herod. V, 76. Strab. p. 392—393. Paus. I, 39, 4. The expedition was made under the conduct of Aletes, Conon. 26. Schol. Pind. Nem. VII, 155.

9) Upon the death of Mnestheus, who had deprived Theseus of the sovereignty at Athens (see p. 11, obs. 20), the Theseidæ came back to the throne, and of this line there ruled in succession Demophon,

Oxyntes, Alpheidas, Thymœtes. But the latter was deposed for a display of cowardice upon an invasion of Attica by the Bœotians (see First Period, obs. 27). In his stead the Neleid Melanthus was raised to the throne, who with the rest of the Neleidæ had been driven out of Pylus by the Dorians (see obs. 3), and who now slew the leader of the enemy in a duel. See Paus. II, 18, 7. Strab. p. 393. Herod. V, 65. Ephor. fr. 25. Polyæn. I, 19. He was succeeded by his son Kodrus, who on the expedition of the Dorians against Athens rescued his country at the sacrifice of his life, and thereby at the same time gave occasion for the abolition of the monarchy. The most detailed account in Lykurg. adv. Leokr. p. 158. Cf. Herod. V, 76. Pherekyd. fr. 110. Polyæn. I, 18. Conon 26. Medon, a son of Kodrus, was the first of the archons.

10) According to Thuc. V, 84 the Melians were Λακεδαιμονίων ἄποικοι. According to Conon. 36 in Photius p. 445. Plut. Quæst. Græc. c. 21. Polyæn. VII, 49 the colony was founded by Achæmus, to whom Amyklæ was assigned as a dwelling-place in reward of the treachery of Philonomus. Part of the emigrants went still further to Gortyna in Krete.

11) Tradition in respect to the above mentioned Doric colonies is wavering and uncertain. In Homer we already find dwelling in Krete the Δωριέες τριχάϊκες, Odyss. XIX, 177, and hence the first Doric settlements are referred back to Tektamus or Tektaphus, a son of Dorus, see Diod. V, 80. Strab. p. 475—476. Steph. Byz. s. v. Δώριον. Later, after the death of Kodrus, the Herakleid Althæmenes goes from Megara to Krete, Strab. p. 653. cf. p. 479. This Althæmenes is then said to have gone to Rhodes and dorised it (the three towns Lindus, Kameirus, Ialysus) Ephor. in Strab. p. 479. Conon. 47. Diod. V, 59. Apollodor. III, 2. On the other hand, in Thuc. VII, 57 the Rhodians are called Ἀργεῖοι γένος and according to Strab. 645, simultaneously with the colony of Althæmenes, another colony, also from Megara, goes to Rhodes, Kos, Knidus, and Halikarnassus. Again the colonisation of Kos together with Kalydnus and Nisyrus is referred by Herodotus (VII, 99) to Epidaurus, that of Halikarnassus by the same author (loc. cit. cf. Strab. p. 656. Paus. II, 30, 8) to Trœzen: and the Knidians are called Λακεδαιμονίων ἄποικοι, Herod. I, 174. cf. Diod. V, 61. Paus. X, 11. Strab. p. 653. Of the whole number of Doric colonies mentioned above, the three towns of Rhodes, together with Kos, Knidus, and Halikarnassus, formed a league, the so called Doric Hexapolis, which had a common sanctuary upon the promontory of Triopium and there celebrated an annual alliance-feast: but Halikarnassus was afterwards expelled from it, see Herod. I, 144. Dionys. Hal. IV, 25.

The Age of the Inner Development of the Hellenes.

B.C.	SPARTA.		ARGOS.	COLONIES.	
	Agidæ:	*Eurypontidæ:*		2) *Æolic:*	3) *Ionic:*
1062	Agis.				
1054				Foundation of the 12 towns on the north-west coast of Asia Minor and of the towns on the islands, Lesbos, Tenedos, and Hekatonnesoi[11]).	
1053		.... Sous.			
1050				Kyme (Cumæ) in central Italy[14]).	
1044			Phlius dorised by Rhegnidas[13]).		Foundation of the twelve Ionic towns on the south-west coast of Asia Minor and in Chios and Samos under the conduct of sons of Kodrus[15]).

12) The foundation of the colonies is said to have been already begun by Orestes (on account of a plague, Demo in Schol. on Eurip. Rhes. v. 250), and to have been carried out after many long delays by Gras, the great grandson of Orestes (Orestes—Penthilus—Archelaus—Gras), and by Kloues and Malaus, who are called descendants of Agamemnon; it was to the former that the colonisation of Lesbos in particular ascribed, to the two latter that of Kyme, the most important of the towns on the continent, see Strab. p. 582. 621 (cf. Pind. Nem. XI, 34. Hellanikus in Tzetzes on Lykophr. 1374). The colonisation of Lesbos is placed 130 years after the destruction of Troy, that of Kyme 20 years later, (Ps.-) Plut. V. Homer. 30, cf. Hellan. loc. cit. The colonists stayed on their way in Bœotia, and were here joined by numerous (Æolian) Bœotians; hence the designation of the colonies as Æolic, Strab. p. 204, cf. Thuc. VII, 57. For the colonies themselves the most important notice is Herod. I, 149—151. The names of the twelve towns on the continent, which embrace the whole coast from Kyme to Abydus (see Ephorus in Strab. p. 600), are according to that passage as follows: Kyme, Larissa, Neon Teichos, Temnus, Killa, Notium, Ægiroessa, Pitane, Ægæ, Myrina, Grynela, Smyrna; the last was afterwards wrested from the Æolians by the Kolophonians and attached to the Ionic confederacy, Herod. loc. cit. Strab. p. 633; six towns were founded on Lesbos, Mytilene, Methymna, Antissa, Pyrrha, Eressus, and Arisba; of which the last-named was afterwards reduced to subjection by Methymna; one each on Tenedos and Hekatonnesoi, called by the same name as the island, Herod. loc. cit.

13) Rhegnidas was the son of Phalkes (see obs. 6) and grandson of Temenus. Submission was made by way of a compromise, so that the former inhabitants remained in their homes. See Paus. II, 13, 1. cf. 12, 6.

14) Founded by Kyme in Asia Minor and Chalkis in Eubœa, the oldest of the Hellenic colonies in Italy, and the oldest altogether outside the district of the Ægean sea, see Strab. p. 243. Vellei. Pat. I, n. Euseb. in Synkell. p. 360. (II, p. 60 ed. Schöne).

15) For the time of the foundation of these colonies see the important passages in Eratosthenes and Apollodorus, p. 12, obs. 25. For the colonies themselves and their foundation see esp. Herod. I, 142—148. Strab. p. 632 ff. As leaders of those colonies the sons of Kodrus occupy the most prominent position; Neleus, to whom the foundation of Miletus, is ascribed, Herod. IX, 97. Paus. VII, 2, 1. Ælian. V. H. VIII, 5. Strab. p. 633, and Androklus the founder of Ephesus, Strab. p. 632. Paus. VII, 2, 5. The names of the towns: Miletus, Myus, Priene (these three in the district of Karia), Ephesus, Kolophon, Lebedus, Teos, Klazomenæ, and Phokæa (in Lydia), Erythræ, Samos, and Chios, Herod. I, 142. As taking part in the movement, besides the Ionians from the Peloponnese, there are also mentioned Abantes from Eubœa, Minyæ from Orchomenus, Kadmeians, Dryopes, Phokensians, Molossians, Arkadians, and even Dorians from Epidaurus. Herod. I, 146. cf. Paus. VII, 2, 2. IX, 37, 3. The twelve towns (later, after the addition of Smyrna, thirteen, see obs. 12) formed an alliance with a common sanctuary, the Panionium, which was erected on the slope of the Mykale range and dedicated to Poseidon, Herod. I, 148. For the favourable situation of these towns, which, as regards political and intellectual development, outstripped the motherland, but quickly fell into decay, see Herod. I, 142: Οἱ δὲ μὲν οὗροι, ὧν καὶ τὸ Ἰώνιόν ἐστι, τοῦ μὲν οὐρανοῦ καὶ τῶν ὡρέων ἐν τῷ καλλίστῳ ἐτύγχανον ἱδρυσάμενοι πόλιας πάντων ἀνθρώπων ὧν ἡμεῖς ἴδμεν. Besides those towns, there were numerous other Ionic settlements upon the islands, see Herod. VII, 95. VIII, 48.

14   SECOND PERIOD. 1104—500 B. C.

B. C.	(LEGENDARY) HISTORY.	ART AND LITERATURE.
1031	Echestratus.	
	Eurypon¹⁶).	
996	Labotas.	
978	.... Prytanis.	
	Commencement of hostilities between Sparta and Argos¹⁷).	
959.	Doryssus.	*Epic Poetry flourishes.*
930	Agesilaus.	Homer and Homeridæ. Iliad
929	.... Eunomus.	and Odyssey*).

16) The kings, Soos, Eurypon, and Polydektes are omitted in the passage of Eusebius cited in obs. 4. It is therefore impossible to determine exactly the length of their reigns.
17) According to Paus. III, 2, 2—3 the Spartans had conquered Kynuria in the reign of Echestratus, and entered upon the war with the Argives under Labotas and Prytanis, on the ground of offences, alleged to have been committed by the Argives touching the conquered territory, cf. Id. 7, 2.

a) The accounts given by ancient writers of the age of Homer vary between 1159, *ενοι* in Philostratus Heroic. ch. XVIII, p. 194 and 685, Theopomp. in Clem. Alexand. Strom. I, p. 327. By far the greatest number and the most authoritative writers set him down as contemporary with the immigration of the Ionians into Asia Minor, or later—cotemporary in particular according to Aristotle, (Pseud.-) Plut. Vit. Hom. and Aristarchus, (Ps.-) Plut. loc. cit. Clem. Alex. loc. cit., consequently about 1044, and still later according to the oldest testimony, Herod. II, 53 : Ἡσίοδον γὰρ καὶ Ὅμηρον ἡλικίην τετρακοσίοισι ἔτεσιν δοκέω μευ πρεσβυτέρους γενέσθαι καὶ οὐ πλέοσι, consequently about 850. Hence the account of Apollodorus holds the mean between the date as fixed by Aristotle and as fixed by Herodotus. At a later period various towns laid claim to the honour of passing as Homer's birth-place, see Antip. Sidon. Ep. XLIV. Anthol. Pal. II, p. 716, cf. Ep. Inc. 486 f.: Ἑπτὰ πόλεις μάρναντο σοφὴν διὰ ῥίζαν Ὁμήρου, Σμύρνα, Χίος, Κολοφών, Ἰθάκη, Πύλος, Ἄργος, Ἀθῆναι, cf. Ep. Antipater (Ps.-) Plut. V. Hom. Procl. V. Hom. Of these, two have the best founded claim: Chios, the home of the minstrel-guild of the Homeridæ, Pind. Nem. II, 1: Ὅθενπερ καὶ Ὁμηρίδαι | ῥαπτῶν ἐπέων τὰ πόλλ' ἀοιδοὶ | ἄρχονται. Schol. loc. cit. Ὁμηρίδας ἔλεγον τὸ μὲν ἀρχαῖον τοὺς ἀπὸ τοῦ Ὁμήρου γένους, οἳ καὶ τὴν ποίησιν αὐτοῦ ἐκ διαδοχῆς ᾖδον, Strab. p. 646; and so moreover the blind bard of the Homeric Hymn to Apollo, (whom Thucydides holds to be Homer himself, III, 104), and Simonides regarded Chios as Homer's native town, Anon. Vit. Homer. Equal claim is laid by Smyrna, where a sanctuary Ὁμήρειον with a statue was dedicated to Homer, Strab. p. 646. Cic. pro Arch. 8, and according to the local legend Homer composed his poetry in a grotto by the springs of the river Meles and was called Μελησιγενής, as being born of the river-god, (Ps.-) Plut. V. Hom. Procl. V. Hom. Paus. VII, 5, 6. The island Ios must next be taken into consideration, Aristot. in Gell. III, 11, 6, where the grave of Homer was shown, Paus. X, 24, 3, and the inhabitants of the island brought him sacrifices, Varr. in Gell. loc. cit. From the cultivation of Homeric poetry in these and other towns arose their claim to be accounted birthplaces of the poet. Of the other circumstances of Homer's life the Greeks had no more certain knowledge, than of the time at which he lived. In any case the Homeric poems originated upon the west coast of Asia Minor; from thence they were transplanted to the mother-country in Europe, to Sparta by Lykurgus, as it is asserted, Plut. Lyk. ch. 4, to Argos before the time of Kleisthenes, Herod. V, 67. Ælian. V. H. IX, 15. In Athens they were already naturalized at the time of Solon and Peisistratus, Diog. Laert. I, 57. Ælian. V. H. VIII, 2; passages from these poems were recited publicly at religious festivals, notably so in Athens at the Panathenæa, as ordained by Solon and Hipparchus with precise directions to the various minstrels relieving one another, Diog. Laert. I, 57: Τὰ δὲ Ὁμήρου ἐξ ὑποβολῆς γέγραφε (Σόλων) ῥαψῳδεῖσθαι, οἷον ὅπου ὁ πρῶτος ἔληξεν, ἐκεῖθεν ἄρχεσθαι τὸν ἐχόμενον, ὥς φησι Διευχίδας ἐν τοῖς Μεγαρικοῖς. These minstrels were hence called ῥαψῳδοί, "stitchers of songs," Bekk. Anecd. II, p. 709: συνέρραπτον γὰρ τοὺς κατάλληλον διδοιαν ἀπαρτίζοντας στίχους Ὁμηρικοὺς καὶ ἕκαλλον τὸ ἐφαρμόζον μέλος. Peisistratus about this time appointed a commission of three learned men, Onomakritus of Athens, Zopyrus of Herakleia, and Orpheus of Kroton, to collect and arrange in orderly series the scattered or loosely arranged Homeric ballads, Cramer Anecd. Græc. Paris. I, p. 6. Schol. Plautin. Cod. Rom. sæc. XV. Pausan. VII, 26, 6. Cic. de orat. III, 34. Epigr. Bekk. Anecdot. II, p. 768: ὃς τὸν Ὅμηρον ἤθροισα σποράδην τὸ πρὶν ἀειδόμενον. What poems are to be ascribed to Homer is a point, upon which the ancients were already in doubt. By some scholars a large number of the most heterogeneous poems was attributed to him, Suid. s. v. Ὅμηρος; another school of the old grammarians only allowed the Iliad to be a genuine work of Homer, Procl. Vit. Hom.: Ὀδύσσειαν, ἣν Ξένων καὶ Ἑλλάνικος ἀφαιροῦνται αὐτοῦ (Ὁμήρου), and therefore attributed the Iliad and Odyssey to different authors, and was hence called οἱ χωρίζοντες, "the Separatists." Long before the Iliad and Odyssey, ballads treating of heroic legends, and in particular the cycle of Trojan legend, were sung to the Kithara, as is proved by the passages in both poems, in which performers such as Achilles, Demodokus, and Phemius, sang of the "glories of heroes," Il. IX, 189, of the "strife of Odysseus and Achilles," Od. VIII, 73, of the "deeds and calamities of the Achæans," Od. VIII, 489, of the "fashion of the wooden horse and of Troy's fall," Od. VIII, 492, of the "woeful return of the Achæans," Od. I, 326. Cf. also Herod. II, 23. Also the later origin of certain parts of the Homeric poems was already recognised by Alexandrine scholars; Aristarchus and Aristophanes regarded the conclusion of the Odyssey as spurious from XXIII, 296 onwards, Schol. Eustath.; Aristarchus passed the same judgment upon the twenty-fourth book of the Iliad; further a large number of single verses were marked as later interpolations by the same scholars. The critical investigation

The Age of the Inner Development of the Hellenes.   15

B. C.	(LEGENDARY) HISTORY.	ART AND LITERATURE.
886	Archelaus. Polydektes.	
884[18])	.... Charilaus.	
	Lykurgus, younger son of Eunomus and brother of Polydektes, conducts the government, as guardian of Charilaus[19]): by his legislation he puts an end to the factions and disorders which are rife in Sparta, and lays the foundation of the Spartan constitution and morals, which was to endure for centuries[20]).	Homeric Hymns[b]). Hesiod and his School. "Ερψα καὶ ἡμέραι. Θεογονία[c]).

18) This according to Eratosthenes and Apollodorus is the year, in which Lykurgus entered upon the guardianship, see p. 12, obs. 25, on which too hinge the dates of the reigns of the Spartan kings adopted in Eusebius from Apollodorus. Yet according to Herod. I, 65 Lykurgus was the guardian of Labotas, consequently in the third generation from Eurysthenes; according to Thuc. I, 18 the legislation of Lykurgus must be placed about sixty years later than the date as given above. It must further be remarked, that according to Herod. loc. cit. Lykurgus set about the work of legislation immediately after he had become guardian (ὡς γὰρ ἐπετρόπευσε τάχιστα μετέστησε τὰ νόμιμα πάντα), according to Ephorus in Strab. p. 482, not until Charilaus had been invested with the sovereign power, up to which time he is said to have gone to Krete, to avoid suspicion, and to have stayed there, cf. obs. 19. For other chronological accounts, see Plut. Lyk. 1. According to a frequently repeated account, Lykurgus in conjunction with the Eleian Iphitus organised the Olympic games and instituted the religious peace (ἐκεχειρία) which lasted during the games, see Aristot. in Plut. Lyk.

cf. id. 23. Paus. V, 4, 4. 20, 1. Athen. XI, p. 495 F. For further information on this point see on 776 B. C.

19) Our knowledge of the history of Lykurgus' life rests almost exclusively upon the biography of Plutarch, according to which he travelled before his legislative work (see in opposition to this view the passage of Herodotus in the preceding note) to Krete, Asia Minor, and Egypt; and in his task relied throughout upon the oracle at Delphi (for the latter circumstance cf. Herod. I, 65).

20) For the ἀνομία before Lykurgus see Herod. I, 65. Thuc. I, 18. Plut. Lyk. 2. For the legislation of Lykurgus in general the chief passages are, besides Plutarch, Aristot. Pol. II, 6. Xenoph. de Rep. Lac. Ephorus in Strab. p. 481 ff. and the exhaustive judgment upon it in Polyb. VI, 48—50. The constitution appears in general a more precise embodiment of the political conditions in Homer. At the head stand the two kings, for whom see obs. 1, For their privileges and honours see especially Herod. VI, 56—60. At their side stands the

of modern times, instigated in particular by Fr. A. Wolf (Prolegomena ad Homerum, 1795) has proceeded further in this direction, and denied, both in the case of the Iliad and Odyssey, the unity of the authorship and also of the date of composition. In the case of the Iliad in particular, by the side of the ancient belief two different views of capital interest have been propounded concerning the origin of the poem. According to one, the Iliad is the concretion of a number of smaller ballads, which were woven together, the gaps being filled by inserted passages, and the traces of the process removed in revision; Homer is therefore no historical personage, but only the personified conception and expression of all poetry of this type. According to the other view, a great and surpassing poet-genius, Homer, selected from the older ballads concerned with the Trojan cycle of legend the narrative of the wrath of Achilles (Il. I, 1), and composed with unity of design an Achilleis, an Iliad of smaller compass. This poem was elaborated with greater breadth and fulness by brotherhoods of minstrels, akin in spirit, not only within the limits of the original design, but also by the insertion of passages and rhapsodies, which were not confined within those limits. In regard to the Odyssey, modern investigation has brought forward preponderating reasons to show that it is of a later origin than the Iliad, but that, in being built with, it was originally planned with a definite unity of design from the store of older ballads dealing with the return home of the Achaean princes, then worked out with greater fulness, and extended by later interpolations and additions. The worth of the Homeric poetry was already appropriately pointed out by the ancients. So Aristotle in Plut. de Pyth. Orac. p. 398 A : 'Αριστοτέλης μὲν οὖν μόνον Ὅμηρον ἔλεγε κινοῦμενα

ὀνόματα ποιεῖν διὰ τὴν ἐνέργειαν, and Cic. Tusc. V, 39, 114: Traditum est etiam Homerum caecum fuisse. At eius picturam, non poesin videmus. Quae regio, quae ora, qui locus Graeciae, quae species formaeque pugnae, quae acies, quod remigium, qui motus hominum, qui ferarum non ita expictus est, ut, quae ipse non viderit, nos ut videremus, effecerit. The different character of the two poems in the Iliad and Odyssey is defined in Aristot. Poet. 24, 3: ἡ μὲν 'Ἰλιὰς ἀπλοῦν καὶ παθητικόν, ἡ δὲ 'Ὀδύσσεια πεπλεγμένον, ἀναγνώρισις γὰρ διόλου καὶ ἠθική.

b) The so-called Homeric hymns, thirty-three in number, may be traced to very different times. The older and longer hymns, to the Delian and Pythian Apollo, to Aphrodite, Hermes, and Demeter, belong to the age of the Homeridae. Thucyd. III, 104. Schol. Pind. Nem. II, 1. Paus. IX, 30, 6. Athen. I. p. 22 B: 'Ὅμηρος ἢ τῶν τις 'Ὁμηριδῶν ἐν τοῖς εἰς 'Ἀπόλλωνα ὕμνοις. Later in origin are the 'Ἐπιγράμματα handed down under Homer's name, and two parody epics, the lost Μαργίτης and the extant Βατραχομυομαχία, about the author of which the ancients were themselves very doubtful. Aristot. Poet. 4. Harpocr. v. Μαργίτης. Suid. v. Πίγρης. Plut. De Malign. Herod. 43. p. 873 f. Tzetzes Exeg. II. p. 37.

c) Hesiod was born at Askra in Boeotia, to which place his father had emigrated from the Aeolic Kyme. With regard to the time at which he lived, accounts differ, Tzetzes Chil. XII, 165 ff : 'Ἡσίοδος ὁ πρότερος κατὰ τινας 'Ὁμήρου, | κατά τινας δ' ἰσόχρονος, ὕστερος καθ' ἑτέρους. He was looked upon as older than Homer, amongst others by Ephorus, Gell. III, 11, 2, and Nikokles, Schol. Pind. Nem. II, 1, as contemporary with Homer by Herodotus, II, 53, Hellanikus and Pherekydes,

SECOND PERIOD. 1104—500 B.C.

B. C.	(LEGENDARY) HISTORY.	ART AND LITERATURE.
826	Teleklus.	
824	.... Nikandrus.	

council of old men, γερουσία, which, including the two kings (the latter had only one vote each, see Thuc. I, 20, cf. Herod. VI, 57), consisted of thirty members, see Plut. L. 26. By the side of these powers in the state the five ephors (instituted according to Herod. I, 65. Xen. de Rep. L. VIII, 3 by Lykurgus himself, according to Plut. Legg. III. p. 692. Arist. Pol. VIII, 11. Plut. L. 7, 27 only by Theopompus) raised themselves little by little to an authority which grew steadily; they were chosen from the people (ἐκ τοῦ δήμου, Arist. Pol. II, 6, hence called οἱ τυχόντες ib.) for one year only, and finally usurped almost all the powers of government. Lastly, the popular assembly (ἀλία Herod. VII, 134, ἀπελλάζειν, Plut. L, 6) could only accept or reject the measures of the council of elders (and afterwards of the ephors), but could not itself propose measures. The members of this assembly consisted only of Spartiatæ, the descendants of the Dorian conquerors, who were the masters of the country, and alone possessed of full civic rights. They were divided into three tribes, the Hylleis, Pamphyli, and Dymanes (see p. 10, obs. 10), into (probably 30) Obæ, see Plut. Lyk. 6, and were originally equal in rank and privileges (ὅμοιοι Xenoph. De Rep. L. x, 70. Isocrat. Areop. § 61); whilst at a later period the καλοὶ κάγαθοί, Arist. Pol. II, 6, 15, or γνώριμοι id. V, 6, 7, are elevated above the rest (ὑπομείονες, Xenoph. Hell. III, 2, 6?) as a higher class of Spartiatæ. Besides the Spartiatæ there were still the two subordinate classes of the population : Περίοικοι, also called Λακεδαιμόνιοι, and Εἴλωτες (so called either from the town Helos, Plut. L, 2. Ephorus in Strab. p. 365, or from the verbal stem ἙΛΟ); the persons of the former were free, but they had no right of voting in the public assembly or share in honourable privileges; the latter were bondsmen, not of the individual Spartiatæ, to whose service they were only appointed by the state, but of the state, see especially Ephorus loc. cit., and were chiefly employed to cultivate the lands of the Spartiatæ and to accompany them as light-armed soldiers in war, see Herod. IX, 28, where it is stated that at Plataeae the 5000 Spartiatæ had with them 35,000 Helots as light-armed troops, (Νεοδαμώδεις, freedmen, see e.g. Thuc. V, 34. VII, 19, 58. Xenoph. Hell. III, 1, 4. 4, 2. μόθακες, the children of Helots, who were brought up with children of the Spartiatæ and afterwards generally set free, see Phylarch in Athen. VI, 271, the κρυπτεία, Plut. Lyk. 28, an instance of atrocity practised on Neodamodes, Thuc. IV, 80. Rough statement of the comparative numbers in the three classes at the time of Sparta's greatest prosperity: 40,000 Spartiatæ, 120,000 Periœci, 200,000 Helots.) In regard to the character of the Lykurgean constitution in general see Aristot.

Pol. II, 3 : Ἔνιοι μὲν οὖν λέγουσιν, ὡς δεῖ τὴν ἀρίστην πολιτείαν ἐξ ἁπασῶν εἶναι τῶν πολιτειῶν μεμιγμένην· διὸ καὶ τὴν τῶν Λακεδαιμονίων ἐπαινοῦσιν. εἶναι γὰρ αὐτὴν οἱ μὲν ἐξ ὀλιγαρχίας καὶ μοναρχίας καὶ δημοκρατίας φασί, λέγοντες τὴν μὲν βασιλείαν μοναρχίαν, τὴν δὲ τῶν γερόντων ἀρχὴν ὀλιγαρχίαν, δημοκρατεῖσθαι δὲ κατὰ τὴν τῶν ἐφόρων ἀρχὴν διὰ τὸ ἐκ τοῦ δήμου εἶναι τοὺς ἐφόρους, and in greater detail Polyb. VI, 10.—But Lykurgus especially aimed at the formation of mind and morals in the Spartiatæ, by means of specially adapted institutions in harmony with his legislation, and particularly at the development, to the highest possible degree, of the νεώδαχεῖν and the καρτερεῖν. Hence the distribution of the soil, by which a fixed landholding was assigned to every head of a family among the Spartiatæ, of which he had not the free disposition, either by sale or purchase, by deed of gift or legacy (the latter rule was in force till the law of the Ephor Epitadeus after the Peloponnesian war, see Plut. Ag. 5); to this end the lands of the Spartiatæ were distributed into 9000 lots (κλᾶροι; to begin with, however, perhaps only 4500 or 6000, the full number only after the conquest of Messenia) Plut. Lyk. 6. cf. Heracl. Pont. ch. 2. Hence the public education, ἀγωγή, which was also extended to females, Xen. de Rep. L. I, 4, but in which the boys and young men in particular were obliged to take part from their seventh to their thirtieth year, if they did not wish to lose their full civic rights, Arist. Pol. II, 6, and in the course of which the boys were distributed into Ἴλαι and ἀγέλαι (dor. βοῦαι), under special superintendents (παιδονόμοι, βοναγοί), exercised chiefly in gymnastics, and further hardened by peculiar contrivances (the διαμαστίγωσις at the altar of Artemis Orthia, stealing, Plut. L. 18. Xen. De Rep. L. II, 6), and accustomed to the practice of obedience by the subordination of the younger to the elder in various gradations (σιδεῖναι, μελλείρενες, πρωτείραι, σφαιρεῖς, εἴρενες). The principle of the training was, Thuc. I, 84 : κράτιστον εἶναι ὅστις ἐν τοῖς ἀναγκαιοτάτοις παιδεύεται, its effect Xen. de Rep. L. III, 4. Arist. Pol. V, 4. Hence, finally, the συσσίτια (φιδίτια, ἀνδρεῖα) of the men, with the standing dish of black soup (called αἱματία or βαφά), the ἐνωμοτίαι in war, Herod. I, 65. Thuc. V, 68, the banishment of the noble metals, Plut. Lyk. 9, 10. Lys. 17. Pol. VI, 49, the restrictions upon intercourse with foreigners (ξενηλασία), Thuc. I, 144. II. 39, and other regulations.—To compel the Spartiatæ to maintain these laws, Lykurgus exacted an oath from them, that they would not alter anything until his return; he travelled to Delphi, but never returned back, Plut. Lyk. 29, 31, and thus the laws were actually retained up to the time of the Peloponnesian war essentially unaltered.

Procl. Vit. Hom., and also in the inscription of a tripod on Mt. Helikon, Dio Chrysost. T. I. p. 76, ed. Reiske: Ἡσίοδος Μούσαις Ἑλικωνίσι τόνδ' ἀνέθηκεν | ὕμνῳ νικήσας ἐν Χαλκίδι θεῖον Ὅμηρον, as later by Philochorus and Xenophanes, Gell. III, 11, 2, Eratosthenes, Strab. p. 23, and Apollodorus, Strab. p. 298. 299. The latter supposition is supported by the character of the poems attributed to the poet. The accounts of Hesiod's life are mythical and wavering, Paus. IX, 31, 5; his tomb with its epitaph was shown at Orchomenus, Paus. IX, 38, 3. Great difference of opinion ruled amongst the Greeks as to what poems were the genuine work of Hesiod. Only the Ἔργα καὶ

ἡμέραι, a poem upon the daily duties of husbandry and housekeeping, was unanimously ascribed by all to Hesiod, with the exception of the first ten lines, Paus. IX, 31, 4. Yet this poem was already at an early date enlarged and mutilated in various ways by interpolations and additions. The Θεογονία, an epic collection of the legends of the generation and struggles of the gods, giants, and heroes, is indeed suspected, Paus. VIII, 18, 1. IX, 31, 4, but still regarded as the work of Hesiod, in conformity with the universal opinion of Greek antiquity, and in particular of the Alexandrine scholars. The Theogony also suffered great changes at an early period in its component parts, and was

The Age of the Inner Development of the Hellenes. 17

B. C.	(LEGENDARY) HISTORY.		ART AND LITERATURE.
786	Alkamenes.	Theopompus.	Epic treatment of the Greek legendary material by the Cyclic poets[d]).

reduced in form to loosely connected patchwork. The 'Ασπὶς 'Ηρακλέους, a description of the shield of Herakles on occasion of the fight between Herakles and Kyknos, was already disclaimed as the work of Hesiod by Alexandrine scholars, Bekk. Anecdot. p. 1165: εἰσὶ γάρ καὶ ἐν αὐτοῖς ὁμώνυμα βιβλία ψευδῆ οἷον ἡ 'Ασπὶς 'Ησιόδου καὶ τὰ Θηριακὰ Νικάνδρου· ἑτέρων γάρ εἰσι ποιητῶν. Further, a number of poems now lost were by some scholars attributed to Hesiod. Thus the Κατάλογοι. γυναικῶν, Ἠοῖαι, Αἰγίμιος, Μελαμποδία, Κήυκος γάμος, but nothing certain is known of the authors of these poems.

d) Κυλικοί ποιηταί was the name given to the Epic poets, who were later than Homer and in particular handled the heroic legend, which borders upon Homer's legendary material. Schol. Clem. p. 104: Κυλικοὶ δὲ καλοῦνται ποιηταὶ οἱ τὰ κύκλῳ τῆς Ἰλιάδος ἢ τὰ μεταγενέστερα ἐξ αὐτῶν τῶν Ὁμηρικῶν συγγράψαντες. Their poems are, except unimportant fragments, entirely lost; for our knowledge of them we depend chiefly upon an epitome, which the grammarian Proklus made of them (in Phot. cod. 239), and further upon the works of plastic art, the so-called tabula Iliaca (in Rome) and the marmor Borgianum (in Naples). The Trojan cycle of legend was handled in the following poems: Κύπρια, from the origin of the Trojan war to the beginning of the Iliad, Herod. II, 117. Athen. VIII, p. 334. c. XV, p. 682. D. E., Αἰθιοπὶς by the Milesian Arktinus, from the close of the Iliad to the death of Achilles, Procl. Chrestom. Phot. Bibl. Cod, 239. Suid. v. Ἀρκτῖνος; Ἰλιὰς μικρά by the Lesbian Leschos, Pausan. X, 25. 3, or by another poet, Schol. Eur. Troad. 821. Pausan. III, 26, 7, from the contest for Achilles' arms to the conquest of the town; Ἰλίου πέρσις by Arktinus, Procl. Chrest. loc. cit. Hieron. Ol. 4. p. 50, the conquest and destruction of the town; Νόστοι by Agias of Troezen, Procl. loc. cit. and by other poets, Suid. v. Νόστος, the return home of the Greek chiefs, Τηλεγονία by Eugammon of Kyrene about 560 B.C., Clem. Alex. Strom. VI. p. 751. Procl. loc. cit, the final fortunes and the death of Odysseus. To other legendary cycles belonged the Θηβαΐς, Paus. IX, 9, 3, Ἐπίγονοι, Herod. IV, 32, Οἰδιπόδεια, by Kinaethon, Marmor Borgianum, or by another poet, Pausan. IX, 5, 5; Οἰχαλίας ἅλωσις by Kreophylus of Samos, Pausan. IV, 2, 2; Πράκλεια by Kinaethon, Schol. Apollon, I, 1357; Μινυάς by the Phokaean Prodikus, Pausan. IV, 33, 7, etc. Of a genealogical character, like the Theogony, were: Τιτανομαχία, Clem. Al. Strom. I. p. 361; Ναυπάκτια ἔπη by Karkinus of Naupaktos(?), Pausan. X, 38, 6; Φορωνὶς (Ἀργολικά), Schol. Apoll. I, 1129; Ἀτθίς by Hegesinus, Paus. IX, 29, 1, etc. Apart from the Cyclic poets stands Peisandrus of Kameirus in Rhodes, who flourished probably about 647, Suid. v. Πείσανδρος. In his epic poem Ἡράκλεια he was the first to furnish Herakles with the club in his labours, Pausan. II, 37, 4. VIII, 22, 4. Strab. p. 688. Schol. Apoll. I, 1195. Suid. loc. cit. Theokrit. Epigr. II, 6. ed Ahr. The age of the Epic poet Asius of Samos is uncertain, Athen. III. p. 125.

SECOND SECTION.

776—500 B.C.

FROM THE FIRST OLYMPIAD TO THE BEGINNING OF THE PERSIAN WARS. EXTENSION OF THE GREEKS BY COLONIES; RISE AND FALL OF TYRANNY IN THE MAJORITY OF GREEK STATES"); GROWTH OF SPARTA TILL IT OBTAINS THE HEGEMONY IN GREECE.

Olympiad.	B. C.	HISTORY.
I, 1	776	Korœbus, victor in the Olympic games, the first whose name is recorded: Commencement of the Olympiads["]).

21) The τυραννίς (omnes habentur et dicuntur tyranni, qui potestate sunt perpetua in ea civitate, quæ libertate usa est, Corn. Milt. 8. cf. Arist. Pol. VI, 10, 4) generally arises from the rebellion, or at least discontent and hostility, kindled amongst the people by the pressure of the oligarchic rule; these circumstances some individual then utilises to make himself tyrant by the agency of the people. In the mixed Doric states, in which the citizens consisted in part of Non-Dorians, it generally happened, that the Non-Dorians rose up against the privileged Dorian population, and stripped them of the sovereignty. The chief passages in regard to tyranny in general are Plut. de rep. VIII. & IX. Xenoph. Hiero, and particularly Aristot. Pol. VIII, 10—11. See id. 10, 3: ὁ δὲ τύραννος (καθίσταται) ἐκ τοῦ δήμου καὶ τοῦ πλήθους ἐπὶ τοὺς γνωρίμους, ὅπως ὁ δῆμος ἀδικῆται μηδὲν ὑπ' αὐτῶν. Φανερὸν δ' ἐκ τῶν συμβεβηκότων. Σχεδὸν γὰρ οἱ πλεῖστοι τῶν τυράννων γεγώνασιν ἐκ δημαγωγῶν, ὡς εἰπεῖν, πιστευθέντες ἐκ τοῦ διαβάλλειν τοὺς γνωρίμους. For the measures, by which the tyrants generally attempted to establish their power, see id. 11, 5: Ἔστι δὲ τά τε πάλαι λεχθέντα πρὸς σωτηρίαν ὡς οἷόν τε τῇ τυραννίδι, τὸ τοὺς ὑπερέχοντας κολούειν καὶ τοὺς φρονήματας ἀναιρεῖν καὶ μήτε συσσίτια ἐᾶν μήτε ἑταιρίαν μήτε παιδείαν μήτε ἄλλο μηδὲν τοιοῦτον, ἀλλὰ πάντα φυλάττειν, ὅθεν εἴωθε γίνεσθαι δύο, φρονήματά τε καὶ πίστεις. Besides the tyrants of Sikyon, Corinth, Megara, and Athens, for whom see infra, we further find recorded Prokles of Epidaurus at the time of Periander, Herod. III, 50, Panætius at Leontium, Kleander at Gela, Anaxilaus at Rhegium, Aristot. Pol. VIII, 12, 13 (where all these are counted amongst the tyrants of the earlier time, i. e. somewhere about the sixth century, with the additional statement, καὶ ἐν ἄλλαις πόλεσιν ὡσαύτως), Hippokrates and Gelon at Gela, Herod. VII, 154, 155, Telys at Sybaris, Herod. V, 14. Diod. XII, 9. 10, Aristodemus at Cumæ, Dionys. Hal. VII, 2—11, Syloson at Samos, Herod. III, 39. 139—149, Polykrates at the same place, Herod. III, 39—56. 120—125, cf. Polyæn. VI, 44. I. 23, 1, Lygdamis at Naxos, Herod. I, 61. 64. Arist. Pol. VIII, 6. 1, and others. Their rule was generally (though not always) violent and cruel, and for that very reason of short duration, see Arist. Pol. VIII, 12, 1: πασῶν ὀλιγοχρονιώτεραι τῶν πολιτειῶν εἰσὶν ὀλιγαρχία καὶ τυραννίς. πλεῖστον γὰρ ἐγένετο χρόνον ἡ περὶ Σικυῶνα τυραννίς, ἡ τῶν Ὀρθαγόρου

παίδων καὶ αὐτοῦ Ὀρθαγόρου· ἔτη δ' αὕτη διέμεινεν ἑκατόν. To show the disposition of the Hellenes towards the tyrants at a later period, Eurip. Suppl. 429 may suffice: Οὐδὲν τυράννου δυσμενέστερον πόλει, | ὅπου τὸ μὲν πρώτιστον οὐκ εἰσὶν νόμοι | κοινοί, κρατεῖ δ' εἷς, τὸν νόμον κεκτημένος | αὐτὸς παρ' αὑτῷ. The Spartans were especially active in expelling the tyrants, see Arist. Pol. VIII, 10, 30. Plutarch. de Herod. Mal. ch. 21. p. 859, and in this very policy, aided by many other favourable circumstances, found a chief means of establishing their hegemony in Greece.

22) For the traditional institution of the Olympic games by Herakles see Paus. V, 7, 4. Pind. Ol. II, 3, 4. III, 21, etc. Polyb. XII, 26, 2; for the renovation of the games by Klymenus, Pelops, Amythaon etc., Paus. V, 8, 1. According to Strabo p. 354 Oxylus was the founder, cf. Paus. V, 8, 2; after Oxylus the games are said to have fallen into oblivion, until Iphitus in common with Lykurgus restored them in the year 884 B. C., see obs. 18. But the victors are only recorded, and the Olympiads reckoned, from the year given above and onwards, see Phlegon. Trall. fr. 1. 12 (ed. Müller). According to Aristot. in Plut. Lyk. 1 the name of Lykurgus was inscribed upon a discus, existing at Olympia, together with that of Iphitus, as founder of the Olympic games, cf. Pausan. V, 20, 1; and according to Phleg. fr. 1 the organisation of the Olympic games was recorded on this same discus. If, then, according to Paus. VIII, 26, 3 the inscription on the tomb of Korœbus stated, that Korœbus was the first victor of all, some probability accrues to the theory, that Korœbus was victor at the first celebration of the Olympic games reorganised by Lykurgus and Iphitus; and hence that Lykurgus belongs to the time of the first Olympiad, and the earlier date rests upon false premises of later chronologists, notably of Timæus, see Plut. loc. cit. For the place of the celebration and its remarkable sights, Paus. V, 10—27. At first the contest consisted only of the footrace over the single stadium (= 600 feet, Gell. N. A. I, 1. Herod. II, 149); in Ol. XIV the double course, δίαυλος, was added; in Ol. XV the long course, δόλιχος (the length of which is variously stated at 7, 12, 14, 20, and 24 stadia, see Suid. s. v. δίαυλος and δόλιχος); in Ol. XVIII the πένταθλον (ἅλμα, δίσκος, δρόμος, πάλη and πυγμή, or later ἀκόντισις) and the wrestling;

The Age of the Inner Development of the Hellenes. 19

Olympiad.	B. C.	DORIC STATES.	ATHENS.	COLONIES.	
				In Italy, etc.	in the Eastern Sea[23].
II, 3	770	....	....	....	Sinope by Miletus[24]).

in Ol. XXIII the boxing; in Ol. XXV the race with the four-horse chariot (ἵππων τελείων); in Ol. XXXIII the Pankratium and the race on horseback (ἵππος κέλης), etc., see Paus. V, 8, 3, Euseb. Chron. The olivebranch was the prize of victory from Ol. VII, see Phleg. Tr. fr. 1; cf. the pleasing narrative Herod. VIII, 26 (a Persian there says to Mardonius: τοιαῦτα Μαρδόνιε, κοίους ἐπ' ἄνδρας ἤγαγες μαχεσομένους ἡμέας οἱ οὐ περὶ χρημάτων τὸν ἀγῶνα ποιοῦνται ἀλλὰ περὶ ἀρετῆς). The celebration of the festival took place every four years, on the tenth to the sixteenth day of the first month in the year, which coincided with the first month of the Athenian year, Hekatombæon, and consequently began with the first new moon after the summer solstice (according to another theory with the new moon which lay nearest the summer solstice); therefore approximately in the first half of July, see Schol. on Pind. Ol. III, 80. 85. V, 6. 8. The employment of the Olympiads as a chronological era is found in isolated instances in Thucydides (III, 8. V, 49) and Xenophon (Hellen. I, 2, 1. II, 3, 1), but only becomes the rule in Timæus and of extant writers in Polybius, Diodorus, and Dionysius of Halikarnassus. In placing the years reckoned by Olympiads parallel with the years reckoned before the birth of Christ in the tabular columns, the Olympiad year has been assumed to correspond to that year of the Christian era, in the course of which the Olympiad commences; so that e.g. Ol. I, 1 and the year 776 B.C. have been placed together as corresponding to one another, whilst the former properly extends from July 776 to July 775; consequently, if an event falls in the half-year prior to the festival, the Olympiad year immediately preceding must be assumed. Orsippus is mentioned as the first, who ran in the footrace naked, a custom which from that time became the rule for contests of all species, Paus. I, 44, 1, or Akanthus, Dionys. Hal. VII, 72, in the 15th Olymp. Dion. H. loc. cit. Distinctions awarded to the Olympian victors: the entry into their native town (εἰσελαύνειν), celebrated with rejoicings, at which, to do honour to the occasion, a breach was not unfrequently made in gate and walls, see Plut. Symp. II, 5, 2. Dio. Cass. LXIII, 20. Suet. Ner. 25, the presidency at public games and festivals, Xenophon in Athen. XI. p. 414; at Athens, the privilege of dining in the Prytaneium, Plut. Apol. Socr. p. 36. D, at Sparta, the honour of fighting in battle near the king, Plut. Lyk. 22; and statues were often erected to them in their native town, Lykurg. Leokr. p. 151. Paus. VI, 13, 1, etc. Moreover the victors were permitted to have their statues placed in the sacred grove Altis at Olympia, which was frequently done at the expense of the state, to which they belonged, Paus. V, 21, 1. VI, ch. 1—18, after Ol. LIX, see Paus. VI, 18, 5. Of the ἐπιδείξεις (showdeclamations), which were delivered at the games, the most celebrated is that of Herodotus, see Lucian. Herod. I, 2. Quomodo hist. sit conscr. § 42. Suid. s. v. Θουκυδίδης. Phot. Cod. 60. Marcellin. Vit. Thuc. p. 32; for that of Gorgias, see Paus. VI, 17, 5. For the universal significance of the games see Lysias in Dionys. Hal. de Lys. Jud. c. 30. (cd. Reiske V. p. 520): ἀγῶνα μὲν σωμάτων ἐποίησε (Herakles), φιλοτιμίαν δὲ πλούτου, γνώμης δὲ ἐπίδειξιν ἐν τῷ καλλίστῳ τῆς Ἑλλάδος, ἵνα τούτων ἁπάντων ἕνεκα ἐς τὸ αὐτὸ ἔλθωμεν τὰ μὲν ὀψόμενοι τὰ δὲ ἀκουσόμενοι· ἡγήσατο γὰρ τὸν ἐνθάδε σύλλογον ἀρχὴν γενέσθαι τοῖς Ἕλλησι τῆς πρὸς ἀλλήλους φιλίας.—Similar to the Olympic games, though not of equal repute, were the Pythian games at Delphi, which were said to have been instituted by Apollo, but only attained a wider

extension and significance after Ol. XLVIII, 3, see especially Paus. X, 7, 3. Strab. p. 418—423. Schol. Pind. Pyth. Arg. of. Soph. El. v. 681—750, and obs. 67: the Nemean in honour of Zeus, said to have been founded by the Seven on occasion of their expedition against Thebes, see Apollod. III, 6, 4: the Isthmian at the isthmus of Corinth, the foundation of which is attributed to Sisyphus in honour of Molikertes, Paus. II, 1, 3; or to Theseus, Plut. Thes. 25; the two latter dating their historical commencement according to Euseb. Chron. p. 94 f. from Ol. LI. 3 (Arm., LII, 1 Hieron.) and L, 1 (Arm., XLIX, 4 Hieron. Cf. however in regard to the Isthmian Plut. Sol. 23); both were celebrated every two, not like the others every four years.

23) The Colonies in the eastern sea—subsequent to the earlier colonies which followed upon the migration of the Dorians and Herakleidæ and prior to the naval supremacy of Athens—proceed chiefly from Chalkis and Eretria in Eubœa and from Miletus. The numerous colonies of Chalkis and Eretria cover the whole of the peninsula of Chalkidike; for these see Strab. p. 447, and the names of the greater part in Herod. VII, 122. 123. Mende, for example, is mentioned as having been founded by Eretria, Thuc. IV, 123, Torone by Chalkis, id. 110. But Potidæa was a Corinthian colony, Thuc. I, 56, and the towns Makistus, Stageira, Argilus, and Sane were founded by Andros, Thuc. IV, 84. 88. 103. 109. The colonies of Miletus extended in great numbers from the Hellespont to the remote interior of the Pontus Euxinus, Scymn. Ch. v. 734 : πλείστας ἀποικίας γὰρ ἐξ Ἰωνίας (οἱ Μιλήσιοι) ἐστείλαν εἰς τὸν Πόντον, ὃν πρὶν ἄξενον διὰ τὰς ἐπιθέσεις λεγόμενον τῶν βαρβάρων προσηγορίαs ἐποίησαν εὐξεῖνον τυχεῖν. Strab. p. 365 : πολλὰ δὲ τῆς πόλεως ἔργα ταύτης, μέγιστον δὲ τὸ πλῆθος τῶν ἀποικιῶν· ὅ τε γὰρ Εὔξεινος πόντος ὑπὸ τούτων συνῴκισται πᾶς καὶ ἡ Προποντὶς καὶ Ἴκαρον τὴν νῆσον καὶ Λῆρον Μιλήσιοι συνῴκισαν καὶ περὶ Ἑλλήσποντον ἐν μὲν τῇ Χερρονήσῳ Λίμνας, ἐν δὲ τῇ Ἀσίᾳ Ἄβυδον Ἀρίσβαν Παισόν, ἐν δὲ τῇ Κυζικηνῶν γῇ Ἀρτάκην Κύζικον· ἐν δὲ τῇ μεσογαίᾳ τῆς Τρῳάδος Σκῆψιν. In addition to these, there are further mentioned as colonies of Miletus in those parts: Lampsakus, Strab. p. 589, Kardia, Scymn. 699, Apollonia, id. 730, Odessus, id. 748, Tomi, id. 765, Istrus, id. 769, Tyras, id. 830, Olbia or Borysthenes, id. 833, Kepus, id. 890, Sinope, id. 947, Phasis, Steph. Byz. s. v., Pantikapæum, Strab. p. 310. Besides the colonies of Miletus, there were a number of colonies from Megara (Chalkedon, Byzantium, Selymbria, Mesembria), and from Lesbos (Sestos, Madytus, Ænus). The date of their foundation is generally unknown; the majority must be placed in the 7th, and a considerable number in the 8th century B.C.; those only are cited in the tables, the date of which can be, at least approximately, determined.

24) Sinope was twice founded from Miletus, the second time according to Hieron. Chron. in 630 B.C. (= 1387 Abr.) p. 89; the first foundation must be placed somewhere about the year as given above, as Trapezus together with Kotyora and Kerasus was founded from Sinope, see obs. 25. Its relationship to Miletus is mentioned, besides Scymn. 947, in Xen. Anab. V, 9, 15. Diodor. XIV, 31. Strab. p. 545.

SECOND PERIOD. 1104—500 B.C.

Olympiad.	B.C.	DORIC STATES.	ATHENS.	COLONIES.	
				in Italy.	in the Eastern Sea.
V, 4	757				Trapezus together with Kotyora and Kerasus by Sinope[26]); Artake and Kyzikus by Miletus[26]).
VII, 1	752		Archons holding office ten years[27]).		
VIII, 1	748	Pheidon, tyrant of Argos[28]).			
IX, 2	743	Alkamenes and Theopompus, kings of Sparta[29]). The Spartans surprise Amphcia in Messenia; first Messenian war[31]).		Rhegium by Chalkidians and Messenians[30]).	

25) See Xenoph. Anab. IV, 8, 22. V, 5, 3. 3, 3. The date fixed in accordance with Euseb. Chron. (Arm) p. 80.

26) Strab. p. 635. The date fixed in accordance with Euseb. Chron. in Hieron. p. 81. Kyzikus, according to Euseb. Chron. Arm. p. 86, was founded anew, and that by Megara in 676 B.C., Jo. Lyd. de Mag. Rom. III, 70.

27) Dion. Hal. I, 71, 75. Vell. Pat. I, 8. Euseb. Chron. Arm. Ol. VI, 2. Hieron. Ol. VI, 4 p. 80 f. The headship of the Medontidæ, the descendants of Kodrus, lasted till about 714, when, in consequence of the barbarous conduct of the archon Hippomenes, it was abolished, see Suid. s. v. Ἱππομένης, cf. Paus. IV, 13, 5. Alkmæon was the last of the archons, who held office for life; Charops the first, who held the decennial office.

28) Pheidon is quoted by Aristotle, Pol. VIII, 10, 6, as an instance of the tyranny, which arises from monarchy. He recovered the supremacy over the towns of Argolis, and also sought to extend his rule beyond Argolis; he was the first to coin money, and introduced standard weights and measures, the so called Æginetan, probably to be referred to Babylon; he further deprived the Eleians of the agonothesy at Olympia, and himself filled the office of president at the games. Important passages: Ephor. in Strab. p. 358. Herod. VI, 127. Paus. VI, 22, 2. The date assigned to Pheidon rests on the passage cited from Pausanias, as there the 8th Olympiad is given as the one in which Pheidon usurped the presidency. At variance with this, his date is given on the Marm. Par. and by Syncellus about 100 years earlier, while according to Herod. loc. cit. it would have to be placed about 600 B.C.

29) The above mentioned kings are recorded by Pausanias (IV, 5, 3. 6, 2) as the ones, in whose reign the first Messenian war was commenced. Alkamenes died before the fifth year of the war, see Paus. IV, 7, 3; whilst according to Paus. IV, 6, 2, it appears as if Theopompus had brought the war to a conclusion. This certainly does not fully harmonize with Eusebius (see obs. 2, Müller fr. Hist. Gr. I. p. 444), according to whom Alkamenes and Theopompus came to the throne in 786 B.C. and the former reigned 36, the latter 43 years. The following kings up to Leonidas are known by name, but we are ignorant of the length of their reigns: the list of Eusebius breaks off with Alkamenes and Theopompus. The successors of Alkamenes, of the line of the Agidæ, are: Polydorus, Eurykrates, Anaxandrus, Eurykrates, Leon, Anaxandridas; of the line of the Eurypontidæ: Zeuxidamus, Anaxidamus, Archidamus, Agasikles, Ariston; see the passages cited from Pausanias in obs. 2. The second Messenian war broke out under Anaxandrus and Anaxidamus, see Paus. IV, 15, 1.

30) With regard to the colonies in Italy our knowledge is chiefly drawn from Strab. p. 252—265. 278—280. Besides the chief colonies mentioned in the tables, some others are mentioned as already founded by the Achæans on their way home at the time of the Trojan war, e.g. Petelia, Strab. p. 254, Krimissa, id. Skyllakion, id. p. 261. Lagaria, id. p. 263, Metapontium, id. 264 (but in regard to this last other legends were also current, id. p. 265) etc. For Rhegium see Strab. p. 257. Herael. Pont. fr. XXV (ed. Müller).

31) The causes of the war: the pretended deceit of Kresphontes when drawing lots for the conquered territories (see obs. 1), the murder of the Spartan king Teleklos, and the refusal of the Messenians to surrender Polychares, who had slain several Spartans, see Paus. IV, c. 4—5, cf. Iustin. III, 4. Diod. XV, 66. VI—X. fr. XXII, (vol. III. p. 104. Dind.). The outbreak of the war falls in the reign of Antiochus and Androkles. The latter wished Polychares to be surrendered to the Spartans, but was slain in an uproar caused by the proposal; Antiochus died soon afterwards, and thus Euphaes as king succeeded to the conduct of the war, Paus. IV, 5, 2. Strab. p. 257. The sources of the narrative in Pausanias are Myron of Priene and Rhianus of Bene in Krete (the latter for the second war), for whom see Paus. IV, 6. (Myron was a late historian; Rhianus, an Alexandrine writer, composed an epic poem, of which Aristomenes was the hero. Their accounts are, however, in many points contradictory, and the authority of the prose writer is depreciated by Pausanias himself); the fragments of Tyrtæus are especially valuable; for this poet see obs. 1.

The Age of the Inner Development of the Hellenes.

Olympiad.	B. C.	DORIC STATES.	ATHENS	COLONIES.			
				in Italy.	in Sicily.	on the coast of Epirus, etc.	in the Eastern Sea.
X, 2	739	The Messenians, after two indecisive battles, retire to the mountain stronghold Ithome[32]).					
XI, 2	735	....	....	....	Naxos by Chalkis[33]).		
XI, 3	734	....	....	....	Syracuse by Corinth[35]).	Korkyra by Corinth[34]).	
XII, 3	730	....	....	....	Leontini and Katana by Naxos[36]).		
XIII, 1	728	....	....	....	Megara Hyblaea by Megara[37]).		
XIV, 1	724	Messenia subdued, and the inhabitants made Helots[38]).					

32) The first battle in the year 740 B.C., Paus. IV, 7, 2; the second in the year 730, Paus. IV, 7, 3—c. 6. The reason, why the country was abandoned, is said to have been exhaustion of pecuniary means and a pestilence, Paus. IV, 9, 1.

33) For the colonies in Sicily the most important passage is Thuc. VI, 3—5. In the same book, c. 1 and 2, information is given about the former inhabitants of the island. For Naxos see id. 3 and Strab. p. 267. The founder is Theokles, an Athenian; for the date fixed see obs. 35.

34) Corinth was then the richest and most prosperous naval state in Greece (the first triremes built there, Thuc. I, 13), and accordingly about this time commenced the foundation of colonies in Sicily, see obs. 33 and 35; to this end the occupation of Korkyra, as a station for ships on the voyage, was an indispensable requisite; and this was followed by the establishment of the other colonies, which commanded the coast of Akarnania and Epirus (Epidamnus, Apollonia, Ambrakia, Anaktorium, Leukas). For the foundation of Korkyra by Chersikrates on the voyage to Syracuse see Strab. p. 269. Timm. fr. 53 (ed Muller.) This town in 644 B.C. made itself independent of Corinth in a sea-fight, the oldest of all sea-fights amongst the Greeks; asserted its independence till the time of Periander, recovering it again after his death, Herod. III, 49—53; it then persisted in a hostile attitude towards the mother city, so that it even neglected all the pious duties, which colonies owed to their mother cities, s. Thuc. I, 25. In all probability the colonies Molykreium and Chalkis were founded cotemporaneously with Korkyra at the mouth of the inner Corinthian gulf, Thuc. III, 102. I, 108.

35) The founder Archias. See Thuc. VI, 3. Strab. p. 269—270. 380. Athen. IV, p. 167. d. The date fixed for the foundation of Syracuse, on which the dates of the Sicilian colonies for the most part depend, rests on Euseb. Chron. and on grounds of probability.

36) "Five years after the foundation of Syracuse," Thuc. VI, 3. cf. Polyaen. V, 5, 1. The celebrated lawgiver Charondas belongs to the town Katana, for whom s. Arist. Pol. II, 12, 6. 7. Diodor. XII, 11—19. Stob. Floril. XLIV, 40. His laws were also transplanted to Rhegium, Heraclid. Pont. fr. XXV, to Mazaka in Cappadocia, Strab. p. 539, to Thurii, Diod. loc. cit., and to several other towns in Italy and Sicily, s. Arist. Pol. II, 12, 6.

37) Thuc. VI, 3. 4. About the same time Zankle (afterwards Messana), which had been founded at a still earlier period by pirates from Kyme (Cumae), was organised as a colony by immigrants from Chalkis and the rest of Euboea under an Œkist from Kyme and one from Chalkis, Thuc. VI, 4. Paus. IV, 23, 3. With the six colonies hitherto mentioned the Hellenic colonisation of Sicily came to an end for some forty years, see 690 B.C.

38) After the retreat to Ithome another indecisive battle was fought in 731 B.C., in which king Euphaes fell: whereupon Aristodemus was chosen king, Paus. IV, 10. The latter fought another battle with the Spartans, the Arcadians and a number of Argives and Sikyonians on the side of the Messenians, and in this the Messenians were victorious, Paus. IV, 11. Nevertheless some years after this, chiefly in consequence of evil omens and other tokens of the displeasure of the gods, Ithome was given up, after Aristodemus had fallen by his own hand, Paus. IV, 9. 11—13. We learn from the following verses of Tyrtaeus, that the war lasted nineteen years: 'Ἀμφ' αὐτὴν δ' ἐμάχοντ' ἐννεακαίδεκ' ἔτη, νωλεμέως αἰεὶ ταλασίφρονα θυμὸν ἔχοντες, αἰχμηταὶ πατέρων ἡμετέρων πατέρες· εἰκοστῷ δ' οἱ μὲν κατὰ πίονα ἔργα λιπόντες φεῦγον Ἰθωμαίων ἐκ μεγάλων ὀρέων, Strab. p. 279. Paus. IV, 15, 1. 13, 4. The beginning of the war Ol. 9, 2=743 B.C. is recorded by Paus. IV, 5, 4, in agreement with which is the record of the victory gained by the Polychares already mentioned at Olympia, Ol. IV, Paus.

SECOND PERIOD. 1104—500 B.C.

Olympiad.	B. C.	DORIC STATES.	ATHENS.	COLONIES.			ART AND LITERATURE.
				in Italy.	in Sicily.	in the Eastern Sea.	
XIV, 4	721			Sybaris by Achæans*).			
XVI, 2	715					Abydus by Miletus*).	
XVII, 3	710			Kroton by Achæans⁴).			
XVIII, 4	705			Tarentum by Sparta⁴).			
XX, 1	700						Lyric Poetry*) rises and flourishes: Kallinus of Ephesus¹); Archilochus of Paros⁸); Simonides of Samos, the Iambographist^h)(Elegiac writer).

IV, 4, 5. The fate of the Messenians, so far as they remained in the country, is described by Tyrtæus: Ὥσπερ ὄνοι μεγάλοις ἄχθεσι τειρόμενοι, δεσποσύνοισι φέροντες ἀναγκαίῃ ὑπὸ λυγρῇ ἥμισυ πᾶν, ὅσσον καρπὸν ἄρουρα φέρει, δεσπότας οἰμώζοντες ὁμῶς ἄλοχοί τε καὶ αὐτοί, εὖτέ τιν' οὐλομένη μοῖρα κίχοι θανάτου. 39) Strab. p. 362—363. Arist. Pol. VIII, 3, 11. For the date s. Scymn. Ch. v. 360 cf. Diod. XI, 90. XII, 10. The great power of the town s. Strab. p. 263: Τοσοῦτον δ' εὐτυχίᾳ διήνεγκεν ἡ πόλις αὕτη τὸ παλαιόν, ὡς τεττάρων μὲν ἐθνῶν τῶν πλησίον ὑπῆρξε, πέντε δὲ καὶ εἴκοσι πόλεις ὑπηκόους ἔσχε, τριάκοντα δὲ μυριάσιν ἀνδρῶν ἐπὶ Κροτωνιάτας ἐστράτευσαν, πεντήκοντα δὲ σταδίων κύκλων συνεπλήρουν οἰκοῦντες ἐπὶ

τῷ Κράθιδι. For the luxury of the town s. Athen. XII, p. 519—522. It was destroyed by the Krotoniates 511 B.C., Scymn. loc. cit. Diod. XI, 90. XII, 9—10. Founded from Sybaris; Poseidonia, Strab. p. 251, Laos, id. 253.
40) Strab. p. 590; ἐπιτρίψαντος Γύγου τοῦ Λυδῶν βασιλέως.
41) Dionys. Hal. II, 59. Herod. VIII, 47. Strab. p. 262. Founded from Kroton, Terina, Steph. Byz. s. v., Scymn. Ch. v. 306.
42) Antiochus and Ephorus in Strab. p. 278—280. Cf. Arist. Pol. VIII, 7, 2. Justin. III, 1. Diod. XV, 66. The date is fixed in accordance with Hieronymus p. 85 (705 B.C. = 1312 Abr.). Founded from Tarentum, Herakleia (on the Siris) Strab. p. 264.

e) Lyric poetry at this period took two chief directions, which may be distinguished by their rhythmical and metrical form: firstly, the elegiac and iambic poetry, the chief forms of which are the dactylic distich and the iambic trimeter, specially peculiar to the Ionic race, and hence always composed in the Ionic dialect; and, secondly, the melic poetry of the Dorians and Æolians. Μέλος signifies a song set to music, sung to the lute or flute on festive occasions, often to the cyclic dance, in various and often partly strophic rhythms, Plat. Rep. III. p. 398: τὸ μέλος ἐκ τριῶν ἐστὶ συγκείμενον, λόγου τε καὶ ἁρμονίας καὶ ῥυθμοῦ. Such songs had in part, especially in the earliest times, a religious significance, as νόμοι, ὕμνοι, παιᾶνες, hymns of praise and chorals; προσόδια, processional hymns; ὑπορχήματα, festal songs to accompany mimic dances; διθύραμβοι, Bacchic choral songs with cyclic dance, etc.; others were of a secular character, as the ἐγκώμια, songs in praise of human beings; ἐπινίκια, songs of victory; σκόλια, παροίνια, drinking songs; ἐρωτικά, love songs; ἐπιθαλάμια, ὑμέναιοι, wedding songs; θρῆνοι, dirges; ἐπικήδεια, funeral songs, etc.

f) Kallinus, usually designated the oldest elegiac poet, Strab. p. 633. Orion. p. 58. Schol. Cic. pro Arch. 10, 3. Terentian. v. 1721; yet his date is uncertain. According to Strab. p. 647, 648 cf. Clem. Al. Strom. I, p. 333, B, he is older than Archilochus. A large fragment is preserved of a war song of his, Poet. Lyr. Th. Bergk. ed. II, fr. 1.

g) Archilochus, son of Telesikles, lived about 700 B.C., Herod. I, 12. Cic. Tusc. I, 1. Syncell. p. 181, emigrated to Thasos on account of poverty, Ælian. V. H. X. 13. Warrior and poet alike, Athen. XIV, 627, he attacks his opponents in biting satirical poems, Pind. Pyth. II, 55. Bergk. fr. 92, notably so Lykambes and his daughters, Hor. Epod. VI, 13. Epist. I, 19, 25. Ovid. Ib. 53. After a life full of passion and tribulation, Bergk. fr. 9. 13. 19. 65. 67. 68. 84, he fell in a battle with Naxos, Suid. v. Ἀρχίλοχος. Divine honours were paid to him by the Parians, Arist. Rhet. II, 23, 11. By reason of his poetical gifts and his perfect language he was ranked by the ancients with Homer, Pindar, and Sophokles, was reputed the inventor of the iambic trimeter, of the trochaic tetrameter, and various compound metres, and regulated the melody and delivery in recitative of his poems, Mar. Vict. p. 2586. ed. Putsch. Plut. d. Mus. p. 1134. D. 1140 extr. Of his poems, Ἐλεγεῖα, Ἴαμβοι, Τετράμετρα, Ἐπῳδοί, Ὕμνοι εἰς Ἡρακλέα, Ἴοβακχοι, only short fragments are preserved, Bergk. p. 536 f.

h) Simonides, the iambographist, a younger cotemporary of Archilochus, led a Samian colony to Amorgos, Suid. v. Σιμωνίδης, v. Σιμμίας Ῥόδιος. Clem. Al. Strom. I, p. 339. B, composed elegiac and iambic poems; it is of the latter only that fragments are preserved, in particular two of considerable length, Bergk. fr. 1, 7.

The Age of the Inner Development of the Hellenes. 23

Olympiad.	B. C.	DORIC STATES.	ATHENS.	COLONIES.			ART AND LITERATURE.
			Archons.	in Italy.	in Sicily.	in the Eastern Sea.	
XXII, 3	690				Gela by Rhodes and Krete[43]).		
XXIII, 4	685	The Messenians rise under Aristomenes; second Messenian War[44]).					Tyrtæus at Sparta[i]) (Elegiac poet); Terpander of Lesbos[k]); Alkman from Sardes[l]) (Melic poetry).
XXIV, 2	683		Nine Archons appointed for one year. Kreon[45]).				
XXIV, 4	681		Tlesias.				
XXV, 2	679	The Messenians retreat to Eira[46]).					

43) Thuc. VI, 4: "44 years after Syracuse." Cf. Diod. Exc. Vat. XIII. Paus. VIII, 46, 2. Herod. VII, 143. The names of the founders are Antiphemus of Rhodes and Entinus of Krete.

44) Paus. IV, c. 14, 4—c. 24. Iustin. III, 5. Diod. XV, 66. The allies of the Messenians; Arcadians, Argives, Pisatans and Sikyonians; of the Spartans; Corinthians, Eleans, and Lepreatans; Paus. IV, 15, 1. 16, 2. Strab. p. 355. 362. According to Paus. IV, 15, 1. the rebellion took place 39 years after the ending of the first war; according to Iustin. III, 5 the second war began 80 years after the first; according to Euseb. Chron. Arm. p. 88 not until 635 B.C. The passage of Tyrtæus (πατέρων ἡμετέρων πατέρες) cited in obs. 38, and the circumstance, that according to Paus. VI, 22, 2 the Pisatans under their king Pantaleon had the conduct of the Olympian games, whilst, according to Strabo p. 355, immediately after the ending of the second Messenian war, the Eleans with the help of the Spartans completely subdued the Pisatans, make it probable that the second war is placed too early by Pausanias.

45) African. in Sync. p. 212. B. Euseb. Chron. p. 84. The first in the board of the nine Archons was styled Archon par excellence, and the year was called after him (hence ἐπώνυμος; for the commencement of the year s. obs. 22); the second was styled βασιλεύς; the third πολέμαρχος; the rest together θεσμοθέται, cf. Polluc. Onom. 85—91. For the power of the Archons at that period see Thuc. I, 126: τότε δὲ τὰ πολλὰ τῶν πολιτικῶν οἱ ἐννέα ἄρχοντες ἔπρασσον. The first ἄρχων ἐπώνυμος, holding office for one year, was Kreon; the last, who held the decennial office, was Eryxias.

46) This happened after the loss of a battle (at the great Trench), which is placed by Pausanias in the third year of the war. But he contradicts himself; for according to 17, 6 and 20, 1 the war lasted 11 years more after this battle, and, according to 23, 2, 17 years altogether. Besides this battle (for which cf. Paus. IV, 17, 2—5; it was lost owing to the treachery of the Arcadian king Aristokrates), mention is further made of an indecisive battle fought in the earlier years of the war at Deræ, see Paus. IV, 15, 21, and of a great victory at Boar's Grave ἐν Στενυκλήρῳ, see ibi. § 4. f. Polyb. IV, 33. For the rest, the whole narrative of Pausanias (or rather of Rhianus, whom he everywhere follows) is nothing but a glorification of Aristomenes, a second Achilles, as he himself calls him, IV, 6, 2. On the side of the Spartans Tyrtæus is the only prominent figure, who by his songs continually restored and rekindled their sinking spirits, see obs. i.

i) Tyrtæus, son of Archembrotus, commonly styled an Athenian of Aphidnæan, Paus. IV, 15, 3. Strab. p. 362. Plat. leg. 1, 629 a. 630, but also a Laconian or Milesian, Suid. s. v., at the time of the second Messenian war reconciled by his lays the striving factions at Sparta, Arist. Pol. VIII, 7, 4. Paus. IV, 18, 2, and fired the war spirit of the youth, Plut. Cleom. 2. Hor. A. P. 402. Hence, even at a later period, his war songs were sung in the field, Lyk. Leokr. p. 162. Athen. XIV, p. 630 f. Fragments of an elegiac poem Εὐνομία are preserved, in praise of the Doric customs and constitution, Plut. Lyc. 6. Bergk. fr. 2—7; three considerable fragments of his war elegies, Bergk. fr. 10. 11. 12, and scanty remnants of his anapæstic marching songs (ἐμβατήρια μέλη), Bergk. fr. 15. 16.

k) Terpander, probably of Antissa in Lesbos, Suid. v. Τέρπανδρος, conquered about 676 B.C. in the musical contest at the Karneian festival at Sparta, Athen. XIV, p. 635. E, and four times in the Pythian games at Delphi, Plut. d. Mus. p. 1132. E. He is called the inventor of the seven-stringed Kithara, which he substituted for that with four strings, Strab. p. 618; and composed songs for this instrument, which he set to various tunes, Plut. d. Mus. p. 1132. C. 1133. B, and thus as poet and composer was the founder at once of Doric music and melic poetry at Sparta, Plut. d. Mus. p. 1134. B. 1146. B. Like his successor Thaletas, who was invited to Sparta from Krete, and Tyrtæus, he too is said to have tranquillised the party quarrels at Sparta, Plut. d. Mus. 1146. B. Amongst the scanty fragments of his poems two verses are preserved in praise of Sparta, Plut. Lyc. 21. At an early period such songs were indigenous in Krete with the usual armed dances, Schol. Pind. Pyth. II, 127. Hymn. Hom. Apoll. 518. f., the composition of which was ascribed above all to Thaletas, Strab. p. 481. Thaletas sang also at Sparta, Plut. Lyc. 4, and his compositions were sung still later at the festival of the Gymnopædia, Athen. XV, p. 678. C. For similar poets and musicians cf. Plut. de Mus. p. 1132 C. 1133. A. 1134 B.

l) Alkman circa 671—657, settled at Sparta, Suid. v. Ἀλκμάν. Euseb. Chron. arm. Olymp. 30, 3 (Hier. 30, 4) p. 86 f. ed. Schöne. cf. Alex. Æthol. Plan. 1, p. 207. He composed hymns and set them to music, Bergk. fr. 1. 2. 8. 17. 18. Pæans, fr. Banqueting-songs, fr. 25, Love-songs, fr. 28. 29; for the most part short songs in the Doric dialect with varying, in part strophic, rhythms

Second Period. 1104—500 b.c.

Olympiad.	b. c.	DORIC STATES.	ATHENS.		COLONIES.	
			Archons.	in Italy.	in Sicily.	in the Eastern Sea.
XXV, 4	677	....	....	....	....	Chalkedon by Megara[47].
XXVI, 4	673	....	....	Lokri by the Lokrians[48].		
XXVII, 2	671	....	Leostratus.			
XXVII, 3	670	Orthagoras, the first tyrant of Sikyon[49].				
XXVII, 4	669	The Spartans defeated by the Argives at Hysiæ[50].	Peisistratus.			
XXVIII, 1	668	Eira taken by the Spartans, and the Messenians again completely subdued[51].	Autosthenes.			
XXIX, 1	664	....	Miltiades.	....	Akræ by Syracuse[52].	
XXX, 1	660	....	....	....	....	Byzantium by Megara[53].
XXX, 2	659	....	Miltiades.			
XXXI, 2	655	Kypselus, tyrant of Corinth[54].				

47) Thuc. IV, 25. Strab. p. 820. Herod. IV, 144; "17 years before Byzantium." According to Hieron. chron. p. 85 in 685 b.c. (= Abr. 1332).

48) Strab. p. 259. Arist. ap. Polyb. XII, 5—11. According to Ephor. in Strab. l. c. Lokri (surnamed Epizephyrii) was a colony of the Opuntian, according to others of the Ozolian Lokrians. For Zaleukus the law-giver of Lokri, circ. 660, see Ephor. ap. Strab. p. 260, Schol. on Pind. Ol. XI, 17. Diod. XII, 20 ff. Arist. Pol. II. xii, 6. 7. Hipponium (Vibo Valentia) and Medma were founded by Lokri, Strab. p. 225.

49) See Arist. Pol. VIII, 12, 1. Orthagoras was succeeded by (Andreas?) Myron, Aristonymus, Kleisthenes, see Herod. VI, 126. Paus. II, 8, 1. Arist. Pol. VIII, 12, 12.—Arist. Pol. VIII, 12, 1: πλεῖστον γὰρ ἐγένετο χρόνου ἡ περὶ Σικυῶνα τυραννὶς ἡ τῶν Ὀρθαγόρου παίδων καὶ αὐτοῦ Ὀρθαγόρου· ἔτη δ᾽ αὕτη διέμεινεν ἑκατόν· τούτου δ᾽ αἴτιον, ὅτι τοῖς ἀρχομένοις ἐχρῶντο μετρίως καὶ πολλὰ τοῖς ἀρχομένοις ἐδούλευον· καὶ διὰ τὸ πολεμικὸς γενέσθαι οὐκ ἦν εὐκαταφρόνητος Κλεισθένης, καὶ τὰ πολλὰ ταῖς ἐπιμελείαις ἐδημαγώγουν. For chronology see obs. 74.

50) Paus. II, 24, 8. According to Paus. III, 75 Kynuria was conquered by the Spartans under Theopompus; but probably the conquest was not made till after the battle of Hysiæ.

51) Paus. IV, 20—24. Aristomenes died at Ialysus in Rhodes. The Messenians, who remained behind, were again made Helots, Paus. IV, 23, 1.

52) Thuc. VI, 5; "70 years after Syracuse." According to Steph. Byz. s. v. Enna was also founded in the same year by settlers from Syracuse.

53) Herod. IV, 144. Scymn. Ch. 717. Steph. Byz. s. v. The date as given by Euseb. Chron. Arm. p. 86 (660 b.c. = 1357 Abr.; Hieron. 658 = 1359). Shortly before Byzantium, Selymbria was also founded by Megara, Scymn. Ch. 715.

54) See Herod. V, 92. For the previous state of affairs and the descent of Kypselus see Id. § 2: ἦν ὀλιγαρχίη καὶ οὗτοι Βακχιάδαι καλεόμενοι ἔνεμον τὴν πόλιν, ἐδίδοσαν δὲ καὶ ἤγοντο ἐξ ἀλλήλων. Ἀμφίονι δὲ ἐόντι τούτων τῶν ἀνδρῶν γίνεται θυγάτηρ χωλή, οὔνομα δέ οἱ ἦν Λάβδα. ταύτην, Βακχιαδέων γὰρ οὐδεὶς ἤθελε γῆμαι, ἴσχει Ἠετίων ὁ Ἐχεκράτεος, δήμου μὲν ἐκ Πέτρης ἐών, ἀτὰρ τὰ ἀνέκαθεν Λαπίθης τε καὶ Καινείδης. This Eetion was the father of Kypselus, himself a descendant of Melas, who had come with Aletes to Corinth, see Paus. V, 18, 2. To commemorate the preservation of Kypselus, the chest was consecrated at Olympia, in which, according to tradition, Kypselus was concealed; this Pausanias saw and described, V, c. 17—19. According to Arist. Pol.

The Age of the Inner Development of the Hellenes. 25

Olympiad.	B. c.	DORIC STATES.	ATHENS.	COLONIES			ART AND LITERATURE.
			Archons.	in the Western Sea.		in the Eastern Sea.	
				in Sicily.	Elsewhere.		
XXXI, 3	654	....	....	....	....	Akanthus and Stageira by Andros ; Abdera by Klazomenæ; Istros, Lampsakus, Borysthenes by Miletus⁵⁵).	
XXXIII, 1	648	....	....	Himera by Zanklo ;			
XXXIV, 1	644	....	Dropides.	Kasmenæ by Syracuse⁵⁶).			
XXXV, 2	639	....	Damasias.				
XXXVII, 2	631	....	....	....	Kyrene by Thera⁵⁷).		
XXXVII, 3	630	....	....	....	Naukratis by Miletus⁵⁸).	....	Mimnermus of Kolophon ᵐ). (Elegiac poet).
XXXVIII, 1	628	....	....	Selinus by Megara Hyblæa⁵⁹).			

VIII, 12, 4 Kypselus was δημαγωγός, and κατὰ τὴν ἀρχὴν ἐτέλεσεν ἀδωροφόρητος; with which however Herod. l. c. § 8 does not agree. The date is settled from the fact, that the rule of the Kypselidæ according to Arist. Pol. l. c. lasted 73½ years (Kypselus 30 years, see id. and Herod. l. c. § 9, Periander 40 years, see Diog. Laert. I, 98, Psammetichus, the son of Gordias 3 years, Arist. l. c.), and that Periander, according to Diog. Laert. I, 95, died in the year 585 B.c. (Ol. XLVIII, 4).

55) See Euseb. Chron. p. 86 ff., who places the foundation of the first four Colonies in the years 657—652 (Abr. 1360—1365). Borysthenes, according to Hieron., was founded in the year 645 B.c. (Abr. 1372). For Abdera see further Solin. Pol. c. 16. This latter town was restored in B. c. 543 by the Teians, who fled from the Persians, see Herod. I, 168. Strab. p. 344.

56) For Himera see Thuc. VI, 5. Diod. XIII, 62. According to Thuc. l. c. fugitives from Syracuse also took part in the colony, so that in consequence the language spoken there was a mixture of Doric and Chalkidic. For Kasmenæ see Thuc. VI, 5: "twenty years after Akræ."

57) Chief notice is Herod. IV, 150—157. The date is fixed by Euseb. Chron. p. 88. Cf. Theophrast. Hist. Plant. VI, 3. Schol. on Pind. Pyth. IV, 1. From Kyrene Barka was founded about the year 550 B.c., Herod. IV, 160.

58) Strab. p. 801. Cf. Herod. II, 154. 178. (The date is only approximate.)

59) Thuc. VI. 4: "a hundred years after the foundation of Megara Hyblæa."

---

m) Mimnermus, Suid. v. Μίμνερμος, lived circa 630, Strab. p. 643, at once flute-player and poet. A collection of his Elegies was known, called after his love Ναννώ, Strab. p. 633. 634. Athen. XIII. p. 597. a. XI. p. 470. a., and an elegy on the battle of the Smyrnæans against the Lydian king Gyges, Paus. IX, 29, 2, and other songs besides. He was preeminently esteemed as a bard of the tender lovesong, Hermesian. in Athen. XIII. p. 597, f. v. 35. Propert. I, 9, 11, Bergk. fr. I. For the subjects and character of his other poetry cf. Bergk. fr. 1. 2. 4. 5. 6. 7.

SECOND PERIOD. 1104—500 B. C.

Olympiad.	B.C.	DORIC STATES.	ATHENS.		COLONIES.		ART AND LITERATURE.
			Archons.		In the Western Sea.		
					In Sicily.	Elsewhere.	
XXXVIII, 4	625	Periander tyrant of Corinth⁶⁰). Theagenes makes himself master of Megara⁶¹).				Epidamnus, Amprakia, Anaktorium, Leukas, Apollonia, by Corinth and Kerkyra⁶¹).	
XXXIX, 4	621		Drakon.	Drakon's Legislation⁶²).			
XL, 1	620			Kylon's attempt to make himself master of Athens⁶⁴.)			
XLI, 2	615		Heniochides.				
XLII, 3	610						Arion of Methymna⁵);

60) Of Periander we are told Arist. Pol. XII, 3, 4: ἐγένετο μὲν τυραννικός, ἀλλὰ πολεμικός, and id. II, 4 it is said of him, that he made most use of the precautionary measures, which tyrants usually employ (see obs. 21). According to Herod. V, 92, § 9 he did not display his cruelty, until after receiving the well known counsel of Thrasybulus, the tyrant of Miletus, cf. Arist. III, 13, 17 (where it is Periander, who gives the advice to Thrasybulus). See further concerning him Herod. III, 47—54. Amongst other proofs, that under him and the Kypselidæ generally the power and the wealth of Corinth increased to a considerable extent, is the fact that, according to Plutarch, De Sera Numinis Vind. c. 7, the colonies Apollonia, Anaktorium, and Leukas were founded in his reign (cf. obs. 61).

61) The founders of Epidamnus were drawn chiefly from Kerkyra, but they were under a Corinthian leader (οἰκιστής), and Corinthians also took part in it, Thuc. I, 24. Strab. p. 316. The foundation of all the other colonies mentioned above is ascribed as a rule to Corinth, Thuc. I, 30. Herod. VIII, 45. Scymn. Ch. v. 459. 465. Plut. Tim. 15. Steph. Byz. s. v. Ἀπολλωνία; but the Kerkyræans took part at all events in Anaktorium and Leukas, Thuc. I, 55. Plut. Them. 25; and probably in Apollonia, like its neighbour Epidamnus, the Kerkyræan element was predominant. The date here given for Epidamnus rests on Euseb. Chron. p. 89. f.; with regard to Amprakia, Leukas, and Anaktorium, we are told that they were founded under Kypselus, Strab. p. 325, 452. Scymn. Ch. v. 454, or under Periander, cf. obs. 60; with regard to Apollonia (Steph. Byz. s. v. Paus. V, 22, 2), we have only the testimony of Plutarch, cited in obs. 60, to fix the date of the colony.

62) Arist. Pol. VIII, 5, 9. Rhet. I, 2, 7. Of the measures, which he adopted, the πολιτεία is alone mentioned by Plutarch, i.e. the demand for repayment of interest paid, Plut. Quæst. Græc. c. 18. The date can only be fixed approximately by the circumstance, that it was with his assistance, that Kylon made himself tyrant of Athens, Thuc. I, 126. Obs. 64. After the fall of Theagenes many changes took place in the political situation; but of these we hear only in general terms, see Arist. Pol. VI, 14, 4. VIII, 5, 4, and the elegies of Theognis, in which this poet, in the period after the fall of Theagenes, complains of the oppression of the nobles by the base rich, cf. obs. 66.

63) The year is only approximately determined: according to Suid. s. v. Δράκων, Tatian. p. 140. Clemens. Alex. Strom. I. p. 309. B. Hieron. Chron. p. 91, he belongs to the 39th Olympiad, according to Euseb. Chron. Arm. p. 90, to the 40th. Plut. Sol. 17. Arist. Pol. II, 12, 13: Δράκοντος δὲ νόμοι μὲν εἰσι, πολιτείᾳ δὲ ὑπαρχούσῃ τοὺς νόμους ἔθηκεν (i.e. his laws made no alteration in the existing constitution). ἴδιον δ' ἐν τοῖς νόμοις οὐδὲν ἐστιν, ὅ τι καὶ μνείας ἄξιον, πλὴν ἡ χαλεπότης διὰ τὸ ζημίας μέγεθος.

64) With regard to the chronology, we can only say with certainty that the occurrence took place somewhere about this time, and in an Olympic year; this latter is told us by Thucydides. Chief notice: Thuc. I, 126. The attempt failed. Kylon escaped; his followers were put to death contrary to express promise, part in holy places. Hence the murderers, amongst whom the Alkmeonids are specially mentioned, were ἐναγεῖς καὶ ἀλιτήριοι, Thuc. l. c. Paus. VII, 25, 1. Plut. Sol. 12.

n) Arion flourished circa 625—609. Herod. I, 23. Euseb. Chron. Arm. Ol. XLII, 3, p. 90, regulated the Bacchic 'double dance,' for which he composed songs and set them to music, naming them διθύραμβοι, Suid. s. v. Ἀρίων, Herod. l. c. His wonderful preservation, see Herod. l. c. Gell. N. Att. XVI, 19. Ælian. V. h. XII, 45. The hymn to Poseidon, which goes under his name, Bergk. p. 602, is the product of a later age.

The Age of the Inner Development of the Hellenes.   27

Olympiad.	B. C.	DORIC STATES.	ATHENS.	COLONIES.			ART AND LITERATURE.
					in the Western Sea.		
			Archons.		in Sicily.	Elsewhere.	
XLII, 3	610	....	....	....	....	....	Alkæus of Mytilene°); Sappho^p) and Errina^q) at Lesbos; Stesichorus at Himera^r) (Melic Poetry).
XLIII, 4	605	....	....	Aristokles.			
XLIV, 1	604	....	....	Kritias.			
XLV, 1	600	....	....	....	....	Massalia by Phokæa^{65}).	The Philosopher Thales of Miletus, founder of the Ionian Philosophy^s).
XLV, 2	599	....	....	Megakles.	Kamarina by Syracuse^{66}).		
XLVI, 2	595	to Ol. XLVIII, 3 = 586. The first Sacred (or Kirrhæan) War^{67}).		Philombrotus.			

65) Aristot. in Athen. XIII, 576. Strab. p. 179—181. Iust. XLIII, 3—5. Herod. I, 163: οἱ δὲ Φωκαέες οὗτοι ναυτιλίῃσι μακρῇσι πρῶτοι Ἑλλήνων ἐχρήσαντο καὶ τόν τε 'Αδρίην καὶ τὴν 'Ἰβηρίην καὶ τὸν Ταρτησσὸν οὗτοί εἰσιν οἱ καταδέξαντες.

66) Thuc. VI, 5: "135 years after Syracuse."

67) The war lasted 10 years, see Kallisthenes in Athen. XIII, 560. c, and was brought to an end in the archonship of Damasias, Schol. Pind. Pyth. Argum. The war was occasioned by Kirrhæan outrages;

Kirrha was destroyed 591 B. C., but probably the war was only brought to a conclusion five years later with the total annihilation of the Kirrhæans, see Schol. Pind. l. c. Strab. p. 418, Plut. Sol. 11. Paus. II, 9, 6. X, 37, 4. Polyæn. III, 5, 1. Solon (Plut. l. c.) and Kleisthenes, tyrant of Sikyon, are specially named as taking part in it (Paus. and Polyæn. l. c.). This war, moreover, led to the extension of the Pythian games; and the Pythian ora begins with the year, in which the war was brought to a close (or with Ol. XLI, 3, as in the celebration of this year an ἀγὼν στεφανίτης first took place), see obs. 22 and Marm. Par.

o) Alkæus, of noble birth, lived circ. 610—595. Suid. v. Σαπφώ. Strab. p. 617. Euseb. Chron. Arm. Ol. XLVI, 2 p. 92, fought with disaster in the struggle between the Mytilenæans and the Athenians for Sigeium, Herod. V, 94. 95, Involved in the political broils of his native city, he as an aristocrat opposed the tyrants Melanchrus, Myrsilus, and others. He led an unsettled life in banishment, continually fighting; he made an attack on the Æsymnete Pittakus, Bergk. fr. 37. Anthol. Pal. IX, 184, and vainly attempted to secure his restoration by force at the head of political exiles, Strab. l. c. Diog. Laert. I, 74, 76. As we see from the fragments preserved to us, he composed hymns, Bergk. fr. 1. 5. 9. 11, political songs and war songs (στασιωτικά), fr. 15. 18. 25, a panegyric on his brother Antimenidas, fr. 33, drinking songs, fr. 34. 35. 36. 39. 41. 45, and love songs, fr. 55. 59. 60. 63, fresh and lively outpourings of an active, passionate, pleasure-loving nature, in dactylic, logaœdic, iambic, choriambic and Ionic metres.

p) Sappho, a contemporary of Alkæus, born at Eresus or Mytilene in Lesbos, Strab. p. 617. Euseb. Chron. Arm. Ol. XLVI, 2 p. 92, Suid. s. v. Σαπφώ, Athen. XIII, p. 599. c. Anth. Pal. VII, 407. Anth. Plan. I, p. 196, daughter of Skamandronymos and Kleïs, Herod. II, 135, lived and wrote in a circle of matrons and maidens, (Ov.) Her. XV, 15. Philostr. vit. Apollon. I, 30. Suid. l. c., some of whom she celebrated in song, as Atthis, Bergk. fr. 33. 41, Mnasidika, Gyrinna, fr. 75. etc. cf. fr. 11. Alkæus' love for her is testified by the fragment of a love song addressed to her, Bergk. Alk. fr. 55; a younger lover was refused by her, fr. 75. On the other hand, the passion for Phaon, traditionally attributed to her, and her leap from the Loukadian rock

are inventions of a later period, Menander in Strab. p. 452. Suid. l. c. (Ovid.) Her. XV. 220. Stat. Silv. V, 3, 155. Other tales and scandalous rumours about her were devised by Attic comedy, Athen. XIII, p. 599. c. d. Suid. l. c. Max. Tyr. XXIV, p. 472. Her love songs, in short strophes composed of iambic dipodies, dactyls, and choriambi, exhibit, together with softness and grace, the glow of passion and freshness of sensuous feeling, Bergk. fr. 2. 3. 52. 53. 54. Plut. Erot. p. 762. Hor. Od. IV, 9, 10; she is therefore highly praised as a poetess by the ancients, Strab. p. 617. Antip. Sid. Anth. Plan. II, p. 25.

q) Erinna, probably an associate of Sappho, Suid. v. Ἤριννα. Eustath. Il. II, 726. Anthol. Pal. VII, 710, composed Epigrams, Bergk. fr. 118—120, a poem Ἠλακάτη, and Epopœa, Suid. l. c., which are frequently praised by old writers, Anth. Pal. VII, 11. 12. 13. 710. 712. 713. IX, 190. Damophyle was also a contemporary poetess, Philostr. v. Apollon. I, 30.

r) Stesichorus, the oldest and greatest poet of Sicily, lived at Himera circ. 632—553, Suid. v. Στησίχορος. Euseb. Chron. Arm. Ol. XLIII, 2. Hieron. Ol. XLII, 1 p. 90. f. Of his life nothing was known except legends, a. g. the nightingale, which sang on the mouth of the boy, Anth. Plan. I, 128. Plin. H. N. X, 29, 43, his fable of the horse and stag, Arist. Rhet. II, 20. Conon. narr. 42, the loss of his eyesight, Plat. Phædr. 243, A. Pausan. III, 19, 11. Isokr. Hel. Enc. p. 218. For his dying strains, Hieron. Ep. 34, and for his death by a robber's hand, Suid. v. ἐνετήσειμα. Of his lyric-epic poems, as Ἀθλα ἐπὶ Πελίᾳ, Γηρυονηΐς, Ἐρίφυλα, Κύκνος, Ἰλίου πέρσις, Νόστοι, Ἑλένα, Ὀρέστεια, only scanty remnants are preserved, chiefly in dactylic-logaœdic metres.

SECOND PERIOD. 1104—500 B. C.

Olympiad.	B. C.	DORIC STATES.	ATHENS.	COLONIES.	ART AND LITERATURE.
			Archons.	in the Western Sea. in Sicily. Elsewhere.	
XLVI, 3	594		Solon. Legislation of Solon[68].		Solon[1]) (political Elegy, Gnomic poetry).

68) Up to the time of Solon the basis of the political organism consisted merely of the 4 tribes (see p. 9, obs. 13), which were divided each into 3 phratries, these again each into 30 clans, and the clans each into 30 houses; see Polluc. VIII, 111: ὅτε μέντοι τέσσαρες ἦσαν αἱ φυλαί, εἰς τρία μέρη ἑκάστη διῄρητο, καὶ τὸ μέρος τοῦτο ἐκαλεῖτο τριττὺς καὶ ἔθνος καὶ φρατρία· ἑκάστου δὲ ἔθνους γένη τριάκοντα ἐξ ἀνδρῶν τοσούτων, ἃ ἐκαλεῖτο τριακάδες, καὶ οἱ μετέχοντες τοῦ γένους γεννῆται καὶ ὁμογάλακτες, γένει μὲν οὐ προσήκοντες, ἐκ δὲ τῆς συνόδου οὕτω προσαγορευόμενοι. But of all those who belonged to these tribes, the Eupatridæ (p. 11, obs. 20) were the only ones, who shared in the sovereignty, Plut. Thes. 25. Dion. Hal. II, 8. Polluc. l. c., and besides them there was certainly a large number of persons, who were not included in the tribes. From the Eupatridæ were chosen the archons, see obs. 45; likewise the Areopagus, which, already in existence before the time of Solon, supported the Archons as a board of advice (Plut. Sol. 19), and at the same time formed the highest tribunal; further the ναύκραροι, for whom see Polluc. VIII, 108. Herod. V, 71; and the ἐφέται, who were instituted by Drakon to try charges of homicide, Polluc. VIII, 125. The constitution was therefore thoroughly aristocratic, and at this period had become more and more oppressive from the merciless employment of the laws concerning debt on the part of the aristocrats, so that many of the citizens had mortgaged their lands, others had given up themselves or their children to serfdom, or left the country, Plut. Sol. 13, 15. But the discontent at this state of affairs had given rise to the formation of three parties at enmity with one another, the Διάκριοι (Democrats), πεδιεῖς or πεδιαῖοι (Oligarchs), and πάραλοι (who stood midway between the other two), Plut. Sol. 13. Thus, as Drakon's legislation had not led to the desired result, the task of remedying the existing evils by new laws was allotted to Solon, the son of Exekestides, of the race of Kodrus (Diog. Laert. III, 1), when Archon for the year 594. The chief source of our knowledge about him is Plut. Solon. His good service in the conquest of Salamis, which had fallen into the hands of Megara, id. 8—10, his participation in the first sacred war, id. 11, cf. obs. 67. The banishment of the Alkmæonids, and the purification of the city as a preparation for the new legislation, id. 12, cf. obs. 64. The work of legislation was inaugurated by the σεισάχθεια, by which, according to Solon's own account (in his verses preserved in Plut. Sol. 15 and Aristid. II. p. 536. Dind.; ὅρους ἀνεῖλον πολλαχῇ πεπηγότας—πολλοὺς δ' Ἀθήνας πατρίδ' ἐς θεόκτιτον ἀνήγαγον πραθέντας), the mortgage-pillars were removed, serfdom for debt abolished, and the exiles restored; which measure in all these cases, as regards the poor, must necessarily have consisted, as Dionys. Hal. V, 65 expressly says, in a cancelling of debts, whilst to the creditors it only afforded in other ways some relief, by a depreciation of the currency (in a proportion of 100 : 73), Plut. Sol. 15. He next divided the people according to their property into 4 classes: πεντακοσιομέδιμνοι, whose property annually yielded at least 500 modimni (about one bushel and a half) of corn, or 500 metretæ (about 9 gallons) of oil; ἱππεῖς with 300; ζευγῖται with 200 (or 150, Dem. adv. Makart. p. 1067) medimni or metretæ; θῆτες with an income falling below this last standard, Plut. Sol. 18. Arist. Pol. II, 9, 6. Polluc. VIII, 130. These classes furnished the scale, by which the taxes (the proportion of the I classes being 1 Talent, ½ talent, 10 minæ, nothing, Polluc. l. c.) and other burdens, but also at the same time participation in the exercise of civil rights, were regulated; thus the constitution was a "timokracy," or, as Aristotle also called it, an ὀλιγαρχία πολιτική, i.e. midway between an oligarchy and democracy, Arist. Pol. 11, 12, 2. The most important points to notice in this constitution, which perhaps was not completely organised in the one year 594 B.C., but gradually in a number of years, are as follows: Archons and Areopagus were retained, both for the administration of justice; but the latter was likewise entrusted with the supervision of the whole state administration, Isokr. Areop. p. 147. Philochor. fr. 17 and 141. h. ed, Müller, cf. Æschyl. Eum. 666 ff., both boards accessible to citizens of the 1st Class alone, Plut. Arist. I. Sol. 19; for the management of public affairs he instituted the βουλή, consisting of 400 members, 100 out of each tribe, whose decrees were partly absolute, partly preliminary decrees (προβουλεύματα) prepared for the final decision of the public assembly (ἐκκλησία). Only citizens of the first 3 classes were admitted to the βουλή, but all citizens to the ἐκκλησία. Finally a popular tribunal, the ἡλιαία, was also instituted, consisting of (no at least later) 6000 citizens. See Plut. Sol. 18—19. Arist. Pol. II, 12. For criticism of Solon see Arist. l. c. § 4: Σόλων γε ἔοικε τὴν ἀναγκαιοτάτην ἀποδιδόναι τῷ δήμῳ δύναμιν, τὸ τὰς ἀρχὰς αἱρεῖσθαι καὶ εὐθύνειν, and Solon's own words, Plut. Sol. 18: δήμῳ μὲν

He perfected the choral song by adding the Epode to the Strophe and Antistrophe. Suid. s. v. Τρία Στησιχόρου. For his fame as an artist see Cic. Verr. II, 35, 87. Anth. Pal. VII, 75.

a) The Ionian philosophy sought to solve the problem of the first cause of things. The first Ionian philosopher, and at the same time the first Greek philosopher, is Thales, circ. 639—549 B.C., Euseb. Chron. Arm. Ol. XXXV, 2. LVIII, 2 p. 88. 95. Herod. I, 170. Diog. L. I, 22 f. Suid. s. v.; he was also counted amongst the seven wise men. In his capacity of statesman he gave advice to the Ionian towns, Diog. L. I, 95. Herod. I, 170, and diverted the Halys, Herod. I, 75. As a student of natural science, mathematics, and astronomy, Diog. L. I, 22, 23, 24, he foretold an eclipse of the sun, Herod. I, 74; see also Arist. Pol. I, 11, 8 f. As a philosopher he saw in water the origin of all things, Arist. Metaph. I, 3, Cic. de nat. d. I, 10. He left no writings behind him in the opinion of most ancient authors, Diog. L. I, 23, Themist. or XXVI, p. 317.

1) With regard to Solon's poems, mention is made of the elegy 'Salamis' in 100 verses, by which he stirred up his fellow citizens to recover Salamis, Bergk. fr. 1, 2, 3, further of elegies on the Athenian state, fr. 4. For his constitution, fr. 5, cf. obs. 68. For the tyranny of Peisistratos, fr. 10, 3. He also composed in elegiac metre 'Ὑποθῆκαι εἰς ἑαυτόν, fr. 13, πρὸς Φιλόκυπρον, fr. 19, πρὸς Μίμνερμον, fr. 20, πρὸς Κριτίαν, fr. 22, and others, fr. 23—27; trochaic tetrameters πρὸς Φῶκον, fr. 32—35; iambic trimeters, fr. 36 etc. His poetry is praised by Plato Tim. p. 21, c. Moreover the statesmen, for such we understand by the wise men, worked by poetry, as Solon did; so Periander, Diog. L. I, 97. Suid. v. Περίανδρος, Cheilon, Diog. L. I, 68, Bias, id. I, 85, Pittakus, id. 78, 79, Kleobulus, id. I, 91, cf. Plut. Protag. p. 343, a. Diog. L. 41, 42.

The Age of the Inner Development of the Hellenes.

Olympiad.	B.C.	DORIANS.	ATHENS.	COLONIES			ART AND LITERATURE.
					in the Western Sea. in Sicily.	Elsewhere.	in the Eastern Sea.
			Archons.				
XLVI, 4	593	....	Dropides.				
XLVII, 1	592	....	Eukrates.		....	....	Odessus by Miletus⁶⁸).	Anaximander of Miletus ᵘ) (Philosopher).
XLVII, 3	590	....	Simon.				
XLVIII, 1	588	....	Philippus.				
XLVIII, 4	585	Periander dies: Psammetichus the last tyrant of Corinth⁶⁹).	Damasias I ?		....	....	....	Sakadas of Argos ᵛ) (melic poetry).
XLIX, 3	582	....	Damasias II	Akragas by Gela⁷¹).			
XLIX, 4	581	Tyranny in Corinth overthrown by the Spartans⁷²).					
L, 2	579	....	....	Lipara by Knidus and Rhodes⁷³).			
L, 4	577	....	Archestratides.				
LII, 3	570	Kleisthenes dies: end of the tyranny at Sikyon⁷⁴).	Aristomenes.	....	....	....	Æsopus ʷ) (fable-poet).

γὰρ ἔδωκα τόσον κράτος ὅσσον ἐπαρκεῖ, τιμῆς οὔτ' ἀφελὼν οὔτ' ἐπορεξάμενος. οἱ δ' εἶχον δύναμιν καὶ χρήμασιν ἦσαν ἀγητοί, καὶ τοῖς ἐφρασάμην μηδὲν ἀεικὲς ἔχειν· ἔστην δ' ἀμφιβαλὼν κρατερὸν σάκος ἀμφοτέροισι, νικᾶν δ' οὐκ εἴασ' οὐδετέρους ἀδίκως. Other remarkable laws: the prohibition of neutrality, Plut. Sol. 20, the arrangement about heiresses, id., the command not to speak ill of the dead, id. 21, the prohibition of idleness, id. 22. etc. All the laws were written upon ἄξονες or κύρβεις, id. 25. Pollux VIII, 28. To prevent the Athenians from making any immediate changes, he made them swear to retain the laws unaltered for ten years, and then went to travel abroad, Herod. I, 29. Plut. Sol. 25, visiting Ægypt, Kyprus (and king Krœsus of Lydia? Herod. I, 30—31); but returned to Athens, and died there, either two years after Peisistratus had made himself tyrant, or still later, Plut. Sol. 32. According to another tradition, Solon first began his travels during the tyranny of Peisistratus, and died, not at Athens, but at Soli in Kyprus, see esp. Diog. Laert. I, 50, 62.

69) "Under Astyages." Scymn. Ch. v. 748.
70) Of Psammetichus nothing further is known, than that he was nephew of Periander, see Nicol. Damasc. fr. 60 ed. Müller, a Kypselid, and son of Gordias (or Gordius), see Arist. Pol. VIII, 12, 3. In general see obs. 54.
71) Thuc. VI, 4; "108 years after Gela."
72) Plut. de Herod. Mal. c. 21. p. 859.
73) Diod. V, 9. Strab. p. 275. Paus. X, 11, 3.
74) For the measures, which Kleisthenes took to assure his rule, and at the same time to satisfy the revengeful feelings of his fellow clansmen against their Dorian rulers, see Herod. V, 67—68: most

u) Anaximander, pupil of Thales circ. 611—547, Apollod. ap. Diog. L. II, 2. Procem. 14, Student of natural science, astronomy, and geography, manufactured, as the story goes, sun-dials, maps and globes; taught that "the infinite" (τὸ ἄπειρον Diog. L. l. c.) was the first cause (ἀρχή) of all things, and is said to have set forth his views in a work περὶ φύσεως (the first philosophical writing).

v) Sakadas, poet and composer, conquered thrice with the flute at the Pythian games, 586—578. Plut. Mus. p. 1134. a. b. Amongst his known works were songs and elegies, Paus. X, 7, 3. VI, 14, 4. II, 22, 9. IV, 27, 4, and an Ἰλίου πέρσις, Atheu. XIII, p. 610 C.

w) The oldest fable, in which animals are introduced, is that in Hesiod. Op. et D. 202 f. Æsopus, of Phrygian descent, lived circ. 572 B.C., Diog. L. I, 72. Suid v. Αἴσωπος, Herod. II, 134; he is said to have been at first a slave, afterwards to have lived at the Court of Krœsus, Plut. Sol. 28, finally to have been slain by the Delphians, Herod. l. c. Plut. ser. num. vind. p. 556 f. The best part of Babrius'

SECOND PERIOD. 1104—500 B.C.

Olympiad.	B.C.	DORIANS.	ATHENS.	COLONIES.			ART AND LITERATURE.
			Archons.	in the Western Sea.		in the Eastern Sea.	
				in Sicily.	Elsewhere.		
LIII, 3	566		Hippokleides.				
LIV, 1	564					Alalia by Phokæa[75])	
LIV, 2	563						Amisus by Phokæa[76]).
LV, 1	560	Anaxandridas and Ariston, kings of Sparta[77]).	Komias.	Peisistratus tyrant[78]).			Krœsus, king of Lydia[79]), subdues the Greeks on the continent of Asia Minor[80]).	The Philosophers Anaximenes of Miletus[x]); Pherekydes of Syros[y]). (Rise of Greek Prose).

characteristic of them all is the alteration of the names of the Doric tribes, to which he gave the new names 'Ύλλεις, 'Ονεᾶται, Χοιρεᾶται. A proof of his wealth and great consequence is afforded by the festivities, with which he celebrated the marriage of his daughter Agariste to the Athenian Megakles, Herod. VI, 126—130. After the death of Kleisthenes the insulting epithets were still applied to the Dorian tribes for a period of 60 years, after which time a reconciliation was effected and the old names restored; at this time we may perhaps set the tyranny of Æschines, Plut. de Herod. Malign. c. 21. p. 859. The dates thus given rest partly on Aristotle's account of the duration of the Orthagorid dynasty (obs. 49), partly on the fact, that Myron is recorded as victor in the Olympic games of Ol. XXXIII (648 B.C.), and last of all, on the fact, that Kleisthenes took part in the first sacred war, obs. 67, and in 582 B.C. conquered in the Pythian games, see Paus. X, 7, 8.

75) Herod. I, 165—166.

76) Scymn. Ch. v. 918: "4 years before Herakleia."

77) According to Herod. I, 67 the rule of these sovereigns was contemporaneous with that of king Krœsus. In their reign the Tegeatans were subdued, see obs. 63.

78) The party struggles of the Diakrians, Parali, and Pedimans (obs. 68) had at this time broken out afresh; the leaders were Peisistratus (of the Diakrians), the Alkmæonid Megakles (of the Parali), and given above.

80) Herod. I, 6: πρὸ δὲ τῆς Κροίσου ἀρχῆς πάντες Ἕλληνες ἦσαν ἐλεύθεροι. For their subjection to Krœsus, see id. 26—27.

Lykurgus (of the Pedimans). Peisistratus first craftily obtained himself a bodyguard, and then by means of it raised himself to supreme power, Herod. I, 59. Plut. Sol. 30. The character of his rule, Herod. l. c.: Ἔνθα δὴ ὁ Πεισίστρατος ἦρχε Ἀθηναίων οὔτε τιμὰς ἰούσας συνταράξας οὔτε θέσμια μεταλλάξας, ἐπί τε τοῖς κατεστεῶσι ἔνεμε τὴν πόλιν κοσμέων καλῶς τε καὶ εὖ, cf. Thuc. VI, 54 and the instances of his mildness, Arist. Pol. VIII, 12, 2. Plut. Sol. 31. He was twice driven out by the coalition of his adversaries, the first time probably 554 B.C., the other time 547, but both times returned and again possessed himself of the tyranny; first (probably 548 B.C.) by his reconciliation with Megakles, next (537) by force, Herod. I, 60—64. Arist. Pol. VIII, 12, 5. The time and duration of the Peisistratid dynasty in general, also the year in which Peisistratus died and Hipparchus was murdered, are perfectly established, see Herod. V, 55. 65. Arist. Pol. VIII, 12, 5. Thuc. VI, 59. Eratosth. ap. Schol. on Aristoph. Vesp. 500; with regard to the interruptions in the rule of Peisistratus, caused by his expulsion on two occasions, this much only is certain, that his second exile came to an end in its eleventh year, Herod. I, 26, and that both periods of banishment together lasted 16 years, Arist. l. c.

79) His reign lasted 14 years, Herod. I, 86, and as his fall happened in 546 B.C., obs. 85, it follows that he came to the throne in the year given above.

collection of fables must be referred to Æsopus, who does not appear to have committed his fables to writing.

x) Anaximenes, pupil of Anaximander, astronomer and philosopher, held air to be the origin of things, Diog. L. II, 3. Prœm. 14. Arist. Metaph. I, 3.

y) Pherekydes, circ. 596—540, Diog. L. I, 121. Cic. Thuc. I, 16,

said to have been the teacher of Pythagoras, Diog. L. Prœm. 13. 15. I, 119. Iamblich. v. Pyth., and acquainted with the learning of the Phœnicians, as also of the Egyptians and Chaldæans, Suid. v. Φερεκύδης. Euseb. Præp. Ev. X, 7, 5; was one of the oldest Greek prose writers, wrote Περὶ φύσεως καὶ θεῶν, Theopomp. ap. Diog. L. I, 116. Suid. l. c., and taught the migration of souls.

The Age of the Inner Development of the Hellenes.

Olympiad.	B.C.	DORIANS.	ATHENS.	COLONIES.	ART AND LITERATURE.
LV, 2	559		Archons. Hegestratus.	Herakleia (in Pontus) by Megara and Boeotia[81]).	
LVI, 1	556		Euthydemus.	Kyrus founds the Persian Empire[82]).	
LVI, 3	554	Tegea compelled to acknowledge the hegemony of Sparta[83]).			
LVIII, 1	548		Erxikleides.		
LVIII, 3	546	The Argives defeated by the Spartans[84]).		The Lydian Empire conquered by Kyrus[85]). Subjection of the Greeks in Asia Minor and the islands to Persia[86]).	
LIX, 2	543			The Phokæans found Velia in lower Italy: the Teians fly to Abdera[87].	Anakreon of Teos[z]); Ibykus of Rhegium[aa]); Theognis of Megara[bb]);

81) Seymn. Ch. v. 972 ff. 975: καθ' οὓς χρόνους ἐκράτησε Κῦρος Μηδίας. Cf. Xenoph. Anab. V, 10, 1. Paus. V, 26, 6. Diod. XIV, 31.

82) He was king 29 years, Herod. I, 214 (or 30 years, according to Dinon ap. Cic. de div. I, 23. Iustin. 1, 6, 14). Cf. obs. 89.

83) The Spartans had always been unfortunate in their former operations against Tegea; they now conquered it, after they had, in obedience to an oracle, fetched home the bones of Orestes, Herod. I, 65—68. Paus. III, 3, 5. But the Tegeatans were, nevertheless, always peculiarly honoured allies of Sparta. The prosperous termination of the war falls in the period immediately preceding the embassy of Krœsus to Sparta, which probably took place in 554 B.C., see Herod. I. 69.

84) The war arose in consequence of an attempt on the part of the Argives to win back the lost territory of Kynuria. Both parties agreed to leave the decision to a picked body of 300 men from each side. But as the result of this combat was not altogether free from doubt, it ended in a battle, in which the Spartans were victorious, Herod. I, 82. Strab. p. 376. This happened, when Krœsus was already besieged by Kyrus, see Herod. l. c., cf. obs. 85.

85) Solin. Polyb. c. 7. Sosikrates ap. Diog. Laert. I, 95. Dion. Hal. Ep. ad Cn. Pomp. p. 773. de Thuc. iud. p. 820.

86) Herod. I, 141. 152—153, 161—171; also of the islands, id. 171. The conquest took place in the years immediately following the fall of the Lydian empire.

87) Herod. I, 167. For Abdera see obs. 55.

z) Anakreon lived circ. 560—531, Athen. XIII, p. 599 C. Suid. s. v., attained the age of 85, and, after the Teians fled before Kyrus to Abdera, stayed at the court of Polykrates at Samos, Strab. p. 638, then at Athens with Hipparchus, Plat. Hipparch. p. 228 C. Ælian. V. H. VIII, 2; after his fall, again at Teos, and, after the failure of the Ionian revolt, at Abdera, Suid. v. Ἀνακρ. Numerous poems pass under his name, written in his manner by later poets of different ages, cf. Bergk. Anacreontica, p. 807—862; the genuine poems are for the most part fragments. Amongst them are invocations of deities, Bergk. fr. 1. 2; love songs, fr. 4. 14. 46. 47. 48. 75; lampoons, fr. 21; drinking songs, fr. 63. 64. 90; elegies, fr. 94; epigrams, fr. 100. 108. 111. 112. 113, 115, etc., chiefly in logaœdic metre. The poet himself says of his poetry fr. 45: χαρίεντα μὲν γὰρ ᾄδω, χαρίεντα δ᾽ οἶδα λέξαι. Kritias praises him in Athen. XIII, 600 D (ᾠδῶν Ἀνακρείοντα).

aa) Ibykus flourished circ. 560—540. He emigrated to Polykrates at Samos, and was murdered, as the story goes, by robbers at Corinth, Suid. v. Ἴβυκος. Anth. Pal. VII, 745, whilst an epitaph states that he died in his native city, Anth. Pal. VII, 714. He wrote, taking Stesi-

chorus especially as his model, seven books of lyric poems in the Doric dialect with choral systems of rhythm, in particular fiery love-songs (ἐρωτομανέστατος περὶ μειράκια), Suid. l. c. Bergk. fr. 1. 2. 26.

bb) Theognis lived circ. 540, after the fall of Theagenes, Steph. Byz. s. v. Μέγαρα. Suid. s. v. Θέογνις. In the struggles between the aristocratic and democratic party he threw in his lot with the former, Bergk. Theogn. v. 219 f. 949 f., was attacked by both parties as a moderate aristocrat, v. 367 f., betrayed by friends, v. 813. 861, lost his property by plundering, v. 677. 1200, and wandered about in banishment in Sicily, Euboea, and Sparta, v. 783 f. Being homesick, he returned to Megara, v. 787 f. 1123 f., and lived through the Persian wars, v. 787 f. 1223 f. He composed a crown of elegies addressed to Kyrnus in 2800 verses, Suid. l. c., which at an early period were abbreviated, mutilated, transposed, and interpolated. Together with the elegies addressed to other persons, the total number of the poet's verses preserved amounts to 1380, Bergk. l. c. In these he upholds the claims and principles of the Dorian nobility, v. 26. 31 f. 53 f. 183 f. 319 f. 609 f., and, full of contempt and bitterness for the ruling democracy,

SECOND PERIOD. 1104—500 B. C.

Olympiad	B.C.	DORIANS.	ATHENS.	COLONIES.	ART AND LITERATURE.
LXI, 4	533	....	Archons. Therikles.		
LXII, 1	532	....	....	....	Polykrates, tyrant of Samos[dd]).	Phokylides of Miletus[cc]) political elegy and gnomic poetry; Hipponax of Ephesus[dd])(Choliambics); Pythagoras of Samos[ee]), Mathematician, Philosopher, Statesman; Xenophanes of Kolophon[ff]), founder of the Eleatic philosophy.
LXII, 4	529	....	....	....	Death of Kyrus; Kambyses succeeds[89]).	
LXIII, 2	527	....	....	Death of Peisistratus; his son Hippias succeeds him[90]).		
LXIV, 1	524	....	Miltiades.		

88) The date assigned to the commencement of his rule is from Euseb. Chron. Arm. p. 96, cf. Polyæn. I, 23, 2 and Herod. I, 64. His fall took place at the time when Kambyses was ill, therefore shortly before his death, Herod. III, 120. For him see Herod. III, 39—60. 120—125, cf. Arist. Pol. VIII, 11, 9. According to Herod. III, 139, in his reign Samos was the greatest of all Hellenic and barbarian towns, and the naval power of Samos seems to have been at that time the greatest in the Hellenic world, Herod. III, 39. Thuc. I, 13. After the death of Polykrates Samos was subdued by the Persians, and made over to Syloson, the brother of Polykrates, who had been banished by

.... ces in its rabble government the ruin of the state and the dissolution of the good old customs, v. 42 f. 53 f. 287 f. 315 f. 675 f. 833 f. 1109, and, as its result, tyranny v. 39 f. 52 f. 1081 f. 1181 f. He thinks full licence should be given to mere pretence of friendliness, v. 61 f., perfidy, v. 283 f., and violence towards the common citizens, v. 847 f.

cc) Phokylides, the contemporary of Theognis, Suid. v. Φωκυλίδης, Cyrill. adv. Julian. VII, p. 225, well off, Bergk. fr. 7 f. 10, of moderate political views, fr. 12 (μέσος θέλω ἐν πόλει εἶναι), composed moral proverbs and rules for conduct under the title Κεφάλια, of which only few fragments are preserved, Bergk. p. 357—360. A ποίημα νουθετικόν, which was ascribed to Phokylides, is of later origin.

dd) Hipponax lived circ. 546—537, at Klazomenæ, having been banished by the tyrants Athenagoras and Komas from his native city, and composed bitter lampoons, in particular against the sculptors Bupalus and Athenis, who had caricatured his ungainly figure, Plin. XXXVI, 5. Suid. s. v. Ἱππῶναξ. Procl. ap. Phot. Bibl. Cod. 239. Athen. XII, p. 552. Ælian. V. H. X, 6, in choliambics or skazons, which were his invention, Bergk. fr. 11. 12. 13. 14. 83. The external circumstances of his life, as also his disposition and poetry, make him appear the proletariate amongst the Greek lyric poets, Bergk. fr. 17. 14. 19. 42.

ee) Pythagoras, pupil of Pherekydes and Anaximander, lived circ. 580—500, educated himself whilst travelling abroad, especially in Egypt, and emigrated from Samos on account of the tyranny of Polykrates to Kroton in lower Italy, Diog. Laert. VIII, 1—4. 15. Suid. s. v. Πυθαγόρας.

the tyrant and obtained help and support from Dareius, see Herod. III, 139—149.

89) Kambyses reigned 7 years, 5 months, Herod. III, 66. Pseudo-Smerdis 7 months, Herod. III, 67, Dareius 36 years. Herod. VII, 4. These accounts, in conjunction with the established date of Dareius' accession to the throne in 485 B.C., are the basis, on which rest the dates connected with the kings Kyrus, Kambyses, Smerdis, and Dareius.

90) For the rule of Hippias, the murder of Hipparchus, and the expulsion of the Peisistratids, see Thuc. I, 20. VI, 54—59. Herod. V, 55—56. 62—65.

Here he gave the constitution an aristocratic form, Diog. L. VIII, 3. By his many-sided learning as philosopher, mathematician, and inventor of the system called by his name, as astronomer, student of medicine, and musician, he gathered round him a circle of numerous pupils, Diog. L. 7, 12. 14. These he organised into a secret league closely knit together by community of goods, with religious rites of initiation and different grades and classes of members, Suid. l. c.; its aim being the cleansing and improvement of the moral and religious life, as is shown by the Pythagorean apophthegms and moral precepts (ἠθικὰ δόγματα, Diog. L. VIII, 22, 8; σύμβολα, Suid. etc.). Pythagoras either met with a violent death at the hands of the democratic party in Kroton, Diog. L. VIII, 14. Suid. l. c., or he died at Metapontium, Diog. L. VIII, 39. As a philosopher (he is said to have been the first to call himself φιλόσοφος, Diog. L. I, 12), he saw in number the essence of things; the best known of his doctrines is that of the migration of souls (Xenophon. ap. Diog. L. VIII, 36 f.). The accounts of writings by him are as dubious as the numerous legends and tales about his person, which were widely propagated at a later time, especially amongst the Neo-Platonists. The most prominent of the Pythagoreans are Philolaus, who reduced the doctrines of the school to a scientific system and committed them to writing, contemporary with Sokrates; and Archytas, contemporary with Plato.

ff) Xenophanes flourished circ. 540—477, Diog. L. IX, 20. Timæus ap. Clem. Strom. 1, p. 301, Euseb. Præp. Ev. XIV, p. 757, and lived at least to the age of 92 years, Bergk. fr. 7. Being banished, he wandered

The Age of the Inner Development of the Hellenes. 33

Olympiad.	B. C.	DORIANS.	ATHENS.	COLONIES.
LXIV, 4	521			Death of Kambyses; Pseudo-Smerdis; Dareius, son of Hystaspes[91]).
LXVI, 2	515			Expedition of Dareius against the Scythians[92]).
LXVI, 3	514		Murder of Hipparchus[93]).	
LXVII, 3	510	Kleomenes and Demaratus, kings of Sparta[94]).	Hippias overthrown[95]).	
LXVII, 4	509		Expansion of the Solonian constitution by Kleisthenes[96]).	

91) See obs. 89.

92) The date of the Scythian expedition cannot be determined with certainty. (Herod. IV, 1—144.) That it was undertaken before 514, we infer from Thuc. VI, 59, cf. with Herod. IV, 138. It cannot well have taken place earlier than 515, as up to that time Dareius was employed in the reduction of the rebellious satraps and provinces, in particular of Orœtes, the Medes and the Babylonians. On his return, Dareius left Megabazus behind him in Thrace to effect its conquest, Herod. IV, 143. V, 1. 2. 15. For the service rendered by Histiæus to Dareius, see id. IV, 136—139, and his recompence, id. V, 11.

93) Although Hipparchus was not tyrant, but brother to him, and so his death did not secure the liberation of Athens—nay, its immediate consequence was that the tyrant's rule pressed still more heavily (see the passages quoted in obs. 90)—nevertheless his murderers, Harmodius and Aristogeiton, lived in the minds of the Athenians as the liberators of Athens, and were extolled as such. So in the famous skolium ap. Athen. XV, p. 695: Ἐν μύρτου κλαδὶ τὸ ξίφος φορήσω, | ὥσπερ Ἀρμόδιος κ' Ἀριστογείτων, | ὅτε τὸν τύραννον κτανέτην, | ἰσονόμους τ' Ἀθήνας ἐποιησάτην, κ. τ. λ.

94) That these two kings, the successors of Anaxandridas and Ariston, were reigning in this year, follows from the fact that both took part in the expedition for the liberation of Athens, Herod. V, 64. Paus. III, 7, 7. From Herod. VI, 108, cf. Thuc. III, 68, it is probable that Kleomenes was already king in 519 B.C., cf. Herod. III, 148.

95) The Alkmæonids first collected an army and marched against the Peisistratids, but were defeated at Leipsydrium, Herod. V, 62; then by the repeated exhortations of the Delphic oracle, the support of which had been won for the Alkmæonids by their restoration of the Delphic temple (burnt down in 548 B.C., Paus. X, 5, 5. Herod. I, 50. II, 180), the Spartans were induced to take upon themselves the expulsion of the Peisistratids; accordingly they first sent Anchimolius against them; but he was defeated: then the king Kleomenes. Hippias retired to the Acropolis, but came to terms with Kleomenes, as his sons had fallen into the Spartan's power, and betook himself to Sigeium. See the passages quoted in obs. 90: cf. Herod. VI, 123. Aristoph. Lysistr. 665 ff., and for Sigeium, which Peisistratus had conquered, Herod. V, 94.

96) Kleisthenes belonged to the family of the Alkmæonids, and was a grandson of Kleisthenes, tyrant of Sikyon, Herod. VI, 131. He had been especially active in the expulsion of the Peisistratids, id. V, 66, but after his return to Athens became involved in a quarrel with another Eupatrid, who, however, was not a member of the Alkmæonid family; being in danger of succumbing to his adversary, he ranged himself with the popular party (so at least Herodotus), and advanced to his exceedingly important reforms, so pregnant with influences in the future, the fundamental principles of which are contained in the following passages. Herod. V, 66: μετὰ δὲ τετραφύλους ἐόντας Ἀθηναίους δεκαφύλους ἐποίησε, τῶν Ἴωνος παίδων, Γελέοντος καὶ Αἰγικόρεος καὶ Ἀργάδεω καὶ Ὅπλητος ἀναλλάξας τὰς ἐπωνυμίας, ἐπιχωρίων δ' ἑτέρων ἡρώων ἐπωνυμίας ἐξευρὼν πάρεξ Αἴαντος· τοῦτον δὲ ὅτε ἀστυγείτονα καὶ σύμμαχον ξεῖνον ἐόντα προσέθετο, cf. id. 98: further Arist. Pol, VII, 4, 18: Ἔτι δὲ καὶ τοιαῦτα κατασκευάσματα χρήσιμα πρὸς τὴν δημοκρατίαν τὴν τοιαύτην, οἷς Κλεισθένης τε Ἀθήνησιν ἐχρήσατο βουλόμενος αὐξῆσαι τὴν δημοκρατίαν —· φυλαί τε γὰρ ἕτεραι ποιητέαι πλείους καὶ φρατρίαι καὶ τὰ τῶν ἰδίων ἱερῶν συνακτέον εἰς ὀλίγα καὶ κοινά καὶ πάντα σοφιστέον. ὅπως ἂν ὅτι μάλιστα ἀναμιχθῶσι πάντες ἀλλήλοις, αἱ δὲ συνήθειαι διαζευχθῶσιν αἱ πρότεραι, and id. III, 2, 3: πολλοὺς γὰρ ἐφυλέτευσε (Κλεισθένης) ξένους καὶ δούλους μετοίκους, i.e. he abolished the 4 old tribes, by which a part of the citizens was excluded from the exercise of civil rights, and instituted 10 altogether new tribes, in which he enrolled, not only the excluded citizens, but also moties and manumitted slaves (Arist.

about in Hellas, Sicily, and lower Italy; and resided in Zankle, Katana, and Elea, Bergk. fr. 7. Diog. Laert. IX, 18, 20. He wrote epics on the foundation of Kolophon and the settlement of the Phokæans in Elea; elegies, iambics, and a didactic poem. As a student of natural science and philosopher he combated the faith in Gods and legends taught by

Homer and Hesiod, Diog. Laert. IX, 18. Karsten Xen. Rel. fr. 1. 5. 7. Bergk. fr. 1, v. 22 (πλάσματα τῶν προτέρων); and taught that God is the oneness of the universe, Arist. Metaph. 1, 5, Diog. Laert. IX, 19. Cic. Acad. IV, 37, 118.

C.   5

34 SECOND PERIOD. 1104—500 B.C.

Olympiad.	B.C.	ATHENS.	HISTORY.	ART AND LITERATURE.
		Archons.		
LXVIII, 1	508	Isagoras.	Kleisthenes expelled from Athens at the instigation of his opponent Isagoras, but recalled after a short time[97]).	
LXVIII, 2	507	....	March of the Peloponnesians, under Kleomenes and Demaratus, together with the Thebans, and Chalkidians against Athens. The Peloponnesian army is disbanded owing to the dissension of its leaders and the opposition of the Corinthians; and the Thebans and Chalkidians are defeated[98]).	
LXIX, 1	504	Akestorides.	....	The Philosophers Herakleitus of Ephesus[gg]); Parmenides of Elea[hh]).
LXIX, 4	501	....	The disastrous undertaking of Aristagoras against Naxos[99]).	

l. c.). The names of the tribes are: Erectheis, Ægeis, Pandionis, Leontis, Akamantis, Œneis, Kekropis, Hippothoontis, Æantis, and Antiochis, Paus. I. 5. [Demosth.] Epit. p. 1397 f. The number of the demes, into which the tribes were distributed by Kleisthenes, was originally 100, Herod. V, 69, afterwards 174, Pol. ap. Strab. p. 396. As a result of this new distribution the number of the βουλή was increased from 400 to 500 (50 from each phyle); and the 50 senators of each phyle managed current affairs for the tenth part of the year, that is for 35 or 36, and in a leap year 38 or 39 days (πρυτανεία, πρυτάνεις); one was always president, ἐπιστάτης, and had the conduct of business, and 9 deputies from the other 9 phylæ usually supported the πρυτάνεις, (πρόεδροι), Suid. v. πρυτανεία, Liban. Arg. to Demosth. adv. Androt. p. 590. It must be added, that ostracism was introduced by Kleisthenes, Thuc. VIII, 73 (διὰ δυνάμεως καὶ ἀξιώματος φόβον). Arist. Pol. III, 13, 15. Diod XI, 55. Plut. Arist. 7. Alkib. 13. Them. 22. etc. Pollux VIII, 19—20.

97) The Spartans by a herald demanded the expulsion of the Alkmæonids (see abs. 64), and consequently also that of Kleisthenes; the Athenians obeyed, and Kleomenes himself came to Athens; but when he tried to abolish the βουλή and hand over the government to a corporation of 300 followers of Isagoras, an outbreak occurred; Kleomenes with his followers occupied the acropolis, and on the third day retired by virtue of a convention, Herod. V, 70—72; cf. Arist. Lysistr. 272. The Athenians were now for a short time so apprehensive, that they applied for help from the Persians, Herod. V, 73.

98) Herod. V, 74—78. 4000 Athenian citizens were sent as κληροῦχοι into the Chalkidian territory, id. 77. For the elevated tone of the Athenians at that time, see id. 78: Ἀθηναῖοι μέν νυν ηὔξηντο· δηλοῖ δὲ οὐ κατ' ἓν μοῦνον ἀλλὰ πανταχῇ ἡ ἰσηγορίη ὡς ἐστὶ χρῆμα σπουδαῖον, εἰ καὶ Ἀθηναῖοι τυραννευόμενοι μὲν οὐδαμῶν τῶν σφέας περιοικεόντων ἦσαν

τὰ πολέμια ἀμείνους, ἀπαλλαχθέντες δὲ τυράννων μακρῷ πρῶτοι ἐγένοντο· δηλοῖ ὦν ταῦτα ὅτι κατεχόμενοι μὲν ἐθελοκάκεον ὡς δεσπότῃ ἐργαζόμενοι, ἐλευθερωθέντων δὲ αὐτὸς ἕκαστος ἑωυτῷ προεθυμέετο κατεργάζεσθαι. The Thebans now contracted an alliance with the Æginetans, whereby the Athenians became involved in a war with Ægina, for the indecisive events of which at its outset, see Herod. V, 79—90. The Spartans, in order to revenge themselves on the Athenians for the injury, which they thought they had suffered in the ejection of Kleomenes, (Herod. l. c. 74. 91), and to prevent the rise of Athens, at this time actually formed the plan of restoring Hippias to power; but their design was wrecked on the opposition of their allies, in particular of the Corinthians, Herod. V, 90—93; hereupon Hippias, who had been summoned to Greece for the said purpose, retired again to Sigeium and left no stone unturned to induce the Persians to march against Athens, id. 94—96. The dates assigned to events from 509—492 B.C. rest purely upon considerations of probability, as we have no firm standing ground; other, but insufficient, chronological data are brought forward, each in its proper place.

99) Histiæus was summoned from Myrkinus, which Dareius had given him, and under some complimentary pretext detained in Susa against his will, Herod. V, 23—24. His son-in-law, Aristagoras, who had been made tyrant in his stead, seduced by Naxian exiles, persuaded Artaphernes, the satrap of Sardis, to embark in an attempt against Naxos, which failed, Herod. V, 30—34. Moved by fear of the vengeance of Artaphernes, by the burden of debts, which he had contracted by the expedition, lastly by the urgent appeals of the discontented Hiatiæus, Aristagoras was driven to the resolution of revolting from the Persian King, Herod. V, 35. It follows from Herod. V, 36, that the revolt took place immediately after the expedition against Naxos.

gg) Heraklcitus flourished circ. 504—501, Diog. Laert. IX, 1. He taught that the essence of all things consists in a constant becoming, or flux (πάντα ῥεῖ); that the becoming is brought about by the strife (πόλεμος, ἔρις) of the elements; and that in this movement fire is the active, over-changing principle. As his teaching, which he laid down in a work, styled περὶ φύσεως or Μοῦσαι, and which he designated as his own exclusive property (id. § 5), often seemed obscure to the ancients, he was called ὁ σκοτεινός, (Aristot.) De Mund. 5. Cic. De Nat. D. I, 26.

hh) Parmenides lived circ. 519—454, Diog. Laert. IX, 21. Alex. Aphrod. Schol. Arist. 536. Plat. Parm. p. 127 A. Theæt. p. 183 E. Sophist. 217 C, pupil of Xenophanes, Arist. Metaph. I, 5. Sext. Emp.

The Age of the Inner Development of the Hellenes. 35

Olympiad.	n. c.	ATHENS.	HISTORY.	ART AND LITERATURE.
LXX, 1	500	Archons. Myrus.	The revolt of Aristagoras and his journey to Greece, in order to solicit help from Sparta and Athens against the Persian king [100]).	Rise of historical composition: The Logographers Hekatæus [ii]), and Dionysius of Miletus [kk]).

100) Aristagoras first set free the Greek towns of Asia Minor from their tyrants, hoping thus to induce them to take part in the revolt, Herod. V, 38; he then went, first to Sparta, to beg for help there; but in vain, Herod. V, 38, 49—51: next to Athens, where it was resolved to send 20 ships to his aid, id. 55. 57, "αὗται δὲ αἱ νέες ἀρχὴ κακῶν ἐγένοντο Ἕλλησί τε καὶ βαρβάροισι." The twenty ships sent by Athens were joined by 5 from Eretria, id. 99.

adv. Mathem. VII, 111. Clem. Al. Strom. I, 301. He wrote a didactic poem in the Ionic dialect and epic metre περὶ φύσεως, in which he taught the unity and immutability of being as the fundamental essence of things, and asserted that thought directed to the pure unified existence was true knowledge; he was the legislator of his native city, Diog. L. l. c. Plut. adv. Col. p. 1126.
ii) Λογογράφοι is the name given to the first Greek historians, who recorded in simple and unadorned prose, for the most part uncritically, the legends of former ages, especially of the foundation of cities and sanctuaries, which up to that time had been orally transmitted. Thuc. I, 21. Dionys. Jud. de Thuc. 5. Diodor. Sic. I, 37. Strab. I. p. 18. Omitting the apocryphal Kadmus of Miletus, Hekatæus is the first of these writers. He flourished circ. 520—500, travelled much, especially in Egypt, dissuaded his fellow citizens from revolt; but when in spite of this it was resolved upon, he exhorted them to shew perseverance and energy in the struggle, Herod. II, 148. V, 36. 125, Suid. v. Ἑκαταῖος. He wrote a geographical work, Περίοδος γῆς (περιήγησις), and a collection of legends, Γενεαλογίαι (Ἱστορίαι), both in prose and in the Ionic dialect, Suid. v. Ἑλλάνικος (l. Ἑκαταῖος). Athen. X, 447 C. D. IX, 410 E. IV, 148 F.

kk) Dionysius, a contemporary of Hekatæus, Suid. s. v. Ἑκαταῖος, wrote a Persian history, Suid. v. Διονύσιος. Accounts of other works from his pen are doubtful.

THIRD PERIOD.

500—431 B.C.

THE HELLENIC RACE IN ITS PRIME.

As a result of the wonderful victories, by which the Persian king's attacks upon the independence of Greece are beaten back, power and consciousness of power are rapidly developed in the Hellenes, and culminate at the highest possible pitch. Amongst all Hellenic states, Athens has already developed the greatest energy during the wars with Persia; it is under her leadership that subsequently the struggle is still further continued, with the object of freeing the rest of the Hellenes in the islands and the coast towns of the Ægean sea from the Persian yoke. The fruits of these victories and glorious exertions redound chiefly to the good of Athens. She makes herself the first Hellenic naval power, and obtains not merely the hegemony by sea, but even for some long time disputes with Sparta the hegemony by land. With regard to home affairs, the last bounds, which confined the democracy, are gradually removed, and thus the whole nation in all its members is raised to the freest and most active participation in public life. Art and literature spring rapidly into the bloom of perfect beauty, whilst master-pieces of skill are produced in the casting of metals, in sculpture, and in architecture, as well as in tragedy. Yet in the soreness and hostile collisions between Sparta and Athens there appear increasing signs of the long and bloody struggle, which in the next period shattered the power and independence of Greece.

Obs. For the period up to the battles of Platæa and Mykale we possess in the last four books of Herodotus a connected and detailed statement of events; from this point onwards Thucydides, in the introduction to his great historical work, is our guide; here he gives a sketch of the period between the Persian wars and the Peloponnesian which, though short, is both trustworthy and instructive. By the side of these historical works of the first rank, other works, chiefly of a much later period, afford us little help, only dealing with single episodes. To this class belong a short epitome in Photius of the Persian histories of Ktesias (circ. 400 B.C.); Diodorus Siculus, whose eleventh book (the preceding five have been lost) commences with the year 480 B.C.: Plutarch in the Lives of Themistokles, Aristeides, Kimon, and Perikles: lastly Cornel'us Nepos and Justin, for whom see Chronological Tables of Roman History, p. 75 k and 93 b.

37

FIRST SECTION.

THE PERSIAN WARS.

500—479 B.C.

Olympiad.	B. C.	HISTORY.
LXX, 2	499	The Ionians together with the auxiliary troops from Athens and Eretria surprise Sardis and burn it[1]; but are defeated on their retreat at Ephesus[2]. The towns on the Hellespont and Karia and Kyprus join the revolt[3].
LXX, 3	498	Kyprus reconquered by the Persians[4]; gradual conquest of the towns on the continent[5]. Flight and death of Aristagoras[6].

1) Herod. V, 99—101. The chronology of this period down to 490 rests on the following data. For 490 B.C. as the year of the battle at Marathon, see obs. 16; 2 years before the expedition of Mardonius took place, that is in 492 B.C., see Herod. VI, 95, cf. id. 46 and 48; 2 years earlier the reduction of Miletus, Herod. VI, 31 and 43; whilst the reduction of Miletus happened in the 6th year of the revolt, Herod. VI, 18. Our information about the course of the revolt is not so perfect, that we can assign events, each to its particular year.

2) Herod. V, 102. The Athenians hereupon left Asia Minor, and abstained from all farther participation in the war, id. 103. Notwithstanding, it was against them that the anger of the Persian king was specially directed, id. 105: βασιλεὺς δὲ Δαρεῖος ὡς ἐξηγγέλθη Σάρδις ἁλούσας ἐμπεπρῆσθαι ὑπό τε 'Αθηναίων καὶ 'Ιώνων—, πρῶτα μὲν λέγεται αὐτόν, ὡς ἐπύθετο ταῦτα, 'Ιώνων οὐδένα λόγον ποιησάμενον, εὖ εἰδότα ὡς οὗτοί γε οὐ καταπροΐξονται ἀποστάντες, εἰρέσθαι οἵτινές εἶεν οἱ 'Αθηναῖοι, μετὰ δὲ πυθόμενον αἰτῆσαι τὸ τόξον, λαβόντα δὲ καὶ ἐπιθέντα οἰστὸν ἄνω ἐς τὸν οὐρανὸν ἀπεῖναι καί μιν ἐς τὸν ἠέρα βαλόντα εἰπεῖν· ὦ Ζεῦ, ἐκγενέσθαι μοι 'Αθηναίους τίσασθαι· εἴπαντα δὲ ταῦτα προστάξαι ἑνὶ τῶν θεραπόντων δείπνου προκειμένου αὐτῷ ἐς τρὶς ἑκάστοτε εἰπεῖν· δέσποτα, μέμνεο τῶν 'Αθηναίων. Accordingly the Ionian revolt, through the share which the Athenians had in it, became a chief occasion of the Persian wars, cf. however obs. 8. 13, 20.

3) Herod. V, 103. 104. (But only the greater part of Karia took part in the revolt, and in Kyprus Amathus held aloof, id. l. c.)

4) Artybius with an army and the Phœnician fleet were sent against Kyprus. The fleet was worsted by the Ionians, who had been summoned to the rescue; but, on the other hand, the Kyprians themselves suffered a complete defeat on land; whereupon the island was roduced to subjection, Herod. V, 108—115. The Kyprians had enjoyed their freedom for the space of a year, Herod. V, 116.

5) Daurises conquers Abydos, Perkote, Lampsakus; and Pæsus on the Hellespont, Herod. V, 117; then turns his arms against Karia, where at first he wins two battles, but is then surprised and destroyed with the whole of his forces, Herod. V, 117—121. At the same time Kios on the Propontis and what was once the Trojan territory, now in the possession of the Æolians, are subdued by Hymeas; also Klazomenæ and Kyme by Artaphernes and Otanes, id. 122—123.

6) Aristagoras deserts the Ionian cause, and retires to Myrkinos, where he and his army are destroyed by the Thracians, Herod. V, 124—126. After the flight and death of Aristagoras, nothing further is recorded with reference to the events of the Ionian war, except that Histiæus arrives in Asia Minor, commissioned by the Persian king to assume the command in chief against the rebels, but intending to betray the Persian army to their enemies: that he was unmasked by Artaphernes, and afterwards turning pirate roamed about the islands of the Archipelago and the coasts of Asia Minor, Herod. VI, 1—5; in which occupation he met with his death in 494 or 493 B.C., id. 26—30.

THIRD PERIOD. 500—431 B.C.

Olympiad	B.C.	ATHENS.	HISTORY.
		Archon.	
LXXI, 1	496	Hipparchus.	
LXXI, 2	495	Philippus.	
LXXI, 3	494	Pythokritus.	The Ionian fleet defeated at Miletus, and Miletus conquered [7]). Defeat of the Argives by the Spartans at the grove of Argus [8]).
LXXI, 4	493	Themistokles.	The islands of the Archipelago and the towns on the north coast of the Hellespont and the Propontis again brought into subjection [9]).
LXXII, 1	492	Diognetus.	The first expedition of the Persians against Greece under Mardonius; Fleet and army almost totally destroyed on Mt. Athos, or in the neighbourhood [10]).
LXXII, 2	491	Hybrilides.	New preparations of Darius: at his summons a large number of the Greek states acknowledge his supremacy [11]).

7) The Persians unite their land and sea force, for an attack upon Miletus, as the hotbed of the war, τἆλλα πολίσματα περὶ ἐλάσσονος ποιησάμενοι, Herod. VI, 6: the number of their ships, which were chiefly furnished by the Phœniclans, but in part also by the Kyprians, Kilikians, and Egyptians (see id.), amounted to 600, id. 9. The Ionians, restricting the war on land to the defence of Miletus, collected their fleet at Lade, an island lying in the neighbourhood of Miletus, intending to venture an engagement with the enemy, id. 7. Their fleet consisted of 80 ships from Miletus, 12 from Priene, 3 from Myus, 17 from Teos, 100 from Chios, 8 from Erythræ, 3 from Phokæa, 70 from Lesbos, 60 from Samos, altogether 353, id. 8. The Persians did not venture a battle, until they had succeeded in corrupting the Samians, id. 9—13. So when the fight began, the Samians (all except 11 ships) took to flight, after them the Lesbians and also most of the other Ionians; the few that made any resistance, amongst whom the Chians chiefly distinguished themselves by their bravery, had to yield to overwhelming force, id, 14—16. Miletus was then taken, and the inhabitants were exiled to Ampe on the Tigris, id. 19—20; "Μίλητος μὲν νῦν Μιλησίων ἠρήμωτο," id. 22. Then, in the same year, Karia was subdued by the Persians, id. 25. (Part of the Samians, ill-pleased with the treachery of their fleet, went with a number of Milesians to Sicily, where they made themselves masters of the town Zankle, id. 22—25. Thuc. VI, 4. Arist. Pol. VIII, 3, 12. However, not long afterwards, Zankle was lost to them again; for Anaxilaus, tyrant of Rhegium, expelled them from the town, to which he gave another population "ξυμμίκτων ἀνθρώπων," Thuc., and at the same time the name Messana, Thuc. VI, 5; cf. Paus. IV, 23, 5.)

8) Herod. VI, 76—83. Cf. Paus. II, 20, 7—8. Plut. De Viri. Mul. p. 245 D—F. Kleomenes defeated the Argives, and then set fire to the grove of Argus, in which the routed had taken refuge. By this means 6000 Argive citizens perished, Herod. VII, 148; and hereby the nation was so weakened, that for the space of a generation the Perioeks, or according to Herodotus the slaves, were masters of the state, Herod.

VI, 83. Arist. Pol. VIII, 3, 7. The date rests on the circumstance, that in Herod. VI, 19. 77 an oracle comprised both the fall of Miletus and the defeat of Argos, and that in Herod. VII, 148 the latter event, at the time of the approach of the second Persian war, is designated as having taken place shortly before.

9) Herod. VI, 31—42. (The inhabitants of Byzantium and Kalchedon fled and found a home, but only for a time, in Mesambria, id. 33, a colony of Megara, Strab. p. 319.) The Ionians had to suffer all the calamities attendant on an enemy's conquest, Herod. l. c. 31—32, but were afterwards treated by Artaphernes with relative mildness and justice, id. 42.

10) Herod. VI, 43—45. For the object of the expedition see id. 43: ἐπορεύοντο ἐπί τε 'Ερέτριαν καὶ 'Αθήνας' αὗται μὲν ὧν σφι πρόσχημα ἦσαν τοῦ στόλου. ἀτὰρ ἐν νόῳ ἔχοντες ὅσας ἂν πλείστας δύναιντο καταστρέφεσθαι τῶν 'Ελληνίδων πολίων—. By a storm the fleet lost 300 ships and 20,000 men on the promontory of Athos, whilst the army was surprised by the Brygians, and a great part of it destroyed. Mardonius therefore relinquished the expedition and returned, after revenging himself on the Brygians.

11) Herod. VI, 48—49. 49: τοῦτι ἥκουσι ἐς τὴν 'Ελλάδα κήρυξι πολλοὶ μὲν ἠπειρωτέων ἔδοσαν τὰ προΐσχετο αἰτέων ὁ Πέρσης, πάντες δὲ νησιῶται ἐς τοὺς ἀπικοίατο αἰτήσοντες. Amongst the latter also Ægina, which had for a long time past been at war with Athens (see p. 38, obs. 98), and which—so at least the Athenians feared—joined the Persian king, in order to overpower Athens with the help of Persia. Accordingly the Athenians sent ambassadors to Sparta, and accused Ægina of treason to the whole Hellenic race; after many delays the Æginetans were compelled to furnish 10 hostages, who were given over to the Athenians, Herod. VI, 50. 73. In consequence, war broke out afresh between Athens and Ægina, id. 87—93. For the reception and treatment of the Persian heralds in Athens and Sparta, see Herod. VII, 133—137.

LXXII, 2	491	Archon.	Demaratus is dethroned, Kleomenes dies: Leotychidas and Leonidas kings of Sparta [12]).
LXXII, 3	490	Phaenippus.	First Persian war [13]). The Persians under Datis and Artaphernes [14]) sail through the Ægean Sea and come to Euboea, take Eretria [15]), and then land on the plain of Marathon; where they are defeated by the Athenians and Plataeans under the command of Miltiades [16]).
LXXII, 4	489	Aristeides.	The disastrous undertaking of Miltiades against Paros: his condemnation and death [17]).
LXXIII, 1	488	Anchises.	

12) Demaratus and Kleomenes were always at feud with one another: Demaratus had thwarted and opposed Kleomenes in the affair of Ægina (see obs. 11), and for this reason Kleomenes compassed his deposition; whereupon Demaratus fled to king Dareius, Herod. VI, 50. 61—70. Kleomenes died soon afterwards, id. 74—75. For the successors of both see id. 71 and VII, 204—205.

13) Herod. VI, 91—121. Cf. Ctes. Pers. § 18 (ed. Bähr). Iustin. II, 9. Cornel. Nep. Them. 4—5. Vengeance on Athens and Eretria was again declared to be the object of the expedition, but at the same time Dareius intended to subdue the whole of Hellas, Herod. VI, 94.

14) Herodotus only states the number of the Persian triremes (600), VI, 95, but not the size of the army. According to Iustin. l. c., the latter amounted to 600,000 men; according to Plato Menex. p. 240 A and Lysias Epitaph. p. 192. § 21, 500,000 men; according to Val. Max. V, 3. Paus. IV, 25, 2. 300,000, according to Corn. Nep. Milt. 5, only 110,000 men.

15) Herod. VI, 95—101. On the voyage Naxos was plundered and destroyed, but Delos spared; troops and hostages were taken from other islands; in Euboea Karystos and Eretria were taken, the latter by treachery after a six days' siege; whereupon the temples were burnt down in revenge for the burning of Sardis, and the inhabitants led away as captives. For the fate of Eretria cf. Plat. Legg. III, p. 698. C. Menex. p. 240. B. Diog. Laert. III, 33. Strab. p. 448.

16) To the plain of Marathon the Persians were conducted by Hippias, as the best use could be there made of the cavalry. The Athenians marched against them under the command of the 10 strategi and the polemarch Kallimachus; the Spartans promised assistance, but delayed, as they dared not march out before the full moon (Herod. l. c. 105—106. 120); the Plataeans, on the other hand, came to the rescue with the whole of their forces (1000 men). According to Iustin. II, 9 the Athenian numbers reached 10,000 men, but counting the Plataeans; according to Corn. Nep. Milt. 4. Paus. IV, 25, 2. X, 20, 2 the total of both armies was 10,000. Owing to the successful exertions of Miltiades the attack was made without delay, Herod. l. c. 109. The number of the fallen: 6400 Persians, 192 Greeks, id. 117. For the nature of the attack and the bravery of the Greeks see id. 112: πρῶτοι μὲν γὰρ Ἑλλήνων τῶν ἡμεῖς ἴδμεν δρόμῳ ἐς πολεμίους ἐχρήσαντο, πρῶτοι δὲ ἀνέσχοντο ἐσθῆτά τε Μηδικὴν ὁρῶντες καὶ ἄνδρας τοὺς ταύτα ἐσθημένους· τέως δὲ ἦν τοῖσι Ἕλλησι καὶ τὸ οὔνομα τὸ Μήδων φόβος ἀκοῦσαι. The day of the battle was the 6th of Boedromion (corresponding roughly to the last few days of September) Plut. Cam. 19. Mor. p. 861 (De Mal. Herod. c. 26). p. 305 (De Glor. Athen. c. 7). In opposition to these accounts of Plutarch, Böckh (Jahnsche Jahrb., Supplement b. 1 N. F. S. 64 ff.) on many grounds, in particular that the battle according to Herod. VI, 105. 120 must have taken place on one of the days immediately following the new moon, has made it probable that the day of the battle must be placed shortly after the middle of the preceding month of Metageitnion, that is about the 17th of this month (= the 12th of September). According to Plut. Arist. 5, Aristeides was one of the 10 strategi, and perhaps Themistokles: at all events, according to this passage, the latter was present at the battle. For the sepulchral mounds raised in honour of the Μαραθωνομάχοι see Paus. I, 32, 4—5. The year of the battle of Marathon is positively established by the testimony of various writers that 10 years intervened between it and the battle of Salamis, Herod. VII, 1. 3. 4. 7. 20 Thuc. I, 18. Platt. Legg. III, p. 698 C. Marm. Par.

17) Herod. VI, 132—136. Corn. Nep. Milt. 7. Herod. l. c. 132—133: αἰτήσας νέας ἐβδομήκοντα καὶ στρατιήν τε καὶ χρήματα Ἀθηναίους, οὐ φράσας σφι ἐπ' ἣν ἐπιστρατεύσεται χώρην, ἀλλὰ φὰς αὐτοὺς καταπλουτιεῖν, ἤν οἱ ἕπωνται—. Ἀθηναῖοι δὲ τούτοισι ἐπαρθέντες παρέδοσαν· παραλαβὼν δὲ ὁ Μιλτιάδης τὴν στρατιὴν ἔπλεε ἐπὶ Πάρον, πρόφασιν ἔχων ὡς οἱ Πάριοι ὑπῆρξαν πρότεροι στρατευόμενοι τριήρεϊ ἐς Μαραθῶνα ἅμα τῷ Πέρσῃ· τοῦτο μὲν δὴ πρόσχημα λόγου ἦν, ἀτὰρ τινα καὶ ἔγκοτον εἶχε τοῖσι Παρίοισι διὰ Λυσαγόρεα τὸν Τισίεω, ἐόντα γένος Πάριον, διαβαλόντα μιν πρὸς Ὑδάρνεα τὸν Πέρσην. He effected nothing, and after his return was accused by Xanthippus, the father of Perikles, and sentenced to pay a fine of 50 talents: but he died from a hurt in the foot, which he had got before Paros. His son Kimon discharged the fine in his stead.

40   THIRD PERIOD. 500—431 B.C.

Olympiad.	B. C.	ATHENS.	HISTORY.	ART AND LITERATURE.
		Archon.		
LXXIII, 4	485	Philokrates.		
LXXIV, 1	484	Leostratus.		
LXXIV, 2	483	Nikodemus.	Aristeides ostracised[18]).	
LXXIV, 3	482	Themistokles.	Themistokles lays the foundation of the maritime power of Athens, by persuading them to expend the revenues from the silver mines of Laureium on the building of triremes, and to construct the harbour Peiræus[19]).	
LXXV, 1	480	Kalliades.	Second Persian war[20]). Xerxes[21]) sets out against Greece at the head of a fleet of 1207 vessels of war and an army of 1,700,000 infantry and 80,000	The Lyric Poets: Simonides[a]),

18) Plut. Arist. 7. Corn. Nep. Arist. 1. The date is given from Plut. Arist. 8, according to which he was recalled in the third year; according to Corn. Nep. l. c. his recall took place in the 6th year, so that his banishment would belong to 486 B.C.
19) With regard to Themistokles, who from this time forward plays a prominent part as the director in chief of Athenian affairs, see in general the character given him by Thucydides (I, 138): ἦν γὰρ ὁ Θεμιστοκλῆς βεβαιότατα δὴ φύσεως ἰσχὺν δηλώσας καὶ διαφερόντως τι ἐς αὐτὸ μᾶλλον ἑτέρου ἄξιον θαυμάσαι. οἰκείᾳ γὰρ συνέσει καὶ οὔτε προμαθὼν ἐς αὐτὴν οὐδὲν οὔτ' ἐπιμαθὼν τῶν τε παραχρῆμα δι' ἐλαχίστης βουλῆς κράτιστος γνώμων καὶ τῶν μελλόντων ἐπὶ πλεῖστον τοῦ γενησομένου ἄριστος εἰκαστής· καὶ ἃ μὲν μετὰ χεῖρας ἔχοι καὶ ἐξηγήσασθαι οἷός τε, ὧν δ' ἄπειρος εἴη κρῖναι ἱκανῶς οὐκ ἀπήλλακτο· τό τε ἄμεινον ἢ χεῖρον ἐν τῷ ἀφανεῖ ἔτι προεώρα μάλιστα· καὶ τὸ ξύμπαν εἰπεῖν, φύσεως μὲν δυνάμει μελέτης δὲ βραχύτητι κράτιστος δὴ οὗτος αὐτοσχεδιάζειν τὰ δέοντα ἐγένετο. Fear of a renewed attack by the Persians showed him the need, but the Æginetan war was his immediate pretext for effecting the building of 200 triremes (the number given by Herodotus) out of the revenue of the Laureian mines, Herod. VII, 144: ὅτε 'Αθηναίοισι γενομένων χρημάτων μεγάλων ἐν τῷ κοινῷ, τὰ ἐκ τῶν μετάλλων σφι προσῆλθε τῶν ἀπὸ Λαυρείου, ἐμέλλον λάξεσθαι ὀρχηδὸν ἕκαστος δέκα δραχμάς, τότε Θεμιστοκλέης ἀνέγνωσε 'Αθηναίους τῆς διαιρέσιος ταύτης παυσαμένους νέας τούτων τῶν χρημάτων ποιήσασθαι διηκοσίας ἐς τὸν πόλεμον, τὸν πρὸς Αἰγινήτας λέγων· οὗτοι γὰρ ὁ πόλεμος συστὰς ἔσωσε τότε τὴν Ἑλλάδα, ἀναγκάσας 'Αθηναίους γενέσθαι 'Αθηναίους, cf. Plut. Them. 4. Corn. Nep. Them. 2. Polyæn. I, 30, 5 (according to all these latter passages only 100 ships were built). In connexion with this undertaking he brought about the construction of the harbour Peiræus, to replace Phalerum with its insufficient accommodation, Thuc. 1, 93. cf. Paus. 1, 1, 2. For the result of the alteration see Plut. Them. 4: ἐκ δὲ τούτου—ἀντὶ μονίμων ὁπλιτῶν, ὡς φησι Πλάτων (Legg. IV, p. 706 B)], ναυβάτας καὶ ἐπιθαλασσίους ἐποίησε καὶ διαβολὴν καθ' αὐτοῦ παρέσχεν, ὡς ἄρα Θεμιστοκλῆς τὸ δόρυ καὶ τὴν ἀσπίδα τῶν πολιτῶν παρελόμενος εἰς ὑπηρέσιον καὶ κώπην συνέστειλε τὸν τῶν 'Αθηναίων δῆμον. The date of these measures cannot be certainly fixed, as the account given in Thuc. I, 93 is of doubtful interpretation. The date given above rests chiefly on Thuc. I, 14; according to which the Athenians in the period up to the death of Dareius, that is up to 485 B.C., had only a few ships of war, and those for the most part only pentekonters; further on Herodotus' whole

account of the matter (VII, 143—144), where e.g. Themistokles in 481 B.C. is called ἀνὴρ ἐς πρώτους νεωστὶ τιμώμενος; on these and other grounds the question has been settled, being worked out in detail, above all by Krüger (hist. phil. Studien I. p. 13 f), in opposition to Böckh (De Arch. Pseudon. in der Abh. der Berl. Acad. 1827. p. 131 f) who places the archonship of Themistokles together with all his other measures in the year 492 B.C.
20) Herod. VII. VIII. IX. Cf. Ctes. Pers. § 23—27. Diod. VI, 1—37. Plut. Them. and Arist. On the present as on the former occasion the chief object was the conquest of the whole of Greece (cf. obs. 13), Herod. VII, 139: ἡ δὲ στρατηλασίη ἡ βασιλέος οὔνομα μὲν εἶχε ὡς ἐπ' 'Αθήνας ἐλαύνει, κατίετο δ' ἐς πᾶσαν τὴν Ἑλλάδα, cf. id. 157. The preparations had continued the whole time since the first war, almost without interruption, first under Dareius, Herod. VII, 1, then under Xerxes, id. 20. Moreover the way was paved for the expedition by digging through the isthmus of Athos, id. 21—24, and bridging over the Strymon, id. 24, and the Hellespont, id. 25. 33—36. Xerxes had also made an alliance with the Carthaginians, that they might make an attack on Sicily and the Greeks there, Diod. XI, 1, 20. cf. Herod. VII, 165. Besides Demaratus (obs. 12), the Aleuadæ of Thessaly and the Peisistratidæ followed in the train of Xerxes, Herod. VII, 6. The Greeks on their side, when they heard of the arrival of Xerxes at Sardis, that is towards the end of the year 481 B.C., held a congress at the Isthmus, in which they first of all renounced all intestine war and dissension, and resolved to send ambassadors to Gelon, tyrant of Akragas in Sicily, further to Krete, Kerkyra, and Argos, to beg for assistance, id. 145; but they nowhere met with success, 148—171. No part was taken in this congress by those, who had at the summons of the Persian king given him earth and water; namely the Thessalians, Dolopes, Ænianes, Perrhæbi, Lokrians, Magnetes, Malians, the Achræans of Phthiotis, the Thebans, and the rest of the Bœotians with the exception of Thespiæ and Platææ, 132. Athens distinguished herself above all by her patriotism, see 139 : 'Αθηναίους ἄν τις λέγων σωτῆρας γενέσθαι τῆς Ἑλλάδος οὐκ ἂν ἁμαρτάνοι τἀληθέος—ἑλόμενοι δὲ τὴν Ἑλλάδα περιεῖναι ἐλευθέρην τοῦτο τὸ Ἑλληνικὸν πᾶν τὸ λοιπόν, ὅσον μὴ ἐμήδισε, αὐτοὶ οὗτοι ἦσαν οἱ ἐπεγείραντες καὶ βασιλέα μετά γε θεοὺς ἀνωσάμενοι. The "wooden walls," 140—144.
21) Xerxes had succeeded to the throne after the death of Dareius in 485 B.C. Herod. VII, 1—4. 20. Sync. p. 208. B.

a) Simonides, of Iulis in Keos, lived from 556 to 468 B.C., Marm. Par. Suid. a. v. Strab. p. 486, in close intercourse with the most eminent men of his time; at the court of Hipparchus, Plat. Hipparch. p. 228 d,

and of the Aleuadæ and Skopadæ in Thessaly, Plat. Protag. p. 339 B. Cic. de orat. II, 86. Bergk Lyr. fr. 5. After the battle of Marathon he at first resided in Athens, where he enjoyed the intimacy of Themis-

Olympiad.	B. C.	HISTORY.	ART AND LITERATURE.
LXXV, 1	480	cavalry [22]). The Spartan king Leonidas takes up his position with 300 Spartiates and some other troops	Pindar[b]), Bakchylides[c]). The epic poet Panyasis[d]).

22) The army assembled in the course of the year 481 B.C. at Kritalla in Kappadokia, and marches from there to Sardis, where it passes the winter together with Xerxes himself, Herod. VII, 26—32; the fleet collected in the harbours of Kyme and Phokæa, Diod. XI, 2. At the beginning of spring the army marches to Abydos, Herod. VII, 40—43, from thence to two bridges over the Hellespont, id. 54—55, which it required 7 days and 7 nights to cross, id. 56: the advance is resumed both by water and land as far as Doriskos, a plain on the Hebrus, id. 58, where a muster of the army and the fleet was held, id. 60—80. The numbering or rather appraising of the army showed a total of 1,700,000 infantry and 80,000 cavalry, id. 60. 87; the fleet comprised 1207 triremes, amongst which were 300 Phœnician, 200 Egyptian, 150 Kyprian, 100 Kilikian vessels, etc., besides 3000 other craft, id. 89. 148: to these must still be added 120 ships and 300,000

tokles and won prizes in poetical contests, Herod. VI, 103. Vit. Æsch. Western. p. 119. Plut. Them. 1. 5; last of all, at the court of Hiero of Syracuse, whom he reconciled to Thero of Agrigentum, Bergk. fr. 142. Cic. Nat. D. I, 22. Schol. Pind. Ol. II, 29. By composing for money, he incurred the reproach of avarice, Pind. Isthm. II, 5 and Schol. on Aristoph. Pac. 698; on account of his powerful memory he was esteemed the inventor of mnemonics, Marm. Par. Cic. de orat. II, 74. 86. Quint. IX, 2, 11. He was an extraordinarily fertile poet and recognised throughout Hellas; he composed chiefly Ἐπινίκοι, Ὕμνοι, Παιᾶνες, Διθύραμβοι, Τωρχήματα, Θρῆνοι, Ἐλεγεῖαι, Bergk. fr. 1—89, Ἐπιγράμματα, Bergk. fr. 90—170, of which numerous fragments are preserved. For the history of the period the fragments of his poems are of importance; as in many elegies and epigrams he celebrates the exploits of the Persian wars: thus the heroes of the battle of Marathon, Vit. Æsch.; Thermopylæ, Bergk. fr. 4. 92. 93. 95. 96. 97. 98; Salamis, Bergk. fr. 1. 100. 101. 102; Plataeæ, Bergk. fr. 84; and of the battles of Kimon, fr. 107. 108. 109, cf. fr. 110. 111. He also composed epigrams on dedicatory offerings of Harmodios and Aristogeiton, fr. 134, of Miltiades, fr. 86, of the Athenians after the battle of Artemisium, fr. 138, of the Hellenes from the Persian spoils, fr. 141, cf. fr. 144. 145, and of Pausanias, fr. 143. etc. The grace of his poems procured him the epithet Μελικήρυτι (διὰ τὸ ἡδύ, Suid.), Plato says of him: σοφὸς καὶ θεῖος ὁ ἀνήρ, Rep. I, p. 331 E.

b) Pindar, son of Daïphantus, born circ. 521—518 B.C. in the Theban borough Kynoskephalæ, of the family of the Ægidæ, Suid. s. v. Eust. Proem. 25. Vit. Pind. Pyth. V, 71, composed at first under the guidance of Lasos of Hermione, Eustath. l. c., and of Korinna, Plut. glor. Athen. p. 347. 348; by the latter he was fifty times conquered in musical contests, Paus. IX, 22, 3. Æl. V. H. XIII, 24. Suid. s. v. Κόριννα: the first time that he came forward independently was in his 20th year with the 10th Pythian ode. That the poet travelled much, chiefly to conduct the performance of his songs at festival gatherings, is shewn by his residence at Delphi, Paus. X, 24, 4, at Olympia, Pind. Ol. X, at Anthedon, Paus. IX, 22, 5, at Argos, Pr. Eust. 16. Vit., at Syracuse at Hiero's court in company with Simonides and Bakchylides, Pr. Eust. 17. Vit., where he also formed a connexion with Thero of Agrigentum, Pind. Ol. II. III. According to his poems he enjoyed intimacy, amongst others, with Arkesilaus of Kyrene, Pyth. IV, V, and especially with the Æginetans, Ol. VIII. Pyth. VIII. Nem. III. IV, V. VI. VII. Isthm. IV. VII. In praise of Athens he sang, Pseudo-Æschin. Ep. 4: αἵ τε λιπαραὶ καὶ ἀοίδιμοι Ἑλλάδος ἐρείσμ' Ἀθᾶναι, for which the Thebans imposed a fine upon him; but the Athenians paid him twice the amount of the fine, and set up his statue in brass. Besides his songs, he approved his orthodox piety by the consecration of shrines, Pyth. III, 77. Paus. IX, 16, 1. 17, 1; but the poet took no active part in politics or war. He is said to have died a painless death in the theatre at Argos at the age of 80, Pr. Eust. 16. Plut. Cons. ad Apoll. p. 109. Suid. l. c.; Alexander the Great honoured his memory by sparing his house alone at the destruction of Thebes, Arr. Anab. I, 29. Of his various lyric poems we have preserved to us four books of Ἐπινίκοι, 14 Olympic, 12 Pythian, 11 Nemean, and 7 (8?) Isthmian triumphal songs to victors in the chariot race with horses, mules or fillies, in the single course, long course, double course and armour race, in wrestling, boxing, the pancratium, and flute-playing; they were sung by choirs to the lute or flute, in Dorian, Æolian, or Lydian harmony and the most varied strophic rhythms: the compositions of the poet of which fragments are still preserved were Ὕμνοι, cf. Böckh fr. 1. 2, Διθύραμβοι, fr. 3. 4, Ἐγκώμια, fr. 2, Σκόλια, fr. 1. 2. Ὀρθῖοι, fr. 1. 2. 3, Προσόδια, fr. 1, Τωρχήματα, fr. 3. 4. Of his poetry Quintilian says, X, 1, 6: Novem lyricorum longe Pindarus princeps spiritus magnificentia, sententiis, figuris, beatissima rerum verborumque copia et velut quodam eloquentiae flumine. Cf. Hor. Carm. IV, 2.—Timokreon of Ialysus in Rhodes was a contemporary of Pindar. Athlete and poet, first he was the friend of Themistokles; then banished on account of alleged sympathies with Persia, he attacked Themistokles and Simonides in lampoons, after he had in vain invoked the Athenian's intercession, Bergk. Tim. fr. 1. 5. Suid. s. v. Plut. Them. 21. Athen. X, p. 415 f., for which Simonides revenged himself by a biting epitaph, Bergk. Sim. fr. 171. Of his poems (Μέλη, Σκόλια, Ἐνυγράμματα) only a few fragments are preserved. Contemporary with the lyric poets enumerated, there were three poetesses: Korinna of Tanagra, nicknamed Μυῖα, Suid. v. Paus. IX, 22, 3, who wrote songs in the Æolic dialect from legendary materials, of which only scanty relics are preserved, Bergk. fr. 2. 14. 18. 20; Telesilla of Argos, who by her bravery and songs rescued her native city from the Spartans, Plut. mul. virt. d. 235 C. Paus. II, 20, 7. 8. Suid. s. v.; Praxilla of Sikyon, Euseb. Chron. Ol. LXXXII, 2 p. 105, of whose poems, Ὕμνοι, Διθύραμβοι, Παροίνια, Σκόλια, only a few remnants are still preserved, B. fr. 1—5.

c) Bakchylides of Iulis in Keos, nephew of Simonides, with whom he lived at the court of Hiero, was at feud with Pindar, Strab. p. 486, Steph. v. Ἰουλίς. Schol. Pind. Ol. II, 154. Nem. III, 143. Pyth. II, 97. He flourished in his prime according to Eusebius Chron. Arm. p. 102 in Olymp. LXXVIII, 3. Of his most considerable poems, Ἐπινίκοι, Ὕμνοι, Παιᾶνες, Διθύραμβοι, Προσόδια, Τωρχήματα, Ἐρωτικά, Ἐνυγράμματα, only few fragments of any length are preserved, B. fr. 13. 27,

d) Panyasis of Halikarnassus, nearly related to Herodotus, flourished circ. 500—460, and met with his death from Lygdamis, the tyrant of his native city, Suid. s. v. Clem. Alex. Strom. VI, p. 206. Hieron. Ol.

THIRD PERIOD. 500—431 B.C.

Olympiad.	B.C.	HISTORY.	ART AND LITERATURE.
LXXV 1	480	from the rest of Greece in the pass of Thermopylæ, but is surrounded and overpowered after a heroic resistance²³): the Greek fleet fights two engagements with the	Upgrowth of dramatic Poetry°). The tragic poets Phrynichus^f), Æschylus^g).

men from the islands and the Greek towns, with which Xerxes came into contact on his way, from all of which he demanded contingents, so that the total of fighting men, including the ships' crews, amounted to 2,041,010, id. 184—187. Such are the really incredible numbers given by Herodotus. According to Ctes. § 22, the army consisted of 800,000 men, the fleet of 1000 ships; according to Diod. XI, 2, 3. 5, there were 1200 ships and 800,000, or with the auxiliary forces added, 1,000,000 men; according to Corn. Nep. Them. 2, 1200 ships, but 700,000 infantry and 400,000 cavalry; according to Iustin. II, 10 the same number of ships and a total of 1,000,000 men. From Doriskus the army marched in 3 parallel lines (Herod. VII, 121), first to Therma, where it was again met by the fleet, Herod. VII, 108—126; and from here into the land of the Malians, where Xerxes pitched his camp at Trachis, id. 196—201: the fleet sailed from Therma, first to the coast of Magnesia between Sepias and Kastanæa, and, after it had here lost 400 ships in a storm, to Aphetæ on the Pagasæan gulf, id. 179—195. The Greeks first decided to defend the entrance into Thessaly, and to this end occupied the pass of Tempe with 10,000 men under the Spartan Eunænetos and Themistokles, but gave up this plan for fear of being surrounded, id. 172—173, and resolved to post an army at Thermopylæ (for which see Introd. p. 2. obs. 1) and to occupy Artemisium, that is the north coast of Eubœa, with the fleet, in order to hinder the advance of the Persians into Central Greece both by land and sea, id. 175—177.
23) Herod. VII, 202—238. The fighting force of the Greeks consisted, in addition to the 300 Spartans, of 500 Tegeatans, 500 Mantineans, 120 men from Orchomenus in Arcadia, 1000 from the rest of Arcadia, 400 Corinthians, 200 from Phlius, 80 from Mykenæ; further 700 from Thespiæ, 400 from Thebes (who according to Herod. VII, 222 joined the army under compulsion, according to Diod. XI, 4 belonged to a non-Medising party), the whole force of Opuntian Lokrians, and 1000 Phokians, id. 202. Xerxes first sends a spy, who finds the Spartans busied with their gymnastics and combing their hair, 208—209; then, after waiting 4 days in the expectation that they would take to flight of themselves, he kept up the attack for three days in vain, first with the Kissians and Medes, then with the 10,000 immortal Persians (for whom cf. Herod. VII, 83), 210—213; after this by the treachery of Ephialtes, the Greeks were surrounded, 213—218, and the last struggle followed, 219—227; in which, however, only the Spartans, Thespians, and Thebans—these last under compulsion—took part, as Leonidas had dismissed all the rest on receiving the news that they were surrounded, 219—221. 228: Θαφθεῖσι δὲ σφι αὐτοῦ τῇ περ ἔπεσον καὶ τοῖσι πρότερον τελευτήσασι ἢ ὑπὸ Λεωνίδεω ἀποπεμφθέντας οἴχεσθαι, ἐπιγέγραπται γράμματα λέγοντα τάδε· Μυριάσιν ποτὲ τῇδε τριηκοσίαις ἐμάχοντο ἐκ Πελοποννάσου χιλιάδες τέτορες· ταῦτα μὲν δὴ τοῖσι πᾶσι ἐπιγέγραπται· τοῖσι δὲ Σπαρτιήτῃσι ἰδίῃ· ὦ ξεῖν', ἀγγέλλειν Λακεδαιμονίοις ὅτι τῇδε κείμεθα τοῖς κείνων ῥήμασι πειθόμενοι. According to Herod. VIII, 24, 20,000 of the Persians had fallen at Thermopylæ. According to Herod. VII, 206 the Olympian games were being celebrated at the very time that the battle was fought.

e) Tragedy was originally a mere choral song with cyclic Dance at the wine feasts of Dionysus, and was called τραγῳδία (goat-song) from the goat sacrificed to the god, Diog. Laert. III, 56: τὸ παλαιὸν ἐν τῇ τραγῳδίᾳ πρότερον μὲν μόνος ὁ χορὸς διεδραμάτιζεν, Arist. Poet. IV, 15; γενομένη οὖν ἀπ' ἀρχῆς αὐτοσχεδιαστικὴ καὶ αὐτὴ (sc. τραγῳδία) καὶ ἡ κωμῳδία, καὶ ἡ μὲν ἀπὸ τῶν ἐξαρχόντων τὸν διθύραμβον, ἡ δὲ ἀπὸ τῶν τὰ φαλλικά. In addition to the choral song in praise of the god, an actor declaiming was next introduced, who narrated stories of Dionysus. When other narratives were intermingled, there arose the proverb: Οὐδὲν πρὸς τὸν Διόνυσον, Suid. s. v. Οὐδὲ κ.τ.λ. Zenob. V, 40. With the introduction of a second actor the dialogue assumed chief importance; with the addition of the third, tragedy reached its perfection, see infr. and obs. g. k. The Satyric drama, an offshoot of Tragedy, arose from the introduction of a chorus in Satyr masks upon the stage, just as it appeared in the revels and mummeries of the Dionysian festivals and sang dithyrambs. Suid. s. v. Ἀρίων. Athen. XIV, p. 630 C. The oldest tragic poets were: Thespis, circ. 536—533, of the Attic district Ikaria, Suid. s. v. Plut. Sol. 29, at once poet, composer, and actor, Athen. I,

22. Hor. A. P. 275. Anthol. Pal. VII, 410. 411, who is looked upon as the founder of tragedy from his having added to the choral song an actor, who declaimed his part, Diog. Laert. III, 56; further, Pratinas of Phlius (circ. 500 B.C.), who is said to have been the first to produce Satyric dramas, Suid. s. v. Paus. II, 13. 5.

f) Phrynichus of Athens circ. 511—476, Suid. s. v. Plut. Them. 5. Schol. Arist. Ran. 941, the first tragic poet of importance, who furnished μύθους καὶ πάθη, Plut. Symp. I. 1 p. 615. The most famous amongst the tragedies exhibited by him were the Μιλήτου ἅλωσις, which, in consequence of the painful impression that it made on the Athenians, brought upon the poet a fine of 1000 drachmas, Herod. VI, 21, and Φοίνισσαι, a glorification of the victory of Athens at Salamis, and accordingly brought out by Themistokles in 477 B.C., Plut. l. c. Athen. XIV, p. 635 C. Only a few verses from his dramas are preserved, Nauck. Trag. Gr. fr. 5. 6. 10. 14. In these the lyric chorus was still predominant, for which Aristophanes praises him, Av. 750: Φρύνιχος ἀμβροσίων μελέων ἀπεβόσκετο καρπόν, ἀεὶ φέρων γλυκεῖαν ᾠδάν. Cf. Schol. Vesp. 220. Ran. 1299 f.

g) Æschylus, son of Euphorion of Eleusis, born 525 B.C., Marm. Par., first came forward with dramas at the age of twenty-five as a rival of Pratinas, Suid. v. Pratinas, but only obtained his first dramatic victory

The Hellenic Race in its Prime. 43

Olympiad.	B. C.	HISTORY.	ART AND LITERATURE.
LXXV, 1	480	Persian at Artemisium of doubtful issue, but retires, on hearing the news of the loss of Thermopylæ, to Salamis[24]). Pleistarchus succeeds Leonidas as king of Sparta under the guardianship of Kleombrotus and afterwards of Pausanias[25]).	The Sicilian Comedy[h]). Epicharmus[i]).

24) Herod, VIII, 1—22. The Greek fleet, commanded by the Spartan Euryblades, consisted of 127 triremes from Athens (partly manned by Plataeans), 40 from Corinth, 20 from Megara, 20 from Chalkis (the ships themselves were lent to the Chalkidians by Athens), 18 from Ægina, 12 from Sikyon, 10 from Sparta, 8 from Epidaurus, 7 from Eretria, 5 from Troezen, 2 from Styra, 2 from Keos; together 271 triremes; in addition, 2 pentekonters from Keos and 7 such vessels from the Opuntian Lokrians; in all 280 ships, id. 1. 2. From the Persian fleet 200 ships were sent to blockade the Euripus and cut off the retreat of the Greeks, id. 7. The Greeks then ventured the first battle, 9—11, and after the 200 Persian ships had gone down in a storm, 12—13, and they themselves had been reinforced by 53 fresh Athenian vessels, 14, the second, 15—17. Both battles proved indecisive, and the Greeks had suffered, if less than the Persians, still very considerably; they were therefore already thinking of retreat, when, to clinch the matter, they received the news of the events at Thermopylæ, by which the defence of their position at Artemisium was rendered utterly useless, 18—22.

25) Herod. IX, 10.

(over 13) in 485, Marm. Par. His poetry was inspired by the great period of the struggle with Persia, in the battles of which he took part with glory, first at Marathon, where he received several wounds, then at Artemisium, Salamis, and Platæa, Marm. Par. Pans. I, 21, 3. I, 14, 4. Phot. s. v. Μαραθῶνιον ποίημα. He added the second actor, and gave the dialogue of the actors a more prominent place than the chorus, (τὸν χορὸν πρωταγωνιστὴν παρεσκεύασεν, Arist. Poet. IV, 15. Diog. I, III, 56), and by splendour of costume and decoration lent lustre to the tragic stage, Vit. Æsch. Philostr. v. Soph. I, 9, Hor. A. P. 278: it was probably he, who introduced the tetralogic form of tragedy. His life was not without its trials; for Simonides conquered him in a poetical contest with his elegy on Marathon, Vit. Æsch., the young Sophoklos with the first play that he brought on the stage, Plut. Cim. 8. Marm. Par.; and he was even accused of impiety, for having disclosed on the stage the secret doctrines of the mysteries, and was only acquitted by the Areopagus on the score of his former services, ÆI. V. H. V, 19. Arist. Eth. Nicom. III, 2. In displeasure the poet repeatedly retired to Sicily, Paus. I, 2, 3. Plut. De Exil. p. 604, where he produced dramas at Hiero's court, and died at Gela, in 456 B.C., Marm. Par. Vit. Æsch, Suid. ÆI. V. H. VII, 16. That his renown as a soldier was dearer to him than his renown as a poet, is proved by his epitaph, which he composed himself, Athen. XIV, p. 627 D. Vit. Æsch. But the Athenians honoured his memory by a decree that his dramas should be performed after his death, Schol. Arist. Ach. 10. Of at least 70 tragedies, which he composed, Vit. Æsch. Suid. s. v., only seven have been preserved in a perfect form; they are: Προμηθεὺς Δεσμώτης, Ἑπτὰ ἐπὶ Θήβας (according to the didaskalia performed in 467 B.C.), Πέρσαι (performed 472 B.C.), (the three connected plays 'Αγαμέμνων, Χοηφόροι, Εὐμενίδες, as a trilogy also called 'Ορέστεια, Aristoph. Ran. 1135. Schol., the poet's masterpiece, triumphantly produced in 458 B.C.,' Ικετίδες. Only scanty fragments are preserved of other dramas, the most important being from the tragedies, Δαναΐδες, Nauck. Gr. fr. 43, Νιόβη, fr. 153. 154. 156. 157, Προμηθεὺς ὁ λυόμενος, fr. 186. 189. 190, 193, Φρύγες, fr. 259, cf fr, 275. 297, 310, But little has come to us of his elegies and epigrams, Ilermann, Reseh. fr. 460 f. That his poetry an ancient critic says, Vit. Æsch.: Κατὰ δὲ τὴν σύνθεσιν τῆς ποιήσεως ζηλοῖ τὸ ἁδρὸν ἀεὶ πλάσμα καὶ ὑπέρογκον ὀνοματοποιΐαις τε καὶ ἐπιθέτοις, ἔτι δὲ καὶ μεταφοραῖς καὶ

πᾶσι τοῖς δυναμένοις ὄγκον τῇ φράσει περιθεῖναι χρώμενος· αἱ τε διαθέσεις τῶν δραμάτων οὐ πολλὰς αὐτῷ περιπετείας καὶ πλοκὰς ἔχουσιν ὡς παρὰ τοῖς νεωτέροις· μόνον γὰρ σπουδάζει τοῖς χαρακτῆρσι τὸ βάρος περιθεῖναι τοῖς προσώποις, ἀρχαῖον εἶναι κρίνων τουτὶ τὸ μέρος, τὸ μεγαλοπρεπὲς καὶ τὸ ἡρωικόν...ὥστε διὰ τὸ πλεονάζειν τῷ βάρει τῶν προσώπων κωμῳδεῖται παρ' Ἀριστοφάνους. Cf. Aristoph. Ran. 814 f, Dio Chrys. Or. LII, p. 267. (Of Chœrilus, the contemporary of Æschylus, we have not one single perfect verse, Suid. s. v. Nauck. fr. 1—3.)

h) Comedy sprang from the songs of raillery and improvised jests of peasants and vine-dressers at the vintage feasts of Bacchus, Aristoph. Pol. IV, 14. Περὶ κωμῳδίας Proleg. Aristoph. ed. Bergk. III, 1—4. The germs of comedy are seen amongst the Dorians in the Spartan pantomimes, Athen. XIV p. 621, and the Megarian farce, Arist. Poet. 3. Eth. IV, 2. Suid. s. v. γέλως Μεγαρικός. This latter is said to have been first brought into metrical form and introduced into Attica by Susarion of Tripodiskos in Megaris, circ. 578 B.C. Marm. Par. Anon. Περὶ κωμ. VIII, 6, 10 p. 535 Mein. Schol. Dion. Thr. p. 748.

i) Epicharmus of Kos lived circ. 500—477, migrated to Megara in Sicily, and was the first to produce comedies in Syracuse shortly before the Persian wars, Suid. v. Ἐπίχαρμος, Diog. Laert. VIII, 78. Schol. Pind. Pyth. I, 98, reducing the indigenous farce of the Sikeliots to an artistic form, Περὶ κωμ. III, 5. Being attached to the doctrine of Pythagoras, he looked with disfavour on the absolute despotism of Hiero, Iambl. v. Pyth. 266. Plut. Num. 8. He attained an age of not less than 90 years, Diog. Laert. l. c. He composed at least some 30 comedies in the Dorian dialect, Suid. l. c. Iambl. V. Pyth. 241, often in trochaic tetrameters (metrum Epicharmium). The number of fragments preserved is very small. Of his poetry it is said, Περὶ κωμ. III, 5: τῇ δὲ ποιήσει γνωμικὸς καὶ εὑρετικὸς καὶ φιλότεχνος. On account of the wisdom of his apophthegms he was ranked high by philosophers, especially by Plato, Iambl. V. Pyth. 166, Plat. Theaet. p. 151 E. Amongst Sicilian comic poets, his contemporaries and successors, are Phormis and Deinolochus; further Sophron of Syracuse, the founder of the mime written in prose (Suid. s. v.), and his son Xenarchus, likewise a writer of mimes, Arist. Poet. I, 8. Suid. s. v. 'Ρηγίνους.

THIRD PERIOD. 500—431 B.C.

Olympiad.	B. C.	ATHENS.	HISTORY.
		Archon.	
LXXV, 1	480		The battle of Salamis on the 20th of Boedromion. Xerxes flees, leaving 300,000 men under the command of Mardonius[26]).
LXXV, 1	479	Xanthippus.	On the 4th of Boedromion[27]) victory of the Hellenes under Pausanias and Aristeides at Plataeae, by which an end was made of the Persian attacks[28]), and victory at Mykale, the first step towards the assumption of the offensive by the Hellenes and towards the liberation of the islands and the towns on the coasts of the Ægean Sea[29]).

26) The Greek fleet retired to Salamis, Herod. VIII, 40; the Persian fleet followed it, and took up its station at Phalerum, id. 66. Now that the road through Thermopylae was opened, Xerxes pressed into central Greece, where all tendered their submission, except Phokis, Plataeae, Thespiae, and Athens. The expedition to Delphi, 35—39; Athens deserted by its inhabitants, 41, and occupied by Xerxes 50—55. The Peloponnesians post themselves on the Isthmus, and endeavour to protect the Peloponnese by a wall built across the Isthmus, 71—73. Doubt and wavering of the Greeks in the fleet, 49. 56—63. 74—80, at last overcome by the perseverance and craft of Themistokles and by Aristeides ἀνὴρ (Ἀθηναῖος μέν, ἐξωστρακισμένος δὲ ὑπὸ τοῦ δήμου, τὸν ἐγὼ νενόμικα πυνθανόμενος αὐτοῦ τὸν τρόπον ἄριστον γενέσθαι ἐν Ἀθήνησι καὶ δικαιότατον, 79.) Battle of Salamis, 83—95, cf. Æsch. Pers. 353—514. The number of the Greek ships was, according to Herodotus, 378 (with which however the numbers of the several contingents do not exactly agree, only giving 366), VIII, 43—48; according to Æschylus 310, Pers. 339; according to Thuc. I, 74 nearly 400; of these the Athenians furnished 200 (including the 20, which had been lent to and manned by the Chalkidians, see obs. 24); the Persian fleet is said to have repaired its losses with the fresh contingents furnished by Greeks, and to have again reached the former total of 1207 ships, Herod. VIII, 66, so too Æsch. Pers. 341; but according to Ctes. 26 there were over 1000 Persian against 700 Greek ships. For the day of the battle see Plut. Cam. 19. Polyæn. III, 11, 2. Instead of the 20th. of Boedromion Böckh (Jahnsche Jahrb. Supplementb. N. F. 1. p. 73 f.) adopts the 19th and makes it correspond, not, as is usually done, to the 22nd but to the 20th of September, because in Plutarch's account, De Glor. Ath., the moon was shining brightly on the day of battle; which, as the full moon fell on the 18th of September, could not well be said of a day later than the 20th. For the flight of Xerxes see Herod. VIII, 97—107. 113—120. Mardonius accompanies the king to Thessaly and winters there, after choosing 300,000 of the bravest soldiers from the army, id. 113. Artabazus also returned to the same place, after he had accompanied the king further on his way as far as Thrace, first taking Olynthus and vainly besieging Potidaea, id. 126—129. The Greek ships pursue the enemy's routed fleet as far as Andros, but here relinquish the pursuit and besiege Andros, though without success, id. 106—112. The proceedings at the Isthmus in reference to the prize of valour, id. 123—125.

27) See Plut. Arist. 19; τῇ τετράδι τοῦ Βοηδρομιῶνος ἱσταμένου κατὰ Ἀθηναίους, κατὰ δὲ Βοιωτοὺς τετράδι τοῦ Πανέμου φθίνοντος. According to Plut. Cam. 19, on the 3rd. Both battles on one day, that at Plataea in the morning, that at Mykale in the evening, Herod. IX, 90. 100—101. Plut. Cam. l. c. Here also Böckh takes the 3rd or 4th of Boedromion not for the day of the battle, but for that on which the battle was celebrated, and places the battle some time earlier, Jahnsche Jahrb. Supplementb. N. F. 1. p. 67 f.

28) Herod. IX, 1—89. Mardonius returns to central Greece early in the spring, id. 1, and occupies Athens for the second time (in the summer, id. 3 : ἢ δὲ βασιλέος αἵρεσις ἐς τὴν Μαρδονίου δεκάμηνος ἐγίνετο). When the Spartans after long delay take the field, id. 6—9. Plut. Arist. 10 (contrast the heroic constancy of the Athenians in spite of the offers of Mardonius, Herod. VIII, 136. 140—144. IX, 4—5), the Persian retires to Bœotia, where he pitched his camp by the side of the Asopus, reaching from Erythrae beyond Hysiae up to the neighbourhood of Plataea, 300,000 strong; to which must be added 50,000 Medising Hellenes, Herod. IX, 32. The Hellenic army encamped opposite, at the foot of Kithaeron, 110,000 strong, viz. 38,700 hoplites, 69,500 light-armed, and 1800 Thespians altogether unarmed; of these 5000 were Spartans, 5000 Lacedaemonians, and 35,000 light-armed Helots, 8000 heavy armed Athenians, etc. 28—30. After both armies had lain opposite each other for 11 days and had already once changed their camps, the Persians begin the attack, when the Hellenes had a second time broken up their camp in order to change their position; the Spartans and Tegeatans engage the Persians, the Athenians the Medising Hellenes; the rest of the Hellenes only come upon the scene, when the victory is already won. The Persian army was almost totally destroyed with the exception of 40,000 men, who made good their escape under Artabazus, id. 70. (Ἁμιστόδημος λωσσῶν, id. 71.) Pausanias' arrogant inscription over the offering dedicated at Delphi, Thuc. I, 132. The pedestal of the tripod, which was at this time set up in honour of Apollo at Delphi, formed by a coiled serpent of brass, was dug up in 1856 at Constantinople, and in place of the inscription of Pausanias, cancelled by the Spartans, it contains the names of the Greek peoples who took part in the battles of Plataea and Salamis, viz. the Lacedaemonians, Athenians, Corinthians, Tegeatans, Megarians, Epidaurians, Orchomenians, Phliasians, Troezenians, Hermionians, Tirynthians, Plataeans, Thespians, Mykenaeans, Keans, Melians, Tenians, Naxians, Eretrians, Chalkidians, Styreans, Eleans, Potidaeans, Leukadians, Anaktorians, Kydnians, Siphnians, Amprakiotans, Lepreatans.

29) In spring the Persian fleet first sails from its winter quarters at Kyme to Samos, where they "ἐφύλασσον τὴν Ἰωνίην μὴ ἀποστῇ, νέας ἔχοντες σὺν ᾕσι Ἰάσι τριηκοσίας", Herod. VIII, 130. The Greek fleet, 110 ships strong (250 according to Diod. XI, 34), sailed first to Ægina, then to Delos, id. 131—132, from thence to Samos; and when they found that the enemy's fleet was not there, to the coast by Mykale, where the Persians had taken refuge under the protection of an army of 60,000 men, Herod. IX, 90—92. 96—98. Revolt of the Ionians, 99. 103—104. The Greeks land, attack the enemy, and win the victory, 102—106, chiefly through the good service of the Athenians, 105. 101 : οἱ μὲν δὴ Ἕλληνες καὶ οἱ βάρβαροι ἐσπευδον ἐς τὴν μάχην, ὡς σφι καὶ αἱ νῆσοι καὶ ὁ Ἑλλήσποντος ἄεθλα προέκειτο.

The Hellenic Race in its Prime.   45

Olympiad.	B. C.	HISTORY.
LXXV, 2	479	Sestos besieged and taken by the Hellenic fleet under the command of Xanthippus[30])

SECOND SECTION.

478—431 B.C.

MARITIME HEGEMONY OF ATHENS; GRADUAL SUBJECTION OF THE ALLIES; HER ATTEMPTS TO WIN THE HEGEMONY BY LAND; SORENESS AND HOSTILE COLLISIONS WITH SPARTA AND THE OTHER PELOPONNESIANS[31]).

Olympiad.	B. C.	ATHENS.	HISTORY.
		Archon.	a) Up to the breach with Sparta, 461 B.C.
LXXV, 3	478	Timosthenes.	Athens rebuilt, and in spite of Sparta's opposition surrounded with a wall[32]).

---

30) Herod. IX, 106—121. 106: ἀπικόμενοι δὲ ἐς Σάμον οἱ Ἕλληνες ἐβουλεύοντο περὶ ἀναστάσιος τῆς Ἰωνίης καὶ ὅκη χρεών εἴη τῆς Ἑλλάδος κατοικίσαι, τῆς αὐτοὶ ἐγκρατέες ἦσαν, τὴν δὲ Ἰωνίην ἀπεῖναι τοῖσι βαρβάροισι· ἀδύνατον γὰρ ἐφαίνετό σφι εἶναι ἑωυτούς τε Ἰώνων προκατῆσθαι φρουρέοντας τὸν πάντα χρόνον, καὶ ἑωυτῶν μὴ προκατημένων Ἴωνας οὐδεμίαν ἐλπίδα εἶχον χαίροντας πρὸς τῶν Περσέων ἀπαλλάξειν· πρὸς ταῦτα Πελοποννησίων μὲν τοῖσι ἐν τέλει ἐοῦσι ἐδόκεε τῶν μηδισάντων ἐθνέων τῶν Ἑλληνικῶν τὰ ἐμπόρια ἐξαναστήσαντας δοῦναι τὴν χώρην Ἴωσι ἐνοικῆσαι, Ἀθηναίοισι δὲ οὐκ ἐδόκεε ἀρχὴν Ἰωνίην γενέσθαι ἀνάστατον οὐδὲ Πελοποννησίοισι περὶ τῶν σφετερέων ἀποικιέων βουλεύειν. At first the Peloponnesians gave way and joined in the expedition to the Hellespont to help in destroying the bridges of Xerxes: but when they found the bridges already destroyed and the Athenians turned to the siege of Sestos, Leotychidas left the fleet together with the Peloponnesians, id. 114. Thuc. 1, 89. Sestos was taken in the course of the winter. Herod. 1. c. 117—118. Thuc. 1, c. His words: Σηστὸν ἐπολιόρκουν—καὶ ἐπιχειμάσαντες εἷλον αὐτήν, may be reconciled with Herodotus, for they do not necessarily mean that Sestos was not taken till after the end of the winter.

31) The period embraced in this section, on account of Thuc. I, 118 where its duration is given in round numbers as 50 years, is usually termed the πεντηκονταετία of Thucydides (1, 89—118): so first by that author's Scholiast on I, 18. 42. 75. 97. For the course of events in this period, see Thuc. 1, 18; κοινῇ τε ἀπωσάμενοι τὸν βάρβαρον ὕστερον οὐ πολλῷ διεκρίθησαν πρός τε Ἀθηναίους καὶ Λακεδαι-μονίους οἵ τε ἀποστάντες βασιλέως Ἕλληνες καὶ ξυμπολεμήσαντες· δυνάμει γὰρ ταῦτα μέγιστα διεφάνη· ἴσχυον γὰρ οἱ μὲν κατὰ γῆν, οἱ δὲ ναυσίν· καὶ ὀλίγον μὲν χρόνον ξυνέμεινεν ἡ ὁμαιχμία, ἔπειτα δὲ διενεχθέντες οἱ Λακεδαιμόνιοι καὶ οἱ Ἀθηναῖοι ἐπολέμησαν μετὰ τῶν ξυμμάχων πρὸς ἀλλήλους, καὶ τῶν ἄλλων Ἑλλήνων εἴ τινές που διασταῖεν, πρὸς τούτους ἤδη ἐχώρουν. ὥστε ἀπὸ τῶν Μηδικῶν ἐς τόνδε ἀεὶ τὸν πόλεμον τὰ μὲν σπενδόμενοι τὰ δὲ πολεμοῦντες ἢ ἀλλήλοις ἢ τοῖς ἑαυτῶν ξυμμάχοις ἀφισταμένοις εὖ παρεσκευάσαντο τὰ πολέμια καὶ ἐμπειρότεροι ἐγένοντο μετὰ κινδύνων τὰς μελέτας ποιούμενοι, cf. id. I, 118. For the chronology of this period we are dependent upon Thucydides (I, 89—118, 128—138) and Diodorus (XI, 39—XII, 37); but although the latter has arranged his narrative throughout by years, yet from his uncritical and superficial method he has been guilty of many contradictions and manifest errors; and Thucydides, on the other hand, though here, as everywhere, he has laboured to attain the greatest accuracy, and that too in the matter of dates (c. 97), with the exception of a few isolated remarks has omitted to give an accurate statement of the years. In many instances, therefore, dates are only founded on conjecture and grounds of more or less probability. The most important passages for the combinations which must consequently be made, are Thuc. I, 101. cf. IV, 102, and I, 112. 115. 87; see the years 465 and 445 B.C.

32) Thuc. I, 89—93. Plut. Them. 19. Corn. Them. 6—7. Thuc. l. c. 92: οἱ δὲ Λακεδαιμόνιοι ἀκούσαντες ὀργὴν μὲν φανερὰν οὐκ ἐποιοῦντο τοῖς Ἀθηναίοις—τῇ μέντοι βουλήσει ὡς ἁμαρτάνοντες ἀδήλως ἤχθοντο.

Olympiad.	B. C.	ATHENS.	HISTORY.
		Archon.	
LXXV, 4	477	Adeimantus.	The harbour of Peiræus completed and surrounded with a wall[33]). On the motion of Aristeides a law is passed at Athens abolishing the limitation, which excluded the citizens of the fourth class from the public offices and dignities[34]). The Hellenic fleet under the command of Pausanias conquers the greater part of the towns in Kyprus and Byzantium[35]).
LXXVI, 1	476	Phaedon.	Treachery of Pausanias[36]); transference of the hegemony by sea to Athens[37]).
LXXVI, 2	475	Dromokleides.	
LXXVI, 3	474	Akestorides.	
LXXVI, 4	473	Menon.	
LXXVII, 1	472	Chares.	
LXXVII, 2	471	Praxiergus.	Themistokles ostracised[38]).
LXXVII, 3	470	Demotion.	The Persians expelled from Eion and the Dolopes from Skyros by the allied fleet under Kimon; Karystus conquered by the Athenians[39]).

33) Thuc. I, 93. Plut. Them. 19. For the commencement of the harbour's construction see obs. 19. The circuit of the wall comprised 60 stadia, Thuc. II, 13. The building of the wall round the town and round the Peiræus is assigned to two consecutive years on the authority of Diod. XI, 41; id. 43; we are informed further, that the Athenians had now resolved to build 20 new triremes every year.

34) Plut. Arist. 22: Ἀριστείδης—ἅμα μὲν ἄξιον ἡγούμενος διὰ τὴν ἀνδραγαθίαν ἐπιμελείας τὸν δῆμον ἅμα δὲ οὐκέτι ῥᾴδιον ἰσχύοντα τοῖς ὅπλοις καὶ μέγα φρονοῦντα ταῖς νίκαις ἐκβιασθῆναι, γράφει ψήφισμα, κοινὴν εἶναι τὴν πολιτείαν καὶ τοὺς ἄρχοντας ἐξ Ἀθηναίων πάντων αἱρεῖσθαι. cf. Arist. Pol. VIII, 3, 7. With regard to the date, we only know thus much generally, that the law was made shortly after the victory at Plataeae.

35) Thuc. I, 94. Diod. XI, 44.

36) Thuc. I, 95. 128—134. Pausanias first of all roused general discontent by his arrogant and tyrannical behaviour. He was accordingly recalled by the Ephors to Sparta to answer for his conduct, and though acquitted of the charge of treason from defective evidence was nevertheless deprived of his command, id. 128—134. The condemnation and death of Pausanias cannot have taken place before 471 B. C., as the Spartans accused Themistokles of complicity in the plot, at the time when he was already living in banishment at Argos, see Thuc. I, 135, and obs. 38.

37) Thuc. I, 95—97. Plut. Arist. 22—24. The Lacedaemonians, after deposing Pausanias, sent Dorkis to assume the command; but the allies had meanwhile attached themselves to Athens, and in consequence refused to acknowledge Dorkis as commander-in-chief; whereupon ἄλλους οὐκέτι ὕστερον ἐξέπεμψαν οἱ Λακεδαιμόνιοι, φοβούμενοι μὴ σφίσιν οἱ ἐξιόντες χείρους γίγνωνται, ὅπερ καὶ ἐν τῷ Παυσανίᾳ ἐνεῖδον, ἀπαλλαξείοντες δὲ τοῦ Μηδικοῦ πολέμου καὶ τοὺς Ἀθηναίους νομίζοντες ἱκανοὺς ἐξηγεῖσθαι καὶ σφίσιν ἐν τῷ τότε παρόντι ἐπιτηδείους, Thuc. I, 95. cf. Diod. XI, 50. For the organisation of the hegemony (which was settled by Aristeides, Plut.) see Thuc. l. c. 96—97. Plut. l. c. 24.

38) Thuc. I, 135, Plut. Them. 22. Diod. XI, 55. When ostracised he first went to Argos, but fled thence when the Spartans accused him of complicity in the treason of Pausanias (according to Plut. l. c. 23, Pausanias first made overtures to him when he was living in banishment at Argos), and finally betook himself to the king of Persia, who received him with honour and gave him the towns Magnesia, Lampsakus, and Myus. He died at Magnesia, as Thucydides assures us (l. c. 138. cf. Cic. Brut. c. 11), by a natural death. See Thuc. I, 135—138. Plut. Them. 23—31. Diod. XI, 55—59. On the passage to Asia he passed by Naxos, when that place was held in siege by the Athenians, Thuc. 137, therefore in 466 B. C., see obs. 42; and when he had arrived in Asia and from thence wrote to the king of Persia, Artaxerxes had recently succeeded to the throne, Thuc. l. c. cf. Plut. Them. 27.

39) Thuc. I, 95. Diod. XI, 60. With the dates thus determined on the authority of Diodorus there certainly remains a large gap,

The Hellenic Race in its Prime.

Olympiad.	B. C.	ATHENS.	HISTORY.
LXXVII, 4	469	Archon. Apsephion.	Leotychidas is banished; Archidamus king of Sparta [40]).
LXXVIII, 1	468	Theagenides.	Death of Aristeides [41]): beginning of Perikles' influence [42]).
LXXVIII, 2	467	Lysistratus.	
LXXVIII, 3	466	Lysanias.	Naxos made subject by the Athenians [43]). Double victory of Kimon over the Persians at the Eurymedon [44]).
LXXVIII, 4	465	Lysitheus.	Xerxes dies: Artaxerxes I. (Longimanus) king of Persia [45]). Athens at war with Thasos [46]).
LXXIX, 1	464	Archedemides.	Earthquake at Sparta and revolt of the Messenian Helots: beginning of the third Messenian war [47]).
LXXIX, 2	463	Tlepolemus.	Thasos made subject by Athens [48]).
LXXIX, 3	462	Konon.	

Inasmuch as the years from 476 B. C. onwards are not occupied with any undertaking against the Persians; but probably numerous other conquests must be placed within this period from 476—466 B. C., which are mentioned neither by Thucydides nor Diodorus; for the whole of Thrake and the Hellespont had been subdued by Persia, according to Herod. VII, 106. 107. 108, and had therefore to be reconquered by the Greeks. For Eion cf. Herod. VII, 107 : for Skyros Plut. Thes. 36.

40) Herod. VI, 72. Paus. III, 7, 8. cf. Diod. XI, 48. Leotychidas was banished for allowing himself to be defeated by the Thessalians in a campaign against Thessaly.

41) Corn. Arist. 3 ("in the fourth year after the banishment of Themistokles"). Plut. Arist. 26.

42) According to Plut. Per. 7 he first came forward after the death of Aristeides. According to the passage id. 16 and Cic. De Or. III, c. 34 he was at the head of the Athenian state for the space of forty years. As he died in 429 B.C., this would lead us to 469; but we must probably regard the time as stated in round numbers at 40 years, and therefore not place too much stress upon it.

43) Thuc. I, 98. The date rests simply on the statement of Thucydides c. 100, which makes the battle at the Eurymedon and the beginning of the war against Thasos follow immediately upon the reduction of Naxos. Thuc. l.c.: πρώτη τε αὕτη πόλις ξυμμαχὶς παρὰ τὸ καθεστηκὸς ἐδουλώθη, ἔπειτα δὲ καὶ τῶν ἄλλων ὡς ἐκάστῃ ξυνέβη. The causes, which led to its subjection, id. 99 : αἰτίαι δ' ἄλλαι τε ἦσαν τῶν ἀποστάσεων καὶ μέγισται αἱ τῶν φόρων καὶ νεῶν ἐκδειαι καὶ λειποστράτιον εἴ τῳ ἐγένετο. But the allies were themselves to blame for the fact that their subjection was possible, id. : διὰ γὰρ τὴν ἀπόκνησιν ταύτην τῶν στρατειῶν οἱ πλείους αὐτῶν, ἵνα μὴ ἀπ' οἴκου ὦσιν, χρήματα ἐτάξαντο ἀντὶ τῶν νεῶν τὸ ἱκνούμενον ἀνάλωμα φέρειν, καὶ τοῖς μὲν Ἀθηναίοις ηὔξετο τὸ ναυτικὸν ἀπὸ τῆς δαπάνης ἣν ἐκεῖνοι ξυμφέροιεν, αὐτοὶ δὲ ὁπότε ἀποσταῖεν, ἀπαράσκευοι καὶ ἄπειροι ἐς τὸν πόλεμον καθίσταντο. Consequently the ξύμμαχοι gradually became metamorphosed into ὑποτελεῖς or ὑπήκοοι.

44) Thuc. I, 100. Diod. XI, 60. First the Phœnician fleet was defeated with a loss of 200 ships (Thuc.); the Greek crews then landed and inflicted a further defeat on the Persian army. (For the so-called peace of Kimon often assigned to this time, see year 449 B.C.)

45) Diod. XI, 69. Syncell. p. 206, D.

46) Thuc. I, 100. The quarrel arose "περὶ τῶν ἐν τῇ ἀντιπέρας Θρᾴκῃ ἐμπορίων καὶ τοῦ μετάλλου, ἃ ἐνέμοντο," Thuc. For these Thasian mines on the opposite Thrakian coast cf. Herod. VI, 46—47. It was probably these mines, which induced the Athenians in this same year to plant a colony on the site afterwards occupied by Amphipolis; but it was shortlived, for the 10,000 soldiers were soon afterwards slain by the Edonians, Thuc. l.c. According to Thuc. IV, 102, Amphipolis was founded 29 years after this first attempt; as the foundation of Amphipolis took place in 437 B.C., this gives 465 (or possibly 466) as the year of this first attempt and likewise as the year in which the war with Thasos began.

47) The Spartans had given the Thasians a solemn promise in answer to their prayers to aid them against Athens by an invasion of Attica, when the pressure of a two-fold danger, the Earthquake and Helotic rebellion, arose and prevented them. Thuc. I, 101. Plut. Cim. 16. Diod. XI, 63—64. The rebel Helots were mostly of Messenian descent and were therefore collectively styled Messenians; they were also joined by Perioeki from Thuria and Æthæa (Thuc.). They meant to surprise Sparta itself in the first moment of consternation; but king Archidamus had immediately summoned to arms all the rest of the Spartans who had not perished in the earthquake, Diod. and Plut. l. c. The rebels therefore retired and established themselves on Ithome, where they were then blockaded. The passages Herod. IX, 35 and 64 point to two battles between the Spartans and Messenians. Both Paus. IV, 24, 2 and Plut. Cim. 16 agree with the date deduced from Thucydides.

48) Thuc. I, 101: Θάσιοι δὲ τρίτῳ ἔτει πολιορκούμενοι ὡμολόγησαν Ἀθηναίοις τεῖχός τε καθελόντες καὶ ναῦς παραδόντες, χρήματά τε ὅσα ἔδει

Olympiad.	B. C.	ATHENS.	HISTORY.
		Archons.	
LXXIX, 4	461	Euthippus.	The Athenians, sensitive of the affront put upon them by the Spartans before Ithome [47]), banish Kimon [48]), renounce the alliance with Sparta, and conclude a counter-alliance with Argos, which is joined by Thessaly, and soon afterwards by Megara [51]).
			b) Up to the thirty year's truce between Athens and Sparta, 445 B. C.
LXXX, 1	460	Phrasikleides.	By Perikles and Ephialtes the Areopagus is stripped of its preeminent influence, and the operation of the popular tribunals is enlarged [52]). Introduction of pay to jurors [53]).

ἀποδοῦναι αὐτίκα ταξάμενοι καὶ τὸ λοιπὸν φέρειν, τήν τε ἤπειραν καὶ τὰ μέταλλα ἀφέντες. Surrender of ships, demolition of walls, defrayal of war-costs, were the usual conditions, which accompanied the subjection of the allied towns.

49) When the siege of Ithome made no progress, in addition to their other allies (Æginetans, Thuc. II, 27. IV, 56, Platæans, id. III, 54, Mantineans, Xen. Hell. V, 2, 3), the Spartans appealed to the Athenians, who sent them troops under Kimon. But *δείσαντες τῶν Ἀθηναίων τὸ τολμηρὸν καὶ τὴν νεωτεροποιίαν καὶ ἀλλοφύλους ἅμα ἡγησάμενοι, μή τι ἦν παραμείνωσιν ὑπὸ τῶν ἐν Ἰθώμῃ πεισθέντες νεωτερίσωσι, μόνους τῶν ξυμμάχων ἀπέπεμψαν, τὴν μὲν ὑποψίαν οὐ δηλοῦντες, εἰπόντες δ' ὅτι οὐδὲν προσδέονται αὐτῶν ἔτι.* Thuc. I, 102: "Καὶ διαφορὰ ἐκ ταύτης τῆς στρατείας πρῶτον Λακεδαιμονίοις καὶ Ἀθηναίοις φανερὰ ἐγένετο," id. According to Plut. Cim. 16. 17, the Athenians must have made two expeditions to assist Sparta, one at the time of the first danger, the other in 461 B. C.; but this seems to rest on a misconception of Aristoph. Lysistr. 1138.

50) He was ostracised for 10 years on account of his inclination to Sparta, and because he was chiefly accountable for the despatch of the expedition, Plut. Cim. 17, cf. 16.

51) Thuc. I, 102: δεινὸν ποιησάμενοι καὶ οὐκ ἀξιώσαντες ὑπὸ Λακεδαιμονίων τοῦτο παθεῖν, εὐθὺς ἐπεὶ ἀνεχώρησαν, ἀφέντες τὴν γενομένην ἐπὶ τῷ Μήδῳ ξυμμαχίαν πρὸς αὐτοὺς Ἀργείοις τοῖς ἐκείνων πολεμίοις ξύμμαχοι ἐγένοντο καὶ πρὸς Θεσσαλοὺς ἅμα ἀμφοτέροις οἱ αὐτοὶ ὅρκοι καὶ ξυμμαχία κατέστη. Megara joined the alliance, id. 103, and the Athenians accordingly built the long walls from the town to the harbour of Nisæa, id. (Since their defeat by the Spartans, obs. 8, the Argives had gradually recovered their strength, and just before this time had enlarged their power by the subjection of Ornea, Midea, and Tiryns, and the destruction of Mykenæ, Strab. p. 342. Paus. IV, 17, 4. 25, 5. 7. Diod. XI, 65.)

52) See Arist. Pol. II, 12, 2 : Καὶ τὴν μὲν ἐν Ἀρείῳ πάγῳ βουλὴν Ἐφιάλτης ἐκόλουσε καὶ Περικλῆς. Plut. Cim. 15 : οἱ πολλοὶ συγχέαντες τὰ καθεστῶτα τῆς πολιτείας κόσμον Ἐφιάλτου προεστῶτος ἀφείλοντο τῆς ἐξ Ἀρείου πάγου βουλῆς τὰς κρίσεις πλὴν ὀλίγων ἁπάσας καὶ τῶν δικαστηρίων κυρίους ἑαυτοὺς ποιήσαντες εἰς ἄκρατον δημοκρατίαν ἐνέβαλον τὴν πολιτείαν, ἤδη καὶ Περικλέους δυναμένου καὶ τὰ τῶν πολλῶν φρονοῦντος. Up to this time the Areopagus at all events in connexion with its

general censorship of morals (p. 28. obs. 68), had jurisdiction "περὶ πάντων σχεδὸν τῶν σφαλμάτων καὶ παρανομιῶν," Androt. and Philochor. in Müller Fr. Hist. Græc. I, p. 387 (fr. 17 of Philochorus): this was completely withdrawn, excepting in the case of capital charges, Philochor. 141: μόνα κατέλιπε τῇ ἐξ Ἀρείου πάγου βουλῇ τὰ ὑπὲρ τοῦ σώματος. According to Plut. Per. 9. Perikles made use of Ephialton only as his tool; but at all events it was the latter, who became the chief object of the opposite party's hate, so that he was actually murdered by them, Plut. Per. 9. Diod. XI, 77. The date rests on Diod. XI, 77, cf. Plut. Cim. 15. The supervision of the state administration in general, which the Areopagus had hitherto exercised, was transferred to the seven democratic νομοφύλακες, who were now first instituted, l. c. : whilst the juridical functions fell to the ἡλιαία (see p. 28. obs 69), the influence and operation of which were thus considerably extended. By this means, the last aristocratic element in the constitution was removed, and thus the fabric of Athenian democracy was brought to completion: at the same time the influence of Perikles reached its height, so that from this time forwards the conduct of public affairs at Athens lay almost altogether in his hand; see Thuc. II, 65 : ἐγίγνετό τε λόγῳ μὲν δημοκρατία, ἔργῳ δὲ ὑπὸ τοῦ πρώτου ἀνδρὸς ἀρχή.

53) The payment of the jurors (μισθὸς δικαστικὸς or ἡλιαστικός) was introduced by Perikles, Arist. Pol. II, 12, 3. Plut. Per. 9, and amounted at first to only 1 obol, but was afterwards raised by Kleon to 3 obols, Aristoph. Eq. 51. Schol. on Aristoph. Plut. 330. In addition to this, Perikles also introduced the θεωρικόν, originally intended to defray the entrance-money at the theatre and amounting to 2 obols, but afterwards distributed on other festive occasions, and by degrees raised in value, so that Demades actually promised every citizen half a mina, see Liban. Arg. Demosth. Olynth. I, Plut. Per. 9. Ἡαρροκραt. s. v. θεωρικά. Plut. Mor. p. 818 (Præc. Reip. Ger. ch. 25). (Other similar payments and donatives were the ἐκκλησιαστικόν—but this was not introduced in the life-time, or at all events the earlier years, of Perikles, and probably amounted first to 1, afterwards to 3 obols, see especially Aristoph. Eccles. 300—310: Kallistratus and Agyrrhius are named as its inventors, see Paræmiogr. ed. Leutsch et Schneid. p. 488. Schol. Arist. Eccl. 102 —further the μισθὸς βουλευτικός, συνηγορικός, etc.). For the injurious influence of these donatives see Arist. Pol. II, 7, 19. Plut. Per. 9. Plat. Gorg. 515, E :

The Hellenic Race in its Prime.

Olympiad.	B. C.	ATHENS.	HISTORY.
		Archons.	
LXXX, 1	460	Phrasikleides.	Athenian expedition to Egypt for the support of the satrap Inarus, who had rebelled against the Persian king[54].
LXXX, 2	459	Philokles.	
LXXX, 3	458	Bion.	The Athenians at war with Corinth, Epidaurus, and Ægina. On land they are defeated at Halieis, but then win a naval victory at Kekryphaleia, and a second, still more decisive, at Ægina; Ægina besieged[55].
			The Corinthians invade Megaris, in order to relieve Ægina, but are defeated by Myronides at the head of the youngest and oldest of the Athenian citizens[56].
LXXX, 4	457	Mnesitheides.	The Spartans at the head of a Peloponnesian army in central Greece defeat the Athenians in the battle of Tanagra[57]. Kimon recalled[58].
LXXXI, 1	456	Kallias.	The Athenians under Myronides conquer the Bœotians at Œnophyta; whereupon Bœotia, Phokis, and Opuntian Lokris join the Athenian alliance[59].
			Completion of the long walls from Athens to the Peirœus and Phalerum[60]. Ægina reduced to subjection[61]. The expedition of Tolmides round the Peloponnese[62].
LXXXI, 2	455	Sosistratus.	The third Messenian war ended by the capture of Ithome; the Athenians assign Naupaktus, lately conquered by them, as a dwelling place to the Messenians[63].
			Athenian army and fleet in Egypt annihilated[64].

ταῦτα γὰρ ἔγωγε ἀκούω, Περικλέα πεποιηκέναι Ἀθηναίους ἀργοὺς καὶ δειλοὺς καὶ λάλους φιλαργύρους εἰς μισθοφορίαν πρῶτον καταστήσαντα, so that thus with the completion of the democracy (see abv. 52) there were at the same time planted the seeds of degeneration into ochlocracy, which, though checked by Perikles, after his death gradually broke out and spread in an ever widening circle. The date, as regards the introduction of the juror's pay, is only approximate.

54) Thuc. I, 104. Diod. XI, 77.

55) Thuc. I, 105. In the battle of Ægina the Æginetans lost 70 ships, and their naval power was thereby annihilated.

56) Thuc. I, 105—106 (105: τῶν δ' ἐκ τῆς πόλεως ὑπολοίπων οἵ τε πρεσβύτατοι καὶ οἱ νεώτατοι ἀφικνοῦνται ἐς τὰ Μέγαρα Μυρωνίδου στρατηγοῦντος). Lys. Epitaph. p. 195. Diod. XI, 79. Two battles were fought, both in the vicinity of Megara (the second ἐν τῇ λεγομένῃ Κιμωλίς, Diod.), as the Corinthians, jeered by the old at home after their first expedition, attempted a second, which had a still more disastrous issue than the first. There is still preserved one of those tables, which contained the register of the Athenians, who fell in this year (ἐν Κύπρῳ, ἐν Αἰγύπτῳ, ἐν Φοινίκῃ, ἐν Ἁλιεῦσιν, ἐν Αἰγίνῃ, Μεγαροῖ τοῦ αὐτοῦ ἐνιαυτοῦ), and which were put up in the Kerameikos, Böckh. Corp. Inscr. Græc. I. p. 292 f. nr. 165.

57) The Spartans had marched to the aid of their relations, the inhabitants of Doris, who had been illtreated by the Phokians. When they found the way over the mountain range Gerania occupied by the Athenians, they marched to Bœotia, where the Athenians, with their allies, in all 14,000 strong, offered them battle. Thuc. I,

107—108. Plat. Menex. p. 242 B. The only result of the combat was, that the Spartans retired home unmolested, Thuc. 108.

58) Plut. Kim. 17. Per. 10. Kimon's recall was the effect of the noble patriotism, which Kimon displayed before the battle of Tanagra (cf. Thuc. I, 107), and of the enthusiasm, which seized upon all parties at Athens after this battle, and afterwards found its expression in the battle of Œnophyta.

59) Thuc. I, 108. The battle was fought on the 62nd day (Thuc.) after that at Tanagra; but must be placed in 456 B. C., as the battle of Tanagra, as is proved by Plut. Kim. 17. Per. 10, took place at the end of the previous year. The result, which the loss of the battle had for the Thebans, was that the ruling aristocratic party was overthrown, the democratic took its place, and concluded an alliance with Athens. The example of Thebes was followed by Phokis and Opuntian Lokris— though not without pressure on the side of Athens—so that now the hegemony of Athens, on land as well as by sea, comprised no small part of Greece.

60) Thuc. I, 108. The building had been begun in the previous year, id. 107. The wall to the Peirœus was 40, the other 35 stadia in length, Thuc. II, 13.

61) Thuc. I, 108. (Diod. XI, 78).

62) Thuc. I, 108. Diod. XI, 84. He burnt Gytheium, took Methone, Chalkis and Naupaktus, and won over Zakynthus and Kephallenia to the Athenian alliance.

63) Thuc. I, 103.

64) Thuc. I, 109—110.

Third Period. 500—431 B.C.

Olympiad.	B. C.	ATHENS.	HISTORY.	ART AND LITERATURE.
		Archons.		
LXXXI, 3	454	Ariston.	Enterprise of Perikles in the Krissœan gulf; Achaia joins the Athenian alliance[65].	
LXXXI, 4	453	Lysikrates.		
LXXXII, 1	452	Chœrephanes.		
LXXXII, 2	451	Antidotus.		
LXXXII, 3	450	Euthydemus.	Five years' truce between Athens and Sparta[66]. Thirty years' peace between Sparta and Argos[67].	The Tragic poets Sophokles[k], Euripides[l].

65) Thuc. I, 111. (Diod. XI, 85). We infer from the words of Thuc. l. c. *εὐθὺς παραλαβόντες*, that Achaia now joined the Athenian alliance, although they might mean, that the Achæans, as members of the alliance, were summoned to take part in the campaign; in which case the Achæans entered on the alliance in the previous year, cf. Thuc. I, 115. (Before this campaign, another, but fruitless, expedition had been made to Thessaly, Thuc. I, 111.) Diod. l. c.: οἱ μὲν οὖν 'Αθηναῖοι κατὰ τοῦτον τὸν ἐνιαυτὸν πλείστων πόλεων ἦρξαν, ἐν' ἀνδρείᾳ δὲ καὶ στρατηγίᾳ μεγάλην δόξαν κατεκτήσαντο. According to Plut. Per. 11. Diod. XI, 88 at the instigation of Perikles Athenian Kleruchs were

k) Sophokles, the son of Sophillus, born circ. 496 B. C. in the Athenian deme of Kolonus, and carefully instructed, especially in music and gymnastics, Vit. Soph. Plut. De Mus. 31, led, when a youth, the festive song and triumphal dance around the trophies from Salamis, Athen. I, p. 20. Vit. Soph. Plut.; at the age of 28 he conquered Æschylus in the contest for the tragic prize, Marm. Par. Plut. Cim. 5, and often afterwards carried off the first or second, never the third prize. Vit. Soph. Suid. s. v. In the organisation of the stage he effected numerous changes; he relinquished a connected ground-work in the plays of a trilogy; he distinctly gave chief importance to the dialogue; he increased the chorus from 12 to 15 performers; he introduced the third actor; he departed from the custom, which brought the poet on the stage as an actor in his dramas; and made many alterations in costume, Vit. Soph. Suid. s. v. After the production of the Antigone the people elected him general with Perikles for the campaign against Samos, Vit. Soph. Plut. Per. 8. Strab, p. 638. In the activity of political life he appears as probonlus, Arist. Rhet. III, 18, 6, and as such uses his influence to promote the institution of the Four Hundred; but he gained no distinction, either as general, or statesman, Athen. XIII, p. 603. 604. He persistently refused invitations of princes to their courts, so great was his devotion to his native city (φιλαθηναιότατος ἦν, Vit. Soph.), where he was a general favourite. l. c. In consequence of a preference for his grandson Sophokles, son of Ariston, who was born to Sophokles by his mistress Theoris, the poet is said to have been summoned by his son Iophon before a family tribunal and charged with being in his dotage, but to have been acquitted upon his reading a passage from the Œdipus at Kolonus, Vit. Soph. Athen. XIII, p. 592. Cic. De Sen. 7, 22. Plut. De Rep. Sen. Ger. II, p. 508. He died in 406 B. C. after a happy life at the age of 91. Vit. Soph. Marm. Par. Argum. 3 Œd. Col. Various tales were current concerning the manner of his death, Diod. Sic. XIII, 103. Vit. Soph. Paus. I, 21, 2 f. The Athenians paid divine honours to their greatest tragic poet after his death, Vit. Soph. Plut. Num. 4. Etym. M. s. v. *Δεξίων*. Of the 113 dramas, which Sophokles probably composed, only seven are preserved in a perfect state; viz. 'Αντιγόνη, the poet's masterpiece (produced 441 B. C.), 'Ηλέκτρα, Οἰδίπους (τύραννος), Οἰδίπους ἐπὶ Κολωνῷ,

at this time sent to the Thrakian Chersonese and Naxos, likewise to Andros and the coast of Thrake.

66) Thuc. I, 112: *Ὕστερον δὲ* (i. e. after the expedition of Perikles) *διαλιπόντων ἐτῶν τριῶν σπονδαὶ γίγνονται Πελοποννησίοις καὶ 'Αθηναίοις πεντάετεῖς, καὶ Ἑλληνικοῦ μὲν πολέμου ἔσχον οἱ 'Αθηναῖοι*. According to Diod. XI, 86. Plut. Kim. 18. Theopomp. fr. 92, it was Kimon, who was the prime mover in securing the truce, his object being to divert the quarrels between Athens and Sparta by a foreign war.

67) Thuc. V, 14.

Αἴας, Φιλοκτήτης (produced 409 B. C.), Τραχίνιαι. Of the rest, some 1000, for the most part short, fragments are in existence, Nauck. Trag. Græc. fr. p. 103 f. The longest are from the dramas 'Αλκαῖαι, N. fr. 86, 'Αληγης, fr. 104, 'Αχιλλέως ἐρασταί, fr. 154, Οὐλυσσης, fr. 235, Κρίουσα, fr. 327, Ναύπλιος, fr. 306, Πολυξένη, fr. 470, Τηρεύς, fr. 521, Τυρώ, fr. 503, cf. fr. 736. 556. Further, mention is made of elegies, pœans, and a work on the chorus by Sophokles, Suid. s. v. The younger Phrynichus praises Sophokles, Argum. III. Œd. Col. : μάκαρ Σοφοκλέης, ὃς πολὺν χρόνον βιοὺς | ἀπέθανεν εὐδαίμων ἀνὴρ καὶ δεξιός, | πολλὰς ποιήσας καὶ καλὰς τραγῳδίας, | καλῶς δ' ἐτελεύτησ', οὐδὲν ὑπο-μείνας κακόν. Of the characteristics of his poetry it is said in Dio. Chrys. Or. LII, p. 272 : ὁ δὲ Σοφοκλῆς μέσος ἔοικεν ἀμφοῖν εἶναι, οὔτε τὸ αὔθαδες καὶ τὸ ἁπλοῦν τὸ τοῦ Αἰσχύλου ἔχων οὔτε τὸ ἀκριβὲς καὶ δριμὺ καὶ πολιτικὸν τὸ τοῦ Εὐριπίδου, σεμνὴν δέ τινα καὶ μεγαλοπρεπῆ ποίησιν τραγικωτάτα καὶ εὐπρεπέστατα ἔχουσαν, ὥστε πλείστην ἡδονὴν μετὰ ὕψους καὶ σεμνότητος ἐνδείκνυσθαι.

l) Euripides, the son of Mnesarchus, born in the island of Salamis 480. B. C., on the day, so it is said, of the battle of Salamis, Vit. Eur. α'. β'. γ'. Western., enjoyed a careful bringing up. As a boy, he gained such distinction in gymnastic arts, that he won a prize in a contest. Vit. α'. Gell. XV, 20; he also had some talent for painting Vit. α'. β'. In his youth, he devoted himself zealously to philosophy, especially ethics, in intercourse with Anaxagoras and Sokrates, and attended the lectures of the Sophists Prodikus and Protagoras on rhetoric, Vit. α'. β'. γ'; his dramas in consequence showed traces of those teachings, especially of Anaxagoras (cf. Troad. 886 : Ζεὺς, εἴτ' ἀνάγκη φύσεως εἴτε νοῦς βροτῶν), and rhetorical artifices (Vit. α': προσεῦρε λέγουσ φυσιο-λογίας, ῥητορείας); and the comic poets jeeringly intimated, that Sokrates assisted Euripides in his tragedies, Vit. α'. Athen. IV, 131 C. Diog. Laert. II, 18. A stern, gloomy, and meditative man, the poet lived retired from company and political life, Vit. β'. γ', conscious of his own powers and little troubled about the verdict of the public, Val. Max. III, 7. His first appearance on the stage was with the drama Πελιάδες (in 456 B. C.), and in spite of the number of his tragedies he only won the first prize five times, Vit. γ'. Suid. s. v. cf. Varro ap. Gell. XVII, 4, 3. However, though the poet was the subject of many

The Hellenic Race in its Prime. 51

Olympiad.	B. C.	ATHENS.	HISTORY.	ART AND LITERATURE.
LXXXII, 4	449	Archon. Pedieus.	The Athenians resume the war against Persia under the conduct of Kimon, and after Kimon's death win a double victory at Salamis in Kyprus, by land and by sea[68]).	The Comic poets Krates[m]), Kratinus[n]).

68) Thuc. I, 112. According to Diod. XIII, 3 it is Kimon himself, who wins the victory. According to this same author (c. 4) the so-called peace of Kimon (according to Demosth. De F. leg. p. 428, Plut. Kim. 13, cf. Herod. VII, 151 more properly named the peace of Kallias) was concluded after this victory, by which, it was said, the Persian king bound himself to grant complete independence to all Hellenic towns in Asia, and to that end never to sail with his fleet west of Phaselis or the neighbouring Chelidonian isles to the south, to the east never beyond the Kyanean rocks at the entrance of the Pontus Euxinus, and to keep his army at the least three days' march from the west coast of Asia Minor. By Plutarch (Kim. 13) this peace is placed after the battle at the Eurymedon; no mention at all of it is found in Thucydides; and the orators are the first to quote it, at first referring to it in general terms, then with increasing exactness of detail, see Isokr. Paneg. p. 65, Areop. p. 150, Panath. p. 244. Demosth. De F. Leg. p. 458, cf. De Rhod. Lib. p. 199. Lykurg. Leokr. p. 199: in later rhetoricians

hostile attacks (Vit. a'. : ὑπὸ γὰρ Ἀθηναίων ἐφθονεῖτο), yet at the date of the Sicilian expedition his poems lived in the mouths of all men, Plut. Nic. 29. Among the innovations, which Euripides made on the stage, first and foremost are the introduction of the prologue, Vit. β'. Aristoph. Ran. 946, 1177, and of monodies or arias, Aristoph. Ran. 1330 f. 944. 951, and the severance of the choral songs from any connexion with the play, Schol. Arist. Ach. 442. He showed great aptitude in delineating states of the soul, in particular the passion of love, but is often too rhetorical. He was not spared bitter experiences. The infidelity of both his wives called forth sharp and illnatured utterances about women in his tragedies, and was not without influence on the delineation of his female characters, Vit. α'. β'. γ'. Aristoph. Thesm. 82 f. This domestic unhappiness and the gibes of the comic poets, which culminate in the Frogs and Thesmophoriazusæ of Aristophanes, induced him to leave the city of his birth, Vit. β'. γ'. He betook himself to Pella to the court of king Archelaus of Macedonia, who treated him with great honour, and to whom the poet showed his gratitude by his last drama Ἀρχέλαος, Vit. α'. There he died in 406 B. c. shortly before Sophokles, who sincerely mourned his loss, Vit α'. β'. γ'. The Athenians honoured his memory with a cenotaph. Paus. I, 2, 2. He wrote at least 75 dramas, Vit. γ'. Varro ap. Gell. XVIII, 4. Suid. l. c., of which 16 tragedies are preserved perfect: Ἑκάβη, Ὀρέστης, Μήδεια, Φοίνισσαι, Ἱππόλυτος στεφανηφόρος, Ἀνδρομάχη, Ἱκετίδες, Ἰφιγένεια ἡ ἐν Αὐλίδι, Ἰφιγένεια ἡ ἐν Ταύροις, Τρῳάδες, Βάκχαι, Ἡρακλεῖδαι, Ἴων, Ἑλένη, Ἡρακλῆς μαινόμενος, Ἠλέκτρα, a satyric drama, Κύκλωψ, and a play filling the place of a satyric drama, Ἄλκηστις (Argum.: τὸ δὲ δρᾶμά ἐστι σατυρικώτερον). The Ῥῆσος, preserved under his name, is not from his pen. Of the rest, nearly 1100 fragments are preserved, the more important from the dramas Ἀλέξανδρος, Nauck. fr. 53, Ἀντιόπη fr. 187, 188, 219, 220, Ἀρχέλαος, fr. 230, Αὐτόλυκος, fr. 284, 287, 288, Δανάη, fr. 318—332, Δικτύς, fr. 336, 339, 349, Ἐρεχθεύς, 362, 363, Ἰνώ, fr. 406, 407, Κρεσφόντης, fr. 452, Κρῆτες, fr. 475, Οἰνόμαος, fr. 575—577, Παλαμήδης, fr. 582, Πλεισθένης, fr. 628, Ῥαδαμανθύς, fr. 660, Φαέθων, fr. 779, 781, Φοῖνιξ, fr. 809, 813, 816, Χρύσιππος, fr. 835, cf. fr. 839, 890. For Euripides as a poet see the criticism of Aristotle Poet. 13, 9. 10: καὶ ὁ Εὐριπίδης, εἰ καὶ τὰ ἄλλα μὴ εὖ οἰκονομεῖ, ἀλλὰ τραγικώτατός γε τῶν ποιητῶν φαίνεται. Cf. Longin. 15, 3: ἔστι μὲν οὖν φιλοπονώτατος Εὐριπίδης δύο ταυτὶ πάθη μανίας τε καὶ ἔρωτας ἐκτραγῳδῆσαι κἄν τούτοις ὡν οὐκ οἶδ᾽ εἰ τισιν ἑτέροις ἐπιτυχέστατος· οὐ μὴν ἀλλὰ καὶ ταῖς ἄλλαις ἐπιτίθεσθαι φαντασίαις οὐκ ἄτολμος. (Of the numerous other tragic poets about the time of Sophokles and Euripides the most prominent are: Aristarchus of Tegea, Suid. s. v. Nauck. trag. Gr. fr. 1—6; Ion of Chios, Suid. s. v. Schol. Arist. Pac. 835. N. fr. 1—68 ; Achæus of Eretria, Suid. s. v. Athen. X, p. 451. N. fr. 1—54, distinguished for his satyr-plays, Diog. L. II, 133; and later Agathon, the friend of Plato, Sympos. ridiculed by Aristophanes for the effeminate, over-refined character of his poetry (as ὁ καλός), Thesm. 25 f. 60 f. 100. 130 f. 150 f. cf. Schol. N. fr. 1—29. Of the mass of tragic poets of his time Aristophanes says, Ran. 89: οὔκουν ἔσθ᾽ ἔστ᾽ ἐνταῦθα μειρακύλλια | Εὐριπίδου πλεῖν ἢ σταδίῳ λαλίστερα ;| ἐπιφυλλίδες ταῦτ᾽ ἐστὶ καὶ στωμύλματα, | χελιδόνων μουσεῖα, λωβηταὶ τέχνης. The like is true of the great number of later tragic poets, none of whom had any creative genius. The names of some 130 tragic poets, and more than 50 fragments of their works, are still preserved.)

m) The great historians of literature themselves divided Attic comedy into an ἀρχαία κωμῳδία, μέση κωμῳδία and νέα κωμῳδία, Anon. Περὶ κωμ. III. IX, 8. The characteristic marks of the older Attic comedy are: the political satire with masks caricaturing real persons, Platon. περὶ διαφορᾶς κωμῳδιῶν 19, called by their proper names (κωμῳδεῖν ὀνομαστί), Isokr. De Pac. p. 161, Περὶ κωμ. VIII, 8, IX, 7, the 24 members of the chorus in burlesque or phantastic masks, Περὶ κωμ. VIII, 34, and the Παράβασις, the Intermezzo or digression from the subject of the piece, when the chorus, singing or declaiming, turns to the spectators and expresses itself in jest or earnest upon circumstances of public life or the relations of the poet to the public, or gives whimsical vent to his thoughts, Aristid. T. II. p. 523. Platon. Περὶ Διαφ. Κωμ. 11: ὁ χορὸς οὐκ ἔχων πρὸς τοὺς ὑποκριτὰς διαλέγεσθαι ἀπόστροφον ἐποιεῖτο πρὸς τὸν δῆμον· κατὰ δὲ τὴν ἀπόστροφον ἐκείνην οἱ ποιηταὶ διὰ τοῦ χοροῦ ἢ ὑπὲρ ἑαυτῶν ἀπελογοῦντο ἢ περὶ δημοσίων πραγμάτων εἰσηγοῦντο. The older Attic comedy developed with the growth of the democratic constitution, and fell with it. The number of poets and their fertility is extraordinarily great. Chionides is called the oldest comic poet of Athens (circa 460 B.C.). Krates of Athens, circ. 450 B.C., the first important comic poet and likewise actor, substituted for the farce innocent of all laws of composition the attempt to construct of definite material taken from real life, Περὶ κωμ. III, 8. Suid. s. v. Κράτης, Arist. Poet. 5; this poet was sometimes applauded, sometimes hissed off the stage by the public, for which he is derided by Aristophanes, Eq. 537. 549. Short fragments are preserved from nine of his comedies. Fragm. Com. Meineke p. 78 f., the most important from the Θηρία, M. fr. 1—4, Παιδιαί fr. 1. Σάμιοι fr. 1.

n) Kratinus of Athens, flourished circ. 449—423, Περὶ Κωμ. III, 7. Aristoph. Pac. 700 f. Lucian. Macrob. ch. 25, and conquered nine

7—2

THIRD PERIOD. 500—431 B.C.

Olympiad.	B.C.	ATHENS.	HISTORY.	ART AND LITERATURE.
		Archons.		
LXXXIII, 1	448	Philiskus.	Renewal of hostilities between Athens and Sparta through the Sacred war[o].	The philosophers Zeno[o]), Empedokles[p]), Anaxagoras[q]).
LXXXIII, 2	447	Timarchides.	The Bœotians defeat the Athenians at Koroneia, and abandon the Athenian alliance[70]).	
LXXXIII, 3	446	Kallimachus.		

it forms a frequently recurring theme in their panegyrics on Athens. For this reason doubt was thrown on the peace by Kallisthenes, see Plut. Kim. 13, and often by scholars in modern times: however, although the peace is subject to many well-founded suspicions, still the passages Thuc. VIII, 5. 6. 56. Herod. VI, 42 are not, as has been thought, incompatible with it; and practically it had a real existence, as after this time the war against Persia ceased for a considerable period, Plut. Kim. 19.

69) The Lacedæmonians made an expedition to central Greece, in order to restore the oracle to the possession of the Delphians, who had had it wrested from them by the Phokians; after their departure

timos with great applause, Suid. s. v. Arist. Eq. 526. 330; his most brilliant victory of all being gained at an advanced age (in 424 B.C.) with the Πυτίνη (wine-flask) against the Clouds of Aristophanes, Arist. Argum. Nub. V. ed. Bergk, when the latter had shortly before ridiculed him as worn out and decayed, Eq. 531—536. He is said to have fixed the number of actors appearing on the stage in comedy at three, Περὶ κωμ. V, 3. Of 26 of his comedies fragments, short for the most part, are preserved, Frag. Com. Græc. Meineke p. 7 f., the most important being from the comedies Ἀρχίλοχοι, Βουκόλοι, Θρᾷτται, Μαλθακοί, Νέμεσις, Ὀδυσσῆς, Πυτίνη, Τροφώνιος, Χείρωνες. His political satire was sharp and bitter, Arist. Acharn. 849. Platon. Περὶ διαφορᾶς χαρακτήρων 1, 3. Anon. Περὶ κωμ. V, 3: ὥσπερ δημοσίᾳ μάστιγι τῇ κωμῳδίᾳ κολάζων. This is also clear from his attacks on Perikles, cf. Thra. M. fr. 1: σχινοκέφαλοι τηδείον ἐπὶ τοῦ κρανίου ἔχων, Cheir. fr. 3: τύραννος, κεφαληγερέταν, and on Aspasia, Cheir. fr. 4: παλλακὴν κυνώπιδα, as opposed to Kimoon, of whom he says, Archil. fr. 1: οὐκ ἀνδρὶ θείῳ καὶ φιλοξενωτάτῳ καὶ πάντ᾽ ἀρίστῳ τῶν Πανελλήνων κρόμμῳ Κίμωνι. He is denoted as having a poetical nature, fond of life, by Suid. s. v.: λαμπρὸς τὸν χαρακτῆρα φιλοτάτῃ δὲ καὶ παιδικῶν ἠττημένος, cf. Περὶ κωμ. III, 7: γέγονε δὲ ποιητικώτατος, κατασκευάζων εἰς τὸν Αἰσχύλου χαρακτῆρα. Cf. Platon. Περὶ διαφ. χαρ. II, 1. Aristoph. Pac. 700 f.—Pherekrates of Athens, was his contemporary, and in 437 B.C. won a prize, Περὶ κωμ. III, 9. To him belong for certain 13 comedies, of which fragments are in existence, the most important being Ἄγριοι, fr. 1. 2. 4. 11. Αὐτόμολοι, fr. 1. Δουλοδιδάσκαλοι, fr. 1—5. Κοριαννώ, fr. 1—5. His personal satire he seems to have shrunk, like Krates, yet he ridicules Alkibiades, Inc. Fab. fr. 5: οὐκ ὢν ἀνὴρ γὰρ Ἀλκιβιάδης, ὡς δοκεῖ, ἀνὴρ ἀπασῶν τῶν γυναικῶν ἐστι νῦν. He is praised for the invention of new stage materials, Περὶ κωμ. l. c. The refinement of his language is denoted by the epithet Ἀττικώτατος, Athen. VI, p. 268 c. Steph. Byz. p. 43; the metrum Pherecrateum is called after him.

o) Zeno, born at Elea, a town of Lower Italy, flourished circ. 468—433 B.C., Diog. Laert. IX, 25. Suid. s.v. Cyrill. Iulian. I, p. 23. A pupil of Parmenides, Plat. Parm. p. 127. Diog. I. l.c. Athen. XI, p. 505, he came repeatedly to Athens, where he met with Sokrates, Plat. Soph. p. 217. Parm. l.c. Theæt. p. 217. Diog. L. IX, 28, and lectured on his doctrines to Perikles and Kallias for 100 minæ, Plat. Alkib. I, p. 119. Plut. Perikl. 4. He improved the laws of his native city, Diog. L. IX,

the Athenians sent a force under Perikles and put the Phokians in possession again. Thuc. I, 112. Plut. Per. 21.

70) Thuc. I, 113. Diod. XII, 6. The Athenians had marched to Bœotia under Tolmides, inasmuch as exiles from Chæronea and Orchomenus (at all events the aristocrats banished in consequence of the battle of Œnophyta, see obs. 59) had made themselves masters of these towns. After the Athenians had conquered Chæronea, on their return they were assailed by the exiles from Orchomenus, who had been joined by exiles from Eubœa and Lokris, and defeated: whereupon, in order to recover the prisoners, they gave up all the towns of Bœotia, i. e. they gave them up to the aristocratical party, which opposed Athens.

33, and attempted to free it from a tyrant. It is uncertain, whether his enterprise succeeded or resulted in his death, Plut. adv. Col. p. 1126. Diog. L. IX, 26—28. Cic. Tusc. II, 22. De Nat. D. III, 33. With regard to his writings, which were composed in prose, partly in the form of dialogues, Plat. Parm. l.c. Diog. L. III, 47 we hear of Ἔριδες (polemical writings) and Ἐξηγήσεις τῶν Ἐμπεδοκλέους πρὸς τοὺς φιλοσόφους περὶ φύσεως, Suid. l.c. He developed the doctrines of his master Parmenides and was looked on as the originator of dialectic, the proof which advances to the truth by refutation of the apparent, Plat. Parm. p. 128. Plut. Per. 4. Diog. L. IX, 25. (Melissus of Samos must also be mentioned, as belonging to the Eleatic school, Diog. L. IX, 24. Plut. Per. 26.)

p) Empedokles of Agrigentum, adherent of the teaching of Pythagoras, pupil of Xenophanes and Parmenides, and contemporary of Zeno, flourished circ. 445—433, Cyrill. Iulian. I, p. 23. Diog. L. VIII, 51. 52. 54. 55. 56. He taught rhetoric and found in Gorgias a distinguished Scholar, l.c. 57. 58. Suid. s.v.; as a statesman laboured for the introduction of the democratic constitution, Diog. L. 72. 73, and traversed the towns of Sicily in great pomp as physician, worker of miracles, wizard, and prophet, l.c. 59—63. 67. 70. 73. Amongst the legends of his death his voluntary leap into the crater of Ætna is the most famous. Nothing certain is known about it, l.c. 67. 69. 70—73. His chief work, Τὰ φυσικά or Περὶ φύσεως, was written in hexameters in the Ionian dialect; of these about 400 are preserved, l.c. 77. Suid. l.c. He served the Roman poet Lucretius as a model, De Ror. Nat. 1, 77 ff. He taught that through the two motive forces of blending friendship (φιλία) and severing discord the four primary elements were mingled and endowed with form.

q) Anaxagoras, born at Klazomenæ, lived from 500—428 B.C., Diog. Laert. II, 6, 7, spending a considerable time at Athens, where he was connected with Perikles and other important men, awakened an interest in philosophy, and exercised considerable influence. Shortly before the beginning of the Peloponnesian war he was accused of impiety (Diod. IX, 38 f. Plut. Per. 32), and was only rescued from death at the intercession of Perikles; but he was obliged to leave Athens, and retired to Lampsakus, where he is said to have died at the age of seventy, Diog. L. II, 12—15. Suid. s.c. Plut. Per. 4. 32. Cic. De Nat. D. I, 11. He wrote a work περὶ φύσεως, of which several

The Hellenic Race in its Prime.

Olympiad.	B. C.	ATHENS.	HISTORY.	ART AND LITERATURE.
LXXXIII, 4	415	Archon. Lysimachides.	Eubœa and Megara revolt from the Athenian alliance; the Peloponnesians under the Spartan king Pleistoanax invade Attica, but retire without inflicting any damage upon the Athenians[71]).	Herodotus the father of History[r]). Plastic art flourishes[s]) —Myron[t]).

71) By his retreat Pleistoanax incurred the suspicion of having allowed himself to be bribed by Perikles. Thuc. I, 144. II, 21. V, 16. Plut. Per. 22. 23. Diod. XII, 6. The battle of Koroneia took place χρόνου ἐγγενομένου μετὰ ταῦτα i. e. after the Sacred war: the revolt of Eubœa occurred οὐ πολλῷ ὕστερον, 14 years before the outbreak of the Peloponnesian war, Thuc. I, 113. 114. II, 21.

---

fragments are preserved; and taught that a single spirit (νοῦς) created the world out of the primitive material, and in consequence received the name Νοῦς. Diog. L. II, 6. Suid. s. v. Archelaus of Miletus the master of Sokrates, was his pupil, who is designated the last Ionian physicist and also the forerunner of Sokrates in Ethics, Suid. s. v. Diog. L. II, 6.

r) Following the fashion of the old compilers of legends (λογογράφοι), Pherikydes of Leros, a settler at Athens, called ὁ γενεαλόγος, wrote circ. 450 B. C, his work Αὐτόχθονες, which treated of family legends, especially Attic, Eratosth. ap. Diog. Laert. 1, 119. Strab. p. 487. Suid. s. v. Dion. Hal. A. R. I, 13. The transition from tale-telling to history is made by Hellanikus of Mytilene in Lesbos, whose earliest years coincide with the beginning of the Persian wars, Thuc. I, 97. Vit. Eurip. Gell. XV, 23. Suid. s. v. Of the numerous writings, which are ascribed to him, those genuine are: Δευκαλιώνεια, Φορωνίς, Ἀτλαντιάς, Τρωικά, which recounted family legends; the histories of single countries formed the subjects of Ἀτθίς, Αἰολικά, Περσικά, whilst Ἱέρειαι τῆς Ἥρας and Καρνεονῖκαι were chronological writings. Herodotus, born at Halikarnassus, of an influential family, a cousin of Panyasis, Suid. s. v., born between 490 and 480 B.C., died between 428 and 424 B.C., Gell. XV, cf. Herod. III, 15. V, 77. VI, 98. VII, 137. I, 130. To avoid the tyrant Lygdamis, he went abroad to Samos, Suid. l. c. As is proved by his history, he visited in the course of extensive travels the mainland of Greece, the islands of the Ægean sea, Asia Minor, Krete, Kyprus, Phœnicia, Syria, Babylonia, Assyria, Media, Egypt, as far as its southern boundary, and Italy. He read in public single sections of his work before the completion of the whole, e. g. at Olympia, see p. 23 obs. 22, at Athens, Plut. De Mal. Herod. 25, at Corinth, Dio Chrys. Or. XXXVII, T. II, p. 103, and at Thebes, Plut. l. c. 31. In 443 B. C. he took part in the foundation of Thurii by the Athenians, Suid. l. c. Strab. p. 790. Schol. Arist. Nub. 331, where he finished his work and died. Plin. N. H. XII, 18. Suid. l. c. In his historical work, Ἱστορίαι, now divided into nine books, each of which bears the name of a muse for its title, his aim was to relate the causes and events of the struggle between the Hellenes and barbarians; he begins with the subjection of the Asiatic Greeks by the Lydian King Krœsus, the first injury inflicted upon the Hellenes by barbarians, and carries his history, interwoven with numerous comprehensive episodes, which contain the history of the Lydians, Egyptians, Scythians, and other nations, up to the conquest of Sestos by the Hellenes. Of the verdicts of ancient critics on Herodotus we may cite in particular: Dion. Hal. Ep. ad Cn. Pomp. 3: ἡδονῇ δὲ καὶ πειθοῖ καὶ τέρψει καὶ τὰς ὁμοιογενεῖς ἀρετὰς εἰσφέρεται μακρῷ Θουκυδίδου κρείττοσιν Ἡρόδοτος, Quint. IX, 4, 18: In Herodoto vero cum omnia (ut ego quidem sentio) leniter fluunt, tum ipsa διάλεκτος habet eam iucunditatem, ut latentes etiam numeros complexa videatur.

s) Legend ascribed old statues, especially wooden figures of gods, to Dædalus; the artists Epeius and Dibutades are likewise mythical names. At an early period art-schools existed in the islands of Ægina, Chios, Samos, and Krete. Thus statues in Æginetan style are ascribed to Smilis of Ægina, Paus. VII, 4, 4. 5. V, 17, 1. Plin. XXXVI, 90. Glaukus of Chios, Herod. I, 25, or Samos, Steph. Byz. s. v. Αἰθάλη, invented circ. 695 (?) the art of soldering metals, Euseb. Chron. 81 f. Herod. l. c. Steph. Byz. l. c. Paus. X, 16, 1; his successors formed a school of statuary in Chios, which already worked in marble, Plin. XXXVI, 11. Dipœnus and Skyllis of Krete, famed for their works in marble circa 572 B. C. Paus. II, 15, 1. III, 17, 6. Plin. XXXVI, 9, 14, were also founders of an art-school. Rhoekus and Theodorus of Samos, architects and sculptors, discovered the casting of metals about 580—540, Herod. III, 60. Paus. VIII, 14, 5. IX, 41, 1. X, 38, 3. The ancients knew of both buildings and statues by both masters. The invention of the square, the level, the turning-lathe, and the key, is also attributed to Theodorus, Plin. VII, 198. The subjects treated in the statuary of the oldest period are gods and divine beings; art appears tied down to the service of religion. Bhoekus and Theodorus of Samos, architects and sculptors, discovered the casting of metals about 580—540, Herod. III, 60. Paus. VIII, 14, 5. IX, 41, 1. X, 38, 3. About the time of the Persian wars there were schools of statuary at Argos, Sikyon, Ægina, and Athens; in which the most eminent masters were Ageladas of Argos, the teacher of Myron, Phoidias and Polyklcitus, Paus. VI, 14, 5. IV, 33, 3. VIII, 42, 4, Kanarchus of Sikyon, Paus. IX, 10, Kallon, Paus. II, 32, 4, Quint. XII, 10, 7. Cic. Brut. 13, and Onatas, Paus. VIII, 42, 4 of Ægina. Besides gods, heroes and Olympian victors were represented by these artists. Amongst the statues preserved of this archaic or hieratic style, the most noticeable are: the Æginetan statues from the pediments of the temple of Pallas at Ægina, the Pallas of the Villa Albani, at Dresden, and at Herkulanum, the Herkulanean Artemis, the Apollo of the Museo Chiaramonti, the Giustinianian Vesta, etc.: and of the old reliefs; the altar of the 12 gods, the tripod-theft, the Samothrakian relief, etc. Forerunners of the great sculptors, who brought their art to perfection, appear in Kalamis circ. 460 B.C., Paus. IX, 16, 1, and Pythagoras of Ithegium about the same time, Paus. VI, 4, 2. 13, 1.

t) Myron, born at Eleutherœ, settled at Athens, a pupil of Ageladas, Plin. XXXIV, 57. Paus. VI, 2, 1. 8, 3. 13, 1, worked chiefly in bronze, and devoted himself especially to the forms of heroes and athletes, and of animals. Of his works the most famous were the diskus-thrower (of which copies are still preserved, the best in the palace Massimi at Rome), Plin. XXXIV, 57. Lukian. Philopseud. 18. Quint. II, 13, and the cow, Plin. l. c., which was often celebrated in epigrams, Anthol. Pal. Ind. Auson. Epigr. 58—68. Tzetz. Chil. VIII, 94. Cic. Verr. IV, 60. He overcame the stiffness of the old style by a living truthfulness to nature; in the representation of the hair and

Third Period. 500—431 B.C.

Olympiad.	B.C.	HISTORY.	ART AND LITERATURE.
LXXXIII, 4	445	Eubœa reconquered by Perikles[u]). Thirty years' peace	Pheidias[u]). Polykleitos[v]). Architecture flourishes[w]).

72) Thuc. I, 114. Diod. XII, 7, 22. Plut. Per. 23. To ensure their possession, the Athenians expelled the aristocrats (styled ἱπποβόται) from Chalkis, and the whole free population from Hestiaea: to which latter town they sent a thousand Athenian Kleruchs.

u) Pheidias, of Athens, son of Charmides, lived from about 500 to 438 B. C., Plut. Per. 31. Plin. XXXIV, 49, instructed by Hegias and Ageladas, Schol. Arist. Ran. 504. Suid. s. v. Γελάδας. Tzetz. Chil. VII, 154. VIII, 192. From the booty taken in the Persian wars he executed various works of art, especially the colossal brazen statue of Athene Promachos on the Akropolis, Herod. V, 77. Paus. I, 28, 2, the statue of Athene Areia at Platæa, made of wood and marble, Paus. IX, 4, 1, and a statue-group as an offering for Delphi, Paus. X, 10, 1. He was then entrusted by Perikles with the chief direction of his great buildings, Plut. Per. 12. 13, and completed the statue of Athene Parthenos for the Parthenon, Max. Tyr. Dissert. XIV, p. 260. Paus. I, 24, 5. 7. Plin. XXXIV, 54. XXXVI, 10. Plut. Per. 31, of gold and ivory, which was consecrated in 438 B. C. Schol. Arist. Pac. 604. s, Euseb. Chron. Arm. p. 106. He then went in connexion with several pupils to Elis, and executed the statue of Zeus for the temple at Olympia, likewise of ivory and gold, Plin. XXXV, 54. Paus. V, 10, 2. V, 11. 14. 5. Strab. p. 353 f. Dio. Chrys. Or. XII, p. 248, Emp.: ἥμερον καὶ σεμνὸν ἐν ἀλύπῳ σχήματι, τὸν βίον καὶ ζωῆς καὶ συμπάντων δοτῆρα τῶν ἀγαθῶν, κοινὸν ἀνθρώπων καὶ πατέρα καὶ σωτῆρα καὶ φύλακα, ὡς δυνατόν ἦν θνητῷ διανοηθέντα μιμήσασθαι τὴν θείαν καὶ ἀμήχανον φύσιν. After his return he was accused by Perikles' enemies, in the first place of embezzlement of a part of the gold intended for the Athene Parthenos, and secondly of impiety in having introduced his own likeness and that of Perikles on the shield of the goddess; and he died in prison, Schol. Arist. Pac. 605. Plut. Per. 31. Diod. XII, 39. Of his artistic idealism, with which he united perfect technical acquirements, Cicero speaks in the following terms, Or. II, 3: Nec vero ille artifex, cum faceret Jovis formam aut Minervæ, contemplabatur aliquem, e quo similitudinem duceret, sed ipsius in mente insidebat species pulchritudinis eximia quædam, quam intuens in eaque defixus, ad illius similitudinem artem et manum dirigebat. We can judge of his works from the fragments of the pediment statues and the reliefs of the metopes and of the frieze of the cella of the Parthenon. To the same period belong the reliefs of the temple of Nike Apteros at Athens, the reliefs of the metopes of the temple of Zeus at Olympia, and of the frieze of the temple of Apollo at Phigalia, and the lately discovered statues from the pediments of the temple of Olympia, and the statue of Nike discovered on the same spot, a work of Paeonius. The most important among the pupils and fellow-workers of Pheidias are Alkamenes, Plin. XXXVI, 16, Agorakritus, Paus. IV, 34, 1. Plin. l. c. 17, Kolotes, Plin. XXXV, 54, and Theokosmus, Paus. I, 40, 3.

v) Polykleitus of Sikyon, a contemporary of Pheidias, residing at Argos, a pupil of Ageladas, Plin. XXXIV, 49. Paus. VI, 6, 1. cf. Thuc. IV, 133. His most celebrated statue representing a god was the Hera of Argos, Paus. II, 17, 4. Strab. p. 372; his Amazon was also exceedingly famous, with which he gained the prize in competition with other artists, and even with Pheidias, Plin. XXXIV, 53. But for the most part he worked at figures of boys and youths and Olympian victors. Specially famous amongst the latter was the Diadumenus, a youth, who is binding the victor's wreath round his head (an imitation may be seen in the Palace Farnese at Rome), and the Doryphorus, a boy with a spear, Plin. XXXIV, 55. Cic. Brut. 86. Orat. 11, 5. He laid down in a treatise the harmony and relative proportions of the limbs in the human body, and illustrated them in a figure, which was taken as a universal model, both from nature and figure being named Kanon, Plin. l. c. He rested the centre of gravity in his statues on one leg, l. c., perfected Toreutike, the chiselling of noble metals for smaller works of art, Plin. XXXIV, 54. 56, and excelled preeminently in gold and ivory work, Strab. p. 372. He was also famous as an architect, having built the theatre at Epidaurus, Paus. II, 27, 5. Quintilian has the following criticism, XII, 10, 7: Diligentia ac decor in Polycleto supra ceteros, cui quamquam a plerisque tribuitur palma, tamen, ne nihil detrahatur, deesse pondus putant. Nam ut humanæ formæ decorem addiderit supra verum, ita non explevisse deorum auctoritatem videtur. Quin ætatem quoque graviorem dicitur refugisse, nihil ausus ultra leves genas.—To the same period belongs Kallimachus, Paus. I, 26, 7. 7, and is called Κατατηξίτεχνος on account of his care in the expression of the smallest and most delicate details. Pliny enumerates a long series of pupils of Polykleitus, XXXIV, 50.

w) The oldest Greek structures are the giant walls surrounding the akropolis in various towns, often called Cyclopean walls (Κυκλώπεια οὐράνια τείχη, Soph. Electr. 1167), remains of which are seen in the ruins of Tiryns, Mykenæ with its lion-gate, Orchomenus, Lykosura, Larissa, etc. Amongst the oldest buildings too must be reckoned the so-called treasure-houses of the princes, and especially the dome-shaped treasure-house of Atreus at Mykenæ. After the immigration of the Dorians architecture was developed in the building of temples, and it was the Doric style which was thus first formed, the buildings being originally of wood, Paus. VIII, 10, 2; its special characteristics are the fluted pillars without a base, the simple capital, and the triglyphs or triple grooves of the frieze. The Doric style then appears in Corinth richly developed (and here was invented the ornamentation of the pediments with reliefs of earthenware, and likewise of the front tiles with figured decorations), especially after Byzes of Naxos had invented the artistic carving of the marble blocks Pind. Ol. 13, 21. Plin. XXXV, 152. By the side of the simple and severe Doric, there was developed in Ionia the lighter and more ornamented Ionic style, which already appears in its perfect form in the 6th century in the temple of Diana at Ephesus, distinguished from the Doric by the slimmer shafts of the pillars, and the volutes of the capital, Herod. I, 92. Plin. XVI, 212. XXXVI, 95 f. Vitruv. IV, 1. After the time of Perikles the Corinthian style also came into prominence, now that Kallimachus had invented

The Hellenic Race in its Prime.

Olympiad.	B. C.	HISTORY.	ART AND LITERATURE.
LXXXIII, 4	445	between Athens and Sparta, by which the former utterly relinquishes the hegemony by land[78]).	Rise of painting: Polygnotus[x]); vase-painting[y]).

78) Thuc. 1, 115. Diod. XII, 7. Thuc.: ἀναχωρήσαντες δὲ ἀπ' Εὐβοίας οὐ πολλῷ ὕστερον σπονδὰς ἐποιήσαντο πρὸς Λακεδαιμονίους καὶ τοὺς ξυμμάχους τριακοντούτεις ἀποδόντες Νίσαιαν καὶ Πηγὰς καὶ Τροιζῆνα καὶ Ἀχαΐαν. In Thuc. I, 67. II, 2 it is distinctly stated that this peace was concluded 14 years before the Peloponnesian war.

the vase-shaped capital with intertwining volutes and acanthus leaves Vitruv. IV, 1, 9. Paus. I, 26, 27: moreover at this time other buildings, besides temples, began to be erected and decorated in an artistic method. The most noticeable remains of buildings in the pure Doric style, which are still in existence, are the temples at Syracuse, Akragas, Selinus, Pæstum, Corinth, Ægina, Phigalia in Arcadia (built by Iktinus, Paus. VIII, 41, 7), and at Athens the Parthenon, built by Iktinus and Kallikrates under the supervision of Pheidias, Plut. Per. 13. Schol. Aristoph. Pac. 606. Strab. p. 396. Paus. VIII, 41, 5, the Propylæa built by Mnesikles, Plut. l. c. Philochorus ap. Harpocr. V. Προπύλαια Corp. Inscr. Att. 1. obs. 314 (begun 437 B.C., completed in 5 years, Harpocr. p. 159 Bk., fragments of the bill of Expenditure, Cf. A. n. 315), the temple of Nemesis at Ilhamnus, and of Pallas at Sunium. The noblest buildings in the Ionic style are the Erechtheium, the temple of Nike Apteros on the Athenian acropolis, the Didymæon at Miletus, and the temple of Pallas Polias at Priene. The buildings in the Corinthian style are of later origin: of these, ruins still exist at Athens, in particular of the temple of Olympian Zeus, which was begun on a magnificent scale by Peisistratus and after many vicissitudes completed by Hadrian. Of the artistic works of the time of Perikles Plutarch says, Per. 13: κάλλει μὲν γὰρ ἕκαστον εὐθὺς ἦν τότε ἀρχαῖον, ἀκμῇ δὲ μέχρι νῦν πρόσφατόν ἐστι καὶ νεουργόν.

x) The accounts of the origin of painting are thoroughly untrustworthy and fabulous, Plin. XXXV, 15, 55. VII, 205. It is said of Eumarus of Athens, that he was the first to distinguish man and woman represented with the pencil, Plin. XXXV, 56; Kimon of Kleonæ, an elder contemporary of the poet Simonides, Inc. anal. 1. n. 77 f., perfected the drawing of the profile, especially of the eye in profile, the representation of the joints of the body, and the drapery folds, Plin. XXXV, 56. Æl. V. H. VIII, 8; Aglaophon of Thasos, father and teacher of Polygnotus and Aristophon, lived circ. 500—470 B.C., Paus. X, 27, 2. Suid. s. v. Πολύγνωτος, Cic. de orat. III, 7, 26. Polygnotus, a Thasian by birth, actively followed his profession as a painter chiefly at Athens, where he occupied the same position with Kimon, that Pheidias did with Perikles, and in reward for his paintings received the civic rights of an Athenian burgess, Suid. s. v. Plin. XXXV, 59. Plut. Cim. 4. Paus. IX, 4, 1. The most important and famous of his works, nearly all of which represented scenes from the world of heroes, are the paintings in the Lesche of the Knidians at Delphi, Plin. l. c. 59. Paus. X, 25, 31, which depicted the destruction of Troy and the lower world. Polygnotus further painted part of the pictures in the Stoa Pœkile at Athens, Paus. I, 15, 2. Plin. l. c., in the temple of the Dioskuri at Athens Paus. I, 16, 1, in the temple of Theseus, Harpocr. s. v., in the Pinakotheka of the Propylæa, Paus. I, 22, 6, in the vestibule of the temple of Athene Areia at Platææ, Paus. IX, 4, 1; also wall-paintings at Thespiæ, Plin. XXXV, 123. He was praised for the delicacy of the drapery in his paintings, which allowed the shape of the body to appear through it, the animation of facial expression,

Plin. XXXV, 59, Luk. Imag. 7, and excellent drawing together with simple colouring, without effects produced by light and shade, Cic. Brut. 18. Qaint. XII, 10: the similarity of the grouping in his compositions is vouched for by the description of the paintings at Delphi, Paus. l. c. He was also famous as a sculptor, Plin. XXXIV, 85. Mikon was his contemporary, Schol. Aristoph. Lysistr. 679; he painted in company with Polygnotus in the Pœkile, the Theseium, and the temple of the Dioskuri, Plin. XXXV, 59. Harpocr. v. Μίκων. Arr. Anab. VII, 13, 10. Suid. Harpocr. s. v. Πολύγνωτος. Paus. I, 18, 1. He was celebrated as a painter of horses, Æl. V. H. IV, 50, and as a sculptor besides, Plin. XXXIV, 88. Panænus, a relation of Pheidias, Strab. p. 354. Paus. V, 11, 2. Plin. XXXV, 54. 57. XXXVI, 177, painted with Polygnotus and Mikon in the Pœkile; he was then engaged with Pheidias on the statue of Zeus at Olympia, partly with the colouring of the statue of Zeus, partly with paintings in the temple; and also painted in the temple of Athena at Elis and coloured the statue of the goddess. Other important painters of this period are Dionysius of Kolophon, an imitator of Polygnotus, Æl. V. H. IV, 3 (πλὴν τοῦ μεγέθους), Arist. Poet. 2. Plut. Timol. 36; Pauson, who made his figures more ugly than those of real life, Arist. l. c. Pol. V, 5, Acharn. 854. Thesmoph. 949; Agatharchus, a decorative painter circ. 450 B.C., Vitruv. VII. præf. § 10. Plut. Alcib. 16. Per. 13; Aristophon, brother of Polygnotus, Plin. XXXV, 138.

y) On the subject of Greek vase-painting our knowledge is not derived from ancient authors, but from the unearthing of painted fictile vases. The chief centres of their discovery are, in Greece: Athens, Corinth, Sikyon, Megara, Ægina, Melos, Thera: but the vessels found in the graves of Italian and Sicilian burying-grounds are much more numerous; so especially in Etruria at Volci, where alone some 6000 have been brought to light, Cære, Tarquinii, Volî, Clusium, Volaterræ; further at Hadria, in Campania at Nola, Cumæ, Plistia, and Surrentum, in Apulia at Rubi, Canusium, Barium, Gnathia, Uria, in Lucania at Pæstum and Anxia, in Sicily at Agrigentum, Syracuse, Gela, Kamarina, Panormus, Akræ. These fictile vessels may be divided into three classes according to the painting: 1) the oldest vases with pale yellow ground and blackish, brown, violet, or red figures, for the most part phantastic forms of animals, flowers, and branches in a clumsy stiff style; 2) vessels with red ground and black figures, chiefly human shapes in old-fashioned drawing with strong prominence given to the chief lines of the body; 3) vases with black ground and red figures, with regular or beautiful drawing, of a later period than the two first classes. Most of the vases found in Etruria belong to the period from the Persian wars to the Peloponnesian war, and do not exhibit the alphabet of Eukleides: most of the Sicilian and Campanian vessels are of later origin, especially those of Nola: most modern of all are the Apulian and Lucanian. By the inscriptions on the vessels the names of some 84 vase-painters or potters have

THIRD PERIOD. 500—431 B.C.

Olympiad.	B. C.	ATHENS.	HISTORY.
		Archons.	c) To the outbreak of the Peloponnesian War.
LXXXIV, 1	444	Praxiteles.	Perikles in solo possession of the government at Athens[74]). Another wall is built from Athens to the Peiræus[75]).
LXXXIV, 2	443	Lysanias.	Thurii founded by the Athenians[76]).
LXXXIV, 3	442	Diphilus.	
LXXXIV, 4	441	Timokles.	
LXXXV, 1	440	Morychides.	The Samian war: Samos and Byzantium reduced to subjection[77]).
LXXXV, 2	439	Glaukinus.	
LXXXV, 3	438	Theodorus.	
LXXXV, 4	437	Euthymenes.	Amphipolis founded by the Athenians[78]).
LXXXVI, 1	436	Lysimachus.	
LXXXVI, 2	435	Antiochides.	
LXXXVI, 3	434	Krates.	Outbreak of the war between Corinth and Kerkyra on account of Epidamnus[79]). Naval victory of the Kerkyræans at Aktium[80]).
LXXXVI, 4	433	Apseudes.	Athens forms an alliance with Kerkyra[81]). Sea-fight between the

74) After Kimon's death (obs. 68) Thucydides, the son of Melesias, became the head of the aristocratic party opposed to Perikles; but in 444 B. C. he was ostracised, after which Perikles remained the sole leader of the nation, Plut. Per. 11—16. The year, when Thucydides was banished, is fixed from Plut. Per. 16, according to which Perikles ruled at Athens "not less than 15 years" after his rival's fall.

75) For greater security a second wall was built from the town to the Peiræus, parallel with the already existing wall and to the south of it (between the first wall to the Peiræus and that to Phalerum, see obs. 60), Plut. Per. 13. Plat, Gorg. p. 456 A. Andok. De Pac. p. 25. Æschin. De F. L. p. 51 ("τὸ μακρὸν τεῖχος τὸ νότιον"). The existence of this second wall is also proved by Thuc. II, 13.

76) Diod. XII, 9—11. The date from (Plut.) Vit. Dec. Or. p. 835 D. Dionys. Lys. p. 435. It was founded in the place of Sybaris, which had been destroyed by the Krotoniates.

77) The war arose in consequence of a dispute between Samos and Miletus about the possession of Priene; the Samians paid no heed to the Athenians, when ordered by them to resign their claims: in consequence the aristocracy in power was first overthrown and a democratic constitution established: when the aristocrats again possessed themselves of the government, the town was besieged by Perikles and "after nine months" forced to surrender, Thuc. I, 115—117. Plut. Per. 24—28. Diod. XII, 27—28. The war began in the 6th year after the thirty years' peace, Thuc. I, 115; for its difficulty see Thuc. VII, 76; according to Thuc. I, 41 the Peloponnesians intended to go to the aid of the Samians, but were dissuaded by the Corinthians. The result of the war was, that the Samians and the Byzantians, who had joined the Samians, became subjects instead of allies, so that now only the Chians and Lesbians remained free allies, Thuc. II, 9. As a sequel of the altered position of Athens towards her former allies, the treasury of the league was removed from Delos to Athens, Plut. Per. 12. Iustin. III, 6. cf. Plut. Arist. 25, probably in 454 B. C., see Corp. Inscr. Att. I. n. 226 ff.

78) Diod. XII, 32. Thuc. IV, 102. Cf. obs. 46.

79) Thuc. I, 24—28.

80) Thuc. I, 29—30. The Corinthians together with their allies had 75 ships, the Kerkyræans 80. According to Thuc. I, 31 after the battle two years were spent by the Corinthians in fresh preparations; the battle therefore may also be suitably placed in 435 B.C. On the same day as the battle Epidamnus was compelled to surrender, Thuc. I, 29.

81) Both parties sent ambassadors to Athens, in order to secure her assistance for themselves. Their speeches Thuc. I, 32—43. Athens decided in favour of Kerkyra, Thuc. I, 44, chiefly for the reason that the alliance with Kerkyra promised great advantages for the voyage across to Italy and Sicily, to which the minds of the Athenians at that time were already directed, Thuc. l. c.: ἅμα δὲ τῆς τε Ἰταλίας καὶ Σικελίας καλῶς ἐφαίνετο αὐτοῖς ἡ νῆσος ἐν παράπλῳ κεῖσθαι, cf. Diod. XII, 54. However the alliance only amounted to an ἐπιμαχία, not a συμμαχία, i. e. it only bound the Athenians to the defence of Kerkyra and its territory, but not to take part in the offensive war with Corinth.

become known to us, Corp. Inscr. Græc. Vol. IV, Fasc. I, Præf. p. XIV; but no trace is found to show that painters of importance occupied themselves with vase-painting, as it was regarded more as a trade than an art, cf. Aristoph. Eccl. 99 ff. Plut. Per. 12 (λημυθουργοί). The largest potteries of Greece were at Corinth, Plin. XXXV, 151. Pind. Ol. XIII, 24, and at Athens, as is proved by the name of the town-quarter Κεραμεικὸς and express statements to that effect, Kritias ap. Athen. I, 28. Plin. XXXV, 155. VII, 198. Suid. s. v. Κωλιάδος κεραμῆες. Both towns carried on a trade with Etruria and Magna Græcia in painted earthenware. As regards Corinth, this is proved by a number of older vases with the Doric alphabet found in Sicily or Italy: the extensive trade of Athens, besides the account of Herodotus, V, 88, is proved by the numerous vases from Volci, Hadria, Sicily, Campania, Apulia, with Attic characters, word-forms, and subjects, and also by the Panathenaic prize vases found at Volci, Nola, and Cyrenaica. But there were also native manufactories in Italy, where Greek vases could be executed under the direction of masters imported from Greece, Plin. XXXV, 152. 155 f.

The Hellenic Race in its Prime.

Olympiad.	B. C.	ATHENS.	HISTORY.
LXXXVI, 4	433	Archon.	Kerkyræans and Corinthians at Sybota, in which the Athenians also take part[82]).
LXXXVII, 1	432	Pythodorus.	The revolt of Potidæa from the Athenian alliance[83]). The war resolved on at Sparta[84]), and by the advice of Perikles at Athens also[85]).

82) Thuc. I, 45—55. The Eleans, Megarians, Leukadians, Amprakiotans and Anaktorians fought on the side of the Corinthians; and the number of their ships amounted to 150, id. 46, whilst the Kerkyræans had only 110 besides the 10 Athenian vessels, id. 47. The result of the battle was indecisive, and though the Corinthians had rather the advantage, they retired in fear of 20 more Athenian vessels, which just then appeared on the scene of action. It is rightly inferred from the inscription Corp. Inscr. Att. I. n. 179, that the battle took place in 433, not 432 B. C.

83) The Athenians demanded that the Potidæans should dismiss the magisterial personages received from Corinth, their mother city, and pull down their walls; whereupon they, in connexion with the Chalkidians and Bottiæans, and confiding in the promise of support from the Corinthians and the rest of the Peloponnesians, revolted from Athens. The Athenians sent an army against the town, and after gaining a victory blockaded it by land and water. Thuc. I, 56—65. We still possess 3 epitaphs, each in two distichs, on the Athenians who fell before Potidæa, see Corp. I. A. I, n. 442. — A third and further cause of the war was the exclusion of Megara from all harbours under the jurisdiction of Athens, which probably took place soon after the revolt of Megara in 445 B. C., see Thuc. I, 42. 67. 139. Plut. Per. 29—30. Præc. Gerend. Reip. (c. 15) p. 812 D, Ar. Acharn. 515—536.

84) The Corinthians caused the other allies of Sparta to send ambassadors with them to Sparta, with the object of bringing about the resolve to declare war against Athens. The war was first resolved upon by the Spartans, Thuc. I, 67—68. The resolution was then adopted by the majority of the allies in a congress held for the purpose, id. 119—125. Of the speeches, which were made at these meetings, those of the Corinthians, 68—71, 120—124, and of King Archidamus, 80—85, are especially instructive from the clear light, which they throw on the character of the Spartans and Athenians (see esp. c. 70) and on the circumstances of the time. "Less than a year" (Thuc. I, 25) had passed since the last meeting, when the war was openly begun with the invasion of Attica. During this time three embassies were sent to Athens, of which the first demanded the expulsion of the Alkmæonidæ, the second the abolition of the Megarian psephism and the raising of the siege of Potidæa, the third the restoration of the independence of all Hellenic towns throughout the Athenian empire, Thuc. I, 126. 139. For the real reason, why the war was resolved upon by Sparta, see Thuc. I, 88: 'Εψηφίσαντο δὲ οἱ Λακεδαιμόνιοι τὰς σπονδὰς λελύσθαι καὶ πολεμητέα εἶναι οὐ τοσοῦτον τῶν ξυμμάχων πεισθέντες τοῖς λόγοις ὅσον φοβούμενοι τοὺς 'Αθηναίους μὴ ἐπὶ μεῖζον δυνηθῶσιν, ὁρῶντες τὰ πολλὰ τῆς 'Ελλάδος ἤδη ὑποχείρια ὄντα, cf. id. 23. For other accounts of the origin of the war, but very unhistorical and altogether unworthy of Perikles, see Ephorus ap. Diod. XII, 38—40. Plut. Per. 31—32. The Corinthians, Æginetans, and Megarians, showed themselves the most vehement opponents of Athens and the most zealous instigators of the war, Thuc. I, 67.

85) Thuc. I, 140—146 (Speech of Perikles, 140—144). The resolution runs (145): ἀνεκρίνατο τῇ ἐκείνου γνώμῃ καθ' ἕκαστά τε ὡς ἔφρασε καὶ τὸ ξύμπαν, οὐδὲν κελευόμενοι ποιήσειν, δίκῃ δὲ κατὰ τὰς ξυνθήκας ἑτοῖμοι εἶναι διαλύεσθαι περὶ τῶν ἐγκλημάτων ἐπ' ἴσῃ καὶ ὁμοίᾳ.

FOURTH PERIOD.

431—338 B.C.

THE INCIPIENT DECLINE.

First Section. The Peloponnesian war, 431—404 B.C. The evils, out of which the Peloponnesian war had arisen—the jealousy cherished by Sparta and its allies of the power of Athens, and the hostile opposition of the aristocratic and democratic principle, which affected not merely the inner life of the Greek states, but also the mutual relations of individual states—grow in sharpness and intensity owing to the war, and develope results increasingly destructive. After a duration of 27 years the war is brought to a close; Athens is conquered and its glory destroyed, but at the same time the force and independence of the other Greek states is broken.

Second Section. Arrogance and humiliation of Sparta, 404—362 B.C. Sparta upholds the supremacy, which it had won in the Peloponnesian war, with severity and arbitrariness. A first attempt on the part of the other important Greek states to shake off the Spartan yoke (in the Corinthian war) is frustrated by Sparta's successful application for Persian support, by means of which it again reduces its foes to subjection. New severities and acts of violence, however, on the part of the Spartans lead to the uprising first of Thebes, then of Athens; in the Theban war, which was the sequel, the importance of Sparta is destroyed and an end made of its sovereignty even in the Peloponnese, not merely in the rest of Greece. For a short time Thebes under the leadership of Epameinondas wins the first place amongst the Greek states, but proves unable to maintain it.

Third Section. The struggle with king Philip, to 338 B.C. Philip of Macedon utilises the weakness and dissensions of Greece, first to render the Greek towns on the Thrakian coast subject to his rule, with but weak and disorganised resistance from Athens; and then, when thus strengthened, to bring Greece itself under his sway. When Philip's designs become more and more apparent, Athens, fired by the eloquence of Demosthenes, once more unites a considerable number of Greek states to do battle with him. But these last efforts end with the battle of Chæroneia, in which the independence and freedom of Greece were lost for ever.

During the whole period literature and art are richly developed. After poetry has put forth in comedy the last of its branches, the golden era of prose follows, in which the most perfect masterpieces are produced in the province of philosophy, history, and oratory. In art, sculpture and architecture maintain themselves at the high excellence of the previous period; for in both provinces, what is lost in power, is replaced by a greater refinement and technical perfection; at the same time painting attains a progressively higher development.

Obs. Thucydides is the chief authority for the Peloponnesian war till towards the end of the year 411 B.C. Xenophon in his Hellenic Historics carries forward the narrative from this point up to the battle of Mantineia: and this writer, though of far less value than Thucydides, and following a very narrow conception of history, ranks first amongst our authorities. Besides these, single supplementary notices and further details are derived from Plutarch (in the biographies of Perikles, Nikias, Alkibiades, Lysander, Artaxerxes, Agesilaus, and Pelopidas), from Diodorus (Book XII—XV), and from passages in Aristophanes and the orators Andokides, Lysias, and Isokrates; but in all cases great caution must be used with these writers, as Plutarch does not always proceed with the necessary criticism in the choice of his sources of information, and Diodorus makes use of his with great carelessness and superficiality, whilst Aristophanes and the orators only mention the events of the day on occasion, and, as a rule, colour them to suit their own immediate object. For isolated portions of history use must further be made of the Agesilaus, probably composed by Xenophon, which however for the most part only repeats the words of the Hellenic histories, with here and there small additions, and the excellent Anabasis of the same author. After the battle of Mantineia we are restricted solely to Diodorus and Plutarch's biographies of Demosthenes and Phokion for a connected narrative; but the more inadequate these sources of information, the more fortunate the chance that just at this very time contemporary orators, before all Demosthenes, supply rich and valuable materials to supplement the defect.

FOURTH PERIOD. 431—338 B. C.

FIRST SECTION.

431—404 B.C.[1]

THE PELOPONNESIAN WAR.

Olympiad.	B. C.	ATHENS.	HISTORY.
		Archon.	a) The Archidamian war[2]), to the peace of Nikias, 431—421 B.C.
LXXXVII, 2	431[a])	Euthydemus.	The Thebans open the war in the spring with the surprise of Plataeae[4]). The Peloponnesian allied army under the Spartan king Archidamus invades Attica[5]). The Athenians revenge themselves for the plundering of their territory by a naval expedition, in which they land and harass the coasts of the Peloponnese; conquer Sollium and Astakus and win

---

1) For the causes which occasioned the war see obs. 79—85 of former period. For its extent and the forces which both sides brought to the combat our chief source of information is Thuc. II, 9. cf. Diod. XII, 42. By these accounts the Spartans had on their side: the whole of the Peloponnese, except Argos and Achaia, both of which remained neutral (but Pellene ranged itself with Sparta, and according to Aristoph. Pac. 475 Argos furnished mercenary troops to both parties), further Megara, Phokis, Lokris, Boeotia, Amprakia, Leukas, Anaktorium. Of these allied states Corinth, Megara, Sikyon, Pellene, Elis, Leukas, and Amprakia possessed ships of war. But in the force on the side of Sparta, as compared with that of Athens, on the whole the land troops were far the most preponderant factor, see Thuc. I, 80: according to Plut. Per. 33 the army could be raised to 60,000 hoplites. However, it was hoped that the Greek towns in lower Italy and Sicily would in virtue of their relationship furnish money and ships, and that so a fleet of 500 vessels would be got together, Thuc. II, 7. Diod. XII, 41. On the side of Athens there were in the character of ξύμμαχοι: Chios and Lesbos, Plataeae, Naupaktos, the greater part of Akarnania, Kerkyra, Zakynthus (and after a short time Kephallenia, see obs. 6), and the Thessalian towns Larissa, Pharsalus, Krannon, Pyrasos, Gyrton, Pherae, for which see Thuc. II, 22 (for the difference between the position of Chios and Lesbos and the rest of the allies see Thuc. VI, 85. VII, 57); in the character of ὑποτελεῖς: the towns on the Asiatic and Thrakian coasts of the Aegean sea, and all the islands as far as Krete, with the exception of Thera and Melos, which remained neutral. From these subject towns Athens drew a yearly tribute of 600 talents, Thuc. II, 13, which shortly before the peace of Nikias was raised to 1200 talents, Andoc. De Pac. p. 24, § 9. Aesch. De Fals. Leg. p. 51, § 175. Plut. Arist. 24, and in place of which after 413 B.C. a duty was levied, Thuc. VII, 28: further 6000 talents were stored up in the treasury,

Thuc. II, 13. The Athenian sea-force consisted of 300 triremes, its land-force of 13,000 hoplites, not counting the 16,000 hoplites who served for the defence of the Attic territory, Thuc. l. c. cf. id. 31, and as regards the fleet see esp. III, 17.—For the feeling of Greece see Thuc. II, 8: ἡ εὔνοια παρὰ πολὺ ἐποίει τῶν ἀνθρώπων μᾶλλον ἐς τοὺς Λακεδαιμονίους, ἄλλως τε καὶ προειπόντων, ὅτι Ἑλλάδα ἐλευθεροῦσιν—οὕτως ὀργῇ εἶχον οἱ πλείους τοὺς Ἀθηναίους, οἱ μὲν τῆς ἀρχῆς ἀπολυθῆναι βουλόμενοι, οἱ δὲ μὴ ἀρχθῶσι φοβούμενοι. II, 54: ἐπερρώωσι τοῖς Λακεδαιμονίοις τὸν θεὸν εἰ χρὴ πολεμεῖν ἀνεῖλε κατὰ κράτος πολεμοῦσι νίκην ἔσεσθαι καὶ αὐτὸς ἔφη συλλήψεσθαι, cf. IV, 85.

2) Such is the name given to this part of the war by Lysias (or Deinarchus?), see Harpocr. s. v. Ἀρχιδάμιος πόλεμος. Thucydides calls it ὁ πρῶτος πόλεμος, V, 20, 24, ὁ δεκαετὴς πόλεμος, V, 35, and ὁ πρῶτος πόλεμος ὁ δεκαετής, V, 26.

3) For the events of the first year, see Thuc. II, 1—46. Diod. XII, 41—44. Plut. Per. 33—34.

4) Some 300 Thebans made themselves masters of Plataeae, having been called in by an aristocratic faction, but were overpowered by the Plataeans and cut down, Thuc. II, 2—6. Diod. XII, 41. The date is fixed by Thuc. id. 2: Τέσσαρα μὲν γὰρ καὶ δέκα ἔτη ἐνέμειναν αἱ τριακοντούτεις σπονδαί, αἳ ἐγένοντο μετὰ τὴν Εὐβοίας ἅλωσιν· τῷ δὲ πέμπτῳ καὶ δεκάτῳ ἔτει ἐπὶ Χρυσίδος ἐν Ἄργει τότε πεντήκοντα δυοῖν δέοντα ἔτη ἱερωμένης καὶ Αἰνησίου ἐφόρου ἐν Σπάρτῃ καὶ Πυθοδώρου ἔτι δύο μῆνας ἀρχοντος Ἀθηναίοις, μετὰ τὴν ἐν Ποτιδαίᾳ μάχην μηνὶ ἕκτῳ καὶ ἅμα ἦρι ἀρχομένῳ—

5) Thuc. II, 10—23. Diod. XII, 42. Prior to the invasion, Archidamus sent another herald to Athens; where however he was not admitted. As he left the Athenian territory, he cried out: ὅδε

The Incipient Decline. 61

Olympiad.	B.C.	ATHENS.	HISTORY.
LXXXVII, 2	431	Archon.	over Kephallenia to their alliance⁶): further they make descents on the territory of the Opuntian Lokrians⁷), expel the Æginetans from their island⁸), and in the autumn invade the territory of Megara⁹).
			The siege of Potidæa is continued¹⁰).
LXXXVII, 3	430¹¹)	Apollodorus.	Second invasion of the Attic territory by the Peloponnesians¹²).
			Outbreak of the plague at Athens¹³). Naval expeditions of the Athenians¹⁴). Perikles is fined by the disheartened populace, and for a short time deprived of his office as Strategus¹⁵).
			Fall of Potidæa¹⁶).

ἡ ἡμέρα τοῖς Ἕλλησι μεγάλων κακῶν ἄρξει, Thuc. l. c. 12. The invasion then took place, on the eightieth day after the episode at Platææ, id. 19, and the army, containing two thirds of the contingents from the several states, id. 10, according to Plut. Per., 33 60,000 strong, penetrated to Acharnæ, 60 stadia from Athens, Thuc. l. c. 19. 21. The inhabitants of Attica had transferred themselves and their goods for safety to Athens, id. 13—17 (cf. Arist. Eq. 789 : οἰκοῦσι' ἐν ταῖς πιθάκναισι κἀν γυπαρίοις καὶ πυργιδίοις), and their cavalry, reinforced by the Thessalians, alone left the city to offer some resistance to the enemy, id. 22.

6) Thuc. II, 23—25, 30. The Athenian fleet (100 vessels) was reinforced on this expedition by 50 Kerkyræan ships, id. 25.

7) Thuc. II, 26. They take Thronium, and defeat the Lokrians at Alope. During the course of the summer the island Atlante was occupied and fortified as a point of attack against the Lokrians, id. 32.

8) Thuc. II, 27.

9) Thuc. II, 31. The invasion of the Megarid territory is from this time forward repeated twice in every year, Thuc. IV. 66. cf. Plut. Per. 30. Aristoph. Acharn. 762. Pac. 481.

10) Thuc. II, 29.—At the close of the year came the funeral ceremony in honour of those who had fallen in the course of the year, and the funeral oration of Perikles, id. 34—46.

11) Thuc. II, 47—70. Diod. XII, 45—47. Plut. Per. 34—37.

12) Thuc. II, 47, 55—57. They penetrate to Laureium, id. 55, and lay waste the whole land during 40 days, id. 57.

13) It broke out shortly after the invasion of the Peloponnesians, Thuc. II, 47, and raged first for the space of 2 years; then, after a short intermission, for the further space of one year, Thuc. III, 87. The famous description of the plague is in Thuc. II, 47—54. According to Thuc. III, 87, it swept off 4400 hoplites, and a countless host of other persons besides, cf. Diod. XII, 58; of 4000 hoplites, who were sent under Hagnon against Potidæa (vide. 16), 1050 died in 40 days alone, Thuc. II, 58. For its injurious effect on Athenian morals see especially id. 53 ; Πρῶτόν τε ἤρξε καὶ ἐς τἄλλα τῇ πόλει τὸ νόσημα. ῥᾷον γὰρ ἐτόλμα τις ἃ πρότερον ἀπεκρύπτετο μὴ καθ' ἡδονὴν ποιεῖν, ἀγχίστροφον τὴν μεταβολὴν ὁρῶντες τῶν τ' εὐδαιμόνων αἰφνιδίως θνησκόντων καὶ τῶν οὐδὲν πρότερον κεκτημένων, εὐθὺς δὲ τἀκείνων ἐχόντων· ὥστε ταχείας τὰς ἐπαυρέσεις καὶ πρὸς τὸ τερπνὸν ἠξίουν ποιεῖσθαι, ἐφήμερα τά τε σώματα καὶ τὰ χρήματα ὁμοίως ἡγούμενοι.—ὅ τι δὲ ἤδη τε ἡδὺ καὶ πανταχόθεν ἐς αὐτὸ κερδαλέον, τοῦτο καὶ καλὸν καὶ χρήσιμον κατέστη· θεῶν δὲ φόβος ἢ ἀνθρώπων νόμος οὐδεὶς ἀπεῖργεν, τὸ μὲν κρίνοντες ἐν ὁμοίῳ καὶ σέβειν καὶ μὴ ἐκ τοῦ πάντας ὁρᾶν ἐν ἴσῳ ἀπολλυμένους, τῶν δὲ ἁμαρτημάτων οὐδεὶς ἐλπίζων μέχρι τοῦ δίκην γενέσθαι βιοὺς ἂν τὴν τιμωρίαν ἀντιδοῦναι, πολὺ δὲ μείζω τὴν ἤδη κατεψηφισμένην σφῶν ἐπικρεμασθῆναι, ἣν πρὶν ἐμπεσεῖν εἰκὸς εἶναι τοῦ βίου τι ἀπολαῦσαι.

14) Whilst the Peloponnesian army was still present in Attica, Perikles at the head of a squadron of 100 Athenian ships and 50 from Chios and Lesbos (carrying 300 cavalry on board ἐν ναυσὶν ἱππαγωγοῖς πρῶτον τότε ἐκ τῶν παλαιῶν νεῶν ποιηθείσαις) made descents on the territory, of Epidaurus, Trœzen, Haliæ, Hermione, and Lakonia (where he took and destroyed Prasiæ), Thuc. II, 56: in the following winter Phormio sails with 20 ships to the Krisæan gulf, to keep guard there, id. 69. (The Peloponnesians also made this year their first expedition by sea with 100 ships against Zakynthus, without any material success, id. 66.)

15) Thuc. II, 59—65. The populace was so disheartened, that it actually sued for peace at Sparta id. 59. Its mood was so far changed by a speech of Perikles (id. 60—64), that it thought no more of seeking peace ; notwithstanding Perikles was removed from his generalship and fined (according to Plut. Per. 35, 15 or 50, according to Diod. XII, 45, 80 talents), id. 65.

16) In the course of the summer a second fleet of 40 ships was despatched to Potidæa under Hagnon and Kleopompus, which however performed but little, Thuc. II, 58 ; in the following winter the town surrendered, id. 70. The inhabitants, who had been reduced to the greatest extremities (καὶ τοῦ τινες καὶ ἀλλήλων ἐγέγευντο, Thuc.), were allowed to depart unmolested, whilst town and territory were allotted to Athenian colonists. (A remarkable event happened this year: the Spartans sent ambassadors, to conclude an alliance with the king of Persia; they fell into the hands of the Athenians and were by them put to death, Thuc. II, 67. cf. Herod. VII, 137.)

THIRD PERIOD. 431—338 B. C.

Olympiad.	B. C.	ATHENS.	HISTORY.
LXXXVII, 4	429[17])	Archons. Epameinon.	Platææ besieged by the Peloponnesians [18]). Brilliant naval victories of Phormio[19]). Death of Perikles[20]).
LXXXVIII, 1	428[21])	Diotimus.	Third invasion of Attic territory by the Peloponnesians[22]). Lesbos, with the exception of Methymna, revolts from Athens: Mytilene is blockaded both by land and water by the Athenians[23]).
LXXXVIII, 2	427[24])	Eukles.	Death of King Archidamus; Agis his successor[25]). Fourth invasion of Attic territory by the Peloponnesians[26]). Mytilene compelled to surrender to Athens[27]), and severely punished[28]).

17) Thuc. II, 71—103. Diod. XII, 47—51.

18) Thuc. II, 71—78. There were 480 men able to bear arms in the town, and only 110 women besides; all other inhabitants, old men, children, the rest of the women, and slaves, had left the town, id. 78. The wearisome siege that ensued is the first, of which we have an accurate description, see esp. Thuc. III, 21.

19) At the instance of the Ampraklots 1000 Lakedæmonians with large numbers of the allies invade Akarnania, but are repulsed at Stratus, Thuc. II, 80—82. It was arranged that a fleet should sail from Corinth to Akarnania to support the enterprise: twice it was repulsed (the first time it was 47, the second time 77 ships strong) by Phormio and his 20 ships (obs. 14) owing to the distinguished bravery and skill of the Athenians, id. 83—92 ; after which Phormio assures himself of Akarnania anew by an expedition thither, id. 102.

20) Thuc. II, 65 : ἐπεβίω (τῷ πολέμῳ) δύο ἔτη καὶ ἓξ μῆνας. The judgment of Thucydides upon him, id. : ὅσον τε γὰρ χρόνον προύστη τῆς πόλεως ἐν τῇ εἰρήνῃ, μετρίως ἐξηγεῖτο καὶ ἀσφαλῶς διεφύλαξεν αὐτήν, καὶ ἐγένετο ἐπ' ἐκείνου μεγίστη· ἐπεί τε ὁ πόλεμος κατέστη, ὁ δὲ φαίνεται καὶ ἐν τούτῳ προγνοὺς τὴν δύναμιν.—αἴτιον δ' ἦν ὅτι ἐκεῖνος μὲν δυνατὸς ὢν τῷ τε ἀξιώματι καὶ τῇ γνώμῃ, χρημάτων τε ἀδωρότατος γενόμενος κατεῖχε τὸ πλῆθος ἐλευθέρως καὶ οὐκ ἤγετο μᾶλλον ὑπ' αὐτοῦ ἢ αὐτὸς ἦγεν, διὰ τὸ μὴ κτώμενος ἐξ οὐ προσηκόντων τὴν δύναμιν πρὸς ἡδονήν τι λέγειν, ἀλλ' ἔχων ἐπ' ἀξιώσει καὶ πρὸς ὀργήν τι ἀντειπεῖν. ὁπότε γοῦν αἴσθοιτό τι αὐτοὺς παρὰ καιρὸν ὕβρει θαρσοῦντας, λέγων κατέπλησσεν ἐπὶ τὸ φοβεῖσθαι καὶ δεδιότας αὖ ἀλόγως ἀντικαθίστη πάλιν ἐπὶ τὸ θαρσεῖν. ἐγίγνετό τε λόγῳ μὲν δημοκρατία, ἔργῳ δὲ ὑπὸ τοῦ πρώτου ἀνδρὸς ἀρχή· οἱ δὲ ὕστερον ἴσοι αὐτοὶ μᾶλλον πρὸς ἀλλήλους ὄντες καὶ ὀρεγόμενοι τοῦ πρῶτος ἕκαστος γίγνεσθαι ἐτράποντο καθ' ἡδονάς τῷ δήμῳ καὶ τὰ πράγματα ἐνδιδόναι. In the last words reference is made to the so-called demagogues, and most of all to Kleon, who had already won influence about this time, and was coming more and more to the front, Plut. Per. 33. 35. (Aristophanes has sketched him for us, especially in the Knights, though it is a very exaggerated caricature ; see esp. 61. 809. 834. 900 ff. ; the names of other demagogues are;

before Kleon, Lysikles ὁ προβατοπώλης and Eukrates ὁ στυππειοπώλης, id. 129 ff.; later than Kleon, Hyperbolus, Thuc. VIII, 73. Plut. Alc. 13. Nic. 11. Arist. Pac. 655 ff. 921. 1319, Lysikrates, id. Av. 513, Peisander, id. Lysistr. 490, Kleophon, obs. 129, etc.)

21) Thuc. III, 1—25. Diod. XII, 52—53. 55—56.

22) Thuc. III, 1.

23) Thuc. III, 2—19. The Mytilenæans are first blockaded by 40 ships under Kleippides, and then by 1000 hoplites under Paches by land as well.

24) Thuc. III, 26—88. Diod. XII, 53—57.

25) According to Diod. XI, 48. XII, 35 he reigned 42 years. The chief proof, that he died in this year, is the fact that the invasion of Attica in 428 was made under his command, Thuc. III, 1 ; whilst in 426 his son Agis, Thuc. III, 89, and in 427 Kleomenes, the guardian of Pausanias of the other royal house, was in command of the troops, Thuc. III, 26. The real king of the other house was Pleistoanax. But he was banished in 445 and not recalled till about 426. During his banishment his son Pausanias reigned, or rather, as he was a minor, his guardian Kleomenes, Thuc. II, 21. V, 16.

26) Thuc. III, 26.

27) Thuc. III, 27—28. The Peloponnesians, whose aid had been invoked by the Mytilenæans, sent a fleet of 42 sail to their assistance under Alkidas, id. 26 ; but it effected nothing owing to the hesitation and incapacity of its leader, id. 29—33.

28) More than 1000 of the most eminent Lesbians were executed, the walls of Mytilene pulled down, their ships taken from them, and the landed possessions of all the Lesbians, with the exception of the Methymnæans, confiscated to the Athenian people : the land was then distributed into 3000 lots, and cultivated by the Lesbians as tenants in fief, who had to pay a rent to their Athenian lords. A public decree was first passed, chiefly at the instigation of Kleon, actually condemning all the Mytilenæans to death : on the next day, however, it was cancelled through the exertions of Diodotus. Thuc. III, 35—50.

The Incipient Decline. 63

Olympiad.	B. C.	ATHENS.	HISTORY.
		Archon.	
LXXXVIII, 2	427		Plataeae taken and destroyed by the Peloponnesians[29]). Bloody faction-fights at Kerkyra[30]). War between the Doric and Ionic towns in Sicily: to the aid of the latter the Athenians send a fleet of 20 ships under Laches and Charoeades[31]).
LXXXVIII, 3	426 *)	Euthynus.	The Spartans found the colony Herakleia in Trachinia[32]). Naval expeditions of the Athenians under Nikias[33]) and Demosthenes; the latter makes descents on the coasts of the Peloponnese and the island Leukadia, and, after an unsuccessful enterprise against Ætolia, inflicts a severe defeat on the Amprakiots and Spartans at Argos Amphilochikum[34]).

---

29) 212 of the besieged had escaped in the previous year, climbing over the enemy's works with great boldness in the night time, Thuc. III, 20—24. The scanty remnant, consisting of 225 men, surrendered in this year, after being promised a fair and equitable trial on the part of the Lacedaemonians; notwithstanding, they were all executed, id. 52—68.

30) This civil war is the prelude to similar bloody struggles in other Greek towns and for that reason is described in detail by Thucydides, III, 70—85. 82: οὕτως ὠμὴ στάσις προὐχώρησε καὶ ἔδοξε μᾶλλον, διότι ἐν τοῖς πρώτη ἐγένετο, ἐπεὶ ὕστερόν γε καὶ πᾶν ὡς εἰπεῖν τὸ Ἑλληνικὸν ἐκινήθη, 83: πᾶσα ἰδέα κατέστη κακοτροπίας διὰ τὰς στάσεις τῷ Ἑλληνικῷ καὶ τὸ εὔηθες, οὗ τὸ γενναῖον πλεῖστον μετέχει, καταγελασθὲν ἠφανίσθη. It was caused by the return of the Kerkyroeans, taken prisoners in the battles of 434 and 433 B. C., who during their stay at Corinth had been won over to the side of the Peloponnesian alliance and aristocratic principles. It was they who raised the dispute and first shed blood, id. 70. The aristocrats had first of all the upper hand, id. 71, they attacked their opponents and conquered them in a battle, 72—73; then the democrats were again victorious, 74. For a short time an arrangement was effected by the exertions of the Athenian Nikostratus, who arrived with a fleet of 12 ships, 75; a few days afterward the fleet of Alkidas also arrived (obs. 27), now 53 ships strong, whereby the democratic party was brought into great peril, 76—80. Their superiority was, however, fully restored by a fresh Athenian fleet of 60 sail, and most of the aristocrats were now murdered, 80—81, with the exception of 500, who at first had taken refuge on the mainland, and who, when the Athenians retired, returned to the island, and entrenched themselves on the mountain Istone, from which they plundered and infested the neighbourhood, 85.

31) On the one side was ranged Syracuse with all the Doric towns in the island, except Kamarina and Lokri in lower Italy: on the other side there were all the Chalkidian towns and Kamarina and Rhegium in lower Italy; the war had arisen from a feud between

Syracuse and Leontini, Thuc. III, 86. The latter sent Gorgias to Athens to beg for assistance, Diod. XII, 53. Paus. VI, 17, 5, and the Athenians granted the request τῆς μὲν οἰκειότητος προφάσει, βουλόμενοι δὲ μήτε σῖτον ἐς τὴν Πελοπόννησον ἄγεσθαι αὐτόθεν, προπεῖραν τε ποιούμενοι εἰ σφίσι δυνατὰ εἴη τὰ ἐν τῇ Σικελίᾳ πράγματα ὑποχείρια γενέσθαι, Thuc. l. c. Their enterprise in this year, id. 88, and also in the following year, id. 90. 99. 115, were of little importance.

32) Thuc. III, 89—116. Diod. XII, 58—60. The Peloponnesians did not invade the Attic territory this year; for when they had already reached the Isthmus under the command of Agis, they were induced to return owing to an earthquake, Thuc. III, 89. Diod. XII, 59.

33) Thuc. III, 92—93. Diod. XII, 59. The colony was founded at the request of the Trachinians and Dorians (in Doris) as a protection against the neighbouring Œtaeans: but at the same time it was hoped that the place would afford great advantages for the war, as the voyage from thence to Euboea, and even to the Thrakian coast, seemed to present no difficulties. However, this, the last of the Greek colonies, and also the first purely military colony, did not thrive, as it was continually attacked by the neighbouring Ænianians, Dolopians, Melians, and several Thessalian tribes, and it was badly governed, Thuc. l. c. and V, 51. 52. According to Diodorus l. c. the number of colonists at its foundation amounted to no fewer than 10,000.

34) Nikias first sailed with 60 ships to Melos, laid the island waste, then invaded the territory of Tanagra in Boeotia, defeated, in conjunction with an army sent from Athens, the Tanagraeans and the Thebans who had come to their aid, and lastly made descents on Lokris, Thuc. III, 91.

35) Thuc. III, 91. 94—98. 100—102. 105—114. The enterprise against Ætolia was undertaken at the instigation of the Messenians at Naupaktus, who told Demosthenes (Thuc. 94): μέγα μὲν εἶναι τὸ τῶν Αἰτωλῶν καὶ μάχιμον, οἰκοῦν δὲ κατὰ κώμας ἀτειχίστους, καὶ ταύτας διὰ πολλοῦ, καὶ σκευῇ ψιλῇ χρώμενον οὐ χαλεπὸν ἀπέφαινον πρὶν ξυμβοηθῆσαι

Olympiad.	B. C.	ATHENS.	HISTORY.
		Archon.	
LXXXVIII, 4	425ᵃ)	Stratokles.	Fifth and last invasion of Attic territory by the Peloponnesians³⁷).

Reinforcements sent by Athens under Sophokles and Eurymedon to Sicily³⁸). On the voyage round the Peloponnese, Demosthenes, who accompanies the fleet, establishes himself at Pylos in Messenia³⁹), maintains it against the assaults of the Spartan army and fleet⁴⁰), and upon the return of the Athenian fleet, the Spartans are beaten at sea⁴¹): a number of distinguished Spartiates are in consequence cut off in the island of Sphakteria, and after fruitless peace proposals, are either killed or taken prisoners by Kleon and Demosthenes⁴²).

The faction struggles at Kerkyra ended by the extermination of the aristocrats⁴³).

καταστραφῆναι, ἐπιχειρεῖν δ' ἐκέλενον πρῶτον μὲν 'Ακαρνᾶσιν, ἔπειτα δὲ 'Οφιονεῦσι, καὶ μετὰ τούτους Εὐρυτᾶσιν, ὅπερ μέγιστον μέρος ἐστὶ τῶν Αἰτωλῶν, ἀγνωστότατοι δὲ γλῶσσαν καὶ ὠμοφάγοι εἰσίν, ὡς λέγονται. However, it ended with heavy loss and retreat on the part of the Athenians and Naupaktians, Thuc. III, 94—98. Hereupon the Ætolians plucked up courage, and invited 3000 Peloponnesians to come and conquer Naupaktus; upon the failure of the attempt, at the demand of the Ampraklots they turned against Argos Amphilochikum, where they and the Ampraklots suffered a very bloody defeat from the inhabitants of Argos and the Akarnanians under the command of Demosthenes, Thuc. III, 100—102, 105—114.

36) Thuc. IV, 1—51. Diod. XII, 61—63. 65. Plut. Nik. 6—8.

37) Thuc. IV, 2. On account of the course of events at Pylos it lasted only 15 days, id. 6. And it was owing to the affair of Pylos, that the invasions of Attica were not repeated, as heretofore, obs. 42.

38) After the petty results of the years 427 and 426 (obs. 31) the Athenians resolved, at the request of their Sicilian allies, to send 40 fresh ships to Sicily, Thuc. III, 115; ἅμα μὲν ἡγούμενοι θᾶσσον τὸν ἐκεῖ πόλεμον καταλυθήσεσθαι, ἅμα δὲ βουλόμενοι μελέτην τοῦ ναυτικοῦ ποιεῖσθαι. These set sail in the spring of 425, Thuc. IV, 2. For the further (but not important) events in Sicily up till the arrival of the Athenians, see Thuc. IV, 1. 24—25.

39) Thuc. IV, 3—5. The situation of Pylos and the island Sphakteria, Thuc. id. 8; ἡ νῆσος ἡ Σφακτηρία καλουμένη τόν τε λιμένα παρατείνουσα καὶ ἐγγὺς ἐπικειμένη ἐχυρὸν ποιεῖ καὶ τοὺς ἔσπλους στενούς, τῇ μὲν δυοῖν νεοῖν διάπλουν κατὰ τὸ τείχισμα τῶν 'Αθηναίων καὶ τὴν Πύλον, τῇ δὲ πρὸς τὴν ἄλλην ἤπειρον ὀκτὼ ἢ ἐννέα, ὑλώδης τε καὶ ἀτριβὴς πᾶσα ὑπ' ἐρημίας ἦν καὶ μέγεθος περὶ πεντεκαίδεκα σταδίους μάλιστα. When the rest of the fleet continued its voyage, Demosthenes remained behind with 5 ships at Pylos, id. 5.

40) Thuc. IV, 6. 8—12.,

41) Thuc. IV, 13—14.

42) A detachment of the Spartan army had been landed on the island, to maintain it against the Athenians, Thuc. IV, 8, and was now cut off by the victory of the Athenian fleet, which had left the latter masters of the sea, id. 14. 15. There were 420 hoplites, and amongst them many of the foremost Spartiates, id. V, 15; ἦσαν γὰρ οἱ Σπαρτιᾶται αὐτῶν πρῶτοί τε καὶ ὁμοίως σφίσι ξυγγενεῖς. In order to rescue their beleaguered citizens, the Spartans endeavoured to conclude a peace; but this was frustrated, chiefly through Kleon, id. IV, 16—23. Kleon, that is (ἀνὴρ δημαγωγὸς κατ' ἐκεῖνον τὸν χρόνον ὢν καὶ τῷ πλήθει πιθανώτατος, id. 21), misled the people to demand the restoration of Nisæa, Pagæ, Trœzen, and Achaia, as the price of the peace, id. 21. cf. Aristoph. Equit. v. 801; ἵνα μᾶλλον | σὺ (Κλέων) μὲν ἁρπάζῃς καὶ δωροδοκῇς παρὰ τῶν πόλεων, ὁ δὲ δῆμος | ὑπὸ τοῦ πολέμου καὶ τῆς ὁμίχλης ἃ πανουργεῖς μὴ καθορᾷ σου, id. v. 804. Pac. 609 : ὁ τοῖς γὰρ ὑμῶν ἦν τότ' ἐν τοῖς σκύτεσιν. When the capture of the beleaguered Spartans was delayed, Kleon insisted upon greater efforts being made to attain this end; he was chosen commander by the populace in a fit of wantonness, but actually succeeded by the help of Demosthenes in bringing the undertaking to a prosperous issue; in an attack upon the island a part of the 420 hoplites were killed, the rest, 292 men, amongst them 120 Spartiates, were taken prisoners and carried to Athens, where they were retained as security for the peace, and security against the repetition of the invasions, which had been hitherto made into the Attic territory, Thuc. IV, 26—41. Plut. Nic. 7—8. cf. Arist. Equit. 64 (said by Demosthenes of Kleon): καὶ πρώην γ' ἐμοῦ | μᾶζαν μεμαχότος ἐν Πύλῳ Λακωνικὴν | πανουργότατά πως περιδραμὼν ὑφαρπάσας | αὐτὸς παρέθηκε τὴν ὑπ' ἐμοῦ μεμαγμένην. A garrison was then posted at Pylos itself, chiefly composed of Messenians from Naupaktus, who inflicted great damage on the Spartans by their raids and the shelter they afforded to runaway Helots, Thuc. IV, 41.

43) Thuc. IV, 2. 44—46. This was accomplished with the help of the Athenian fleet, when it continued its voyage from Pylos to Sicily by way of Kerkyra.

The Incipient Decline.

Olympiad.	B. C.	ATHENS.	HISTORY.
LXXXVIII, 4	425	Archon.	The Athenians make hostile landings on the Corinthian territory[44]), establish themselves on Methone[45]), and take Anaktorium[46]).
LXXXIX, 1	424 [47])	Isarchus.	Nikias takes Kythera, and, making it his head-quarters, plunders the Lakonian coast and other parts of the Peloponnese[48]).
			In Sicily peace is established by the reconciliation of the belligerents; the Athenians return home from thence[49]).
			Nisæa taken by the Athenians[50]).
			The fortunes of Athens at their culminating point; despondency of Sparta[51]).
			Brasidas marches to the Thrakian coast[52]), and there brings about the revolt of most of the towns on the Chalkidic peninsula from the Athenian alliance[53]).
			The Athenians in an invasion of Bœotia totally defeated at Delium[54]).

44) Thuc. IV, 42—45.
45) Thuc. IV, 45.
46) Thuc. IV, 49.
47) Thuc. IV, 52—116. Diod. XII, 66—70.
48) Thuc. IV, 53—54. The enterprise was conducted by Nikias and Nikostratus and was of great importance, as by it the Athenians gained a second station from which they could harass Laconia and the rest of the Peloponnese, id. 54—57. Starting from this point, they also landed in Kynuria, conquered Thyrea, and took prisoners the Æginetans, who had found a refuge there after their expulsion from Ægina (obs. 8), and were now all put to death, id. 56—57.
49) Thuc. IV, 58—65. The settlement was effected chiefly at the instigation of the Syracusan Hermokrates, id. 58, to the great chagrin of the Athenians, id. 65.
50) Thuc. IV, 66—69. They would also have taken Megara, had not Brasidas been in the neighbourhood and prevented it, id. 70—74.
51) See esp. Thuc. IV, 55: γεγενημένου μὲν τοῦ ἐπὶ τῇ νήσῳ πάθους ἀνελπίστου καὶ μεγάλου, Πύλου δ' ἐχομένης καὶ Κυθήρων καὶ πανταχόθεν σφᾶς περιεστῶτος πολέμου ταχέος καὶ ἀπροφυλάκτου, ὥστε παρὰ τὸ εἰωθὸς ἱππέας τετρακοσίους κατεστήσαντο καὶ τοξότας, ἔς τε τὰ πολεμικὰ εἴπερ ποτὲ μάλιστα δὴ ὀκνηρότεροι ἐγένοντο, ξυνεστῶτες παρὰ τὴν ὑπάρχουσαν σφῶν ἰδέαν τῆς παρασκευῆς ναυτικῷ ἀγῶνι καὶ τοῦτο πρὸς Ἀθηναίους, οἷς τὸ μὴ ἐπιχειρούμενον ἀεὶ ἐλλιπὲς ἦν τῆς δοκήσεώς τι πράξειν. καὶ ἅμα τὰ τῆς τύχης πολλὰ καὶ ἐν ὀλίγῳ ξυμβάντα παρὰ λόγον αὐτοῖς ἔκπληξιν μεγίστην παρεῖχεν.
52) The expedition was undertaken at the invitation of the Chalkidians and Perdikkas, king of Macedonia, Thuc. IV, 79. (Perdikkas is the first Macedonian king that exercises any influence

on the affairs of Greece. Before the Peloponnesian war he was in alliance with the Athenians, but then became hostile to them; and after that sided, now with the Athenians, now with their opponents, Thuc. I, 56—63. II, 29. 80. 95—101. IV, 79: πολέμιοι μὲν οὐκ ὢν ἐκ τοῦ φανεροῦ, φοβούμενοι δὲ καὶ αὐτὸν τὰ παλαιὰ διάφορα τῶν Ἀθηναίων.) For the object of the expedition see Thuc. IV, 80: τῶν γὰρ Ἀθηναίων ἐγκειμένων τῇ Πελοποννήσῳ καὶ οὐχ ἥκιστα τῇ ἐκείνων γῇ ἤλπιζεν ἀποστρέψαι αὐτοὺς μάλιστα, εἰ ἀντιπαραλυποίην πέμψαντες ἐπὶ τοὺς ξυμμάχους αὐτῶν στρατιάν, ἄλλως τε καὶ ἑτοίμων ὄντων τρέφειν τε καὶ ἐπὶ ἀποστάσει σφᾶς ἐπικαλουμένων, cf. id. 81. With great boldness Brasidas led the expedition by land; he was at the head of 1700 hoplites, of whom 700 were Helots (afterwards manumitted, Thuc. V, 34), Thuc. IV, 78—80.
53) The first to revolt were Akanthus and Stageirus, Thuc. IV, 84—88; then in the winter Amphipolis, id. 102—106; next Torone and other towns. (The historian Thucydides, who was stationed at Thasos with a small fleet, hurried up to the support of Amphipolis, but was only able to save Eion, id. 107; and was on this account banished, id. V, 26; for the importance of Amphipolis, see id. IV, 108.) For the feeling of the towns see Thuc. IV, 108: αἱ πόλεις—αἱ τῶν Ἀθηναίων ὑπήκοοι—μάλιστα δὴ ἐπήρθησαν ἐς τὸ νεωτερίζειν καὶ ἐπεκηρυκεύοντο πρὸς αὐτὸν κρύφα, ἐπιπαρεῖναί τε κελεύοντες καὶ βουλόμενοι αὐτοὶ ἕκαστοι πρῶτοι ἀποστῆναι, (or Brasidas, Id. 81: τὸ γὰρ παραυτίκα ἑαυτὸν παρασχὼν δίκαιον καὶ μέτριον ἐς τὰς πόλεις ἀπέστησε τὰ πολλά, 108: καὶ ἐν τοῖς λόγοις πανταχοῦ ἐδήλου ὡς ἐλευθερώσων τὴν Ἑλλάδα.
54) The invasion of Bœotia was part of a concerted plan for the reduction of Bœotia; Demosthenes was to make his way into the country from Siphæ on the Corinthian gulf, whilst Hippokrates invaded it by way of Oropus. Both reckoned on the support of a democratic party devoted to Athens. But Demosthenes began the

FOURTH PERIOD. 431—338 B. C.

Olympiad.	B. C.	ATHENS.	HISTORY.	ART AND LITERATURE.
		Archons.		
LXXXIX, 2	423⁵⁵)	Amynias.	Armistice between Sparta and Athens for a year⁵⁶). But the war is continued on the Thrakian coast, where the Athenians again make some progress⁵⁷).	
LXXXIX, 3	422⁵⁸)	Alkaeus.	The Bœotians wrest Panaktum from Athens⁵⁹).	
			Kleon is sent to Thrake and fights the battle of Amphipolis with Brasidas; the Athenians are defeated: Kleon and Brasidas fall⁶⁰).	
LXXXIX, 4	421⁶¹)	Aristion.	Peace of Nikias⁶²).	
			b) The period of a half peace between Sparta and Athens with the continuance of hostilities between the rest of the Greek states up to the open breach of the treaty stipulations and the end of the Sicilian expedition, 421—413⁶³).	
LXXXIX, 4	421		Discontent of the Spartan allies at the peace,	The Comic Poets Eupolis*),

enterprise too soon, and as simultaneous action on the part of both was thus rendered impossible, Demosthenes was foiled at Siphæ and Hippokrates suffered a severe defeat, in which nearly 1000 hoplites fell. Thuc. IV, 76—77. 89—101. For the part taken by Sokrates and Alkibiades in the battle see Plat. Apol. Sokr. p. 28 B. Lach. p. 181 B. Symp. p. 221 A. B. Plut. Alc. 7. Strab. p. 403.

55) Thuc. IV, 117—135. Diod. XII, 72.

56) Thuc. IV, 117—119. Both parties were inclined for it; the Athenians, in order to check the advances of Brasidas; the Spartans, in order to recover their prisoners by a peace to be concluded in continuation of the armistice, id. 117. The conditions were, that both parties should retain what they held on the conclusion of the armistice, id. 118. But as Brasidas refused to restore Skione, which had gone over to him two days after the armistice had been concluded, id. 122, the war was still carried on on the Thrakian coast: at home peace was preserved till after the expiration of the armistice, id. 134.

57) The result of the enterprise, which was conducted by Nikias and Nikostratus, was that Mende, which had followed Skione and gone over to the enemy, Thuc. IV, 123, was reconquered and Skione blockaded, Thuc. IV, 129—131.

58) Thuc. V, 1—13. Diod. XII, 73—74.

59) Thuc. V, 3.

60) Thuc. V, 2—3. 6—11.

61) Thuc. V, 13—38. Diod. XII, 74—76.

62) Thuc. V, 14—20. The peace was concluded on the 24th of Elaphebolion ('Ελαφηβολιῶνος μηνὸς ἕκτῃ φθίνοντος), Thuc. V, 19, cf. id. 20: ἅμα ἦρι ἐκ Διονυσίων εὐθὺς τῶν ἀστικῶν, αὐτόδεκα ἐτῶν διελθόντων καὶ ἡμερῶν ὀλίγων παρενεγκουσῶν ἢ ὡς τὸ πρῶτον ἡ ἐσβολὴ ἐς τὴν 'Αττικὴν καὶ ἡ ἀρχὴ τοῦ πολέμου τοῦδε ἐγένετο, i. e. about the end of March. Nikias and Pleistoanax were especially active in promoting the peace, id. 16; the chief incentives were on the side of the Athenians, the disastrous battles of Delium and Amphipolis and the apprehension that the revolt of the allies would spread still further; on the side of the Spartans, the prisoners taken at Pylos, the hostile stations at Pylos and Kythera, further the treaty with Argos now at the point of expiration, id. 14—16. An additional motive at Athens was the financial exhaustion; for they had not only consumed the treasure of 6000 talents (obs. 1), all except the reserve fund of 1000 talents (for which see obs. 103), but had also borrowed considerable sums from the temples, Corp. Inscr. Gr. I, n. 76. The sum and substance of the convention, communicated to us by Thucydides, id. 18, was that both parties should restore what they had won in the war, that it is all prisoners and all conquered places. Accordingly Pylos and Kythera were to be given up by the Athenians, Panaktum, Amphipolis and the rest of the Thrakian towns by their enemies. Nisæa was to be left to Athens (in compensation for Plataea), id. 17. All allies of both parties were to be independent.

63) Thuc. V, 25: ἐξ (ἐντὰ? id. VI, 105) ἕτη μὲν καὶ δέκα μῆνας ἀπέσχοντο μὴ ἐπὶ τὴν ἑκατέρων γῆν στρατεῦσαι, ἐξωθεν δὲ μετ᾽ ἀνακωχῆς οὐ βεβαίου ἔβλαπτον ἀλλήλους τὰ μάλιστα· ἔπειτα μέντοι—αὐθις ἐς πόλεμον φανερὸν κατέστησαν, id. V, 26: τὴν διὰ μέσου ξύμβασιν εἴ τις μὴ ἀξιώσει πόλεμον νομίζειν, οὐκ ὀρθῶς δικαιώσει.

a) Eupolis, named with Kratinus and Aristophanes as the most important poet of the old comedy, born at Athens in 446, came forward with his first comedy in 429, and met with his death before the end of the Peloponnesian war, probably in a sea-fight, Suid. s. v. Anon. Περὶ κωμ. Bergk. Prol. Com. III, 1. VIII, 24. The titles of 14 of his comedies have been handed down to us with certainty; those, from

Olympiad.	B. C.	HISTORY.	ART AND LITERATURE.
LXXXIX, 4	421	especially of the Bœotians, Corinthians, and Megarians, and their refusal to accede to it⁶⁴).	Aristophanes ᵇ).

64) The Bœotians were discontented, because they had to give up Panaktum, the Megarians because they were not to recover Nisaea, Thuc. V, 17. 20, the Corinthians, because Sollium and Anaktorium were withheld from them, id. 30, and the Eleans, because they had to grant the Lepreatans their independence again, id. 31.

which the most important fragments are preserved, are: 'Αστρατοι ἤ 'Ανδρόγυνοι, Mein. Fr. Com. Græc. Eup. fr. 1, Δῆμοι, fr. 2. 3. 15, Είλωτες, fr. 3, Κόλακες, fr. 1. 10. 11. 18, Μαρικᾶς, fr. 5. 6, Πόλεις, fr. 7. 8. 10, Χρυσοῦν γένος, fr. 1—3. His political comedy was full of bitter personal sallies, as the fragments testify. Thus, for example, he attacks Kleon, Chrys. Gen. fr. 1—4. Inc. fab. fr. 10: Κλέων Προμηθεύς ἐστι μετὰ τὰ πράγματα, the demagogue Hyperbolus in the Marikas, Quint. I, 10, 18. Πόσιγχ. v. Ἱερεὺς Διονύσου, the poltroon Peisander, Astrat. fr. 1. Marik. fr. 6. Schol. Aristop. Av. 1556, the debauchee Kallias, Kol. fr. 5. Schol. Aristoph. Av. 284, Alkibiades on account of his loose living, Kol. fr. 16, and in the Βάπται, Περὶ κωμ. VIII, 24, and even Nikias on account of his weakness towards sycophants, Marik. fr. 5, and Kimon on account of his Spartan sympathies, Pol. fr. 10, although elsewhere he recognises the merits of the two last. Platonius says of the genius of Eupolis, Περὶ Διαφ. Χαρ. II, 2: Εὔπολις δὲ εὐφάνταστος μὲν εἰς ὑπερβολήν ἐστι κατὰ τὰς ὑποθέσεις...ὥσπερ δέ ἐστιν ὑψηλός, οὕτω καὶ ἐπίχαρις καὶ περὶ τὰ σκώμματα λίαν εὔστοχος.

b) Aristophanes, an Athenian of the phyle Pandionis and the deme Kydathenæum, son of Philippus, flourished circ. 427—388, Vit. Aristophan. Περὶ κωμ. III, 12. Bergk. Prol. de Com. We know neither the year of his birth nor of his death, and of the circumstances of his life little more than is disclosed by the production of his comedies. The young poet had his first play brought upon the stage in the name of the actor Kallistratus; this was the Δαιταλῆς, Aristoph. Nub. 524, Schol., with which he won the second prize. Early in 426, during the presence of many ambassadors from the allies at Athens, he produced his Βαβυλώνιοι in which he ridiculed the election of officials by lot and by show of hands, and first attacked Kleon. He was thereupon accused by the wrathful Kleon of libel and underhand acquisition of civic rights, but acquitted, Acharn. 377, Schol. 502. Schol. 632. In 425 he won the first prize in competition with Kratinus and Eupolis with the Ἀχαρνῆς, Argum. Acharn., in which he recommends peace and covers the war-loving Lamachus with ridicule, v. 566 f.: 'Ιὼ Λάμαχ', ὦ βλέπων ἀστραπάς, |...ὦ γοργολόφα, and also Perikles, as the originator of the war, v. 530 f.: 'Εντεῦθεν ὀργῇ Περικλέης οὑλύμπιος | ἤστραπτ', ἐβρόντα, ξυνεκύκα τὴν Ἑλλάδα, and Aspasia, v. 527. In 424 he conquered Kratinus and Aristomenes with the 'Ιππῆς, Argum. Eq. II. 315, in which he lashes Kleon's demagogy, v. 310: Τὴν πόλιν ἅπασαν ἡμῶν ἀνατετυρβακώτ, | ὅστις ἡμῶν τὰς Ἀθήνας ἐκκεκώφηκας βοῶν, v. 795: Τὴν εἰρήνην ἐξενεκτέωσαν, τὰς πρεσβείας τ' ἀνελωκυίαν, v. 892: βύρσης κάκιστον ὄζων, cf. v. 75 f. 802 f., and Kleon's assistant Hyperbolus, v. 1304; 'Ανδρα μοχθηρὸν πολίτην, ὀξίνην Ὑπέρβολον, cf. v. 978. Eupolis travestied and distorted the play, when he brought Hyperbolus on the stage in his Marikas, Nub. 551—556. Schol. The Νεφέλαι, in 423 B. C., found little applause, for Kratinus won the first, and Ameipsias the second prize, Argum. Nub. V. Schol. Nub. 549. 552.

Schol. Vesp. 1033. 1039; it is a satire on the groundless and strawsplitting subtleties of the Sophists, v. 360: μετεωροσοφιστῶν, v. 401: μεριμνοφροντισταί, v. 103 : τοὺς ὠχριῶντας, and also on the dialectics and the supposed atheism of Sokrates, v. 359: λεπτοτάτων λήρων ἱερεῦ, v. 104: ὁ κακοδαίμων Σωκράτης, v. 1477: ἐξέβαλλον τοὺς θεοὺς διὰ Σωκράτην, v. 247. 365. 367, who is brought on the stage as the representative of the whole movement, v. 103 f. When the piece was altered and produced a second time, it was still unsuccessful, Argum. Nub. V. In 422 the poet won the second prize with the Σφῆκες, Arg. Vesp., in which he laughs at the litigiousness of the Athenians, v. 505: 'Ορθροφοιτοσυκοφαντοδικοταλαιπώρων τρόπων, v. 1108, and their representative Kleon, v. 595 f. ; ὁ Κλέων ὁ κεκραξιδάμας, v. 342 : Δημολεγοκλέων, cf. v. 62. 409. 758. 1224 f. 1285 f. After the death of Brasidas and Kleon in the battle of Amphipolis the poet (in 421) in his comedy Εἰρήνη, with which he won the second prize, recommended the peace just inaugurated, Argum. Pac. II, and attacked the heads of the war party; thus Sophists, v. 608: Ἱερὶν παθεῖν τι δεινόν αὐτὸς ἐξέφλεξε τὴν πόλιν, | ἐμβαλὼν σπινθῆρα μικρὸν Μεγαρικοῦ ψηφίσματος | ἐξεφύσησεν τοσοῦτον πόλεμον, Phoidias, v. 605, Lamachus, v. 303 : Ἡμέρα γὰρ ἐξέλαμψεν ἥδε μισολάμαχος, v. 473 f., Kleon, v. 49. 270 : Ὁ βυρσοπώλης ὃς ἐκύκα τὴν Ἑλλάδα, v. 652 f. : πανοῦργος ἦν δ᾽ εἴη | καὶ λῃστὴς καὶ συκοφάντης | καὶ κύκηθρον καὶ τάρακτρον, v. 753 f., and Hyperbolus, v. 680 f. 921. 1319. The next play of the poet preserved to us is the Ὄρνιθες, which won the second prize on its production in 414, during the Sicilian expedition, Argum. Av. II. Schol. Av. 998. Prompted by the venturesome enterprise against Syracuse, he represents in the foundation of Cloud-cuckoo-town, Νεφελοκοκκυγία, v. 551 f. 819 f., and the bird-republic the high-soaring bubble-enterprise of Athenian policy and the immoderate arrogance of the demagogy, v. 1284: 'Ορνιθομανοῦσι, πάντα δ᾽ ὑπὸ τῆς ἡδονῆς ποιοῦσιν, v. 1289: Εἶτ᾽ ἀτενέμων᾽ ἐνταῦθα τὰ ψηφίσματα᾽ | ὠρνιθωμάνουν δ᾽ οὕτω περιφανῶς etc., and ridicules the demagogues Kleonymus, v. 289. 1470 f., and Peisander, v. 1556. The Λωσιστράτη was produced shortly after the disastrous issue of the war in Sicily and the fall of the democratic constitution in 411, Schol. Lys. 173. 1095, in which the poet again recommends peace, v. 1266: νῦν δ᾽ αὖ | φιλία τ᾽ αἷες εὔπορος εἴη | ταῖς συνθήκαις, | καὶ τῶν αἱμυλῶν ἀλωπέκων | παυσαίμεθα. The Θεσμοφοριάζουσαι, produced in the same year, Thesm. 1060, exposes the corrupt morality of the Athenian women, and ridicules the poetry of Euripides and Agathon, v. 29 f. In the Βάτραχοι, with which the poet won the first prize, Argum. Ran. I, in 405, he parodies the poetry of Æschylus and Euripides, v. 824 f., and gives the older poet the preference. The Ἐκκλησιάζουσαι, produced in 392, Schol. Eccl. 193, is a satire upon a democratical state with community of goods and women, v. 590 f. 613 f. The poet's last play is the second Πλοῦτος, produced in 388, Arg. Plut. III, in which the god of wealth recovers his sight and from

9—2

Olympiad	B. C.	HISTORY.	ART AND LITERATURE.
LXXXIX, 4	421	Fifty years alliance between Sparta and Athens⁶⁵). Alliance between Corinth, Argos, Mantineia, Elis, and the Chalkidic towns in Thrake⁶⁶).	The Philosophers Leukippus⁰), Demokritus⁴). The Sophists⁰) Protagoras⁴),

65) Thuc. V, 22—24 : αὕτη ἡ ξυμμαχία ἐγένετο μετὰ τὰς σπονδὰς οὐ πολλῷ ὕστερον.
66) Thuc. V, 27—31. The discontent of Sparta's allies was intensified by the stipulation contained in the treaty between Sparta and Athens: ἣν τι δοκῇ Λακεδαιμονίοις καὶ Ἀθηναίοις προσθεῖναι καὶ ἀφελεῖν περὶ τῆς ξυμμαχίας, ὅ τι ἂν δοκῇ, εὔορκον ἀμφοτέροις εἶναι, id. 23.

29. In general κατὰ τὸν χρόνον τοῦτον ἥ τε Λακεδαίμων μάλιστα δὴ κακῶς ἤκουσε καὶ ὑπερώφθη διὰ τὰς ξυμφοράς, id. 26: consequently οἱ πολλοὶ ὥρμηντο πρὸς τοὺς Ἀργείους καὶ αὐτοὶ ἕκαστοι ξυμμαχίαν ποιεῖσθαι, id. However, Tegea could not be induced to join the alliance, and Thebes and Megara still observed for the time a waiting policy, id. 31.

this time forwards distributes his bounties to the deserving. Besides those plays of Aristophanes preserved in a perfect state, short fragments from some 30 dramas are extant, the most important being from the Βαβυλώνιοι, Mein. fr. 1. 17, Γεωργοί, fr. 1. 13, Δαιταλῆς, fr. 16, Θεσμοφοριάζουσαι δεύτεραι, fr. 3. 6. 15. When Dionysius of Syracuse wished to become acquainted with the Athenian state, it is said that Plato sent him the comedies of Aristophanes and declared them the truest mirror of the life of state and people at Athens, Vit. Arist. 9. Plato was also the reputed author of the epigram, Thom. Mag. Vit. Arist. 5: Αἱ Χάριτες τέμενός τι λαβεῖν ὅπερ οὐχὶ πεσεῖται | ζητοῦσαι ψυχὴν εὗρον Ἀριστοφάνους. Cf. Antipater Thessal. Anth. Pal. IX, 186: Ὦ καὶ θυμὸν ἄριστε, καὶ Ἑλλάδος ἤθεσιν ἶσα | κωμικὲ καὶ στύξας ἄξια καὶ γελάσαι. The most prominent contemporary poets of the older comedy are: Phrynichus, Aristoph. Nub. 548. Schol. Ran. 13. Suid. v. Περὶ Κωμ. III. Bergk. Prol. de Com., who won the second prize with his play Μοῦσαι, when Aristophanes conquered with the Frogs, Argum. Ran. 1. Fragments of 10 of his comedies have come down to us, especially Ἐφιάλτης, Moin. fr. 1, Μονότροπος, fr. 1. 4, Μοῦσαι, fr. 1. cf. Inc. fab. fr. 1. 3; Plato of Athens, Suid. s. v. Diog. Laert. III, 109. Cyrill. adv. Iul. I, p. 13. 6, an excellent comic poet. Fragments are preserved of nearly thirty of his comedies, thus in particular : Ἕλλας ἢ νῆσοι, fr. 1, Ζεὺς κακούμενος, fr. 1, Λάκωνες ἢ ποιηταί, fr. 1, Πείσανδρος, fr. 2, Σοφισταί, fr. 1. 3, Ὑπέρβολος, fr. 1. 2. 3, Φάων, fr. 1. 2. Altogether, fragments are preserved of some 40 poets of the older comedy; besides those mentioned, the most numerous from Telekleides, Hermippus, Ameipsias, Archippus, Strattis, Theopompus, etc. Cf. Mein. Fragm. Com. Graec.

c) Leukippos, reputed a pupil of Eleatic philosophers, Diog. Laert. IX, 30 f. Tzetz. Chil. II, 90, cf. Arist. De Gener. et Corr. I, 8, was the founder of the atomic system, according to which the world was a concretion of an infinite number of indivisible and qualitatively similar atomic bodies, Diog. L. l. c.: πρῶτος τε ἀτόμους ἀρχὰς ὑπεστήσατο, Cic. De Nat. D. I, 24. Acad. IV, 37. He wrote λόγοι and περὶ νοῦ, Stob. Ecl. Phys. I. p. 100.

d) Demokritus of Abdera, born circ. 460, is said to have lived to the age of 109 years, Diog. L. IX, 34. 41. 43. He spent his property on extensive travels to Babylon, Persia, and the Red Sea, Egypt, and Meroe, also to Greece, where he visited Athens, l. c. 35. 36. 49. Strab. p. 703. He deposited the rich treasure of the knowledge he had

amassed in numerous writings, composed in the Ionic dialect, which handled materials in every branch of science; in Ethics, physics, mechanics, mathematics, astronomy, medicine, grammar, philosophy of language, geography, military science, jurisprudence, music, poetry and painting, as is proved by the register of his works in Diogenes Laertius, IX, 45—49. He perfected the atomic system of Leukippus, l. c. 44 f. Of his writings only scanty fragments are extant; but Cicero praises his style, Or. 20, De Divin. II, 64. De Orat. I, 11.

e) The Sophists, leaving the track of former philosophers, do not occupy themselves with nature and theoretical science as such; they profess to be teachers of virtue, i. e. of practical wisdom in matters of state and private life, and of oratory; but, as their teaching has no positive character, they apply themselves to merely formal education and often take their chief task to be mere declamation about the subjects dealt with. They travelled round the Greek towns, where they delivered lectures and imparted instruction for money, and they exercised considerable influence on their time. Plat. Soph. 218 c. F. 231 E. F. 261 A. F. Phaedr. 267 A. Prot. 310 D. 315 A. Rep. X, 600 E. Aristot. Metaph. IV, 2. Soph. Elench. I, 2: ἔστι γὰρ ἡ σοφιστικὴ χρηματιστική ἀπὸ φαινομένης σοφίας, ἀλλ᾽ οὐκ οὔσης, Plut. Them. 2: τὴν καλουμένην σοφίαν, οὕτως δὲ πεινότητα πολιτικὴν καὶ δραστήριον σύνεσιν.

f) Protagoras of Abdera, an elder contemporary of Sokrates, born circ. 485, Diog. L. IX, 50. 56. Plat. Prot. 309 c. 320 c. 361 E, for 10 years went the round of the Greek towns (from about 443 B. C. onwards) teaching for money, Plat. Prot. 310 E. 349 A. Hipp. Mai. 282 E. Athen. V, p. 218 B. C. XI, p. 506 A. Diog. L. IX, 52, and in particular was the first to discuss disputed questions conversationally, Suid. s. v., as he was also the first to receive the epithet σοφιστής, Plat. Prot. 349 A. He was in close intercourse with Perikles, Plut. Per. 26. Cons. ad Apoll. p. 430, and was employed as legislator at Thurii, Diog. Laert. IX, 50. On account of his verdict: Περὶ μὲν θεῶν οὐκ ἔχω εἰδέναι, εἴθ᾽ ὡς εἰσίν εἴθ᾽ ὡς οὐκ εἰσίν, his books were publicly burnt, and he was himself banished from Athens as a denier of god, Diog. L. IX, 51. 52. Suid. s. v., and perished on the voyage to Sicily, being 70 years old at the least, Diog. L. IX, 55. Out of his numerous writings of a dialectical, ethical, and political character, l. c., only a few doctrines are preserved; thus his chief doctrine, Plat. Theaet. 152 A: πάντων χρημάτων μέτρον ἄνθρωπον εἶναι, cf. Cratyl. 385 E. Aristot. Metaph. IV, 4, 5. X, 1. Cic. Acad. II, 46: id cuique verum esse, quod cuique videatur.

The Incipient Decline.

Olympiad.	B.C.	ATHENS.	HISTORY.	ART AND LITERATURE.
XC, 1	420[a])	Archons. Astyphilus.	Alliance between Sparta and Thebes[e]); Alkibiades[f]) brings about a counter-alliance between Athens, Argos, Elis, and Mantineia[g]).	Gorgias[x]), Hippias[h]), Prodikus[i]), Sokrates, opponent of the Sophists[k]).
XC, 2	419[n])	Archias.	Alkibiades marches to the Peloponnese and wins over Patræ to the Athenian-Argive league[m]).	Thucydides, historian[l]).

67) Thuc. V, 39—51. Plut. Alc. Diod. XII, 77. (In consequence of the hostile disposition of the Eleans towards Sparta the Spartans are excluded from this year's celebration of the Olympic games, Thuc. V, 49—50.)
66) The Athenians did not restore Pylos, as they failed to recover Panaktum and the Chalkidian towns. The Spartans accordingly made overtures to the Bœotians, in order to persuade them to deliver up Panaktum, Thuc. V, 35. But a further reason for the turn which events took was, that at Sparta with the change of the year warlike Ephors had come into office, id. 36. As the Bœotians refused to surrender Panaktum, unless the Spartans would conclude an alliance with them, an alliance was effected "πρὸς ἕαρ", id. 39. At this the Athenians were provoked in a high degree, partly because they perceived in it an infraction of the terms of their agreement with Sparta, id. 42, partly

g) Gorgias, of Leonti in Sicily, lived circ. 480—375, Plin. II. N. XXXII, 83. Suid. s.v., and died over a hundred years old, Plat. Phædr. 261 c. Apollod. ap. Diog. L. VIII, 58. Paus. VI, 15, 5. Cic. Sen. 5. Quint. III, 1, 9. Athen. XII, p. 548 D. A pupil of Empedokles, Diog. L. l. c. ('Αριστοτέλης ἐν τῷ Σοφιστῇ φησιν πρῶτον Ἐμπεδοκλέα ῥητορικὴν εὑρεῖν, Ζήνωνα δὲ διαλεκτικήν). Quint. l. c. Suid. s.v., he came forward in various towns in Greece as a teacher of oratory and philosophy. In his own home he gave practical proof of his powers as statesman and popular orator, and in 422 B. c., when sent as ambassador of Leontini to Athens, he won the support of the Athenians for the city of his birth against Syracuse, Diod. XII, 53. Plat. Hipp. Mai. 282 D, then came again to Athens, Plat. Men. 71 c, and in later years lived at Larissa in Thessaly, l. c. At an advanced age he retained his mental powers, Quint. XII, 11, 21. Athen. XII, p. 548, and died a gentle death with soul at peace, Æl. V. H. II, 35. A master of impromptu speaking, Cic. De Fin. II, 1. De Orat. I, 22. III, 32, and of ornate prettiness (καλλιλογία), Dion. Hal. Demosth. 4, he excercised an important influence on the development of Attic eloquence, Dion. Hal. Lys. 3: 'Ἵλγατο καὶ τῶν Ἀθήνησι ῥητόρων ἡ ποιητική καὶ τροπική φράσις Γοργίου ἄρξαντος. Of his philosophical writings the most important was Περὶ τοῦ μὴ ὄντος ἢ περὶ τῆς φύσεως, preserved partly in Aristotle, De Melisso, Xenophane et Gorgia, and in Sextus Empiricus Adv. Math. VII, 55 f. His famous declamations (ἐπιδείξεις) are lost. The ἀπολογία Παλαμήδους attributed to him, as also the ἐγκώμιον Ἐλένης, is not from his pen.

h) Hippias of Elis, Suid. s.v., a contemporary of Protagoras, Sokrates, etc., statesman and diplomatist, Plat. Hipp. Mai. 281 A. Philostr. Vit. Soph. I, 11, p. 495, rhetor, sophist, grammarian, mathematician, astronomer, musician, Plat. Hipp. Mai. 285 D.c. D. Protag. 315 c, poet, painter, sculptor, art-connoisseur, the universal artist, Hipp. Min. 368 B—D. Cic. De Or. III, 32, a man of many-sided but superficial knowledge, Xen. Mem. IV, 4, 0, πολυμαθής, vain and boastful, Plat. l. c. Cic. l. c., and as a philosopher not nearly so important as the two sophists above mentioned. Of his numerous declamations and poems, Hipp. Min. 368 c. Paus. V, 25, I. Plut. Num. 1, only one epigram has come down to us.

because Panaktum, instead of being restored by the Bœotians, was destroyed by them, id. 39, 40, 42.
69) For the youth of Alkibiades and for his character in general see Plat. Alc. 1—13. 23. cf. Plat. Symp. p. 216 ff. Prot. p. 309. 320. etc. He first came into prominence on the present occasion by the part which he played in the public affairs of Athens, and that as an opponent of the Spartans, by whom he felt himself hurt in his pride and ambition, Thuc. V, 43. He was the son of Kleinias, who fell in the battle of Koroneia; by his mother Deinomache a grandson of Megakles and connected with Perikles, who had filled the post of guardian to him in virtue of his relationship, Plut. 1,
70) Thuc. V, 40—47. Plut. Alc. 14.
71) Thuc. V, 52—57. Diod. XII, 78.
72) Thuc. V, 52.

i) Prodikos of Keos, Suid. s.v., appeared as a diplomatist and orator at Athens in the interest of his native city, Plat. Hipp. Mai. 282 c: highly respected for his wisdom (hence the proverb σοφώτερος Προδίκου Apostol. XVI, 62), he like the other Sophists delivered lectures for a fee, Plat. Cratyl. 384 D, in which amongst other things he treated of the meaning of words and the usages of language, l. c. Prot. 341 c. He was a friend of Sokrates and bore a part in his conversations, Hipp. Mai. l. c. Amongst his auditors were Xenophon, Philostr. V. Soph. I, 12, Kritias, Plat. Charm. p. 163, Theramenes, Suid. s.v. Athen. V, p. 220 D, Thucydides, Vit. Marc. 36, Euripides, Gell. XV, 20 etc. Only reports of his declamations and doctrine have come down to us: his tale of the young Herakles at the cross-roads, entitled Ὥραι, became famous, Xenoph. Memor. II, 1, 21. Suid. s.v. Cic. Off. I, 32. Quint. IX, 2, 36. Maxim. Tyr. Diss. XX, 232 f.

k) See below obs. w.

l) Thucydides, son of Olorus, born probably circ. 460—453 (472 according to the untrustworthy account of Pamphila in Gell. XV, 23) in the Attic deme Halimus, of an influential family, and related to Miltiades, Thuc. IV, 104. Plut. Kim. 4. Thuc. Vit. Marcell. 2, 15. 16. 34. 55. Suid. s.v., is said to have been present on one occasion when Herodotus recited a portion of his history, Vit. Marc. 54. Suid. l. c., and to have been a pupil of the orator Antiphon and the philosopher Anaxagoras, Vit. Marc. 22. Vit. Anon. 2. Suid. l. c. s.v. 'Αντιφῶν, r. 'Αντυλλος. He possessed gold-mines in Thrake, Thuc. IV, 105. Plut. Kim. 4, and married a Thrakian wife from Skapte Hyle, Vit. Marc. 19. At the beginning of the Peloponnesian war he was ill of the plague, Thuc. II, 48; some years later he commanded an Athenian squadron, with which he saved Eion, the port of Amphipolis, but was unable to protect Amphipolis itself against the attack of Brasidas, obs. 53. In 423, he was in consequence accused by Kleon and banished, Vit. Marc. 4. 23. 26. 46. 55. Cic. De Orat. II, 13. Plin. H. N. VII, 111, lived 20 years in banishment, for the most part at Skapte Hyle, Thuc. V, 26. Vit. Marc. 25, 46, where he wrote his history, and only returned to Athens circ. 403, Vit. Marc. 31. 32. 45. 55. Vit. Anon. 10. Plut. Kim. 4. Neither the time nor the manner of his death is established; probably

Olympiad.	B.C.	ATHENS.	HISTORY.	ART AND LITERATURE.
XC, 3	418[73])	Archons. Antiphon.	War between Sparta and Argos[74]). Battle of Mantineia[75]). Argos and Mantineia compelled to conclude a peace and alliance with Sparta[76]).	Hippokrates, Physician[m]).
XC, 4	417[77])	Euphemus.	The democracy overthrown at Argos[78]), but soon restored, and at the same time the alliance with Athens renewed[79]).	The Painters, Apollodorus[n]),

73) Thuc. V, 57—81. Diod. XII, 78—80.
74) The occasion which led to the war was that the Argives, in connexion with the Athenians, had in the previous year repeatedly invaded the territory of Epidaurus, in order to compel the Epidaurians to join their alliance, Thuc. V, 53—56. The Spartans had already in 419 marched out twice to the aid of the Epidaurians, but were on both occasions compelled to return by unfavourable sacrifices, id. 54. 55. In this year a large army from Sparta and all its allies (the Spartans αὐτοὶ καὶ οἱ Εἴλωτες πανδημεί, the Bœotians 5000 hoplites, 5000 light-armed, and 500 horsemen strong, 2000 Corinthian hoplites, Tegeatans, Sikyonians, Pellenians, Phliasians, Megarians, id, 57, στρατόπεδον γὰρ δὴ τοῦτο κάλλιστον Ἑλληνικὸν τῶν μέχρι τοῦδε ξυνῆλθεν, id. 60) mustered under the command of Agis at Phlius, and from thence penetrated by three different ways into Argos, id. 57—59; and the Argives, who were surrounded by their foes and cut off from their town, were in a most critical situation: at this juncture Agis allowed himself to be persuaded by two Argives, who, just like Agis himself, conducted the negotiation on their own private authority alone, to conclude a four months' armistice, with which both parties were discontented, Argives as well as Spartans, id. 60, 63. (In consequence the Spartans ordained, that the king should be accompanied in military expeditions from this time forward by ten commissioners, ξύμβουλοι, id. 63.)
75) Up to this time the Eleans and Mantineians were the only allies of Argos who had taken part in the war; a further force of

he was murdered circ. 400—401, according to some at Athens, according to others at Skapte Hyle, Marc. Vit. Thuc. 32. Plut. Kim. 4. Paus. I, 23, 11. 2, 23. Vit. Anon. 10. His history, Συγγραφὴ περὶ τοῦ πολέμου τῶν Πελοποννησίων καὶ Ἀθηναίων, begun during the war, Cic. l. c. Plin. l. c. Vit. Marc. 23, 47, but not completed till after its conclusion, Thuc. I, 13. 18. II, 54. V, 26, comprises the first 21 years of the war in 8 books; the last of which, however, was never revised. See for the history and the speeches invoven into the narrative, Thuc. I, 20—22 and especially 22—3: κτῆμά τε ἐς ἀεὶ μᾶλλον ἢ ἀγώνισμα ἐς τὸ παραχρῆμα ἀκούειν ξύγκειται. Quintilian passes this criticism on Thucydides, comparing him with Herodotus, X, 1, 73: Densus et brevis et semper instans sibi Thucydides, dulcis et candidus et fusus Herodotus; ille concitatis, hic remissis affectibus melior; ille contionibus, hic sermonibus; ille vi, hic voluptate. Cf. Cic. Brut. 7, 29. (Contemporary historians, writing upon the same periods as Herodotus and Thucydides, are: Kratippus, who supplemented and continued the work of Thucydides, Dion. Hal. De Thuc. Iud. 16, Plut. glor. Athen. I, p. 345, and Stesimbrotus of Thasos, Plut. Kim. 4. Athen. XIII, p. 580 D, who interpreted the Homeric poems at Athens in the manner of the Sophists, Tatian. Or. Adv. Gr. 48. Xen. Symp. III, 6. Vit. Hom. p. 31. Westerm., and composed a treatise Περὶ Θεμιστοκλέους καὶ Θουκυδίδου καὶ Περικλέους, of which Plutarch made use, Athen. l. c. Plut. Them. 2. 24. Kim. 4. 14. 16. Per. 8. 13. 26. 30, and also another Περὶ τελετῶν, Etym. M. p. 465. About the same time Antiochus of Syracuse wrote

1000 hoplites and 300 cavalry now arrived from Athens, and the Athenians (accompanied by Alkibiades as ambassador) prevailed upon the allies to sanction the immediate resumption of the war, Thuc. V, 61. They accordingly attacked and took Orchomenus, id., and then turned to attack Tegea: but from this enterprise the Eleans held themselves aloof, id. 62. The Spartans, summoned to the rescue by Tegea, march out under Agis (who promises to make good his former error, id. 63), and cut their Arkadian allies, and fight the victorious battle of Mantineia with the enemy, id. 68—64. Five-sixths of the whole fighting population of Sparta took part in the battle, id. 64, the number of which according to O. Müller's computation based on Thuc. V, 68 amounted to 4784 men. Id. 75: τὴν ὑπὸ τῶν Ἑλλήνων τότε ἐπιφερομένην αἰτίαν ἔς τε μαλακίαν—καὶ ἐς τὴν ἄλλην ἀβουλίαν καὶ βραδυτῆτα, ἐνὶ ἔργῳ ἂν ἐλύσαντο.
76) Thuc. V, 76—79. 81.
77) Thuc. V, 82—83. Diod. XII, 80—81.
78) Thuc. V, 81. This took place before the end of the winter, but towards spring, id., chiefly through a chosen body of 1000 men, whom the Argives maintained at the cost of the state, Diod. XII, 80.
79) Thuc. V, 82. The record of the alliance Corp. Inscr. Att. n. 50. It was in consequence of this treaty that Argos was connected with the son by long walls, so that the Athenians could bring them help at any time. This gave rise to a fresh campaign against Argos on the part of Sparta, which had no important results, id. 83.

a history of the Sicilians, Diod. XII, 71, and a work Περὶ Ἰταλίας, Strab. V, p. 242. VI, p. 252 ff.)
m) Hippokrates of Kos, the founder of scientific medicine, was sprung from the family of the Asklepiads, in which the art of medicine was hereditary, and flourished circ. 436, Hieron. Ol. 86, 1. p. 107. Gell, XVII, 21, 18. He was a pupil of Demokritus and of the Sophists Gorgias and Prodikus, Suid. s. v., and appears from the intimations given in his writings to have undertaken travels, especially to the countries on the Black Sea, as well as to Thrake and Macedonia. Many kinds of untrustworthy accounts and tales are found of his life; all that is certain is, that he finally practised at Larissa in Thessaly and also died there, Suid. s. v. Amongst the numerous writings attributed to Hippokrates many are from the pen of later authors; the most important of those held to be genuine are: Περὶ ἐπιδημιῶν (concerning epidemics), Προγνωστικά (concerning the diagnosis of diseases), Ἀφορισμοί (short medical precepts), Περὶ διαίτης ὀξέων (concerning the diet in feverish diseases), Περὶ ἀέρων, ὑδάτων, τόπων (concerning the influence of soil and climate on the origin of diseases), Περὶ τῶν ἐν κεφαλῇ τρωμάτων, Περὶ ἀγμῶν (concerning fractures), Περὶ ἱερῆς νούσου (concerning epilepsy). His fame and his teaching reached as far as Persia and Arabia, and the writings attributed to him are translated into Persian and Arabic.
n) Apollodorus of Athens, an elder contemporary and precursor of Zeuxis, Plin. N. H. XXXV, 60. Plut. glor. Athen. p. 362 n, was called

The Incipient Decline. 71

Olympiad	B.C.	ATHENS.	HISTORY.	ART AND LITERATURE.
XCI, 1	416⁸⁰)	Archon. Arimnestus.	Melos taken by the Athenians⁸¹).	Zeuxis^o), Parrhasius^p), Timanthes^q).
XCI, 2-4	415–413		Sicilian Expedition, at the instance of an embassy from the Egestæans, which begged for help against Selinus and Syracuse⁸²).	

80) Thuc. V, 84—VI, 7. Diod. XII, 80—83.
81) Thuc. V, 84—116. In the first years of the war Melos had remained neutral, obs. 1, but after the attack of Nikias in 426 B.C. (obs. 34) it had adopted a hostile attitude, Thuc. V, 84. Especial interest attaches to the present attack as on this occasion the Athenians, in the course of lengthy negotiation with the Melians, lay down their political principles, the sum of which is contained in the words (89): δίκαια μὲν ἐν τῷ ἀνθρωπείῳ λόγῳ ἀπὸ τῆς ἴσης ἀνάγκης κρίνεται, δυνατὰ δὲ οἱ προὔχοντες πράσσουσι καὶ οἱ ἀσθενεῖς ξυγχωροῦσι. The issue of the war is, that the Melians surrender after an obstinate resistance, the males capable of bearing arms are put to death, the rest of the population is sold into slavery, and the territory is divided amongst Athenian citizens, id. 116.
82) The Egestæans were hard pressed by Selinus and Syracuse, Thuc. VI, 6. Their ambassadors (they came to Athens in the winter of 416—415) represented to the Athenians, that the Syracusans, who had already annihilated the town of Leontini (cf. Thuc. V, 4), would subdue the whole of the island, and then lend their support to their kinsfolk, the Spartans; at the same time they promised large pecuniary subsidies, id. An Athenian embassy, which was sent to Egesta to ascertain the truth as to the value of those promises, returned (tricked by the Egestæans, VI, 46) with favourable tidings, and thus the undertaking was determined upon in spite of the opposition of Nikias (his speech VI, 9—14), chiefly at the instigation of Alkibiades (his speech VI, 16—18): a second speech of Nikias, in which he gave prominence to

σκιαγράφος, because he discovered the gradation of colours obtained by distribution of light and shade, Plut. l. c. Schol. II. X, 265. Hesych. s. v. σκιά.

o) Zeuxis of Herakleia (in lower Italy ?), a younger contemporary of Apollodorus, Plin. H. N. XXXV, 61. Æl. V. H. IV, 12, flourished at the time of Sokrates, Plat. Gorg. 453 c. Xen. Memor. I, 4, 3. Œcon. 10. 1, and painted at various places, especially at Ephesus, Tzetz. Chil. VIII, 196. Famous amongst his pictures was the Centaur family, Luc. Zeux. 4 f.; his Helena for the temple of Lakinian Hera, Plin. XXXV, 64. Cic. De Inv. II, 1. Æl. V. H. IV, 12. XIV, 17; an Eros crowned with roses at the temple of Aphrodite at Athens, Schol. Aristoph. Acharn. 991; bunches of grapes so true to nature, that the birds flew to them, Plin. H. N. XXXV, 65; and a boy with bunches of grapes, l. c. 66. He also decorated the palace of Archelaus, king of Macedonia, with paintings, Æl. V. H. XIV, 17. His pictures were characterised by uncommon situations, sensuous beauty, and picturesque illusions produced by effects of light and shade on the colour tones, Aristot. Poet. 6. Plin. XXXV, 61. Cic. l. c. Quint. XII, 10, 5. Many traits are preserved of his pride as an artist, Plin. XXXV, 63. Plut. Per. 13. Æl. l. c.

p) Parrhasius of Ephesus, Suid. s. v. Harpocr. s. v. Athen. XII, p. 543. Strab. p. 462. Plin. XXXV, 60. 67, a rival of Zeuxis at the time of

the difficulties of the undertaking (20—23), had only the effect of kindling still more the zeal of the Athenians, and it was resolved to furnish and provide all that the generals should think necessary, Thuc. VI, 8—26. For the whole Sicilian expedition see Thuc. VI. VII. Diod. XII, 83—XIII, 35, Plut. Nic. 12—30. For the ultimate cause of the undertaking see especially the continuation of the passage cited in obs. 20, Thuc. II, 65 : ἐξ ὧν (viz. in consequence of the corrupting influence of the demagogues on the character of the Athenian people) ἄλλα τε πολλὰ, ὡς ἐν μεγάλῃ πόλει καὶ ἀρχὴν ἐχούσῃ, ἡμαρτήθη καὶ ὁ ἐς Σικελίαν πλοῦς. For the motives of Alkibiades as the prime mover of the expedition see id. VI, 15: ἐνῆγε δὲ προθυμότατα τὴν στρατείαν Ἀλκιβιάδης ὁ Κλεινίου, βουλόμενος τῷ τε Νικίᾳ ἐναντιοῦσθαι, ὧν καὶ ἐς τἆλλα διάφορος τὰ πολιτικὰ καὶ ὅτι αὐτοῦ διαβόλως ἐμνήσθη, καὶ μάλιστα στρατηγῆσαί τε ἐπιθυμῶν καὶ ἐλπίζων Σικελίαν τε δι' αὐτοῦ καὶ Καρχηδόνα λήψεσθαι καὶ τὰ ἴδια ἅμα εὐτυχήσας χρήμασί τε καὶ δόξῃ ὠφελήσειν. Alkibiades himself at a later period represents the Athenian plans to the Lacedæmonians in the following way, id. 80: ἐπλεύσαμεν ἐς Σικελίαν πρῶτον μέν, εἰ δυναίμεθα, Σικελιώτας καταστρεψόμενοι, μετὰ δὲ ἐκείνους αὖθις καὶ Ἰταλιώτας, ἔπειτα καὶ τῆς Καρχηδονίων ἀρχῆς καὶ αὐτῶν ἀποπειράσοντες· εἰ δὲ προχωρήσειε ταῦτα ἢ πάντα ἢ καὶ τὰ πλείω, ἤδη τῇ Πελοποννήσῳ ἐμέλλομεν ἐπιχειρήσειν, κομίσαντες ξύμπασαν μὲν τὴν ἐκεῖθεν προσγενομένην δύναμιν τῶν Ἑλλήνων, πολλοὺς δὲ βαρβάρους μισθωσάμενοι καὶ Ἴβηρας κ. τ. λ., and that the Athenians from the very beginning aimed at least at the whole of Sicily, is expressly attested by Thucyd. VI, 6; such were the plans, with which they busied the Peloponnesian war, Quint. XII, 10, 4, lived a considerable time at Athens, Senec. Controv. V, 10. Acron. Hor. Od. IV, 8, 6. Xenoph. Memor. III, 10. Famous amongst his pictures were the Athenian Demus, Plin. XXXV, 69, and a curtain, so deceptively painted, that Zeuxis took it for an actual curtain, and gave it the preference over his own grapes, l. c. 65. His pictures are praised for delicate individualisation of characters, correctness of drawing, exactness of proportions, as also for the delicate handling of light effects, l. c. 67. Acron. Hor. l. c. His presumption and vanity as an artist were notorious, Plin. XXXV, 71, Æl. V. H. IX, 11. Athen. XII, p. 543 c. XV, p. 687 b.

q) Timanthes, probably of Kythnus, was a contemporary of Parrhasius, over whom he obtained a brilliant victory with his picture of the contest between Aias and Odysseus for the arms of Achilles, Plin. XXXV, 72. Æl. V. H. IX, 11. Athen. XII, p. 543. He likewise carried off the prize against Kolotes of Teos with his famous picture of Iphigeneia standing at the sacrificial altar, where the artist depicted Agamemnon with veiled countenance, not delineating the father's grief, but leaving it to the imagination, Plin. XXV, 73. Cic. Orat. 22. Quint. II, 13. Some of the motives of this picture of Timanthes are reproduced in a wall painting of Pompeii, Müller and Oesterley, Denkmäler I, no. 200. His genius chiefly proved itself in the circumstance that his pictures expressed more than his brush had actually depicted, Plin. l. c.

FOURTH PERIOD. 431—338 B.C.

Olympiad.	B.C.	ATHENS.	HISTORY.
		Archons.	
XCI, 2	415[86])	Chabrias.	The Athenians sail with a fleet of 134 ships and numerous troops to Sicily under the command of Nikias, Alkibiades, and Lamachus[84]), but at first owing to the disunion amongst the commanders[85]) and the recall of Alkibiades, which took place soon afterwards[86]), they make but little progress[87]). Victory of the Athenians at Syracuse, with no important result[88]).
XCI, 3	414[89])	Teisandrus.	After the arrival of reinforcements from Athens[90]) Nikias advances upon Syracuse, takes Epipolæ, the height commanding the town, and after gaining the upper hand in the open field begins from this point to

themselves, although most of them were totally unacquainted with the size and circumstances of Sicily, id. 1. It is further a remarkable circumstance in this connexion, that at this time, as is proved by the inscription cited in obs. 62, not only had the sums borrowed from the temples been repaid, but 3000 talents had also been again deposited in the state treasury.

83) Thuc. VI, 8—93. Diod. XII, 83—XIII, 6. Plut. Nic. 12—16. Alc. 17—23.

84) Of the 134 triremes 100 were furnished by Athens, 34 by the allies; besides the rowers, there were on board 5100 hoplites (2200 from Athens, 500 from Argos etc.), 480 bowmen, 700 Rhodian slingers, only 30 horsemen. The departure from Athens took place in the middle of the summer; the ships and crews of the allied forces put in at Kerkyra, Thuc. VI, 30, 42—43. The Athenian fleet was fitted out with extraordinary care and magnificence, id. 30—31.

85) The fleet sailed from Kerkyra to Italy and along the coast, without being received by any of the Italian towns, as far as Rhegium, where the inhabitants likewise refused to receive the army into the town, Thuc. VI, 44. There they gained intelligence of the trick played upon them by the Egestæans, id. 46, cf. obs. 82; in the council of war, which then followed, Nikias proposed to sail to Egesta, adjust its quarrel with Selinus, and then return home. Alkibiades insisted that they should first establish themselves in Sicily by intriguing with the rest of the towns and then attack Syracuse; whilst Lamachus declared for an immediate attack upon Syracuse while still unprepared, id. 47—49. Lamachus, however, went over to the opinion of Alkibiades, which accordingly prevailed: thereupon the Athenians sailed to Naxos, which joined them voluntarily, and won over Katana as well by trickery, id. 50—51,

86) Thuc. VI, 27—29, 53, 60—61. Andoc. de myst. p. 2—9 (§ 11—69 Bekk.). Plu'. Alc. 18—22. Already before the departure of the fleet the Hermes-pillars at Athens were mutilated in one night, and the opponents of Alkibiades utilised this opportunity to make him suspected with the populace. However, the charge, when Alkibiades came openly forward to meet it, was for the time withdrawn. After his departure the popular agitation induced by the occurrence was yet further heightened by the announcement that the Eleusinian mysteries had been mocked and desecrated by being parodied in private

houses. It was generally thought that these proceedings were connected with traitorous plans for the overthrow of the democracy (Thuc. VI, 28. 60: τῶντα αὐτοῖς ἐδόκει ἐπὶ ξυνωμοσίᾳ ὀλιγαρχικῇ καὶ τυραννικῇ πεπρᾶχθαι). The prosecution of Hermokopidæ was now, it is true, brought to an end by the information furnished by Andokides, Thuc. VI, 60. Andoc. de myst. p. 5—9 (§ 34—69). de red. s. p. 20 (§ 7—9). Plut. Alc. 21: nevertheless the prosecution on account of the mysteries was continued, and Alkibiades recalled in consequence, Thuc. VI, 61, Plut. Alc. 22. Alkibiades obeyed the summons of the Salaminian vessel despatched for the purpose, but seized an opportunity for escape during a landing at Thurii: the Athenians then condemned him to death in his absence, Thuc. VI, 61. Plut. Alc. 22.

87) The summer passed, and they had only made a fruitless attempt to win over Kamarina, Thuc. VI, 52; after which they sailed along the north coast of the island to Egesta, took a small town, Hykkara, but on the other hand made unsuccessful attacks on Himera and Hybla, id. 62.

88) Thuc. VI, 63—71. The battle was won in the winter by a stratagem; after it the Athenians returned back to Naxos and Katana, to winter there, id. 72. Subsequently the Athenians were again disappointed in a design upon Messene, id. 74. But the Syracusans utilised the delay of the Athenians, above all at the instigation of Hermokrates, who had at an earlier period called attention to the danger threatening from Athens and recommended energetic measures (id. 32—41); by reducing the number of generals from 15 to 3 they obtained greater unity in the conduct of the war, id. 73, they extended the town walls so as to include the quarter Temenites, id. 75, and sent ambassadors to Corinth and Sparta, to beg for assistance; there they found a zealous advocate in Alkibiades, id. 73. 88—93 (who had gone from Thurii by way of Kyllene to Sparta, id. 88). Meanwhile the Athenians gained some support from the Sicilians living in the interior of the island, id. 88 : besides which they were actually suing for the alliance of Carthage and Tyrrhenia, id.

89) Thuc. VI, 94—VII, 18. Plut. Nic. 17—20. Diod. VIII, 7—9.

90) Thuc. VI, 74. 98. 94. The reinforcements consisted of 250 horsemen (without horses), 30 mounted bowmen, and 300 talents, 94. The cavalry was soon afterwards further strengthened by 300 horsemen from Egesta and 100 from Naxos and other Sicilian towns, id. 98.

Olympiad.	B. C.	ATHENS.	HISTORY.
		Archon.	
XCI, 3	414		shut in the town with walls[91]). But, when the circumvallation is nearly completed[91]), the Spartiate Gylippus comes with help from the Peloponnese[93]), defeats the Athenians and throws them back on the defensive[94]).
			The Athenians harass the coast of Lakonia with hostile landings, and thus lead up to the renewal of open and direct war with Sparta[95]).
XCI, 4	413[96])	Kleokritus.	Dekeleia in Attic territory occupied by the Spartans[97]).

91) Thuc. VI, 96—103. Epipolæ was an elevated plain, which immediately adjoined the town to the westward, rising in the form of a triangle, of which Euryelus was the apex to the west, and falling precipitously on every side (ὠνόμασται ὑπὸ τῶν Συρακοσίων διὰ τὸ ἐπιπολῆς τοῦ ἄλλου εἶναι Ἐπιπολαί), id. 96. The Athenians forestalled the Syracusans in occupying the height, to the importance of which the attention of the latter was only drawn when too late, defeated a detachment of Syracusans, which at the last moment attempted to dispute the possession, id. 96—97, then began to build the wall of circumvallation, defeated the Syracusans in a cavalry encounter, id. 98, destroyed a line of cross-works, by which the Syracusans tried to intercept the Athenian wall, and inflicted fresh losses upon them on the occasion, id. 99—100; when they had completed more than half the wall on Epipolæ, and had further gained a new victory over the Syracusans, (in which Lamachus was killed), and their fleet had entered the great harbour, they then continued the walls southwards on the low ground toward the great harbour, id. 101—102. Their success procured them increasing numbers of allies: for not only did many of the Sicilian appear in their camp, but 3 pentekonters also arrived from Tyrrhenia (cf. obs. 89), id. 103.

92) Thuc. VII, 2: ἐντὰ μὲν ἢ ὀκτὼ σταδίων ἤδη ἐτετέλεστο τοῖς Ἀθηναίοις ἐς τὸν μέγαν λιμένα διπλοῦν τεῖχος, πλὴν κατὰ βραχύ τι τὸ πρὸς τὴν θάλασσαν, τοῦτο δ' ἔτι ᾠκοδόμουν· τῷ δὲ ἄλλῳ τοῦ κύκλου πρὸς τὸν Τρώγιλον ἐπὶ τὴν ἐτέραν θάλασσαν λίθοι τε παραβεβλημένοι τῷ πλέονι ἤδη ἦσαν, καὶ ἔστιν ἃ καὶ ἡμίεργα, τὰ δὲ καὶ ἐξειργασμένα κατελείπετο. παρὰ τοσοῦτον μὲν Συράκουσαι ἦλθον κινδύνου. Thus the Syracusans were already beginning to negotiate amongst themselves and with Nikias about surrender, id. VI, 103, VII, 2.

93) Thuc. VI, 93. 104. VII, 1—2. 7. Gylippus precedes with 4 ships, at first only with the intention of protecting the towns in Italy; for, from the intelligence he had received about Syracuse, circumstances there were hopeless, id. 104; he then continues his voyage to Himera, (Nikias omitted to prevent him, id.), lands there, draws some 2000 men to his standard from Himera, Selinus, Gela, and other towns, and with these and his own troops (700 men) marches for Syracuse, into which he forces his way at the spot not yet fortified by the Athenians, id. VII, 1—2. Before this event, the Corinthian Gongylus had already entered the harbour of Syracuse with a single trireme and had brought the news of the aid approaching, id. 2; still later there came 12 more ships, for the most part Corinthian, id. 7.

94) Gylippus upon his entry into Syracuse, as soon as he had united his troops with the Syracusans, prepared to offer battle to the Athenians, but neither army would begin the attack: on the next day he took fort Labdalum, an important Athenian position, Thuc. VII, 3; he then began to build a cross wall to cut the Athenian fortifications, id. 4, and though he was defeated in the next battle, id. 5, he made a fresh attack upon the Athenians, defeated them and now completed the wall he had begun, which rendered it impossible for the Athenians to complete the circumvallation, id. 6. Gylippus next traversed the other Sicilian towns, to stir them up to the warm support of Syracuse, id. 7.; and the result was that nearly the whole of Sicily rose against the Athenians, id. 15; applications were again made to Corinth and Sparta, id. 7. 17, and Syracuse itself began to fit out its ships to try conclusions with the Athenians by sea as well as by land, id. 7. Nikias fortified Plemmyrium at the entrance of the harbour, προσεῖχέ τε ἤδη μᾶλλον τῷ κατὰ θάλασσαν πολέμῳ, ὁρῶν τὰ ἐκ τῆς γῆς σφίσιν, ἐπειδὴ Γύλιππος ἧκεν, ἀνελπιστότερα ὄντα, id. 4, and sent messengers with a letter to Athens, in which he described his distressed situation (see esp. id. 11: ξυμβέβηκέ τε πολιορκεῖν δοκοῦντας ἡμᾶς ἄλλους αὐτοὺς μᾶλλον ὅσα γε κατὰ γῆν τοῦτο πάσχειν), and begged the Athenians either to recall him and the whole of the army or send considerable reinforcements id. 8. 10—15. The Athenians chose the latter alternative, and during the winter sent Eurymedon with 10 ships and 20 talents in advance. Demosthenes was to follow with the main force in the spring, id. 16. The further prayer of Nikias, that he might be released from the command, was not granted, but Menander and Euthydemus were appointed joint commanders with him; later Eurymedon and Demosthenes were to share the command with him, id. 16.

95) Thuc. VI, 105. cf. V, 25, VII, 18, and obs. 63.

96) Thuc. VII, 19—VIII, 6. Plut. Nic. 20—30. Diod. XIII, 10—33.

97) This was done at the advice of Alkibiades. Thuc. VI, 91. 93. VII, 18, at the very beginning of the spring, id. 19. Dekeleia was only 120 stadia distant from Athens, ἐπὶ δὲ τῷ πεδίῳ καὶ τῆς χώρας τοῖς κρατίστοις ἐς τὸ κακουργεῖν ᾠκοδομεῖτο τὸ τεῖχος, ἐπιφανὲς μέχρι τῆς τῶν Ἀθηναίων πόλεως, id. For the losses thus inflicted on the town (the total devastation of the country, desertion of slaves, obstruction of supplies from Euboea, etc.), id. 27—28. 28: τῶν τε πάντων ὁμοίως ἐπακτῶν ἐδεῖτο ἡ πόλις καὶ ἀντὶ τοῦ πόλις εἶναι φρούριον κατέστη.

Olympiad.	B.C.	ATHENS.	HISTORY.
XCI, 4	413	Archon.	Demosthenes arrives with a fleet of 73 ships and an army before Syracuse to the support of Nikias[98]). He makes an attack upon the Syracusan fortifications on Epipolæ, which fails[99]); the fleet is defeated in the harbour, and itself blockaded there in consequence; after which the whole Athenian army upon its retreat into the interior is either cut down or captured[100]).
			c) The Dekeleian War[101]). The last efforts of Athens up till the surrender of the city, 412—404.
XCII, 1	412[102])	Kallias.	Most of the former allies of Athens, in particular Euboea, Lesbos, Chios, Erythræ, solicit alliance with Sparta[103]). Sparta, in alliance with the

---

98) For the expedition of Demosthenes s. Thuc. VII, 20. 26. 31. 33. 35. His arrival with 73 triremes and 5000 hoplites, furnished partly by Athens, partly by allies, and numerous light-armed troops, id. 42. Meanwhile the Peloponnesians also had made preparations to send aid to the Syracusans, id. 17. 19. 31, and a part of those auxiliaries had already reached Syracuse, id. 25, the others came somewhat later, id. 50; further Gylippus had returned to Syracuse with numerous reinforcements from the Sicilian towns, id. 21, cf. n. 94; the Syracusan fleet had ventured to defy the Athenians, and had been worsted in a first battle, id. 21—23, but had afterwards won a brilliant victory, id. 37—41. In addition to this, Gylippus made an attack upon Plemmyrium simultaneously with the first sea-fight, which resulted in its capture, id. 23. 24. The consequence of all which was that the Syracusans τὴν ἐλπίδα ἤδη ἐχυρὰν εἶχον ταῖς μὲν ναυσὶ καὶ πολὺ κρείσσους εἶναι, ἐδόκουν δὲ καὶ τὸν πεζὸν χειρώσεσθαι, id. 41. The arrival of Demosthenes restored the balance of power, at least for the moment, and reduced the Syracusans from their sense of superiority to their old doubts and apprehensions.

99) Thuc. VII, 43—45.

100) The advice of Demosthenes, to set sail and return to Athens with the fleet and army immediately after the failure of the attack on Epipolæ, frustrated by the unhappy procrastination of Nikias, Thuc. VII, 46—49; sickness amongst the Athenians, id. 47; fresh reinforcements on the side of the Syracusans, id. 50; resolution to set out for Thapsus or Katana, and frustration of the plan by an eclipse of the moon (on August 27th 413 B.C.) and the superstition of Nikias, id.; naval victory of the Syracusans, id. 51—54; blockade of the harbour, id. 56. 59; unsuccessful attempt of the Athenians to break through, id. 61—71; after a delay of two days, again caused by the procrastination of Nikias, a start made by land, to seek a place of refuge in the interior of the island, and after six days wandering up and down, the whole army overpowered, id. 72—85. Nikias and Demosthenes executed, id. 86—87. Plut. Nic. 28—29. (At its departure from Syracuse the army was still 40,000 strong, Thuc. VII, 75; the number of prisoners brought to Syracuse amounted to

7000, id. 87. The states, which sent help to the one or the other party, are enumerated id. 57—58; they are, on the side of the Athenians: Lemnos, Imbros, Ægina, Hestiæa, Eretria, Chalkis, Styra, Karistos, Kos, Andros, Tenedos, Miletus, Samos, Chios, Methymna, Ænus, Rhodes, Kythera, Argos, Kephallonia, Zakynthos, Korkyra, Naupaktus, Mantineia, Kreta, Thurii, Metapontium, Naxos, Katana, and in addition, Plataeans, Æolians, Akarnanians, Sicilians, Tyrrhenians; on the side of the Syracusans: the Greek towns in Sicily with the exception of Naxos and Katana; further Sparta, Corinth, Sikyon, Leukas, Ambrakia, the Boeotians, Arcadian mercenaries and Sicilians.)

101) So called according to Diod. XIII, 9. Harpocr. s. v. Δεκελεικὸς πόλεμος. Pomp. Trog. Prol. lib. v. So in Isokr. 166 D. Demosth. Androt. § 15, p. 597. de Cor. 96.

102) Thuc. VIII, 7—60. Diod. XIII, 34. 36. 37.

103) For the position of Athens in general after the Sicilian disaster s. Thuc. VIII, 1: Πάντα δὲ πανταχόθεν αὐτοὺς ἐλύπει τε καὶ περιειστήκει ἐπὶ τῷ γεγενημένῳ φόβος τε καὶ κατάπληξις μεγίστη δή· ἅμα μὲν γὰρ στερόμενοι καὶ ἰδίᾳ ἕκαστοι καὶ ἡ πόλις ὁπλιτῶν τε πολλῶν καὶ ἱππέων καὶ ἡλικίας οἵαν οὐχ ἑτέραν ἑώρων ὑπάρχουσαν, ἐβαρύνοντο, ἅμα δὲ ναῦς οὐχ ὁρῶντες ἐν τοῖς νεωσοίκοις ἱκανὰς οὐδὲ χρήματα ἐν τῷ κοινῷ οὐδ' ὑπηρεσίας ταῖς ναυσὶν ἀνέλπιστοι ἦσαν ἐν τῷ παρόντι σωθήσεσθαι, τούς τε ἀπὸ τῆς Σικελίας πολεμίους εὐθὺς σφίσιν ἐνόμιζον τῷ ναυτικῷ ἐπὶ τὸν Πειραιᾶ πλευσεῖσθαι, ἄλλως τε καὶ τοσοῦτον κρατήσαντας—καὶ τοὺς ξυμμάχους σφῶν μετ' αὐτῶν ἀποστάντας· ὅμως δὲ ἐκ τῶν ὑπαρχόντων ἐδόκει χρῆναι μὴ ἐνδιδόναι—. A commission of 10 persons was chosen to conduct affairs at this extraordinary juncture, id., and, to remedy the deficiency of supplies, it was determined (in the summer) that a sum of 1000 talents, which had been set aside at the beginning of the war to meet any desperate emergency, should be put in use, id. VIII, 15, cf. II, 24. For the inclination of the allies to revolt generally s. id. VIII, 2, and for the embassies sent from Euboea, Lesbos, Chios, Erythræ to Agis or Sparta, id. 5. Moreover, both the Persian satraps in Asia Minor, Tissaphernes and Pharnabazus, vied with one another in their efforts to secure the Spartan alliance, id. 5. 6.

The Incipient Decline.

Olympiad.	B.C.	ATHENS.	HISTORY.	ART AND LITERATURE.
XCII, 1	412	Archon.	Persian satrap Tissaphernes[104], gradually brings Chios, Erythræ, Klazomenæ[105], Teos[106], Miletus[107], Lebedos, Eræ[108], Lesbos[109], and also Rhodes in the course of the winter[110], to revolt from Athens. Athens, by degrees collecting a fleet to oppose the Spartans of more than 100 ships[111], retakes Teos, Lesbos, and Klazomenæ[112], and attacks Chios[113]). Alkibiades, who had taken refuge with Tissaphernes from the machinations of the Lacedæmonians[114], negotiates with the Athenians at Samos for his recall[115]). Preparations for the overthrow of the democracy at Athens[116]).	
XCII, 2	411[117])	Theopompus.	Oropus wrested from the Athenians by the Bœotians[118]).	Artistic political

---

104) They first decided in favour of Tissaphernes, Thuc. VIII, 6, and by the end of the winter 411 B.C. three conventions were concluded with him, id. 18. 37. 58. The two first of these ceded back to the king all that he and his forefathers possessed: afterwards the Spartans thought this unworthy of them (id. 43: δεινὸν εἶναι εἰ χώρας ὅσης βασιλεὺς καὶ οἱ πρόγονοι ἦρξαν πρότερον, ταύτης καὶ νῦν ἀξιώσει κρατεῖν· ἐνῆν γὰρ καὶ νήσους ἀπάσας πάλιν δουλεύειν καὶ Θεσσαλίαν καὶ Λοκροὺς καὶ τὰ μέχρι Βοιωτῶν, καὶ ἀντ' ἐλευθερίας ἂν Μηδικὴν ἀρχὴν τοῖς Ἕλλησι τοὺς Λακεδαιμονίους περιθεῖναι), and therefore made the third convention, by which, however, the whole of Asia was still made over to the king. In return Tissaphernes promised to furnish them with pay.
105) Thuc. VIII, 11—14. This important acquisition (for the power and flourishing condition of Chios at that time, id. 15. 24. 45) was won for the Spartans chiefly through Alkibiades, owing to whose successful interposition the Spartans sailed in advance with 5 ships and induced the Chians to revolt, when the rest of the fleet destined to cooperate with them was detained by the Athenians, id. 7—11.
106) Thuc. VIII, 16.
107) Thuc. VIII, 17.
108) Thuc. VIII, 19.
109) Thuc. VIII, 22—23.
110) Thuc. VIII, 44.
111) Little by little the Athenians sent against the enemy in the archipelago, first 8 ships under Strombichides, Thuc. VIII, 15. 16, then 10 under Thrasykles, id. 17, 16 under Diomedon, id. 19, 10 under Leon, id. 23, 48 under Phyrnichus, Onomakles, and Skironides, together with 3500 hoplites (1000 from Athens, 1500 from Argos, 1000 from other allies), id. 25, and lastly 35 under Charminus, Strombichides, and Euktemon, id. 30. After all these detachments had been sent, on one occasion 104 ships appear united at one point, id. 30.
112) Thuc. VIII, 20. 23.
113) Thuc. VIII, 24. 30. 38. 40. 55. The Athenians are in possession of several strongholds in the island, from which they press the town hard. They have their headquarters at this time regularly at Samos, id. 21.

114) Thuc. VIII, 45. Plut. Alc. 24.
115) Thuc. VIII, 45—52. Plut. Alc. 24—26. Alkibiades induced Tissaphernes to hang back in his support of the Spartans, and, instead of aiding them to conquer Athens by his assistance, to allow both belligerents mutually to exhaust themselves with the war: then he deluded the Athenians at Samos with the hope of Persia's aid, which he promised to obtain for them, if they would only change the constitution, Thuc. VIII, 48: ὁ Ἀλκιβιάδης, ὅπερ καὶ ἦν, οὐδὲν μᾶλλον ὀλιγαρχίας ἢ δημοκρατίας δεῖσθαι ἐδόκει αὐτῷ (τῷ Φρυνίχῳ) ἢ ἄλλο τι σκοπεῖσθαι ἢ ὅτῳ τρόπῳ ἐκ τοῦ παρόντος κόσμου τὴν πόλιν μεταστήσας ὑπὸ τῶν ἑταίρων παρακληθεὶς κάτεισι.
116) Peisander is sent to Athens by the fleet at Samos, which is inclined to fall in with the proposals of Alkibiades, in order to bring about the recall of Alkibiades and the change in the constitution, Thuc. VIII, 49. The populace, which also on its part was not unfavourable, gives him plenary power to negotiate with Alkibiades and Tissaphernes, id. 53—54. 54: καὶ ὁ μὲν Πείσανδρος τάς τε ξυνωμοσίας, αἵπερ ἐτύγχανον πρότερον ἐν τῇ πόλει οὖσαι ἐπὶ δίκαις καὶ ἀρχαῖς, ἁπάσας ἐπελθὼν καὶ παρακελευσάμενος ὅπως ξυστραφέντες καὶ κοινῇ βουλευσάμενοι καταλύσουσι τὸν δῆμον, καὶ τἆλλα παρασκευάσας ἐπὶ τοῖς παροῦσιν ὥστε μηκέτι διαμέλλεσθαι, αὐτὸς μετὰ τῶν δέκα ἀνδρῶν τὸν πλοῦν ὡς τὸν Τισσαφέρνην ποιεῖται. Alkibiades is at first able to put off the Athenians with false hopes, id. 56. (Tissaphernes, not to estrange the Spartans too widely, concludes with them the third convention mentioned above in obs. 104.)
117) Thuc. VIII, 61 to the end. Xen. Hell. I, 1. The events related from § 11 of the first chapter of the Hellenika up to the end must be placed towards the end of the winter 411/0, see obs. 129, and therefore according to the Thucydidean method of reckoning the years, which Xenophon too follows in both the first two books, still belong to the year 411, but according to calendar years to the year 410. Diod. XII, 38—46. Plut. Alc. 26—27. In Diodorus the events of this year are distributed over two archonships: the case is the same with regard to the occurrences of the year 406: conversely under the years 400 and 408 are comprehended the events of two years.
118) Thuc. VIII, 60: τελευτῶντος ἤδη τοῦ χειμῶνος.

10—2

Olympiad.	B.C.	HISTORY.	ART AND LITERATURE.
XCII, 2	411	The democracy overthrown at Athens by Peisander, Antiphon, Phrynichus, and Theramenes; and an oligarchic council of 400 members instituted [119]). Split between the town and fleet, which latter declares in favour of the democracy [120]). Alkibiades recalled by the fleet [121]). The oligarchy in the town is overthrown again	Oratory: Antiphon [r]), Andokides [s]), Lysias [t]).

119) Thuc. VIII, 63—69. Lys. adv. Eratosth. p. 126 (§ 65—67). The appointment of the 400 took place, after the people had been intimidated by the Hetaeriae (Thuc. l. c. 66, cf. obs. 116), the method being as follows: 5 πρόεδροι are appointed; they choose 100 members, and the hundred 3 members each, Thuc. l. c. 67. The 400 were further to institute a popular assembly of 5000 citizens; but this was never done, id. The heads and leaders of the revolution named above are described id. 68. By these same men the revolution was

carried out in several of the allied states; the result of which was, that several of these states, in particular Thasos, immediately upon the institution of the oligarchy, revolted and went over to Sparta, id. 64.
120) Thuc. VIII, 72—77. In bringing about this alteration in the feelings of the fleet and its return to democracy Thrasyllus and Thrasybulus displayed the greatest activity, id. 75.
121) Thuc. VIII, 81—82.

r) Antiphon, of the deme Rhamnus in Attica, born circ. 480 B.C., Suid. v. Harpocr. v. Antiph. Vit. a'. Westerm., instructed by his father the sophist Sophilus, Ant. Vit. a'. β'. IV, opened a school of oratory at Athens, Plut. de glor. Athen. p. 350, where Thucydides was one of his pupils and admirers, Ant. Vit. a'. β'. Thuc. VIII, 68, and took fees for composing forensic speeches for defendants, Phot. Bibl. Cod. 300, on which account he was ridiculed by the comic poet Plato, Ant. Vit. a'. Philostr. Ant. Vit. XV. p. 498. He never spoke in the popular assembly on questions of state, nor as attorney in the law-courts, except once in his own behalf, when accused of high treason, Thuc. l. c. Cic. Brut. 12; it is said that in the Peloponnesian war he distinguished himself, not only as a diplomatist and ambassador, but also as a general and admiral, and that he fitted out ships of war at his own expense, Ant. Vit. a'. Philostr. l. c. He was the mainspring of the movement that overthrew the democratic constitution and set up the select board of 400 citizens, Thuc. l. c. Ant. Vit. β'. Philostr. l. c. cf. obs. 119. After the restoration of the democracy he was charged with high treason at the instance of Theramenes, and in spite of his able defence was condemned and executed; his property was confiscated, his house pulled down, and his children punished with atimia, Ant. Vit. a'. Lysias adv. Eratosth. p. 427. Thuc. l. c. Cic. l. c. The ancients knew a τέχνη ῥητορική by Antiphon and 35 speeches esteemed genuine, Ant. Vit. a'. Quint. III, 1, 11. Of his speeches 15 are preserved, three probably written for actual criminal suits (the most famous of them Περὶ τοῦ Ἡρώδου φόνου); the other twelve are model speeches on fictitious cases, each set of four speeches comprising two speeches for the prosecution and two for the defence on one and the same case. On account of his eloquence he received the name of Nestor, and he was the oldest of the 10 Attic orators adopted in the canon of the Alexandrines, Ant. Vit. a'. Philostr. l. c. For the character of his eloquence cf. Dion. Hal. de Is. 20: 'Αντιφῶν γε μὴν τὸ αὐστηρὸν μόνον καὶ ἀρχαῖον, ἀγωνιστὴς δὲ λόγων οὔτε δικανικῶν οὔτε συμβουλευτικῶν ἐστιν.

s) Andokides, son of Leogoras, born 444—441 B.C. (de redit. 7. de myst. 117 ff. 148, 448 as the year of his birth is incorrect), was closely identified with the political events of his time. He commanded the Athenian flotilla, which aided the Kerkyraeans against the Corinthians, l. c. Thuc. I, 51, was afterwards implicated in the prosecution of the Hermokopidae, and in. spite of his denunciation of the guilty parties was punished with the loss of civic rights, obs. 86. He

then undertook sea voyages in the course of commercial speculations, And. Vit. de myst. § 137. Ps.-Lys. c. Andoc. § 6. And. de red. § 11 f; but returned to Athens during the rule of the 400, was imprisoned, escaped out of prison to Elis, and did not return home till after the downfall of the thirty in company with Thrasybulus, And. Vit. But his ill success in an embassy to Sparta during the Corinthian war brought down banishment upon him anew, in which he probably died, l. c. Four speeches have come down to us under his name, which are not without importance for the history of the time: Περὶ τῆς ἑαυτοῦ καθόδου, Περὶ τῶν μυστηρίων, Περὶ τῆς πρὸς Λακεδαιμονίους εἰρήνης, of which however the genuineness is doubted, and the speech κατ' 'Αλκιβιάδου, which is decidedly not from his pen. He belonged to the canon of the ten Attic orators. Of the style of his speeches it is said, And. Vit.: ἔστι δ' ἁπλοῦς καὶ ἀκατάσκευος ἐν τοῖς λόγοις, ἀφελὴς τε καὶ ἀσχημάτιστος.

t) Lysias, son of the Syracusan Kephalus, who came and settled at Athens, born 459 B.C. ([Plut.] Vit. Lys., according to modern critics 432) at Athens, at the age of 15 joined the Athenian colony sent to Thurii, where he enjoyed the instruction of Tisias, and lived for 32 years. After the defeat of the Athenians at Syracuse he was obliged to leave Thurii on account of his Athenian sympathies, returned to Athens, and laboured there as an orator and teacher of rhetoric, Vit. Lys. a'. β'. Western. Imprisoned under the rule of the thirty as an enemy of the government, he saved himself by escaping to Megara; but his property was confiscated, obs. 153. He then supported the undertaking of Thrasybulus against the tyrants by contributions of money, and after their downfall lived at Athens in retirement from the activity of public life, as civic rights had not been conferred upon him. He died 379 B.C. Vit. Lys. β'. Phot. bibl. cod. 262. Cic. Brut. 12. The ancient critics recognised 233 speeches by him as genuine, Vit. Lys. β', Phot. l.c. Of these, 35 are preserved (amongst them some not genuine), chiefly forensic speeches, but nevertheless very important in part for the history of the time, and fragments of from fifty to sixty of the rest, cf. Or. Att. Bekker I, p. 399 f.; probably the speech against Eratosthenes was the only one that he himself delivered. Cicero says of him, Brut. g: egregie subtilis scriptor atque elegans, quem jam prope audeas oratorem perfectum dicere. Cf. Quint. X, 1, 78. XII, 10, 24. Dionys. Hal. περὶ τῶν ἀρχαίων ῥητόρων ὑπομνηματισμοί.

The Incipient Decline.

Olympiad.	B.C.	ATHENS.	HISTORY.
		Archon.	
XCII, 2	411		from its being suspected of traitorous relations with Sparta[122], and the democracy restored[123]). Euboea is lost to Athens[124]). The Spartan fleet, renouncing its connexion with Tissaphernes, betakes itself to the Hellespont to Pharnabazus[125]). The Athenians follow[126]) and win two naval victories at Kynossema[127]).
XCII, 3	410[128])	Glaukippus.	The Spartan fleet is totally annihilated by the brilliant victory of the Athenians gained under the command of Alkibiades at Kyzikus[129]). The Athenians masters of the sea[130]).

122) Immediately after the institution of the oligarchic senate, ambassadors were sent to Agis and to Sparta to negotiate a peace, but without success, Thuc. VIII, 70—71. And when after this the rupture between town and fleet had taken place, and an attempt at mediation had come to nothing, id. 72. 86. 89, the oligarchs tried to secure peace with Sparta at any price for the sake of their own safety, and with this object built the fort Eetioneia at the entrance of the Peiraeus, to give them, as it was universally believed, the command of the harbour and enable them to admit into it with security a Spartan fleet for their support, id. 90—92. 91: ἐκεῖνοι γὰρ μάλιστα μὲν ἐβούλοντο ὀλιγαρχούμενοι ἄρχειν καὶ τῶν ξυμμάχων, εἰ δὲ μή, τάς τε ναῦς καὶ τὰ τείχη ἔχοντες αὐτονομεῖσθαι, ἐξειργόμενοι δὲ καὶ τούτου μὴ οὖν ὑπὸ τοῦ δήμου γε αὖθις γενομένου αὐτοὶ πρὸ τῶν ἄλλων μάλιστα διαφθαρῆναι, ἀλλὰ καὶ τοὺς πολεμίους ἐσαγαγόμενοι ἄνευ τειχῶν καὶ νεῶν ξυμβῆναι καὶ ὁπωσοῦν τὰ τῆς πόλεως ἔχειν, εἰ τοῖς γε σώμασι σφῶν ἄδεια ἔσται.

123) An opposition party had been formed in the ranks of the oligarchs themselves, which, with Theramenes for its chief leader, taking advantage of the popular discontent, now effected the counter-revolution, Thuc. VIII, 89—94. Lys. adv. Eratosth. p. 126. In consequence of this the council of 500 was restored, and the popular assembly of the 5000 was instituted, Thuc. l. c. 97. id.; καὶ οὐχ ἥκιστα δὴ τὸν πρῶτον χρόνον ἐπί γ' ἐμοῦ Ἀθηναῖοι φαίνονται εὖ πολιτεύσαντες (i. e. the Athenians displayed excellent management in their political affairs). μετρία γὰρ ἥ τε ἐς τοὺς ὀλίγους καὶ τοὺς πολλοὺς ξύγκρασις ἐγένετο καὶ ἐκ πονηρῶν τῶν πραγμάτων γενομένων τοῦτο πρῶτον ἀνήνεγκε τὴν πόλιν. The full democracy was either soon restored, of which, however, mention is nowhere made, or the constitution now newly adopted was held to be such, as at this time there can hardly have been more than 5000 citizens at Athens; at least in Lys. adv. Eratosth. p. 124. § 43 it is said of the period shortly before the battle of Aegospotami: δημοκρατίας ἔτι οὔσης. According to Andoc. de myst. § 95—99 the old constitution was restored after the lapse of less than one year. The recall of Alkibiades now followed in the regular logal method, id.

124) A Spartan fleet under Agesandridas, which had for a considerable time stayed at various places in the neighbourhood of Athens, in understanding, as it was thought, with the oligarchs, when the counter-revolution had taken place at Athens, sailed against Euboea

and defeated at Eretria an Athenian fleet under Thymochares, which had been hastily collected and sent in pursuit; whereupon the whole of Euboea revolted, with the single exception of Oreus, Thuc. VIII, 94—96. (cf. Xen. Hell. I, 1, 1, which is probably a second account of this same battle.) For the severity of the loss, Thuc. l. c. 95: Εὔβοια γὰρ αὐτοῖς ἀποκεκλῃμένης τῆς Ἀττικῆς πάντα ἦν, 96; οὔτε γὰρ ἡ ἐν Σικελίᾳ ξυμφορά, καίπερ μεγάλη τότε δόξασα εἶναι, οὔτ' ἄλλο οὐδέν πω οὕτως ἐφόβησεν.

125) (The Spartiate Dorkyllidas had already at the beginning of the summer marched with a small force to the satrapy of Pharnabazus, and there induced the towns Abydos and Lampsakus to revolt from Athens: but the latter was soon afterwards retaken by the Athenians, Thuc. VIII, 61—62.) The Spartan fleet under Astyochus lay the greater part of the summer in the harbour of Miletus, without achieving anything of importance, waiting for the Phoenician fleet promised by Tissaphernes; but as this fleet failed to arrive, and Tissaphernes on no single occasion furnished their pay, Mindarus, who was the successor of Astyochus in the command, set sail with the whole of his fleet for the Peloponnese, Thuc. VIII, 63. 78—79. 83—85. 87—88. 99—103. (A small squadron had already sailed in advance, which had effected the revolt of Byzantium, id. 80.)

126) Thuc. VIII, 100. 103.

127) The first battle, Thuc. VIII, 104—106. Diod. XIII, 39—40, the second, Xen. Hell. I, 1, 4—7. Diod. XIII, 45—46. Plut. Alc. 27. In both Thrasyllus and Thrasybulus were the Athenian leaders, but the second was won chiefly owing to the arrival of Alkibiades during the fight. The time of the second ἀρχομένου χειμῶνος, Xen. l. c. § 2.

128) Xen. Hell. 1, 2. Diod. XIII, 49—53. 64. Plut. Alc. 28—29.

129) Xen. Hell. 1, 1, 11—26. Diod. VIII, 49—51. The time of the victory, λήγοντος τοῦ χειμῶνος, Diod. l. c. 49. Mindarus himself fell. The remarkable announcement of the battle by the Spartan lieutenant-general Hippokrates in the following words: Ἔρρει τὰ καλὰ (κᾶλα?). Μίνδαρος ἀπέσσυα· πεινῶντι τὤνδρες, ἀπορίομες τί χρὴ δρᾶν. Xen. Hell. l. c. § 23. Plut. Alc. 23. According to Diod. l. c. 52—53. Aeschin. de f. leg. p. 38. § 76 the Spartans were so disheartened by this defeat, that they sent ambassadors to Athens with proposals for peace, which were however frustrated by the demagogue Kleophon.

130) Plut. Alc. 28 says (though with some exaggeration): οἱ Ἀθηναῖοι—οὐ μόνον τὸν Ἑλλήσποντον εἶχον βεβαίως, ἀλλὰ καὶ τῆς ἄλλης

FOURTH PERIOD. 431—338 B.C.

Olympiad.	B.C.	ATHENS.	HISTORY.
		Archons.	
XCII, 4	400[131]	Diokles.	Chalkedon and Byzantium taken by the Athenians[132].
XCIII, 1	408[133]	Euktemon.	Cyrus governor of Asia Minor[134]. Alkibiades at Athens[135].
			Death of the Spartan king Pleistoanax : Pausanias his successor[136].
XCIII, 2	407[137]	Antigenes.	Lysander, the Spartan commander-in-chief, defeats the Athenian fleet at Notium in the absence of Alkibiades[138]. Alkibiades deposed from his command[139].
XCIII, 3	406[140]	Kallias.	Kallikratidas, the Spartan commander-in-chief[141], takes Methymna, defeats the Athenian admiral Konon, and shuts him up in the harbour of Mytilene[142].

θαλάσσης ἐξήλασαν κατὰ κράτος τοὺς Λακεδαιμονίους, cf. obs. 132. Immediately after the battle a fleet was stationed at Chrysopolis at the entrance of the Bosporus, to command this important sea-way and to levy a tithe from the passing vessels, Hell. I, 1, 22. In Attica itself Thrasyllus, who had been sent to Athens to announce the victory, gained some advantages over Agis, id. 33, and was then equipped with 50 ships, 1000 hoplites, and 100 horsemen, id. 34; with which he made several landings on the coast of Asia Minor, and then effected a junction with Alkibiades, id. 2, 1—13 ; after which Pharnabazus was attacked and defeated at Abydos, id. § 15—19. On the other hand the Messenians were this year driven out of Pylos, which they had hitherto held with a garrison, id. § 18. Diod. VIII, 64; also the Megarians recovered Nisaea, Diod. l. c. 65.

131) Xen. Hell. I, 3. Diod. XIII, 65—67. Plut. Alc. 29—31.

132) Xen. Hell. I, 3, 2—22. The conquest of Byzantium more fully in Plut. Alc. 31. Diod. XIII, 66—67. In the following year Thasos and the Thrakian towns were reunited to the Athenian alliance, Xen. Hell. I, 4. 9. Diod. XIII, 64. cf. Xen. l. c. 1, 32, and also about the same time (in 409 or 408 B.C.) according to Diod. XIII, 86 all the towns on the Hellespont except Abydos were again reduced to subjection by the Athenians. At the surrender of Chalkedon, Pharnabazus, with whom a convention was concluded on this occasion, was obliged to bind himself amongst other conditions to conduct Athenian ambassadors to the Persian king, Xen. Hell. I, 3, 8. 13 : but on the way (in the spring of 408) Pharnabazus met Cyrus, obs. 134, and, at his request, instead of leading the ambassadors to the king, retained them in captivity for three years (from 408—405 B.C.), Xen. l. c. 4, 5—7.

133) Xen. Hell. I, 4. Plut. Alc. 32—35. Diod. XIII, 68—69.

134) Xen. Hell. I, 4, 2—7. He was appointed by the king, his father, κάρανος τῶν ἐς Καστωλὸν ἀθροιζομένων, id. § 3, and was bound by his father's charge, and still more by his own wish and intention, to lend Sparta most emphatic support, id. 5, 3. In the spring of this year he arrived at Gordium in Phrygia.

135) Xen. Hell. I, 4, 8—20. Plut. and Diod. l. c. He arrived at Athens at the time of the Plynteria, Xen. l. c. § 12, on the 25th of Thargelion (in June), Plut. l. c. 34, and remained there till the Eleusinian mysteries, which were celebrated on the 30th of Boedromion (September), Xen. l. c. § 20. 21. Plut. l. c. He then sailed with a fleet of 100 ships to Andros, defeated the Andrians, but failed to take their town, Xen. l. c. § 21—22. Plut. l. c. 35. He had been chosen στρατηγὸς αὐτοκράτωρ, Xen. § 20.

136) Diod. XIII, 75. XIV, 89. cf obs. 25.

137) Xen. Hell. I, 5. Diod. XIII, 70—74. Plut. Alc. 35—36. Lys. 4—5.

138) Lysander had by his skilful address won the particular favour of Cyrus, and raised his fleet by means of the liberal support of Cyrus to 90 triremes, Xen. Hell. I, 5, 1—10. Plut. Lys. 4. The Athenian subordinate commander Antiochus ventured a battle against the express order of Alkibiades, and was defeated, Xen. l. c. § 11—14. Alkibiades then hurried up and offered Lysander battle, which the latter declined, id. § 15.

139) Xen. Hell. I, 5, 16—17. He escapes ἐς Σηρρόνησον ἐς τὰ ἑαυτοῦ τείχη, id. § 17. Ten generals were appointed to fill his place, viz. Konon, Diomedon, Leon, Perikles, Erasinides, Aristokrates, Archestratus, Protomachus, Thrasyllus, Aristogenes, id. § 16.

140) Xen. Hell. I, 6, 1—II, 1, 9. Diod. XIII, 76—79. 97—103.

141) Xen. Hell. I, 6, 1. He increases the Spartan fleet from 90 to 140, id. § 3, and later to 170 sail, id. § 16. His proud Spartan self-respect in his dealings with Cyrus and his genuinely Hellenic patriotism, id. § 6—7 (ὁ δὲ αὐτῷ εἶπε δύο ἡμέρας ἐπισχεῖν· Καλλικρατίδας δὲ ὀχθεσθεὶς τῇ ἀναβολῇ καὶ ταῖς ἐπὶ τὰς θύρας φοιτήσεσιν ὀργισθεὶς καὶ εἰπὼν ἀθλιωτάτους εἶναι τοὺς Ἕλληνας, ὅτι βαρβάροισι κολακεύουσιν ἕνεκα ἀργυρίου, φάσκων τε, ἢν σωθῇ οἴκαδε, κατά γε τὸ αὑτῷ δυνατὸν διαλλάξειν Ἀθηναίους καὶ Λακεδαιμονίους ἀπέπλευσεν, id.); his great moral influence on the allies, id. § 8—12; his mildness, id. § 14—15.

142) The conquest of Methymna, id. 6, 12—15. Diod. XIII, 76. Konon (who had only 70 ships, with which to oppose him, Xen. l. c. 5, 20) defeated and shut in, id. 6, 16—18. Diod. XIII, 77—79.

The Incipient Decline.

Olympiad.	B. C.	ATHENS.	HISTORY.	ART AND LITERATURE.
XCIII, 3	406	Archon.	Victory of the Athenian fleet at Arginusæ[143]). Condemnation of the Athenian generals[144]).	
XCIII, 4	405[145])	Alexias.	Lysander again takes the command[146]). The Athenian fleet annihilated at the battle of Ægospotami[147]). The allies of Athens made subject[148]). Athens blockaded by land and sea[149]).	
XCIV, 1	404	Anarchia.	Athens compelled to surrender: its walls	Epic Poets: Antimachus[u]), Chœrilus[v]).

143) The Athenians, informed by Konon of the posture of affairs, with the utmost exertion fit out 110 ships (Diod. XIII, 97), which were swollen by 40 from Samos and other allies, Xen. Hell. I, 6, 19—25. Kallikratidas goes to meet the Athenian fleet with 120 ships (he left 50 behind to blockade Konon), id. 26. Battle of Arginusæ, id. 27—38. cf. Diod. XIII, 97—100. The Spartans lost 77 ships, Diod. l. c. 100. cf. Xen. l. c. § 34, the Athenians 25, Xen. id. Kallikratidas was killed, id. 33.

144) Xen. Hell. I, 7. Diod. XIII, 101—103. Owing to a storm the Athenian commanders had been unable to save the crews drifting on the wrecks of the vessels shattered by the enemy or to bury the dead, Xen. l. c. 6, 35. On this charge they were accused and condemned by the agitated populace, whose excitement was chiefly due to Theramenes (id. 7, 5 cf. II, 3, 35) and the demagogues Kallixenus and Kleophon (Xen. Hell. I, 7, 8. 35). Two of them (Protomachus and Aristogenes) had saved themselves by flight, six (Perikles, Diomedon, Lysias, Aristokrates, Thrasyllus, Erasinides, id. § 2) were actually executed; Konon and Archestratus had not been present at the battle. The proceedings in their condemnation were illegal: but Sokrates was the only one of the Prytanes, who had the courage to oppose them, id. § 15. cf. Xenoph. Mem. I, 1, 18. Plut. Apol. Socr. p. 32. n. The sentence falls in the month of October, as it was passed at the time of the festival of the Apaturia, Xen. Hell. I, 7, 8, which was celebrated in October.

145) Xen. Hell. II, 1, 10—2, 9. Diod. XIII, 104—107. Plut. Lys. 7—14.

146) After the death of Kallikratidas the allies begged the Spartans to place Lysander again in command: whereupon the Spartans, though they could not make him navarch—as re-election to this post was illegal—appointed him Epistoleus, but practically with the power of the chief in command, Xen. Hell. II, 1, 6—7. The commanders of the Athenians were Konon, Adeimantus, Philokles, Menander, Tydeus, Kephisodotus, Xen. id. I, 7, 1. II, 1, 16. Lysander was most liberally supplied with money by Cyrus, who at this time left Asia Minor, id. II, 1, 11—14.

147) After some unimportant enterprises on both sides (Xen. Hell. II, 1, 15—16) Lysander sailed to the Hellespont and there took the town of Lampsakus, id. § 17—19; the Athenian fleet of 180 sail followed the enemy to the Hellespont and took up its station at Ægos-potami, opposite Lampsakus, id. § 20—21, where it was surprised by Lysander and captured without resistance, id. 22—28. cf Plut. Lys. 10—11. Diod. XIII, 105—106. Only Konon with 8 ships and the Paralus escaped: the latter announced the disaster at Athens. Konon fled to Euagoras at Kyprus, Xen. l. c. § 28—29. The crews of the rest of the ships wore for the most part made prisoners, and put to death to the number of 3000 (Plut. Lys. 11); the other commanders also fell into the hands of the conqueror and were likewise executed, with the exception of Adeimantus, Xen. l. c. § 30—32. Suspicion of treachery against the commanders, especially Adeimantus, Xen. l. c. § 32. Paus. IV, 17, 2. IX, 36, 6. X, 9, 5. Lys. adv. Alc. A. p. 143. § 38. For the time of the battle see obs. 150.

148) Xen. Hell. II, 2, 1—2. 5—6: εὐθὺς δὲ καὶ ἡ ἄλλη Ἑλλὰς ἀφειστήκει Ἀθηναίων μετὰ τὴν ναυμαχίαν πλὴν Σαμίων. The Athenians, who were found in the allied towns and elsewhere, were all sent to Athens, so that in consequence of the increase in population scarcity might be felt all the sooner, Xen. l. c. § 2.

149) At the instance of Lysander, who with an army comprising contingents from all the Peloponnesian states with the solitary exception of Argos king Pausanias posted himself before the walls of Athens, whilst Lysander blockaded the harbour with 150 ships, Xen. Hell. II, 2, 7—9.

u) Antimachus of Kolophon, flourished towards the end of the Peloponnesian war, Cic. Brut. 51. Diod. XIII, 108, in intercourse with Panyasis and Stesimbrotus, Suid. s. v., as well as with Plato, who is said to have admired his poems, Plut. Lys. 18. Procl. Plat. Tim. p. 28. He wrote an elegiac poem Λύδη, dedicated to his deceased love, in which he strung together mythical love-stories, and so furnished the Alexandrians with a model, Athen. XIII, p. 597. Plut. Consol. ad Apoll. p. 403. Phot. bibl. cod. 213, and a comprehensive Θηβαΐς, Cic. l. c. Hor. A. P. 146. Schol. His poetry was admired by Hadrian and the Alexandrians, Spart. 15. Suid. s. v. Ἀδριανός, but was also censured as learned, forced, showy and prolix, without grace and ill composed, Quint. X, 1, 53. Plut. Timol. 36. (ἐκβεβιασμένοι καὶ κατατόνοις ἔοικε). Dion. Hal. de verb. comp. 22.

v) Chœrilus of Samos, reputed a slave by birth who had gained his freedom by running away. He carried on the history of Herodotus in verse, was advanced by Lysander, whose victories he was to celebrate, and then lived at the court of king Archelaus of Macedonia, Suid. s. v. Plut. Lys. 18. He sang of the victory of Athens over Xerxes, Suid. l. c. in an epic poem (Περσῇτ or Περσικά), of which no considerable fragment is extant.

Olympiad.	B. C.	HISTORY.
XCIV, 1	404	pulled down, and its ships surrendered to Sparta.[150]); the rule of the Thirty instituted[151]).

150) In spite of the pressure of want, the Athenians offered an energetic resistance for a considerable period, and at the same time by a comprehensive amnesty they removed all occasion of domestic disunion, Xen. Hell. II, 2, 10—11. Andoc. de myst. p. 10. § 73—79. (The decree to that end, Andoc. l. c. § 77—79.) They then sent ambassadors to Agis and to the Spartans to beg for peace on condition that they should confine themselves to the town and Peiræus and join the Spartan league. But when the Spartans demanded that the long walls should be pulled down for the distance of 10 stadia, the negotiations were broken off, Xen. l. c. § 11—15. Lys. adv. Agor. p. 130. § 8. After the intrigues and machinations of the aristocratic heteriæ had already spread confusion and insecurity in Athens, Lys. adv. Erat. p. 124. § 43—44, Theramenes volunteered to go first of all to Lysander, in order to ascertain the actual intentions of Sparta with regard to Athens, but stayed there over three months, and when the Athenians, who had meanwhile been reduced to the uttermost extremity by his delay, despatched him to Sparta on his return with full and unconditional powers, he brought back peace on the terms, that the long walls and the fortification works of the Peiræus should be destroyed, the ships be surrendered, all but 12, the exiles be recalled, and the Athenians themselves be bound to follow the Spartans everywhere as allies; and the Athenians now could not help submitting to these conditions, Xen. Hell. II, 2, 15—23. Lys. adv. Agor. p. 130. § 9—33. adv. Erat. p. 125. § 62—70. The decree of the ephors in reference to the conditions of peace ran (Plut. Lys. 14): Τάδε τὰ τέλη τῶν Λακεδαιμονίων ἔγνω· Καββαλόντες τὸν Πειραιᾶ καὶ τὰ μακρὰ σκέλη καὶ ἐκβάντες ἐκ πασῶν τῶν πόλεων τὰν αὐτῶν γᾶν ἔχοντες, ταῦτά κα δρῶντες τὰν εἰράναν ἔχοιτε ἁ χρὴ δόντες (αἱ χρήδοιτε?) καὶ τοὺς φυγάδας ἀνέντες. Περὶ δὲ τᾶν ναῶν τῷ πλήθεος ὀκοῖόν τί κα τηνεῖ δοκέῃ, ταῦτα ποιέντε. The Thebans and Corinthians were actually of the opinion that Athens must be destroyed, Xen. l. c. § 19. Andoc. de pac. p. 26. § 21. "Λακεδαιμόνιοι δὲ οὐκ ἔφασαν πόλιν Ἑλληνίδα ἀνδραποδιεῖν μέγα ἀγαθὸν εἰργασμένην ἐν τοῖς μεγίστοις κινδύνοις γενομένοις τῇ Ἑλλάδι," Xen. l. c. § 20. According to Plut. Lys. 15 the walls of Athens were destroyed on the 16th of Munychion i. e. the 25th of April, with which Thuc. V, 26. II, 2 is in agreement. The battle of Ægospotami must accordingly be placed at the latest in the month of August of 405 B. C., as it is only thus that the time is adequate for the events which happened in the interval (obs. 149).

151) The Thirty are appointed shortly after the destruction of the walls, Xen. Hell. II, 3, 11, and that under the personal cooperation of Lysander, who had sailed for Samos after the conclusion of peace, but was fetched back to Athens some months later for this purpose, Diod. XIV, 3. Lys. adv. Erat. p. 126. § 71. The manner of their choice, Lys. l. c. p. 126. § 71—77. Their names, Xen. Hell. III, 3, 2, their pretended object: "οἱ τοὺς πατρίους νόμους ξυγγράψουσι, καθ᾽ οὓς πολιτεύσουσι," id. § 2, but τούτους μὲν ἀεὶ ἔμελλον ξυγγράφειν τε καὶ ἀποδεικνύναι, βουλὴν δὲ καὶ τὰς ἄλλας ἀρχὰς κατέστησαν ὡς ἐδόκει αὐτοῖς, id. § 11.—Paus. III, 7, 10: καὶ ὁ πόλεμος οὗτοι τό τὴν Ἑλλάδα ἔτι βεβηκυῖαν διέσεισεν ἐκ βάθρων καὶ ὕστερον Φίλιππος ὁ Ἀμύντου σαθρὰν ἤδη καὶ οὐ παντάπασιν ὑγιῆ προσκατήριψεν αὐτήν.

SECOND SECTION.

404—362 B.C.

FROM THE END OF THE PELOPONNESIAN WAR TO THE BATTLE OF MANTINEIA. SPARTA'S ARROGANCE AND HUMILIATION [152].

Olympiad.	B. C.	ATHENS.	HISTORY.
			a) Up to the outbreak of the Corinthian War, 894 B.C.
XCIV, 1	404	*Anarchia.*	Tyranny of the Thirty at Athens [153]; Athenian exiles under Thrasybulus make an inroad into Attica and there maintain themselves [154].

152) This conception of the history of the section is clearly expressed by Xenophon at the turning point of Sparta's good fortune (when the Spartans were expelled from the Kadmeia in 879 B. c.) in the following words: Προκεχωρηκότων δὲ τοῖς Λακεδαιμονίοις, ὥστε Θηβαίους μὲν καὶ τοὺς ἄλλους Βοιωτοὺς ὑπηκόους ὑπ' ἐκείνοις εἶναι, Κορινθίους δὲ πιστοτάτους γεγενῆσθαι, Ἀργείους δὲ τεταπεινῶσθαι, Ἀθηναίους δὲ ἠρημῶσθαι, τῶν δ' αὖ συμμάχων κεκολασμένων, εἰ δυσμενῶς εἶχον αὐτοῖς, παντάπασιν ἤδη καλῶς καὶ ἀσφαλῶς ἡ ἀρχὴ ἐδόκει αὐτοῖς κατεσκευάσθαι. Πολλὰ μὲν οὖν ἄν τις ἔχοι καὶ ἄλλα λέγειν καὶ Ἑλληνικὰ καὶ βαρβαρικά, ὡς θεοὶ οὔτε τῶν ἀσεβούντων οὔτε τῶν ἀνόσια ποιούντων ἀμελοῦσιν· νῦν γε μὴν λέξω τὰ προκείμενα. Λακεδαιμόνιοί τε γὰρ οἱ ὁμόσαντες αὐτονόμους ἐάσειν τὰς πόλεις, τὴν ἐν Θήβαις ἀκρόπολιν κατασχόντες ὑπ' αὐτῶν μόνων τῶν ἀδικηθέντων ἐκολάσθησαν, Hell. V, 3, 29. 4, 1. For the severity and arrogance of the Spartans see the speech of the Thebans at Athens, id. III, 5, 8—15, especially § 12—13: Τοὺς μὲν εἵλωτας ἁρμοστὰς καθιστᾶναι ἀξιοῦσι, τῶν δὲ ξυμμάχων ἐλευθέρων ὄντων, ἐπεὶ εὐτύχησαν, δεσπόται ἀναπέφηναν. Ἀλλὰ μὴν καὶ οὓς ὑμῶν ἀπέστησαν φανεροί εἰσιν ἐξηπατηκότες· ἀντὶ γὰρ ἐλευθερίας διπλῆν αὐτοῖς δουλείαν παρεσχήκασιν, ὑπό τε γὰρ τῶν ἁρμοστῶν τυραννοῦνται καὶ ὑπὸ δέκα ἀνδρῶν, οὓς Λύσανδρος κατέστησεν ἐν ἑκάστῃ πόλει. Cf. Plut. Lys. 14: κατέλυε τὰς πολιτείας (Λύσανδρος) καὶ καθίστη δεκαδαρχίας, πολλῶν μὲν ἐν ἑκάστῃ σφαττομένων, πολλῶν δὲ φευγόντων. Not only their lust for dominion, their avarice also developed its pernicious effects, having been first chiefly kindled by the 470 talents, which Lysander brought home with him as the surplus of the donations of Cyrus, Xen. Hell. II, 3, 8, and also by the 1000 talents and more, which flowed every year from the allies into Sparta's exchequer, Diod. XIV, 10, cf. Plut. Lys. 17.

153) At first the Thirty showed themselves moderate, only bringing to trial and condemning those who had incurred well founded hatred as informers (συκοφάνται), or otherwise objectionable persons, Xen. Hell. II, 3, 12. But in a short time, when they had provided for their own security by a Spartan body-guard, granted by Lysander at their request, they also put to death men who were suspected by them merely on account of their political views, or men whose wealth excited their avarice, id. § 13—21. From the number of the citizens they had chosen out 3000, who together with the Spartan body-guard were to form their support; all the rest of the citizens they had disarmed, id. § 17—20. Theramenes ("κόθορνος" Xen. l. c. § 31), who was discontented with these measures, was executed, chiefly at the instigation of Kritias, id. § 15—56. (Speech of Kritias, § 24—34, of Theramenes, § 35—49.) Examples of their cruelty: the execution of 300 citizens of Eleusis and Salamis, Xen. Hell. II, 4, 8—10. Lys. adv. Erat. p. 125. § 32. adv. Agor. p. 133. § 44; the ill-usage of Lysias and murder of his brother Polemarchus, Lys. adv. Erat. p. 120. § 4—24; the murder of Leon, Nikeratus, Antiphon, Xen. Hell. II, 3, 39—40. cf. Plat. Apol. Socr. p. 93 c. According to Isocr. Areop. p. 153. § 67. Æschin. de f. leg. p. 38. § 77 they put to death 1500 citizens without trial or verdict; more than 5000 were compelled to save themselves by flight, Isocr. l. c. The name, 'thirty tyrants,' first in Diodorus (XIV, 2, 3 etc.), Cornelius Nepos (Thrasyb. 1), Iustin. (V, 10), etc.

154) Xen. Hell. II, 4, 2—7. The exiles, 70 in number, starting from Thebes, made themselves masters of the fortress Phyle in Attic territory, id. § 2: the Thirty with the 3000 (obs. 153) make a fruitless effort to expel them, § 2—3; a detachment of troops, which they left behind them, is surprised by the exiles and driven off with loss, § 4—7. This happened in the winter, as is proved by § 3.

Olympiad.	B.C.	ATHENS.	HISTORY.
		Archons.	
XCIV, 2	403	Eukleides.	Victory of the exiles over their opponents[155]; their return to Athens through the mediation of the Spartan king Pausanias[156]; universal amnesty[157]; establishment of the democracy in the archonship of Eukleides[158].
XCIV, 3	402	Mikon.	
XCIV, 4	401	Xenænetus.	Campaign of the younger Cyrus against his brother Artaxerxes with an army of 11,000 Hellenic hoplites, 2000 peltasts, and 100,000 Asiatics[159].

155) The exiles, whose numbers had now been swollen to 1000, starting from Phyle, made themselves masters of the Peiræus, and here (at Munychia) fought a victorious battle with the Thirty, who advanced to the attack; in it fell Kritias, Xen. Hell. II, 4, 10—19; on the fifth day after the successful surprise of Phyle (obs. 154), id. § 13, so still in the winter: in perfect agreement with which is the fact that id. § 21 (: τοῖς ἀνοσιωτάτοις τριάκοντα, οἳ ἰδίων κερδέων ἕνεκα ὀλίγου δεῖν πλείους ἀπεκτόνασιν Ἀθηναίων ἐν ὀκτὼ μησὶν ἢ πάντες Πελοπον- νήσιοι δέκα ἔτη πολεμοῦντες) the duration of the rule of the Thirty up to this time is stated at 8 months.

156) The victory won by the exiles, and the intercourse which was afterwards in many cases maintained between them and the citizens in Athens, and the continually increasing numbers and strength of the exiles led to an outbreak of the discontent that reigned in the town, and the Thirty were obliged to leave the town and hand over the sovereignty to a newly elected board of ten persons, Xen. Hell. II, 4, 20—27; which, however, instead of mediating with the exiles, as was hoped, showed itself no less hostile to them than the Thirty, Lys. adv. Erat, p. 125, § 53—61. Diod. XIV, 42, Iustin. V, 9. Accordingly the Ten, like the Thirty, who had gone to Eleusis, sent ambassadors to Sparta, to pray for help; and through the efforts of Lysander 100 talents were supplied to them, whilst he himself was commissioned to go to the aid of the oligarchs at Athens with an army, and his brother Libys with a fleet, Xen. l. c. § 28—29, 39: ὥστε ταχὺ μάλιν ἐν ἀπορίᾳ ἦσαν οἱ ἐν Πειραιεῖ, οἱ δ' ἐν τῷ ἄστει πάλιν αὖ μέγα ἐφρόνουν ἐπὶ τῷ Λυσάνδρῳ. But in their distress the exiles were aided by the ill-will and jealousy which had at that time grown up against Lysander in consequence of his violence and arrogance, not merely in the other Greek states, but even in Sparta itself. The measures enumerated in obs. 152, which were imposed on the Greek states, had come from him, and it was also his doing, that the Spartans prohibited all Greek states from receiving the Athenian fugitives, Lys. adv. Erat. p. 129, § 97. Diod. XIV, 6; at Sparta jealousy had been excited chiefly by the exaggerated honours, which were everywhere paid him, Plut. Lys. 18, and the suspicion was even harboured, that he intended to make himself king, Plut. Lys. 24—26, 30. Diod. XIV, 13. In this way the feeling against Athens in those very states which had displayed the greatest hostility, namely Corinth and Thebes (obs. 150), underwent a total change, so that the exiles found at Thebes, not only a welcome, but even support, and both Thebes and Corinth refused to take part in further hostilities against Athens, Xen. Hell. II, 4, 30. At Sparta the king Pausanias won over three ephors to his side, φθονήσας Λυσάνδρῳ, εἰ κατειργασμένος ταῦτα ἅμα μὲν εὐδοκιμήσει, ἅμα δὲ ἰδίας ποιήσοιτο τὰς Ἀθήνας, Xen.

id. § 29: he followed Lysander with an army to Attica, where he at first joined in the operations against the exiles, but secretly entered into negotiations with them and with the better disposed party in the town, and brought about the convention, ἐφ' ᾧ τε εἰρήνην μὲν ἔχειν ὡς πρὸς ἀλλήλους, ἀπιέναι δὲ ἐπὶ τὰ ἑαυτῶν ἑκάστους πλὴν τῶν τριάκοντα καὶ τῶν ἕνδεκα καὶ τῶν ἐν Πειραιεῖ ἀρξάντων δέκα, Xen. id. § 38: after which Thrasybulos entered the town, and soon afterwards the oligarchs, who still maintained themselves at Eleusis, were conquered. For the whole of the events subsequent to the march of Pausanias see Xen. Hell. II, 4, 29—43. That the Spartan expedition lasted till late in the summer of 403 B.C., must be inferred from Xen. l. c. § 25, where it is said of the exiles, that they made raids from the Peiræus upon the Attic territory and collected ξύλα καὶ ὀπώραν: according to Plut. Mor. p. 349 f. (de glor. Athen. c. 7), which is in perfect agreement, the return of the exiles took place on the 12th of Boedromion, i.e. in the month of September.

157) Xen. Hell. II, 4, 43. Andoc. de myst. p. 12, § 90—91. The oath, which all the exiles took upon their return, ran : καὶ οὐ μνησικα- κήσω τῶν πολιτῶν οὐδενὶ πλὴν τῶν τριάκοντα καὶ τῶν ἕνδεκα, οὐδὲ τούτων ὃς ἂν ἐθέλῃ εὐθύνας διδόναι τῆς ἀρχῆς ἧς ἦρξεν, id. § 90; and similar oaths were also for the future invariably taken by the senate and the board of jurors, id. § 91.

158) Most important authority, Andoc. de myst. p. 11, § 81—90. A commission was appointed to draw the laws up anew on the basis of Solon's and Drakon's legislation ; these were then examined by the senate and by 500 Nomothetæ elected by the people; after which a law expressly provided, τὰς δίκας καὶ τὰς διαίτας κυρίας εἶναι, ὁπόσαι ἐν δημοκρατουμένῃ τῇ πόλει ἐγένοντο, τοῖς δὲ νόμοις χρῆσθαι ἀπ' Εὐκλείδου ἄρχοντος, id. § 87. The newly constituted democracy is everywhere associated with the name of the Archon Eukleides. During his year of office state recognition of the new Ionic alphabet (introduction of Η and Ω, Χ, Ψ, etc.) was also first made.

159) The expedition, presented to us by Xenophon in his well known and admirable narrative, the Κύρου ἀνάβασις (with which we must compare the account of Diodorus, XIV, 19—31, 37, drawn seemingly for the most part from Ephorus and Theopompus), was undertaken by Cyrus, to dispossess his elder brother Artaxerxes of the throne, Xen. Anab. I, 1, 1—4. The leaders of the Greek mercenaries were Klearchus, Proxenus, Sokrates, Menon, Cheirisophus; for the numbers of the Greek and likewise of the barbarian troops see id. I, 7, 9 cf. 2, 3, 6, 9, 25, 4, 3. The point of departure was Sardes,

The Incipient Decline. 83

Olympiad.	B.C.	ATHENS.	HISTORY.	ART AND LITERATURE.
		Archons.		
XCIV, 4	401		Battle of Kunaxa and retreat of the Ten Thousand[160]).	
XCV, 1	400	Laches.	The Spartans send Thimbron with an army to Asia Minor, to protect the Greek towns there against Tissaphernes[161]).	
XCV, 2	399	Aristokrates.	The remnant of the Ten Thousand, taken	Death of Sokrates[w]).

id. I, 2, 1: the march lasts, including the days of rest, 180 days up to the battle of Knaxa, as may bo seen from the statements, id. I, 2—7: it was begun in the spring of 401 B.C. see obs. 160. For the significance of the enterprise for the history of Greece see obs. 161.

160) The Hellenes are victorious, but Cyrus falls, and his barbarian troops are routed, Xen. Anab. I, 8—10. The Hellenes now begin their retreat, the narrative of which occupies the remaining six books of the Anabasis of Xenophon, at first under the conduct of the Persians as far as the river Zapatas in Media (now the great Zab); from this point, after the Persians had broken their agreement, and the chief leaders together with 20 lochages had been treacherously murdered by Tissaphernes (id. II, 5—6), alone and harassed by continual attacks from the Persian army and the inhabitants of the country. The departure of the expedition is correctly placed by Diod. XIV, 19, Diog. L. II, § 55 in 401 B.C., but in the archonship of Xenaenetus, and therefore in the second half of the year. But it follows that this latter is incorrect from the fact that the whole retreat up to Kotyora on the Black Sea lasted 8 months,

Xen. Anab. V, 5, 4, and that it is the depth of winter whilst they are still in Armenia, id. IV, 5, 12; for from this it follows, that the battle of Kunaxa must have been fought in the autumn, and accordingly the departure from Sardes, as it took place 180 days before the battle (obs. 159), must be placed in the spring.

161) Xen. Hell. III, 1, 3: Ἐπεὶ μέντοι Τισσαφέρνης πολλοῦ ἄξιος βασιλεῖ δόξας γεγενῆσθαι ἐν τῷ πρὸς τὸν ἀδελφὸν πολέμῳ σατράπης κατεπέμφθη, ὧν τε αὐτὸς πρόσθεν ἦρχε καὶ ὧν Κῦρος, εὐθὺς ἠξίου τὰς Ἰωνικὰς πόλεις ἁπάσας ἑαυτῷ ὑπηκόους εἶναι· αἱ δὲ ἅμα μὲν ἐλεύθεραι βουλόμεναι εἶναι, ἅμα δὲ φοβούμεναι τὸν Τισσαφέρνην, ὅτι Κῦρον δἰ ἐξὸν ἀντ' ἐκείνου ᾑρημέναι ἦσαν (s. Xen. Anab. I, 1, 6), ἐς μὲν τὰς πόλεις οὐκ ἐδέχοντο αὐτόν, ἐς Λακεδαίμονα δ᾽ ἔπεμπον πρέσβεις καὶ ἠξίουν, ἐπεὶ πάσης τῆς Ἑλλάδος προστάται εἰσίν, ἐπιμεληθῆναι καὶ σφῶν, τῶν ἐν Ἀσίᾳ Ἑλλήνων, ὅπως ἥ τε χώρα μὴ δῃοῖτο αὐτῶν καὶ αὐτοὶ ἐλεύθεροι εἶεν. Hereupon the Spartans sent Thimbron with 1000 Neodamodes and 4000 Peloponnesians, Xen. Hell. III, 1, 4—5. cf. Diod. XIV, 35—36; who at first achieves but little success. (There were 300 Athenian horsemen in Thimbron's army, who were furnished by Athens at the call of Sparta, Xen. l. c. § 4.)

w) Sokrates, son of the sculptor Sophroniskus and the midwife Phaenarete born 469 B.C., Apollod. ap. Diog. Laert. II, 44. Plat. Apol. 17 D, at first pursued his father's art, Diog. Laert. II, 19, and learnt the kithara from Konnus, Plat. Euthyd. 272 c. Monex. 235 E. He cultivated his powers in personal intercourse with distinguished men, Xen. Œc. II, 16. Plat. Apol. 21, e. g. with Prodikus, Meno 96 D, and by studying the works of poets and philosophers, Plat. Phaed. 97 D. Xen. mem. II, 1, 21. I, 6, 14. In form and face ugly as a Silenus, Xen. Symp. 5, 2 f. 4, 19 f. 2, 19. Plat. Symp. 215. Theaet. 143 E. Meno 80 A, wretchedly poor, Plat. Apol. 23 c (ἐν πενίᾳ μυρίᾳ) 38 B. Xen. Oec. 2, 2 f. mem. I, 2, 1, 6, 5 f. Aristoph. Nub. 103 f., hardened and troubled with no wants, Plat. Symp. 219 E. 220 A. Phaed. 229 A. Xen. l. c. 6, 10. Oec. II, 10, Sokrates is praised by Plato and Xenophon as a model of piety and justice, of disinterestedness and self-command, of steadfastness, intrepidity and tranquillity of soul, of true friendship and patriotism, Plat. Phaed. Xen. mem. I, 1, 11. IV, 8, 10—12. I, 2, 1 f. Thus he bore with serenity and playfulness the humours of his wife Xanthippe, Xen. mem. II, 2. Diog. Laert. II, 36; he unselfishly admitted every one to his company, without asking for remuneration, Plat. Apol. 31 c. Euthyphr. 3 D. Xen. mem. I, 6, 11: also in his pleasures he preserved his discretion and self-command, Plat. Symp. 176 c. 213 E. 223 D. Xen. mem. I, 2, 1 f. Symp. 2, 24 f. In his public life he everywhere showed himself upright, steadfast,

brave, see obs. 54. 144. He taught conversationally in the most unconstrained intercourse, Plat. an sen. resp. s. gor. p. 796: Σωκράτης γοῦν οὔτε βάθρα θείς ποτ' εἰς θρόνον καθίσας οὔτε ὥραν διατριβῆς ἢ περιπάτου τοῖς γνωρίμοις τεταγμένην φυλάττων ἀλλὰ καὶ παίζων, ὅτε τύχοι, καὶ συμπίνων καὶ συστρατευόμενος ἐνίοις καὶ συναγοράζων, τέλος δὲ καὶ συνδεδεμένος καὶ πίνων τὸ φάρμακον, ἐφιλοσόφει. His highest vocation seemed to him to be the spiritual and moral education of men, Plat. Phaed. 32 D f. 28 D f. Theaet. 150 c f., for which the Delphic oracle praises him as the wisest of mortals, Plat. Apol. 21. Xen. Apol. 15. He thought he perceived the voice of a divine revelation in his breast, τὸ δαιμόνιον, a presentiment, whether an action should be undertaken, whether it would be salutary and productive of the wished for result, Plat. Apol. 31 D. Theaet. 151 A. Xen. mem. I, 1, 4. IV, 8, 5. etc. He had this in common with the Sophists, that he did not inquire into nature, as presented to our senses, or its creative cause, but only into the spiritual and moral condition of man: he was opposed to them, in that he looked upon conceptual knowledge, to which he held all virtue to consist, as the goal of philosophy, Plat. Prot. 329 D f. 349 D f. Xen. mem. III, 9. IV, 6. Symp. 2, 12. Aristot. Eth. Nic. III, 11. VI, 13. Eth. Eud. I, 5. III, I. VII, 13. etc.; he looked upon the consciousness of ignorance as the stepping-stone to knowledge, Plat. Apol. 21 D. 23 D. Theaet. 150 c: this consciousness he woke in others by his method of questioning (εἰρωνεία), Plat.

11—2

84   FOURTH PERIOD.   431—338 B. C.

Olympiad.	B. C.	HISTORY.	ART AND LITERATURE.
XCV, 2	399	into pay by Thimbron, joins in the struggle against the Persians¹⁶²). Thimbron is recalled, and Derkyllidas put in his place¹⁶³). Campaign of the Spartans against Elis¹⁶⁴).	Sokratic school: Eukleides of Megara*), Antisthenes, the cynic⁷), Aristippus, the

162) The Ten Thousand reach the Black Sea at Trapezus, Xen. Anab. IV, 7, 21—27. 8, 22 : from here they proceeded, partly by land, partly by water, by way of Kerasus, Kotyora, Sinope, Herakleia, and Kalpe, to Chrysopolis, then crossed over to Byzantium, and finally, after various annoyances on the part of the harmost at Byzantium (first Anaxibius, then Polus), took service with the Thrakian prince Seuthes. This happened in the winter, id. VII, 3, 13. 42. etc., and two months afterwards, that is sometime in the spring of 399 B.C., they entered Thimbron's service at his request, id. VII. 6, 1. Their number at that time still amounted to a total of 6000, VII, 7, 23. cf. V, 5, 3. 10, 16. Their arrival enabled Thimbron to act on the offensive against Tissaphernes, so that the Spartans made some progress, Xen. Hell. III, 1, 6—7.

163) Xen. Hell. III, 1, 8: Δερκυλλίδας—ἀνὴρ δοκῶν εἶναι μάλα μηχανικός, καὶ ἐκαλεῖτο δὲ Σίσυφος. He subdued Æolis, id. 1, 9—2, 1 ; then wintered in Bithynia, id. 2, 1—5; in the following spring crossed over to the Chersonese, and there occupied his army till the autumn with the building of a wall across the isthmus, id. § 6—10; upon its completion he returned to Asia and took Atarneus after a siege of 8 months, id. § 11; then (in the summer of 397 B. c.)

undertook at the bidding of the ephors a campaign against Karia, but soon afterwards, on his way back from Karia, concluded an armistice with Tissaphernes and Pharnabazus, which the Persians offered him at the moment when both armies were posted opposite each other in battle array in the vicinity of the Meander, id. § 12—20. With reference to the chronology, it follows from this account, that up to the armistice Derkyllidas had spent three summers and two winters, 399—397 B. c., in Asia. It is proved by Xen. l. c. 4, 6, that he also remained during the following winter till the arrival of Agesilaus and even after that.

164) Xen. Hell. III, 2, 21—29. Paus. III, 8, 2. Diod. XIV, 17. The causes of the war, Xen. id. § 21—22. A first invasion resulted in nothing, as Agis returned home on account of an earthquake, when he had entered the enemy's territory, id. § 24; on the occasion of a second invasion, which according to Xenophon took place in the same year (περιιόντι τῷ ἐνιαυτῷ, id. § 25. cf. Thuc. 1, 30), but according to Pausanias a year later, while Diodorus only mentions one invasion altogether, the whole of Elis, with the exception of the capital, was taken and plundered. For evidence as to date see obs. 163.

Apol. 21 c. 22 B f. 23 B f. At the same time he set up no definite system, Cic. Acad. I, 4, 18, but only supplied a general impulse to others, Plat. Mem. p. 98. Further, he wrote nothing, Cic. de orat. III, 16, so that for our knowledge of his teaching we are dependent on the works of his pupils, Plato and Xenophon. But his method of teaching excited much displeasure at Athens, especially in the party, which, like Aristophanes, was unfavourable generally to the new philosophical movement, or wished to restore the old Attic democracy. Consequently Sokrates was accused by the democrats Meletus, Anytus, and Lykon: 'Ἀδικεῖ Σωκράτης, οὓς μὲν ἡ πόλις νομίζει θεοὺς οὐ νομίζων, ἕτερα δὲ καινὰ δαιμόνια εἰσηγούμενος, ἀδικεῖ δὲ καὶ τοὺς νέους διαφθείρων, Diog. L. II, 40. Plat. Apol. 24 B. Xenoph. mem. I, 1, 1. Without making use of the ordinary legal means, Sokrates defended himself with the pride of innocence. Diog. L. l. c., and was found guilty by a small majority of the votes, Plat. Apol. 36 A, but when, upon being called on to fix the extent of punishment due, he declared himself worthy of the honour of maintenance in the Prytaneion, he was condemned to death by a greater majority of the votes, Apol. 36 D. On account of the fatal embassy to Delos a reprieve of 30 days intervened before the execution of the sentence, Plat. Phæd. 58. Xen. mem. IV, 8, 2, which Sokrates disdained to make use of for escape, Plat. Phæd. 99 A. Apol. 37 c. Kriton. After its expiration he drank the cup of poison with the unruffled calm and cheerfulness of soul, which Xenophon, mem. IV, 8, and more especially Plato, Phæd. 115 D ff., pourtray in a touching narrative.

x) Euklcides of Megara, a faithful pupil of Sokrates : Plat. Theæt. 142 cf. Phæd. 59 c, after the latter's death afforded a shelter to his

pupils, Diog. Laert. II, 106, and became the founder of the Megarian school or the Dialectics, and the composer of 6 dialogues. He united the teaching of Sokrates, that knowledge is the essence of virtue, with the teaching of the Eleatics on the unity of being, Diog. L. l. c. Cic. Acad. II, 42. There were six dialogues by him, though doubt was already cast on them in ancient times; but of these nothing has been preserved, Diog. L. II, 64, 108. Suid. s. v. Amongst his pupils the most famous were Diodorus, Diog. L. II, 111, and Stilpo, l. c. 113 f. The Elean-Eretric school was a lateral branch of the Megaric, founded by Phædon of Elis, the friend of Sokrates, Diog. L. l. c. II, 105. Suid. s. v. Gell. II, 18, Plat. Phædon.

y) Antisthenes of Athens, at first pupil of Gorgias, subsequently a faithful follower of Sokrates, Diog. L. VI, 1, 2. Xen. mem. III, II, 17. II, 5. III, 4, 4. Symp. II, 10. III, 7. IV, 34, after his master's death collected pupils around him in the gymnasium Kynosarges. Owing to the neglect of outward appearances and ruling customs he himself was called 'Ἀπλοκύων, and his pupils Κυνικοί, Diog. L. VI, 13. His chief dogma was, l. c. 11 : αὐτάρκη—τὴν ἀρετὴν εἶναι πρὸς εὐδαιμονίαν, μηδενὸς προσδεομένην. Of his numerous writings, l. c. 15, only scanty fragments are preserved. Two declamations, which were ascribed to him, Αἴας and 'Ὀδυσσεύς, are hardly genuine. The best known of his pupils is Diogenes of Sinope, called ὁ Κύων (died 323 B. c., Diog. L. VI, 79), who carried to extremes the teaching of his master to the complete renunciation of the most ordinary needs and conveniences of life and neglect of prevailing custom. Numerous anecdotes and characteristic traits are preserved of the bizarre eccentricities of this proletarian among philosophers, Diog. L. VI, 20—81, amongst them his meeting with Alexander the Great, Cic. Tusc. V, 32.

Olympiad.	B.C.	ATHENS.	HISTORY.	ART AND LITERATURE.
		Archon.		
XCV, 3	398	Ithykles.	Elis submits to the demands of Sparta[165]). Death of the Spartan king Agis: Agesilaus his successor[166]).	Cyrenaic[z]), Plato the Academic[aa]).

---

165) Xen. Hell. III, 2, 30—31. Paus. III, 8, 2. Diod. XIV, 34. The Eleans were obliged to pull down the walls of their capital, and renounce the sovereignty, which they had hitherto maintained over the other towns and races of the district. This result was arrived at in the summer following the Spartan invasion. (At the same time according to Diod. l. c. the Spartans also expelled the Messenians from Kephallenia and Naupaktus.)

166) Xen. Hell. III, 3, 1—4. Plut. Lys. 22. Ages. 3. Paus. III. 8, 4—5. Agis died after the conclusion of peace with Elis, Xen. l. c. § 1. Agesilaus, his brother, succeeded him, chiefly through Lysander's support, although Agis left a son behind him, Leotychides, whose nearer relationship gave him the better title.

---

z) Aristippus of Kyrene came to Athens to hear Sokrates, Diog. L. II, 65. Plat. Phaed. 59 c, travelled much and lived at Syracuse in intercourse with the elder Dionysius, Diog. L. II, 66 f: he was the first of the Sokratics to teach for money, l. c. 72. 74. 80, and became the founder of the Cyrenaic school. He taught that pleasure, ἡδονή, is the highest good, Diog. L. II, 75: τὸ κρατεῖν καὶ μὴ ἡττᾶσθαι ἡδονῶν, Xen. mem. II, 1. III, 8; whence the Cyrenaics were also called 'Ἡδονικοί. The accounts of his writings are uncertain and contradictory, l. c. 64. 83 f.

aa) Plato, son of the Athenian Ariston, whose family derived its lineage from Kodros, and of Periktione his mother, who was descended from Solon and therefore also from Kodrus, was born probably in the year of Perikles' death, 429 B.C. (or 427 ?), Phaed. III, 1. 2. 3. Vit. α′. β′. Westerm. Vit. min. p. 382. 388. Suid. s. v. Besides stories of his birth, the biographers inform us of his instruction in grammar, music, and gymnastics, of a wrestling prize, which he is said to have carried off, and of poetical attempts, Diog. I. l. c. 4. 5. Vit. α′, and also of military service, Diog. l. c. 8. Through Kratylus he became acquainted with the philosophy of Herakleitus, Arist. Metaph. I, 6. Vit. α′. p. 385. When about 20 years old, he became connected with Sokrates, Diog. L. III, 6. Vit. β′. p. 391. Suid. s. v., who regarded him with affection, Xen. mem. III, 6, 1; but he was absent at the death of Sokrates through sickness, Plat. Phaed. 59 B. Apol. 38 B. Diog. L. III, 36. Of the Sokratics, Antisthenes and Aristippus were his opponents, Plat. Phaed. 59 A. Soph. 251 E. Diog. L. III, 35. 36. After the death of Sokrates he betook himself together with other followers of that philosopher to Eukleides at Megara, and then undertook journeys to Kyrene, Egypt, Lower Italy, and Sicily, in which he made nearer acquaintance with the Cyrenaic Theodorus and the Pythagoreans, in particular Philolaus and Archytas, l. c. 6. 9. Vit. β′. p. 392. α′. p. 385. At the court of the elder Dionysius in Syracuse he excited such offence by his frankness, that the tyrant gave him to the Spartan ambassador Pollis to be sold as a slave at Ægina, where Annikeris of Kyrene is said to have purchased his freedom, Plut. Dion. 5. Diog. L. III, 18—21. Vit. α′. p. 385 f. Upon his return he delivered lectures to numerous pupils in the gymnasium 'Ακαδήμεια, situate hard by Athens, and so called from a hero 'Ακάδημος, Diog. L. III, 7. 41: ὅθεν καὶ 'Ακαδημαϊκὴ προσηγορεύθη ἡ ἀπ' αὐτοῦ αἵρεσις, cf. Vit. δ′. p. 387. He is said to have come a second time to Sicily after the death of Dionysius at Dion's invitation (368), and after Dion's banishment a third time (361) without any favourable result for the political circumstances of Syracuse, l. c. 21 f. With his mental powers unimpaired Plato attained his 81st year and died 348 B.C. Hermipp. ap. Diog. L. III, 2. Cic. de sen. 5. The purity and loftiness of his character are highly extolled by the ancients, Diog. L. l. c. 44 : τὸν τις καὶ τηλόθι ναίων | τιμᾷ ἀνὴρ ἀγαθὸς θεῖον ἰδόντα βίον. There are extant, passing under his name, 41 philosophical dialogues, a collection of philosophical definitions and 13 letters, l. c. III, 57 f, of which however the definitions, the letters, and likewise a number of the smaller dialogues, in particular Minos, Hipparchus, the second Alkibiades, Anterastae, Theages, Klitophon, and Epinomis, are generally esteemed spurious. The ancients had already attempted to connect the dialogues of Plato in tetralogies or trilogies, l. c.; modern scholars have arranged and grouped them in various ways according to chronology and internal relationship. The dialogues of preeminent importance for Plato's teaching are: Φαῖδρος, on love as a yearning after the idea; Πρωταγόρας, on the teachableness and unity of virtue and its origin from knowledge; Γοργίας, on the worthlessness of the principles of happiness taught by the sophists, and of the unity of virtue and happiness; Θεαίτητος, on the distinction between knowledge and the perceptions and notions of sense; Σοφιστής a refutation of the views of the Eleatic school about being and non-being; Παρμενίδης, Plato's peculiar doctrine of supersensible, uncreated, unchangeable and indestructible essences as prototypes of the things of sense and becoming, Ἰδέαι, εἴδη; Κρατύλος, on the relation of speech to cognition; Συμπόσιον, on philosophic love; Φαίδων, on the soul and its immortality; Φίληβος, on the highest good, and the different kinds of being ; Πολιτεία, on the realisation of justice in the state, together with a description of a model state; Τίμαιος, on the origin and disposition of the world. The 'Απολογία Σωκράτους and Κρίτων are important above all as historical accounts of the work and fate of Sokrates.

FOURTH PERIOD. 431—338 B.C.

Olympiad.	B.C.	ATHENS.	HISTORY.	ART AND LITERATURE.
XCV, 4	397	Archons. Suniades.	Conspiracy of Kinadon at Sparta[167]).	Historians: Xenophon[bb]), Ktesias[cc]), Philistus[dd]).
XCVI, 1	396	Phormion.	Agesilaus in Asia Minor; his successful enterprises against the Persian satraps[168]).	

167) Xen. Hell. III, 3, 4—11. cf. Arist. Pol. VIII, 7, 3. The conspiracy was in existence till οὔπω ἐνιαυτὸν ὄντος ἐν τῇ βασιλείᾳ 'Αγησιλάου, Xen. l. c. § 4. Of Kinadon, its originator, it is said, id. § 5: οὗτος δ' ἦν καὶ τὸ εἶδος νεανίσκος καὶ τὴν ψυχὴν εὔρωστος, οὐ μέντοι τῶν ὁμοίων (for the ὅμοιοι cf. Xen. de Rep. Lac. X, 7. XIII, 1, 7. Anab. IV, 16, 14, and Arist. l. c.; the ὑπομείονες stood opposed to these, Xen. l. c. § 6); the object of his enterprise he stated to be, μηδενὸς ἥττων εἶναι ἐν Λακεδαίμονι, id. § 11. What is most worthy of note besides the great danger which menaced Sparta, is that on this occasion a revelation is first made of the extraordinarily small number of Spartiates in the enjoyment of full rights. The informer, who brought the conspiracy to light, recounts ὅτι ὁ Κινάδων ἀγαγὼν αὐτὸν ἐπὶ τὸ ἔσχατον τῆς ἀγορᾶς ἀριθμῆσαι κελεύοι ὁπόσοι Σπαρτιᾶται εἶεν ἐν τῇ ἀγορᾷ· καὶ ἐγώ, ἔφη, ἀριθμήσας βασιλέα τε καὶ ἐφόρους καὶ γέροντας καὶ ἄλλους ὡς τετταράκοντα, ἠρόμην, τί δή με τούτους, ὦ Κινάδων, κελεύεις ἀριθμῆσαι; ὁ δὲ εἶπε, Τούτους, ἔφη, νόμιζέ σοι πολεμίους εἶναι, τοὺς δ' ἄλλους πάντας συμμάχους πλέον ἢ τετρακισχιλίους ὄντας τοὺς ἐν τῇ ἀγορᾷ· ἐπιδεικνύναι δ' αὐτόν, ἔφη, ἐν ταῖς ὁδοῖς ἔνθα μὲν ἕνα, ἔνθα δὲ δύο πολεμίους ἀπαντῶντας, τοὺς δ' ἄλλους ἅπαντας συμμάχους, καὶ ὅσοι δὲ ἐν τοῖς χωρίοις Σπαρτιατῶν τύχοιεν ὄντες, ἕνα μὲν πολέμιον τὸν δεσπότην, συμμάχους δ' ἐν ἑκάστῳ πολλούς, id. § 7. For the hatred against the Spartiates cherished by the Helots, Neodamodes, ὑπομείονες, and Perioeki, see id. § 6. The plot was frustrated, as has been said, by the confession of an informer, and a most fearful vengeance was wreaked on all the accomplices, id. § 11. cf. Polyaen. II, 14, 1.

168) Xen. Hell. III, 4, 1—15. After the suppression of Kinadon's conspiracy (id. § 1), Agesilaus, upon receipt of the intelligence that the Persian king was making great preparations, offered to take the command in Asia in person, and in the spring of 396 B.C. commenced his journey to that country with 30 Spartiates, 2000 Neodamodes, and 6000 allies, id. § 2. Upon his arrival in Asia Tissaphernes offered him an armistice, on the pretext that he was anxious to bring about a peace acceptable to Sparta at court: this Agesilaus agreed to for 3 months. After the expiration of that time he invaded Phrygia, whilst Tissaphernes, deceived as to his plans, massed his forces in Karia for the defence of that district, id. § 11—15. It is certain that the expedition of Agesilaus was entered on in the spring of 396 B.C., from the following considerations. His return from Asia took place in the summer of 394 B.C., the preparations for which were begun in the spring, see obs. 177: but according to Xen. Ages. I, 34. Plut. Ages. 14, 15, his operations in Asia comprehended a period of two years, and in Xen. Hell. III, 4, 20 it is expressly noticed in the spring of 395 B.C., that one year had elapsed since the departure of Agesilaus from Sparta (see id. § 16). The narrative of events in Xenophon is also in complete accordance with this assumption: for after the events of 396 B.C. the approach of spring is remarked, Hell. III, 4, 10; then follows the march of Agesilaus into Lydia and Phrygia, the latter ἅμα μετοπώρῳ, id. IV, I, 1; then the winter quarters in Phrygia (that it is winter during his stay there, is proved in particular by the passage, id. § 14); and in the following spring (id. § 41) he is busied with preparations for a campaign in the interior of Asia at the very moment when he receives orders to return, id. 2, 1—2.

bb) Xenophon of Athens, son of Gryllus, born circ. 444, Diog. Laert. II, 48 f (according to others circ. 431), companion and pupil of Sokrates, also of Prodikus, Philostr. Vit. Soph. I, 12, after the end of the Peloponnesian war, betook himself to Cyrus at Sardes, Diog. L. II, 55. Anab. III, 1, 4, accompanied his Grecian mercenaries, and after the battle of Kunaxa and the murder of the Grecian captains conducted the 10,000 back to Thrake. In consequence of this he was banished from Athens and fought under Agesilaus; the Spartans presented him with an estate near Skillus, which they had wrested from the Eleans; and here he employed himself with agriculture, hunting and riding, and the composition of his works, Diog. L. II, 51. 52. Anab. V, 3, 7. Paus. V, 6, 4. When expelled from his property by the Eleans, Diog. l. c. 53, though meanwhile recalled by the Athenians, he betook himself to Corinth, where he passed the rest of his days, l. c. 56. After bearing with composure the death of his son Gryllus, l. c. 53, he died probably circ. 353 B.C. His writings, for the most part of an historical or political character, are: Κύρου παιδεία, 'Ανάβασις, 'Ελληνικά, a Greek history of the time from where the work of Thucydides ends to the battle of Mantineia, Λακεδαιμονίων πολιτεία, 'Αθηναίων πολιτεία (the three last suspected), Πόροι ἢ περὶ προσόδων, on the resuscitation of the Athenian finances, 'Ιέρων,

Περὶ ἱππικῆς, Ἱππαρχικός, Κυνηγετικός—partly of a philosophic character: 'Απομνημονεύματα Σωκράτους, Σωκράτους ἀπολογία πρὸς τοὺς δικαστάς, Συμπόσιον φιλοσόφων, Οἰκονομικός λόγοι. His language was esteemed a model of the purest Attic, and he was therefore called 'Αττικὴ μέλιττα. Cf. Dion. Hal. Ep. ad Cn. Pomp. 4. Cens. de vet. script. III, 2. Cic. orat. 19, de orat. II, 14. Brut. 35. Quint. X, 1, 82.

cc) Ktesias of Knidus a contemporary of Xenophon, was at the time of the battle of Kunaxa physician in ordinary to the Persian King Artaxerxes Mnemon, but left the Persian Court in 399 B.C., and returned home to his native country, Diod. II, 32. Anab. I, 8, 27. Suid. s. v. He wrote in the Ionic dialect a history of the great monarchies of the east, in part drawn from native sources, under the title Περσικά in 23 books, Suid. l. c., from which extracts are preserved in Photius, Bibl. Cod. 72, Diod. I, II, etc. Plutarch Vit. Artax., etc., and a smaller work 'Ινδικά, from which Photius likewise gives extracts, together with some other writings, which have been altogether lost.

dd) Philistus of Syracuse, born before the attack made by Athens upon Syracuse, Plut. Nic. 19, a relative and adherent of the elder Dionysius, Diod. III, 91. XIV, 8. Plut. Dion. 11, 36. Corn. Nep. Dion.

The Incipient Decline.

Olympiad.	B. C.	ATHENS.	HISTORY.
XCVI, 2	395	Archons. Diophantus.	Agesilaus invades Lydia and overthrows the Persian cavalry[169]. Tissaphernes is deposed in consequence: his successor Tithraustes sends Timokrates to Greece, to stir up war against Sparta by means of bribery[170]. The war opens in Phokis: Lysander is defeated at Haliartus and killed[171]. The Spartan king Pausanias deposed; his successor Agesipolis[172]. Agesilaus occupies winter quarters in Phrygia[173]. b) The Corinthian War 394—387 B.C.
XCVI, 3	394	Eubulides.	The allied Thebans, Athenians, Corinthians, and Argives are conquered by the Spartans at Corinth[174].

---

169) Schooled by the injury, which he had suffered from the enemy's cavalry in the previous year, he had strengthened his mounted troops, Xen. Hell. III, 4, 15, and had made use of the winter generally to train and discipline his forces, id. 16—19 ; the favourable results of this year were also produced by the success of a stratagem, id. § 20—24.

170) Xen. Hell. III, 4, 25, 5, 1—2. Thebes, Corinth, and Argos were the states, in his dealings with which Timokrates employed bribery; Athens was also inclined to war, without however receiving any bribe. (Otherwise in regard to the Athenians, Paus. III, 9, 4. Plut. Ages. 15.).

171) On the occasion of a territorial dispute between the Phokians and Lokrians (according to Xen. Hell. III, 5, 3 they are the Opuntian, according to Paus. V, 9, 4 the Ozolian Lokrians of Amphissa) the Thebans supported the latter: thereupon the Phokians applied for help at Sparta, and Lysander was despatched to call out the Œtæans, Malians, Ænianes and Herakleotes, and to commence the war against the Thebans with these forces and the Phokians; the king Pausanias was to follow after with a Peloponnesian army, Xen. Hell. III, 5, 3—7 ; Lysander penetrated into Bœotia and invested Haliartus, but was defeated and killed in a sally of the Haliartians, supported by a Theban contingent, id. 17—21, cf. Plut. Lys. 28. Pausanias came too late to help Lysander, and returned without venturing a battle against the united Thebans and Athenians (the latter had been won over by the Thebans to join in the war as their allies, Xen. l. c. § 8—16), Xen. l. c. § 21—24. The war is called, Diod. XIV, 81. Plut.

Lys. 27, the Bœotian, and is at first merely a war between Sparta and Thebes, the latter having Athenian support; it must therefore be distinguished from the Corinthian war following.

172) Pausanias was condemned to death for the cowardice which he displayed in the circumstances described in obs. 171, but also at the same time for the favour which he had shown the Athenian democrats in 403 B. C. (obs. 156); he anticipated the sentence and saved himself by flight. Xen. Hell. III, 5, 25. He left behind him two sons under age, Agesipolis and Kleombrotus, of whom the former became his successor, at first under the protectorate of Aristodemus, id. IV, 2, 9. Paus. III, 5, 7.

173) Tithraustes had concluded an armistice (for 6 months, Diod. XIV, 80) with him, Xen. Hell. III. 4, 25—29. For his winter quarters see id. IV, 1, 1—40.

174) After the Bœotian war the league was formed between the above mentioned states, Diod. XIV, 82. cf. Xen. Hell. IV, 2, 1, and was also joined by the Eubœans, the Lokri Ozolæ, and the Akarnanians, Diod. l. c. Xen. l. c. § 17. After this the Thessalians were also compelled to join the league, though they had hitherto stood on the side of Sparta; Herakleia on Œta was taken, and thus the alliance of the neighbouring tribes was also secured, Diod. l. c. cf. Xen. id. 3, 3. In the spring the allies mustered at Corinth, the Spartans marched to oppose them; Paus. V, § 52, according to Diod. l. c. XIV, 83 on the river Nemeas) in which the Spartans were victorious, Xen. Hell. IV, 2 (according to Diod. l. c. the issue was doubtful). The forces on both sides : 6000

3, afterwards lived in banishment at Adria, Plut. d. exil. 14, p. 605 c, and was probably recalled by the younger Dionysius in 357 B.C., Plut. l. c. Corn. Nep. l. c. In a sea fight with Dion and the Syracusans he was taken prisoner and executed, when admiral of the fleet of Dionysius, Plut. Dion. 35. Diod. XVI, 11, 16. He wrote Σικελικά, Plut. Dion. 11, a history of Sicily from the oldest times down to the

younger Dionysius, Diod. XIII, 103. XV, 89. Dion. Hal. ep. ad Pomp. 6, and perhaps other works as well, Suid. s. v. Only very scanty fragments of his work have come down to us, Fragm. Histor. Græc. ed. C. Muller I, p. 185 f. Plutarch calls him, Dion. 36 : Φιλοτυραννό-τατος ἀνθρώπων. Cf. Quint. X, 1, 74 : Imitator Thucydidis, et ut multo infirmior ita aliquando lucidior.

88   FOURTH PERIOD. 431—338 B.C.

Olympiad.	B.C.	ATHENS.	HISTORY.
		Archon.	
XCVI, 3	394		The Spartan fleet under Peisander defeated at Knidus by Konon and Pharnabazus[174] Agesilaus recalled from Asia[175]; his victory over the allies at Koroneia[176].
XCVI, 4	393	Demostratus.	Corinth the central point of the war and the mustering place of the allied forces[178]. The long walls of Athens restored by Konon[177].

hoplites from Sparta, 3000 from Elis, 1500 from Sikyon, 3000 from Epidaurus, Trœzen, Hermione and Halis, 600 Lacedæmonian horsemen, 300 Kretan bowmen, 400 slingers: on the other side, 6000 hoplites from Athens, 7000 from Argos, 5000 from Bœotia, 3000 from Corinth, 3000 from Eubœa, besides 1550 horsemen from Bœotia, Athens, Eubœa, and the Opuntian Lokrians, and also light-armed Arcadians, Lokrians, Melians, Xen. l. c. § 16—17 (according to Diodorus the Spartans numbered 23,000 infantry and 500 cavalry, the allies 15,000 infantry and 500 cavalry, XIV, 82, 83). The battle had no further result, than that the allies were obliged to renounce their design of penetrating into Laconia. For the time see Xen. Hell. IV, 3, 1. cf. obs. 177.

175) Konon (for whose flight from Ægospotami to Kypros see obs. 147) had already in 397 or 396 B. c. been provided with money by the Persian king at the instance of Pharnabazus for the equipment of a fleet, but up to the present time had achieved but little, chiefly for the reason that pay was not furnished by the Persian monarch, Diod. XIV, 39. 70. Isocr. l'aneg. p. 70, § 142. Philipp. p. 94, § 62—64. cf. Xen. Hell. III, 4, 1. In order to obtain warmer support from the Persian king, he travelled himself to the court at Babylon, Diod. XIV, 81. Corn. Nep. Con. 3, cf. Ctes., Pers. fr. 63. When in consequence the strength of his fleet had received considerable additions, together with Pharnabazus he fought the battle of Knidus with Peisander (who had been appointed navarch by Agesilaus in 395 B. c. Xen. Hell. III, 4, 27—29), by which an end was made for the present of Sparta's naval supremacy, Xen. Hell. IV, 3, 10—12. Diod. XIV, 83. The Spartan harmosts were now expelled from all the islands and from the coast-towns: in Abydos and Sestos alone the Spartan rule was upheld by Derkyllidas, Xen. l. c. 8, 1—11. Isocr. Phil. l. c. § 63 : νικήσας τῇ ναυμαχίᾳ (Κόνων) Λακεδαιμονίους μὲν ἐξέβαλεν ἐκ τῆς ἀρχῆς, τοὺς δὲ Ἕλληνας ἠλευθέρωσεν. According to Diod. l. c. Konon and Pharnabazus had about 90 ships, Peisander 85; but from Xen. l. c. § 12 the disproportion between the combatants seems to have been greater. According to Xen. id. § 7 Konon had Hellenes under his command, but according to Plut. Money. p. 245 A. they were only φυγάδες καὶ ἐθελονταί. As for the time, the battle must be placed towards the end of the month of July or in the first few days of August, Xen. id. § 10. obs. 177.

176) On the approach of spring Agesilaus marched from Phrygia (obs. 173) to the coast, and there made preparations for a campaign in the interior of the Persian empire, "νομίζων ὁπόσα ὀπισθεν ποιήσαιτο ἔθνη, πάντα ἀνυστερήσειν βασιλέως," Xen. Hell. IV, 1, 41. Here he was found by the message from home ordering his return; and to this, in spite of the brilliant prospects which opened to his view, he

yielded instant and unmurmuring obedience, only allowing himself sufficient time to complete his preparations, Xen. id. 2, 1—8. Ages. I, 35—36. Plut. Ages. 15.

177) Agesilaus took the same way, which Xerxes had done on his expedition against Greece, but, instead of consuming 6 months as the Persian did, he traversed the distance in 1 month, Xen. Hell. IV, 2, 8. Ages. II, 1. When he was at Amphipolis, he received tidings of the Spartan victory at Corinth, Xen. id. 3, 1; and, when he was on the point of invading Bœotia, news reached him of the death and defeat of Peisander, and at the same time an eclipse of the sun took place, id. § 10. Plut. Ages. 17. For the battle of Koroneia (in which the hostile forces were composed of Bœotians, Athenians, Argives, Corinthians, Ænianians, Eubœans, and the Ozolian and Opuntian Lokrians, id. § 15) see id. § 15—21. As the eclipse of the sun just mentioned occurred on the 14th of August 394 B. c., it follows that the battles of Corinth and Knidus must be placed somewhere about the same time, the first about the middle, the latter towards the end of July in this year: this eclipse affords us at the same time firm standing ground on which to base our chronological computations from 401 B. c. onwards, all of which rest on this date and the combinations connected with it.

178) Xen. Hell. IV, 4, 1 : Ἐκ δὲ τούτου ἐπολέμουν Ἀθηναῖοι μὲν καὶ Βοιωτοὶ καὶ Ἀργεῖοι καὶ σύμμαχοι αὐτῶν ἐκ Κορίνθου ὁρμώμενοι, Λακεδαιμόνιοι δὲ καὶ οἱ σύμμαχοι ἐκ Σικυῶνος. Hence too the name "Corinthian war," Diod. XIV, 86. Paus. III, 6, 6. Of the further events of the war only two occurrences, besides the conclusion of peace, can be determined with chronological certainty, obs. 180 and 183; all other dates rest merely on combinations, and can all the less lay claim to anything more than mere probability, as Xenophon (who first relates the war by land, IV, 4—7, and then the war by sea, IV, 8—1) has here almost wholly abstained from giving any indications in regard to the time of the events.

179) Xen. Hell. IV, 8, 7—10. Konon and Pharnabazus sail out at the beginning of spring (id. § 7), first plunder the coast of Laconia, take Kythera, subsidize the allies at Corinth; Konon then goes to Athens, to set up the walls with Persian money: and on this account he is often celebrated by the orators as the second founder of the Athenian hegemony, Demosth. Lept. p. 477, § 68: θεῖὁ' ἐλθὼν Ἀντάγρας τὰ τείχη καὶ πρῶτος πάλιν περὶ τῆς ἡγεμονίας ἐνάψας τῇ πόλει τὸν λόγον πρὸς Λακεδαιμονίους εἶναι, cf. Isocr. Phil. p. 95, § 64. Areop. p. 153. § 65. About this time, probably in 202 B. c., the Spartans send Antalkidas to the Persian satrap Tiribazus, to offer him an alliance, Xen. Hell. IV, 8, 12—16; although the alliance was not

The Incipient Decline.

Olympiad.	B. C.	ATHENS.	HISTORY.
		Archous.	
XCVII, 1	392	Philokles.	Victory of the Spartans at Lechæum[180]).
XCVII, 2	391	Nikoteles.	Agesilaus invades the territory of Argos[181]), the Spartans masters of the territory of Corinth and of the Corinthian gulf[182]).
XCVII, 3	390	Demostratus.	Iphikrates restores the ascendancy of the allied powers[183]). The naval enterprises of the Spartans under Teleutias, and of the Athenians under Thrasybulus[184]).

effected, still the negotiations had this result, that Konon was taken prisoner by Tiribazus, and the satrap furnished the Spartans with money to fit out a fleet, id. § 16. Diod. XIV, 85. Whether Konon was put to death or escaped, is doubtful, Corn. Nep. Con. 5. cf. Lys. de bon. Aristoph. p. 165. § 89. Isocr. Paneg. p. 73. § 154: at all events to the great loss of Athens he took no further part in the war.

180) After a bloody party-struggle at Corinth the Spartans are admitted by the opposition party into the long walls between the town and the harbour Lechæum, and inflict a severe defeat on the allies, who try to drive them out again, Xen. Hell. IV, 4, 2—12: the long walls are then destroyed, and later Sidus and Krommyon are also taken, id. § 13. (Lechæum itself was probably also taken, Diod. XIV, 86, cf. Xen. l. c. § 12. 17.) From Aristides Or. XLVI. vol. II, p. 276 (Jebb) τῆς δ' ἐν Κορίνθῳ μάχῃ καὶ τῆς ἐν Λεχαίῳ μάσοι ἀρχων Εὐβουλίδης it follows that the battle of Lechæum occurred in the year following the archonship of Eubulides, therefore in the second half of 393, or in the first half of 392 B. C.: the latter is the more probable, as it fits in better with the chain of events. That the manner, in which the war was conducted after the battle, it is said, Xen. l. c. § 13 : Ἐκ δὲ τούτου στρατιαὶ μὲν μεγάλαι ἑκατέρων διεπέπαυντο, φρουροὺς δὲ πέμπουσαι αἱ πόλεις, αἱ μὲν ἐς Κόρινθον αἱ δὲ ἐς Σικυῶνα, ἐφύλαττον τὰ τείχη· μισθοφόρους γε μὴν ἑκάτεροι ἔχοντες διὰ τούτων ἐρρωμένως ἐπολέμουν. Iphikrates especially distinguished himself in this war with mercenary troops (the use of which began at this time, Demosth. Phil. I, p. 45, § 23. Isocr. Phil. p. 101. § 96. Harpocr. s. v. ξενικόν); he improved the equipment of the light-armed forces (πελτασταί) Corn. Nep. Iphicr. I. Diod. XV, 54, and now won several advantages over the allies of Sparta by their means, Xen. l. c. § 14—17.

161) Xen. Hell. IV, 4, 19.

162) The long walls of Lechæum (obs. 180) had been meanwhile rebuilt by the Athenians (and Lechæum had probably been occupied by them at the same time), Xen. Hell. IV, 18; Agesilaus now took them once more, id. § 19, and his brother Teleutias, who at this same time commanded the Corinthian gulf with 12 triremes, id. 8, 11, came and took the ships and docks of the Corinthians, making himself master of the harbour Lechæum, id. 4, 19.

183) Agesilaus again invaded the territory of Corinth at the time of the Isthmian games, Xen. Hell. IV, 5, 2, and there made himself master of Peiræum, id. § 3—6. At this same time, however, Iphikrates

with his peltasts attacked a division (μόρα) of Spartan hoplites and almost totally destroyed them, id. § 9—17, see esp. § 12, according to which only a few of the whole division, 600 strong, made good their escape. (The number of the slain given at 250, id. c. 17, is therefore certainly too small.) After this, with regard to enterprises by land, we are only informed of another campaign of Agesilaus against Akarnania, id. c. 6, and an invasion of Argos by Agesipolis, id. 7, 2—7. For the great impression made by this success of Iphikrates (like that made by the capture of the Spartiates on Sphakteria) see id. 5, 10. However, Iphikrates was soon recalled from Corinth, as by his brilliant exploits he had excited the jealousy of the other allies, id. 8, 34; according to Diod. XIV, 92, cf. Aristid. Panath. I, p. 108 (Jebb), because at Corinth he had made himself master of the town, and the Athenians themselves were displeased with his conduct. The Isthmian games were always celebrated in the spring of the 2nd and 4th year of each Olympiad, and the annihilation of the Spartan mora must therefore be placed in 392 or 390 B. C. That the latter date is the more correct, is plain from the consideration that the occurrence of the war can hardly be brought under the period up to 392, see in particular obs. 180 and 182; a further proof in favour of the later date is furnished by the speech of Andokides on the Peace, that is, presupposing its genuineness, which can hardly be doubted. This speech was delivered in 391 B. C. see p. 25. § 20, and whilst mention is made in it of the battles of Corinth, Koroneia, and Lechæum, § 18, it is expressly noticed that the Spartans have never yet been defeated in a single battle, § 19. Further, the lively wish of the Thebans for peace is recorded in § 20, which according to Xen. Hell. IV, 5, 6 existed before the destruction of the mora, whilst after that incident the Thebans were anything but inclined to peace, id. § 9. We may add that just at this time, as we learn from the same speech, negotiations for peace were also pending between Athens and Sparta, and ambassadors came from Sparta to Athens about the peace, but went away again without effecting their object, see Philochor. in the argument of the speech.

184) The Spartans had already at an earlier date (in 391 B.C.) despatched Ekdikus as navarch with 8 ships, to reestablish the aristocrats at Rhodes, who had been driven out by the democratic party (Diod. XIV, 79, 97): but he had failed to accomplish anything, Xen. Hell. IV, 8, 20—22. They then sent Teleutias, who collected a fleet of 27 ships, and established himself in Rhodes, carrying on war with the democratic party in power, id. 23—24. 25. At this same time Thrasybulus was sent out by the Athenians with 40 ships, and he made himself master of Byzantium and Chalkedon, defeated at Lesbos

C.   12

Olympiad.	B.C.	ATHENS.	HISTORY.
		Archons.	
XCVIII, 2	387	Theodotus.	The Spartans through their ambassador Antalkidas win over the Persian king to impose a peace in harmony with their own interests, to which all the other belligerent states submit under compulsion[185].
XCVIII, 3	386	Mystichides.	c) The violent conduct of Sparta towards Mantineia, Thebes, Olynthus and Phlius up to the expulsion of the Spartans from the Kadmeia, 386—379 B.C.
XCVIII, 4	385	Dexitheus.	Mantineia destroyed by the Spartans[186].
XCIX, 1	384	Diotrephes.	
XCIX, 2	383	Phanostratus.	
XCIX, 3	382	Euandrus.	Commencement of the Olynthian War[187].
			The Kadmeia occupied by the Spartans[188].

the Spartan harmost, Therimachus of Methymna, but afterwards when on the point, as it appears, of attacking Teleutias at Rhodes, he was killed at Aspendus, id. 25—30, cf. Diod. XIV, 94. Lys. ad Ergocl. Demosth. Lept. p. 475. § 60. Teleutias was succeeded by Hierax as navarch, Xen. Hell. V, 1, 5, and he by Antalkidas, id. § 6. Of the undertakings by sea, attention must also be drawn to the defeat which Iphikrates inflicted on the harmost Anaxibius of Abydon (probably in 389 B.C.), Xen. Hell. IV, 8, 34—39, and to the war between Ægina and Athens, id. V, 1, 1—24, which was carried on from 390 B.C. onwards, id. § 1. 2, and in which (in 388 or 387 B.C.) Teleutias obtained a great advantage by surprising the Peiræus, id. § 13—24. Antalkidas placed his lieutenant Nikolochus in command of the fleet; he, however, is shut up in Abydon by the Athenian leaders, Iphikrates and Diotimus, id. § 6—7. 25. Antalkidas himself makes a journey to the Persian Court.

185) Antalkidas, after winning over the Persian king, returned to the scene of the war, and with support from Persia collected a fleet of 80 sail, with which he commanded the sea, Xen. Hell. V, 1, 25—28. With Sparta in such overwhelming superiority, the allies could not help accepting the peace which Antalkidas had brought with him from the Persian king. Accordingly they submitted to it: yet it was only when compelled by the threats of Sparta, that Thebes consented to vouchsafe independence to the other Bœotian towns, and also Corinth to dismiss the Argive garrison and take back her exiles, bl. 29—34. The peace ran (id. § 31): Ἀρταξέρξης βασιλεὺς νομίζει δίκαιον, τὰς μὲν ἐν τῇ Ἀσίᾳ πόλεις ἑαυτοῦ εἶναι καὶ τῶν νήσων Κλαζομενὰς καὶ Κύπρον· τὰς δὲ ἄλλας Ἑλληνίδας πόλεις καὶ μικρὰς καὶ μεγάλας αὐτονόμους ἀφεῖναι πλὴν Λήμνου καὶ Ἴμβρου καὶ Σκύρου· ταύτας δὲ ὥσπερ τὸ ἀρχαῖον εἶναι Ἀθηναίων· ὁπότεροι δὲ ταύτην τὴν εἰρήνην μὴ δέχονται, τούτοις ἐγὼ πολεμήσω μετὰ τῶν ταύτα βουλομένων καὶ πεζῇ καὶ κατὰ θάλατταν καὶ ναυσὶ καὶ χρήμασιν. For the advantages which the peace gave to Sparta, cf. Isocr. Paneg. id. § 86: Ἐν δὲ τῷ πολέμῳ μᾶλλον ὑπερρόνει τοῖς ἐναντίοις πράττοντες οἱ Λακεδαιμόνιοι, πολὺ ἐπικυδέστεροι ἐγένοντο ἐκ τῆς ἐπ' Ἀνταλκίδου εἰρήνης καλουμένης. προστάτας γὰρ γενόμενοι τῆς ὑπὸ βασιλέως καταπεμφθείσης εἰρήνης—; the ignominy of this peace is an oft-recurring theme for blame and accusation in the Attic orators, see esp. Isocr. Paneg. p. 64—67. § 115—128. Plat. Menex. p. 245. For the date see Polyb. I, 6: ἔτει ἐπιστήσει μετὰ τὴν ἐν Αἰγὸς ποταμοῖς ναυμαχίαν ἐννεακαιδέκατον, πρὸ δὲ τῆς ἐν Λεύκτροις μάχης ἑκκαιδέκατον. (In consequence of this peace Plataea was restored, Paus. XI, 1, 3, but was again destroyed by the Thebans in 374 B.C. (or 373? Paus.); Paus. l.c. Xen. Hell. VI, 3, 1. Diod. XV, 46, Isocr. Plataic., and was only rebuilt by Alexander the Great.)

186) Xen. Hell. V, 2, 1—7. Diod. XV, 5. 12. The Spartans required the Mantineians to pull down their walls (their reasons, Xen. l.c. § 2, especially ἔτι δὲ γιγνώσκειν ἐφασαν φθονοῦντας μὲν αὐτοῖς, εἴ τι σφίσιν ἀγαθὸν γίγνοιτο, ἐφηδομένους δ' εἴ τις συμφορὰ προσπίπτοι, id.), and when they refused, the Spartans besieged the town, and in the end compelled the inhabitants to pull them down, and to settle as of old in 4 villages: from this measure followed of itself the restoration of the aristocratic constitution. The date assigned rests in this instance, as in the majority of the events immediately following, upon Diodorus; here again no definite accounts of the time are found in Xenophon, and thus only isolated and chance indications as to chronology can be turned to account from that writer.

187) The Olynthians, utilising the straitened situation of the Macedonian kings, had united the Greek towns in the vicinity of the coast in a league, to which even Pella belonged: according to Xenophon the Akanthians and Apolloniates now came to Sparta, and begged for its support against the preponderant power of Olynthus; according to Diod. XV, 19 (cf. Isocr. Paneg. p. 67. § 126) it was Amyntas, king of Macedonia, who applied for Sparta's assistance, and the Spartans first sent Eudamidas with 2000 men against Olynthus; a larger force was to follow as soon as possible, Xen. Hell. V, 2, 11—24.

188) This was effected by Phœbidas, the brother of Eudamidas; he had to conduct the reinforcements sent after his brother to the scene of the war, and whilst on his way thither made himself master of the Kadmeia through the treachery of a Theban party friendly to Sparta, Xen. Hell. V, 2, 25—36. Though the Spartans imposed a fine on Phœbidas, still they left the garrison in the Kadmeia, Polyb. IV, 26. Plut. Pelop. 6. Diod. XV, 22. According to Diod. l.c. this cannot have happened before 382 B.C.; and with this Aristid. or. XIX,

Olympiad.	B. C.	ATHENS.	HISTORY.
XCIX, 4	381	Archons. Demophilus.	Teleutias, the Spartan commander, is defeated by the Olynthians and falls in the battle[189].
C, 1	380	Pytheas.	King Agesipolis, leader of the Spartans against Olynthus, dies[190]. Kleombrotus King of Sparta in his stead[191]). Phlius besieged by the Spartans under Agesilaus[192]).
C, 2	379	Nikon.	Olynthus[193]) and Phlius[194]) reduced to subjection. The liberation of Thebes and the Kadmeia[195]).

1. p. 258 (Jehh) is also in agreement; according to which passage the occupation of the Kadmeia happened at the time of the Pythian games, i.e. in the first months of the third year of the Olympiad: Xenophon only tells us, that it took place in the summer, l. c. § 20. The succession of events, which must be settled in agreement with Xenophon, is not opposed to the adoption of this year as the date.

189) Teleutias led (certainly still in 382 B c.) the larger army, fixed at 10,000 men, into the territory of Olynthus: he strengthened himself with mercenary troops from Amyntas and a Thrakian prince Derdas, and won (still in the same year) a victory over the enemy, Xen. Hell. V, 2; 39—43: but in the following year (Xen. l. c. 3, 1) he was totally defeated, and himself lost his life, id. 3, 1—6.

190) Xen. Hell. V, 3, 8—9. 18—19. From Xen. l. c. § 3, cf. § 18, it is clear that Agesipolis cannot have conducted the war in the same summer, in which Teleutias fell; and, besides that, this is improbable on account of the great preparations, which were made for the campaign under Agesipolis, id. § 8. However, it does not follow from that passage, that the beginning of the war must be placed in 383 B. c.: Polybiades, the successor of Agesipolis, could join the army in a short time, and then very easily bring the war to an end by the summer of 379 B. c.

191) Diod. XV, 23. Paus. III, 6, 1.

192) Shortly after the destruction of Mantineia, probably in 384 B.c., the Phliasians had been obliged to take back their exiles at the demand of Sparta and to restore them to their property, Xen. Hell. V, 2, 8—10. The result, as was easy to foresee, was that disputes arose between them; whereupon Agesilaus marched into their territory and invested the town, id. 3, 10—18. According to Xen. l. c. § 10, the disputes, which resulted in war, broke out at the time when Agesipolis was conducting the war against Olynthus.

193) Xen. Hell. V, 3, 26. Diod. XV, 23. The Olynthians were overcome by Polybiades, the successor of Agesipolis; they were obliged to renounce their league, and join the Spartan alliance.

194) Xen. Hell. V, 3, 21—25. According to id. § 25 the affair with Phlius (τὰ μὲν περὶ Φλιοῦντα) lasted altogether 1 year and 8 months. The town was obliged to surrender unconditionally, and Agesilaus appointed a commission, half being composed of exiles, to punish the guilty and introduce a new legislation; for the better security of which he left a garrison behind him.

195) Xen. Hell. V, 4, 3—12. Plut. Pelop. 7—12. de gen. Socr. p. 575—598. Diod. XV, 25—26. The leaders of the bold enterprise, by which the liberation was effected, were Mellon, Charon, Phyllidas, and above all Pelopidas (the last not named by Xenophon); by them the heads of the party which had betrayed Thebes to Sparta, Archias, Philippus, Leontiades, Hypates, were murdered, and thus the town itself was freed; on the following day, with help from the rest of the exiles and Athenian volunteers, who had been summoned from the borders of Attica, the Kadmeia was assaulted by storm, and the garrison immediately surrendered on the condition of a free departure being granted them. For the time of this event, so important in its consequences, see Plut. Ages. 24, according to which it took place shortly after the reduction of Phlius, whilst according to Plut. Pelop. 9. Xen. l. c. § 14, it took place in the winter (379/8). (For the turning-point marked in the history of this period by the liberation of Thebes, see obs. 152: cf. also the Panegyric of Isokrates, composed in 380 B.c., which everywhere discloses to us the arrogance of Sparta, the pressure with which that arrogance weighed on the other Greek states, and in particular the evil case of the Greek towns in Asia Minor, which Sparta had given up to the Persians, see esp. p. 65. § 117: Τοσοῦτον δ' ἀνέχουσι τῆς ἐλευθερίας καὶ τῆς αὐτονομίας, ὥσθ' αἱ μὲν ὑπὸ τυράννοις εἰσί, τὰς δ' ἁρμοσταὶ κατέχουσιν, ἔνιαι δ' ἀνάστατοι γεγόνασι, τῶν δ' οἱ βάρβαροι δεσπόται καθεστήκασιν, further Isocr. de pac. p. 179. § 97—101. etc.)

FOURTH PERIOD. 431—338 B.C.

Olympiad.	B. C.	ATHENS.	HISTORY.
		Archons.	d) The Theban War. 378—362 B.C.
C, 3	378	Nausinikus.	Kleombrotus and Agesilaus make successive invasions of Bœotia, but without important result[196].
			Athens unites with Bœotia against Sparta[197]) and recovers the hegemony by sea[198]).
C, 4	377	Kallias.	Second invasion of Bœotia by Agesilaus[199]).
CI, 1	376	Charisandrus.	Unsuccessful attempt of Kleombrotus to penetrate again into Bœotia[200]).
			Naval victory of the Athenians under Chabrias over the Spartans at Naxos[201]).

196) Xen. Hell. V, 4, 13—18. 35—41. The first expedition of Kleombrotus was undertaken in the second half, and before the end of, the winter 379/8, see Xen. l.c. § 14; on the second expedition of Agesilaus the Athenians had already come to the aid of the Thebans under the command of Chabrias, and it was they chiefly who kept Agesilaus from venturing a battle through the imposing attitude of their peltasts, Diod. XV, 32—33. Corn. Nep. Chabr. 1.

197) After the liberation of the Kadmeia the Athenians had at first attempted to appease and pacify the Spartans for the help, which they had lent the Thebans on that occasion (obs. 195), by condemning to death the two generals who had been concerned in the affair, Xen. Hell. V, 4, 19. Plut. Pel. 14. (It is also worthy of note as a proof of the fear which was universally entertained of Sparta, that even the Thebans after the liberation of the Kadmeia still sent an embassage to Sparta, offering to remain under Sparta's hegemony as heretofore. Isocr. Plat. p. 301. § 29.) But soon after this Sphodrias, whom Agesilaus had left behind as harmost at Thespiæ, made an inroad into Attica, Xen. l.c. § 20—24, which the Spartans left unpunished, id. § 25—33. This induced the Athenians to take part openly with the Thebans, id. § 34.

198) Diod. XV, 28. 29—30. The Athenians summoned the islands and the towns on the Thrakian coast, to unite in a league with them; in which, little by little, some 70 towns (Diod. l.c. Æsch. de f. leg. p. 37. § 70) came to participate. The alliance was established with very fair conditions for those who joined it (e.g. the Athenians bound themselves never to acquire possessions in foreign territory, and generally showed no wish to prejudice in any way the independence of the allies. Diod. l.c. Isocr. Plat. p. 300. § 18. p. 305. § 44), and the conditions were embodied in a record, which was signed by the members, and which happily is still preserved in an inscription found in 1851, see Meier Comment. epigr. II, p. 53 ff. The first to join the alliance were, as we are told, Chios, Byzantium, Rhodes, Mytilene, Diod. l.c. 28, then Eubœa, with the exception of the town Hestiæa, Skiathos and Peparethus, id. 30; numerous other names are found in the inscription mentioned, e.g. Perinthus, Maroneia,

Paros, Andros, Tenos, Antissa, Eresus, Keos, Amorgos, Selymbria, Siphnos, Zakynthus: Thebes also joined this league, id. and Diod. l.c. 20. The common concerns were discussed in a συνέδριον at Athens, id. 28, and the contributions of the allies were styled συντάξεις, in order to avoid the name φόροι, which had become odious; so in Isocr. de pac. p. 165. § 29. p. 166. § 36. Xenophon does not mention this alliance, but he at least intimates its existence, Hell. V, 4, 35, and presupposes it in his later narrative. That it was concluded in this year, we learn from the inscription, already referred to, in which the archon of the year 378/7 is named Nausinikus; when in line 4 mention is made of the seventh Prytany of this year, i.e. February or March 377 B.C., this only refers to the composition of the document, which, as is shown by line 24, did not take place till after the alliance had been concluded with several states. Diodorus places it, as he does the events of this period generally, a year too late.

199) Xen. Hell. V, 4, 47—55. The time is given definitely id. § 47. On the way home he was attacked by an illness, which arose from a sore in the foot: this prevented him for a considerable time from taking any part in the war, id. 58. Plut. Ages. 27.

200) Xen. Hell. V, 4, 59. The Thebans and Athenians had occupied Kithæron, and Kleombrotus vainly endeavoured to expel them from their position, and so open up the way into Bœotia.

201) The Peloponnesians had fitted out a fleet of 60 ships, with which they harassed and commanded the sea in the neighbourhood of Athens; accordingly the Athenians went on board their vessels, and gave them battle at Naxos, when the Spartans were totally defeated, Xen. Hell. V, 4, 60—61. Diod. XV, 34—35. Plut. Phoc. 6. Demosth. Lept. p. 480. § 77—78. (According to Demosthenes Chabrias took 49 ships, according to Diodorus 24 were scuttled, 8 taken.) The time of the battle, the 16th of Boedromion (September), Plut. l.c. Cam. 19. After the battle many islands in the archipelago were won over to the Athenian alliance, Plut. Phoc. 7. Dem. l.c. (According to Dem. Phil. III, p. 119. § 23 the prostasy of the Lacedæmonians ceased with this battle.)

The Incipient Decline.   93

Olympiad.	B. C.	ATHENS.	HISTORY.
		Archons.	
CI, 2	375	Hippodamas.	The Athenians under Timotheus extend their naval supremacy over the Ionian sea[202]). The Thebans restore the Bœotian league, formed under their own headship, and compel the Bœotian towns to join it[203]).
CI, 3	374	Sokratides.	The Thebans invade Phokis[204]); but are compelled to retire by Kleombrotus, who had been sent by the Spartans with an army to the aid of the Phokians[205]). A short peace, soon ruptured again, between Athens and Sparta[206]).
CI, 4	373	Asteius.	Successful naval expedition of Iphikrates to Kerkyra, by which the supremacy of Atheus in the Ionian sea is restored and fortified[207]).
CII, 1	372	Alkisthenes.	

202) Xen. Hell. V, 4, 62—66. Diod. XV, 36. Timotheus defeated the Peloponnesian fleet under Nikolochus at Alyzia, Xen. l. c. § 65, and won over Kerkyra to the Athenian alliance, id. § 64, likewise Kephallenia, the towns in Akarnauia, and Alketas, king of the Molossians, Diod. l. c. cf. Xen. id. (For Timotheus generally cf. Isocr. de permut. § 109—130. Dem. Lept. p. 480. § 78.)

203) Xen. Hell. V, 4, 63: Ἄτε δὲ εἰς τὰς Οὐρβας οὐκ ἐμβεβληκότων τῶν πολεμίων οὔτ᾽ ἐν ᾧ Κλεόμβροτος ἦγε τὴν στρατιὰν ἔτει οὔτ᾽ ἐν ᾧ Τιμόθεος περιέπλευσε, θρασεῖαι δὴ ἐστρατεύοντο οἱ Θηβαῖοι ἐπὶ τὰς περιοικίδας πόλεις καὶ πάλιν αὐτὰς ἀνελάμβανον. At all events much was contributed to this result by a victory, which the Thebans under Pelopidas gained over a troop of enemies, superior in number, at Tegyra, Plut. Pelop. 16—17. Diod. XV, 37. (It is not mentioned by Xenophon.) Orchomenos alone still remained unsubdued. The passage cited from Xenophon is of great importance for the chronology, as in it the year in which Kleombrotus made his fruitless attempt to invade Bœotia (376 B. c.) is expressly distinguished from the year in which Timotheus sailed round the Peloponnese and the Thebans reduced the Bœotians to subjection. Now if for the year 375 B. c. the advance of the Thebans was limited to this, and it is not till below VI, 1, 1 that it is noted as a further advance, that they invaded Phokis, then it follows at the same time, that this invasion cannot well be placed earlier than 374 B. c.

204) Xen. Hell. VI, 1, 1.

205) Xen. Hell. VI, 2, 1.

206) Xen. Hell. VI, 2, 1—3. The causes which led to the peace on the side of Athens, id. § 6: εἰ δ᾽ Ἀθηναῖοι αὐξανομένους μὲν ὁρῶντες τοὺς Θηβαίους, χρήματα τε οὐ συμβαλλομένους εἰς τὸ ναυτικόν, αὐτοὶ δὲ ἀποκναιόμενοι καὶ χρημάτων εἰσφοραῖς καὶ λῃστείαις ἐξ Αἰγίνης καὶ φυλακαῖς

τῆς χώρας, ἐπεθύμησαν τῆς εἰρήνης καὶ πέμψαντες πρέσβεις εἰς Λακεδαίμονα εἰρήνην ἐποιήσαντο. They now immediately recalled Timotheus, who still remained with the fleet in the western sea; but the war soon broke out again: for on his way back Timotheus reestablished some fugitives (the expelled democratic party) in Zakynthos, and the Spartans on their side sent a fleet again to the western sea, in order to expel these fugitives, id. § 2—3. cf. Diod. XV, 45.

207) The Spartan fleet (obs. 206), 60 ships strong, sails under the command of Mnasippus to Kerkyra and besieges the town, Xen. Hell. VI, 2, 2—9: the Athenians, applied to for help by the Kerkyreans, first send 600 hoplites under Kiesikles by the land route, id. 10—11, and then fit out a fleet of 60 ships, and again appoint Timotheus to the command; he however, in order first to obtain sufficient hands to man the ships, sails eastward to the islands, instead of to Kerkyra, id. 11—12. Diod. XV, 47. In the speech of Demosthenes (or Apollodorus?) against Timotheus p. 1186. § 6 we find the welcome account which fixes the time of this event in the month of Munychion in the archonship of Sokratides; from the same speech we learn, that he was accused for his conduct and that the case was tried in the month of Maimakterion (November) in the archonship of Asteius, id. p. 1190. § 22. In consequence the Athenians replaced him in the command by Iphikrates, who then (as it appears, not till after the trial of Timotheus in the winter of 373/2 or perhaps in the spring of 372 B. c.?) proceeded to Kerkyra, Xen. l. c. § 13—14. 27—38. But before he arrived there, Mnasippus had been already defeated and slain, and Kerkyra liberated, id. § 15—27. Iphikrates at first remained in those waters, continually widening the boundaries and strengthening the foundations of the Athenian supremacy, id. § 37—38.

FOURTH PERIOD. 431—338 B.C.

Olympiad.	B.C.	ATHENS.	HISTORY.	ART AND LITERATURE.
		Archons.		
CII, 2	371	Phrasikleides.	The Greek states conclude peace with one another, all except Thebes, which refuses to accede to it[208]). Kleombrotus invades Bœotia, to compel the Thebans to accept the peace, but is totally defeated by Epameinondas in the battle of Leuktra[209]). Kleombrotus himself falls: his successor on the throne is Agesipolis II, and after the death of the latter, which took place shortly afterwards, Kleomenes II[210]).	
CII, 3	370	Dysnikctus.	Mantineia rebuilt[211]); the whole of Arcadia united into one common state with Megalopolis for its capital[212]).	Middle Comedy[ee]): Antiphanes[ff]), Alexis[gg]).

208) Xen. Hell. VI, 3. The conditions of peace, see id. § 18; ἐψηφίσαντο καὶ οἱ Λακεδαιμόνιοι δέχεσθαι τὴν εἰρήνην, ἐφ᾽ ᾧ τούς τε ἁρμοστὰς ἐκ τῶν πόλεων ἐξάγειν, τά τε στρατόπεδα διαλύειν καὶ τὰ ναυτικὰ καὶ τὰ πεζικά, τὰς τε πόλεις αὐτονόμους ἐᾶν· εἰ δέ τις παρὰ ταῦτα ποιοίη, τὸν μὲν βουλόμενον βοηθεῖν ταῖς ἀδικουμέναις πόλεσι, τῷ δὲ μὴ βουλομένῳ μὴ εἶναι ἔνορκον συμμαχεῖν τοῖς ἀδικουμένοις. The Thebans were excluded from the peace, because they were not willing to sign it for themselves separately, but only for the whole Bœotian league, id. § 19—20. Plut. Ages. 28. Date of the peace: the 14th of Skirophorion (June), Plut. id.

209) Xen. Hell. VI, 4, 2—15. Diod. XV, 51—56. Plut. Pel. 20—23. Paus. IX, 13. According to Diod. l. c. 52 the Thebans were 6,000 men strong, the Spartans, according to Plut. l. c. 20, 11,000 strong. The victory was chiefly due to the oblique order of battle adopted by Epameinondas, Diod. l. c. 55: λοξὴν ποιήσας τὴν φάλαγγα, cf. Plut. l. c. 20, and to the fact that this general gave his left wing a depth of 50 men, and with this threw himself on the right wing of the enemy, where Kleombrotus was stationed with the most distinguished of the Spartiates, Xen. l. c. § 12: λογιζόμενος ὡς εἰ νικήσειαν τὸ περὶ τὸν βασιλέα, τὸ ἄλλο πᾶν εὐχείρωτον ἔσοιτο. Of the 700 Spartiates, who were present in the battle, 400 fell with the king Kleombrotus, besides 1,000 Lacedæmonians, id. § 15. cf. Diod. l. c. 56. Dionys. Hal. Arch. II, 17. Plut. Ages. 24. Paus. IX, 13, 4. Of the Thebans only 300, Diod. l. c., or actually only 47, Paus. l. c., are said to have fallen. For the important share of Pelopidas and the sacred band in the victory, Plut. Pel. 23 (for the sacred band generally see id. 18—19): The time of the battle: on the 5th of Hekatombæon (July), 20 days after the peace,

ee) The special characteristics of middle comedy, the writers of which embrace the period from the end of the Peloponnesian war up to Alexander, are stated in particular as follows: instead of the unfettered personal and political satire of the old comedy, the ridicule under feigned names (αἰνιγματωδῶς κωμῳδεῖν), Περὶ κωμ. VIII, 8, 9. IV, 4. IX, 9. Schol. Dion. Thrac. p. 749. Arist. Poet. 9. Eth. Nicom. IV, 8; the preponderance of parodies on serious poems, Platon. Περὶ διαφ. κωμ. I, 16. Athen. XI, p. 472 E; and the travesty of myths (Eubul. Antiop. fr. 2); the absence of the costly chorus and of the lively play of fantasy, which was an element in the old comedy, Περὶ κωμ. VIII, 15; and the introduction of standing masks or characters. For the style see Περὶ κωμ. III, 9: τῆς δὲ μέσης κωμῳδίας οἱ ποιηταὶ πλάσματος μὲν οὐχ ἥψαντο ποιητικοῦ, διὰ δὲ τῆς συνήθους ἰόντες λαλιᾶς λογικὰς ἔχουσι τὰς ἀρετάς, ὥστε σπάνιον ποιητικὸν εἶναι χαρακτῆρα παρ᾽ αὐτοῖς.

Plut. Ages. 28. Cam. 19. Paus. VIII, 27, 6, in the archonship of Phrasikleides, Dionys. Hal. Lys. p. 479. Marm. Par. For the firmness of the Spartans on receiving intelligence of the disaster, see Xen. l. c. § 16, especially τῇ δὲ ὑστεραίᾳ ἦν ὁρᾶν, ὧν μὲν ἐτέθνασαν οἱ προσήκοντες, λιπαροὺς καὶ φαιδροὺς ἐν τῷ φανερῷ ἀναστρεφομένους, ὧν δὲ ζῶντες ἠγγελμένοι ἦσαν, ὀλίγους ἂν εἶδες, τούτους δὲ σκυθρωποὺς καὶ ταπεινοὺς περιιόντας. They immediately equipped a new army and despatched it under the command of Archidamus: but meanwhile a convention had been arrived at through the mediation of Jason (obs. 224) between the Spartans and Thebans, which allowed the Spartans to depart freely: Archidamus thus met the retiring army at Megara, and returned back in its company, Xen. l. c. § 17—26. Cic. de off. I, § 84: Illa (plaga) pestifera, qua cum Cleombroto invidiam timens temere cum Epaminonda confixisset, Lacedæmoniorum opes corruerunt. Further, for the ruinous results of the battle to Sparta, cf. Isocr. Phil. p. 91. § 47—50.

210) Diod. XV, 60. Paus. III, 6, 1. Plut. Ag. 3.

211) Xen. Hell. VI, 5, 3—5. Cf. obs. 186. The restoration was but one manifestation of the universal effort to obtain independence of Sparta, which was awakened in many parts of the Peloponnese by the battle of Leuktra. In regard to the time, thus much only is proved by the passage cited from Xenophon, that the rebuilding took place shortly after the battle of Leuktra; according to Paus. VIII, 8, 6, IX, 14, 2 it did not follow until the occasion of a Theban invasion of the Peloponnese, obs. 213.

212) Xen. Hell. VI, 5, 6—9. Diod. XV, 59. Paus. VIII, 27, 1—6. According to Paus. l. c. the foundation of Megalopolis took place in the

ff) Antiphanes, born it is uncertain whether at Smyrna, Rhodes, or Chios, lived circ. 404—328, and wrote numerous comedies at Athens, Suid. s. v. Περὶ κωμ. III, 14 (εὐφυέστατον εἰς τὸ γράφειν καὶ δραματοποιεῖν). Of these, titles and fragments of some 280 plays have come down to us, the most important from the comedien Ἀγροικός, Ἀλιευομένη, Ἀφροδίσιοι, Ἀφροδίτης γοναί, Βουτάλιων, Γανυμήδης, Δίδυμοι, Κνοισθιδεὺς ἢ Γάστρων, Κύκλωψ, Λήμνιαι, Οἰνόμαος ἢ Πέλοψ, Παράσιτος, Πλούσιοι, Ποίησις, Πρόβλημα, Σαπφώ, Στρατιώτης ἢ Τύχων, Φιλοθήβαιοι. Cf. Meineke fr. com. med. p. 3 f. The refinement of his style is praised, Athen. I, p. 27 D, IV, p. 156 C. 168 D.

gg) Alexis, born at Thurii, then an Athenian citizen, Suid. s. v. Steph. Byz. p. 510, lived over a century, from about 390 to 288 B.C.

The Incipient Decline. 95

Olympiad.	B.C.	HISTORY.	ART AND LITERATURE.
CII, 3	370	First invasion of the Peloponnese by Epameinondas; he penetrates into Laconia, and marches through the country as far as Gytheium and Helus[213]. Messenia restored[214]. Alliance between Athens and Sparta[215].	Orators: Isokrates[hh]), Isæus[ii]).

same (Olympiad.) year, and only a few months after the battle of Leuktra; Xenophon and Diodorus l. c. only inform us of the Arcadian rising: the foundation of Megalopolis is placed by Diodorus in another passage (XV, 72) in the year 368/7. The decision of common concerns lay with the Ten Thousand (οἱ μύριοι), who met together at Megalopolis as the representatives of the united communes, Diod. l. c. cf. Xen. Hell. VII, 1, 38. 4, 2. 33. 34. Demosth. de f. leg. p. 344. § 11. p. 403. § 198.

213) In consequence of the Arcadian movement the Spartans under Agesilaus undertook an expedition against that country, without achieving any important success, Xen. Hell. VI, 5, 10—21, "in the middle of the winter" (370—369), id. § 20. After the Spartans had retired, the Boeotians arrived (Orchomenus had at this time joined the league Diod. XV, 57), reinforced by Phokians, Euboeans, Lokrians, Akarnanians, also Herakleiotes, Malians, and Thessalian cavalry, Xen. l. c. § 23, according to Diod. XV, 62 over 50,000 strong, according to Plut. Pel. 24. Ages. 31 actually 70,000 men strong. They united with the Arcadians, Argives, and Eleans, and then invaded Laconia, Xen. l. c. § 23—32. Diod. XV, 62—67, the first time for 500 years that the country had been invaded by an enemy (Diod. l. c. § 65. Xen. id. § 28 : τῶν δὲ ἐκ τῆς πόλεως αἱ μὲν γυναῖκες οὐδὲ τὸν καπνὸν ὁρῶσαι ἠνείχοντο, ἅτε οὐδέποτε ἰδοῦσαι πολεμίους). The Orchomenians, Phliasians, Corinthians, Epidaurians, Pellenians, Haliaeans, and Hermioneans, who remained true to their alliance, came to the help of

Sparta, Xen. id. § 29. cf. VII, 2, 2, and the Athenians also sent at their request an auxiliary force under Iphikrates, id. VI, 5, 33—49. Diod. l. c. 63. Epameinondas however not only marched through Laconia, but also returned without hindrance, Xen. id. § 50—52. It was still winter at the time, id. 50. (He, together with the rest of the Boeotarchs, had retained his command beyond the legal period, and is said to have been charged with this offence upon his return to Thebes, but to have vindicated his conduct with brilliant success, Plut. Pel. 25. Paus. IX, 14, 2—4. Corn. Nep. Epam. 7—8.)

214) Diod. XV, 66. Plut. Pel. 24. Paus. IV, 27, 5. IX, 14, 2, cf. VI, 2, 5. The restoration took place in connexion with the expedition of Epameinondas, see the passages quoted, esp. Paus. IV, 27, 5 : In Xenophon it is not mentioned on this occasion, but in the following year he takes the fact for granted, see Hell. VII, 1; 27, cf. 29. 36.

215) Xen. Hell. VII, 1, 1—14. Diod. XV, 67. With regard to the hegemony it was determined, that both by land and sea it should be held alternately by Athens and Sparta for the space of 5 days, Xen. l. c. § 14. The conclusion of the alliance took place certainly not long after the Athenians had as a matter of fact already lent aid to the Spartans, obs. 213, that is, as this event had happened in the winter of 370/69, before the expiration of 369 B. C., and when Xenophon (l. c. § 1) says that it was concluded τῷ ὑστέρῳ ἔτει, the official year or the year from spring to spring can only be meant.

Plut. d. defect. orac. p. 420. Περὶ κωμ. III, 316. Aristot. ap. Strab. Floril. CXVI, 47, and is said to have written 245 comedies. The most considerable fragments preserved are from the plays Αἴωνιος, Ἀντυλλανκωμένος, Ἀσωτοδιδάσκαλος, Δημήτριος ἢ Φιλέταιρος, Ἰσοστάσιον, Κρατεύας ἢ Φαρμακοπώλης, Λέβης, Λίνος, Μανδραγοριζομένη, Μιλησία, Ὀλυνθία, Παννυχὶς ἢ Ἔριθοι, Ταραντῖνοι, Φαίδροι, cf. Meineke fragm. com. med. p. 382 f. He is praised for his wit, Athen. II, p. 59. Athenæus knew over 800 plays of the middle comedy, VIII, p. 336 n : the names and fragments of 59 poets have come down to us. Besides those already named, the most numerous and important fragments preserved are from the comedies of Anaxandrides of Kamirus, and Eubulus of Athens. Mein. l. c. p. 161. 203.

hh) Isokrates of Athens, the master of epideiktic eloquence, born 436 B.C., Isocr. vit. Western. Vit. min. p. 245 f. Vit. β'. γ', enjoyed a careful training, and attended the lectures of Tisias, Gorgias, Prodikus, and Sokrates (Plat. Phædr. p. 278 E. 279 B.). Vit. α'. β'. γ'. Suid. s. v. As timidity and bodily weakness prevented him from coming forward in public, Isocr. Panath. § 9. Philipp. § 81. Vit. α'. β' (: ἰσχνόφωνός τ' ὢν καὶ εὐλαβὴς τὸν τρόπον). γ', he founded a school of rhetoric, first in Chios, then at Athens, Vit. β', wrote speeches for parties at law, for which he took payment, and made a large fortune, so that he could discharge the trierarchy, Vit. α'. β'. Isocr. Περὶ ἀντιδ.

§ 5. An opponent of the sophists, he gave prominence to the practical ethical side of political oratory, Isocr. Κατὰ τῶν σοφ. § 19. Ἑλένης ἐγκωμ. § 1—13. Πρὸς Νικοκλ. § 6. Περὶ ἀντιδ. § 3. Vit. α', and educated numerous pupils, e.g. Theopheus, Theopompus, Ephorus, Isæus, Lykurgus, Demosthenes (?), Hypereides, etc. Vit. β'. γ'. Cic. de orat. II, 22, 94. He was a zealous patriot and committed suicide through grief at the defeat of Chæroneia, Vit. α'. β'. γ'. Paus. 1, 17. Of his speeches, about the number of which the ancients themselves differed in opinion, Vit. β'. γ'. Suid. l. c., 21 are still preserved, 8 forensic and 13 political declamations (ἐπιδείξεις); amongst them of special prominence and also historical importance are the Πανηγυρικός and the Παναθηναϊκός, panegyrics on Athens; further Ἀρεοπαγιτικός, Περὶ εἰρήνης ἢ συμμαχικός, Πρὸς Νικοκλέα, Φίλιππος, Ἀρχίδαμος, Πλαταϊκός. Also ten letters have come down to us bearing his name, Bekk. Oratt. Att. II, p. 482 f.; and a treatise on oratory, τέχναι (τέχνη), was ascribed to him, Vit. β'. Cic. de invent. II, 2. Quint. II, 15, 4. Western. I, p. 298. Cicero calls Isokrates "pater eloquentiæ", de orat. II, 2, 10: cf. Dion. Hal. Isocr. 3: θαυμαστὸν γὰρ καὶ μέγα τὸ τῆς Ἰσοκράτους κατασκευῆς ὕψος, ἡρωικῆς μᾶλλον ἢ ἀνθρωπίνης.

ii) Isæus of Chalkis in Euboea, lived circ. 420—348, and settled at Athens, where he became the pupil of Isokrates and Lysias, established

FOURTH PERIOD. 431—338 B.C.

Olympiad.	B.C.	ATHENS.	HISTORY.	ART AND LITERATURE.
CII, 4	369	Archons. Lysistratus.	Second invasion of the Peloponnese by Epameinondas[216].	Sculptors: Skopas[kk]), Praxiteles[ll]).
CIII, 1	368	Nausigenes.	The Arcadians defeated by the Spartans[217]).	
CIII, 2	367	Polyzelus.	Fruitless attempt on the part of Thebes to establish peace by means of Persian influence[218]).	

216) Xen. Hell. VII, 1, 15—22. Diod. XV, 67—69. The Athenians and Spartans had occupied the Oneium range, in order to close the entrance into the Peloponnese against the Thebans: but the Thebans defeat the Spartans, and so open the way, Xen. l.c. § 15—17. They next win over Pellene and Sikyon to join their league, and lay waste the territory of Epidaurus, id. § 18. cf. 2, 11: then return back again, without achieving any further important success. It is also worthy of notice, that at this time auxiliary troops were sent to the Spartans by Dionysius, tyrant of Syracuse, Xen. l.c. I, 20—22; as also on two future occasions, the last time in the reign of Dionysius the younger, id. 1, 28. 4, 12. From Xenophon and also from Diodorus it is probable that the second expedition, as well as the first, took place in 369 B.C. But considering the nature of our sources of information this cannot be looked upon as fully proved, and it is not impossible that the expedition was not undertaken till 368 B.C. In point of fact, for the chronology of the whole period up to the battle of Mantineia, not counting the fixed points secured to us by the celebration of the Olympic games, obs. 223, and by an eclipse of the sun, obs. 224, we are dependent merely on Diodorus and on combinations, as Xenophon only yields us few and inadequate landmarks. Now Diodorus is in the habit of classing together all the events of the Olympiad year (or, what is nearly the same thing, of the year calculated by the archonship at Athens), i.e. of the time from the middle of summer in one year to the same time in another (not to mention that he very

often combines the events of two years under one, and generally proceeds in a very incorrect and superficial manner), and consequently it always remains uncertain, where we are confined to his testimony, whether the events are to be placed a year earlier or later.

217) In the consciousness of the increase in their strength produced by their union, the Arcadians had made several successful enterprises on their own account, Xen. Hell. VII, 1, 22—26. Accordingly Archidamus, the son of Agesilaus, undertook a campaign against them in connexion with the auxiliaries from Syracuse, and by a bold attack, when the Arcadians attempted to surround him, won a brilliant victory, in which many Arcadians fell, but not a single Spartan lost his life, Xen. l.c. § 28—32. Diod. XV, 72. Plut. Ages. 33, hence called the ἄδακρυς μάχη, Plut. l.c. Owing to the growth of their self-esteem just referred to, the Arcadians had already at this time become more and more estranged from Thebes, Xen. l.c. § 24. 39: also the disputes with Elis were already beginning, § 26. 32.

218) Xen. Hell. VII, 1, 33—40. Plut. Pelop. 30. Artax. 22. The conditions of peace (for these see Xen. l.c. § 36), in the negotiation of which Pelopidas, who had been sent by the Thebans as ambassador to Susa, was mainly instrumental, were dictated by the Persian king, but not accepted by the rest of the Greek States. An attempt to establish peace, made a year previously by Philiskus, the ambassador of the satrap Ariabazanes, had been shipwrecked on the refusal of

a school of rhetoric, which was visited by Demosthenes, and, as counsel, wrote speeches for his clients to deliver in the courts, Is. vit. α'. β'. γ'. Westerm. Vit. min. p. 266 f. Suid. s. v. Plut. Glor. Athen. p. 350 c., all on cases relating to inheritances. We know the titles of 55 of his speeches, but only 11 are extant. Mention is also made of a theoretical work of his, ἰδίαι τέχναι, Vit. β'. It is said of the style of Isaeus in comparison with Lysias, Vit. γ': διαφέρει δ' ὅτι τῇ μὲν πολὺ τὸ ἀφελὲς καὶ τὸ ἠθικὸν καὶ ἡ χάρις, ἡ δ' Ἰσαίου τεχνικωτέρα δόξειεν ἂν εἶναι καὶ ἀκριβεστέρα καὶ σχηματισμοῖς διειλημμένη ποικίλοις etc.

kk) Skopas of Paros flourished between 392 and 348 B.C., Strab. p. 604. Paus. VIII, 45, 3. 4, worked specially in Karian marble, and enriched Greece, Ionia, and Karia with numerous representations of gods, demigods, and heroes, notably those of the circle of Dionysus and Aphrodite. The most famous of his statues were the raving Bacchante, Callistrat. Stat. 2. Anthol. Pal. IX, 774. Anth. Jac. I, 75, his gods of love Eros, Himeros, and Pothos in the temple of Aphrodite at Megara, Paus. I, 43, 6, and the group Poseidon, Thetis, and Achilles, Plin. XXXVI, 26. He was employed as architect on the temple of Athene Alea at Tegea, the most beautiful in the Peloponnese,

Paus. VIII, 45, 4, and on the tomb of Mausolus, Plin. XXXIV, 30, 31. The living truth to nature and the beauty, with which he expressed in marble human passions and violent emotions of the soul, filled the beholder with admiration.

ll) Praxiteles of Athens flourished circ. 368—336 B.C. Corp. Inscr. Gr. no. 1604. Plin. XXXIV, 50, and, like Skopas, worked chiefly in marble, Plin. XXXIV, 69: marmore felicior ideo et clarior fuit. Especially famous among his many masterpieces were the resting Satyr (περιβόητος) Plin. XXXIV, 69. Paus. I, 20, 1, the Knidian Aphrodite, Plin. XXXVI, 20: ante omnia est non solum Praxitelis verum in toto orbe terrarum Venus, and the Eros at Thespiae, Paus. IX, 27, 3. Plin. XXXVI, 22: propter quem Thespiae visebantur. In the delineation of sensuous charms and the grace of bodily form he was a master unsurpassed, Luc. amor. 13. imag. 4. Pliny says of him, l.c. 20: marmoris gloria supernuit etiam semet. Whether the famous group of the dying children of Niobe was the work of Skopas or Praxiteles, the ancients were themselves doubtful, Plin. XXXVI, 28. Amongst extant statues, from which we can gain an intuition as to the artistic style of the period of Skopas and Praxiteles, are the Niobidae at Florence, the so-called Niobide at Paris, the so-called Ilioneus at Munich, and the reliefs on the monument of Lysikrates.

The Incipient Decline.

Olympiad.	B.C.	ATHENS.	HISTORY.
		Archons.	
CIII, 3	366	Kephisodorus.	Third invasion of the Peloponnese by Epameinondas[218]). Alliance between Arcadia and Athens[219]). Phlius and Corinth conclude a peace with Thebes[221]).
CIII, 4	365	Chion.	War between Elis and Arcadia[222]).
CIV, 1	364	Timokrates.	The Arcadians in possession of Olympia: under their protection the Pisatans arrange the celebration of the Olympic games instead of the Eleans[223]). Pelopidas is killed in battle with Alexander of Pherae[224]). The

---

218) Thebes to accept a peace, which did not recognise the independence of Messenia (Xen. l. c. § 27. Diod. XV, 70).

219) Xen. Hell. VII, 1, 41—43. Diod. XV, 75. The expedition was directed against Achaia. The towns there were, it is true, compelled to join the Bœotian alliance; but when the Thebans in these towns at the instigation of the Arcadians and contrary to the wish of Epameinondas forcibly established the democratic constitution and expelled those opposed to it, they not only revolted again, but even openly espoused the side of Sparta.

220) Occasion for this alliance was furnished by Oropus, which, having been wrested from Athens in 411 B.C. (obs. 118), and having lapsed again to Athens in the first years of the Theban war, was now taken possession of once more by the Thebans, Xen. Hell. VII, 4, 1. Diod. XV, 76. The Athenians, namely, were irritated with the allies, because they refused them the required assistance for the recovery of Oropus; and the Arcadians made use of the opportunity, to induce Athens to conclude an alliance with themselves, Xen. l. c. § 2—3. Accordingly the Athenians were now at one and the same time in league with the Spartans and their enemies, the Arcadians, just as the Arcadians were with the Thebans and their enemies, the Athenians; a relation, which is explained by the position of the Arcadians at that time (obs. 217), but one which naturally could not be lasting. For the misunderstandings hence arising between Athens and Corinth, Xen. l. c. § 4—6.

221) Xen. Hell. VII, 4, 6—11. Diod. XV, 76. The Corinthians together with the Phliasians and other allies (who, however, are not named) concluded peace (which according to Diodorus was dictated by the king of Persia), because they were exhausted by the hardships and losses of the war, from which Phlius in particular had suffered severely (Xen. Hell. VII, 2). They first called on Sparta to share in the peace: but the Spartans could not make up their minds to do so, as they were unwilling to recognise the independence of Messenia. (This was the situation, when the Spartans were called on to conclude peace and recognise the independence of Messenia, to which the speech of Isokrates refers, that bears the name of Archidamus.)

222) Xen. Hell. II, 4, 12—18. Diod. XV, 77. The Eleans had surprised Lasium, which belonged to the Arcadian league; whereupon the Arcadians, after defeating the Eleans at Lasium, invade Elis, lay the country waste, and take several towns, amongst them Pylos. The result of the war was that the Eleans enrolled themselves amongst the

allies of Sparta, Xen. l. c. § 19: on the present occasion support was lent them by the Achæans, id. § 17, who were Spartan allies (obs. 219).

223) Xen. Hell. VII, 4, 19—33. Diod. XV, 78. The Arcadians invade Elis anew and defeat the Eleans, Xen. l. c. § 19. At the request of the Eleans the Spartans under Archidamus invade Arcadia and take Kromnus: in consequence the Arcadians return back from Elis, invest Kromnus and compel the garrison, such, that is, as had not made their escape, to surrender, id. § 20—25. 27. The Arcadians now renew their invasion of Elis, and get the Pisatans to undertake the management of the Olympic games under their protection; and this is done in spite of a brave attack made by the Eleans, id. 28—32: for that reason this Olympiad was not counted by the Eleans, as being an 'Ἀνολυμπιάς, Paus. VI, 22, 2.

224) (In Thessaly Jason of Pherae, already mentioned in obs. 209, had in 374 B.C. gained possession of the sovereignty as Ταγός, Xen. Hell. VI, 1: after the battle of Leuktra he was just on the point of marching into Greece, and his power was so great, that much apprehension was entertained there, when he was murdered in the summer of 370 B.C., about the time of the Pythian games, id. VI, 4, 27—32. His immediate successors were Polydorus and Polyphron; and when Polydorus had been murdered by Polyphron and Polyphron by Alexander, the latter ascended the throne, id. § 33—35; and he maintained his sovereignty for the space of 11 years, from 369—358 B.C., Diod. XV, 61. Owing to his cruelty the Aleuadæ of Larissa first applied to the king of Macedonia, and then the Thessalian towns applied to Thebes for assistance, Diod. XV, 61, 67. Plut. Pel. 26.) Pelopidas, probably in 369 B.C., made a first invasion of Thessaly, in which he liberated the Thessalian towns and at the same time compelled the Macedonian king Alexander to yield up Larissa, of which he had taken possession, Plut. Pel. 26. In the following year he returned to Thessaly as an ambassador without an army, but was treacherously held prisoner by Alexander of Pherae, until the Thebans under the command of Epameinondas, after the failure of a first expedition under another commander, restored him to freedom (probably in 368 B.C.), Plut. Pel. 27—29. Diod. XV, 71. 75. Both times (so according to Plut. l. c., according to Diodorus only the first time) Pelopidas made his way as far as Macedonia and so obtained the conclusion of an alliance between the Macedonian king and Thebes. In the present instance it again remains doubtful (cf. obs. 215) whether the expeditions must be placed as stated or a year later.

C. 13

FOURTH PERIOD.   431—338 B.C.

Olympiad.	B. C.	ATHENS.	HISTORY.
		Archons.	
CIV, 1	364		Thebans extend their hegemony over Thessaly[225], and even attempt to win the hegemony by sea[226].
CIV, 2	363	Charikleides.	Schism amongst the Arcadians[227].
CIV, 3	362	Molon.	Battle of Mantineia and death of Epameinondas[228]. The belligerent parties conclude peace, in which Sparta refuses to share[229].

In 364 B.C. Pelopidas was again invoked by the Thessalians to their aid against Alexander of Pherae, and defeated him at Kynoskephalae, but fell himself in the battle, Plut. Pel. 31—32. Diod. XV, 80. The precise date of this expedition is established by an eclipse of the sun, which according to Plutarch and Diodorus happened immediately before it, and which fell on the 13th of July 364 B.C.

225) On the intelligence of Pelopidas' death the Thebans immediately undertook a Greek expedition to Thessaly (with an army of 7000 hoplites and 700 horsemen under command of Malkitas and Diogeiton, Plut.), and compelled Alexander of Pherae to free the Thessalian towns, as also the Magnesians, Phthiotians, and Achaeans, to confine himself to Pherae, and to join the Boeotian league, Plut. Pel. 35. Diod. XV, 80.

226) At the instance and under the command of Epameinondas a voyage was made, which was extended as far as Byzantium, but remained without further consequences owing to the death of Epameinondas occurring soon afterwards, Diod. XV, 78—79, cf. Isocr. Phil. p. 93. § 53. Æsch. de f. leg. p. 42. § 105: 'Επαμεινώνδας στρατηγὸς οὐχ ὑποπτήξας τὸ τῶν 'Αθηναίων ἀξίωμα εἶπε διαρρήδην ἐν τῷ πλήθει τῶν Θηβαίων, ὡς δεῖ τὰ τῆς 'Αθηναίων ἀκροπόλεων προπύλαια μετενεγκεῖν εἰς τὴν προστασίαν τῆς Καδμείας. The expedition to Thessaly, obs. 225, and the voyage of Epameinondas are in all probability synchronous; else, it may be presumed, Epameinondas would have held the command in the former, but whether both should be placed in 364 or 363 B.C. cannot be determined with certainty.

227) The schism arose out of the possession of Olympia and of the temple-treasures there, which were applied by the common Arcadian board to the payment of the troops (the so-called 'Επάρετοι). The Mantineians were the first to declare against this proceeding, and their example was followed by other Arcadians (it was the aristocratic party, it appears, that made the opposition, and the states, where the aristocrats were in the ascendant, went over to this side, Xen. Hell. VII, 4, 34. 35, 5, 1), and this party now concluded peace with the Eleans, Xen. l. c. 4, 35, and sent ambassadors to Athens and Sparta to pray for assistance, id. 5, 3, whilst the other party called the Thebans to their aid, id. 4, 34. For the whole of these events, id. 4, 33—5, 3. Diod. XV, 82. In the Peloponnese there were now ranged on the one side, the Spartans, Eleans, Achaeans (obs. 222), and one half of the Arcadians with Mantineia at their head; on the other side, the Argives, the Messenians, and the other half of the Arcadians with Tegea at their head: Corinth and Phlius remained neutral (obs. 221).

228) Xen. Hell. VII, 5, 4—27 (i. e. to the end of the work). Diod. XV, 83—88. Plut. Ages. 34. The army of Epameinondas comprised the whole force of Boeotia, the Euboeans, and many Thessalians; in the Peloponnese his ranks were swollen by the peoples named in obs. 227, Xen. l. c. § 4—5: the Phokians had refused to accompany him id. § 4. The strength of the two armies is stated by Diodorus (84), at 30,000 infantry and 2000 cavalry on the side of the Thebans, and 20,000 infantry and 2000 cavalry on that of Sparta. Before the battle Epameinondas made an attempt to surprise, first Sparta, and then Mantineia: both attempts failed in consequence of unfavourable accidents, Xen. l. c. § 9—17. Polyb. IX, 8. The battle, like that of Leuktra, was won by the oblique formation of the Theban ranks, Xen. l. c. § 23: 'Ο δὲ τὸ στράτευμα ἀντίπρωρον ὥσπερ τριήρη προσῆγε νομίζων, ὅπῃ ἐμβαλὼν διακόψειε, διαφθερεῖν ὅλον τὸ τῶν ἐναντίων στράτευμα, but after the fall of Epameinondas (for his death see Paus. VIII, 11, 4—5. Diod. XV, 87. Plut. Mor. [Apophth. reg.] p. 194 c. Corn. Nep. Epam. 9. Cic. de finn. II, § 97. ad div. V, 12) the Thebans did not follow up their victory any further, Xen. l. c. § 25, 'Ἐπεὶ γε μὴν ἐκεῖνοι ἔπεσεν, οἱ λοιποὶ οὐδὲ τῇ νίκῃ ὀρθῶς ἔτι ἐδυνάσθησαν χρήσασθαι, ἀλλὰ φυγούσης μὲν αὐτοῖς τῆς ἐναντίας φάλαγγος οὐδένα ἀπέκτειναν οἱ ὁπλῖται οὐδὲ προῆλθον ἐκ τοῦ χωρίου, ἔνθα ἡ συμβολὴ ἐγένετο. For the time of the battle see Plut. Mor. p. 845 E. (Vit. X. or. 27) p. 350 A. (de glor. Ath. 7), according to which it took place on the 12th of Skirophorion (June), 362 B.C.— Diod. XV, 87: Παρὰ μὲν γὰρ ἑκάστῳ τῶν ἄλλων ἓν ἂν εὕροι (τις) προτέρημα τῆς δόξης, παρὰ δὲ τούτῳ ('Επαμεινώνδᾳ) πᾶσαι τὰι ἀρετὰι ἠθροισμέναι.— ῥωμαλεότητι σώματος καὶ λόγου δεινότητι, ψυχῆς λαμπρότητι, μισαργυρίᾳ, ἐπιεικείᾳ, τὸ δὲ μέγιστον ἐν τοῖς πολεμικοῖς ἀγῶσιν ἀνδρείᾳ καὶ στρατηγίᾳ.— τοιγαροῦν ἡ πατρὶς αὐτοῦ ζῶντος μὲν ἐκτήσατο τὴν ἡγεμονίαν τῆς Ἑλλάδος, τελευτήσαντος δὲ ταύτην ἀστερήθη.

229) Diod. XV, 88. Plut. Ages. 35. Polyb. IV, 33. The Spartans excluded themselves from the peace, because they were unwilling to recognise the independence of Messenia. In Arcadia several of the towns united in Megalopolis wished to separate themselves again, but they were retained by force, Diod. XV, 94.

The Incipient Decline.   99

THIRD SECTION.

361—338 B.C.

THE STRUGGLE WITH KING PHILIP.

Olympiad.	B.C.	ATHENS.	HISTORY.
		Archons.	a) The war of the allies and the Sacred War and the advances of Philip up to his first expedition against Greece in 346 B.C.[230].
CIV, 4	361	Nikophemus.	Death of Agesilaus, Archidamus III king of Sparta[231].
CV, 1	360	Kallimedes.	
CV, 2	359	Eucharistus.	Philip, king of Macedonia[232]. He rids himself of his rival aspirants to the throne[233], and concludes peace and an alliance with Athens[234].

---

230) The war of the allies serves to rob Athens of the means to oppose Philip, and by the sacred war the power, which Thebes had just lately won, was broken. The chief reason, however, why Greece succumbed, must be sought in the degeneration of the Greeks, and accordingly Demosthenes, the most vigorous and noble of Philip's opponents, directed his chief efforts to kindle greater energy in the Athenians. Of the other states, in particular of Thebes, we are without detailed information: for Athens, see Dem. Phil. I, p. 41, § 4: βούλεσθε (viz. for the future as for the past) περιιόντες αὐτῶν πυνθάνεσθαι, λέγεταί τι καινόν; cf. id. p. 53. § 44. p. 45. § 20: ὅπως μὴ ποιήσετε ἃ πολλάκις ὑμᾶς ἔβλαψε, πάνθ' ἐλάττω νομίζοντες εἶναι τοῦ δέοντος καὶ τὰ μέγιστ' ἐν τοῖς ψηφίσμασιν αἱρούμενοι, ἐπὶ τῷ πράττειν οὐδὲ τὰ μικρὰ ποιεῖτε, thus their line of action in opposition to Philip p. 51, § 40: ὥσπερ οἱ βάρβαροι πυκτεύουσιν—ὑμεῖς ἐὰν ἐν Χερρονήσῳ πύθησθε Φίλιππον, ἐκεῖσε βοηθεῖν ψηφίζεσθε, ἐὰν ἐν Πύλαις, ἐκεῖσε, ἐὰν ἄλλοθί που, συμπαραθεῖτε ἄνω κάτω καὶ στρατηγεῖσθε μὲν ὑπ' ἐκείνου, βεβούλευσθε δὲ οὐδὲν αὐτοὶ συμφέρον περὶ τοῦ πολέμου οὐδὲ πρὸ τῶν πραγμάτων προοράτε οὐδέν, πρὶν ἂν ἢ γεγενημένον ἢ γιγνόμενόν τι πύθησθε. Cf. also Olynth. II, p. 25. III, p. 29. § 3. Phil. II, p. 66, § 3—4. The want of money, which was a bar to all enterprises, was chiefly caused by the practice of distributing the surplus of the public exchequer amongst the people in the form of the so-called θεωρικά (see third period, obs. 53); and these, like all other pernicious measures, proceeded for the most part from the demagogues, who flattered the people: see for the θεωρικά Olynth. III, p. 31, § 11, and for the demagogues in particular id. p. 36. § 29—31. Finally a great evil lurked in the fact, that wars were now, as a rule, carried on exclusively with mercenaries, obs. 240.

231) Plut. Ages. 36, 40. Diod. XV, 93. Xen. Ages. II, 28—31. He went after the battle of Mantineia in the spring of 361 B.C. to Egypt, having been called by Nektanebus, the king of that country, to his assistance, and died on his way home in the winter of 361/0 B.C.

232) (For the origin of the royal house in Macedonia see Herod. VIII, 137—139. V, 22. The Macedonian kings are mentioned in Greek history, beginning with Amyntas, a contemporary of the Peisistratids, onwards, id. V, 94: he was succeeded by Alexander, who reigned at the time of the Persian wars, see id. V, 137. VIII, 136. 140. IX, 44, 45. etc., and this monarch by Perdikkas, who reaches down to the second half of the Peloponnesian war (to 413 B.C.), and often came into contact with the Greeks during its continuance, obs. 32: Archelaus then reigns till 399; Orestes till 397; Acropus, the son of Aeropus, till 393, when he was murdered by Amyntas II, who then maintains the sovereignty with interruptions till 370, when he died, leaving behind him three sons, Alexander, Perdikkas, and Philip. Alexander reigned till 368; then his murderer Ptolemaeus of Alorus till 365; then the second brother Perdikkas till 359, when he fell in a battle with the Illyrians.) Philip came to the throne in 359 B.C. (Diod. XVI, 2), at the age of 23, as is shown by Paus. VII, 7, 4. Justin. IX, 8, after passing 3 years previously as a hostage at Thebes, Justin. VII, 5, cf. Diod. XVI, 2. Plut. Pel. 26 etc. (It appears from Æsch. de f. leg. p. 31, § 26—29, that he did not come to Thebes till after the death of his brother Alexander, and likewise it is proved by Speusipp. ap. Athen. XI. p. 506 z, that he returned to Macedonia, not after the death of Perdikkas, but whilst he was still on the throne.) He succeeded to the sovereignty under the most difficult circumstances, as the empire was threatened in the north and north-west by the Paeonians and Illyrians, of whom the latter had just defeated Perdikkas, and by several rivals for the throne within the kingdom itself: but he overcame these difficulties mainly by the shrewdness with which, over and above his many distinguished qualities, he succeeded in isolating his enemies and conquering them one by one: his mode of procedure may be gathered in greater detail from the accounts following. First he rid himself of

Olympiad.	B.C.	ATHENS.	HISTORY.
		Archons.	
CV, 2	359		Philip subdues the Pæonians and Illyrians²³⁵).
CV, 3	358	Kephisodotus.	Eubœa recovered by the Athenians²³⁶).
CV, 4	357	Agathokles.	Philip conquers Amphipolis²³⁷) and Pydna²³⁸): his alliance with Olynthus²³⁹).

the rival claimants of the throne, then, quieting Athens with a peace, an alliance, and promises, he conquered the Pæonians and Illyrians; after which he strengthened himself by contracting an alliance with Olynthus and the Thrakian towns, in the hope of wresting from Athens its possessions on the Thrakian coast; he next annihilated Olynthus, and finally, with the support of Thebes, pushed his way into Greece. For his introduction of the phalanx see Diod. XVI, 3. Polyb. XVIII, 12—15. For his character as contrasted with the inactivity of the Athenians, see Dem. Ol. II, p. 24. § 23 : οὐ δὴ θαυμαστόν ἐστιν, εἰ στρατευόμενος καὶ πονῶν ἐκεῖνος αὐτὸς καὶ παρῶν ἐφ' ἅπασι καὶ μηδένα καιρὸν μηδ' ὥραν παραλείπων ἡμῶν μελλόντων καὶ ψηφιζομένων καὶ πυνθανομένων περιγίγνεται. (According to Justin. VII, 5 he at first undertook the duties of sovereign only as the guardian of Amyntas, the son of his brother Perdikkas, but was soon compelled by the people to assume the royal title.)

233) His rivals were Pausanias, who was supported by the Thrakian King Kotys; and Argæus, supported by Athens; the former was put aside owing to negotiations with Kotys, Diod. XVI, 2. 3. Theop. fr. 33, the latter was defeated, Diod. XVI, 3. Justin. VII, 6. Mention is made of a third pretender in the person of Archelaus, Theop. fr. 32.

234) Dem. adv. Aristocr. p. 660. § 121 : Φίλιππος—'Αργαῖον κατάγοντας λαβὼν τῶν ἡμετέρων τινὰς πολιτῶν ἀφῆκε μὲν αὐτούς, ἀπέδωκε δὲ πάντα ὅσ' ἀπώλεσαν αὐτοῖς, πέμψας δὲ γράμματα ἐπηγγέλλετο ἕτοιμος εἶναι συμμαχίαν ποιεῖσθαι καὶ τὴν πατρικὴν φιλίαν ἀνανεοῦσθαι, cf. Diod. XVI, 4. Justin. VII, 6. The alliance was actually concluded, and Philip secretly promised the Athenians, that he would help them with the conquest of Amphipolis, Theop. fr. 189. Dem. Ol. II, p. 19. § 6. 7.

235) Diod. XVI, 4. 8. Justin. VII, 6. Since according to Diod. l. c. 8, the conquest of Amphipolis followed immediately upon the subjection of the Illyrians, and this cannot have taken place before 357 B. c., obs. 236 and 240, the campaign against the Pæonians and Illyrians cannot be placed earlier than the year 358 B. c.

236) Eubœa, which previously belonged to the Athenian alliance, obs. 228, had gone over to that of Thebes after the battle of Leuktra, Xen. Hell. VI, 5, 23. VII, 5, 4. Eretria was now threatened by other Eubœan towns and the Theban allies of the latter, and in its distress turned to Athens: Athens very readily granted the aid implored, defeated the opponents of Eretria together with the Thebans, and then brought over the whole of Eubœa to its side once more, Diod. XVI, 7. Dem. adv. Androt. p. 597. § 14. pro Megalop. p. 205. § 14. Olynth. I, p. 11. § 8. de Chersones. p. 108. § 74—75. Isocr. Phil. p. 93. § 53. Æsch. adv. Ctes. p. 65. § 85. The eagerness with which the

Athenians pursued the matter is shown in particular from Dem. de Chers. l. c. ἔστε γὰρ δήπου τοῦτ', ὅτι Τιμόθεός ποτ' ἐκεῖνος ἐν ὑμῖν ἐδημηγόρησεν ὡς δεῖ βοηθεῖν καὶ τοὺς Εὐβοέας σώζειν, ὅτε Θηβαῖοι κατεδουλοῦντο αὐτούς, καὶ λέγων εἶπεν οὕτω πως· "εἰπέ μοι, βουλεύεσθε" ἔφη "Θηβαίους ἔχοντες ἐν νήσῳ, τί χρήσεσθε καὶ τί δεῖ ποιεῖν; οὐκ ἐμπλήσετε τὴν θάλατταν, ὦ ἄνδρες 'Αθηναῖοι, τριήρων; οὐκ ἀναστάντες ἤδη πορεύσεσθε εἰς τὸν Πειραιᾶ; οὐ καθέλξετε τὰς ναῦς;" οὐκοῦν εἶπε μὲν ταῦτα ὁ Τιμόθεος, ἐποιήσατε δ' ὑμεῖς; and from Æsch. l. c. ἐπειδὴ διέβησαν εἰς Εὔβοιαν Θηβαῖοι καταδουλώσασθαι τὰς πόλεις πειρώμενοι, ἐν πέντε ἡμέραις (cf. Dem. adv. Androt. l. c.) ἐβοηθήσατε αὐτοῖς καὶ ναυσὶ καὶ πεζῇ δυνάμει, καὶ πρὶν τριάκονθ' ἡμέρας διελθεῖν ὑποσπόνδους Θηβαίους ἀφήκατε, κύριοι τῆς Εὐβοίας γενόμενοι, καὶ τάς τε πόλεις αὐτὰς καὶ τὰς πολιτείας ἀπέδοτε ὀρθῶς καὶ δικαίως τοῖς παρακαταθεμένοις—and in consequence the orators are pleased to make frequent mention of this enterprise to the renown of the Athenians. The actual conclusion of an alliance is proved, partly by Dem. pro Megalop. l. c., partly, and that more particularly, by a record found in modern times, Rangabé Ant. Hell. II, no. 391 and 392. According to the inscription just mentioned the alliance was resolved upon in the archonship of Agathokles, 357/6; according to Dem. Ol. I, l. c. the ambassadors from Amphipolis came to Athens to beg for help, just at the time when the operations in Eubœa had been brought to a close.

237) Diod. XVI, 8. The people of Amphipolis sent ambassadors begging for help and offering to make over town and territory to the Athenians, Theop. fr. 47, Dem. Ol. I, p. 11. § 8 : but the Athenians allowed themselves to be deceived by Philip's assurance, that he would fulfil his promise (obs. 234) and give up the town to them, Dem. Ol. II, p. 19. § 6. (Dem.) de Halon. p. 83. § 27 : whereupon Philip stormed the town (according to Dem. Olynth. I, p. 10, § 5 being assisted by treachery), and retained it for himself, Epist. Phil. p. 164. § 21. The inhabitants were mildly treated on the whole, but Philip's opponents were banished, Diod. l. c. Corp. Inscr. Gr. II, no. 2008. Upon this war between Athens and Philip broke out, and lasted up to the peace of 346 B. c.

238) Pydna together with Potidæa, Methone, and the whole region round about the Thermaic gulf belonged to Athens, Dem. Phil. I, p. 41. § 4. For its conquest see Diod. XVI, 8. Dem. Lept. p. 475. § 63. According to the latter passage it was taken by treachery, cf. Olynth. I, p. 10. § 5.

239) Dem. adv. Aristocr. p. 656. § 108. Olynth. II, p. 22, § 14. Phil. II, p. 70. § 20. He contracts the alliance to prevent his being hindered at first in his enterprises by the powerful Olynthians, and, in order to win them over, gives them Anthemus, which had long been

The Incipient Decline.

Olympiad.	B. C.	ATHENS.	HISTORY.
		Archons.	
CV, 4	357		Chios, Byzantium, Rhodes and Cos revolt from the Athenian alliance: beginning of the war of the allies[238]. The Athenians defeated at Chios: Chabrias falls in the battle[239].
CVI, 1	356	Elpines.	Philip subdues Potidæa[240]. Foundation of Philippi[243].
CVI, 2	355	Kallistratus.	The war of the allies ends with the grant of independence to the revolted allies[244].

---

a bone of contention between Olynthus and Macedonia, Dem. Phil. II, l. c., and also promises to subdue Potidæa for them, obs. 242.

240) The outbreak was chiefly owing to the fact, that the Athenians did not remain faithful to the principles of equity and mildness, which they professed at the reestablishment of their hegemony, and also at first practised (obs. 198); thus, in particular, they had begun to partition property in foreign countries amongst Athenian Kleruchs, as at Samos, Philochor. fr. 131. Strab. p. 638. Heraclid. Pont. X, 7, of. Diod. XVIII, 18. Isocr. de permut. § 111. Dem. de Rhod. lib. p. 193. § 9, at Potidæa, obs. 242, and elsewhere, Isocr. l. c. §103. Another principal subject of complaint consisted in the mode in which Athens habitually carried on its wars. It was the regular practice, that is, to employ mercenaries only, and, as the leaders usually got no pay from Athens, they were obliged to extort money from the allies, see Dem. Phil. I, p. 53. § 45: ὅποι δ' ἂν στρατηγὸν καὶ ψήφισμα κενὸν καὶ τὰς ἀπὸ τοῦ βήματος ἐλπίδας ἐκπέμψητε, οὐδὲν ὑμῖν τῶν δεόντων γίγνεται, ἀλλ' οἱ μὲν ἐχθροὶ καταγελῶσιν, οἱ δὲ σύμμαχοι τεθνᾶσι τῷ δέει τοὺς τοιούτους ἀποστόλους, id. p. 46. § 24: ἐξ οὗ δ' αὐτὰ καθ' αὑτὰ τὰ ξενικὰ ὑμῖν στρατεύεται, τοὺς φίλους νικᾷ καὶ τοὺς συμμάχους, οἱ δ' ἐχθροὶ μείζους τοῦ δέοντος γεγόνασιν, cf. id. § 46. 47. etc. According to Dem. de Rhod. lib. p. 191. § 3 the occasion of the war was the fear of the Rhodians, Chians, and Byzantians, that Athens would make an attack upon their independence, and the promise of support from Mausolos, the prince of Karia, a dependency of the Persian empire, cf. Diod. XVI, 7. According to Diod. l. c. the beginning of the war belongs to the archonship of Kephisodotos, 358/7 ; but according to Dionys. Hal. Lys. p. 480 the whole of the war belongs to the archonships of Agathokles and Elpines, i. e. from the summer of 357 to that of 355 B. c.: according to Diod. XVI, 7, cf. 22, the war lasted three years. The outbreak of this war was the reason why the Athenians were at first prevented from undertaking any undertaking in opposition to Philip.

241) The Athenians made an attack on Chios: Chabrias fell, whilst attempting to force his way into the harbour with the fleet; whereupon the Athenians were beaten back, Diod. XVI, 6. Corn. Nep. Chabr. 4. Plut. Phoc. 6.

242) Diod. XVI, 8. The help from Athens came too late, Dem. Phil. I, p. 50. § 35. The Athenian Kleruchs there were expelled, the rest of the inhabitants were sold into slavery, Diod. l. c. Dem. Phil. II, p. 70. § 20. (Demosth.) de Hal. p. 79. § 10: town and territory

were handed over to the Olynthians, Diod. l. c. Dem. Olynth. II, p. 19. § 7. adv. Aristocr. p. 656. § 107. And this was done in spite of an alliance, which Philip had previously made with the town, (Demosth.) de Hal. l. c. The time of the capture of Potidæa is fixed with the greater precision, as according to Plut. Alex. 3. Consol. ad Apoll. p. 105 A. § 6. Justin. XII, 16 there arrived immediately after the occupation of the town the joyful intelligence of three events, the birth of Alexander at Pella, the victory of Philip's racehorse at Olympia, and the defeat of the Illyrians by Parmenion : now the birth of Alexander is placed by Plut. Alex. l. c. on the 6th of Hekatombæon (21st of July) 356 B. C.

243) Diod. XVI, 8. Philip was invoked by the inhabitants of the town Krenides, situated on this spot, to aid them against the Thrakians, and after repulsing the Thrakians, founded Philippi, and peopled it with the inhabitants of Krenides and Datus, which latter had shortly before been established by the Thasians on the coast, Artemid. ap. Steph. Byz. s. v. Φίλιπποι. Appian. B. C. IV, p. 105. Strab. p. 323. 333. fr. 33. 34. 36. 41. 43. The most important gain secured by this measure to Philip was, that he extended his conquests from Philippi to the Nestos, Strab. p. 323, and that from Philippi he was able to work the mines in the Pangæum range, the annual yield of which he brought up to 1000 talents, Diod. l. c.

244) Of the further course of the 'war of the allies' all that we know is as follows. When Chares had already been despatched with 60 ships, the Athenians fitted out a second fleet, with an equal number of vessels, under Iphikrates, Timotheus, and Mnestheus (Isocr. de permut. § 129. Corn. Nep.). Both fleets united; and when the enemy who had entered on the siege of Samos relinquished it upon receiving news of the approach of the Athenian ships, Chares insisted upon giving battle to the enemy's fleet, whilst the other commanders considered this impracticable owing to a storm. Hereupon Chares attacked the enemy alone, but without success (in the Hellespont, Diod., at Embata, Polyæn., at Samos, Corn. Nep.), Diod. XVI, 21. Corn. Nep. Tim. 3. Polyæn. III, 9, 29, and then entered into relations with the Persian satrap Artabazus, who had revolted against the Persian king. But at the menace of the Persian king, that he would support the foes of Athens with 300 ships of war, the Athenians recalled Chares and granted complete independence to the allies, Diod. XVI, 22. Timotheus, Iphikrates and Mnestheus were for their conduct in the battle arraigned by Chares and Aristophon, according to Dionys. Hal. de Din. p. 668 in 354 B. C.; the first was condemned

FOURTH PERIOD. 431—338 B.C.

Olympiad.	B.C.	ATHENS.	HISTORY.
		Archons.	
CVI, 2	355		Commencement of the (second) Sacred War[245].
CVI, 3	354	Diotimus.	
CVI, 4	353	Thudemus.	Philip conquers Methone[246]. He marches to Thessaly to support the Thessalian towns against the tyrants Lykophron and Peitholaus of Pheræ, and is twice defeated by the Phokians allied with Lykophron under the command of Onomarchus[247].

to pay a fine of 100 talents, the other two were acquitted, Diod. XVI, 21. Corn. Nep. Tim. 3. Iaocr. de permut, § 129. Timotheus thereupon fled from Athens, and died in the same year: Iphikrates retired from all concern in public affairs, and thus Cornelius Nepos rightly says (Timoth. 4): Hæc extrema fuit ætas imperatorum Atheniensium Iphicratis, Chabriæ, Timothei, neque post illorum obitum quisquam dux in illa urbe fuit dignus memoria. (The revolted allies after this fell under the sway of the Karian prince, Dem. de pac. p. 63. § 25: and, except for Euboea, the Athenian alliance was confined to a number of small islands, so that the contributions of its members amounted to no more than 45 talents, Dem. de Cor. p. 305. § 234.)

245) The origin and progress of the sacred war are most closely bound up with the Amphiktyonic league (hence too the name 'sacred war': it is called the second with reference to the war of 595 B. C. see p. 27. obs. 67; the war of 448, see p. 52. obs. 69, is usually not counted). It is upon this occasion that the league first assumes prominent historical importance, whilst according to the legend it had been founded of old by Amphiktyon, the son of Deukalion: it was composed of 12 races (Thessalians, Bœotians, Dorians, Ionians, Perrhæbians, Magnesians, Lokrians, Œtæans or Ænianians, Phthiotic Achæans, Malians, Phokians, Dolopians), the representatives of which (Πυλαγόραι and Ἱερομνήμονες) assembled twice each year (in the spring and autumn), at Delphi or Anthela: each of the 12 peoples named had two votes, see the chief notices Æschin. de F. Leg. p. 43. §§ 115—117. Strab. p. 420. The principal object of the league was the administration and protection of the temple and the public games: but besides this it was also laid down, that none of the Amphiktyonic towns should be razed to the ground, that none should have its water cut off, and that no brazen trophies should be erected, Æschin. l. c. § 116. Cic. de Inv. II, § 69, cf. Plut. Mor. p. 278. (Quæst. Rom. 37). The Thebans now made use of the preponderant influence, which they still possessed at this time, to have the Phokians condemned by the Amphiktyons to pay a heavy fine, on the charge that they had tilled sacred territory, and when the fine was not paid, to have the whole of Phokis consecrated to the Delphian god (the true ground must certainly be sought in the ancient hatred of the Thebans towards the Phokians, which was also shared by the Thessalians, Pausan. X, 2, 1, cf. Herod. VII, 176. VIII, 27 ff., and which in the case of the Thebans had lately been intensified by the refusal of Phokis in 362 B. C. to join in the expedition to the Peloponnese, obs. 228): Philomelus now placed himself at the head of his countrymen and made himself master of the temple at Delphi, Diod. XVI, 23—24. Pausan. X, 2, 1. Justin. VIII, 1. The Phokians found allies in the Spartans and Athenians, of whom the former, probably several years before this date, had likewise been condemned by the Amphiktyons to pay a heavy fine

on account of their occupation of the Kadmeia; the other members of the Amphiktyonic league united to make war against Phokis, Diod. XVI, 27. 29. The war lasted 10 years, Æschin. de F. Leg. p. 45. § 131. adv. Ctesiph. p. 74. § 148, and as it was ended in 346 n. c., obs. 255, it must therefore have begun in 356 or 355 B. c. Diodorus places the beginning of the war in the latter year, and also states its duration, XVI, 59, at 10 years: but he contradicts himself, inasmuch as in XVI, 14 he places the conquest of Delphi, with which the war opens, in 357 B. c., and in the same passage assigns the war a duration of eleven years, and of nine years in XVI, 23. The Phokians supported the expenses of the struggle by plundering the temple-treasures of Delphi (from which Philomelus according to Diod. XVI, 24. 27. 28. 56 as yet abstained, but cf. id. 36), by which they were placed in a position to levy fresh relays of mercenary troops, Isocr. Phil. p. 93. § 53; this, however, was doubly detrimental to Greece, firstly because by the mass of money thus put into circulation (according to Diod. XVI, 56 over 10,000 talents were stolen) venality and extravagance were fostered, Diod. XVI, 37, and secondly because the gangs of mercenaries increased in number, see e. g. Isocr. Phil. p. 101, § 96. As regards the course of the war, Diodorus, on whom we are almost entirely dependent, informs us of a number of battles lost and won; but we can nowhere gain any clear and definite knowledge beyond the facts quoted in the following observations. For the hostilities passing in the Peloponnese along with the Phokian war proper see obs. 251.

246) Diod. XVI, 31. 34. The town was destroyed, Dem. Phil. III, p. 117. § 26. The Athenians again came too late to the rescue, Dem. Phil. I, p. 50. § 35. (It was at the siege of Methone, that Philip lost his right eye by a wound from an arrow, Dem. de Cor. p. 247. § 67. Strab. p. 330. fr. 22. p. 374. Justin. VII, 6. Plin. H. N. VII, 37,)

247) In Thessaly the immediate successor to Jason of Pheræ (obs. 224) was Alexander, and after his murder in 359 n. c. Tisiphonus; Lykophron and Peitholaus followed, and both the two were now in possession of the sovereignty, subsequently to the death of Tisiphonus, Xen. Hell. VI, 4, 35—37. Plut. Pel. 35. Diod. XVI, 14. The Phokians had contracted an alliance with them, Diod. XVI, 35. 35; on the other hand the Aleuadæ applied to Philip for aid against the tyrants, Diod. XVI, 35. (According to Diod. XVI, 14. Justin. VII, 6 this had already happened once in 357 or 356 B. c. and Philip had at that time made an expedition to Thessaly, in which he is said to have liberated the Thessalian towns.) In the war, which thus arose, Onomarchus (who was now, after the death of Philomelus in 354 n. c. Diod. l. c. 31, at the head of the Phokians, and in 353 B. c. had made great progress against his foes, id. 33) first sends Phayllus to Thessaly, and then, when he is defeated, comes in person with the whole of the army and defeats Philip in two battles, id. 35. Polyæn. II, 38, 2.

The Incipient Decline.

Olympiad.	B. C.	ATHENS.	HISTORY.
		Archons.	
CVII, 1	352	Aristodemus.	The Phokians defeated by Philip; Onomarchus falls[248]). Philip's attempt to penetrate through Thermopylæ into Greece, frustrated by the Athenians[249]). He possesses himself of Pagasæ and Magnesia[250]). Struggles in the Peloponnese[251]).
CVII, 2	351	Thessalus.	
CVII, 3	350	Apollodorus.	Eubœa lost to Athens[252]).
CVII, 4	349	Kallimachus.	Philip against Olynthus[253]).

---

248) Diod. XVI, 35. Dem. de F. Leg. p. 443. § 319. Paus. X, 2, 3. The army of Onomarchus was annihilated, Diod. l. c. 37 : Phayllus was appointed commander in the place of Onomarchus, id. 36. Diodorus places the three battles of Onomarchus under one (Olympiad-) year, cf. also Dionys. Hal. de Din. p. 665 : but it is probable that the two first are separated from the last by an intermediate winter ; and these two battles must therefore be placed in 352 B.C., as after them Philip had first to return to Macedonia and make new preparations.

249) Diod. XVI, 37. 38. Dem. Phil. I, p. 44. § 17. p. 52. § 41. De F. Leg. p. 443. § 319. de Cor. p. 236. § 32.

250) Dem. Olynth. I, p. 15. § 22. II, p. 21. § 11. The tyrants were expelled, Diod. XVI, 37. Dem. Olynth. II, p. 22. § 14. Phil. II, p. 71. § 22.

251) When the Thebans were involved in the sacred war, the Spartans attempted to reduce Messenia to its former subjection and generally to regain their hegemony in the Peloponnese. Accordingly the Messenians, probably in 355 B.C., applied at the very first to Athens for assistance, and the Athenians concluded a defensive alliance with them, Paus. IV, 28, 1—2. Dem. de Megal. p. 204. § 9. The Spartans then menaced Megalopolis : but in 352 B.C. the Thebans sent an army to the Peloponnese and in conjunction with the Megalopolitans, Messenians, Argives, and Sikyonians fought several engagements with the Spartans, but without any decisive result, Diod. XV, 39. Paus. VIII, 27, 7. After that the war slumbers for a time, or is confined to mutual hostilities with no important consequences. At a later period, the Megalopolitans also, when once more hard pressed by Sparta, applied to Athens, on which occasion Demosthenes (probably in the first months of the year 352 B.C., cf. Dionys. Hal. ad Amm. I, 4 p. 725) delivered the speech Ὑπὲρ Μεγαλοπολιτῶν, in which he so far supported their prayer for aid, as to recommend the Athenians not to allow the town to be overpowered by Sparta. Of the general aim of the Spartans he says in this speech (p. 207. § 22), ὁρῶ γὰρ αὐτοὺς καὶ νῦν οὐχ ὑπὲρ τοῦ μὴ παθεῖν τι κακὸν πόλεμον ἀραμένους, ἀλλ' ὑπὲρ τοῦ κομίσασθαι τὴν προτέραν οὖσαν ἑαυτοῖς δύναμιν, and for the means, which they employed to effect their object (p. 206, § 16) : νυνὶ γάρ φασιν ἐκείνοι, Θεοῖ Ἠλείους μὲν τῆς Τριφυλίας τινὰ κομίσασθαι, Φλιασίους δὲ τὸ Τρικάρανον, ἄλλοις δέ τισι τῶν Ἀρκάδων τὴν αὐτῶν καὶ τὸν Ὠρωπὸν ἡμᾶς, οὐχ ἵν' ἑκάστους ἡμῶν ἴδωσιν ἔχοντας τὰ ἑαυτῶν, οὐδ' ὀλίγου δεῖ· ὀψὲ γὰρ ἂν φιλάνθρωποι γεγονότες εἶεν· ἀλλ' ἵνα πᾶσι δοκῶσι συμπράττειν ὅπως ἂν ἕκαστα κομίσωνται ταῦθ' ἃ φασιν αὐτῶν εἶναι, ἵν' ἐπειδὰν ἴωσιν ἐπὶ Μεσσήνην αὐτοί, συστρατεύωσιν πάντες αὐτοῖς οὗτοι. Demosthenes, however, was unable to secure the adoption of his policy.

252) Party struggles had broken out in Eubœa, which was again in alliance with Athens, from 358 B.C. (obs. 236), at the instigation, as it appears, or at least with the cooperation of Philip, Plut. Phoc. 12. Dem. Phil. I, p. 51, § 37 : Plutarchus, the tyrant of Eretria, had sought aid at Athens against his enemies, and Phokion had been despatched with an army to Eubœa. But although that general won a victory at Tamynæ, yet the Athenians could not bear down the resistance of all the other inhabitants of the island ; Plutarchus himself proved false and untrustworthy, and so the Athenians were obliged to leave the island with ignominy and loss: and after that time it showed increasing favour to Philip, Plut. Phoc. 12—14. Æsch. adv. Ctes. p. 66. § 86—88. Cf. Dem. De Pac. p. 58, § 5. obs. 261. The date as determined rests on Dem. in Bœot. p. 999. § 16, cf. Dionys. Hal. de Din. p. 656.

253) After the war had been ended in Thessaly, Philip marched in 352 to Thrake (infr. obs. 262), and was then for a long time engrossed by a sickness, and also, it seems (Dem. de Hal. p. 84. § 32), by a campaign in Epirus ; at the same time he employed his marine force, just newly organised, on all kinds of voyages, in the course of which he actually landed on Attic territory, Dem. Phil. I, p. 49. § 34, cf. Æsch. De F. Leg. p. 37. § 72. (Dem.) adv. Neær. p. 134. § 3 : in the summer or the autumn of 349 B.C. he next turned against Olynthus, for which the time had come in pursuance of Philip's plans, cf. obs. 230. For the progress of his conquests up to this point see Dem. Olynth. I, p. 12. § 12 : τὸ πρῶτον Ἀμφίπολιν λαβών, μετὰ ταῦτα Πύδναν, πάλιν Ποτίδαιαν, Μεθώνην αὖθις, εἶτα Θετταλίας ἐπέβη· μετὰ ταῦτα Φεράς, Παγασάς, Μαγνησίαν, πάνθ' ὃν ἐβούλετο εὐτρεπίσας τρόπον ᾤχετ' εἰς Θρᾴκην· εἶτ' ἐκεῖ τοὺς μὲν ἐκβαλών, τοὺς δὲ καταστήσας τῶν βασιλέων ἠσθένησε· πάλιν ῥαΐσας οὐκ ἐπὶ τὸ ῥᾳθυμεῖν ἀπέκλινεν, ἀλλ' εὐθὺς Ὀλυνθίοις ἐπεχείρησε. τὰς δ' εἰς Ἰλλυριοὺς καὶ Παίονας αὐτοῦ καὶ πρὸς Ἀρύμβαν καὶ ὅσοι τις ἂν εἴποι παραλείπω στρατείας. The Olynthians, who gradually began to conceive apprehensions about their alliance with Philip and about his intentions, had, probably in 352 B.C., concluded peace with Athens, Dem. Aristocr. p. 156. § 109. Olynth. III, p. 30. § 7; these apprehensions were heightened still more, when Philip in 351 B.C. made an expedition into the neighbourhood of the Olynthians against the Disaltians and thus touched the territory of the Olynthian league, Dem. Phil. I, p. 44. § 17. Justin. VIII, 3. This strained relation, during which Philip never ceased to put off the Olynthians with perpetual assurances of friendship, Dem. Ol. III, l. c., lasted till the summer of 349 B.C., when Philip invaded the territory of Olynthus (still repeating his friendly assurances) and took Geira and some other places, cf. Diod. XVI, 52 and the most important accounts of the whole war, Dem. De F. Leg. p. 425. § 263—267. Philoch. fr. 132 (ap.

FOURTH PERIOD. 431—338 B. C.

Olympiad.	B. C.	ATHENS.	HISTORY.	ART AND LITERATURE.
		Archons.		
CVIII, 1	348	Theophilus.	Olynthus taken and destroyed by Philip²³⁴).	
CVIII, 2	347	Themistokles.		
CVIII, 3	346	Archias.	Philip concludes a peace and alliance with Athens, and, being invoked by the Thebans to their aid, penetrates into Greece, subdues	The orators Demosthenes ᵐᵐ),

Dionys. Hal. Ep. ad Amm. I, 9. 11. p. 734—735), which latter passage contains the most exact accounts of the time, as well as of the various occasions, on which succour was despatched by Athens. The Athenians were induced by repeated embassies from Olynthus to send assistance on two occasions, first under Chares, then under Charidemus, but in both instances consisting merely of mercenaries: both the two first Olynthiac orations of Demosthenes, which belong to this the first period of the war, contain for the chief part general appeals to the Athenians to take an active share in the struggle.
234) In the winter Philip had been obliged to undertake an expedition to Thessaly, where at that time serious discontent with his rule was rife, and where Peitholaus (obs. 247) had reestablished himself at Pheræ, Diod. XVI, 52. Dem. Olynth. I, p. 15. § 22, 11, p. 21.

§ 11. After he had restored the country to tranquillity, he again marched in the spring of 348 upon Olynthus; first of all many towns in the territory surrendered to him, for the most part owing to treachery, Dem. De F. Leg. § 266; he then attacked Olynthus itself, and finally captured the town through the treachery of Lasthenes and Euthykrates, Diod. XVI, 53. Dem. De F. Leg. § 267, Phil. III, p. 125. § 56. It was destroyed, and with it 32 other towns in Chalkidike, Dem. Phil. III, p. 117. § 26. Diod. l. c. At the instigation of Demosthenes, who delivered his third Olynthiac oration at the time when Olynthus was already in great distress, the Athenians sent a fresh force under Chares, consisting of 17 ships, 300 horsemen, and 2000 (or 4000 Demosth.) citizen hoplites; which, however, was too late to effect its object, Dem. De F. Leg. § 267. Philochor. l. c.

mm) Demosthenes, born in the deme Pæania in 384 B.C., Dem. Vit. a′, Western. Vit. min. p. 281 (according to Dion. Hal. ad Amm. I, 4 in 381), made oratory his study, stimulated by listening to the eloquence of Kallistratus and the instruction of Isæus, Plut. Dem. 5. Suid. s. v. Vit. a′, p. 281. Feeble in body and defective in voice, Vit. β′, p. 295 : τραυλὸν—τὴν γλῶτταν—, τὸ δὲ πνεῦμα ἀτονώτερον, Vit. γ′, p. 299 : καὶ τὴν ἀκοὴν ἀσθενὴς, by perseverance he overcame all difficulties, l. c. Plut. Dem. 4. 5. Cic. de or. I, 61. Phot. bibl. cod. 265. Vit. β′, p. 295, yet never spoke extempore, Plut. Dem. 8. Vit. a′, p. 290. Deprived of his father's care when eight years old, as soon as he came of age he charged his guardians with embezzlement of his estate, cont. Aphobum I, p. 817. § 12. p. 828. § 49. III, p. 861. § 58. contr. Onet. p. 866. § 15. Vit. a′, p. 282. γ′, p. 299, wrote (as a λογογράφοι) speeches for others, delivered speeches in the law-courts as attorney, and made his first appearance in public life in 355 B.C. with the speeches against Leptines and Androtion, delivered in the popular assembly, Dion. Hal. Ep. ad Amm. I, 4, officiated as senator, c. Mid. p. 551. § 111, and as architheoros, id. p. 552. § 115, but also suffered from the outrageous attacks of his enemy Meidias, id. p. 540. 545. 547. 548. He first spoke on questions of state in 354 B.C. in his speeches Περὶ συμμοριῶν, against the war with Persia, de Rhod. lib. p. 191. § 5. 192. § 6, and in 352 B.C. Ὑπὲρ Μεγαλοπολιτῶν, cf. obs. 251. But his greatest and grandest achievements as statesman, orator, and head of the patriots, were reserved for the struggle with the plans of Philip of Macedonia. It was during the Phokian war, that he first came forward to oppose that prince and to support Olynthus in the speeches Κατὰ Φιλίππου α′ (in 351 B.C.), 'Ολυνθιακοὶ α′, β′, γ′ (in 349), cf. De F. Leg. p. 426. § 256, Dion. Hal. Ep. ad Amm. I, 9, cf. obs. 233, 234. After the fall of this town, however, he acted as ambassador, and spoke in the assembly in 346 B.C. on behalf of peace, Περὶ εἰρήνης, and against Æschines in the indictment Περὶ παραπρεσβείας, Vit. 253 ; both which speeches, however, in their present form were in the opinion of ancient critics only written, not delivered, Plut. Dem. 15.

Argum. Æschin. De F. Leg. p. 314. Argum. De Pac. p. 56. Vit. Æschin. a′. Western. p. 236. Meanwhile the interference of Philip in the disputes of the Peloponnesians gave rise to the second speech Κατὰ Φιλίππου in 344 B.C., cf. obs. 256; then his policy of perfidy and violence in Thrake called forth in 341 the speeches Περὶ τῶν ἐν Χερρονήσῳ and Κατὰ Φιλίππου γ′, cf. obs. 262. 263. In like manner Demosthenes is the soul of all Athenian enterprises and exertions in opposition to Philip up to the battle of Chæronea, cf. obs. 267, where he was carried along in the flight of his countrymen, Æschin. c. Ctes. § 175. 244. 253. Plut. Dem. 20. Vit. a′, p. 284. He was now appointed to deliver the memorial oration over those, who had fallen in this battle, Ἐπιτάφιος λόγος, cf. De Cor. p. 320, § 26 f. He was at this time exposed to the hostile machinations and charges of the Macedonising party, De Cor. p. 310 : in particular Æschines came forward to oppose him, when the proposal was made to crown him publicly, ἀρετῆς ἕνεκα καὶ καλοκαγαθίας, ἧς ἔχων διατελεῖ ἐν παντὶ καιρῷ εἰς τὸν δῆμον τὸν 'Αθηναίων, De Cor. p. 266, § 118 f.; but Demosthenes triumphed over his opponent after delivering his speech Περὶ τοῦ στεφάνου in 330 B.C. Philip's death he hailed as a joyful event, Æschin. c. Ctes. § 77. Plut. Dem. 12. Vit. a′, p. 287 f., and now repeatedly used his influence to promote a rising against Alexander, Plut. Dem. 23. Æschin. c. Ctes. § 160 f., so that after the fall of Thebes that monarch demanded the extradition of Demosthenes and other patriots, a demand from which he however desisted, Diod. XVII, 15. Arr. I, 10, 7. Plut. l. c. Phoc. 17. One consequence of the residence of Harpalus at Athens was, that Demosthenes was charged by the Macedonising party with corruption, and, though innocent (Paus. II, 33), condemned, Plut. l. c. 25. Vit. a′, p. 285. β′, p. 301. Dinarch. c. Demosth. Athen. XIII, p. 592 E. However, he escaped from prison, resided in Trozen and Ægina, Plut. l. c. 26. Vit. a′, l. c. Vit. δ′, p. 308, and on the revolt of Athens after the death of Alexander was recalled and conducted home with festive pomp, Plut. l. c. 27. Vit. a′, l. c. After the disastrous issue of the Lamian war, when Antipater demanded the

The Incipient Decline. 105

Olympiad.	B. C.	HISTORY.	ART AND LITERATURE.
CVIII, 3	346	and lays waste Phokis, and is adopted as a member of the Amphiktyonic league[255].	Lykurgus[nn]), Æschines[oo]), Hypereides[pp]).

255) For the further course of the sacred war after 352 B. c. see Diod. XVI, 36—40. 56—59, where many other incidents of the war are noticed, but without giving us a clear insight into them. At last the Phokians were in possession of Orchomenus, Koroneia, Korsiæ, and Tilphossæum, Diod. l. c. 58. Dem. De F. Leg. p. 385. § 141. p. 387. § 148 ; the Thebans were hard pressed, Dem. l. c. Isocr. Phil. p. 93. § 54—55 : εἰς τοῦτο δ' αὐτῶν περιέστη ἐ τὰ πράγματα, ὥστ' ἐλπίσαντες ἅπαντας τοὺς Ἕλληνας ὑφ' αὑτοῖς ἕσεσθαι νῦν ἐν σοὶ (Φιλίππῳ) τὰς ἐλπίδας ἔχουσι τῆς αὐτῶν σωτηρίας. Accordingly at the invitation of the Thebans Philip came to the rescue, without hindrance on the part of the Athenians, who were tricked by false promises, compelled the capitulation of Phalaikus, who, as the next successor but one to Onomarchus, was now in command of the Phokian army and had hitherto defended Thermopylæ ; then pressed into Phokis, and destroyed all the Phokian

surrender of the heads of the popular party, Demosthenes fled to Ægina, sought protection in the temple of Poseidon at Kalauria, and died by his own act, taking poison before the eyes of Antipater's emissaries, in 321 B. c. Plut. Dem. 29. Vit. α', p. 287. 291. (Lucian) Encom. Dem. 43. Of the 65 speeches of Demosthenes, known to antiquity, Vit. α', p. 289, 60 have come down to us bearing his name, comprising political speeches, forensic speeches, and declamations, several of which are held to be spurious, as Περὶ Ἀλοννήσου, Κατὰ Φιλίππου δ', Περὶ τῶν πρὸς Ἀλέξανδρον συνθηκῶν, Ἐρωτικός, Ἐπιτάφιος &c. It is said of Demosthenes, Suid. s. v. : Δημοσθένης ὁ ῥήτωρ ἀνὴρ ἦν γνῶναί τε καὶ εἰπεῖν ὅσα ἐνθυμηθείη δυνατώτατος γενόμενος· ὅθεν καὶ δεινότατος ἔδοξε τῶν καθ' αὑτόν, οἷα δὴ ἱκανώτατοι τὸ ἀφανὲς εἰκάσαι καὶ τὸ γνωσθὲν ἐξηγήσασθαι, and of the impression made by his oratory, Dion. Hal. de adm. vi dicend. Demosth. 22 : Ὅταν δὲ Δημοσθένους τινὰ λάβω λόγων, ἐνθουσιῶ τε καὶ δεῦρο κάκεῖσε ἄγομαι, πάθος ἕτερον ἐξ ἑτέρου μεταλαμβάνων, ἀπιστῶν, ἀγωνιῶν, δεδιώς, καταφρονῶν, μισῶν, ἐλεῶν, εὐνοῶν, μεταξύ, ὁ θυμούμενος, φθονῶν, ἅπαντα τὰ πάθη μεταλαμβάνων, ὅσα κρατεῖν ἀνθρωπίνης γνώμης. For his ethical standpoint (as opposed to Philip) see Olynth. II, p. 20. § 10: οὐ γὰρ ἔστιν, οὐκ ἔστιν, ὦ ἄνδρες Ἀθηναῖοι, ἀδικοῦντα καὶ ἐπιορκοῦντα καὶ ψευδόμενον δύναμιν βεβαίαν κτήσασθαι, ἀλλὰ τὰ τοιαῦτα εἰς μὲν ἅπαξ καὶ βραχὺν χρόνον ἀντέχει, καὶ σφόδρα γε ἤνθησεν ἐπὶ ταῖς ἐλπίσιν, ἂν τύχῃ, τῷ χρόνῳ δὲ φωρᾶται καὶ περὶ αὑτὰ καταρρεῖ· ὥσπερ γὰρ οἰκίας, οἴμαι, καὶ πλοίου καὶ τῶν ἄλλων τῶν τοιούτων τὰ κάτωθεν ἰσχυρότατα εἶναι δεῖ, οὕτω καὶ τῶν πράξεων τὰς ἀρχὰς καὶ ὑποθέσεις ἀληθεῖς καὶ δικαίας εἶναι προσήκει, τοῦτο δὲ οὐκ ἔνι νῦν ἐν τοῖς πεπραγμένοις Φιλίππῳ.

nn) Lykurgus, born at Athens between 399 and 393 B. c., Libun. Arg. Or. c. Aristog., of the noble clan of the Eteobutadæ, educated under Plato and Isokrates, Diog. L. III, 46. Vit. Lyc. α'. Westerm. Vit. Min. p. 270, rendered great services in the domestic administration of Athens in his twelve years management of the finances, by raising the state revenue, Vit. α', 271. 278, by augmenting the war material and stores of weapons, l. c. p. 271. 279, by his care for state buildings and works of art, festal pomp, the drama, poetry, and science, l. c. p. 271—274, and by his laws enforcing public morality under police supervision, l. c. p. 272. 273. 278. In the law-courts he was victorious alike as accuser and counsel for the defence, l. c. p. 272. 275. In foreign politics he appears only once to have taken an active part as ambassador, l. c. p. 272 ; yet as a tried patriot he was amongst those, whose surrender was demanded by Alexander. His uprightness, irreproachableness, and stedfast character, and also his excellent administration, procured him high honours from the Athenians, l. c. p. 274. 276. 278. 279. He died before 323 B. c., p. 274. Of his 15 speeches only one is extant,

Κατὰ Λεωκράτους. Of his oratory it is said Dion. Hal. Vett. scr. cens. V, 3: Ὁ δὲ Λυκοῦργός ἐστι διαπαντὸς αὐξητικὸς καὶ διηρμένος καὶ σεμνὸς καὶ ὅλος κατηγορικὸς καὶ φιλαλήθης καὶ παρρησιαστικὸς οὐ μὴν ἀστεῖος οὐδὲ ἡδύς, ἀλλ' ἀναγκαῖος.

oo) Æschines, born at Athens in the deme Kothokidæ in 390 B. c., Vit. α', p. 261. Vit. β'. p. 265. Westerm. Vit. Min. Æsch. c. Tim. § 49, of lowly origin, Dem. De Cor. p. 270. § 129. p. 313. § 258. Vit. β', managed to obtain civic rights (ἐνωμότησε), Dem. De Cor. p. 314. § 261, served as a scribe to subordinate magistrates, Vit. γ'. Dem. De Cor. p. 314. § 261. Endowed with a strong body and beautiful voice, he next went upon the stage, Dem. De Cor. 288. § 180. p. 314. § 262. Vit. α'. β'. γ', then became secretary to Aristophon, afterwards to Eubulus, Æschin. De. F. Leg. § 160. Vit. α'. β'. He acted as ambassador for Athens in the Peloponnese, Dem. De F. Leg. p. 344. § 10 f. Vit. β' : and after the first embassy for peace sent to Philip appears to have been won over to his interests, Dem. l. c., cf. obs. 255. He was accused of high treason by Demosthenes and Timarchus for delaying the journey of the second embassage, Dem. l. c. Arg. Or. p. 337, but got rid of one of his accusers by the counter-charge Κατὰ Τιμάρχου, Argum. Æsch. Or. c. Tim. Dem. De F. Leg. p. 341. § 2. p. 433. § 287. Vit. α'. Suid. s. v. As one of the Pylagoræ at Delphi he brought about the sacred war against Amphissa in Philip's interest, cf. obs. 266, and after the battle of Chæroneia came forward to combat Ktesiphon's proposal to crown Demosthenes in the speech Κατὰ Κτησιφῶντος, by which he sought the overthrow of Demosthenes. But when vanquished by his rival's speech Περὶ στεφάνου, he left Athens and betook himself to Asia Minor, and after Alexander's death to Rhodes, where he established a school of rhetoric, то 'Ροδιακὸν διδασκαλεῖον, Vit. α'. γ. Suid. s. v. Philostr. V, I, 18. He died at Samos in 314 B. c., Plut. Dem. 24. Vit. α'. Plut. Bibl. Cod. 61, p. 20. 264, p. 490. Of the three speeches, which have come down to us under his name, Κατὰ Τιμάρχου, Κατὰ Κτησιφῶντος, Περὶ παραπρεσβείας, the last in the opinion of the ancient critics was not spoken, but was only a written defence against the charge of Demosthenes. Other writings attributed to him were already declared spurious in ancient times, Vit. α'. Endowed with all the gifts of a born orator, his free education had procured made him a master of extempore speaking, and after Demosthenes he was the first orator of his time, Vit. α'. Dion. Hal. de adm. vi dicend. Demosth. 35. Suid. s. v : πρῶτοι δὲ πάντων τὸ θεῖον λέγειν ἤκουσε διὰ τὸ σχεδιάζειν ὡς ἐνθουσιῶν.

pp) Hypereides of the Attic deme Kollytus, the contemporary of Lykurgus, educated under Plato and Isokrates, Vit. α'. Westerm. Vit.

106   FOURTH PERIOD. 431—338 B. C.

Olympiad.	B. C.	ATHENS.	HISTORY.
		Archon.	b) Philip strengthens and extends his influence in Greece, and continues his conquests in Thrake, till the second Sacred War affords him the opportunity to annihilate the independence of Greece by the battle of Chæroneia [255]).
CVIII, 4	345	Eubulus.	Philip strengthens his rule in Thessaly [257]).

towns (the Bœotian towns conquered by Phokians he restored to the Thebans), and procured a sentence from the Amphiktyonic tribunal condemning the Phokians to pay annually a sum of 60 talents to the Delphic temple, until the whole of the stolen money was replaced: he himself, besides the two Phokian votes in the Amphiktyonic tribunal, received still further the προμαντεία at Delphi and the conduct of the Pythian games, Diod. XV, 59—60. Dem. De Pac. p. 62. § 21. De F. Leg. p. 359. § 57. For the fearful desolation of Phokis see Dem. l. c. p. 361. § 65. p. 378. § 100: for the time of the capitulation of Phalækus (23rd of Skirophorion = 17th of July), id. p. 359. § 57—59. p. 440. § 327. The behaviour of Athens in the midst of these events attracts our attention all the more, as it forms a chief theme in the speeches of Demosthenes and Æschines and the subject of the hottest contention between the two great orators in their speeches (delivered in 343 B. C. Dion. Hal. Ep. ad. Amm. I, 10. p. 737. Arg. β'. ad Dem. De F. Leg. p. 338) on the false embassy and in the speech of Demosthenes for the crown, and that of Æschines against Ktesiphon. Allured by the arts of Philip, the Athenians first sent in February of 346 B. C. an embassy of 10 persons to him, amongst whom were Demosthenes and Æschines; and these brought back home a letter and promises from Philip, see in particular Æsch. De F. Leg. p. 29. § 12—55. Hereupon a peace and alliance were resolved upon on the 19th of Elaphebolion (April) at the proposal of Philokrates, and sworn to by the Athenians, see id. p. 53. § 56—78. Dem. De F. Leg. p. 359. § 57, and for its provisions (Dem.) de Halon. p. 82. § 24—27. p. 84. § 31. Dem. De F. Leg. p. 365. § 143. p. 444. § 321. But whilst Philip's not gaining time to make further conquests—for the principal article in the peace was to the effect that each party should remain in statu quo—depended upon the peace being now sworn to as soon as possible by Philip, who was at the time carrying on war with Kersobleptes in Thrake, yet the ambassadors were most dilatory, much against the will of Demosthenes (who with Æschines again took part in the mission), so that Philip farther conquered Serreium, Doriskus, Hieron Oros; and when they at last returned home after an absence of 2 months and 10 days on the 13th of Skirophorion, Dem. De F. Leg. p. 389. § 156. p. 390. § 108. p. 359. § 57—58, they deceived the Athenians with the illusive representation, that Philip had no thought of annihilating the Phokians, but on the contrary only of punishing the Thebans, so that Philip was enabled to penetrate into Phokis and annihilate

the Phokians without let or hindrance: see for these events Dem. De F. Leg. p. 346. § 17—71. p. 387. § 150—176. De Cor. p. 230. § 18—52. cf. Æschin. De F. Leg. p. 41. § 97—143; and for the deceitful promises of Æschines, Dem. De Pac. p. 59. § 10. Phil. II, p. 73. § 30. De F. Leg. p. 347. § 20—22. De Cor. p. 231. § 21. etc. cf. Æschin. De F. Leg. p. 46. § 130. The Athenians, in the highest degree irritated at the issue of the matter, at first wished to refuse recognition to the foregoing resolutions of the Amphiktyons, and to come to a rupture with Philip again: but Demosthenes produced an alteration in their frame of mind, representing to them in his speech on the peace, that under existing circumstances they could not resume the war without the greatest detriment to themselves.

256) For the progress, which had been made by treachery in the various Greek States in consequence of bribery on the part of Philip, see Dem. De F. Leg. p. 424. § 259: νόσημα γάρ, ὦ ἄνδρες 'Αθηναῖοι, δεινὸν ἐμπέπτωκεν εἰς τὴν 'Ελλάδα καὶ χαλεπὸν καὶ πολλῆς τινὸς εὐτυχίας καὶ παρ' ὑμῶν ἐπιμελείας δεόμενον· οἱ γὰρ ἐν ταῖς πόλεσι γνωριμώτατοι καὶ προεστάναι τῶν κοινῶν ἀξιούμενοι, τὴν αὑτῶν προδιδόντες ἐλευθερίαν οἱ δυστυχεῖς, αὐθαίρετον αὑτοῖς ἐπάγονται δουλείαν, Φίλιππον ξενίαν καὶ ἑταιρίαν καὶ φιλίαν καὶ τοιαῦθ' ὑποκοριζόμενοι, οἱ δὲ λοιποὶ καὶ τὰ κύρι' ἄττα ποτ' ἐστὶν ἐν ἑκάστῃ τῶν πόλεων, οὓς ἔδει τούτους κολάζειν καὶ παραχρῆμα ἀποκτιννύναι, τοσοῦτ' ἀπέχουσι τοῦ τοιοῦτό τι ποιεῖν, ὥστε θαυμάζουσι καὶ ζηλοῦσι καὶ βούλοιτ' ἂν αὐτὸς ἕκαστος τοιοῦτος εἶναι, cf. De Cor. p. 324. § 365, where the names are given of the traitors in the various states, in Thessaly, Thebes, Arcadia, Messenia, Argos, Sikyon, Elis, Corinth, Megara, Eubœa. At Athens the chief were Æschines, Philokrates, Pytholes, Hegemon, Demades; they were confronted by Philip's opponents Lykurgus, Hypereides, Hegesippus, and above all Demosthenes, who at this time had the conduct of public affairs placed more and more in his control. For the situation and feeling of the Greeks in general, Dem. Phil. III, p. 119. § 33. τὸν αὐτὸν τρόπον ὅνπερ τὴν χάλαζαν ἔμοιγε δοκοῦσι θεωρεῖν, εὐχόμενος μὴ καθ' ἑαυτοὺς ἕκαστος γενέσθαι, κωλύειν δ' οὐδεὶς ἐπιχειρῶν, cf. De Cor. p. 241. § 45. etc.

257) He instituted dekadarchies in the various towns, and also placed garrisons in some, Diod. XVI, 69. Dem. Phil. II, p. 71. § 22. De F. Leg. p. 424. § 260. (Dem.) de Hal. p. 84. § 32. Diodorus places this event a year later; but from Dem. Phil. II, l. c. it seems probable that it belongs to 345 B. C., as the speech was delivered in 344, and the measure is here mentioned as carried out.

Min. p. 312. Suid. s. v., a patriot, but of loose morals, Vit. a'. p. 314, contributed to the expedition to Eubœa, Dem. De Cor. p. 259. § 99. c. Mid. p. 566. § 160. Plut. Phoc. 12. Vit. a', p. 315, went as ambassador to Rhodes, l. c., took part in the expedition to Byzantium Vit. a', p. 312, and was accused of having taken Persian gold, l. c. He then came forward as joint-accuser of Philokrates in the embassy

prosecution, Dem. De F. Leg. p. 376. § 116; after the occupation of Elateia cooperated as ambassador to promote the defensive alliance with Thebes, Dem. De Cor. p. 291. § 187, and after the battle of Chæroneia proposed energetic measures for the defence of the town, Vit. a'. p. 313. Lyc. c. Leocr. § 41. Dem. c. Aristog. p. 803. § 11. He was also an active opponent of Alexander, so that his surrender

The Incipient Decline.   107

Olympiad.	B.C.	ATHENS. Archons.	HISTORY.
CIX, 1	344	Lykiskus.	He makes the Messenians and Argives dependent on himself, by taking them under his protection against Sparta[258].
CIX, 2	343	Pythodotus.	His fruitless attempt to bring Megara into his power[259].
CIX, 3	342	Sosigenes.	His expedition to Epirus and Thessaly[260]: the institution of macedonising tyrants in Euboea[261].
CIX, 4	341	Nikomachus	Expedition to Thrake[262].

258) After the conclusion of the sacred war Philip espoused the cause of the Messenians, Argives, and Arcadians against Sparta (cf. obs. 251), sending troops to their aid and promising to come in person: Demosthenes went as ambassador to the Argives and Messenians, in order to warn them against joining Philip, and after his return delivered (in 344 B.C., Dion. Hal. ad Amm. I, 10, p. 737) the second Philippic, from which details of these circumstances may be drawn; see especially p. 68. § 9. p. 69. § 13. p. 71. § 23, and his speech to the Argives and Messenians there reported, id. p. 70. § 20—25. But his exertions produced no good results: not only the Messenians, Argives, and Arcadians appear from this time forth as the dependents and allies of Philip, but even the Eleans, Paus. V, 4, 5. Dem. Phil. III, p. 118. § 27.

259) Chief authority is Dem. De F. Leg. p. 435. § 294—295. cf. id. p. 368. § 87. p. 404. § 204. p. 446. § 326. p. 446. § 334. Phil. III, p. 115. § 17. p. 118. § 27. De Cor. p. 248. § 71. Plut. Phoc. 15. The incident is quite fresh at the time, when the speech on the false embassy was delivered, that is in 343 B.C., id. § 294. 334. Megara is from this time forward the ally of Athens, Dem. de Chers. p. 94. § 18. Phil. III, p. 130. § 74.

260) In Epirus Arybbas is dethroned, and Alexander, the brother of Olympias, made king in his room, Just. VII, 6. VIII, 8. Diod. XVI, 72. XIX, 88. (Dem.) de Hal. p. 84. § 32. Plut. Pyrrh. I, and at the same time three Elean colonies Pandosia, Buchota, and Elatcia are captured by him, de Hal. l. c. He had concluded an alliance with the Ætolians and intended to march against Ampraka and Akarnania, and even into the Peloponnese, Dem. Phil. III, p. 118. § 27. p. 119. § 34: but this design of his was frustrated by the Athenians, who marched to Akarnania with an armed force, Dem. adv. Olymp. p. 1173. § 24, and sent embassies to call upon the Peloponnesians to resist, Dem. Phil. III, p. 129. § 72. The date is settled by the fact that in the speech on Halonnesus delivered in 342 B.C. mention is made of these events, and

in the third Philippic of 341 B.C. the embassies to the Peloponnese are referred to, as having been sent in the previous year, l.c. Philip then returned from Epirus by way of Thessaly, and here instituted a tetrarchy, to bring the country in this way still more thoroughly under his rule, Dem. Phil. III, p. 117. § 26. For the absolute authority, with which he after this time disposed of Thessaly's armed force, see Dem. id. p. 119. § 33. cf. Arrian. VII, 9, 4.

261) Kleitarchus made himself master of Eretria, and Philistides of Oreus, both being supported by auxiliaries of Philip, Dem. Phil. III, p. 125. § 57—62. p. 128. § 66. p. 117. § 27. p. 119. § 33. De Cor. p. 248. § 71. These auxiliaries were probably despatched by Philip at the time, when he marched with his army through Thessaly, obs. 260: apart from this probability, the date here given rests solely on the fact, that these events are first mentioned in the third Philippic.

262) Athens had her possession of the Thrakian Chersonese continually imperilled by the Thrakian chieftains, in particular by the rulers of the Odrysian empire, which according to Strab. p. 33. fr. 48 stretched from the Hebrus to Odessus. After many previous negotiations and obstructions it was assured to the Athenians in 357 B.C. by a convention with the Odrysian prince Kersobleptes, with the exception, however, of Kardia, Dem. adv. Aristocr. p. 678. § 173. p. 681. § 181: in 353 B.C. Chares conquered the town Sestos, and with this conquest the Athenian occupation of the Chersonese, all except Kardia, was completely effected, Diod. XVI, 34. Philip had already in 353 B.C. made a campaign against Thrake, though without any result of importance, Dem. l. c. § 183; this he repeated in 351, and on this occasion compelled Kersobleptes to subjection, and took his son as a hostage, Dem. Ol. I, p. 12. § 13. III, p. 29. § 4. Isocr. Phil. p. 86. § 21. Æschin. De F. Leg. p. 38. § 81: for a third campaign in 346 B.C. see obs. 255. His intention in these campaigns was, partly to prepare the way for his march to Asia by taking possession of the coast-lands of the Hellespont and the Propontis, partly to inflict damage on the

was demanded with that of his fellows, Vit. a'. p. 312. Arr. I, 10, 7. In spite of this he came forward as prosecutor in the Harpalian suit against Demosthenes, whose political creed he shared, l.c.; again, he was a zealous promoter of the Lamian war, and delivered the funeral oration over the fallen, l. c. p. 315. Plut. Phoc. 23. Diod. XVIII, 3. Accordingly after the battle of Krannon he fled from Athens to Ægina, but was seized by Antipater's myrmidons, and cruelly put to death (in 322 n. c.), Vit. a', p. 315. Plut. Phoc. 29. Dem. 28, ῥήτωρ τῶν πρώτων κεκριμένων ι' εἷς. Suid. s. v. Of his 53

speeches, recognised as genuine by the ancients, up to a short time ago only a few fragments were extant. But lately four of these speeches have been discovered on papyrus rolls in graves at Thebes in Egypt, in a better or worse state of preservation; in 1847 fragments of the speech against Demosthenes in the case of Harpalus, in 1853 the speech for Lykophron almost perfect and that for Euxenippus quite perfect, in 1856 the funeral oration for those who had fallen in the Lamian War, imperfect and defective.

14—2

FOURTH PERIOD. 431—338 B.C.

Olympiad.	B.C.	ATHENS.	HISTORY.
CX, 1	340	Archons. Theophrastus.	With the help of Demosthenes the Athenians rally round their flag a number of allies, comprising Byzantium, Abydos, Euboea, Megara, Corinth, Achaia, Akarnania, Leukadia and Kerkyra[263]. Philip besieges Perinthus and Byzantium; the former is supported by the king of Persia, the latter by the Athenians, Chians, and Rhodians[264].
CX, 2	339	Lysimachides.	Philip is compelled to relinquish the siege of Perinthus and Byzantium[265]. Second (third) sacred war; Philip invoked by the Amphiktyons to their aid against Amphissa[266].

Athenians; for this latter point see Dem. de Chers. p. 100, § 44—45. De Cor. p. 254. § 87. De F. Leg. p. 397. § 180. The present expedition was undertaken in the summer of 342 B.C.; this is proved by the fact, that at the time when the speech of Demosthenes on the Chersonese was delivered, Philip had been ten months in Thrake, id. p. 90. § 2. p. 98. § 35; but the speech in question was delivered in 341 and towards the time of the Etesiae (which prevail in the month of July), Dion. Hal. p. 737. ad Amm. I, 10. Dem. de Chers. p. 99. § 14, after Philip had already spent a winter in Thrake, id. § 35. In the first two years, 342 and 341, Philip subdued Kersobleptes (and Teres), Diod. XVI, 71. Ep. Phil. p. 1f0. § 8: Diopeithes at the head of the Athenian klerucha defended the Chersonese, and carried on war with Kardia, which Philip strengthened by a Macedonian garrison, Dem. de Chers. p. 104. § 58. p. 105. § 64. Phil. III, p. 120. § 35. Ep. Phil. p. 161. § 11. The hostilities of Diopeithes gave Philip a handle for complaint at Athens: but Demosthenes took him under his protection in the speech on the Chersonese. For Diopeithes see further Philochor. ap. Dion. Hal. p. 666. de Din. 13.

263) Megara had been the ally of Athens since 343 B.C., obs. 259: in Euboea Chalkis was the first town to enter into an alliance with Athens; this was brought about by Kallias, Æschin. adv. Ctes. p. 66. § 80—93, probably in 342 B.C.; as in 341 in the speech on the Chersonese and in the third Philippic the Chalkidians together with the Megarians are named as allies of Athens, Dem. de Chers. p. 94. § 18. Phil. III, p. 130. § 74. In the third Philippic, delivered shortly after the speech on the Chersonese, about May in 341 B.C., Demosthenes called on the Athenians to enlist fresh allies in their cause, id. p. 129. § 71, and the alliance with Byzantium and Abydos was now effected (in 341 or 340), Dem. De Cor. p. 326. § 302: ambassadors were even sent to the Persian king, though without any result, Ep. Phil. p. 160. § 6. Æschin. adv. Ctes. p. 81. § 228; in Euboea, the tyrant Philistides was overthrown in Oreus and the tyrant Kleitarchus in Eretria, and so the whole of the island was secured to the alliance, Dem. De Cor. p. 252. § 79. p. 254. § 87. Diod. XVI, 74. The liberation of

Eretria was effected by Phokion, who then sailed to Byzantium, consequently in 340 B.C., see Diod. l.c. The liberation of Oreus on the other hand must be placed in 341 from Æschin. adv. Ctes. p. 68. § 103. For the alliance with the other states mentioned above see what is an exceedingly invidious account, Æschin. adv. Ctes. p. 67. § 94—105, cf. Dem. De Cor. p. 306. § 235. Plut. Mor. p. 581 D. According to Æschin. adv. Ctes. l. c. § 68 the 16th of Anthesterion (February) was fixed as a general meeting-day for the allies, when probably the league was resolved on: this can only be that particular day in 340, as in the third Philippic, delivered in the previous year, § 103. For the alliance with the other states mentioned above see but its existence nowhere spoken of.

264) Diod. XVI, 74—77. Philochor. fr. 135 (ap. Dion. Hal. p. 741. ad Amm. I, 11). Paus. I, 29, 10. Plut. Phoc. 14. Hesych. Mil. Origg. Const. § 27—31 (Müller fragm. histor. graec. Vol. IV. p. 151). The Athenians declared the peace broken and overturned the pillar recording the alliance, Diod. XVI, 77. Philochor. l. c. Æschin. adv. Ctes. p. 61. § 55: they then sent, first Chares, and later Phokion to the rescue, Diod. Plut. Hesych. Mil. l. c. From Philochorus we gather, that the siege of Perinthus was first entered upon in the archonship of Theophrastus, which began in the summer of 340 B.C., whilst Diodorus places it in the previous archonship. Also the Chians, Koans, and Rhodians sent help to Byzantium, Diod. l. c.

265) Diod. XVI, 77. Plut. Phoc. 14.

266) In the Amphiktyonic congress, in the spring of 339, war was declared at the proposal of Æschines against the town Amphissa, for having tilled the sacred territory of Amphissa, see p. 27 obs. 67: the Amphiktyons fail to effect anything against Amphissa and therefore in the autumn meeting invoke Philip to their aid, Æschin. adv. Ctes. p. 68. § 106—129. Dem. De Cor. p. 274. § 140—153. It is proved, that the first Amphiktyonic congress referred to met in the spring of 339 B.C., by the passages Æschin. adv. Ctes. p. 69. § 115. p. 71. § 128.

The Incipient Decline. 109

Olympiad.	B. C.	ATHENS.	HISTORY.	ART AND LITERATURE.
CX, 3	338	Archon. Chærondas.	Philip occupies Elateia; the Athenians, Thebans, and the other allies of Athens rise against him ^{oo}); their defeat at Chæroneia ²⁶⁸).	Historians: Theopompus^{qq}), Ephorus^{rr}). The Philosopher Speusippus (older Academy)^{ss}).

267) Philip came forward at the call of the Amphiktyons, while it was still winter time, and occupied first of all the two towns Kytinium and Elateia, commanding the plain of Bœotia, by which the Greeks had their eyes opened to his further plans, s. Philoch. fr. 135. Dem. de Cor. p. 278. § 152. p. 264. § 108. Æsch. adv. Ctes. p. 73. § 140. Diod. XVI, 84. For the effect, which the news caused in Athens, s. Dem. de Cor. p. 284. § 169: Ἑσπέρα μὲν γὰρ ἦν, ἧκε δ' ἀγγέλλων τις ὡς τοὺς πρυτάνεις, ὡς Ἐλάτεια κατείληπται· καὶ μετὰ ταῦτα οἱ μὲν εὐθὺς ἐξαναστάντες μεταξὺ δειπνοῦντες τούτ' τ' ἐκ τῶν σκηνῶν τῶν κατὰ τὴν ἀγορὰν ἐξεῖργον καὶ τὰ γέρρα ἐνεπίμπρασαν, οἱ δὲ τοὺς στρατηγοὺς μετεπέμποντο καὶ τὸν σαλπιγκτὴν ἐκάλουν καὶ θορύβου πλήρης ἦν ἡ πόλις· τῇ δὲ ὑστεραίᾳ ἅμα τῇ ἡμέρᾳ οἱ μὲν πρυτάνεις τὴν βουλὴν ἐκάλουν εἰς τὸ βουλευτήριον, ὑμεῖς δὲ εἰς τὴν ἐκκλησίαν ἐπορεύεσθε κ. τ. λ. How Demosthenes thereupon came forward in the popular assembly, and urged an alliance with Thebes, and then went himself as ambassador to Thebes, and there overcame all difficulties and hindrances by his eloquence, for this s. Dem. l. c. § 169—187. p. 298. § 211—214. cf. Plut. Dem. 18. Justin. IX, 3. The war was carried on a long time with success (the other allies besides the Thebans, s. obs. 263), and the Greeks even won two battles, Dem. de Cor. p. 300. § 216. At this very time, however, Amphissa was taken by Philip, and a mercenary force of 10,000 men, raised by the allied Greeks, annihilated, s. Æsch. adv. Ctes. p. 74. § 146. Diod. XVIII, 56.

268) Diod. XVI, 84—87. Philip had over 30,000 men, s. id. 86; on the side of the Greeks, besides the citizen soldiers, there were 15,000 mercenaries and 2000 horse, Justin. IX, 3; 1000 Athenians fell upon the field and 2000 were taken prisoners, Dem. de Cor. p. 314. § 264. Lyk. adv. Leokr. p. 108. § 142. Demst. fr. p. 179. § 9. Diod. XVI, 86. 88. The fame of the slain, Lyk. l. c. p. 153. § 46—50; the glorious end of the Theban sacred band, Plut. Pel. 18. Alex. 9. The day of the battle was the 7th Metageitnion (August or September), Plut. Cam. 19. For the dismay, which the defeat spread at Athens, s. Lyk. l. c. p. 152. § 37—45. Athens submitted, and was punished with the loss of her possessions by sea, on the other hand recovering Oropus, s. Paus. I, 25, 3. 34, 1. Diod. XVIII, 56; also the 2000 prisoners were restored without ransom, Demad. fr. p. 179. § 9. Thebes received a Macedonian garrison, Diod. XVI, 87. Justin. IX, 4.—Lyk. l. c. p. 154. § 50: συνετάφη τοῖς τούτων (those slain at Chæroneia) σώμασιν ἡ τῶν ἄλλων Ἑλλήνων ἐλευθερία: Justin. IX, 3: Hic dies universæ Græciæ et gloriam dominationis et vetustissimam libertatem finivit.—Philip marched on after the battle into the Peloponnese, where submission was made by all but Sparta, and where he took and gave portions of territory, as he pleased: see Diod. XVII, 3. Polyb. IX, 28, 33. Paus. VIII, 7, 4.

qq) Theopompus of Chios, born about 380, Phot. Bibl. Cod. 176, p. 203, emigrated with his father, who was suspected of Laconian sympathies, to Ephesus, Diod. XV, 48. Suid. s. v. Ἔφορος. Phot. l. c., and also came on his travels to Athens, where he received rhetorical instruction from Isokrates, Vit. Isocr. γ΄, Westerm. Vit. min. p. 256 f. Suid. l. c. Phot. Bibl. Cod. CCLX, p. 793. Dion. Hal. Ep. ad Pomp. 6, I, and shone in declamations, Phot. l. c. p. 205. Vit. Isocr. l. c. Gell. X, 18. He was then induced to write history by Isokrates, Phot. l. c. Athen. III, p. 85. a. Recalled by Alexander's influence to his native town, after that king's death he was again obliged to flee, and was coldly received even by Ptolemy, Phot. l. c. Of his fortunes after this no record has been handed down to us. His chief works are Ἑλληνικαὶ ἱστορίαι or Ἑλληνικά, a continuation of the narrative of Thucydides down to the battle of Knidos, Diod. XIII. 52. XIV, 84. Thuc. Vit. Marc. 45. Anon. 5. Suid. s. v., and Φιλιππικά, Diod. XVI, 3. Phot. l. c. p. 406. Cf. Fragm. Hist. Græc. ed. C. Th. Müller, Vol. I, p. 278—333. He is unanimously reproached with censoriousness. Polyb. VIII, 12. Dion. Hal. l. c. 6, 8. Nep. Alc. 11. Plut. Lys. 30. Herod. Mal. p. 855. a. Athen. VI, p. 254. b. For his style cf. the following note.

rr) Ephorus of Kyme in Æolia, Suid. s. v., was trained by Isokrates

in company with Theopompus, l. c. Vit. Isocr. α΄, β΄, γ΄, Westerm. Vit. min. p. 248. 252. 256 f., and persuaded to devote himself to writing history, Sence. Tranq. An. c. 6. Quint. X, 1, 74, and lived into the time of Alexander, Clem. Alex. Strom. 1, p. 145. The chief work amongst his writings was Ἱστορίαι in 30 books, which comprised the history of Greece from the return of the Heraklidæ to the siege of Perinthus in 340 B. C., Diod. VI, 1. V, 1. XVI, 26. Suid. s. v., but was only completed by his son, Diod. XVI, 14, the first universal history, Polyb. V, 33, 2. Cf. Fragm. Hist. Græc. ed. C. Th. Müller, Vol. I, p. 234—277. In contrast with Theopompus it is said of him, Suid. s. v.: Ἔφορος ἦν τὸ ἦθος ἁπλοῦς, τὴν δὲ ἑρμηνείαν τῆς ἱστορίας ὕπτιος καὶ νωθρὸς καὶ μηδεμίαν ἔχων ἐπίτασιν, ὁ δὲ Θεόπομπος τὸ ἦθος πικρὸς καὶ κακοήθης, τῇ δὲ φράσει πολὺς καὶ συνεχὴς καὶ φοράς μεστός, φιλαλήθης τε· ὁ γ΄ οὖν Ἰσοκράτης τὸν μὲν ἔφη χαλινοῦ δεῖσθαι, τὸν δ' Ἔφορον κέντρου. Cf. Cic. de orat. II, 13. III, 9. Quint. X, 1, 74.

ss) Speusippus of the Athenian deme Myrrhinus, born somewhere about 395—393, son of a sister of Plato, Diog. L. IV, 1, was trained by Isokrates, l. c. 2, and in particular by Plato, l. c. 1: καὶ ἐμεινε μὲν ἐπὶ τῶν αὐτῶν Πλάτωνι δογμάτων; but he also adopted many of the Pythagorean doctrines, Arist. Eth. Nic. 1, 6. He stood in connexion with prominent men of his time, such as Dionysius, Dion and

Olympiad.	B.C.	ATHENS.	HISTORY.
CX, 4	337	Archon. Phrynichus.	Philip appointed commander against the Persian king by the Hellenes in the national assembly at Corinth [269]).

---

269) Diod. XVI, 89. Justin. IX, 5.

Philippus, l. c. 5, and accompanied Plato to Syracuse, Plut. Dion. 35. After Plato's death he was for eight years president of the academy, l. c. 1. Feeble in body and passionate, he became the prey of melancholy, and put an end to his own life, l. c. 1. 3. 4. Of his numerous writings (Ύπομνήματα, Διάλογοι, Ἐπιστολαί) only the titles, l. c. 4. 5, and a few fragments are still extant. The leading philosophers assigned to the so-called older academy are, besides Speusippus, his successor Xenokrates and the contemporary Herakleides of Pontus, and later Polemon, Krates, and Krantor.

FIFTH PERIOD.

336—146 B.C.

THE EXTINCTION OF GREEK FREEDOM.

Whilst Alexander the Great is subduing the Persian empire and extending his sway over the vast extent of its dominions, thus opening up the East to Greek speech and culture, whilst after his death the huge Macedonio-Persic empire, which he had established, is being split up into several empires amid long, bloody, and desolating struggles between his generals, the so-called Diadochi,—Greece, in spite of repeated attempts to regain its freedom, is kept in a state of dependency on Macedonia, or even drawn into the disputes of the Diadochi to its still greater discomfiture; until Macedonia is so weakened by quarrels about the throne and domestic wars and finally by the Keltic invasion, that it is obliged to relinquish Greece. Greece now raises herself once more to a brief enjoyment of freedom; to secure which there are founded leagues of federal states. In the Peloponnese especially a more active vitality asserts itself: here the Achæan league expels the macedonising tyrants and unites a large number of towns under its protection; and here too about this same time the attempt is made at Sparta to restore the Lykurgean constitution in its purity, and thus to inspire the state with its old energy. But with this upward impulse the old dissension soon returns. Sparta, which employs its newly awakened force in striving to pass its narrow limits and regain its former hegemony, comes into conflict with the Achæan league. The league, in danger of succumbing, invokes the king of Macedonia to its aid; but with this result, that together with Sparta the Achæan league and all the rest of Greece again fall under Macedonian rule. Meanwhile the Roman Empire had grown, until it reached the boundaries of Greece and Macedonia. The struggle between Rome and Macedonia follows. The various states of Greece side with one or other of the belligerent powers; and those, which take part with Rome, at first gain in that state a champion in reserve against Macedonia. Afterwards, when the king of Macedonia is conquered and confined to the ancient limits of his empire, the whole of Greece obtains its freedom as a gift from the conqueror, but only to fall again together with Macedonia under Roman sway after an enjoyment of freedom more apparent than real. When such was the course of history, it was impossible that art and literature should display a vigorous and independent development during this period. Notwithstanding art on the whole maintains itself at its former level and in some branches, particularly in painting, even makes considerable progress towards perfection. In literature, not taking into account oratory, which continues to flourish for some time, and also a certain revival of comedy, the production is throughout confined to imitations and to more learned works, which have only a subordinate value for the Greek race.

Authorities. For the history of Alexander Arrian in his 'Αλεξάνδρου 'Ανάβασις and the 'Ινδική is the chief source of our information. It is true that he only belongs to the second century after Christ, but he has lent his historical works a proportionately high value by the careful and conscientious use which he made of contemporary writers (Ptolemæus, Aristobulus, Nearchus). For the rest of the period it is in Polybius alone, and so far as he is lost, in the parts of Livy drawn from him, that we possess an at all pure and trustworthy source of historical information. For the time of Alexander we have still further a special source in Curtius (De Rebus Gestis Alexandri Magni): but from his want of thoroughness and the partiality of his views set forth with a predominance of rhetoric he, compared with Arrian, only takes a subordinate rank. Besides these writers, for the period as a whole we are dependent merely on Diodorus, whose work, however, breaks off with the 20th book and the year 302 B.C. (of the rest we only possess extracts and fragments); on Plutarch in the biographies of Alexander, Demosthenes, Phokion, Eumenes, Demetrius Poliorketes, Pyrrhus, Agis, Kleomenes, Aratus, and Philopœmen; and on some supplementary notices from Strabo, Pausanias, Justin, etc.

The Extinction of Greek Freedom.   113

FIRST SECTION.

336—323 B.C.

FOUNDATION OF THE VAST MACEDONIO-PERSIC MONARCHY BY ALEXANDER THE GREAT.

Olympiad.	B. C.	ATHENS.	HISTORY.	ART AND LITERATURE.
CXI, 1	336	Archon. Pythodelus.	Philip murdered[1]). Alexander succeeds[2]). Alexander suppresses the movement, which arises in Greece at the news of Philip's death, by	The orators Demades[a]), Deinarchus[b]). The Philosopher Aristotle[c]).

1) Diod. XVI, 91—94. Justin. IX, 6. Plut. Alex. 10. He was 46 years old, Paus. VIII, 7, 4, (47 according to Justin. IX, 8), and had reigned 24 years, Diod. l. c. 95. He was murdered by Pausanias, a captain of the body-guard, to whom he had refused satisfaction for an outrage inflicted upon him by Attalus, cf. Arist. Pol. VIII, 10, 16. But the murder was committed not without the guilty knowledge and complicity of other persons, Plut. l. c.: in particular Olympias is designated the prime mover, Justin. IX, 7, and even Alexander did not remain unassailed by suspicion, Plut. l. c. Justin. l. c.: Alexander himself accused the Persian king of being the arch-contriver of the crime, Arr. II, 14, 5.

a) Demades of Athens, of humble origin, Suid. s. v., the deadly enemy of Demosthenes, Plut. Dem. 28, after he had been taken prisoner at Chaeroneia, was bribed by Macedonian gold to act in Philip's interest, Diod. XVI, 87. Gell. XI. 9. Sext. Empir. I, 13. p. 281, and was in favour with Alexander, whose vengeance he, in community with Phokion, averted from his native city, Plut. Dem. 23. Diod. XVII, 15. The Athenians released him from the civil disability to which he had been condemned, in order to send him to Antipater to beg that the Macedonian garrison might be withdrawn from Munychia, Plut. Phoc. 30. At a later period he was charged by Antipater with traitorous intrigues against him, was seized and put to death (319 or 318 B.C.), Diod. XVIII, 48. Paus. VII, 10. Val. dissipated, and extravagant, Plut. Phoc. 1. 20. 30, Suid. s. v., he was still a born orator, witty and ready, Plut. Dem. 8. 10. Cic. Or. 26. There is no speech by him extant, and even the genuineness of a fragment attributed to him (ὑπὲρ τῆς δωδεκαετίας) is doubted, cf. Cic. Brut. 9. Quint. II, 17, 12.

b) Deinarchus, born at Corinth circ. 361 B.C., Dionys. Din. 4, came at an early age to Athens, where he became intimately acquainted with Theophrastus and Demetrius Phalereus, l. c. 2, and as a stranger won himself fame, in particular by speeches written to be delivered by others in the law-courts, l.c. He spoke as an adherent of the Macedonians in the Harpalian prosecution, l. c. After the liberation of Athens by Demetrius Poliorketes he went into banishment at Chalkis in Euboea, Dion. Hal. l. c. 3. Vit. β'. Westerm. p. 321, from which he first returned in 292 B.C. He pleaded for the first time in the law-courts as an old man against a faithless friend Proxenus, who

2) Plut. Alex. 11: παρέλαβε—τὴν βασιλείαν, φθόνους μεγάλους καὶ δεινὰ μίση καὶ κινδύνους πανταχόθεν ἔχουσαν. For the dangers threatening him from without, see obs. 3 and 4: at home he was menaced by the partisans of Kleopatra, the wife whom Philip had married after divorcing Olympias, and of her uncle Attalus, who had already in 36 B.C. been sent by Philip to Asia in advance, Diod. XVI, 91. XVII. 2. Accordingly Alexander had Attalus put to death, Diod. XVII, 2, 5: and besides that several members of the royal family were executed, (in part only as victims of the hatred and cruelty of Olympias), Paus. VIII, 7, 5. Justin. IX, 7. Ælian. V. H. XIII, 36—Alexander was 20 years old, when he ascended the throne, Plut. l. c. Arr. I, 1, 1. For a

had cheated him of his property, Dion II. l. c. Vit. 3. β'. It is uncertain when he died. Of his speeches, the number of which is variously stated, Vit. β'. Suid. s. v., three are extant, all of them delivered in the Harpalian trial : Κατὰ Δημοσθένους, Κατὰ Ἀριστογείτονος, Κατὰ Φιλοκλέους. Of his oratory it is said, Dion. II. l. c. 5 : οὐδὲν γὰρ οὔτε κοινὸν οὔτ' ἴδιον ἔσχεν οὔτ' ἐν τοῖς ἰδίοις οὔτ' ἐν τοῖς δημοσίοις ἀγῶσιν, ἀλλὰ καὶ τοῖς Λυσίου παραχλήψεσίν ἐστιν ὅπου γίνεται καὶ τοῖς Ὑπερείδου καὶ τοῖς Δημοσθένους λέγοις.

c) Aristotle, born at Stageira in Chalkidike in 384 B.C., the son of a physician Nikomachus, who himself wrote works on natural science (Suid. s. v. Νικόμαχος), Apollod. ap. Diog. L. V, 9, after losing his parents, came to Athens when 17 years old, having received a careful education, and lived there for 20 years, Diog. L. l. c. Arist. Vit. a'. Westerm. Vit. min. p. 498. At Athens he was Plato's most prominent pupil, being called by him τοὺς τῆς διατριβῆς, Diog. L. V, 2. II, 109. Æl. V. H. III, 19. IV, 9. Vit. a'. β'. p. 399. W., and during part of this period imparted instruction in rhetoric in opposition to Isokrates, Cic. de Or. III, 35. Quint. III, 1, 14. On one occasion he also acted as ambassador for the Athenians with Philip, Diog. L. V, 9. After Plato's death he betook himself to his friend Hermeias, tyrant of Atarneus and Assus in Mysia, l. c. 7. 9—11, and after his downfall in 345 B.C. to Mytilene in Lesbos, l. c. Two years later he was summoned by Philip to undertake the education of the young Alexander, and remained for eight years in Macedonia, l. c. It was at this time that he procured from Philip or Alexander the restoration of his native town, which had been destroyed by Philip, l. c. 4. Plut. Alex. 7. He then returned back to Athens, where he taught philosophy for thirteen

Fifth Period. 336—146 B.C.

Olympiad.	B.C.	HISTORY.	ART AND LITERATURE.
CXI, 1	336	his swift appearance in that country, and is appointed in an assembly at Corinth, just as his father had been, commander of the Greeks against the Persians[a].	The sculptor Lysippus[d]. The art of stone-engraving and die-sinking: Pyrgoteles[e].

description of his character see esp. Plut. 8. Diog. L. V, 1, 6. Strab. p. 69. Arr. Ind. XX, thirst for knowledge and Greek education. Plut. 4, thirst for glory. Arr. VII, 14. Plut. 52, enthusiastic friendship, Arr. 5, 2 (οὐ γὰρ χρῆναι—τὸν βασιλέα ἄλλο τι ἢ ἀληθεύειν). Plut. 9, his bravery in his earliest youth. Id. 21, temperance and abstemiousness in the earlier period of his life. Id. 73. 75, adherence to the popular creed. His praise generally see Arr. VII, 28—30. Curt. X, 5. For his degeneration later on see obs. 18.

years (335—322 B.C.) in the Lyceum, Diog. L. V, 5; and delivered strictly scientific lectures to his pupils in a narrower sense (ἀκροατικά), as well as lectures generally intelligible to a larger circle of hearers (ἐξωτερικά), Gell. XX, 5. His relations with his royal pupil became cold in consequence of the incarceration and death of Kallisthenes, Aristotle's nephew, Diog. L. V, 10. Plut. Alex. 55. After Alexander's death he was accused of impiety, Diog. L. l. c., and found a refuge in Chalkis in Euboea under Antipater's protection, l. c. 5. 9. 14. There he died in 322 B. C., shortly before Demosthenes, at the age of sixty-three, l. c. 10. Vit. a', cf. Dion. Hal. ad Amm. I, 5. Of his numerous works, which according to the registers handed down to us, Vit. γ', p. 402—404. W. Diog. L. V, 22—27, embraced all provinces of human knowledge and thought, and laid the foundations of several sciences, as of logic, natural history, the theory of poetry, etc., many have been lost, and those which have come down to us are not all of them genuine. The most important are the following. Those which treat of the laws of thought: Κατηγορίαι, on the most universal classnotions, Περὶ ἑρμηνείας, on speech as expression of thought, Ἀναλυτικὰ πρότερα, on syllogisms, Ἀναλυτικὰ ὕστερα, on demonstrable knowledge and proof by syllogism, Τοπικά, points of view for the invention of reasons and counter-reasons, Περὶ τῶν σοφιστικῶν ἐλέγχων, on fallacies. These works are comprehended under the title Ὄργανον. The things of sense and the essence of things are treated of in: Τὰ μετὰ τὰ φυσικά, on the universal first cause of things; and amongst the works on natural science touching the nature of particular things are Ἀκρόασις φυσική, general view of nature, Περὶ γενέσεως καὶ φθορᾶς, Μετεωρολογικά, Περὶ ζῴων ἱστορία; the treatise Περὶ ψυχῆς, one of the most important, contains his teaching on the soul. Mathematical subjects are handled in Περὶ ἀτόμων γραμμῶν and Μηχανικὰ προβλήματα. His ethical and political doctrines are comprised above all in Ἠθικὰ Νικομάχεια and Πολιτικά (Πολιτικῆ ἀκρόασις), his doctrine on the arts of poetry and speaking in Περὶ ποιητικῆς and Τέχνη ῥητορική. Of Aristotle it is said, Vit. β', p. 401. W.: ἐν φιλοσοφίᾳ δ' ὑπερβέβηκε τὰ ἀνθρώπινα μέτρα, μηδὲν ἐλλιπὲς περὶ αὐτῆς πραγματευσάμενος, ἀλλὰ καὶ πολλὰ αὐτῇ προσθεὶς ἐκ τῆς ἑαυτοῦ ἀγχινοίας τὴν ὅλην κατώρθωσε φιλοσοφίαν. His school is named the Peripatetic, because Aristotle was in the habit of teaching whilst walking up and down (περιπατῶν), Diog. L. V, 2. Cic. Acad. I, 4. Gell. XX, 5. etc. Its leaders after Aristotle were Theophrastus, Eudemus, and Strato.

d) Lysippus of Sikyon flourished at the time of Alexander, Plin. H. N. XXXIV, 51. Paus. VI, 1, 2: was originally a worker in metal, and as an artist self-taught, Plin. l. c. 61, and is said to have executed 1500 statues, for the most part in bronze, l. c. 37. The most famous

3) Diod. XVII, 3—4. Arr. I, 1, 1—3. At Athens Demosthenes first announced the news of Philip's death to the people, Æsch. adv. Ctes. p. 64. § 77. Plut. Alex. 11. Phoc. 16, and the people resolved to bestow a crown of honour on the murderer and to refuse the hegemony to Alexander, Plut. Dem. 22. Diod. XVII, 3. But at Athens, as elsewhere, the arrival of Alexander immediately suppressed the movement, and at Corinth greater concessions were made to Alexander, than had been granted to his father; on this occasion the

of these were: a colossal statue of Zeus in brass at Tarentum, Plin. XXXIV, 40, a four-horse chariot with the sun-god of the Rhodians, l. c. 63, the bronze colossus of Herakles at Tarentum, l. c. 40. Strab. p. 278. Plut. Fab. Max. 22, and an allegorical figure of Καιρός, Jac. anal. II, n. 13. Callistr. stat. 6. Tzetz. Chil. VIII, 200. X, 322. Numerous and highly celebrated in antiquity were his representations of Alexander, Plin. l. c. 63, who refused to allow any one but Lysippus to execute a statue of him, Arr. Alex. I, 16, 17. Plut. de virt. Alex. p. 335. a. Alex. 4: καὶ γὰρ ἃ μάλιστα πολλοὶ τῶν διαδόχων ὕστερον καὶ τῶν φίλων ἀπεμιμοῦντο, τήν τ' ἀνάτασιν τοῦ αὐχένος εἰς εὐώνυμον ἡσυχῇ κεκλιμένου καὶ τὴν ὑγρότητα τῶν ὀμμάτων διατετήρηκεν ἀκριβῶς. He, as opposed to Apelles, represented Alexander with a lance, Plut. Is. et Osir. 24. p. 360, and of such a statue in bronze it is said in an epigram, Anth. Jac. II, 13. p. 50 : Λύσιππε, πλάστα Σικυώνιε, θαρσαλέα χείρ | δαῖε τεχνῖτα, πῦρ τοι ὁ χάλκεος ὁρῇ, | ὃν κατ' Ἀλεξάνδρου μορφᾶς χέεις· οὔτι μεμπτοί, | Πέρσαι· συγγνώμη βουσὶ λέοντα φυγεῖν. Besides this Lysippus was also commissioned by Alexander to execute the portrait statues of the Macedonian knights, who fell by the Granikus, Plin. l. c. Arr. Alex. I. c. Plut. Alex. 17. Criticisms on him may be found in Plin. l. c. 65 : Statuariae arti plurimum traditur contulisse capillum exprimendo, capita minora faciendo quam antiqui, corpora graciliora siccioraque, per quae procerius signorum maior videretur, cf. Propert. III, 7, 9 ; Gloria Lysippi est animosa effingere signa. We still possess imitations of the works of Lysippus in the Apoxyomenos of the Vatican and in the Farnese Herakles.—A whole artistic school at Sikyon and Argos attached itself to Lysippus. After this the development of art ceases for a considerable period in Greece, and continues only in Asia Minor, where at Pergamon and in Rhodes it arrived at a particularly high standard of perfection. The art school of Pergamon had undertaken the task of ennobling by their works the victories of the kings Attalus (241—197) and Eumenes (197—159) over the Gauls (Plin. XXXIV, 84), and thus created historical works of art, of which we still possess imitations in the dying gladiator and in the group of Arria and Paetus at Rome, both scenes from the Gaulish combats. The characteristics of the Rhodian school are the tendency to the colossal and the desire to excite and keep at tension the emotions of the beholder by the action represented : the most prominent works of this school are the groups of the Laokoon and the Farnese bull.

e) Of the art of engraving stones it is said Macrob. VII, 13: Imprimebatur sculptura materio anuli, sive ex ferro, sive ex auro foret —. Postea luxuriantis aetatis usus signaturas pretiosis gemmis coepit insculpere, cf. Plin. XXXVII, 1—9. Glyptica began to flourish, after the precious stones of India had become known at Alexander's

The Extinction of Greek Freedom. 115

Olympiad.	B. C.	ATHENS.	HISTORY.	ART AND LITERATURE.
CXI, 2	335	Archon. Eumœnetus.	The revolted Thrakian, Pæonian, and Illyrian tribes subdued by Alexander[4]). Revolt of the Thebans: Thebes taken and destroyed[5]).	The Painters Apelles[f]), Protogenes[g]).

Spartans alone once more refused to recognise his hegemony, Arr. I, 1, 2: Λακεδαιμονίοις ἀνοκρίνασθαι, μὴ εἶναι σφίσι πάτριον ἀκολουθεῖν ἄλλοις, ἀλλ' αὐτοὺς ἄλλων ἐξηγεῖσθαι. At Corinth a convention was established (called κοινὴ εἰρήνη καὶ συμμαχία), the conditions of which we learn from the speech (Dem.) De Fœd. cum Alex., which, though not from the pen of Demosthenes, may perhaps be from that of Hypereides, and at all events is from the pen of a contemporary (in the year 335 B. c.). The most important clause is that providing for the establishment of a κοινὸν συνέδριον at Corinth, in which affairs of common interest are to be deliberated on, and which remained in existence during the reign of Alexander, see e.g. Diod. XVII, 73. The members of this body are styled in the speech referred to οἱ συνεδρεύοντες καὶ οἱ ἐπὶ τῇ κοινῇ φυλακῇ τεταγμένοι, p. 215. § 15, All Greek states are to be free and independent, p. 213. § 6, no changes are to be made in existing constitutions, no exiles are to be recalled without the knowledge and consent of the Synedrium, no fresh exiles to be made, no distributions of lands are to be set on foot, no slaves to be manumitted for state purposes, etc. p. 214. § 10. p. 215. § 15. p. 216. § 16: all provisions, the object of which was to suppress freedom and independent movement in the individual states, and

time. Most frequent of all are works in amethyst, hyacinth, topaz, garnet, jasper, onyx, agate, cornelian : and these engraved stones are either sunk (intaglios) or raised (cameos), the former being employed for signet-rings, the latter for ornaments. Also the engraving of dies for coins attained perfection at this time, as is shown in particular by coins of the lower Italian and Sicilian towns Tarentum, Herakleia, Thurii, Velia, Metapontum, and the Macedonian coins struck during the reign of Alexander. The names of a number of die engravers are known merely from coin inscriptions.—Pyrgoteles, a contemporary of Alexander, and the most famous gem-engraver of his time, alone had permission to engrave the likeness of the king on gems, Plin. XXXVII, 8 (non dubie clarissimo artis ejus).

f) Apelles, born at Kolophon, Suid. s. v., or at Ephesus, Strab. p. 642. Lucian. De Calumn. non Tem. Cred. 2, or at Kos, Plin. XXXV, 79. Ovid. Ars Am. III, 401. Pont. IV, 1, 29, first the pupil of Ephorus at Ephesus, and then of Pamphilus at Amphipolis, Plin. l. c. 76. Plut. Arat. 13, afterwards lived in Macedonia, where he became the friend of Alexander, who often visited his studio and would allow no other artist to paint him. In the course of his travels he came to Rhodes, where he generously gave his support to Protogenes, Plin. l. c. 81. 88, and also painted at Athens, Athen. III, p. 590 e, Corinth, l. c. 588 D, Smyrna, Paus. IX, 35, 2, Samos, Plin. l. c. 93, as also at Alexandria, where, however, he was exposed to attacks from the jealousy of his fellow artists, Plin. l. c. 89. His most famous pictures were Aphrodite Anadyomene, the goddess rising up from the sea, for the temple of Asklepios at Kos, Plin. l. c. 91. Plin. l. c. 87, Diabole, an allegorical picture of calumny, Lucian. l. c. 5, and amongst the numerous portraits of Philip and Alexander, Plin. l. c. 89, in particular Alexander with the thunder-bolt in his hand (κεραυνοφόρος) for the temple of the Ephesian Artemis, l. c. 92.

to put them in the power of Alexander, who was master of the Synedrium.

4) Arr. I, 1—6. Diod. XVII, 8. Plut. Alex. 11. Strab. p. 301. He marched from Amphipolis over Hæmus and advanced as far as the Ister, and even crossed it: then, after receiving ambassadors from the most distant races, even from the Kelts, with offerings of friendship and gold, Arr. I, 4, 6—8. Strab. l. c., he turned westwards against the Pæonians and Illyrians, and here reached as far as the town Pelion in the neighbourhood of the lake Lychnitis. From these campaigns, besides the subjection of the peoples named, he gained a further advantage, in that he was enabled to draw from those regions light-armed troops, which did him great service in his wars: amongst those the Agrianians are in particular frequently mentioned. Illyrian auxiliaries, see Curt. IV, 13, 31. VI, 6, 35; besides them and the Agrianians, still further Odrysians, Triballians, Thrakians, Pæonians, Diod. XVII, 17.

5) Arr. I, 7—10. Diod. XVII, 8—15. Plut. Alex. 11—13. The revolt was called forth by the false news, that Alexander had fallen, Arr. VII, 2. Demad. fr. p. 180. § 17. Justin. XI, 2. Besides the Thebans the Ætolians, Eleans and Arcadians were also in revolt : and Cic. Verr. IV, 60, of which the king himself said, Plut. de virt. Alex. p. 335 A : ὅτι δυοῖν 'Αλεξάνδρων ὁ μὲν Φιλίππου γέγονεν ἀνίκητος, ὁ δὲ 'Απελλοῦ ἀμίμητος: very celebrated also was his picture of a horse, so true to nature, that a living horse neighed to it, Plin. l. c. 85. It is said of him, Plin. l. c. 69 : Picturæ plura solus prope quam ceteri omnes contulit, Præcipua ejus in arte venustas fuit, cum eodem state maxumi pictores essent, quorum opera cum admiraretur, omnibus conlaudatis dicens illam suam Venerem dicebat, quam Græci Charita vocant. From the numerous anecdotes and traits of character recorded in the authors referred to we catch a clear view, not only of the artist's genius, but also of his amiable, witty, and magnanimous nature. Antiphilus was a rival of Apelles, but equal to him neither in genius nor technical perfection ; his most celebrated work was a boy blowing a fire, Plin. XXXV, 138. 113. Quintilian, XII, 10 gives special praise to his 'facilitas.'

g) Protogenes, either of Kaunus, Plin. XXXV, 101. Paus. I, 3, 4. Plut. Demetr. 22, or of Xanthus in Lykia, Suid. s. v., lived for a long time in poverty and obscurity at Rhodes, is said to have painted ships even up to his fiftieth year, and only worked himself into notice by laborious and persevering industry, Plin. l. c. 101, supported by Apelles, cf. obs. f. His most celebrated painting was the picture of Ialysus, the hero of Rhodes, with the still more famous hound, the foam dripping from its muzzle, l. c. 102; also the resting Satyr with the double-flute in his hand, painted at Rhodes, whilst Demetrius Poliorkeios was taking the town by storm, Strab. p. 652. Plin. l. c. 105. By the most attentive observation of nature he attained to the most minute truth to nature. It is said of him, l. c. Impetus animi ut quædam artis libido in hæc potius cum tulere. Petron. sat. 84: Protogenis rudimenta cum ipsius naturæ veritate non sine quodam horrore tractavi.

15—2

Olympiad.	B. C.	ATHENS.	HISTORY.
		Archon.	
CXI, 3	334	Ktesikles.	Departure of Alexander on his expedition against the Persian empire⁶). He conquers the Persian satraps in the battle of the Granikus and subdues Asia Minor⁷).

the latter had already advanced as far as the isthmus: Athens had resolved on war, but was still delaying. Thebes was taken after a brave resistance, and was destroyed chiefly at the instigation of its enemies in Hellas, the Phokians, Orchomenians, Thespians, and Plataeans: only Pindar's house was spared, Arr. I, 9, 10. Plut. Al. 11. The inhabitants were sold as slaves, to the number of 30,000; 6000 had fallen in the struggle, Diod. XVII, 14. Plut. l. c. From Athens Alexander at first required the surrender of his chief opponents, Demosthenes, Lykurgus, Hypereides, Polyeuktus, Chares, Charidemus, Ephialtes, Diotimus, Mœrokles, but was so far appeased by ambassadors from Athens, as to rest content with the banishment of Charidemus and Ephialtes, Arr. I, 10, 2—6. Diod. XVII, 15. Plut. Phoc. 17. Dem. 23. Justin. XI, 4. Dinarch. adv. Demosth. p. 94. § 32—33. The fall of Thebes happened in October, as follows from the circumstance that the Athenians were celebrating the great mysteries just at the time, when the intelligence arrived at Athens.

6) The start was effected ἅμα τῷ ἦρι ἀρχομένῳ, Arr. I, 11, 3. His army consisted according to Diod. XVII, 17 (the solitary passage, where the various component elements of the army are stated at the commencement of the expedition) of 12,000 Macedonians, 7000 allies, 5000 mercenaries, 5000 Odrysians, Triballians and Illyrians, 1000 Agrianians, together with 30,000 infantry, and 4,500 cavalry, viz. 1500 Macedonians, 1300 Thessalians, 600 Greeks, and 900 Thrakians and Paeonians; with which the statement of the total in Arr. l. c. nearly tallies, where the numbers are given as "not much more than 30,000 infantry, and over 5000 cavalry." Other accounts, for the most part rather higher, Plut. Al. 15. Polyb. XII, 19. Justin. XI, 6. The 12,000 Macedonian foot-soldiers formed the greater part of the phalanx (consisting of 6 τάξεις under the leaders Perdikkas, Koenus, Krateros, Amyntas, Meleager, Philippus: the soldiers belonging to the phalanx were called πεζέταιροι, and were ranged 16 deep in order of battle, being armed with σάρισσαι 21 feet in length); the rest composed the corps of hypaspists (lighter-armed foot-soldiers) under the command of Nikanor, the son of Parmenion. The command in chief over all the Macedonian infantry and also over the 7000 allies and 5000 mercenaries was held by Parmenion. The Macedonian cavalry, ἵππος τῶν ἑταίρων, τὸ ἑταιρικόν, ἵππος ἑταιρική, οἱ ἀμφ' αὐτὸν ἱππεῖς, consisted of 8 ἴλαι, amongst which was the ἴλη βασιλική, also called τὸ ἄγημα, commanded by Philotas, the son of Parmenion. See esp. Arr. I, 14, 1—3. II, 8, 1—4. III, 11, 8—12, 5. Diod. XVII, 57, cf. p. 99. obs. 232. Besides the land force, the king was also accompanied by a fleet of 160 ships, see esp. Arr. I, 11, 6. 18, 4, amongst which were 20 Athenian vessels, Diod. XVII, 22. To protect Macedonia he left Antipater behind him with 12,000 infantry and 1500 cavalry, Diod. l. c.—The king of Persia, with whom he began the war, was Darcius Kodomannus: this monarch had been raised to the throne by Bagoas in 336 B. C. after the murder of Arses: it was this same Bagoas, who had murdered Artaxerxes Ochus in 338 B.C. and made Arses king. Seeing the position of existing affairs, the Persian king sought to strengthen his forces with Greek mercenaries and to enter into relations with the Greek towns; and for their part all the discontented Greeks were inclined to favour the king of Persia. Hence

in all the great battles following Greek mercenaries formed the most serviceable part of the Persian armies; hence several remittances of money sent by the king to Greece, Diod. XVII, 4. Arr. II, 14, 6. Dinarch. adv. Dem. p. 91. § 10. p. 92. § 18. Æsch. adv. Ctes. p. 88. § 239. p. 90. § 250; hence embassies from Greece to Persia, Arr. II, 15, 2, and continual apprehensions on Alexander's part on account of the defection of the Greeks, Arr. I, 18, 8. II, 17, 2, although Alexander left nothing undone to win over the Greeks to his side, and in particular always represented his expedition as undertaken at once in the name and the interest of Greece, see esp. Arr. I, 16, 6. 7. II, 14, 4. III. 6, 2. Plut. Al. 16.

7) Arr. I, 11—29. Diod. XVII, 17—28. Plut. Al. 15—18. Justin. XI, 6. Whilst his army crosses over from Sestos to Abydos, Alexander first goes to Ilium, where he sacrifices to Pallas and exchanges his arms for those of Achilles, μακαρίσας αὐτόν, ὅτι καὶ ζῶν φίλου πιστοῦ καὶ τελευτήσας μεγάλου κήρυκος ἔτυχεν, Plut. 15. Arr. 12, 1. He then joins his army again at Arisbe, and advances by way of Perkote, Lampsakus, the river Praktius, Kolonæ, Hermeius, to the river Granikus, on the eastern bank of which he finds the enemy encamped. The commanders of the enemy, Arr. 12, 8—10. Dangerous advice of Memnon, not to risk a battle, but to confine themselves to the defensive, to waste the land in advance of Alexander and to make descents on Greece and Macedonia with the fleet in his rear, Arr. 12, 9—10. Diod. 18. For the battle on the Granikus, Arr. 13—16. Diod. 18—21. The numbers of the enemy amounted according to Arr. 14, 4 to about 20,000 cavalry and nearly 20,000 Greek foot soldiers (according to Diod. 19 to over 10,000 cavalry and 100,000 infantry, according to Justin. to 600,000 men). For the nature of the battle, Arr. 15, 4: ἦν μὲν ἀπὸ τῶν ἵππων ἡ μάχη, πεζομαχίᾳ δὲ μᾶλλόν τι ἐῴκει· ξυνεχόμενοι γὰρ ἵπποι τε ἵπποις καὶ ἄνδρες ἀνδράσιν ἠγωνίζοντο.— For the danger to Alexander's life averted by Kleitus see Arr. 15, 8. Plut. 16. The Persian infantry had taken no part whatever in the battle; and it was not till the battle was finished, that it was attacked and cut down almost to a man, Arr. 16, 3. Plut. 16. The number of those who fell on the side of the Macedonians amounted according to Arr. 16, 4 only to a total of some 100 men, or even 34 according to Aristobulus ap. Plut. 16. After the battle, which was fought according to Plut. Cam. 19 in the month Thargelion (May), Alexander captured in succession Sardes, Arr. 17, 3—8, Ephesus, id. § 9—12, Magnesia, Tralles and other Ionian and Æolian towns, id. 18, 1—2, and next Miletus, id. 18, 8—19, 11. In the siege of Miletus the fleet still cooperated with the army: after the capture of the town it was disbanded, id. 20, 1 : Χρημάτων τε ἐν τῷ τότε ἀπορίᾳ καὶ ἅμα οὐκ ἀξιόμαχον ὁρῶν τὸ αὑτοῦ ναυτικὸν τῷ Περσικῷ, οὔκουν ἐθέλων οὐδὲ μέρει τινὶ τῆς στρατιᾶς κινδυνεύειν· ἄλλως τε ἐπενόει, κατέχων ἤδη τῷ πεζῷ τὴν Ἀσίαν, ὅτι οὔτε ναυτικοῦ ἔτι δέοιτο, τάς τε παραλίους πόλεις λαβὼν καταλύσει τὸ Περσικὸν ναυτικόν, οὔτε ὁπόθεν τὰς ὑπηρεσίας συμπληρώσουσιν οὔτε ὅπῃ τῆς Ἀσίας προσέξουσιν ἔχοντας. The siege of Halikarnassus, which still remained, was a work of especial difficulty, and was only brought to a successful issue after great obstacles had been overcome, Arr. 20, 2—23, 8. When finally this town had also been taken (the citadel at first still maintained itself), Alexander sent Parmenion

The Extinction of Greek Freedom. 117

Olympiad.	B. C.	ATHENS.	HISTORY.
		Archons.	
CXI, 4	333	Nikokrates.	Memnon's enterprises by sea, and his death[8]. Alexander prosecutes his march and defeats the Persian king Dareius at Issus[9].
CXII, 1	332	Niketes.	Conquest of Syria, Phœnicia, Palestine, and Egypt[10]. Foundation of Alexandria[11].

(it was already winter time, Arr. 24, 1. 5) to march to Phrygia by way of Sardes, id. 24, 3, whilst he himself continued to follow the coast through Lykia and Pamphylia, and then marching in a northerly direction by way of Kelænæ to Gordium effected a junction with Parmenion, id. 24—29. In the Hellenic towns, which submitted to him, he everywhere established a democracy, id. 17, 10, 18, 2: for the rest, he always, if practicable, allowed not only the former laws, institutions, and taxes, but even the rulers, to remain, as he found them, see e. g. id. 17, 24. 23, 7.

8) Arr. II, 1—2. Diod. XVII, 29. Memnon (cf. obs. 7, διαβεβοημένος ἐπὶ συνέσει στρατηγικῇ, Diod. XVII, 18) was appointed by Dareius commander in chief of the entire fleet; he took Chios and Lesbos, except Mytilene, which town he besieged, and entered into relations with Greece, in particular with the Spartans, so that Alexander was menaced by him in Greece and even in Macedonia; his death, which lamed irrecoverably the whole enterprise, εἴπερ τι ἄλλο καὶ τοῦτο ἐν τῷ τότε ἔβλαψε τὰ βασιλέως πράγματα, Arr. 1, 3. Mytilene was now taken by Autophradates and Pharnabazus, Arr. 1, 3—5, likewise Tenedos and several other islands in the archipelago, id. 2, 1—2. 13, 4—7: but in the following year all was reconquered by Hegelochus, which put an end to this section of the war, Arr. III, 2, 3—7. Curt. IV, 5, 14—22.

9) Arr. II, 3—12. Diod. XVII, 30—39. Plut. Al. 18—21. Curt. III. Polyb. XII, 17—22. (The first two books of Curtius are lost.) Before his departure from Gordium the cutting of the Gordian knot, Arr. 3. Plut. 18. Curt. III, I. (According to Plutarch l. c. by this method of undoing the knot is also signified the dismemberment of Alexander's empire after his death, "πολλὰς ἐξ αὐτοῦ κοπέντος ἀρχὰς φανῆναι.") His march passes through Paphlagonia, Kappadokia, Kilikia (where he fell dangerously ill at Tarsus and was saved by the Akarnanian Philippus, Arr. 4, 7—11. Diod. 31. Plut. 19. Curt. 5—6): when on the point of crossing the Amanus and attacking Dareius, who was encamped on the opposite side, he hears that Dareius has marched by a pass situated to the north over the Amanus into the defile between the Amanian and Syrian Gate, and is now in his rear (Arr. 6, 6: καὶ τι καὶ δαιμόνιον τυχὸν ἦγεν αὐτὸν εἰς ἐκεῖνον τὸν χῶρον, οὗ μήτε ἐκ τῆς ἵππου πολλὴ ὠφέλεια αὐτῷ ἐγίνετο πλῆθους αὐτοῦ τῶν τε ἀνθρώπων καὶ τῶν ἀκοντίων τε καὶ τοξευμάτων— id. 7, 1: ὑπερβαλὼν δὴ τὰ ὄρη Δαρεῖος τὰ κατὰ τὰς πύλας τὰς Ἀμανικὰς καλουμένας ὡς ἐπὶ Ἰσσὸν προῆγε): he therefore reverses his march, and fights a battle with him somewhat to the south of Issus by the river Pinarus. The army of Dareius numbered 600,000 μάχιμοι, Arr. 8, 8. Plut. 18, (500,000, Diod. 31): the loss on the Persian side in the battle amounted to 100,000 killed, Arr. II, 8; on the side of Alexander only 300 infantry and 150 cavalry are said to have fallen, Diod. 36. Amongst the prisoners were the mother, the wife, and two daughters of Dareius, Arr. II, 9, who to their good fortune experienced the most generous treatment at Alexander's hands, id. 12, 3—8. The battle was fought in the month Maimakterion (November), id. 11, 11. The rich treasures of Dareius were captured after the battle by Parmenion at Damaskus, id. Curt. 13. Athen. XIII. p. 607 f. Proposals of peace from Dareios shortly after the battle, Arr. 14, and during the siege of Tyre; in these latter he offered to cede to Alexander all countries west of the Euphrates, id. 25. Cf. Curt. IV, 1, 7—14. 5, 1—8. Diod. 39. 54.

10) Arr. II, 13—III, 6. Diod. XVII, 40—51. Plut. Al. 24—28. Curt. IV, 1—8. On the way to Egypt (the reasons, why he at once undertook the expedition, instead of pursuing Dareius, see Arr. II, 17, 1—4) all places voluntarily submitted to him, with the exception of the towns Tyre and Gaza. The former, situated on an island, and separated from the mainland by a channel 4 stadia in breadth (Curt. 2, 7) and 3 fathoms in depth (Arr. 18, 3), with walls 150 feet high (Arr. 21, 4), was only taken after a siege of seven months (Diod. 46. Plut. 24. Curt. 4, 19) by means of a mole, constructed from the mainland to the island, and with the help of a fleet collected by the rest of the Phœnicians, the Kyprians, Rhodians, etc., Arr. 16—24. Diod. 40—47. Curt. 2—4. Plut. 24—25, in the month Hekatombræon (July), Arr. 24, 6. Gaza offered an equally obstinate resistance, and was taken after a siege of two months, Arr. 26—27. Diod. 48. Curt. 6. Plut. 26. Egypt yields without resistance, Diod. 49: οἱ Αἰγύπτιοι τῶν Περσῶν ᾐσεβηκότων εἰς τὰ ἱερὰ καὶ βιαίως ἀρχόντων ἀσμένως προσεδέχοντο τοὺς Μακεδόνας. For his sojourn in the country see Arr. III, 1—5. Diod. 49—52. Curt. 6—8. Plut. 26—27; for his march to the oracle of Jupiter Ammon, Arr. 3—4. Diod. 49—51. Curt. 7—8. Plut. 27. According to Diodorus, Curtius, and Plutarch, from this time he had himself addressed as God.

11) Arr. III, I, 5—2, 2. Diod. XVII, 52. Curt. IV, 8. Plut. Al. 27. For the position and importance of the town see Diod. l. c.: ἀνὰ μέσον οὖσα τῆς τε λίμνης (the lake Mareotis) καὶ τῆς θαλάττης δύο μόνον ἀνὰ τῆς γῆς ἔχει προσόδους στενὰς καὶ παντελῶς εὐφυλάκτους· τὸν δὲ τύπον ἀποτελοῦσα χλαμύδι παραπλήσιον ἔχει πλατείαν μέσην σχεδὸν τὴν πόλιν τέμνουσαν καὶ κάλλει θαυμαστήν.—καθόλου δὲ ἡ πόλις τοσαύτην ἐπίδοσιν ἔλαβεν ἐν τοῖς ὕστερον χρόνοις, ὥστε παρὰ πολλοῖς αὐτὴν πρώτην ἀριθμεῖσθαι τῶν κατὰ τὴν οἰκουμένην.

FIFTH PERIOD. 336—146 B. C.

Olympiad.	B.C.	ATHENS.	HISTORY.
		Archons.	
CXII, 2	331	Aristophanes.	Alexander penetrates into the interior of the Persian empire and defeats Darcius a second time at Gaugamela[12]). Darcius flies to Media[13]). Alexander in Babylon, Susa, and Persepolis[14]).
			The Spartans under king Agis[15]) in connexion with the Eleians, Achæans, and Arkadians (except Megalopolis), in revolt against Macedonia[16]).
CXII, 3	330	Aristophon.	The Spartans and their allies defeated by Antipater[17]).

12) Arrian. III, 6—15. Diodor. XVII, 52—61. Curt. IV, 8—16. Plut. Al. 29—33. The departure from Egypt took place at the beginning of spring, Arrian. 6, 1; the line of march first led over the old route as far as Tyre, from there it turned eastwards to the Euphrates, which was crossed in the month Hekatombæon (July, Arrian. 7, 1) at Thapsakos; they now march first in a northerly direction, then through the north of Mesopotamia, cross the Tigris (with no opposition on the part of the enemy, but with no little difficulty) and keeping to the left bank of the Tigris during a further march of forty days, reach the neighbourhood of the foe (Arrian. 7, 7), who had encamped at Gaugamela, distant 600 stadia westwards from Arbela (Arrian. 8, 7) and about the same distance south-eastwards from Nineveh. After Alexander's passage of the Tigris, an eclipse of the moon took place, Arrian. 7, 6, which falls on the 20th or 13th September, and the battle was also fought in the same month, id. and 15, 7, in the month Pyanepsion, id.; but according to Plutarch Cam. 19, the battle took place on the 26th Boedromion, cf. also Alex. 31, where the eclipse of the moon is placed at the commencement of the great mysteries, and the battle eleven days later. The army of Darcius numbered 1,000,000 infantry and 40,000 cavalry, Arrian. 8, 6, cf. Diodor. 53. Plutarch. 31. Curt. 9, 3; its composition Arrian. 8, 3—6. 11, 3—7; Alexander had now (in consequence of repeated reinforcements) 40,000 infantry and 7000 cavalry, id. 12, 5. According to id. 15, 6, 300,000 Persians fell in the battle, and a still greater number were taken prisoners; of the Macedonians not more than 10 are said to have fallen, id. According to Diodorus (61) the number of Persians slain amounted to 90,000, and that of Macedonians to 500.

13) Arrian. III, 16, 1—2. Diodor. XVII, 64. Curt. V, 1. Plut. Alex. 36. He directed his flight to Media and stayed first of all in Ekbatana, σπεύδων τῷ διαστήματι τῶν τόπων λαβεῖν ἀναστροφὴν καὶ χρόνον ἱκανὸν εἰς παρασκευὴν δυνάμεως, Diodor.

14) Arrian. III, 16—18. Diodor. XVII, 64—72. Curt. V, 1—7. Plut. Al. 34—42. In Babylon he stayed 30 days, Diodor. 64, in Persepolis 4 months, βουλόμενος τοὺς στρατιώτας ἀναλαμβάνειν (καὶ γὰρ ἦν χειμῶνος ὥρα), Plut. 37. The destruction of the royal fortress at Persepolis by fire, Arrian. 18, 11—12, cf. Diodor. 72. Curt. 7. Plut. 38.

15) Agis III had succeeded his father Archidamus III (p. 99. obs.

231) in 338 B. C., when the latter had fallen in Italy in the war, which he was conducting as the ally of the Tarentines against the Messapians, Diodor. XVI, 63. 88. Plut. Ag. 3. Cam. 19.

16) Agis had already in 333 B.C. placed himself in connexion with Autophradates and Pharnabazus (see obs. 8), and from them received 30 talents and 10 triremes, with which he had begun the war in Krete, in order to put himself in possession of the island in opposition to Alexander, s. Arrian. II, 13, 4. 6. Diodor. XVII, 48. And in 331 B. C. the Peloponnese itself was in revolt, as is proved by the circumstance that Alexander in this year despatched Amphoterus with a considerable fleet to the Peloponnese (τὰ ἐν Πελοποννήσῳ ὅτι αὐτῷ νεωτερίσθαι ἀπήγγελτο), to assist the states which supported his cause, Arrian. III, 6, 3. Diodor. XVII, 62. In the following winter he sent 3000 talents from Susa to Antipater for the purposes of this war, Arrian. III, 16, 10.

17) Diodor. XVII, 62—63. 72. Din. adv. Demosth. p. 94, § 34. Æschin. adv. Ctesiph. p. 72. § 133. p. 74. § 165. Curt. VI, 1. The allies besieged Megalopolis, and were on the point of taking it (Æschin. l. c. § 165), when Antipater arrived with 40,000 men (Diodor. 63; the Greeks had 20,000 foot and 2000 horse, id. 62), and in spite of brave resistance totally routed the Greeks. In the battle there fell 5300 Greeks and 3500 Macedonians, Diodor. 63, cf. Curt. l. c. § 16. Hæc victoria non Spartam modo sociosque ejus, sed etiam omnes, qui fortunam belli spectaverant, fregit. id. The punishment of the Eleians and Achæans, s. Curt. l. c. § 21; the Spartans were referred to Alexander for the decision of their fate, and consequently sent ambassadors to him, s. Æschin. l. c. § 133. The battle must be placed, not in 331 B.C., but (with Diodorus) in 330; for when Æschines delivered his speech against Ktesiphon, the aforesaid Spartan ambassadors had not set out, s. id. § 133, and Alexander was ἔξω τοῦ ἄρκτου, whilst this speech was not delivered till the second half of the year 330, see Plut. Demosth. 24. Dionys. Hal. p. 476. (Ep. ad. Amm. 12); it is therefore incorrect to place it, as Curtius does (l. c. § 21), before the battle of Gaugamela; and when Alexander says: ἔοικεν, ὦ ἄνδρες, ὅτε Δαρείῳ ἡμεῖς ἐνιεῶμεν, ἐκεῖ τις ἐν 'Αρκαδίᾳ γεγονέναι μυομαχία, Plut. Ages. 15, these words must not be understood, as if both battles had been exactly simultaneous.

The Extinction of Greek Freedom. 119

Olympiad.	B. C.	ATHENS.	HISTORY.
		Archon.	
CXII, 3	330		Alexander pursues Dareius through Media and Parthia, and after the Persian king's murder by Bessus[18]) continues his march in pursuit of Bessus through Parthia, Areia, Drangiana, Arachosia, to Baktria[19]).
CXII, 4	329	Kephisophon.	He subdues Baktria, and marches over the Oxus to Sogdiana[20]). Bessus taken prisoner[21]). Crossing of the Iaxartes[22]).

---

18) Arr. III, 19—22. Curt. V, 8—13. Plut. Al. 42—43. Diod. XVII, 73. On hearing of Alexander's approach, Dareius flies to the north-east with 3000 cavalry and 6000 infantry (Arr. 19, 5), intending to retreat as far as Baktria, and there to form an army out of the military forces of these districts (id. § 1). Alexander marches first to Ekbatana, then—with only a part of the army for the sake of greater swiftness—in 11 days (id. 20, 2) to Rhagae on the southern slope of Elbur in the neighbourhood of the Caspian gate, afterwards with increasing speed and detachments decreasing in strength along the slope of Elbur through the north of Parthia, till (in the neighbourhood of Hekatompylus, probably in the district of what is now Damaghan, Diod. XVII, 75. Curt. VI, 2, 15) he finds Dareius murdered by Bessus, Nabarzanes, and Barsaentes. That is, they had first thrown Dareius into chains, intending, εἰ μὲν διώκοντα σφᾶς Ἀλέξανδρον πυνθάνοιντο, παραδοῦναι Δαρεῖον Ἀλεξάνδρῳ καὶ σφίσι τι ἀγαθὸν εὑρίσκεσθαι, εἰ δὲ τὸ ἔμπαλιν ἐπανεληλυθότα μάθοιεν, τοὺς δὲ στρατιὰν τε ξυλλέγειν ὅσην πλείστην δύναιντο καὶ διασῴζειν ἐς τὸ κοινὸν τὴν ἀρχήν, Arr. 21, 5, and now put him to death, when they were surprised by Alexander, in the month Hekatombaeon (July), id. 22, 2. Bessus fled to Baktria, and there crowned himself king, id. 25, 3. From this time forward, now that, Dareius being dead, Alexander was able to look on himself as heir to the Persian empire, he began according to the general supposition to incline to debauchery, to adopt Persian customs, and to require divine veneration, Curt. VI, 2, 6. cf. Arr. IV, 7, 3—5. 9, 9. Diod. 77. Plut. 45.

19) He first marched in a north-westerly direction to Hyrkania (the modern Masenderan), where he subdued the Mardians and Tapurians, Arr. III, 23—25, 2. Curt. VI, 4—5. Diod. XVII, 75—76. Plut. Alex. 44. For the further march, Arr. III, 25—29. Diod XVII, 78—83. Curt. VI, 6—VII, 4. (Plutarch has from this point onwards entirely lost the thread of events.) Originally he intended to march straight to Baktria, but turned southwards to Areia (Herat) because of the defection of Satibarzanes, whom he had appointed governor of this province, Arr. 25, 4—6. On the approach of Alexander Satibarzanes took refuge in flight, id. § 7; and Alexander now continued his march in this direction as far as Drangiana (Sedschestan), id. § 8. (Here the trial and execution of Philotas: shortly afterwards the murder of Parmenion at Ekbatana, Arr. 26. Curt. VI, 7—VII, 2. Diod. 79—80. Plut. 48—49.) Then the march through Arachosia, Gedrosia, Arr. 28, 1, through the country of the Paropamisadn, where he founds a new Alexandreia (some miles to the N.E. of Cabul), id. §

4, cf. IV, 22, 4, and across the Paropamisus (Hindukusch) in spite of all the difficulties and hardships incident to winter time, Arr. 28, 1, 9. Bessus fled on his approach to Sogdiana, id. § 9—10.

20) Arr. III, 29, 1—4. Curt. VII, 4—5. Baktria with its chief towns Aornus and Baktra (Balkh) surrender to him without resistance, Arr. § 1. The crossing of the Oxus, which was 6 stadia in width, id. 3, is accomplished within five days on inflated skins, made out of the army's tent coverings, id. § 4. Diodorus XVII, 83 records the entry of Alexander into Baktria, and the capture of Bessus, which according to this author happens in Baktria itself: then follow in the next chapter events, which belong to the winter of 327—326 B.C. and to Alexander's expedition to India: the intermediate portion has been lost.

21) Arr. III, 29, 6—30, 5. Curt. VII, 5. Bessus is betrayed by his comrades Spitamenes and Dataphernes, and taken prisoner by Ptolemy, son of Lagus. Alexander had him brought out as a captive naked and in chains to be scourged, Arr. 30, 4—5, he then had him mutilated at Baktra, and led off to Ekbatana, where he was executed, id. IV, 7, 3. Spitamenes and the rest of those, who had delivered up Bessus, in fear of Alexander continue the war against him, id. IV, 1, 5. Owing to them the rising spreads over a large part of Sogdiana and even as far as Baktria, id., cf. Curt. VI, 6, 15.

22) Alexander founds a new Alexandreia on the banks of the Iaxartes (about the neighbourhood of the modern Kodschend), Arr. IV, 1, 3: ὅ τε γὰρ χῶρος ἐπιτήδειος αὐτῷ ἐφαίνετο αὐξῆσαι τὴν πόλιν ἐπὶ μέγα καὶ ἐν καλῷ οἰκισθήσεσθαι τῇ ἐπὶ Σκύθας, εἴποτε ξυμβαίνοι, ἐλάσεως καὶ τῆς προφυλακῆς τῆς χώρας πρὸς τὰς καταδρομὰς τῶν πέραν τοῦ ποταμοῦ ἐποικούντων βαρβάρων. According to Curtius the foundation of this city caused the appearance of a Skythian army on the further bank, VII, 7, 1: Rex Scytharum, cuius tum ultra Tanaim imperium erat, ratus eam urbem, quam in ripa amnis Macedones condiderant, suis impositam esse cervicibus. But Alexander crosses over the river and repulses them with great loss, Arr. IV, 4—5, 1. Curt. VII, 7—9. Before and after this expedition he has to combat with the rebellion, which continually breaks out afresh at different places in Sogdiana, Arr. IV, 1—3. 5—6. Curt. VII, 6—7, 10. He spends the winter in Baktra, Arr. IV, 7, 1: Ταῦτα δὲ διαπραξάμενος ἐς Ζαρίασπα (the usual name for Baktra in Arrian) ἀφίκετο, καὶ αὐτοῦ κατέμενεν ἔστε παρελθεῖν τὸ ἀκμαῖον τοῦ χειμῶνος.

FIFTH PERIOD. 336—146 B.C.

Olympiad.	B. C.	ATHENS.	HISTORY.
		Archons.	
CXIII, 1	328	Euthykritus.	Continuation of the war in Sogdiana[23]).
CXIII, 2	327	Hegemon.	Subjection of Sogdiana[24]). Departure for India and march to the neighbourhood of the Indus[25]).
CXIII, 3	326	Chremes.	He crosses the Indus, and advances into India across the rivers Hydaspes, Akesines, and Hydraotes as far as the Hyphasis, where he is compelled to return by his discontented army. March back to Hydaspes[26]).

23) Arr. IV, 16—17. Curt. VII, 10—VIII, 3. The complete subjection of Sogdiana was rendered difficult by reason that the greater part of the country, with exception of the fruitful and permanently cultivated districts of the Iaxartes in its upper and middle course and of the Polytimetus (Kohik), consisted of Steppes, and was inhabited by nomads, called Skythians and Massagetæ in Arrian; and in this part the rebellious always found a refuge and gathered new forces. Alexander now marched through the country with his army in five divisions, which reunited in the capital Marakanda (Samarkand), where Alexander granted them some rest, Arr. 16, 1—3. (It was here, at Marakanda, that Alexander, whilst intoxicated, killed his friend Kleitus, Arr. IV, 8—9. Curt. VIII, 1—2. Plut. Alex. 52—53.) New towns were founded to keep the country in check, Arr. 16, 3. 17, 4. Curt. VII, 10, 15. But the greatest advantage, that befell Alexander in this year, was the death of Spitamenes, who was killed by the Massagetæ (according to Curtius by his wife), Arr. 17, 4—7. Curt. VIII, 3. This time he pitched his winter quarters in Sogdiana itself at Nautaka, Arr. 18, 2.

24) Arr. IV, 18—20. Curt. (VII, 11) VIII, 4. The chief undertaking in this year was the conquest of the rock of Oxyartes, esteemed impregnable; his daughter Roxane was then married by Alexander. This brought the conquest of Sogdiana to a close, Arr. 21, 1, Alexander now first marched from Baktra, subduing on his way thither the Paretakæ, and capturing in the course of his operations a second similar stronghold, the rock of Choriencs, Arr. 21—22, 2. (During his stay in Baktra the philosopher Kallisthenes was put to death by the command of Alexander, Arr. IV, 10, 14, cf. 22, 2. Plut. Alex. 53—55. Curt. VIII, 5--8.)

25) Arr. IV, 22—30. Curt. VIII, 9—12. Diod. XVII, 84—85. Alexander started from Baktra at the end of the spring, Arr. 22, 3. His plan, id. 15, 6: αὐτῷ δὲ τὰ Ἰνδῶν ἔφη ἐν τῷ τότε μέλειν, τούτων γὰρ καταστρεψάμενοι πᾶσαν ἂν ἔχειν τὴν Ἀσίαν· ἐχομένης δὲ τῆς Ἀσίας ἐναιέναι ἐς τὴν Ἑλλάδα, ἐκεῖθεν δὲ ἐφ' Ἑλλησπόντου τε καὶ τὴν Προποντίδα ξὺν τῇ δυνάμει πάσῃ τῇ τε ναυτικῇ καὶ τῇ πεζικῇ ἐλάσειν εἴσω τοῦ Ἰόντον. He first marched over the Paropamisus to Alexandreia (oho. 19), and from there to the river Kophen (Kabul), where the Indian prince Taxiles met him on his march, to make submission to him, Arr. 22, 6. He then sent Hephæstion and Perdikkas with a detachment in advance, to march straight to the Indus and to get a bridge ready built over that river, id. § 7. He himself marched with the rest of the army rather more to the north through the southern outlying mountains of the Paropamisus range (Hindukusch), continually fighting with natural obstacles and with the warlike inhabitants of these districts (and here again he conquered a fortress named Aornus, situated on a seemingly inaccessible mountain, id. 29—30. Curt. 11. Diod. 85). It was winter, when Alexander was passing through these mountainous regions, and it was not till the spring, that he descended into the lowlying plains of the Indus; this is definitely attested by Aristobulus, see Strab. p. 691: διαγεψάντων κατὰ τὴν ὀρεινὴν ἔν τε τῇ Ἀσσακανοῦ γῇ τὸν χειμῶνα, τοῦ δ' ἔαρος ἀρχομένου καταβεβηκότων εἰς τὰ πεδία—.

26) Arr. V, 3 to the end of the book, Curt. VIII, 12—IX, 3. Diod. XVIII, 86—95. The modern names of the rivers are: Hydaspes = Dschelum, Akesines = Dschenab, Hydraotes = Rawi, Hyphasis = Sutledsch. The most important battle, which he had to fight on this march, was that with Porus, who had posted himself at the passage of the Hydaspes, and whom he treated with the greatest generosity after his victory, Arr. V, 9—19. Curt. VIII, 13—14. Diod. 87—89. On the eastern bank of the Hydaspes he founds the towns of Nikœa and Bukephala, Arr. 19, 4. His further plans, prevented by the refusal of the army to follow him, id. 26, 1: εἰ δέ τις καὶ αὐτῷ πολεμεῖν ποθεῖ ἀκοῦσαι ὃ τινες ἔσται πέρας, μαθέτω ὅτι οὐ πολλὴ ἔτι ἡμῖν ἡ λοιπή ἔστω ἔστι ἐπὶ τὸν ποταμὸν τὸν Γάγγην καὶ τὴν ἕφαν θάλασσαν· ταύτῃ δὲ λέγω ὑμῖν ξυναφῆς φανεῖται ἡ Υρκανία θάλασσα· καὶ ἐγὼ ἀναδείξω Μακεδόσι τε καὶ τοῖς ξυμμάχοις τὸν μὲν Ἰνδικὸν κόλπον ξύρρουν ὄντα τῷ Περσικῷ, τὴν δὲ Υρκανίαν τῷ Ἰνδικῷ· ἀπὸ δὲ τοῦ Περσικοῦ ἐς Λιβύην περιπλευσθήσεται στόλῳ ἡμετέρῳ τὰ μέχρι Ἡρακλέους στηλῶν· ἀπὸ δὲ στηλῶν ἡ ἐντὸς Λιβύη πᾶσα ἡμετέρα γίγνεται καὶ ἡ Ἀσία δὴ οὕτω πᾶσα, καὶ ὅροι τῆς ταύτῃ ἀρχῆς οὕσπερ καὶ τῆς γῆς ὅρους ὁ θεὸς ἐποίησε. The spot, at which he turned, was marked by 12 altars of towering height, which he caused to be erected, Arr. 29, 1. The passage of the Hydaspes and the battle with Porus took place in the time after the summer solstice, Arr. 9, 3. 4; and this statement is confirmed by the weighty testimony of Aristobulus in Strabo (p. 691) already quoted, according to which the passage of the Hydaspes and the march to the Hyphasis (here called Hypanis) and the return march to the Hydaspes fall in the time of the Etesiæ, whilst the building of the ships and the preparations for the continuation of the expedition made there fall in the period about the setting of the Pleiads (i.e. according to Arr. VI, 21, 2 about the beginning of winter). The statement of Arrian, V, 19, 3, which makes the passage of the Hydaspes take place ἐν' ἄρχοντος Ἀθηναίοις Ηγεμόνος μηνὸς Μουνυχιῶνος (i.e. in April of 326 B.C.) must therefore be erroneous or interpolated.

The Extinction of Greek Freedom. 121

Olympiad.	B. C.	ATHENS.	HISTORY.	ART AND LITERATURE.
		Archons.		
CXIII, 4	325	Antikles.	He proceeds, partly by water, on the rivers Hydaspes, Akesines, and Indus, partly by land, along the banks of these rivers, till he arrives in the vicinity of the mouth of the Indus[27]). From there he marches by land through the territory of the Arabians and Oreitæ and through Gedrosia and Karmania to Persis[28]), whilst Nearchus with the fleet looks for the sea road to the Persian gulf[29]).	
CXIV, 1	324	Hegesias.	His stay at Susa, Opis, and Ekbatana[30]). His attempts to secure the fusion of the Persians and Macedonians[31]).	
CXIV, 2	323	Kephisodorus.	He commands the Greek towns to receive back their exiles[32]).	
			. . . .	New Comedy: Philemon[h]).

27) Arr. Anab. VI, 1—20. Ind. XVIII—XIX. Curt. IX, 3—10. Diod. XVII, 95—104. The number of vessels, which formed the fleet fitted out on the Hydaspes, amounted to 1800, partly triremes, partly ships of burden and transports for the horses, Ind. XIX, 7. The army advanced amid perpetual struggles with the tribes on the route, which were subdued by force, if they refused a voluntary submission; of these the Mallians offered the most obstinate resistance. For the fight with the Mallians see Arr. 6—13, and for the severe wound, which Alexander himself got in the battle owing to his mad rashness, id. 10—13. Curt. 4—6. Diod. 98—99. Plut. Al. 63. The army halted at Pattala, where the Indus branches into two arms, and Alexander himself sailed down both arms as far as the sea, to acquire a knowledge of the locality, Arr. 18—20. Curt. 9—10. The expedition lasted 10 months according to Aristobulus, Strab. p. 692, only 7 months according to Plut. Alex. 66: the latter is the more probable, see obs. 28.

28) Arr. VI, 20—30. Curt. IX, 10—X, 1. Diod. XVII, 104—107. He had previously sent Kraterus in advance with a part of the army, to take the road through Arachosia and Gedrosia to Karmania, Arr. 15, 5. 16, 3. He himself traversed the route above indicated (through the modern Beludchistan) amid extraordinary difficulties, till the description of which see Arr. 24—26. In Karmania he rejoined Kraterus, id. 27, 3, and here Nearchus also sought him out to bring him intelligence of the progress of the fleet, id. 28, 7. Ind. XXXIV—XXXVI. Alexander's expedition was begun before the cessation of the Etesian, i.e. before the month of October, Arr. 21, 1, 3. In 60 days he completes the march to Pura (Bunpur), the capital of Gedrosia, id. 24, 1. It is winter, when he marches through Karmania, id. 28, 7.

29) Arr. Ind. XXI to the end. Alexander had chosen Nearchus, from his great confidence in that general, to conduct this exceedingly dangerous and arduous voyage, id. XX. He waited at Pattala, till the Etesian (the so-called monsoons) blowing from the south-west had ceased, and set sail on the 20th of Boedromion, id. XXI, 1. Anab. VI,

21, 1. He rejoined Alexander at Susa in the following spring, Ind. XLII. Anab. VII, 5, 6.

30) Arr. VII, 4—15, 3. Dion. XVII, 107—111. (Up to the end of the section, in Curtius the greater part of the narrative still preserved is, with the exception of some short fragments, chiefly occupied with the Macedonian revolt and a passage on the death of Alexander; the rest is lost.) In Susa the marriage of Alexander to a daughter of Dareius and of many distinguished Macedonians to Persian ladies, Arr. 4, 4—8. Plut. Alex. 80. From there he sailed down the Pasitigris or Eulæus to the Persian gulf, and then up the Tigris to Opis, Arr. 7. At this place the revolt of the Macedonian army took place; its immediate cause was the proceeding of Alexander, who formed a new phalanx out of 10,000 Persians, and enrolled many Persians in the ranks of the Macedonian cavalry, and even appointed them to posts of command, id. 6, 8—12. Curt. X, 2—4. Diod. 108, 109. Plut. Al. 71. The rebellion was allayed: and then 10,000 Macedonians were despatched home under the command of Kraterus and Polysperchon, Arr. 12, 1—4. Next comes his march to Ekbatana (the mention of which in Arrian has been lost through an hiatus at the end of chap. 12), Diod. 111, where Hephæstion dies, Arr. 14. Diod. 110. Plut. 72. In the winter (Arr. 15, 3) he undertakes another campaign against the mountain tribe of the Kossæi, Arr. 15, 1—3. Diod. 111.

31) In particular the measures made mention of in obs. 30 were directed to this end; viz. his own marriage and that of many distinguished Macedonians with Persian ladies, and the enrolment of numerous Persians in the army. For this mingling of races in the army cf. further Arr. VII, 23, 3—4.

32) Diod. XVII, 109. XVIII, 8. Curt. X, 2, 4. The object of Alexander in adopting this measure, Diod. XVIII, 8: ἅμα μὲν δέξῃ ἕνεκεν, ἅμα δὲ βουλόμενος ἔχειν ἐν ἑκάστῃ πόλει πολλοὺς ἰδίους ταῖς εὐνοίαις πρὸς τοὺς νεωτερισμοὺς καὶ τὰς ἀποστάσεις τῶν Ἑλλήνων. The number of exiles to be recalled is stated at 20,000, id., and the result of this measure must certainly have been to cause an outbreak of party struggles and discord in all the towns, id. cf. obs. 86.

h) The new comedy, which flourished in the time of Alexander and the Diadochi, is a further development of the middle, inasmuch as personal satire and parody retreat still further into the background, and it becomes the comedy of manners and character, drawn from ordinary life, Euanth. de comœd.: Nova comœdia, quæ argumento communi magis et generaliter ad omnes homines, qui mediocribus fortunis

C.   16

FIFTH PERIOD.   336—146 B.C.

Olympiad.	B.C.	HISTORY.	ART AND LITERATURE.
CXIV, 2	323	His plans for further campaigns of conquest[33]). His death at Babylon[34]).	Menander[l]), Diphilus[k]).

33) His next plan was to sail round the Arabian peninsula, Arr. VII, 19, 6. Accordingly he collected a large fleet at Babylon, to which town he had gone in spite of the warnings of the Chaldæans, id. 16, 5: for the fleet he had requisitioned Phœnician sailors, id. 19, 3—5, erected docks at Babylon, id. 21, 1, and made all other necessary preparations for the enterprise. Another plan of his was to have the Caspian sea explored : this, like the Persian gulf, he held to be a gulf of the great Ocean : with a view to the enterprise he had already given orders for the construction of a fleet there, id. 16, 1—4. In addition to which other plans were attributed to him, aiming at nothing less than the subjection of the whole world, id. I, 2. Curt. X, 1, 17—19. Diod. XVIII, 4. Plut. Al. 68. cf. obs. 23.

agunt, pertineret et minus amaritudinis spectatoribus et eadem opera multum delectationis afferret, concinna argumento, consuetudine congrua, utilis sententiis, grata auribus, apta metro. Cic. ap. Donat. Rep. IV, 11 : Comœdiam esse imitationem vitæ, speculum consuetudinis, imaginem veritatis. No play belonging to the new comedy has been preserved in a perfect state, but we can get a good idea of its character from the imitations of Plautus and Terence.—Philemon, either of Soli, Strab. p. 671, or more probably of Syracuse, Περὶ κωμ. III, 15. Bergk, Prol. Arist. Suid. s. v., received civic rights at Athens, and made his debut as a dramatic poet about 330—328 B.C, with the play Τυφθολιμαῖος, Clem. Alex. Strom. VI, p. 267, in which he entered on the track of the new comedy. He was the rival of his rather younger contemporary Menander, over whom he generally carried off the victory, Vit. Aristoph. 10. Gell. XVII, 4, travelled for a long time, Alciphr. Ep. II, 3, Plut. de ira coh. p. 458 A. de virt. mor. p. 449 E, and then returned to Athens, where he died in the year 292 B.C. at least 96 years old, Suid. s. v. Diod. XXIII, 7. Lucian, Macrob. 25. Of the 97 dramas ascribed to him, Περὶ κωμ. l. c. Suid. s. v., we have the titles and short fragments of 57 plays, the most important from the comedies : 'Αδελφοί, 'Έφηβοι, Σάρδιος, Σικελικός, Στρατιώτης, cf. Mein. fr. com. Græc. II. 821—867, ed. min. It is said of him, Apul. Flor. 10 : Reperias apud ipsum multos sales, argumenta lepide inflexa, agnatos lucide explicatos, personas rebus competentes, sententias vitæ congruentes, ioca non infra soccum, seria non usque ad cothurnum.

l) Menander of Athens, born 342 B.C., Strab. p. 526, son of the general Diopeithes (p. 109, obs. 262), brought up by his uncle, the comic poet Alexis, Περὶ κωμ. III, 16. Suid. s. v. 'Αλεξις, led a brilliant life devoted to enjoyment, Suid. s. v. (περὶ γυναῖκας ἐκμανέστατος), and was on intimate terms with the most important personages, as with Epikurus, Strab. l. c., Theophrastus, Alciphr. II, 2, Demetrius of Phalerum, Phædr. VI, 1. Diog. L. V, 79, etc. Before he was twenty years old, he came forward with his first play, 'Οργή, Περὶ κωμ. l. c.

34) Arr. VII, 24 to the end. Plut..Al. 75—77. Curt. X, 5. Diod. XVII, 117—118. He died of a fever in the 114th Olympiad, in the archonship of Hegesias, at the age of 32 years, 2 months, 8 days, after a reign of 12 years and 8 months, Arr. 28, 1, l. c. according to a computation, founded on Plut. Al. 3 and 75, on the 11th or 13th of June, 323 B.C. A story is told of the last moments of his life : ἐρεσθαι τοὺς ἑταίρους αὐτὸν ὅτῳ τὴν βασιλείαν ἀπολείπει· τὸν δὲ ἀποκρίνασθαι ὅτι τῷ κρατίστῳ· οἱ δέ, προσθεῖναι πρὸς τούτῳ τῷ λόγῳ ὅτι μέγαν ἐπιτάφιον ἀγῶνα ὁρᾷ ἐφ' αὑτῷ ἐσόμενον, Arr. 26, 3. cf. Diod. XVIII, 1. Curt. 5, 5. He is said to have given his signet ring to Perdikkas, Diod. XVIII, 2. Curt. 6, 4. His interment at Alexandria, see Diod. XVIII, 16—28. Curt. X, 10. Paus. I, 6, 3.

Euseb. Ol. 114, 4. p. 117, but only conquered 8 times, Gell. XVII, 4. Martial V, 10. He refused to comply with an invitation to Alexandria sent him by king Ptolemy, the son of Lagus, Alciphr. II, 3. 4. Plin. II. N. VII, 29, and stayed in the city of his birth, where he died in 290 B.C., 52 years old, in the prime of his poetical activity, Περὶ κωμ. l. c. Plut. Aristoph. et Men. comp. 2. Of more than a hundred of his dramas known to the ancients, Suid. s. v. Περὶ κωμ. l. c. Gell. l. c., the titles and fragments of 88, besides a number of unnamed fragments, are preserved, the most important from the comedies : 'Αδελφοί, 'Αρρηφόρος ἢ Αὐληρίς, Γεωργός, Δεισιδαίμων, Δύσκολος, 'Επίκληρος, 'Επιτρέποντες, 'Υπνίοχος, Θεοφορουμένη, Κιθαριστής, Κόραξ, Κυβερνῆται, Λευκαδία, Μισογύνης, Μισούμενος, Ναύκληρος, 'Οργή, Περικειρομένη, Περινθία, Πλόκιον, Τροφώνιος, Ψευδολιμαῖος ἢ 'Αγροῖκος, Ψευδηρακλῆς, for the most part comedies of character, cf. Mein. fr. com. Gr. II, 867—1066, ed. min. His imitators amongst the comic poets of Rome were Cæcilius, Afranius, Hor. Ep. II, 1, and above all Terence, Donat. Vit. Ter. p. 754 ; of whose plays preserved to us the Adelphi, Andria, Heautontimorumenos, and Eunuchus are translations of the similarly named plays of Menander. The verdict of a Greek critic on Menander, Περὶ κωμ. IX, 10 : ἐνίσημος δ' ὁ Μένανδρος, ὃς ἄστρον ἐστὶ τῆς νέας κωμῳδίας, and of his plays it is said by Quintilian X, 1 : ita omnem vitæ imaginem expressit, tanta in eo inveniendi copia et eloquendi facultas, ita est omnibus rebus, personis, adfectibus accommodatus.

k) Diphilus of Sinope, Strab. p. 546. Περὶ κωμ. V, 17, was, like Menander, not averse to the enjoyments of life, Athen. XIII, p. 583. Alciphr. Ep. I, 37, and composed 100 comedies, Περὶ κωμ. l. c. He died at Smyrna, l. c. The titles and fragments of 49 of his comedies are preserved, the most important fragments are from the plays : 'Απολιπούσα, 'Εμπορος, Ζωγράφος, Παράσιτος, Πολυπράγμων, Συνωρίς, cf. Mein. fr. com. Gr. II, 1066—1096, ed. min.—Further, names, titles and fragments of plays are preserved from 24 poets of the new comedy, the most important fragments being from Philippides, Sosipater, Euphron, Baton, Damoxenus. Meinek. II, 1096—1160.

SECOND SECTION.

323—280 B.C.

THE WARS OF ALEXANDER'S GENERALS: GREECE WITH SHORT INTERRUPTIONS UNDER MACEDONIAN SWAY.

Olympiad.	B. C.	ATHENS.	HISTORY.
		Archon.	
CXIV, 2	323	Kephisodorus.	The generals of Alexander distribute the provinces of his empire amongst themselves under the nominal sovereignty of Philip Arrhidæus and of Alexander, the son of Roxane, and under the supreme direction of Perdikkas[35]).
			Almost the whole of Greece revolts against the Macedonian rule[36]). The allied Greeks under Leosthenes defeat Antipater, and shut him up

---

[35]) Curt. X, 6—10 (up to the end). Arr. de rebus post Alex. (Photius Bibl. Cod. 92) § 1—7. Diod. XVIII, 1—4. Justin. XIII, 1—4. After the death of Alexander a dispute broke out between the commanders of the cavalry and Meleager, who put himself forward as commander of the infantry: it ended in a compromise, by which Arrhidæus, the son of Philip by his marriage with Philinna, was raised to the throne under the name Philip, as well as Alexander's son by Roxane (obs. 24), who was not yet born. Antipater was appointed commander-in-chief in Europe, Krateros the guardian of Philip Arrhidæus, whilst Perdikkas was to have the supreme direction of the whole in his capacity as chiliarch, Arr. § 3. Meleager was soon afterwards put out of the way together with other malcontents, id. § 4. Curt. 9. The distribution of the provinces amongst the various generals resulted in the following arrangement: Ptolemy, the son of Lagus, received Egypt and Libya; Laomedon Syria; Philotas Kilikia; Peithon Media; Eumenes Kappadokia and Phrygia; Antigonus Pamphylia, Lykia, and Great Phrygia; Kassander Karia; Menander Lydia, Leonnatus Hellespontine Phrygia; Lysimachus Thrake; Krateros and Antipater Macedonia and Greece; in the rest of the provinces the governors appointed by Alexander were allowed to remain unchanged, Arr. § 4—8. Diod. 3. Curt. 10. Justin. 4. (Besides the two new kings mentioned the following members of the royal family were still in existence: Olympias, the mother of Alexander, who was now resident in Epirus, "non mediocre momentum partium," Justin. 6; Herakles, a son of Alexander by Barsine, Plut. Alex. 21. Curt. 6; and the sister of Alexander, Kleopatra, as also his half-sisters Thessalonike and Kynane; finally Adea the daughter of the latter, afterwards called Eurydike; who was married to Philip Arrhidæus, Diod. XVIII, 23. XIX, 35. 52. Justin. XIV, 5. Arr. § 22. In the course of the wars between the Diadochi with the exception of Thessalonike, who married Kassander, they were all put out of the way, Philip Arrhidæus and Eurydike in 317 B. C., Diod. XIX, 11. Justin. XIV, 5; Olympias in 315, Diod. in 311, Diod. XIX, 105; Herakles in 309, Diod. XX, 20, 28; Kleopatra in 308, Diod. XX, 38.)

[36]) (For the whole war see Diod. XVIII, 8—15. 16—18. Hyperid. Epitaph. Plut. Phoc. 22—28. Demosth. 27—30. Justin. XIII, 5.) The revolt was occasioned by the ordinance of Alexander for the recall of the exiles, obs. 32. The Athenians and Ætolians most of all felt great annoyance: accordingly the Athenians on the first rumour of Alexander's death entered into negotiations with Leosthenes, the commander of the mercenary troops, which had been disbanded by the satraps in pursuance of an order from Alexander, and had collected on the promontory of Tænarum; and when the

FIFTH PERIOD. 336—146 B. C.

Olympiad.	B. C.	ATHENS.	HISTORY.
CXIV, 2	323	Archon.	in Lamia (Lamian war)[37]). Leosthenes falls: Antiphilus succeeds to the command of the Greeks[38]).
CXIV, 3	322	Philokles.	Leonnatus comes to succour Antipater, but is defeated by the Greeks in a cavalry engagement and is slain[39]). Still the approach of Leonnatus raised the blockade of Lamia, and Antipater effects a junction with the remnant of Leonnatus' army, as also with Kraterus, who likewise comes to his aid, and defeats the Greeks at Krannon[40]).
			The Greek states are subdued singly by Antipater[41]). Athens is compelled to change its constitution, and to admit a Macedonian garrison into Munychia[42]).

certain intelligence of Alexander's death arrived, they took 8000 of these mercenaries into their service; Leosthenes now betook himself to Ætolia and joined his forces to those of the Ætolians (7000 in number), Lokrians, Phokians, and other neighbouring tribes, Diod. XVII, 100, 111. XVIII, 9—9. Paus. I, 25, 4. V, 52, 2. The Athenians then sent ambassadors and called on a number of other Greek States to take part in the war (in the Peloponnese Argos, Epidaurus, Sikyon, Trœzen, Elis, Phlius and Messene joined their standard; in central Greece, in addition to the peoples mentioned, the Dorians and Akarnanians; further Karystus in Euboea and all the Thessalian tribes); they themselves took the field with an army of 5000 foot and 500 horse, all citizens, and 2000 mercenaries, and in conjunction with Leosthenes defeated the Bœotians at Platæœ: after which the whole army marched to Thermopylæ, to wait for Antipater, Diod. XVIII, 10—11. 12. Paus. I, 25, 4. Hyper. Epitaph. § 10—11.

37) Diod. XVIII, 12—13. Paus. I, 1, 3 (ἔξω τῶν Θερμοπυλῶν). At this time Antipater had only 13,000 infantry and 600 cavalry at his disposal, Diod. 12. When he was shut up in Lamia, he made proposals for peace; but they produced no result, as his enemies required an unconditional surrender, Diod. 18. Plut. Phoc. 26.

38) Diod. XVIII, 13. (The Athenians honoured him with a public funeral, at which Hypereides delivered the funeral oration: for this cf. p. 107 obs. pp.)

39) Diod. XVIII, 14—15. Leonnatus came with 20,000 foot and 2500 horse. Antiphilus had only 22,000 foot and 3500 horse left, as many soldiers of the allied army had gone home: he was therefore constrained to relinquish the blockade of Lamia, in order to go and meet Leonnatus.

40) Diod. XVIII, 16—17. The army of Antipater now numbered 40,000 heavy-armed, 3000 light-armed troops, and 5000 cavalry, Diod. 16. The place, where the battle was fought, is mentioned in Plut. Phoc. 26. Paus. X, 3, 3. The day of battle was the 7th of Metageitnion (August), Plut. Cam. 19. Dem. 28. For Kraterus see p. 121. obs. 30.

41) Diod. XVIII, 17. The proposal of Antiphilus for entering on mutual negotiations was rejected by Antipater and Kraterus; the rest of the allies then submitted singly, as mild conditions were offered them: thus only the Athenians and Ætolians remained, and they were consequently menaced by the whole of the enemy's force, Athens first of all.

42) Diod. XVIII, 18. Plut. Phoc. 26. Dem. 27. The peace was arranged by Phokion and Demades on the condition, that the Athenians paid the costs of the war, that they surrendered the orators hostile to the Macedonians, in particular Demosthenes and Hypereides, that they limited civic rights to such as possessed at least 2000 drachmas, that they evacuated Samos, which was still in the possession of Athenian Kleruchs (p. 101. obs. 240), and that they received a Macedonian garrison in Munychia. This garrison then took up its quarters at Munychia on the 20th of Boedromion (September or October), Plut. Phoc. 28. All citizens, who were not possessed of the aforesaid minimum of property were banished (to the number of 12,000, whilst only 9000 remained at Athens), and for the most part transported to Thrake, id. The orators fled, but were condemned to death by the Athenian people, and sought out by Antipater's emissaries: Hypereides and two others were seized in Ægina, carried before Antipater and executed by his orders: Demosthenes escaped the same fate by a voluntary death in the island of Kalauria, Plut. Dem. 28—30. Vit. V, orr. p. 846 F. Arr. De Reb. Post Alex. § 13. (Lucian.) Encom. Dem.—Antipater and Kraterus then marched against the Ætolians, to reduce them also to subjection, but they were met with an obstinate resistance, and were called away by the war breaking out in Asia, before they could effect their conquest, Diod. XVIII, 24—25 Polyb. IX, 30. cf. obs. 43.

The Extinction of Greek Freedom.

Olympiad.	B.C.	ATHENS.	HISTORY.
		Archons.	
CXIV, 4	321	Archippus.	War of the governors Antigonus, Antipater, Kraterus, and Ptolemy against Perdikkas and Eumenes; Perdikkas deserted and slain by his troops[43]. The war is continued with Eumenes[44]). The growing power of Antigonus[45]).
CXV, 1	320	Neaechmus.	
CXV, 2	319	Apollodorus.	
CXV, 3	318	Archippus.	Death of Antipater: war between Polysperchon and Kassander, the son of Antipater, to dispute the succession to the possession of Macedonia[46]). Kassander makes himself master of Athens[47]).
CXV, 4	317	Demogenes.	The Athenians attempt to regain their freedom by siding with Polysperchon; but are compelled to yield submission to Kassander anew[48]),

43) Diod. XVIII, 23. 25. 29. 33—36. Justin. XII, 6. 8.

44) As the ally of Perdikkas, Eumenes had won a victory in Kappadokia over Kraterus and Neoptolemus, both of whom fell in the battle, Diod. XVIII, 30—32. Plut. Eum. 5—7. Corn. Nep. Eum. 3—4. After the death of Perdikkas he was defeated by Antigonus in consequence of treachery and shut up in Nora (in Kappadokia), but afterwards recovered liberty with the aid of Olympias and Polysperchon, and now carried on an exceedingly chequered war in Kilikia, Phœnicia, Susiana, Persis, Media, and Paraetakene, till he was betrayed in the winter of 316/5 by his own troops, surrendered to Antigonus, and was by him put to death, Diod. XVIII, 40—42. 50, 58. 57—63. 73. XIX, 12—34. 37—44. Plut. Eum, 8 to the end. Corn. Nep. Eum. 5 to the end. Justin. XIV, 1—4.

45) After the fall of Perdikkas Antipater was raised to be ἐπιμελητὴς αὐτοκράτωρ, and at Triparadeisus in Syria a fresh distribution of countries was arranged; in regard to which it is specially noteworthy that Seleukus received Babylonia, Diod. XVIII, 39. Arr. De Reb. Post Alex. § 30—38. At the same time Antigonus was appointed commander-in-chief of the royal forces; in which capacity he continually strengthened his power and by degrees won a totally independent position, Diod. XVIII, 41. 47. 50, 52. 55. He raised his army according to Diod. 50 up to 60,000 infantry and 10,000 cavalry.

46) Diod. XVIII, 47. 48—49. Antipater appointed Polysperchon as his successor, πρεσβύτατον σχεδὸν ὄντα τῷ 'Αλεξάνδρῳ συνεστρατευμένων καὶ τιμώμενον ὑπὸ τῶν κατὰ τὴν Μακεδονίαν, Diod. 48. Kassander was appointed chiliarch by his father, id.; with this he did not rest satisfied, but betook himself to Antigonus, in order to begin the war against Polysperchon with his support, Diod. 54. He first of all established himself in Greece, obs. 47—49, and then, with

Greece as the base of operations, conquered Macedonia in the years 316 and 315, Diod. XIX, 35—36. 49—51. Polysperchon still maintained himself in Greece, but made submission to Kassander in 309 B.C., who in return appointed him strategus of the Peloponnese, Diod. XX, 28.

47) Immediately after the death of his father, and before the news of that event was bruited about, Kassander sent his devoted follower Nikanor to Athens, to take the command of the garrison in Munychia in place of Menylius; and he managed to make himself master of the Peiraeus as well; in both which proceedings the guilty complicity of Phokion cannot be denied. Plut. Phoc. 31—32. Diod. XVIII, 64.

48) Polysperchon, to win over the Greeks to his own side, issued an edict in the name of the kings, in which he proclaimed that all Greek states should have their former constitution restored to them and enjoy complete independence, Diod. XVIII, 55—57. He then sent his son Alexander to Greece and followed himself with a larger army; and whilst the former lay before the walls of Athens, the Athenian exiles (obs. 42), who had returned in great numbers, condemned the ruling authorities and the friends of Kassander either to banishment or to death: part of these fled to Polysperchon, but were surrendered by him to the Athenians, and the capital sentence was carried into effect (also in the case of Phokion), Plut. Phoc. 28 to the end. Diod. XVIII, 65—67. Kassander then put into the Peiraeus with 35 ships of war and 4000 men, and as Polysperchon met with no material success in the contest, either at Athens or elsewhere, the Athenians saw themselves compelled to submit to Kassander, who limited civic rights to the possessors of 1000 drachmas, and secured his sovereignty, partly by the garrison in Munychia, which he continued to support there in the future, partly by the appointment of a πρεστάτης in the person of Demetrius of Phalerum, Diod. XVIII, 68—74. cf. obs. 49.

FIFTH PERIOD. 336—146 B. C.

Olympiad.	B. C.	HISTORY.	ART AND LITERATURE.
CXV, 4	317	who places the government of the town in the hands of Demetrius of Phalerum⁴⁹).	The Philosophers Theophrastus¹), Epikurus™), Zeno the Stoic"). The Orator Demetrius of Phalerum°).

49) Diod. XVIII, 74. His prostasy lasted till 807 B. c., see obs. 56. For him cf. further Polyb. XII, 13. Æl. V. H. III, 43. Diog. L. V, 75—85. Cic. de legg. III, § 14. do rep. II, § 2. Brut. § 37. etc. During his prostasy a census was taken at Athens, which yielded the number of 21,000 citizens, 10,000 metoeks, and 400,000 slaves, Ctesicl. ap. Athen. VI, p. 272 c.

l) Theophrastus of Eresus in Lesbos, born circ. 372 B. c., is said to have originally been called Tyriamus, and only to have had the name Theophrastus given him by Aristotle on account of his eloquence, Diog. L. ¡V, 36. 38. He was a pupil of Leukippus, of Plato, but above all of Aristotle; and after his master's flight from Athens in 322 B.c. undertook the conduct of the Aristotelian school, and is said to have trained 2000 pupils, l. c. 36. 37. 39. cf. Gell. XIII, 5. He was banished with other philosophers from Athens in 305 by the law of Sophokles, which prohibited freedom of teaching, but returned again shortly afterwards on the repeal of the law, Diog. L. V, 38, attained a great age, l.c. 40. cf. 'Ηθικ. χαρ. prœf., and died about 287 B. c., l. c. 58. Of his numerous writings, of which the catalogue, Diog. L. 42—51, bears witness to the wealth and multiplicity of his knowledge, there are extant in particular: 'Ηθικοί χαρακτῆρες, character sketches, Περί φυτῶν ἱστορία, Αἴτια Φυτικά, Περί λίθων, Περί πυρός. The extension and active employment of philosophy in the various fields of empirical knowledge and the foundation of botany are the most eminent of the services, which he rendered to science.—Amongst the pupils of Aristotle besides Theophrastus we must name Dikæarchus of Messana and Aristoxenus of Tarentum; both of whom displayed the many-sidedness and learned zeal for the accumulation of facts peculiar to the Peripatetic school, and employed themselves actively as writers in various branches of science. Dikæarchus, to whom Cicero awards especial praise (de off. II, 15. Tuscul. I, 18), in addition to works on philosophy (περί ψυχῆς, Cic. ad Att. XIII, 12. Tuscul. I, 10. 1, 31. de off. II, 5) and political history, wrote geographical treatises (βίος τῆς Ἑλλάδος), based on preliminary labours of a thorough description, e.g. mensurements of heights (Plin. II, 65) and drawing of maps (Cic. ad Att. VI. 2. Diog. L. V, 51). Aristoxenus was especially valued for his studies in the domain of music; so much so, that as the highest authority of antiquity in this province ho was called ὁ μουσικός, Cic. de fin. V, 19. Suid. s. v. Of his musical works we are still in possession of the three books ἀρμονικῶν στοιχείων, though preserved in a very fragmentary form, and a larger fragment together with extracts from the ῥυθμικά στοιχεία.

m) Epikurus, born in 342 B.C. at Samos, where his father had settled as a kleruch, though as an Athenian belonging to the deme of Gargettus, Diog. L. X, 1, 14, first came to Athens at the age of 10, l. c. 1, and educated himself in the study of the earlier philosophers and sophists, l. c. 2, 3. 4. 12. He now taught in Kolophon, l. c. 1, Mytilene and Lampsakus, l. c. 15, not returning to Athens until 307 B. c., l. c. 2. 15. There he lived and taught in close intercourse with numerous pupils, withdrawn from public life in the retirement of his gardens, l. c. 10. 17. 25. 119. He is praised for his temperate and simple life, for the purity of his morals, his goodness of heart, and his love for his country, l. c. 10. 11 ; yet failed to escape the jeers and calumnies of comic poets and hostile philosophers, l. c. 6. 7. In his old age he was chained to a sick bed by severe bodily sufferings, l. c. 7. 8, but, true to his teaching, he still preserved tranquillity and cheerfulness of soul up to his death in 270 B. c., l. c. 15. 22. Cic. de fin. II, 30. One of the most prolific authors of antiquity (πολυγραφώτατος), he is said to have written 300 volumes, Diog. L. 26. 27. 28. Of his chief work Περί φύσεων alone have single mutilated fragments come down to us in the rolls of Herculanum. He taught after Demokritus that the world, the gods, and the soul arose from atoms, Diog. L. 41 f., and further developed the doctrines of the Cyrenaics, that the spiritual pleasure of the tranquil soul, conditional on knowledge, is the goal of happiness and the essence of virtue, l. c. 128—138. His doctrine, so often misunderstood and refuted, is magnificently enshrined in the poem of Lucretius De Rerum Natura.

n) Zeno, of Kitium in Kypros, lived circ. 340—260, Euseb. Hieron. Chron. ol. 128, 1, p. 120, ol. 129, 1. p. 121, and is said at first to have pursued his father's trade, as a dealer in purple, but to have made an early acquaintance with the writings of the Sokratics, till he came to Athens in consequence of his ship being wrecked, Diog. L. VII, 1—5, 58. 31. Here he applied himself to philosophy, attended the lectures of the Cynic Krates, l.c. 2. 3. 4. VI, 105, the Megaric Stilpo, l. c. 2. 24. II, 120, the Academics Xenokrates and Polemo, l. c. 2. 25. Suid. s. v. Cic. de fin. IV, 6, 8. Acad. I, 9. II, 24, and trained himself by the study of the older philosophers and poets, Diog. L. 3. 4. 31. Cic. nat. deor. I, 14. In the ripeness of manhood he first taught in the στοὰ ποικίλη, whilst walking to and fro, to a large concourse, Diog. L. V. 4. 14 : from which circumstance he himself was called ὁ στωικός, Suid. s. v., and his pupils, at first styled Ζηνώνειοι, began to be called στωϊκοί or οἱ ἀπὸ τῆς στοᾶς φιλόσοφοι l. c. 5, Suid. s. v.: he was held in high honour by his countrymen the Kitians, by the Athenians, l. c. 6. 10, and by Antigonus, l. c. 6. 7. 13. 15. He was repulsively ugly, l. c. 1. 16, indefatigably active, l. c. '15, sparing to the veriest trifle, l. c. 16, proverbial for his temperance (Τοῦ φιλοσόφου Ζήνωνος ἐγκρατέστερος), l. c. 27. Suid. s. v. Ζην. ἐγκ., disinclined to great company, l. c. 14, calm and dignified, l. c. 15. 18, silent, l. c. 20. 21. 23. 24, but a master of short, trenchant repartee and derisive observations, l. c. 17—28. His writings comprehended works on logic as the source of knowledge, physics, and ethics, l. c. 4. Peculiar to him and his school in particular is the doctrine of the single, eternal god, the all-diffused creative soul of the universe (ἕν τε εἶναι θεὸν καὶ νοῦν, l. c. 135, σπερματικοὺς λόγους ὄντα τοῦ κόσμου, l. c. 136, ἄφθαρτός ἐστι καὶ ἀγέννητος δημιουργὸς ὢν τῆς διακοσμήσεως), and of virtue which is happiness in and for itself and must be striven for on its own account, l.c. 89. 127, but finds its active expression more especially in four chief virtues mutually conditional on one another, φρόνησις, ἀνδρεία, δικαιοσύνη, σωφροσύνη, l. c. 92, 102, 125. Of his pupils, special mention must be made of Chrysippus of Kilikia (circ. 282—209), who by his numerous writings reduced the Stoic teaching to an established system.

o) Demetrius, born in Attica of the deme Phalerum, received a learned and many-sided training, in particular under Theophrastus, and entered on a political career at the time of the Harpalian trial,

The Extinction of Greek Freedom.   127

Olympiad.	B. C.	ATHENS.	HISTORY.
		Archons.	
CXVI, 1	316	Demokleides.	
CXVI, 2	315	Praxibulus.	Defeat and death of Eumenes[50]. Restoration of Thebes by Kassander[51].
CXVI, 3	314	Nikodorus.	War of the governors Seleukus, Ptolemy, Kassander and Lysimachus against Antigonus[52]. Peace between Antigonus and Kassander in Greece[53].
CXVI, 4	313	Theophrastus.	
CXVII, 1	312	Polemon.	
CXVII, 2	311	Simonides.	Peace between the governors[54]. Greece is declared free in the peace of the governors[55].

50) Diod. XIX, 40—44. Plut. Eum. 17—19. cf. obs. 44.
51) Diod. XIX, 53—54. Paus. IX, 7.
52) The cause of the war was in part quite general, namely the jealousy of the rest of the governors at the growing power of Antigonus: in part it was stirred up by Seleukus, who feared the machinations of Antigonus, and so fled from his governorship of Babylonia, Diod. XIX, 55—56. App. Syr. 54. For the whole war see Diod. XIX, 57—64. 66—69. 73—75. 77—100. It consists chiefly of isolated enterprises productive of no decisive results, of which, not taking into account the events in Greece (obs. 53), prominence deserves only to be given to the battle of Gaza in which Demetrius Poliorketes, the son of Antigonus, meets with a defeat, Diod. 80—84. Plut. Demetr. 5, and to the return of Seleukus to Babylonia in the same year, with which commences the era of the Seleukids (known to us from the books of the Maccabees, Josephus, and coins), see Diod. 90—92. App. Syr. l. c.

53) Antigonus proclaimed freedom and independence to the Greeks, in order to draw them over to his side, Diod. XIX, 61; and to give emphasis to his proclamation and to drive Kassander out of Greece, he successively sent in the years 314—312 Aristodemus, Dioskorides, Telesphorus, and his nephew Ptolemy with money, troops, and ships; and they succeeded in expelling the garrisons and freeing the towns of the Peloponnese and central Greece, with the exception of Sikyon, Corinth, and Athens, id. 57. 60—61. 63—64. 66—69. 74. 77—78. 87. Ptolemy of Egypt issued the same proclamation, and also sent a fleet of 50 sail in 314 B.C. to Greece, which, however, achieved no successes,

id. 62. 64. Kassander undertook several campaigns against Greece, but without any important result, id. 63. 67. Besides all these, Polysperchon and Alexander also maintained an army in Greece (obs. 48), and the latter at first joined Antigonus, id. 57. 60, then went over again to Kassander, id. 64, but soon died, id. 67; whilst Polysperchon (who had likewise at first joined Antigonus, id. 59) maintained himself independently in possession of Sikyon and Corinth, id. 74. Athens retained its Macedonian garrison: it compelled Demetrius to conclude a convention with the general of Antigonus on his entering the Attic territory, of the provisions of which we have no information given us, id. 78.

54) Diod. XIX, 105. The peace agreed upon provided that the belligerent generals should retain their governorships, but Kassander only until Alexander, the son of Roxane, came of age; this last provision led to Kassander's putting him and his mother to death (which was probably the object of all the parties to the agreement), see obs. 35.

55) Diod. XIX, 105. This condition contained in the peace was afterwards turned to account by the governors, to make war mutually on one another under the pretext of freeing Greek towns. Thus Ptolemy of Egypt in 310 and 309 B.C. overran Kilikia, Lykia, and the islands of the Ægean sea, Diod. XX, 20. 27, and in 308 even made a campaign against Greece itself, where he took Sikyon and Corinth, id. 37; and under a like pretext Demetrius Poliorketes embarked on his enterprises, obs. 56, so that the war never wholly slept, till it again broke fully out in 302 B.C.

Diog. L. V, 75. Strab. p. 398. Cic. de off. I, 1. Brut. 9. de legg. III, 6: for ten years, from 317 to 307 B. C., he stood at the head of the Athenian administration, cf. obs. 49. 56, and raised the revenues and resources of the state, Diog. L. l. c. Cic. de rep. II, 1. Strab. l. c., in gratitude for which the Athenians erected 360 statues to him, Nep. Milt. 6. Diog. L. l. c., but at a later period he excited displeasure by prodigality and extravagances, Athen. XII, p. 542 c, so that on the appearance of Demetrius Poliorketes before the walls of Athens he was obliged to fly and was condemned to death. Diog. L. 77. Plut. Demetr. 8 f. Dion. Hal. Din. 3. He then betook himself to Thebes, cf. obs. 56, and from thence to Egypt, Diog. L. 78. Strab. l. c. Diod. XX, 45,

where he lived for science and was the confidential adviser of Ptolemy Soter, Æl. V. II. III, 17. Cic. de fin. V, 19: but fell into disgrace with his successor and died not long after 283 B. c. in upper Egypt from the bite of a snake, as the story goes, Diog. L. l. c. Cic. pro Rab. Post. 9. A catalogue of the titles of his works is alone preserved, Diog. L. 80 f.; they embraced the province of history, politics, literature, philosophy, and rhetoric. He was looked on as the last Attic orator; and with him the decadence of eloquence already began, Quint. X, 1, 80 : still he is praised for the refinement and grace of his style, Cic. off. I, 1. Or. 27. de or. II, 23. Brut. 9: itaque delectabat magis Athenienses quam inflammabat. c. 82.

FIFTH PERIOD. 336—146 B. C.

Olympiad.	B. C.	ATHENS.	HISTORY.
		Archons.	
CXVIII, 2	307	Anaxikrates.	Demetrius Poliorketes frees Athens [56]).
CXVIII, 3	306	Korœbus.	The governors Antigonus, Demetrius, Seleukus, Ptolemy, Kassander, and Lysimachus assume the royal title [57]).
CXVIII, 4	305	Euxenippus.	
CXIX, 1	304	Pherekles.	
CXIX, 2	303	Leostratus.	
CXIX, 3	302	Nikokles.	
CXIX, 4	301	Kalliarchus.	Battle of Ipsus, in which Antigonus loses empire and life. His empire is divided between Seleukus and Lysimachus [58]).
CXX, 1	300	Hegemachus.	
CXX, 2	299	Euktemon.	
CXX, 3	298	Mnesidemus.	Demetrius conquers Athens and secures his possession by a garrison in the Peiræus, in Munychia, and in the Museum [59]). At the same time he extends his rule in the rest of Greece [60]).

56) Diod. XX, 45—46. Plut. Demetr. 8—14. The day of his arrival was the 26th of Thargelion (June), Plut. 8. He conquered and destroyed Munychia, declared Athens free, restored the democracy (Demetrius of Phalerum, whose prostasy now came to an end, was conducted by him to Thebes), promised the people 150,000 medimni of wheat and timber to build 100 ships—a promise, which was afterwards actually fulfilled by Antigonus—and restored Imbros to them: in return the degenerate Athenians loaded both Antigonus and Demetrius with exaggerated honours; they erected statues to them, named them kings and saviours (θεοὶ σωτῆρες), built altars to them, had their names inwoven together with those of Zeus and Athene on the peplus annually offered to that goddess, and added two new tribes, called Antigonis and Demetrias, to the 10 phylæ, etc. see Plut. 10—13. Diod. 46. Athen. VI, p. 253—254. Philoch. fr. 144. (Dion. Hal. p. 659). Also Megara is taken by Demetrius on this occasion and declared free, Plut. 9. Diod. 46. Philoc. l. c. But he is recalled by his father from further undertakings in Greece, and by his orders carries on the war in Kyprus against Ptolemy, Diod. 47—48. wins a brilliant naval victory over Ptolemy at Salamis, id. 49—52. Plut. 15—16, accompanies his father as commander of the fleet on a fruitless expedition to Egypt, Diod. 73—76, besieges Rhodes for the space of a year, 304—303 B.C., Diod. 81—88. 91—100. Plut. 21—22 (in which he won the epithet Πολιορκητής from his magnificent siege-works, of which the so-called 'Ελέπολις is especially famous, Plut. 21); when the siege was brought to an end by a convention with the Rhodians, who had offered the stoutest resistance, he returned in 303 B.C. to Greece, where Kassander and Polyperchon had meanwhile regained a firm footing: he there completed the liberation of the towns, by relieving Athens, which was besieged by Kassander (Plut. 23), and conquering Sikyon (which was still in the hands of Ptolemy, obs. 55), Corinth, Bura and Skyros in Achaia, and Orchomenus in Arcadia, Diod. 100. 102—108. 110. Plut. Demetr. 23—27. He then resided in Athens, where new honours were heaped upon him; and from here he started in the spring of 301 B.C., in the month of Munychion (April, Plut. 26), to march through Thessaly to attack Kassander, but was called away by his father to take part in the great war, which had meanwhile broken out (obs. 58), see Diod. 110.

57) Diod. XX, 53. Plut. Demetr. 17—18. Antigonus set the example, as on receiving intelligence of the naval victory of Demetrius at Salamis (obs. 56) he assumed the royal title himself, and also bestowed it on Demetrius; thereupon the rest of the governors followed suit.

58) The renewal of the war between Antigonus and his former opponents (obs. 52) was occasioned by the straits to which Kassander had been reduced by Demetrius, obs. 56. When Kassander had secured the union of the Kings against Antigonus, Lysimachus (in 302 B.C.) advanced into Asia as far as Ephesus and Sardes, both which towns were captured by him, Diod. XX, 106—107. But Antigonus, who set his army in motion from Antigoneia, forced him back on the coast of the Pontus Euxinus, where both passed the winter in the district of Herakleia, id. 108—109. In the spring of 301 Antigonus called in Demetrius, obs. 56. For the battle, in which the army of Antigonus, composed of 70,000 infantry, 10,000 cavalry, 400 elephants, and 70 war chariots (Plut. 28), see Plut. Demetr. 28—29. Diod. Exc. XXI. (Exc. Hoeschel., de virt. et vit., Vatic.). Justin. XV, 5. App. Syr. 55 (in which last passage only is the site of the battle mentioned). 301 B.C. must be accepted as the year of the battle, as Diodorus, who forms almost the sole foundation for the chronology of the period after the death of Alexander, places the beginning of the war in 302 B.C., and after next mentioning the winter quarters of the belligerent kings, XX. 111. 113, announces the battle of Ipsus as forming the beginning of the 21st book (which has been lost from all the remaining books).

59) Demetrius escaped from the battle of Ipsus, and was still possessed of a considerable force in his large fleet and a number of towns, which were in his power, Plut. Demetr. 31—32. Immediately after the battle it was his intention to betake himself to Athens, but messengers were sent to meet him and refuse him admittance, id. 30. And at the same time Kassander, turning the overthrow of his adversary to account, again extended his sway in Greece, id. 31 (ἐξέπιπτον γὰρ ἑκασταχόθεν αἱ φρουραὶ καὶ πάντα μεθίστατο πρὸς τοὺς πολεμίους); he secured his position at Athens by setting up Lachares as tyrant there and upholding him by his force, id. 33. Paus. I, 25, 5. Demetrius, however, returned after he had raised his forces to still

The Extinction of Greek Freedom.   129

Olympiad.	b. c.	ATHENS.	HISTORY.
		Archons.	
CXX, 4	297	Antiphates.	
CXXI, 1	296	Nikias.	Death of Kassander. Disputes about the throne in Macedonia[61]).
CXXI, 2	295	Nikostratus.	
CXXI, 3	294	Diotimus?	Demetrius makes himself master of Macedonia[62]).
CXXI, 4	293	Olympiodorus.	
CXXII, 1	292	Philippus.	
CXXII, 3	290	Kallimedes.	
CXXII, 4	289	Thersilochus.	
CXXIII, 1	288	Diphilus.	
CXXIII, 2	287	Diokles.	Demetrius overthrown by Pyrrhus[63]). The Athenians under the leadership of Olympiodorus expel the garrisons of Demetrius, and assert their freedom[64]). Administration of Demochares[65]). Antigonus Gonatas, the son of Demetrius, maintains himself in a part of Greece[66]).
CXXIII, 3	286	Diotimus.	Pyrrhus expelled by Lysimachus out of Macedonia[67]).

---

greater strength by certain other undertakings (the time, at which this took place, cannot be determined with precision; but the connexion of events, as given by Plutarch, makes it necessary to assume an interval of at least 2, perhaps even of 3 years), conquered Athens, and now posted a garrison, not only in the Peiraeus and Munychia, but also in the Museum, Plut. 33—34. Paus. l. c.

60) The only information afforded to us by Plutarch up to the expedition of Demetrius to Macedonia is, that Demetrius had conquered the Spartans, Demetr. 35; but that he in this interval subdued the greater part of the Peloponnese, and Megara in addition to Athens in central Greece, follows from the passage id. 39, where it is said of him immediately after the seizure of Macedonia: ἔχων δὲ καὶ τῆς Πελοποννήσου τὰ πλεῖστα καὶ τῶν ἐντὸς Ἰσθμοῦ Μέγαρα καὶ Ἀθήνας.

61) Plut. Demetr. 36. Paus. IX, 7, 3. Kassander left behind him three sons, Philip, Antipater, and Alexander: the first died very soon, and disputes arose between the two latter, in consequence of which Alexander invoked Pyrrhus of Epirus to his assistance, as well as Demetrius. The date assigned rests on Porphyr. fr. (ed. Müller, vol. III, p. 693 ff.) 3. § 2 and 4. § 2: according to which Kassander died 19 years after the murder of Olympias.

62) Demetrius had Alexander put to death and then made himself master of the throne: Antipater, the brother of Alexander, was put to death by Lysimachus, to whom he had fled for refuge, Plut. Demetr. 36—37. Pyrrh. 7. Justin. XVI, 1. Porphyr. fr. 3 and 4. § 3.

63) Demetrius by his hauteur had made himself hated in the army as well as amongst the people; so when he entered on a war at one and the same time with Lysimachus, Seleukus, Ptolemy, and Pyrrhus, his army deserted him, on his leading it against Pyrrhus, and went

over to that prince, Plut. Demetr. 44. Pyrrh. 11—12. Justin, XVI, 2. Demetrius fled and died after many adventures in 283 B. c., a prisoner of Seleukus, Plut. Demetr. 52. The reign of Demetrius in Macedonia lasted 7 years according to Plut. Demetr. 44, 6 years according to Porphyr. fr. 3 and 4. § 3: according to this latter source (fr. 4. § 3) the sons of Kassander reigned in all 3 years 6 months, and in this case the accession of Demetrius would have to be placed, not in 294, but 293 B.C.

64) The occurrence, as well as the date of the occurrence, rests on the combination of Paus. I, 26, 1—3 with Plut. Demetr. 46. Pyrrh. 12: according to the last passage the liberation was effected with the help of Pyrrhus.

65) Plut. Vitt. X or. p. 847 D. p. 851. Polyb. XII, 13. He was the nephew of Demosthenes and conducted the administration with so much approval that in 270 B. c. a statue was erected to him in pursuance of a popular decree, which is preserved to us in Plut. l. c. p. 851. The date is established as 270 by the decree itself, as in it Pytharatus is named as archon, and he was archon in this year according to Diog. L. X. § 15; it is likewise established by the decree, that Demochares was dead in this year: that he undertook the administration of the state in 287 B. c., may be inferred with probability, partly from the position of affairs in general, partly from the special accounts contained in the decree of his services.

66) In 287 B. c. Pyrrhus had charged Antigonus with the task of maintaining Greece, Plut. Demetr. 44. 51: but a part of the towns were wrested from his grasp by Ptolemy, id. 46. Pyrrh. 11.

67) Plut. Pyrrh. 12. Porph. fr. 3 and 4. § 4. Pyrrhus maintained Macedonia only 7 months, Porph. l. c.

Fifth Period. 336—146 b.c.

Olympiad.	b. c.	ATHENS.	HISTORY.
		Archons.	
CXXIII, 4	285	Ismus.	
CXXIV, 1	284	Euthias.	
CXXIV, 2	283	Kimon?	
CXXIV, 3	282	Menckles.	
CXXIV, 4	281	Nikias.	Lysimachus defeated by Seleukus and slain in the battle[68]). Seleukus murdered by Ptolemy Keraunus[69]).
CXXV, 1	280	Gorgias.	Invasion of Macedonia by the Kelts: Ptolemy Keraunus defeated by them and slain[70]).

THIRD SECTION.

280—221 b.c.

THE ACHÆAN LEAGUE SPREADS AND FLOURISHES, GROWTH OF SPARTAN POWER— UP TO THE WAR BETWEEN THE LEAGUE AND SPARTA AND THE SUBJECTION OF BOTH TO MACEDONIAN INFLUENCE.

Olympiad.	b. c.	HISTORY.	ART AND LITERATURE.
CXXV, 1	280	The first germ of the Achæan league in the union of Dyme, Patræ, Tritæa and Pharæ[71]).	The historian Philochorus[p]).

---

68) Paus. I, 10, 3—5. Justin, XVII, 1—2. Porph. fr. 3 and 4. § 4. His reign over Macedonia lasted 5 years 6 months, Porph. l. c.: the battle was fought at Korupedion (in Hellespontine Phrygia), id. fr. 4.
69) Justin, XVII, 2. Porph. fr. 3 and 4. § 5. (According to Porph. Seleukus was murdered immediately after the victory, according to Justin 7 months after it.)
70) Diod. XXII, 13. Exc. Hoesch. Paus. X, 19, 4. Justin, XXIV, 1—5. According to Porph. fr. 3. § 5, fr. 4. § 6 the rule of Ptolemy lasted 1 year, 5 months: that the invasion of Macedonia by the Gauls cannot be later than 280 follows from the circumstances that attended their inroad into Greece, which took place at least one year later and according to Paus. X, 23, 9 in the 2nd year of the 125th Olympiad. According to Polyb. II, 41 the kings Ptolemy, son of Lagus, Lysimachus, Seleukus and Ptolemy Keraunus, the brother of the Egyptian monarch, all died "about the time of the 124th Olympiad." In Macedonia the last-named was succeeded by Meleager (2 months), Antipater (45 days), and then by Sosthenes (2 years), Porph. fr. 3. § 7. fr. 4. § 6. 7: Καὶ γίνεται ἀναρχία Μακεδόσι.
71) After Tisamenus had taken refuge from the Dorians and Herakleidæ in Achaia, his descendants at first held the sovereignty there, p. 9. obs. 23: but later the monarchy was abolished, as in other places, and a democratic constitution was established in all the towns:

p) Philochorus of Athens lived circ. 306—262, Dion. Hal. d. Dinarch. 3, was a seer and interpreter of signs, Suid. s. v. Procl. Hesiod. Opp. 810, and was put to death as an adherent of Ptolemy Philadelphus after the occupation of Athens by Antigonus Gonatas, Suid. s. v. His most important work is an 'Ἀτθίς in 17 books, a history of Athens from the earliest period up to Antiochus Theos (Ol. 129, 3), Suid. s. v. Dion. Hal. l. c. 3. 13. Mention is made besides of other writings on history and the history of literature from his pen, Suid. s. v.: but of all these nothing but fragments has been preserved to us, Muell. hist. Græc. fragm. I, p. 384—417.

The Extinction of Greek Freedom. 131

Olympiad.	B.C.	ATHENS.	HISTORY.
		Archons.	
CXXV, 2	279	Anaxikrates.	Invasion of Hellas by the Kelts and their defeat[71].
CXXV, 3	278	Demokles.	
CXXV, 4	277	Polyeuktus.	Antigonus Gonatas king of Macedonia[72].
CXXVI, 2	275		Ægium, Bura, and Keryneia join the Achæan league[74].

whilst at the same time the towns, 12 in number, entered into a league, which maintained itself up to the era of the Macedonian supremacy; at which time the various towns were separated, and garrisons were posted in the towns, or tyrants established there, chiefly by Demetrius Poliorketes and Antigonus Gonatas, Pol. II, 41. Strab. p. 384. The names of the 12 towns, Herod. I, 145 : Pellene, Ægeira, Ægæ, Bura, Helike, Ægium, Rhypes, Patræ, Pharæ, Olenus, Dyme, and Tritæa, cf. Paus. VII, 6, 1, where Keryneia is named instead of Patræ. Of these towns, Helike was destroyed by an earthquake in 373 B.C., Diod. XV, 48—40. Paus. VII, 24, 4—5. 25, 2; whilst Olenus, Rhypes, and Ægæ had gradually fallen so low, that they were deserted by their inhabitants, Paus. VII, 18, 1. 23, 4. 25, 7. Strab. p. 386. 387. On the other hand Keryneia and Leontium had so prospered, that they were qualified to become members of the league; and thus Polybius (l. c.) enumerates the following 10 towns: Patræ, Dyme, Pharæ, Tritæa, Leontium, Ægeira, Pellene, Ægium, Bura, Keryneia. For the union of the 4 first mentioned towns as the germ, from which sprang the renovated Achæan league, see Pol. l. c. Strab. p. 384. The revival took place about the 124th Olympiad, at the time when Pyrrhus crossed over to Italy, Pol. and Strab. l. c., 38 years before the battle of the Ægatian isles, Pol. II, 43. For the object of the league see Pol. l. c.: ἐν τέλει—τοῦτο δ᾽ ἦν τὸ Μακεδόνας μὲν ἐκβαλεῖν ἐκ Πελοποννήσου, τὰς δὲ μοναρχίας καταλῦσαι, βεβαιῶσαι δ᾽ ἑκάστοις τὴν κοινὴν καὶ πάτριον ἐλευθερίαν. The supreme direction of the league was at first placed in the hands of two strategi together with a grammateus; after 255 one strategus only was chosen, Pol. l. c.; with him an hipparchus, Pol. V, 95. XXVIII, 6, an hypostrategus, id. IV, 59. V, 94, and 10 demiurgi (also called ἄρχοντες, probably the representatives of the 10 Achæan towns, to which the league was originally confined), Pol. XXIV, 5. V, 1. XXIII, 10. Liv. XXXII, 22. XXXVIII, 30. These last, together with the strategus and perhaps the hipparchus, formed a sort of probouleutic board for the general assembly (ἐκκλησία), in that they convoked the assembly and prepared the resolutions to be adopted, see Pol. and Liv. l. c. The regular general assembly was convened twice a year, in spring and autumn, Pol. IV, 37. V, 1. II, 54. Liv. XXXVIII, 32, at Ægium up to the latest times of the league, when (in 189 B.C.) a change was introduced in the custom, which had made Ægium the sole place of assembly hitherto, Liv. XXXVIII, 30. The strategus and other strategi entered on office at the time of the rising of the Pleiads, i. e. in May, Pol. IV, 37. V, 1. For the league generally cf. Paus. VII, 17, 2: ἔτι ἐκ δένδρου λελωβημένου—ἀνεβλάστησεν ἐκ τῆς Ἑλλάδος τὸ Ἀχαϊκόν, Plut. Arat. 9: οἱ τῆς μὲν πάλαι τῶν Ἑλλήνων ἀκμῆς

οὐδὲν ὡς εἰπεῖν μέρος ὄντες—εὐβουλίᾳ καὶ εὐνοίᾳ—οὐ μόνον αὑτοὺς ἐν μέσῳ πόλεων τηλικούτων καὶ τυραννίδων διεφύλαξαν ἐλευθέρους, ἀλλὰ καὶ τῶν ἄλλων Ἑλλήνων ὡς πλείστους ἐλευθεροῦντες καὶ σώζοντες διετέλουν, Pol. II, 37: τοιαύτην καὶ τηλικαύτην ἐν τοῖς καθ᾽ ἡμᾶς καιροῖς ἔσχε προκοπὴν καὶ συντέλειαν τοῦτο τὸ μέρος, ὥστε μὴ μόνον συμμαχικὴν καὶ φιλικὴν κοινωνίαν γεγονέναι πραγμάτων περὶ αὑτούς, ἀλλὰ καὶ νόμοις χρῆσθαι τοῖς αὐτοῖς, καθόλου δὲ τούτῳ μόνῳ διαλλάττειν τοῦ μὴ μιᾶς πόλεως διάθεσιν ἔχειν σχεδὸν τὴν σύμπασαν Πελοπόννησον, τῷ μὴ τὸν αὐτὸν περίβολον ὑπάρχειν τοῖς κατοικοῦσιν αὐτήν, τἆλλα δ᾽ εἶναι καὶ κοινῇ καὶ κατὰ πόλεις ἑκάστοις ταὐτὰ καὶ παραπλήσια.

72) Paus. I, 4, 1—5. X, 19—23. Diod, (Exc. Hoesch.) XXI, 13. Justin, XXIV, 6—8. After their invasion of Macedonia (obs. 70) the Kelts first return home again, Paus. X, 19, 4 : and it was when at home, that they were induced by Brennus to undertake a fresh expedition, directed on this occasion against Hellas, id. § 5, on which they enter with an army of 152,000 foot and 20,400 horse, id. § 6, in the second year of the 125th Olympiad, id. 23, 9. The Greeks occupy Thermopylæ with a numerous army, consisting of 10,000 hoplites and 500 horsemen from Bœotia, 7000 Ætolian hoplites, 3000 hoplites and 500 horsemen from Phokis, 1000 Athenian hoplites, etc., whilst the whole of the Athenian fleet stationed itself in the neighbourhood of the coast, id. 20, 3. Here the Kelts were defeated in a battle; nevertheless they got past the Hellenes and directed their march against Delphi; but here they suffered a total defeat, partly from the Delphians, partly—so it was imagined—from the miraculous support of the god, who interested himself in the protection of his sanctuary.

73) The reign of Antigonus is said to have lasted 44 years, (Lucian.) Macrob. 11, Porphyr. fr. 3 and 4. § 8, reckoned, that is, from 283 B.C., the year of his father's death (obs. 68) onwards. According to Porphyr. fr. 4 l. c. he ruled 10 years in Greece, before he made himself master of Macedonia, reckoned from the flight of his father in 287 B.C. onwards, obs. 63. Plut. Demetr. 51. In the same passage of Porphyrius Olymp. CXXXV, 1 is stated as the year of his death. It follows from the chronological data cited in obs. 70 touching his predecessors, that he made himself master of Macedonia in 277 B.C.

74) Pol. II, 41. The Ægians expelled the Macedonian garrison " in the fifth year " after the foundation of the league; at the same time the Buriaus slew their tyrant, whilst the tyrant of Keryneia, recognising the force of circumstances, voluntarily abdicated.

132   Fifth Period.   336—146 b. c.

Olympiad.	b. c.	ATHENS.	HISTORY.	ART AND LITERATURE.
CXXVII, 1	272	Archons.	Death of Pyrrhus[75]).	Bucolic Poetry[q]): Theokritus[r]), Bion[s]), Moschus[t]).
CXXVII, 2	271	Pytharatus.		
CXXVII, 3	270	Aristarchus?		
CXXVIII, 3	266	Peithodemus?		
CXXIX, 1	264	Diognetus.		
CXXIX, 3	262	Diomedon?	Athens once more subject to Macedonian rule[76]).	
CXXIX, 4	261	Hermogenes?		
CXXX, 1	260	Arrhenides.		
CXXXI, 4	253	—of Diomeia.		
CXXXII, 1	252	Leochares.		
CXXXII, 2	251	Theophilus.	Aratus frees Sikyon and unites it to the Achœan league[77]).	Alexandrines: Aratus[u]).
CXXXII, 3	250	Ergochares.		
CXXXII, 4	249	Niketes.		

75) Pyrrhus, immediately after leaving Italy (Plut. Pyrrh. 26), consequently in 274 b. c., attacked Macedonia, made himself master of this empire, and then marched against Greece: here he first attacked Sparta, but without success, and then turned against Argos, where he met with his death in an attempt to take the town by storm (as the story goes, he was killed by a roof-tile, whom he had already forced his way into the town), Plut. Pyrrh. 26—34, Paus. I, 13, 5—7. III, 6, 2. Justin, XXV, 3—5. The year of his death is established, partly by the sequence of events, partly by the statement of Oros. IV, 3, that the Tarentines submitted to Rome on receiving the intelligence of the death of Pyrrhus: and this event took place in 272 b. c. according to the triumphal fasti.

76) Paus. III, 6, 3. Justin, XXVI, 2. From the combination of these two passages it becomes clear, that Antigonus, probably soon after the death of Pyrrhus, marched against Greece, where he had to struggle, not only with the Greeks, but also with a fleet of Ptolemy under Patroklus, that this Patroklus and king Areus of Sparta came to the aid of the Athenians, who were besieged by Antigonus (which must have happened prior to 265 b. c., as in this year Areus fell in a battle at Corinth against Alexander of Epirus, Plut. Ag. 3. Diod. XX, 29),

that Antigonus was at first recalled from this war by a fresh Keltic invasion of Macedonia, and then by an attack of Alexander, the son of Pyrrhus, but that finally Athens succumbed after a brave resistance (according to Polyæn. IV, 6, 20 Antigonus succeeded by stratagem). The year of the capture is fixed by the circumstance, that the comic poet Philemon according to Suid. s. v. Φιλ. died immediately before the event, and that his death according to Diod. (Exc. Hoesch.) XXIII, 7 is to be placed in 262 b. c. An inscription discovered in modern times, first published by Pittakis 'Αρχαιολογ. Nr. 1), informs us, that Athens and Sparta, the latter in company with its allies, had about 270 b. c. concluded an alliance with one another and with Ptolemy for the protection of their own Independence and that of the rest of the Greeks; and at the same time affords interesting corroboration of Niebuhr's conjecture, that the war carried on between Antigonus and the Greeks was the Chremonidean war mentioned by Athenæus (p. 250 f), as Chremonides is mentioned in the inscription. Antigonus stationed garrisons in the Peiræus, in Munychia, and in the Museum: but the last was soon afterwards withdrawn again.

77) Pol. II, 43 (where the year is given). Plut. Ar. 2—10. With and through Aratus the league first attained its greater importance and

q) Bucolic poetry is a mixed species between descriptive and dramatic poetry, with pastoral life and pastoral love for its theme, Anon. Περὶ τῶν τῆς ποιήσ. χαρακτ.: τὸ δὲ βουκολικὸν ποίημα μίγμα ἐστὶ παντὸς εἴδους—ἤγουν διηγηματικοῦ καὶ δραματικοῦ—, αὕτη ἡ ποίησις τὰ τῶν ἀγροίκων ἤθη ἐκμάσσεται.—This form of poetry arose principally from popular pastoral songs connected with the service of Artemis in Sicily and Laconia, Anon. Περὶ τῆς εὐρέσεως τῶν βουκολ., to which Theokritus gave an artistic finish.

r) Theokritus of Syracuse flourished at the time of Ptolemy Philadelphus, was a pupil of the poet Philetas of Kos and Asklepiades of Samos, and lived at Kos, Syracuse and Alexandreia, Vit. a', Western. Vitt. min. p. 285. Suid. s. v. Theocr. Id. XV, 56. XV. XVII. Mosch. Id. III; the story of his execution by Hiero for slanderous abuse, Schol. Ovid. Ibis 551, has little probability, compared with Id. XVI. Under the name of Theokritus we possess 30 εἰδύλλια, short poetical sketches of pastoral life or social conditions, and 26 epigrams, for the greater part in the Doric dialect, cf. Ahrens, Bucolicor. Græcor. rell. p. 165—175: but the genuineness of several

of these poems is doubtful. Other poems from his pen have been lost, Suid. s. v. cf. Quint. X, 1, 55: Admirabilis in suo genere Theocritus, sed musa illa rustica et pastoralis non forum modo verum ipsam etiam urbem reformidat.

s) Bion, born at Smyrna, a contemporary of Theokritus, Suid. s. v. Mosch. 'Επιτάφ. Βίων. 70, lived in Sicily, id. V, 55 f. 76 f., and died of poison, which had been administered to him. A poem of his, 'Επιτάφιος 'Αδώνιδος, is preserved in tact, and, besides, fragments of his pastoral and love songs, cf. Ahrens, Bucolicor. Græc. rell. I, p. 179—198. In his epitaph it is said: σὺν αὐτῷ | καὶ τὸ μέλος τέθνακε καὶ ὤλετο Δωρὶς ἀοιδά.

t) Moschus of Syracuse, Suid. s. v., a younger contemporary of Theokritus and Bion, 'Επιτ. Βίων., a friend of Aristarchus, Suid. s. v. Of his extant poems the most important is the Εὐρώπη, Ahrens, Bucolicor. Græc. rell. p. 197—210. The authors of several of the poems ascribed to Moschus, as also to Theokritus, are uncertain, cf. Incert. Idyll. Ahrens, l. c. 213—263.

u) Aratus, probably of Soli in Kilikia, according to others of Tarsus,

The Extinction of Greek Freedom. 133

Olympiad.	B. C.	ATHENS.	HISTORY.	ART AND LITERATURE.
		Archons.		
CXXXIII, 1	248	—s of Erchia.		Kallimachus[v]), Ly-
CXXXIII, 2	247	Diokles.		kophron[w]), Apollo-
CXXXIII, 3	246	Euphiletus.		nius[x]),Eratosthenes[y]).
CXXXIII, 4	245	Herakleitus.		
CXXXIV, 2	243	Antiphilus.	Corinth and Megara united to the Achæan league[78]).	
CXXXIV, 3	242		Disastrous attempt on the part of the Spartan king, Agis IV, to restore the Lykurgean constitution[79]).	
CXXXIV, 4	241	Monekrates.		
CXXXV, 1	240	—on of Alopeke.		

higher aims, Plut. Philop. 8. For Aratus see esp. Plut. Ar. 10: πολέμῳ μὲν καὶ ἀγῶνι χρῆσασθαι φανερῶς ἀθαρσῆς καὶ δύσελπις, κλέψαι δὲ πράγματα καὶ συσκευάσασθαι κρύφα πόλεις καὶ τυράννους ἐπιβουλώτατος, cf. Pol. IV, 8. 60.

78) Pol. II, 43. Plut. Ar. 16—24. A Macedonian garrison lay in Acro-Corinthus, by which Antigonus commanded the whole of the Peloponnese, Plut. l. c. 16. cf. Paus. VII, 7, 3. Aratus conquered Acro-Corinthus and carried over the town, which thus regained its freedom, to the Achæan league. From this time Aratus, who in this year was strategus for the second time, was up to his death the virtual leader of the league, Pol. l. c.: μεγάλην δὲ προκοπὴν ποιήσας τῆς ἐπιβολῆς ἐν ὀλίγῳ χρόνῳ λοιπὸν ἤδη διετέλει προστατῶν μὲν τοῦ τῶν Ἀχαιῶν ἔθνους, Plut. l. c. 24: ὥστ' ἐπεὶ μὴ καθ' ἐνιαυτὸν ἐξῆν, παρ' ἐνιαυτὸν

of noble family, Vit. α', Westerm. Vitt. min. p. 53. Vit. β', l. c. p. 57, Vit. δ', p. 59. Suid. s. v., flourished about 284—276, Vit. α', Suid. s. v., attended the lectures of the Stoic Persæus at Athens, Vit. δ', and went with him to the court of Antigonus Gonatas, with whom he stood in favour, Vit. α', γ', δ', and at whose instigation he composed his chief poem, Φαινόμενα, on the movements of the heavenly bodies with an appendix on weather signs (Διοσημεῖα), written in hexameters. In addition to this he also wrote other works of various descriptions, Suid. s. v. Macrob. Sat. V, 20. Vit. γ' (σφόδρα πολυγράμματος ἀνήρ). His chief work was translated into Latin by Cicero, de nat. d. II, 41, Cæsar Germanicus, and Festus Avienus; and in spite of its learned monotony, Quint. X, 1, 55, was held in high esteem by the Romans, Cic. de orat. I, 16. de rep. I, 14. Ovid. Amor. I, 15, 16: Cum sole et luna semper Aratus erit.

v) Kallimachus, of the family of the Battiadæ at Kyrene, the pupil of the grammarian Hermokrates, then head of a school at Alexandreia, and afterwards appointed by Ptolemy Philadelphus to a place in the Museum and Library there, of which he finally became the director, Suid. s. v. Περὶ κωμ. VIII, 20 f. Bergk, Prol. Aristoph., lived circa 260—230. A learned poet and critic, he is said to have composed 800 works, Suid. s. v. We possess 6 of his hymns and 60 epigrams; of his other writings only fragments are now extant. His elegies were especially prized, Quint. X, 1, 58 (princeps elegiæ), and thus served as the models of Roman poets, as Ovid, Propertius (cf. Eleg. III, 1) and Catullus (LXVI, de coma Berenices); just as his lampoon Ἴβις on Apollonius of Rhodes was copied by Ovid in his poem of the same name. Then we must mention his αἴτια, a learned collection of legends in 4 books, and his πίνακες, in which he catalogued the whole contents of Greek literature, and became the founder of Greek literary history, Suid. s. v. He also

αἱρεῖσθαι στρατηγὸν αὐτόν, ἔργῳ δὲ καὶ γνώμῃ διὰ παντὸς ἄρχειν. Trœzen and Epidaurus also joined the league at this time, Plut. l. c. Paus. II, 8, 4. VII, 7, 1.

79) The decline of Sparta, which begins with the Peloponnesian war and was above all hastened by the influx of large sums of money during and after the war, see p. 81. obs. 152, and which soon afterwards was still further fostered by the rhetra of Epitadeus, p. 16. obs. 20, was specially manifested in the fact that the landed property became more and more concentrated in the hands of a small minority, and the number of citizens in possession of full civic rights continually diminished, Plut. Agis 5: ταχὺ τῆς εὐπορίας εἰς ὀλίγους συρρυείσης πενία τὴν πόλιν κατέσχεν ἀνελευθερίαν καὶ τῶν καλῶν ἀσχολίαν ἐπιφέρουσα —ἀπελείφθησαν ἑπτακοσίων οὐ πλείονες Σπαρτιᾶται καὶ τούτων ἴσως ἑκατὸν

exercised very considerable influence as a teacher: Eratosthenes, Aristophanes, and others were his pupils (Καλλιμάχειοι). It is said of him, Ovid. Amor. I, 15, 14, Dattiades semper toto cantabitur orbe; quamvis ingenio non valet; arte valet.

w) Lykophron, of Chalkis in Eubœa, poet and grammarian, had a post assigned him by Ptolemy Philadelphus in the library of Alexandreia, to arrange the works of the comic poets, Vit. α', Westerm. Vitt. min. p. 142. Suid. s. v. Περὶ κωμ. VIII, 19 f. Bergk, Prol. Aristoph., and was ranked in the seven-starred constellation (Πλειάς) of poets of the Alexandrine period. Of his writings only his epic poem Ἀλεξάνδρα (erroneously entitled Κασσάνδρα) is now extant, Suid. s. v.: τὸ σκοτεινὸν ποίημα. All his other works, and in particular his 20 tragedies, Suid. s. v., are lost.

x) Apollonius of Alexandreia lived about 260—190, but left his native city, on meeting with ill success in the public recitation of his epic poem, Ἀργοναυτικά, owing, it is said, to the envy and slander of other poets, Vit. α', β', Westerm. Vitt. min. p. 50. 51. On this occasion he also took offence at Kallimachus, and attacked him in an epigram, Anthol. Gr. Iac. T. III, p. 67; to which the latter replied with the Ibis. He then went to Rhodes, there opened a school of rhetoric, and won such applause by the public recitation of his poems, that he obtained civic rights and hence too the epithet ὁ Ῥόδιος, Vit. α', β'. He was afterwards recalled to Alexandreia to the Museum, and was head librarian at the library there. Besides his learned epic, Ἀργοναυτικά, and the epigram referred to, nothing of his writings is now extant.

y) Eratosthenes, born at Kyrene in 276 B. C., was educated at Athens, was then promoted by Ptolemy Euergetes to be president of the Alexandrine library, Suid. s. v. Περὶ κωμ. VIII, 21, Bergk. Prol.

Fifth Period. 336—146 b.c.

Olympiad.	b.c.	ATHENS.	HISTORY.
		Archon.	
CXXXV, 2	239		Demetrius II king of Macedonia[80]).
CXXXVI, 2	235		Kleomenes III king of Sparta[81]).
CXXXVI, 3	234		Megalopolis joins the league[82]).
CXXXVII, 3	230	Alexander.	
CXXXVII, 4	229		Antigonus II king of Macedonia[83]).
			Athens freed by Aratus from Macedonian rule[84]).
CXXXVIII, 1	228		Argos, Hermione and Phlius join the league[85]).
CXXXVIII, 2	227		Commencement of the Kleomenean war. Hostilities between S_iarta and the Achæan league in Arcadia[86]).

ἦσαν οἱ γῆν κεκτημένοι καὶ κλῆρον, cf. p. 86. obs. 107. Accordingly Agis entered on a course of active reform with a law, by which debts were remitted; and this was followed by a second law, which provided that a redistribution of the soil should be taken in hand, and that the whole territory should be divided into 4500 lots for the Spartiates and into 15000 for the periœks; whilst the number of the Spartiates was to be supplemented by the adoption of periœks and strangers, Plut. Agis 8. The chief opponent of the new laws, the other king Leonidas, was deposed and banished, id. 11. 12, and the prosperous course of the undertaking seemed fully assured, when the selfishness of one of the ephors, Agesilaus, a kinsman and adherent of Agis, spoilt all by the deferment of the land-distribution, id. 13. 16. So whilst Agis was absent with the army, to aid the Achæans against the Ætolians, a total change in the public feeling took place; Leonidas returned, made himself master of the state, id. 16, and had Agis executed together with his mother Agesistrata and his grandmother Archidameia, id. 18—20. The date, as here determined, is based chiefly on the passage Plut. Agis 13, where it is related, that in the campaign referred to Agis advised Aratus to prevent the Ætolians from penetrating into the Peloponnese by the occupation of the isthmus. This presupposes that the Macedonians were no longer in possession of Corinth, as in the other case nothing could have been said of any occupation of the isthmus: it must therefore have taken place after 243 b.c., obs. 78: but again, on the other hand, an Ætolian inroad could not happen after 239 b.c., as after the death of Antigonus, which took place in this year, the Ætolians and Achæans concluded peace, Polyb. II, 44. The campaign referred to must therefore be placed between 243 and 239, perhaps in the year 241: it then follows that the commencement of Agis' attempts at reform belongs to the year 242 b.c., as between this and the campaign a change of ephors takes place, Plut. Agis 12.

80) He reigned 10 years, Pol. II, 44. Porphyr. fr. 3 and 4. § 9, and died in the year in which the Romans first crossed over to Illyria, i.e. in 229 b.c., Pol. l.c. cf. II, 10. 11.

81) He was the son of Leonidas, obs. 79, and reigned 16 years, Plut. Cleom. 38; thus, presupposing that he died in 219 b.c., obs. 95, it follows that he ascended the throne in the year given above.

82) Pol. II, 44. Plut. Arat. 30. Lydiadas, the tyrant of Megalopolis, voluntarily abdicated, and carried over the town to the league. The date here given rests on the statement of Plut. l.c., that the Achæans appointed Lydiadas strategus after his resignation of the sovereignty, and repeated their choice on two subsequent occasions, and that in alternation with Aratus: now the last occasion on which he filled the office of strategus cannot be placed later than 229 b.c., as Aratus was strategus in 233, Aristomachus in 227, Aratus again in 226, and Lydiadas fell in 226 b.c. in the battle of Leuktra, Plut. l.c. 35. 37. obs. 87; whilst on the other hand the union of Megalopolis with the league must be placed as short a time as possible before the death of Demetrius, as Polybius l.c. says that it took place whilst he was still alive. Accordingly it is rendered at least probable, that Lydiadas was strategus in the years 233, 231, and 229, and consequently that Megalopolis joined the league in 234 b.c.

83) For the time of Demetrius' death see obs. 80. He was succeeded by Antigonus Doson, a nephew of Antigonus Gonatas on a brother's side, at first as guardian of Philip, the son of Demetrius, then as king, Pol. II, 45. Porphyr. fr. 4. § 10. He reigned 9 years according to Diod. ap. Porphyr. fr. 3. § 10, in perfect agreement with which are the passages Pol. II, 70. Plut. Cleom. 27. 30, according to which he died shortly after the battle of Sellasia, whilst the account of Porphyrius himself, fr. 3 and 4. § 10, that he reigned 12 years, is irreconcilable with these passages.

84) Diogenes, the commander of the garrison, was induced to withdraw by a sum of 150 talents, to which Aratus contributed the sixth part out of his own means, Plut. Arat. 24. 34. Cleom. 16. Paus. II, 8, 5. Athens, however, did not join the league. The town was freed Δημητρίου τελευτήσαντος, therefore probably in 229 b.c.

85) Plut. Arat. 35. Aristomachus, who was tyrant of Argos, was induced by Aratus to lay down the tyranny; and in return for this he was appointed strategus for the following year, Plut. l.c. The strategia of Aristomachus must be placed in 227 b.c., obs. 95; and this fixes the year adopted in the Table.

86) Kleomenes wished for war οὐδέμενος ἂν ἐν πολέμῳ μᾶλλον ἢ κατ' εἰρήνην μεταστῆσαι τὰ παρόντα, Plut. Cleom. 3: so too Aratus was

---

Aristoph., and died in 196 or 194 n.c., by voluntarily abstaining from food, it is said, Suid. s. v. Lucian. Macrob. 27. He was nicknamed Βῆτα, because he took the second rank in every department of learning, Suid. He is said to have been the first to call himself Φιλόλογος, Suet. de Grammatt. 10. His great work, Γεωγραφικά (γεωγραφούμενα or γεωγραφία), raised geography to a science, but is lost, all except citations in Strabo. Besides this, his writings extended to the province of philosophy, chronology, history, history of literature, mathematics, astronomy, and grammar. All that is preserved is a solitary epigram on the doubling of the cube, Anthol. Græc. Iac. I, P, 2, p. 315, and a letter to King Ptolemy about this problem, Eratosth. Bernhardy, p. 175 f. The Καταστερισμοί, a catalogue of stars, which has come down to us under his name, is of much later origin.

The Extinction of Greek Freedom.   135

Olympiad.	B. C.	HISTORY.
CXXXVIII, 3	226	The victories of Kleomenes at Mt Lykœum and Leuktra in the territory of Megalopolis[87]).
CXXXVIII, 4	225	The reintroduction of the Lykurgean constitution at Sparta by Kleomenes[88]). Invasion of Achaia by Kleomenes and his victory at Dyme[89]).
CXXXIX, 1	224	Fruitless negotiations for peace[90]). Kleomenes makes a fresh inroad into Achaia. He conquers Pellene and Argos: Kleonæ, Phlius and Corinth voluntarily join his standard[91]).
CXXXIX, 2	223	He besieges Acrocorinthus and Sikyon[92]). King Antigonus, invoked by the Achæans to their aid, penetrates into the Peloponnese[93]).

with him the Achæan league, because Sparta alone opposed his plans, which were directed to the union of the whole of the Peloponnese, id., and because he feared, that the Ætolian league might unite with Sparta and the Macedonian king for the suppression of the Achæan league, Pol. II, 45, 46; an apprehension, which sprang from the circumstance, that about this time the Spartans took away the towns Tegea, Mantineia, and Orchomenus, which were in alliance with the Ætolians, without remonstrance on the part of the Ætolians, Pol. II, 46. The ephors at Sparta, perceiving the hostile intentions of the Achæans, charged Kleomenes with the task of occupying Belmina on the frontier of Laconia and Megalopolis; Kleomenes executed their orders and fortified the Athenæum there; the Achæans then captured Kaphyæ in Arcadia, whilst Kleomenes took Mothydrium, and when the Achæans penetrated into Arcadia with an army of 20,000 infantry and 1000 cavalry, Kleomenes marched to oppose them with 5000 men, and offered them battle; but the Achæans retired. This was the prelude to the Kleomenic war, see Plut. Cleom. 4. Arat. 35. Pol. II, 46. For the chronology of the whole war, of which Polybius only gives a short survey up to the advent of Antigonus, see obs. 95.

87) The Achæans under Aratus had invaded Elis; Kleomenes came to the assistance of the Eleans, and won the first victory at Mt Lykæum, Plut. Cleom. 6. Arat. 36. Pol. II, 51; Aratus then took Mantineia by a bold stroke, Plut. l. c. But Kleomenes again took the field, captured Leuktra near Megalopolis, and inflicted a defeat on the Achæans, when they came to the succour of the distressed Megalopolis, Plut. Cleom. 6. Arat. 36—37. Pol. II, 51 (in which last passage Laodikeia is named as the place of the battle).

88) Kleomenes, who was more energetic than Agis (κέντρον τι θυμοῦ τῇ φύσει προσῆειτο, Plut. Cleom. 1), and sought for the reason of the ill success of Agis principally in the ephors, began with the murder of the ephors, Plut. Cleom. 8. 10, and then carried out the reform, taking in hand a fresh distribution of the land and reintroducing (with the help of the Stoic Sphærus) the ἀγωγή, id. 11. By the admission of perioeks he raised the number of the hoplites to 4000, id. He also appointed his brother, Eukleidas, joint-king, id.: up to this time he alone had filled the royal throne, as his father Leonidas had done after the murder of Agis.

89) Plut. Cleom. 14. Pol. II, 51 (near the Hekatombæum). He had also previously retaken Mantineia, Plut. l. c. Pol. II, 58.

90) Disheartened by his repeated defeats, Aratus had refused the

office of strategus for this year, although his turn had come round, Plut. Cleom. 15. Arat. 38, and the Achæans were disposed to accede to the demand of Kleomenes, that the hegemony should be yielded to him: the negotiations, however, were frustrated, in the first place by chance occurrences, and afterwards by the intrigues of Aratus (who was already in secret treaty with the king of Macedonia, Pol. II, 51. Plut. Arat. 38), see Plut. Cleom. 15. 17. Arat. 30.

91) Plut. Cleom. 17—19. Arat. 39. Pol. II, 52.—Plut. Cleom. 17: Ἐγεγόνει δὲ κίνημα τῶν Ἀχαιῶν, καὶ πρὸς ἀπόστασιν ὥρμησαν αἱ πόλεις, τῶν μὲν δήμων νομήν τε χώρας καὶ χρεῶν ἀνοκοπὰς ἐλπισάντων, τῶν δὲ πρώτων πολλαχοῦ βαρυνομένων τὸν Ἄρατον, ἐνίων δὲ καὶ δι᾽ ὀργῆν ἐχόντων ὡς ἐπάγοντα τῇ Πελοποννήσῳ Μακεδόνας. The capture of Argos was effected on the occasion of the Nemean games, i. e. in the winter of 221/3 B. c., cf. obs. 95.

92) Plut. Cleom. 19. Arat. 40. Pol. II, 52.

93) Aratus, who feared a combination between Sparta, the Ætolian league and the king of Macedonia, and saw, not merely his life's plan of uniting the Peloponnese under the hegemony of the Achæan league, but even the existing constitutions of the individual towns menaced by Kleomenes, had for a considerable time past been in secret treaty with Antigonus; after their repeated defeats the negotiations were conducted openly and with the assent of the league, and were now brought to a satisfactory conclusion; for, now that Corinth had gone over to Kleomenes and Acro-Corinthus was blockaded by him, there was no more hesitation about fulfilling the condition imposed by Antigonus, which had hitherto been the stumbling-block, that Acro-Corinthus should be made over to him, Pol. II, 45—51. cf. Plut. Cleom. 16. Arat. 38. For the cession of Acro-Corinthus Plut. Arat. l. c.: Οὐ γὰρ πρότερον ἐπέβη τοῖς Ἀχαιοῖς δεομένοις καὶ ὑποβάλλουσιν αὐτοὺς διὰ τῶν πρεσβειῶν καὶ τῶν ψηφισμάτων ἢ τῇ φρουρᾷ καὶ τοῖς ὁμήροις· ὥσπερ χαλινουμένους ἀνασχέσθαι. Antigonus came with 20,000 foot and 1400 horse, Plut. Arat. 43. On the approach of Antigonus Kleomenes relinquished the siege of Sikyon and occupied the isthmus: but as Argos in his rear revolted and was occupied by the Achæans, he saw himself compelled to give up this position, and Antigonus now advanced to the frontier of Laconia, where he destroyed the Spartan fortifications at Belmina and Ægæ, Pol. II, 52—54. Plut. Cleom. 20—21. Arat. 43—44. Kleomenes now sought to rely principally on Ptolemy for support, and at this time sent his mother and his son to him as hostages, Plut. Cleom. 22. cf. Pol. II, 51.

136   FIFTH PERIOD. 336—146 B. C.

Olympiad.	B. C.	HISTORY.	ART AND LITERATURE.
CXXXIX, 3	222	Antigonus conquers the Arcadian towns Tegea, Orchomenus, Mantineia, Heræa, and Telphusa⁹⁴).	
CXXXIX, 4	221	Kleomenes totally defeated by Antigonus at Sellasia⁹⁵).	The Alexandrine Grammarians and Critics Zenodotus^z), Aristophanes^{aa}), Aristarchus^{bb}).

94) Pol. II, 54. Plut. Cleom. 23. Kleomenes manumitted all helots, who paid 5 minæ, and after strengthening his army by enlisting these freedmen (according to Plutarch their numbers amounted to 6000, according to Macrob. Sat. I, 11 to 9000), he surprised Megalopolis in the winter-time, took and destroyed it, Plut. Cleom. 23—25. Philop. 5. Pol. II, 55, 61.

95) In the spring, before Antigonus had mustered his troops again, Kleomenes invaded and laid waste the territory of Argos, Pol. II, 64. Plut. Cleom. 26. Then at the beginning of summer he takes up his station at Sellasia (Pol. II, 65), waiting for Antigonus, with a total of 20,000 men. Antigonus marches to meet him with 28,000 foot and 1200 horse; and a battle follows, in which Kleomenes is totally defeated, Pol. II, 65—69. Plut. Cleom. 27—28. Philop. 6. According to Plut. Cleom. 28 the 6000 Spartans, who were present at the battle, are said to have fallen, all but 200. Kleomenes flies to Egypt, where he vainly labours to induce the king to grant him succour for his native land, and where two years later (Pol. IV, 35), when at last he was even treated as a prisoner and an attempt to regain his freedom by exciting a rebellion in Alexandreia had failed, he puts himself to death together with his followers, Plut. Cleom. 32—39. Pol. V, 35—39. Antigonus was admitted without resistance into Sparta and abolished the institutions of Kleomenes, Pol. VI, 70, and then returned to Macedonia, whither he was called by an Illyrian invasion; but left behind a garrison in Corinth and Orchomenus, by which he upheld his sovereignty in the Peloponnese, Pol. IV, 6. Plut. Arat. 45. For the military importance of Corinth cf. Pol. VII, 11. Plut. Arat. 50. Flam. 10. Paus. VII, 7, 8. The Achæans were united with the Epirotes, Phokians, Bœotians, Akarnanians and Thessalians in a league; which in reality stood under the supreme headship of Macedonia, Pol. IV, 9. In like manner the relations between Sparta and Macedonia were firmly established by a special alliance, id. For the complete dependence of the Achæan league on Macedonia see Plut. Arat. 45: Ἐψηφίσαντο δ᾽ ἄλλῳ μὴ γράφειν βασιλεῖ μηδὲ πρεσβεύειν πρὸς ἄλλον ἄκοντος Ἀντιγόνου, τρέφειν τε καὶ μισθοδοτεῖν ἠναγκάζοντο τοὺς Μακεδόνας. That the battle of Sellasia took place in 221 B. C., not as is commonly assumed in 222, is established by this fact, that Antigonus, after the battle and further after settling affairs at Sparta to suit his pleasure, was present at the Nemean games, Pol. II, 70, which, as is proved with especial clearness by Pol. V, 101, were always celebrated in summer-time at the beginning of the third Olympiad year, therefore on this occasion not 222, but 221 B. C. If this is established, it then follows, that Antigonus came to Greece in the summer of 223 B.C., as Pol. II, 54 expressly mentions his winter quarters in the Peloponnese in two different years; and in perfect agreement with this is the fact, that the conquest of Argos by Kleomenes happened on the occasion of the Nemean games, obs. 91, which in winter-time were always celebrated in the first Olympiad year, consequently in this case in 224/3. The other events of the war are fixed by the strategi, under whom they occurred; these are successively, Aristomachus (in 227 B.C.), Plut. Arat. 35. Cleom. 4, Aratus (in 226 B.C.), Plut. Arat. l.c., Hyperbatas (in 225), Plut. Cleom. 14, Timoxenus (in 224), Plut. Arat. 38, cf. Cleom. 15. But the chronology adopted receives further confirmation from the statement of Polybius, II, 57, that the capture of Mantineia by Aratus (obs. 87) took place in the fourth year before

z) Zenodotus of Ephesus, the pupil of Philetas, head director of the library at Alexandreia and tutor to the sons of Ptolemy Philadelphus, busied himself with the grammar and criticism of Greek poets, and prepared the first edition of Homer, Suid. s. v. Περὶ κωμ. Bergk, Prol. Aristoph. VIII, 27.

aa) Aristophanes of Byzantium, critic and grammarian, the pupil of Zenodotus, Kallimachus, and Eratosthenes, and teacher of Aristarchus, and after Apollonius Rhodius director of the library at Alexandreia, Suid. s. v. Ἀρίσταρχος, v. Ἐρατοσθένης. The invention of signs for accents and stops is attributed to him, Villoison. Anecd. Gr. II, p. 131. Apollon. Alex. IV, p. 304, and to him together with Aristarchus the establishment of the Alexandrine canon, Procl. Chrestom. p. 340 f. Quint. X, 1, 46 f. The studies of Aristophanes, like those of all the other Alexandrine scholars, centred in the Homeric poems, which he edited with an apparatus of critical marks, but his labours were also directed to other Greek poets, and moreover he wrote a lexicological work, λέξεις. But of all his books fragments only have been preserved in the scholia on the poets.

bb) Aristarchus of Samothrake, educated at Alexandreia by Aristophanes, became tutor to the young Ptolemy Epiphanes and (after Aristophanes) head librarian, and as the most celebrated of all grammarians and critics (ὁ κορυφαῖος τῶν γραμματικῶν, ὁ γραμματικώτατος) trained numerous pupils, but finally went in his old age to Kypros, where he is said to have died voluntarily of starvation at the age of 72, Suid. s. v. Ἀριστοφάνης, Athen. II, p. 71 D. He occupied himself in particular with the criticism and interpretation of the older poets (see above p. 15. obs. s), Homer, Pindar, Archilochus, Æschylus, Sophokles, Ion, Aristophanes; and according to Suidas wrote over 800 commentaries and several grammatical works, of which fragments alone are preserved in the collections of scholia. His important services in the criticism and interpretation of Homer are rendered most conspicuous by the Homeric scholia and the commentary of Eustathius. His chief opponent was Kratos of Mallus, who taught at Pergamum and replied to the chief work of Aristarchus Περὶ ἀναλογίας by a treatise Περὶ ἀνωμαλίας, Gell. II, 25. cf. XIV, 6, 3. Varro de L. L. IX, 1. He became the founder of the Pergamean school.

FOURTH SECTION.

220—146 B.C.

THE GREEKS ARE DRAWN INTO THE STRUGGLE BETWEEN ROME AND MACEDONIA, AND SIDING WITH ONE OR OTHER OF THE BELLIGERENT STATES AT LAST FALL UNDER ROMAN RULE.

Olympiad.	B.C.	HISTORY.
CXL, 1	220	Philip V. king of Macedonia[96].
CXL, 1-4	220-217	War of the allies; the Achæans, Bœotians, Phokians, Epirotes, Akarnanians, and Messenians, allied with Philip, in conflict with the Ætolians, Spartans, and Eleans[97]).

the advent of Antigonus. It must be confessed, that several obscure points still remain: thus, on the above supposition, it is at least incorrect, when in 219 B.C. at the time of the change in the strategus Polybius reckons 3 years from the flight of Kleomenes to the battle of Sellasia, IV, 35. 37: further the statement of Polybius, II, 43, that Aratus was strategus for the second time in 243 B.C. (obs. 78), and that he filled the strategia every alternate year, is irreconcilable with the fact, that his strategia in 226 B.C. is said to have been the twelfth, Plut. Arat. 38: finally there still remains a difficulty, which is hard to explain, that Timoxenus, who was strategus in 224 B.C., is said to have been again strategus in 223, Pol. II, 53: with which, however, id. 52 and Plut. Arat. 41 must be compared. Still these doubts are not sufficient to overthrow the assumptions adopted above, which are based on certain proofs.

96) For the time of his accession to the throne see obs. 83. He was now 17 years old, Pol. IV, 5, and in the first part of his reign gained universal approbation and love by his justice and mildness, as well as by his bravery and military capacities, Pol. IV, 77. VII, 12 (κοινὸς τις οἷον ἐρώμενος ἐγένετο τῶν Ἑλλήνων διὰ τὸ τῆς αἱρέσεως

εὐεργετικόν), but afterwards degenerated, Pol. VII, 12. 13. X, 26. Plut. Arat. 51.

97) The war (ὁ συμμαχικὸς πόλεμος, Pol. IV, 13) arose out of a plundering raid of the Ætolians through Achaia as far as Messenia, Pol. IV, 1—13. For the date of its commencement, id. 14. 26. On the one side were ranged those who had entered into alliance with Macedonia after the Kleomenic war, obs. 93; only with this difference, that the Spartans went over to the side of the Ætolians, Pol. IV, 16, 35, and, as a set off, the Messenians attached themselves to Philip and the Achæan league, id. 9. 15. 25 : besides their now allies, the Spartans, the Ætolians were still further supported by their old allies, the Eleans, id. 36. For the whole war, which was carried on by both sides merely by plundering inroads into hostile territory without decisive result see Pol. IV, 1—37. 57 to V, 30. 91—105, cf. Plut. Arat. 47—48 : at last, however, Philip and his allies are in the ascendant: notwithstanding, he concludes peace on receiving the news of Hannibal's victory at lake Trasimene, in order to leave himself free to ally himself with Hannibal against Rome, Pol. V, 101—105. cf. Roman Chron. Tables (5th ed.) p. 48. obs. 18;

138   FIFTH PERIOD. 336—146 B.C.

Olympiad.	B. C.	ATHENS.	HISTORY.
		Archons.	
CXLI, 2	215		War between Rome and Macedonia[98].
CXLI, 4	213		Aratus poisoned by Philip[99].
CXLII, 1	212	Anthesterius.	
CXLII, 2	211	Aristodemus.	The Ætolians contract an alliance with the Romans, and are thereby drawn into the struggle between Rome and Macedonia; their example is followed by the Spartans, Eleans, and Messenians: whilst the Achæans, Bœotians, Phokians, Epirotes, Akarnanians, Eubœans, Lokrians, and Thessalians take part in the war on the side of Macedonia[100].
CXLIII, 4	205	Kallistratus.	Peace between Rome and Philip and the allies of both parties[101].
CXLIV, 1	204	Pasiades.	
CXLV, 1	200	Nikias.	Second Macedonian war[102].
CXLV, 3	198		The Achæans go over to the side of Rome[103].
CXLV, 4	197	Achæus.	Defeat of Philip at Kynoskephalæ[104].
CXLVI, 1	196	Athenion.	Peace between Rome and Macedonia[105].
			Greece declared free[106].
CXLVI, 2	195	Ktesikrates.	The Romans and Achæans at war with Nabis of Sparta: Nabis submits and is confined to the possession of the town of Sparta[107].

---

on the condition, ὥστε ἔχειν ἀμφοτέροις, ἃ νῦν ἔχουσι, Plut. l. c. 103,— Pol. V, 105: Τὰς μὲν οὖν Ἑλληνικὰς καὶ τὰς Ἰταλικὰς, ἔτι δὲ τὰς Λιβυκὰς πράξεις οὕτως ὁ καιρὸς καὶ τοῦτο τὸ διαβούλιον συνέπλεξε πρῶτον· οὐ γὰρ ἔτι Φιλιππος οὐδ' οἱ τῶν Ἑλλήνων προεστῶτες ἄρχοντες πρὸς τὰς κατὰ τὴν Ἑλλάδα πράξεις ποιούμενοι τὰς ἀναφορὰς οὔτε τοὺς πολέμους οὔτε τὰς διαλύσεις ἐποιοῦντο πρὸς ἀλλήλους, ἀλλ' ἤδη πάντες πρὸς τοὺς ἐν Ἰταλίᾳ σκοποὺς ἀνέβλεπον.

98) See Roman Chron. Tables. p. 48. obs. 18. 21. Immediately after the conclusion of the war of the allies, Philip had turned against Illyria, which he wished to conquer, in order to be able to lend a helping hand to Hannibal from that country, see Pol. V, 108—110. VIII, 13. Accordingly Illyria was at the very first the chief theatre of the war between Philip and the Romans.

99) Pol. VIII, 14. Plut. Arat. 52—54. Paus. II, 9, 4. After his death Philopœmen came into increasing prominence as director of the affairs of the league, "the last of the Hellenes," Plut. Philop. 1. For him see Plut. Philop. Paus. VIII, 49—52. Pol. X, 22—24. XI, 8—10, etc.

100) See Roman Chron. Tables. p. 49. obs. 31. cf. Pol. XI, 5.

The Messenians who had hitherto sided with Philip had gone over to the enemy in consequence of the ill-treatment and injustice, which they suffered from Philip, Pol. VIII, 10. 14. Plut. Arat. 49—51.

101) See Roman Chron. Tabl. p. 51. obs. 45.

102) See Roman Chron. Tabl. p. 53. obs. 1—5.

103) See Roman Chron. Tabl. p. 53. obs. 5. For the vacillating and ambiguous attitude of Nabis, the tyrant of Sparta see obs. 107.

104) See Roman Chron. Tabl. p. 53. obs. 7.

105) See Roman Chron. Tabl. p. 53. obs. 8.

106) See Roman Chron. Tabl. p. 53. obs. 9.

107) After the death of Kleomenes, Agesipolis III and Lykurgus (the latter a non-Herakleid) were chosen kings at Sparta, Pol. IV, 35; but Agesipolis was expelled by Lykurgus, Liv. XXXIV, 26. Lykurgus now ruled alone as tyrant, after him Machanidas, and when he had been slain by Philopœmen, Pol. XI, 11—18. Plut. Phil. 10, Nabis. War was undertaken against Nabis, partly because, when the Achæans had joined the Romans (obs. 103), he had entered into a coalition with Philip and made himself master of the town of Argos, Liv.

The Extinction of Greek Freedom. 139

Olympiad.	B.C.	ATHENS. Archons.	HISTORY.
CXLVII, 1	192		Murder of Nabis, and union of Sparta with the Achæan league[108].
			Beginning of the Syrian war between Rome and Antiochus, king of Syria[109].
			The Ætolians allies of Antiochus[110].
CXLVII, 4	189	Demostratus.	End of the Syrian war[111].
			The power of the Ætolians broken by the peace dictated to them by the Romans[112].
CXLVIII, 1	188		Philopœmen compels the Spartans to abolish the last remnants of the Lykurgean constitution[113]: then follow continual disputes, fostered by the Romans, between Sparta and the Achæan league[114].
CXLIX, 1	184	Tychandrus.	

XXXII, 38—40; partly with the object of preventing his alliance with Antiochus, with whom war was now impending, Liv. XXXIII, 44. For the war with Nabis, Liv. XXXIV, 22—41. Plut. Flam. 13. The upshot was, that the tyrant was confined to Sparta and its immediate territory, was cut off from all sea-communication, and was condemned to pay a considerable fine, Liv. XXXIV, 35—40. cf. XXXV, 12. With this, however, the Achæans were not satisfied, as in their ophion the war ought only to have been brought to an end with the overthrow of Nabis, Plut. l. c.: διεψεύσατο τὰς τῆς Ἑλλάδος ἐλπίδας, Liv. XXXIV, 41: serva Lacedaemon relicta et lateri adhaerens tyrannus non sincerum gaudium praebebant, cf. id. 48. 49. XXXV, 31.

108) War had again broken out between Nabis and the Achæans, because the former, seduced by the Ætolians, had made an attempt to reconquer the coast of Laconia. Nabis is totally defeated by the Achæans under Philopœmen, and compelled to shut himself up within the walls of Sparta, Liv. XXXV, 12—13. 25—30. Hereupon the Ætolians send a detachment of troops to Sparta, nominally to aid him, but in reality to put him out of the way, and to take possession of the town. Nabis is in fact killed, but the Ætolians neglect to secure the town; and now Philopœmen hurries up and compels the Spartans to join the league, without, however, disturbing the Lykurgean constitution, id. 35—37. Plut. Phil. 15. Paus. VIII, 50.

109) See Roman Chron. Tabl. p. 54. obs. 10—15.

110) The Ætolians were discontented with Rome on account of the peace with Philip, as in their opinion their services had not been sufficiently rewarded, Liv. XXXIII, 11. 12. 13. 31. 35. 49. XXXIV, 22. 23. Pol. XVIII, 17. 21. 22. 23. 31. Plut. Flam. 9; they were likewise ill pleased, not only on account of the war, but also of the peace with Nabis, Liv. XXXIV, 23. 41. Hence their negotiations and alliance with Antiochus, Liv. XXXIII, 43. 44. XXXV, 12. 32—33. 34. 43—45. Pol. XX, 1. Appian Syr. 12.

111) See Roman Chron. Tabl. p. 54. obs. 15.

112) After various unsuccessful negotiations for peace, for which see Liv. XXXVI, 22. 27—29. 34—35. XXXVII, 1. Pol. XX, 9—11, further after both the Scipios had granted them an armistice for six months

in 190 B. C., in order to leave themselves free for the campaign against Antiochus in Asia, Liv. XXXVII, 4—7. Pol. XXI, 1—3, M. Fulvius, the consul of the year 189, recommenced the war, took Amprakia, and threatened to invade Ætolia. Peace was now at last concluded on the following terms: the Ætolians were to pay 500 talents, to cede all towns, which the Romans had taken from them since the time of Flaminius, to furnish hostages, and to bind themselves to carry on war only with the consent of the Romans, etc., Liv. XXXVII, 49. XXXVIII, 1—15. Pol. XXII, 8—15. After this they brought themselves to utter ruin owing to factions, Pol. XXX, 14. Liv. XLI, 25. XLII, 2.

113) Liv. XXXVIII, 30—34. Paus. VII, 8, 4. VIII, 51, 1. Plut. Phil. 16. This measure was occasioned by an attempt on the part of the Spartans to make themselves masters of the coast-towns: Philopœmen (auctor semper Achæis minuendi opes et auctoritatem Lacedaemoniorum, Liv. l. c. 31) demanded the surrender of the authors of this attempt, and when the Spartans not only refused his demand, but also arrived at the resolution to separate themselves from the Achæan league, he marched into Laconia, and now demanded the surrender of those, who had advised the adoption of this resolution; and when the surrender was made, he had them executed to the number of 80, or rather as many as had escaped being slain immediately on their arrival in the Achæan camp (outrage of Kompasion, Pol. XXIII, 1. 7). The Spartans themselves were now obliged to recall the citizens banished by Nabis (cf. Liv. XXXIV, 35. Pol. XX, 12), and on the other hand to banish the citizens enrolled by him, to pull down their walls, to abolish the Lykurgean constitution, etc.— Per haec enervata civitas Lacedaemoniorum Achæis diu obnoxia fuit, Liv. XXXVIII, 34. The full admission of Sparta to the Achæan league did not take place till the year 181 B.C., Pol. XXV, 1—2.

114) In consequence of the frequent revolutions at Sparta there were a number of banished Spartans, who had their adherents in Sparta itself (according to Pol. XXIV, 4 Sparta was split into 4 different factions) and were continually sending embassies to Rome to beg for help: embassies of this kind are mentioned in the year 187, Pol. XXIII, 1, in 185, id. 4. 5. 7. Liv. XXXIX, 33. 35—37, in the year

18—2

Fifth Period. 336—146 b.c.

Olympiad	B.C.	ATHENS.	HISTORY.	ART AND LITERATURE.
		Archons.		
CXLIX, 2	183		War of the Achæan league with Messonia and death of Philopœmen[114]).	
CL, 2	179		Philip of Macedonia dies; he is succeeded by Perseus[115]).	
CLI, 2	171		Third Macedonian war[117]).	
CLIII, 1	168		Perseus defeated at Pydna and taken prisoner[118]).	
CLIII, 2	167	Aristæchmus.	Violent measures adopted by the Romans against the Achæan league: a thousand of the noblest Achæans are summoned to Rome and detained in Italy as prisoners[118]).	
CLIII, 4	165	Xenokles.		
CLIV, 1	164	Nikomenes.		
CLIV, 4	161	Phædrias.		
CLVII, 2	151		Release of the Achæan prisoners[170]).	The poet Nikander[cc]).

182, Pol. XXIV, 10. Liv. XXXIX, 48, in the year 181, Pol. XXV, 2. 8. Liv. XL, 20, in the year 179, Pol. XXVI, 3. The Romans at first return ambiguous and evasive answers, till they think the time has come for active interference. Even during the war, and before Philopœmen invaded Laconia, senatus responsum ita perplexum fuit, ut et Achæi sibi de Lacedæmone permissum acciperent et Lacedæmonii non omnia concessa iis interpretarentur, Liv. XXXVIII, 32: it is not till the occasion of the subsequent embassies in 187 and 185 B.C., that they declare, that, though not satisfied with Philopœmen's proceedings, they will leave matters as they stand, Pol. XXIII, 1, 7. 10: in 182 B.C. they repeat this declaration, but at the same time add a light menace, Pol. XXIV, 10: διὰ τοῖς μὲν ἐκ τῆς Λακεδαίμονος ἀνεκρίθησαν, τοῖς περὶ Σηρανσον, βουλόμενοι μετέωρον ἐᾶσαι τὴν πόλιν, διότι πάντα πεποιήκασιν αὐτοῖς τὰ δυνατά, κατὰ δὲ τὸ παρὸν οὐ νομίζουσιν εἶναι τοῦτο τὸ πρᾶγμα πρὸς αὐτούς· τῶν δὲ Ἀχαιῶν παρακαλούντων, —τούτων μὲν οὐδενὶ προσεῖχον, ἀπεκρίθησαν δὲ διότι οὐδ' ἂν ὁ Λακεδαιμονίων ἢ Κορινθίων ἢ Ἀργείων ἀφίστηται δῆμος, οὐ δεήσει τοὺς Ἀχαιοὺς θαυμάζειν ἐὰν μὴ πρὸς αὐτοὺς ἡγῶνται· ταύτην δὲ τὴν ἀπόκρισιν ἐκθέμενοι, κυρίγματος ἔχουσαν διδόσιν τοῖς βουλομένοις ἔπεκεν Ῥωμαίων ἀφίστασθαι τῆς τῶν Ἀχαιῶν πολιτείας—in 181 and 179 B.C. they make a direct demand for the recall of the banished Spartans, Pol. XXV, 2. XXVI, 3. Liv. XL, 20. For the history of the further relations between Sparta and the Achæan league see obs. 121.

115) Messenia had been compelled in 191 B.C. to join the league, Liv. XXXVI, 31. cf. Pol. XXIII, 10. It now deserts the league, and it appears that Flamininus had knowledge of their determination, Plut. Flam. 17. Pol. XXIV, 5: hence the war with the league, in which

Philopœmen meets with his death, Plut. Philop. 18—21. Pol. XIV, 8. 9. 12, τεσσαράκοντα ἔτη συσχῶν πολεμήσαι, Pol. l. c. 12. The war is brought to an end in the following year with the subjection of the Messenians, id.

116) Roman Chron. Tabl. p. 55. obs. 2.
117) See id. obs. 3—6.
118) See id. p. 56. obs. 7. 8.
119) Notwithstanding many attempts, the Achæans had refused to allow themselves to be seduced into an alliance with Perseus, Pol. XXVIII, 3—7. Nevertheless the patriots of the league, with Lykortas, Archon, and Polybius at their head (Pol. XXVIII, 3), were accused by Kallikrates and Andronidas, of whom the former had been spreading his calumnies and charges ever since 179 B.C. and not without success, Pol. XXVI, 1—3 (for the infamy and degradation of both see id. XXX, 20), on the ground that they had secretly favoured Perseus, and when they had rebutted this accusation and declared themselves ready to justify themselves by all means in their power, they were summoned to Rome, and detained there, Pol. XXX, 10. Liv. XLV, 31. Paus. VII, 10, 2.

120) After the Achæans had repeatedly begged through ambassadors for their liberation to no purpose, Pol. XXXI, 8. XXXII, 7. XXXIII, 1. 2. 13, they were at last released on Cato's representation, that it mattered little περὶ γερόντων Γραικῶν, πότερον ὑπὸ τῶν παρ' ἡμῖν ἢ τῶν ἐν Ἀχαία νεκροφόρων ἐκκομισθῶσι, Plut. Cat. mai. 9: this was in the 17th year of their captivity, when they now scarcely numbered 300, Paus. VII, 10, 2.

cc) Nikander of Kolophon, Vit. a', Western. vitt. min. p. 61. Suid. s.v. Cic. de or. I, 16, lived circ. 160—140, was a priest of the Klarian Apollo, and at the same time grammarian, physician, and poet, Vit. a'. Suid. s. v. Of his poems only two have come down to us: Θηριακά, on poisonous animals and remedies for their bite; and Ἀλεξιφάρμακα, on antidotes to the consumption of poisoned meats and drinks, both full of learning, but of no poetical value. Of his lost poems we must mention the Ἑτεροιούμενα, Ovid's model in his Metamorphoses.

The Extinction of Greek Freedom. 141

Olympiad.	B. C.	ATHENS.	HISTORY.	ART AND LITERATURE.
CLVIII, 2	147	Archon. Hagnotheus.		
CLVIII, 3	146		The Achæans declare war against Sparta and consequently with Rome[121]). Their defeat at	The historian Polybius[dd]).

---

121) The chief authorities for the last catastrophe of Greece are Paus. VII, 11—16 and the fragments Pol. XXXVIII, 1—5. XL, 1—5. 7—11. In addition to the subjects of dispute between Sparta and the Achæan league a fresh quarrel had arisen between Sparta and Megalopolis, a member of the league, on a question of frontier. C. Sulpicius Gallus was in 164 B.C. commissioned by the Roman senate to decide the dispute; and he left the concern to Kallikrates (obs. 119), but at the same time made use of the opportunity to entice such towns, as were members of the league, to revolt, Pol. XXXI, 9. Paus. VII, 11, 1. Thus on the one hand the hostility between Sparta and the league was maintained, and on the other the hostile feeling of the Achæans against the Romans was still further fostered. And the flame was fanned by the prisoners returning home from Rome (obs. 120), who were incensed to the uttermost by the injustice perpetrated on themselves, Zonar. Ann. IX, 31. The immediate occasion of the war, however, was a quarrel between Athens and Oropius. The latter, although standing under the suzerainty of Athens had been unmeritedly plundered by the Athenians, and after many fruitless negotiations (which also gave rise to the despatch of the three celebrated Athenian philosophers Karneades, Diogenes, and Kritolaus as ambassadors to Rome, see Roman Chron. Tabl. p. 56. obs. h) the Oropians had bribed with ten talents Menalkidas, a Spartan, who however was strategus of the league in the present year (150 B.C.), to prevail on the league to procure them justice against Athens, Paus. VII, 11, 2—3. Menalkidas, on being accused by Kallikrates, because the former had withheld the share of the 10 talents, which he had promised him, now bribed Diæus, the strategus of 149 B.C., to secure himself from an adverse verdict. But Diæus, in order to divert the attention of the Achæans from himself and this disgraceful proceeding, brought about the outbreak of the war between the league and Sparta, Paus. VII, 12. 13. Then follows in 147 the embassy of L. Aurelius Orestes, who announced to the Achæans, that Sparta, Corinth, Argos, Orchomenus, and Herakleia by Œta were to be separated from the league: but this announcement excited such a storm of fury in the Achæan assembly, that his very person hardly escaped ill-usage, Paus. l. c. 14, 1—2; next the embassy of L. Julius with easier terms, but with no better success, Paus. id. § 3—4. Pol. XXXVIII, 1—3. The same ill-success attended a further embassy sent to the league by Q. Caecilius Metellus from Macedonia in the spring of the year 146 B.C., Pol. id. 4. Kritolaus, who was appointed strategus for 146 (the election was made towards the end of the year at this time, a deviation from the former custom), had made use of the winter 147/6 to stir up the Achæans by fanatical speeches and revolutionary measures, Pol. id. 3; and now brought about in the assembly at Corinth, the same before which the last Roman embassy had appeared, the declaration of war 'nominally against Sparta, but virtually against Rome,' Pol. id. 5.

dd) Polybius of Megalopolis, son of the Achæan general Lykortas, Suid. s. v. Paus. VIII, 30, 4, born circa 240 B.C., admirer of Philopœmen, Plut. an sen. resp. ger. p. 790 f, whose burial urn he brought home from Messenia, Plut. Philop. 20. In the war between the Romans and Perseus he recommended neutrality, Pol. XXVIII, 3. 6, then acted as commander of the cavalry, l. c. XXVIII, 7, and frequently as ambassador and diplomatist, l. c. XXV, 7. XXVIII, 10 f. XXIX, 8, but was carried off to Rome together with other leaders of the patriotic party, cf. obs. 119. 120. At Rome he was received into the house of Æmilius Paullus, instructed his sons, App. Pun. 132, and became the confidential friend of Scipio Æmilianus, Pol. XXXII, 9. 10. Plut. Symp. IV, 1. Voll. Pat. I, 18. He returned to Greece in 151 B.C. with the other Achæan captives, and from this time forward frequently used his influence at Rome in favour of his countrymen, Pol. XXXII, 7. XII, 5. XXXV, 6. Plut. Cat. mai. 9; afterwards followed Scipio to Africa, to be present at the siege of Carthage, App. Pun. 132. Paus. VIII. 30, 4, and explored with a fleet the north and west coast of Africa, Plin. H. N. V, 9. 26. VI, 199. Returning to Greece shortly after the destruction of Corinth, he was unwearriedly active in his efforts to alleviate the fate of his country and to settle its affairs, Plut. Philop. 20. Pol. XI, 7. 8. 9; in return for which he was loaded with honours by Greeks and Romans alike, l. c. 10. Paus. VIII, 9. 30. 44, 5. 48, 6. With a view to writing his history he undertook journeys to Asia Minor, Pol. XXII. 21, Egypt, l. c. XXXIV, 14, Gaul, Spain, and Africa, id. III, 59; after the completion of the history he returned back to Greece, XXXVII, 2a. XL, 2, where he died in 122 B.C. at the age of 82, in consequence of a fall from his horse, Lucian. Macrob. 22 f. Of the history of Polybius (ἱστορία καθολική) in 40 books the first five are extant in a perfect state, the remainder in fragments and extracts. In this work he had set himself the task of describing the subjection of the countries of the Mediterranean to the Roman rule from the second Punic war to the conquest of Macedonia. He adopted a synchronous arrangement of events, and in his ἱστορία ἀποδεικτική (II, 37), i.e. the careful statement of the causes and consequences of the actions recorded (IX, 1), pursued the practical aim of instructing the πολιτικοί and educating them for the conduct of public affairs (I, 1. IX, 1. 21)

Fifth Period. 336—146 b. c.

Olympiad.	b. c.	HISTORY.
CLVIII. 3	146	Skarphea and Leukopetra: destruction of Corinth, and subjection of Greece to Roman rule[122]).

---

[122] Paus. VII, 15—16. Pol. XL, 1—5. Thebes and Chalkis were allied with the Achæans, Paus. VII, 14, 4. Liv. LII. After the conclusion of the Macedonian war Metellus wished to bring the war in Greece also to a conclusion, and accordingly marched down to Greece, where he defeated Kritolaus at Skarphea (in Lokris). As Kritolaus himself fell in the battle, Diæus assumed the command, and by employment of the most extreme measures and the enlistment of slaves collected an army of 14,000 foot and 600 cavalry, Paus. l. c. 15, 4. Metellus had now to give place to the consul L. Mummius, who with an army of 23,000 infantry and 3500 cavalry posted himself on the isthmus over against the Achæans, id. 16, 1. On this spot a battle followed, which decided the fate of Greece, id. § 6: δημοκρατίας μὲν ἔπαυε, καθίστατο δὲ ἀπὸ τιμημάτων τὰς ἀρχάς, καὶ φόρος τε ἐτάχθη τῇ Ἑλλάδι, καὶ οἱ τὰ χρήματα ἔχοντες ἐκωλύοντο ἐν τῇ ὑπερορίᾳ κτᾶσθαι, συνέδριά τε κατὰ ἔθνος ἕκαστον, τό τ' Ἀχαιῶν καὶ τὸ ἐν Φωκεῦσιν ἢ Βοιωτοῖς ἢ ἑτέροθί που τῆς Ἑλλάδος, καταλέλυντο ὁμοίως πάντα—, §. 7: ἡγεμὼν δὲ ἔτι καὶ ἐπ' ἐμοῦ ἀπεστέλλετο, καλοῦσι δὲ οὐχ Ἑλλάδος, ἀλλ' Ἀχαΐας ἡγεμόνα οἱ Ῥωμαῖοι, cf. Pol. XL, 7—11.

PREPARING FOR PUBLICATION.

CHRONOLOGICAL TABLES OF ROMAN HISTORY

UNIFORM WITH THE PRESENT VOLUME,

BY

CARL PETER.

TRANSLATED FROM THE GERMAN

BY

G. CHAWNER, M.A.
FELLOW AND LECTURER OF KING'S COLLEGE, CAMBRIDGE.

A SELECTION OF GREEK INSCRIPTIONS.

WITH INTRODUCTIONS AND ANNOTATIONS,

BY

E. S. ROBERTS, M.A.
FELLOW AND TUTOR OF CAIUS COLLEGE, CAMBRIDGE.

CAMBRIDGE:
AT THE UNIVERSITY PRESS.

London: C. J. CLAY, M.A. & SON.
CAMBRIDGE UNIVERSITY PRESS WAREHOUSE,
17, PATERNOSTER ROW.

UNIVERSITY PRESS, CAMBRIDGE,
June, 1882.

CATALOGUE OF

WORKS

PUBLISHED FOR THE SYNDICS

OF THE

Cambridge University Press.

London: C. J. CLAY, M.A. AND SON.
CAMBRIDGE UNIVERSITY PRESS WAREHOUSE,
17 PATERNOSTER ROW.

Cambridge: DEIGHTON, BELL, AND CO.
Leipzig: F. A. BROCKHAUS.

250
17.6.82

PUBLICATIONS OF
The Cambridge University Press.

THE HOLY SCRIPTURES, &c.

THE CAMBRIDGE PARAGRAPH BIBLE

of the Authorized English Version, with the Text Revised by a Collation of its Early and other Principal Editions, the Use of the Italic Type made uniform, the Marginal References remodelled, and a Critical Introduction prefixed, by the Rev. F. H. SCRIVENER, M.A., LL.D., Editor of the Greek Testament, Codex Augiensis, &c., and one of the Revisers of the Authorized Version. Crown 4to. cloth. gilt. 21s.

From the Times.

"Students of the Bible should be particularly grateful to (the Cambridge University Press) for having produced, with the able assistance of Dr Scrivener, a complete critical edition of the Authorized Version of the English Bible, an edition such as, to use the words of the Editor, 'would have been executed long ago had this version been nothing more than the greatest and best known of English classics.' Falling at a time when the formal revision of this version has been undertaken by a distinguished company of scholars and divines, the publication of this edition must be considered most opportune."

From the Athenæum.

"Apart from its religious importance, the English Bible has the glory, which but few sister versions indeed can claim, of being the chief classic of the language, of having, in conjunction with Shakspeare, and in an immeasurable degree more than he, fixed the language beyond any possibility of important change. Thus the recent contributions to the literature of the subject, by such workers as Mr Francis Fry and Canon Westcott, appeal to a wide range of sympathies; and to these may now be added Dr Scrivener, well known for his labours in the cause of the Greek Testament criticism, who has brought out, for the Syndics of the Cambridge University Press, an edition of the English Bible, according to the text of 1611, revised by a comparison with later issues on principles stated by him in his Introduction. Here he enters at length into the history of the chief editions of the version, and of such features as the marginal notes, the use of italic type, and the changes of orthography, as well as into the most interesting question as to the original texts from which our translation is produced."

From the Methodist Recorder.

"This noble quarto of over 1300 pages is in every respect worthy of editor and publishers alike. The name of the Cambridge University Press is guarantee enough for its perfection in outward form, the name of the editor is equal guarantee for the worth and accuracy of its contents. Without question, it is the best Paragraph Bible ever published, and its reduced price of a guinea brings it within reach of a large number of students. But the volume is much more than a Paragraph Bible. It is an attempt, and a successful attempt, to give a critical edition of the Authorised English Version, not (let it be marked) a revision, but an exact reproduction of the original Authorised Version, as published in 1611, minus patent mistakes. This is doubly necessary at a time when the version is about to undergo revision... To all who at this season seek a suitable volume for presentation to ministers or teachers we earnestly commend this work."

From the London Quarterly Review.

"The work is worthy in every respect of the editor's fame, and of the Cambridge University Press. The noble English Version, to which our country and religion owe so much, was probably never presented before in so perfect a form."

THE CAMBRIDGE PARAGRAPH BIBLE,

STUDENT'S EDITION, on *good writing paper*, with one column of print and wide margin to each page for MS. notes. This edition will be found of great use to those who are engaged in the task of Biblical criticism. Two Vols. Crown 4to. cloth. gilt. 31s. 6d.

THE LECTIONARY BIBLE, WITH APOCRYPHA,

divided into Sections adapted to the Calendar and Tables of Lessons of 1871. Crown 8vo. cloth. 3s. 6d.

London: Cambridge Warehouse, 17 Paternoster Row.

BREVIARIUM AD USUM INSIGNIS ECCLESIAE SARUM.

Fasciculus II. In quo continentur PSALTERIUM, cum ordinario Officii totius hebdomadae juxta Horas Canonicas, et proprio Completorii, LITANIA, COMMUNE SANCTORUM, ORDINARIUM MISSAE CUM CANONE ET XIII MISSIS, &c. &c. juxta Editionem maximam pro CLAUDIO CHEVALLON ET FRANCISCO REGNAULT A.D. MDXXXI. in Alma Parisiorum Academia impressam: labore ac studio FRANCISCI PROCTER, A.M., ET CHRISTOPHORI WORDSWORTH, A.M. Demy 8vo. cloth. 12s.

FASCICULUS I. In quo continentur KALENDARIUM, et ORDO TEMPORALIS sive PROPRIUM DE TEMPORE TOTIUS ANNI, una cum ordinali suo quod usitato vocabulo dicitur PICA SIVE DIRECTORIUM SACERDOTUM. Demy 8vo. cloth. £1.

"Not only experts in liturgiology, but all persons interested in the history of the Anglican Book of Common Prayer, will be grateful to the Syndicate of the Cambridge University Press for forwarding the publication of the volume which bears the above title, and which has recently appeared under their auspices."—*Notes and Queries.*

"We have here the first instalment of the celebrated Sarum Breviary, of which no entire edition has hitherto been printed since the year 1557... Of the valuable explanatory notes, as well as the learned introduction to this volume, we can only speak in terms of the very highest commendation."—*The Examiner.*

GREEK AND ENGLISH TESTAMENT,
in parallel Columns on the same page. Edited by J. SCHOLEFIELD, M.A. late Regius Professor of Greek in the University. Small Octavo. New Edition, with the Marginal References as arranged and revised by Dr SCRIVENER. Cloth, red edges. 7s. 6d.

GREEK AND ENGLISH TESTAMENT,
THE STUDENT'S EDITION of the above, on *large writing paper.* 4to. cloth. 12s.

GREEK TESTAMENT,
ex editione Stephani tertia, 1550. Small 8vo. 3s. 6d.

THE NEW TESTAMENT IN GREEK
according to the text followed in the Authorised Version, with the Variations adopted in the Revised Version. Edited by F. H. A. SCRIVENER, M.A., D.C.L., LL.D. Crown 8vo. 6s. Morocco boards or limp. 12s.

THE BOOK OF ECCLESIASTES,
With Notes and Introduction. By the Very Rev. E. H. PLUMPTRE, D.D., Dean of Wells. Large Paper Edition. Demy 8vo. 7s. 6d.

"No one can say that the Old Testament is a dull or worn-out subject after reading this singularly attractive and also instructive commentary. Its wealth of literary and historical illustration surpasses anything to which we can point in English exegesis of the Old Testament; indeed, even Delitzsch, whose pride it is to leave no source of illustration unexplored, is far inferior on this head to Dr Plumptre."—*Academy,* Sept. 10, 1881.

THE GOSPEL ACCORDING TO ST MATTHEW
in Anglo-Saxon and Northumbrian Versions, synoptically arranged: with Collations of the best Manuscripts. By J. M. KEMBLE, M.A. and Archdeacon HARDWICK. Demy 4to. 10s.

THE GOSPEL ACCORDING TO ST MARK
in Anglo-Saxon and Northumbrian Versions synoptically arranged: with Collations exhibiting all the Readings of all the MSS. Edited by the Rev. Professor SKEAT, M.A. late Fellow of Christ's College, and author of a MŒSO-GOTHIC Dictionary. Demy 4to. 10s.,

London: Cambridge Warehouse, 17 Paternoster Row.

PUBLICATIONS OF

THE GOSPEL ACCORDING TO ST LUKE, uniform with the preceding, edited by the Rev. Professor SKEAT. Demy 4to. 10s.

THE GOSPEL ACCORDING TO ST JOHN, uniform with the preceding, by the same Editor. Demy 4to. 10s.

"*The Gospel according to St John, in Anglo-Saxon and Northumbrian Versions*: Edited for the Syndics of the University Press, by the Rev. Walter W. Skeat, M.A., Elrington and Bosworth Professor of Anglo-Saxon in the University of Cambridge, completes an undertaking designed and commenced by that distinguished scholar, J. M. Kemble, some forty years ago. His was not himself permitted to execute his scheme: he died before it was completed for St Matthew. The edition of that Gospel was finished by Mr., subsequently Archdeacon, Hardwick. The remaining Gospels have had the good fortune to be edited by Professor Skeat, whose competency and zeal have left nothing undone to prove himself equal to his reputation, and to produce a work of the highest value to the student of Anglo-Saxon. The design was indeed worthy of its author. It is difficult to exaggerate the value of such a set of parallel texts. ... Of the particular volume now before us, we can only say it is worthy of its two predecessors. We repeat that the service rendered to the study of Anglo-Saxon by this Synoptic collection cannot easily be overstated."—*Contemporary Review.*

THE POINTED PRAYER BOOK, being the Book of Common Prayer with the Psalter or Psalms of David, pointed as they are to be sung or said in Churches. Royal 24mo. Cloth. 1s. 6d.

The same in square 32mo. cloth. 6d.

"The 'Pointed Prayer Book' deserves mention for the new and ingenious system on which the pointing has been marked, and still more for the terseness and clearness of the directions given for using it."—*Times.*

THE CAMBRIDGE PSALTER, for the use of Choirs and Organists. Specially adapted for Congregations in which the "Cambridge Pointed Prayer Book" is used. Demy 8vo. cloth extra, 3s. 6d. Cloth limp, cut flush. 2s. 6d.

THE PARAGRAPH PSALTER, arranged for the use of Choirs by BROOKE FOSS WESTCOTT, D.D., Canon of Peterborough, and Regius Professor of Divinity in the University of Cambridge. Fcap. 4to. 5s.

The same in royal 32mo. Cloth 1s. Leather 1s. 6d.

"The Paragraph Psalter exhibits all the care, thought, and learning that those acquainted with the works of the Regius Professor of Divinity at Cambridge would expect to find, and there is not a clergyman or organist in England who should be without this Psalter as a work of reference."—*Morning Post.*

THE MISSING FRAGMENT OF THE LATIN TRANSLATION OF THE FOURTH BOOK OF EZRA, discovered, and edited with an Introduction and Notes, and a facsimile of the MS., by ROBERT L. BENSLY, M.A., Sub-Librarian of the University Library, and Reader in Hebrew, Gonville and Caius College, Cambridge. Demy 4to. Cloth. 10s.

"Edited with true scholarly completeness."—*Westminster Review.*
"Wer sich je mit dem 4 Buche Esra eingehender beschäftigt hat, wird durch die obige, in jeder Beziehung musterhafte Publication in freudiges Erstaunen versetzt werden."—*Theologische Literaturzeitung.*
"It has been said of this book that it has added a new chapter to the Bible, and, starting as the statement may at first sight appear, it is no exaggeration of the actual fact, if by the Bible we understand that of the larger size which contains the Apocrypha, and if the Second Book of Esdras can be fairly called a part of the Apocrypha."—*Saturday Review.*

THEOLOGY—(ANCIENT).

THE PALESTINIAN MISHNA. By W. H. LOWE, M.A. Lecturer in Hebrew at Christ's College, Cambridge. [*In the Press.*

London: Cambridge Warehouse, 17 Paternoster Row.

SAYINGS OF THE JEWISH FATHERS,
comprising Pirqe Aboth and Pereq R. Meir in Hebrew and English, with Critical and Illustrative Notes. By CHARLES TAYLOR, D.D. Master of St John's College, Cambridge, and Honorary Fellow of King's College, London. Demy 8vo. cloth. 10s.

"The 'Masseketh Aboth' stands at the head of Hebrew non-canonical writings. It is of ancient date, claiming to contain the dicta of teachers who flourished from B.C. 200 to the same year of our era. The precise time of its compilation in its present form is, of course, in doubt. Mr Taylor's explanatory and illustrative commentary is very full and satisfactory."—*Spectator.*

"If we mistake not, this is the first precise translation into the English language accompanied by scholarly notes, of any portion of the Talmud. In other words, it is the first instance of that most valuable and neglected portion of Jewish literature being treated in the same way as a Greek classic in an ordinary critical edition... The Talmudic books, which have been so strangely neglected, we foresee will be the most important aids of the future for the proper understanding of the Bible... The *Sayings of the Jewish Fathers* may claim to be scholarly, and, moreover, of a scholarship unusually thorough and finished."—*Dublin University Magazine.*

"A careful and thorough edition which does credit to English scholarship, of a short treatise from the Mishna, containing a series of sentences or maxims ascribed mostly to Jewish teachers immediately preceding, or immediately following the Christian era..."—*Contemporary Review.*

THEODORE OF MOPSUESTIA'S COMMENTARY ON THE MINOR EPISTLES OF S. PAUL.
The Latin Version with the Greek Fragments, edited from the MSS. with Notes and an Introduction, by H. B. SWETE, D.D., Rector of Ashdon, Essex, and late Fellow of Gonville and Caius College, Cambridge. In Two Volumes. Vol. I., containing the Introduction, with Facsimiles of the MSS., and the Commentary upon Galatians—Colossians. Demy 8vo. 12s.

"In dem oben verzeichneten Buche liegt uns die erste Hälfte einer vollständigen, ebenso sorgfältig gearbeiteten wie schön ausgestatteten Ausgabe des Commentars mit ausführlichen Prolegomena und reichhaltigen kritischen und erläuternden Anmerkungen vor."—*Literarisches Centralblatt.*

"It is the result of thorough, careful, and patient investigation of all the points bearing on the subject, and the results are presented with admirable good sense and modesty. Mr Swete has prepared himself for his task by a serious study of the literature and history which are connected with it; and he has produced a volume of high value to the student, not merely of the theology of the fourth and fifth centuries, but of the effect of this theology on the later developments of doctrine and methods of interpretation, in the ages immediately following, and in the middle ages."—*Guardian.*

"Auf Grund dieser Quellen ist der Text bei Swete mit musterhafter Akribie hergestellt. Aber auch sonst hat der Herausgeber mit unermüdlichem Fleisse und eingehender Sachkenntniss sein Werk mit allen denjenigen Zugaben ausgerüstet, welche bei einer solchen Text-Ausgabe nur irgend erwartet werden können... Von den drei Haupthandschriften... sind vortreffliche photographische Facsimile's beigegeben, wie überhaupt das ganze Werk von der *University Press* zu Cambridge mit bekannter Eleganz ausgestattet ist."—*Theologische Literaturzeitung.*

"It is a hopeful sign, amid forebodings which arise about the theological learning of the Universities, that we have before us the first instalment of a thoroughly scientific and painstaking work, commenced at Cambridge and completed at a country rectory."—*Church Quarterly Review* (Jan. 1881).

"Herrn Swete's Leistung ist eine so tüchtige dass wir das Werk in keinen besseren Händen wissen möchten, und mit den sichersten Erwartungen auf das Gelingen der Fortsetzung entgegen sehen."—*Göttingische gelehrte Anzeigen* (Sept. 1881).

VOLUME II., containing the Commentary on 1 Thessalonians—Philemon, Appendices and Indices. 12s.

SANCTI IRENÆI EPISCOPI LUGDUNENSIS
libros quinque adversus Hæreses, versione Latina cum Codicibus Claromontano ac Arundeliano denuo collata, præmissa de placitis Gnosticorum prolusione, fragmenta necnon Græce, Syriace, Armeniace, commentatione perpetua et indicibus variis edidit W. WIGAN HARVEY, S.T.B. Collegii Regalis olim Socius. 2 Vols. Demy 8vo. 18s.

London: Cambridge Warehouse, 17 Paternoster Row.

PUBLICATIONS OF

M. MINUCII FELICIS OCTAVIUS.
The text newly revised from the original MS., with an English Commentary, Analysis, Introduction, and Copious Indices. Edited by H. A. HOLDEN, LL.D. Head Master of Ipswich School, late Fellow of Trinity College, Cambridge. Crown 8vo. 7s. 6d.

THEOPHILI EPISCOPI ANTIOCHENSIS LIBRI TRES AD AUTOLYCUM
edidit, Prolegomenis Versione Notulis Indicibus instruxit GULIELMUS GILSON HUMPHRY, S.T.B. Collegii Sanctiss. Trin. apud Cantabrigienses quondam Socius. Post 8vo. 5s.

THEOPHYLACTI IN EVANGELIUM S. MATTHÆI COMMENTARIUS,
edited by W. G. HUMPHRY, B.D. Prebendary of St Paul's, late Fellow of Trinity College. Demy 8vo. 7s. 6d.

TERTULLIANUS DE CORONA MILITIS, DE SPECTACULIS, DE IDOLOLATRIA,
with Analysis and English Notes, by GEORGE CURREY, D.D. Preacher at the Charter House, late Fellow and Tutor of St John's College Crown 8vo. 5s.

THEOLOGY—(ENGLISH).

WORKS OF ISAAC BARROW,
compared with the Original MSS., enlarged with Materials hitherto unpublished. A new Edition, by A. NAPIER, M.A. of Trinity College, Vicar of Holkham, Norfolk. 9 Vols. Demy 8vo. £3. 3s.

TREATISE OF THE POPE'S SUPREMACY,
and a Discourse concerning the Unity of the Church, by ISAAC BARROW. Demy 8vo. 7s. 6d.

PEARSON'S EXPOSITION OF THE CREED,
edited by TEMPLE CHEVALLIER, B.D. late Fellow and Tutor of St Catharine's College, Cambridge. New Edition. Revised by R. Sinker, B.D., Librarian of Trinity College. Demy 8vo. 12s.

"A new edition of Bishop Pearson's famous work *On the Creed* has just been issued by the Cambridge University Press. It is the well-known edition of Temple Chevallier, thoroughly overhauled by the Rev. R. Sinker, of Trinity College. The whole text and notes have been most carefully examined and corrected, and special pains have been taken to verify the almost innumerable references. These have been more clearly and accurately given in very many places, and the citations themselves have been adapted to the best and newest texts of the several authors— texts which have undergone vast improvements within the last two centuries. The Indices have also been revised and enlarged. ......Altogether this appears to be the most complete and convenient edition as yet published of a work which has long been recognised in all quarters as a standard one."— *Guardian.*

AN ANALYSIS OF THE EXPOSITION OF THE CREED
written by the Right Rev. JOHN PEARSON, D.D. late Lord Bishop of Chester, by W. H. MILL, D.D. late Regius Professor of Hebrew in the University of Cambridge. Demy 8vo. cloth. 5s.

London: Cambridge Warehouse, 17 *Paternoster Row.*

WHEATLY ON THE COMMON PRAYER,
edited by G. E. CORRIE, D.D. Master of Jesus College, Examining Chaplain to the late Lord Bishop of Ely. Demy 8vo. 7s. 6d.

CÆSAR MORGAN'S INVESTIGATION OF THE TRINITY OF PLATO,
and of Philo Judæus, and of the effects which an attachment to their writings had upon the principles and reasonings of the Fathers of the Christian Church. Revised by H. A. HOLDEN, LL.D. Head Master of Ipswich School, late Fellow of Trinity College, Cambridge. Crown 8vo. 4s.

TWO FORMS OF PRAYER OF THE TIME OF QUEEN ELIZABETH. Now First Reprinted. Demy 8vo. 6d.

"From 'Collections and Notes' 1867—1876, by W. Carew Hazlitt (p. 340), we learn that—'A very remarkable volume, in the original vellum cover, and containing 25 Forms of Prayer of the reign of Elizabeth, each with the autograph of Humphrey Dyson, has lately fallen into the hands of my friend Mr H. Pyne. It is mentioned specially in the Preface to the Parker Society's volume of Occasional Forms of Prayer, but it had been lost sight of for 200 years.' By the kindness of the present possessor of this valuable volume, containing in all 25 distinct publications, I am enabled to reprint in the following pages the two Forms of Prayer supposed to have been lost."—*Extract from the* PREFACE.

SELECT DISCOURSES,
by JOHN SMITH, late Fellow of Queens' College, Cambridge. Edited by H. G. WILLIAMS, B.D. late Professor of Arabic. Royal 8vo. 7s. 6d.

"The 'Select Discourses' of John Smith, collected and published from his papers after his death, are, in my opinion, much the most considerable work left to us by this Cambridge School [the Cambridge Platonists]. They have a right to a place in English literary history."—Mr MATTHEW ARNOLD, in the *Contemporary Review*.
"Of all the products of the Cambridge School, the 'Select Discourses' are perhaps the highest, as they are the most accessible and the most widely appreciated...and indeed no spiritually thoughtful mind can read them unmoved. They carry us so directly into an atmosphere of divine philosophy, luminous with the richest lights of meditative genius... He was one of those rare thinkers in whom largeness of view, and depth, and wealth of poetic and speculative insight, only served to evoke more fully the religious spirit, and while he drew the mould of his thought from St Paul."—Principal TULLOCH, *Rational Theology in England in the 17th Century*.
"We may instance Mr Henry Griffin Williams's revised edition of Mr John Smith's 'Select Discourses,' which have won Mr Matthew Arnold's admiration, as an example of worthy work for an University Press to undertake."—*Times*.

THE HOMILIES,
with Various Readings, and the Quotations from the Fathers given at length in the Original Languages. Edited by G. E. CORRIE, D.D. Master of Jesus College. Demy 8vo. 7s. 6d.

DE OBLIGATIONE CONSCIENTIÆ PRÆLECTIONES decem Oxonii in Schola Theologica habitæ a ROBERTO SANDERSON, SS. Theologiæ ibidem Professore Regio. With English Notes, including an abridged Translation, by W. WHEWELL, D.D. late Master of Trinity College. Demy 8vo. 7s. 6d.

London: Cambridge Warehouse, 17 Paternoster Row.

ARCHBISHOP USHER'S ANSWER TO A JESUIT, with other Tracts on Popery. Edited by J. SCHOLEFIELD, M.A. late Regius Professor of Greek in the University. Demy 8vo. 7s. 6d.

WILSON'S ILLUSTRATION OF THE METHOD of explaining the New Testament, by the early opinions of Jews and Christians concerning Christ. Edited by T. TURTON, D.D. late Lord Bishop of Ely. Demy 8vo. 5s.

LECTURES ON DIVINITY delivered in the University of Cambridge, by JOHN HEY, D.D. Third Edition, revised by T. TURTON, D.D. late Lord Bishop of Ely. 2 vols. Demy 8vo. 15s.

ARABIC, SANSKRIT AND SYRIAC.

POEMS OF BEHÁ ED DÍN ZOHEIR OF EGYPT. With a Metrical Translation, Notes and Introduction, by E. H. PALMER, M.A., Barrister-at-Law of the Middle Temple, Lord Almoner's Professor of Arabic and Fellow of St John's College in the University of Cambridge. 3 vols, Crown 4to.
Vol. I. The ARABIC TEXT. 10s. 6d.; Cloth extra. 15s.
Vol. II. ENGLISH TRANSLATION. 10s. 6d.; Cloth extra. 15s.

"Professor Palmer's activity in advancing Arabic scholarship has formerly shown itself in the production of his excellent Arabic Grammar, and his Descriptive Catalogue of Arabic MSS. in the Library of Trinity College, Cambridge. He has now produced an admirable text, which illustrates in a remarkable manner the flexibility and graces of the language he loves so well, and of which he seems to be perfect master.... The Syndicate of Cambridge University must not pass without the recognition of their liberality in bringing out, in a worthy form, so important an Arabic text. It is not the first time that Oriental scholarship has thus been wisely subsidised by Cambridge."—*Indian Mail*.

"It is impossible to quote this edition without an expression of admiration for the perfection to which Arabic typography has been brought in England in this magnificent Oriental work, the production of which redounds to the imperishable credit of the University of Cambridge. It may be pronounced one of the most beautiful Oriental books that have ever been printed in Europe: and the learning of the Editor worthily rivals the technical get-up of the creations of the soul of one of the most tasteful poets of Islâm, the study of which will contribute not a little to save honour of the poetry of the Arabs.— MYTHOLOGY AMONG THE HEBREWS (*Engl. Transl.*), p. 194.
"For ease and facility, for variety of metre, for imitation, either designed or unconscious, of the style of several of our own poets, these versions deserve high praise, ... We have no hesitation in saying that in both Prof. Palmer has made an addition to Oriental literature for which scholars should be grateful; and that, while his knowledge of Arabic is a sufficient guarantee for his mastery of the original, his English compositions are distinguished by versatility, command of language, rhythmical cadence, and, as we have remarked, by not unskilful imitations of the styles of several of our own favourite poets, living and dead."—*Saturday Review*.
"This sumptuous edition of the poems of Behá-ed-dín Zoheir is a very welcome addition to the small series of Eastern poets accessible to readers who are not Orientalists. ... In all there is that exquisite finish of which Arabic poetry is susceptible in so rare a degree. The form is almost always beautiful, be the thought what it may. But this, of course, can only be fully appreciated by Orientalists. And this brings us to the translation. It is excellently well done. Mr Palmer has tried to imitate the fall of the original in his selection of the English metre for the various pieces, and thus contrives to convey a faint idea of the graceful flow of the Arabic. ...... Altogether the inside of the book is worthy of the beautiful arabesque binding that rejoices the eye of the lover of Arab art."—*Academy*.

THE CHRONICLE OF JOSHUA THE STYLITE, composed in Syriac A.D. 507 with an English translation and notes, by W. WRIGHT, LL.D., Professor of Arabic. Demy 8vo. cloth. 10s. 6d.

London: Cambridge Warehouse, 17 Paternoster Row.

NALOPÀKHYÁNAM, OR, THE TALE OF NALA;
containing the Sanskrit Text in Roman Characters, followed by a
Vocabulary in which each word is placed under its root, with references
to derived words in Cognate Languages, and a sketch of Sanskrit
Grammar. By the late Rev. THOMAS JARRETT, M.A. Trinity College,
Regius Professor of Hebrew, late Professor of Arabic, and formerly
Fellow of St Catharine's College, Cambridge. Demy 8vo. 10s.

NOTES ON THE TALE OF NALA,
for the use of Classical Students, by J. PEILE, M.A. Fellow and Tutor
of Christ's College. Demy 8vo. 12s.

GREEK AND LATIN CLASSICS, &c. (See also pp. 24—27.)

A SELECTION OF GREEK INSCRIPTIONS,
With Introductions and Annotations by E. S. ROBERTS, M.A.
Fellow and Tutor of Caius College. [*Preparing.*

THE AGAMEMNON OF AESCHYLUS.
With a Translation in English Rhythm, and Notes Critical and Explanatory. **New Edition Revised.** By BENJAMIN HALL KENNEDY,
D.D., Regius Professor of Greek. Crown 8vo. cloth. 6s.

"One of the best editions of the masterpiece of Greek tragedy."—*Athenæum.*
"It is needless to multiply proofs of the value of this volume alike to the poetical translator, the critical scholar, and the ethical student. We must be contented to thank Professor Kennedy for his admirable execution of a great undertaking."—*Sat. Rev.*
"Let me say that I think it a most admirable piece of the highest criticism..... I like

your Preface extremely; it is just to the point."—*Professor Paley.*
"Professor Kennedy has conferred a boon on all teachers of the Greek classics, by causing the substance of his lectures at Cambridge on the Agamemnon of Æschylus to be published...This edition of the Agamemnon is one which no classical master should be without."—*Examiner.*

THE ŒDIPUS TYRANNUS OF SOPHOCLES by
the same Editor. Crown 8vo. Cloth 6s.

"Dr Kennedy's edition of the *Œdipus Tyrannus* is a worthy companion to his *Agamemnon*, and we may say at once that no more valuable contribution to the study of Sophocles has appeared of late years. Besides the text and notes, the volume contains a most interesting introduction to and analysis of the play, a rhythmical trans-

lation, and three indices. The first of these consists of a list of words and phrases either uncommon in themselves, or employed in unusual ways; in the second we find various particles as exhibited in the play; while the third gives valuable information on grammatical points as illustrated by the usage of Sophocles."—*Saturday Review.*

THE THEÆTETUS OF PLATO by the same Editor.
Crown 8vo. Cloth. 7s. 6d.

PLATO'S PHÆDO,
literally translated, by the late E. M. COPE, Fellow of Trinity College,
Cambridge. Demy 8vo. 5s.

ARISTOTLE.—ΠΕΡΙ ΔΙΚΑΙΟΣΤΝΗΣ.
THE FIFTH BOOK OF THE NICOMACHEAN ETHICS OF
ARISTOTLE. Edited by HENRY JACKSON, M.A., Fellow of Trinity
College, Cambridge. Demy 8vo. cloth. 6s.

"It is not too much to say that some of the points he discusses have never had so much light thrown upon them before...."
Scholars will hope that this is not the only portion of the Aristotelian writings which he is likely to edit."—*Athenæum.*

ARISTOTLE'S PSYCHOLOGY,
with a Translation, Critical and Explanatory Notes, by EDWIN
WALLACE, M.A., Fellow and Tutor of Worcester College, Oxford.
Demy 8vo. cloth. 18s.

London: Cambridge Warehouse, 17 *Paternoster Row.*

1—5

ARISTOTLE.

THE RHETORIC. With a Commentary by the late E. M. COPE, Fellow of Trinity College, Cambridge, revised and edited by J. E. SANDYS, M.A., Fellow and Tutor of St John's College, Cambridge, and Public Orator. With a biographical Memoir by H. A. J. MUNRO, M.A. Three Volumes, Demy 8vo. £1. 11s. 6d.

"This work is in many ways creditable to the University of Cambridge. And while it must ever be regretted that a work so laborious should not have received the last touches of its author, the warmest admiration is due to Mr Sandys, for the manly, unselfish, and unflinching spirit in which he has performed his most difficult and delicate task. If an English student wishes to have a full conception of what is contained in the *Rhetoric* of Aristotle, to Mr Cope's edition he must go."—*Academy.*

"Mr Sandys has performed his arduous duties with marked ability and admirable tact . . . . . . In every part of his work —revising, supplementing, and completing— he has done exceedingly well."—*Examiner.*

PRIVATE ORATIONS OF DEMOSTHENES, with Introductions and English Notes, by F. A. PALEY, M.A. Editor of Aeschylus, etc. and J. E. SANDYS, M.A. Fellow and Tutor of St John's College, and Public Orator in the University of Cambridge.

PART I. Contra Phormionem, Lacritum, Pantaenetum, Boeotum de Nomine, Boeotum de Dote, Dionysodorum. Crown 8vo. cloth. 6s.

"Mr Paley's scholarship is sound and accurate, his experience of editing wide, and if he is content to devote his learning and abilities to the production of such manuals as these, they will be received with gratitude throughout the higher schools of the country. Mr Sandys is deeply read in the German literature which bears upon his author, and the elucidation of matters of daily life, in the delineation of which Demosthenes is so rich, obtains full justice at his hands. . . . . We hope this edition may lead the way to a more general study of these speeches in schools than has hitherto been possible."—*Academy.*

PART II. Pro Phormione, Contra Stephanum I. II.; Nicostratum, Cononem, Calliclem. 7s. 6d.

"To give even a brief sketch of these speeches (*Pro Phormione* and *Contra Stephanum*) would be incompatible with our limits, though we can hardly conceive a task more useful to the classical or professional scholar than to make one for himself. . . . . It is a great boon to those who set themselves to unravel the thread of arguments pro and con to have the aid of Mr Sandys's excellent running commentary . . . . and no one can say that he is ever deficient in the needful help which enables us to form a sound estimate of the rights of the case. . . . . It is long since we have come upon a work evincing more pains, scholarship, and varied research and illustration than Mr Sandys's contribution to the 'Private Orations of Demosthenes'."—*Sat. Rev.*

". . . . the edition reflects credit on Cambridge scholarship, and ought to be extensively used."—*Athenæum.*

DEMOSTHENES AGAINST ANDROTION AND AGAINST TIMOCRATES, with Introductions and English Commentary, by WILLIAM WAYTE, M.A., late Professor of Greek, University College, London, Formerly Fellow of King's College, Cambridge, and Assistant Master at Eton. [*In the Press.*

PINDAR.

OLYMPIAN AND PYTHIAN ODES. With Notes Explanatory and Critical, Introductions and Introductory Essays. Edited by C. A. M. FENNELL, M.A., late Fellow of Jesus College. Crown 8vo. cloth. 9s.

"Mr Fennell deserves the thanks of all classical students for his careful and scholarly edition of the Olympian and Pythian odes. He brings to his task the necessary enthusiasm for his author, great industry, a sound judgment, and, in particular, copious and minute learning in comparative philology. To his qualifications in this last respect every page bears witness."—*Athenæum.*

"Considered simply as a contribution to the study and criticism of Pindar, Mr Fennell's edition is a work of great merit. But it has a wider interest, as exemplifying the change which has come over the methods and aims of Cambridge scholarship within the last ten or twelve years. . . . Altogether, this edition is a welcome and wholesome sign of the vitality and development of Cambridge scholarship, and we are glad to see that it is to be continued."—*Saturday Review.*

THE NEMEAN AND ISTHMIAN ODES. [*In the Press.*

London: Cambridge Warehouse, 17 Paternoster Row.

THE BACCHAE OF EURIPIDES.

with Introduction, Critical Notes, and Archæological Illustrations, by J. E. SANDYS, M.A., Fellow and Tutor of St John's College, Cambridge, and Public Orator. Crown 8vo cloth. 10s. 6d.

"Of the present edition of the *Bacchae* by Mr Sandys we may safely say that never before has a Greek play, in England at least, had fuller justice done to its critical, interpretation, and archæological illustration, whether for the young student or the more advanced scholar. The Cambridge Public Orator may be said to have taken the lead in issuing a complete edition of a Greek play, which is destined perhaps to gain redoubled favour now that the study of ancient monuments has been applied to its illustration."—*Saturday Review.*

"Mr Sandys has done well by his poet and by his University. He has given a most welcome gift to scholars both at home and abroad. The illustrations are aptly chosen and delicately executed, and the *apparatus criticus*, in the way both of notes and indices is very complete."—*Notes and Queries.*

"The volume is interspersed with well-executed woodcuts, and its general attractiveness of form reflects great credit on the University Press. In the notes Mr Sandys has more than sustained his well-earned reputation as a careful and learned editor, and shows considerable advance in freedom and lightness of style..... Under such circumstances it is superfluous to say that for the purposes of teachers and advanced students this handsome edition far surpasses all its predecessors. The volume will add to the already wide popularity of a unique drama, and must be reckoned among the most important classical publications of the year."—*Athenaeum.*

"This edition of a Greek play deserves more than the passing notice accorded to ordinary school editions of the classics. It has not, like so many such books, been hastily produced to meet the momentary need of some particular examination; but it has employed for some years the labour and thought of a highly finished scholar, whose aim seems to have been that his book should go forth *totus teres atque rotundus*, armed at all points with all that may throw light upon its subject. The result is a work which will not only assist the schoolboy or undergraduate in his tasks, but will adorn the library of the scholar.".. "The description of the woodcuts abounds in interesting and suggestive information upon various points of ancient art, and is a further instance of the very thorough as well as scholarlike manner in which Mr Sandys deals with his subject at every point. The commentary (pp. 87—240) bears the same stamp of thoroughness and high finish as the rest of the work. While questions of technical grammar receive due attention, textual criticism, philology, history, antiquities, and elucidation of the poet's meaning. We must leave our readers to use and appreciate for themselves Mr Sandys' assistance."—*The Guardian.*

LECTURES ON THE TYPES OF GREEK COINS.

By PERCY GARDNER, M.A., Disney Professor of Archæology. Royal 4to. *[In the Press.*

M. TULLI CICERONIS DE FINIBUS BONORUM ET MALORUM LIBRI QUINQUE.

The text revised and explained; With a Translation by JAMES S. REID, M.L., Fellow and Assistant Tutor of Gonville and Caius College. *[In the Press.*

M. T. CICERONIS DE OFFICIIS LIBRI TRES,

with Marginal Analysis, an English Commentary, and copious Indices, by H. A. HOLDEN, LL.D. Head Master of Ipswich School, late Fellow of Trinity College, Cambridge, Classical Examiner to the University of London. **Fourth Edition.** Revised and considerably enlarged. Crown 8vo. 9s.

"Dr Holden truly states that 'Text, Analysis, and Commentary in this third edition have been again subjected to a thorough revision.' It is new entirely the best edition extant.... The Introduction (after Heine) and notes leave nothing to be desired in point of fulness, accuracy, and neatness; the typographical execution will satisfy the most fastidious eye."—*Notes and Queries.*

"Dr Holden has issued an edition of what is perhaps the easiest and most popular of Cicero's philosophical works, the *de Officiis*, which, especially in the form which it has now assumed after two most thorough revisions, leaves little or nothing to be desired in the fullness and accuracy of its treatment alike of the matter and the language."—*Academy.*

London: Cambridge Warehouse, 17 *Paternoster Row.*

PUBLICATIONS OF

M. TULLII CICERONIS DE NATURA DEORUM

Libri Tres, with Introduction and Commentary by JOSEPH B. MAYOR, M.A., Professor of Moral Philosophy at King's College, London, formerly Fellow and Tutor of St John's College, Cambridge, together with a new collation of several of the English MSS. by J. H. SWAINSON, M.A., formerly Fellow of Trinity Coll., Cambridge. Vol. I. Demy 8vo. 10s. 6d. [Vol. II. *In the Press.*

"Such editions as that of which Prof. Mayor has given us the first instalment will doubtless do much to remedy this undeserved neglect. It is one on which great pains and much learning have evidently been expended, and is in every way admirably suited to meet the needs of the student.... The notes of the editor are all that could be expected from his well-known learning and scholarship..... It is needless, therefore, to say that all points of syntax or of Ciceronian usage which present themselves have been treated with full mastery..... The thanks of many students will doubtless be given to Prof. Mayor for the amount of historical and biographical information afforded in the commentary, which is, as it should be, supplemented and not replaced by references to the usual authorities."—*Academy.*

P. VERGILI MARONIS OPERA

cum Prolegomenis et Commentario Critico pro Syndicis Preli Academici edidit BENJAMIN HALL KENNEDY, S.T.P., Graecae Linguae Professor Regius. Extra Fcap. 8vo. cloth. 5s.

MATHEMATICS, PHYSICAL SCIENCE, &c.

MATHEMATICAL AND PHYSICAL PAPERS.

By Sir W. THOMSON, LL.D., D.C.L., F.R.S., Professor of Natural Philosophy, in the University of Glasgow. Collected from different Scientific Periodicals from May 1841, to the present time.
[*Nearly ready.*

MATHEMATICAL AND PHYSICAL PAPERS,

By GEORGE GABRIEL STOKES, M.A., D.C.L., LL.D., F.R.S., Fellow of Pembroke College, and Lucasian Professor of Mathematics in the University of Cambridge. Reprinted from the Original Journals and Transactions, with Additional Notes by the Author. Vol. I. Demy 8vo. cloth. 15s.

"The volume of Professor Stokes's papers contains much more than his hydrodynamical papers. The undulatory theory of light is treated, and the difficulties connected with its application to certain phenomena, such as aberration, are carefully examined and resolved. Such difficulties are commonly passed over with scant notice in the text-books...; Those to whom difficulties like these are real stumbling-blocks will still turn for enlightenment to Professor Stokes's old, but still fresh and still necessary, dissertations. There nothing is slurred over, nothing extenuated. We learn exactly the weaknesses of the theory, and the direction in which the completer theory of the future must be sought for. The same spirit pervades the papers on pure mathematics which are included in the volume. They have a severe accuracy of style which well befits the subtle nature of the subjects, and inspires the completest confidence in their author."—*The Times.*

Vol. II. *Nearly ready.*

THE SCIENTIFIC PAPERS OF THE LATE PROF. J. CLERK MAXWELL.

Edited by W. D. NIVEN, M.A. In 2 vols. Royal 4to. [*In the Press.*

A TREATISE ON NATURAL PHILOSOPHY.

By Sir W. THOMSON, LL.D., D.C.L., F.R.S., Professor of Natural Philosophy in the University of Glasgow, and P. G. TAIT, M.A., Professor of Natural Philosophy in the University of Edinburgh. Vol. I. Part I. Demy 8vo. 16s.

"In this, the second edition, we notice a large amount of new matter, the importance of which is such that any opinion which we could form within the time at our disposal would be utterly inadequate."—*Nature.*

Part II. *In the Press.*

London: Cambridge Warehouse, 17 Paternoster Row.

ELEMENTS OF NATURAL PHILOSOPHY.
By Professors Sir W. THOMSON and P. G. TAIT. Part I. Demy 8vo. cloth. *Second Edition.* 9s.

"This work is designed especially for the use of schools and junior classes in the Universities, the mathematical methods being limited almost without exception to those of the most elementary geometry, algebra, and trigonometry. Tiros in Natural Philosophy cannot be better directed than by being told to give their diligent attention to an intelligent digestion of the contents of this excellent *vade mecum.*"—*Iron.*

A TREATISE ON THE THEORY OF DETERMINANTS AND THEIR APPLICATIONS IN ANALYSIS AND GEOMETRY, by ROBERT FORSYTH SCOTT, M.A., of St John's College, Cambridge. Demy 8vo. 12s.

"This able and comprehensive treatise will be welcomed by the student as bringing within his reach the results of many important researches on this subject which have hitherto been for the most part inaccessible to him. . . . It would be presumptuous on the part of any one less learned in the literature of the subject than Mr Scott to express an opinion as to the amount of his own research contained in this work, but all will appreciate the skill with which the results of his industrious reading have been arranged into this interesting treatise."—*Athenæum.*

HYDRODYNAMICS,
A Treatise on the Mathematical Theory of the Motion of Fluids, by HORACE LAMB, M.A., formerly Fellow of Trinity College, Cambridge; Professor of Mathematics in the University of Adelaide. Demy 8vo. 12s.

THE ANALYTICAL THEORY OF HEAT,
By JOSEPH FOURIER. Translated, with Notes, by A. FREEMAN, M.A. Fellow of St John's College, Cambridge. Demy 8vo. 16s.

"It is time that Fourier's masterpiece, *The Analytical Theory of Heat,* translated by Mr Alex. Freeman, should be introduced to those English students of Mathematics who do not follow with freedom a treatise in any language but their own. It is a model of mathematical reasoning applied to physical phenomena, and is remarkable for the ingenuity of the analytical process employed by the author."—*Contemporary Review,* October, 1878.
"There cannot be two opinions as to the value and importance of the *Théorie de la Chaleur.* It has been called 'an exquisite mathematical poem,' not once but many times, independently, by mathematicians of different schools. Many of the very greatest of modern mathematicians regard it, justly, as the key which first opened to them the treasure-house of mathematical physics. It is still *the* text-book of Heat Conduction, and there seems little present prospect of its being superseded, though it is already more than half a century old."—*Nature.*

THE ELECTRICAL RESEARCHES OF THE HONOURABLE HENRY CAVENDISH, F.R.S.
Written between 1771 and 1781, Edited from the original manuscripts in the possession of the Duke of Devonshire, K.G., by J. CLERK MAXWELL, F.R.S. Demy 8vo. cloth. 18s.

"This work, which derives a melancholy interest from the lamented death of the editor following so closely upon its publication, is a valuable addition to the history of electrical research. ... The papers themselves are most carefully reproduced, with fac-similes of the author's sketches of experimental apparatus.
. . . Every department of editorial duty appears to have been most conscientiously performed; and it must have been no small satisfaction to Prof. Maxwell to see this goodly volume completed before his life's work was done."—*Athenæum.*

AN ELEMENTARY TREATISE ON QUATERNIONS,
By P. G. TAIT, M.A., Professor of Natural Philosophy in the University of Edinburgh. *Second Edition.* Demy 8vo. 14s.

London: Cambridge Warehouse, 17 *Paternoster Row.*

PUBLICATIONS OF

A TREATISE ON THE PHYSIOLOGY OF PLANTS,
by S. H. VINES, M.A., Fellow of Christ's College. [*In the Press.*

THE MATHEMATICAL WORKS OF ISAAC BARROW, D.D.
Edited by W. WHEWELL, D.D. Demy 8vo. 7s. 6d.

COUNTERPOINT.
A Practical Course of Study, by Professor G. A. MACFARREN, M.A., Mus. Doc. Third Edition, revised. Demy 4to. cloth. 7s. 6d.

ASTRONOMICAL OBSERVATIONS
made at the Observatory of Cambridge by the Rev. JAMES CHALLIS, M.A., F.R.S., F.R.A.S., Plumian Professor of Astronomy and Experimental Philosophy in the University of Cambridge, and Fellow of Trinity College. For various Years, from 1846 to 1860.

ASTRONOMICAL OBSERVATIONS
from 1861 to 1865. Vol. XXI. Royal 4to. cloth. 15s.

A CATALOGUE OF THE COLLECTION OF BIRDS
formed by the late HUGH EDWIN STRICKLAND, now in the possession of the University of Cambridge. By OSBERT SALVIN, M.A., F.R.S., &c. Strickland Curator in the University of Cambridge. Demy 8vo. £1. 1s.

A CATALOGUE OF AUSTRALIAN FOSSILS
(including Tasmania and the Island of Timor), Stratigraphically and Zoologically arranged, by ROBERT ETHERIDGE, Jun., F.G.S., Acting Palæontologist, H.M. Geol. Survey of Scotland, (formerly Assistant-Geologist, Geol. Survey of Victoria). Demy 8vo. cloth. 10s. 6d.
"The work is arranged with great clearness, and contains a full list of the books and papers consulted by the author, and an index to the genera."—*Saturday Review.*

ILLUSTRATIONS OF COMPARATIVE ANATOMY, VERTEBRATE AND INVERTEBRATE,
for the Use of Students in the Museum of Zoology and Comparative Anatomy. Second Edition. Demy 8vo. cloth. 2s. 6d.

A SYNOPSIS OF THE CLASSIFICATION OF THE BRITISH PALÆOZOIC ROCKS,
by the Rev. ADAM SEDGWICK, M.A., F.R.S., and FREDERICK M^cCOY, F.G.S. One vol., Royal 4to. Plates, £1. 1s.

A CATALOGUE OF THE COLLECTION OF CAMBRIAN AND SILURIAN FOSSILS
contained in the Geological Museum of the University of Cambridge, by J. W. SALTER, F.G.S. With a Portrait of PROFESSOR SEDGWICK. Royal 4to. cloth. 7s. 6d.

CATALOGUE OF OSTEOLOGICAL SPECIMENS
contained in the Anatomical Museum of the University of Cambridge. Demy 8vo. 2s. 6d.

London: Cambridge Warehouse, 17 Paternoster Row.

LAW.
AN ANALYSIS OF CRIMINAL LIABILITY.
By E. C. CLARK, LL.D., Regius Professor of Civil Law in the University of Cambridge, also of Lincoln's Inn, Barrister at Law. Crown 8vo. cloth. 7s. 6d.

"Prof Clark's little book is the substance of lectures delivered by him upon those portions of Austin's work on jurisprudence which deal with the 'operation of sanctions'... Students of Jurisprudence will find much to interest and instruct them in the work of Prof. Clark." *Athenaeum.*

A SELECTION OF THE STATE TRIALS.
By J. W. WILLIS-BUND, M.A., LL.B., Barrister-at-Law, Professor of Constitutional Law and History, University College, London. Vol. I. Trials for Treason (1327—1660). Crown 8vo. cloth, 18s.

"A great and good service has been done to a students of history, and especially to those of them who look to it to a legal aspect, by Prof. J. W. Willis-Bund in the publication of a *Selection of Cases from the State Trials*.... Professor Willis-Bund has been very careful to give such selections from the State Trials as will best illustrate those points in what may be called the growth of the Law of Treason which he wishes to bring clearly under the notice of the student, and the result is, that there is not a page in the book which has not its own lesson.... In all respects, so far as we have been able to test it, this book is admirably done."—*Scotsman.*

"Mr Willis-Bund has edited 'A Selection of Cases from the State Trials' which is likely to form a very valuable addition to the standard literature... There can be no doubt, therefore, of the interest that can be found in the State trials. But they are large and unwieldy, and it is impossible for the general reader to come across them. Mr Willis-Bund has therefore done good service in making a selection that is in the first volume reduced to a commodious form."—*The Examiner.*

"This work is a very useful contribution to that important branch of the constitutional history of England which is concerned with the growth and development of the law of treason, as it may be gathered from trials before the ordinary courts The author has very wisely distinguished these cases from those of impeachment for treason before Parliament, which he proposes to treat in a future volume under the general head 'Proceedings in Parliament.'"—*The Academy.*

"This is a work of such obvious utility that the only wonder is that no one should have undertaken it before.... in many respects therefore, although the trials are more or less abridged, this is for the ordinary student's purpose not only a more handy, but a more useful work than Howell's."—*Saturday Review.*

"Within the boards of this useful and handy book the student will find everything he can desire in the way of lists of cases given at length or referred to, and the statutes bearing on the text arranged chronologically. The work of selecting from Howell's bulky series of volumes has been done with much judgment, merely curious cases being excluded, and all included so treated as to illustrate some important point of constitutional law."—*Glasgow Herald.*

"Mr Bund's object is not the romance, but the constitutional and legal bearings of that great series of *causes célèbres* which in unfortunately not within easy reach of readers not happy enough to possess valuable libraries.... Of the importance of this subject, or of the want of a book of this kind, referring not vaguely but precisely to the grounds of constitutional doctrines, both of past and present times, no reader of history can feel any doubt."—*Daily News.*

VOL. II. In two parts. Price 14s. each.
Vol. III. *In the Press.*

THE FRAGMENTS OF THE PERPETUAL EDICT OF SALVIUS JULIANUS,
collected, arranged, and annotated by BRYAN WALKER, M.A. LL.D., Law Lecturer of St John's College, and late Fellow of Corpus Christi College, Cambridge. Crown 8vo., Cloth, Price 6s.

"This is one of the latest, we believe quite the latest, of the contributions made to legal scholarship by that revived study of the Roman Law at Cambridge which is now so marked a feature in the industrial life of the University.... In the present book we have the fruits of the same kind of thorough and well-ordered study which was brought to bear upon the notes to the Commentaries and the Institutes... Hitherto the Edict has been almost inaccessible to the ordinary English student, and such a student will be interested as well as perhaps surprised to find how abundantly the extant fragments illustrate and clear up points which have attracted his attention in the Commentaries, or the Institutes, or the Digest."—*Law Times.*

London: Cambridge Warehouse, 17 *Paternoster Row.*

THE COMMENTARIES OF GAIUS AND RULES OF ULPIAN. (New Edition, revised and enlarged.)

With a Translation and Notes, by J. T. ABDY, LL.D., Judge of County Courts, late Regius Professor of Laws in the University of Cambridge, and BRYAN WALKER, M.A., LL.D., Law Lecturer of St John's College, Cambridge, formerly Law Student of Trinity Hall and Chancellor's Medallist for Legal Studies. Crown 8vo. 16*s*.

"As scholars and as editors Messrs Abdy and Walker have done their work well. . . . . For one thing the editors deserve special commendation. They have presented Gaius to the reader with few notes and those merely by way of reference or necessary explanation. Thus the Roman jurist is allowed to speak for himself, and the reader feels that he is really studying Roman law in the original, and not a fanciful representation of it."—*Athenæum*.

THE INSTITUTES OF JUSTINIAN,

translated with Notes by J. T. ABDY, LL.D., Judge of County Courts, late Regius Professor of Laws in the University of Cambridge, and formerly Fellow of Trinity Hall; and BRYAN WALKER, M.A., LL.D., Law Lecturer of St John's College, Cambridge; late Fellow and Lecturer of Corpus Christi College; and formerly Law Student of Trinity Hall. Crown 8vo. 16*s*.

"We welcome here a valuable contribution to the study of jurisprudence. The text of the *Institutes* is occasionally perplexing, even to practised scholars, whose knowledge of classical models does not always avail them in dealing with the technicalities of legal phraseology. Nor can the ordinary dictionaries be expected to furnish all the help that is wanted. This translation will then be of great use. To the. ordinary student, whose attention is distracted from the subject-matter by the difficulty of struggling through the language in which it is contained, it will be almost indispensable."—*Spectator*.
"The notes are learned and carefully compiled, and this edition will be found useful to students."—*Law Times*.
"Dr Abdy and Dr Walker have produced a book which is both elegant and useful."—*Athenæum*.

SELECTED TITLES FROM THE DIGEST,

annotated by B. WALKER, M.A., LL.D. Part I. Mandati vel Contra. Digest XVII. 1. Crown 8vo. Cloth. 5*s*.

"This small volume is published as an experiment. The author proposes to publish an annotated edition and translation of several books of the Digest if this one is received with favour. We are pleased to be able to say that Mr Walker deserves credit for the way in which he has performed the task undertaken. The translation, as might be expected, is scholarly." *Law Times*.

Part II. De Adquirendo rerum dominio and De Adquirenda vel amittenda possessione. Digest XLI. 1 and 11. Crown 8vo. Cloth. 6*s*.

Part III. De Condictionibus. Digest XII. 1 and 4—7 and Digest XIII. 1—3. Crown 8vo. Cloth. 6*s*.

GROTIUS DE JURE BELLI ET PACIS,

with the Notes of Barbeyrac and others; accompanied by an abridged Translation of the Text, by W. WHEWELL, D.D. late Master of Trinity College. 3 Vols. Demy 8vo. 12*s*. The translation separate, 6*s*.

London: Cambridge Warehouse, 17 *Paternoster Row.*

HISTORY.

THE GROWTH OF ENGLISH INDUSTRY AND COMMERCE,
by W. CUNNINGHAM, M.A., late Deputy to the Knightbridge Professor in the University of Cambridge. With Maps and Charts. Crown 8vo. Cloth. 12s.

"He is, however, undoubtedly sound in the main, and his work deserves recognition as the result of immense industry and research in a field in which the labourers have hitherto been comparatively few."—*Scotsman*, April 14, 1882.

LIFE AND TIMES OF STEIN, OR GERMANY AND PRUSSIA IN THE NAPOLEONIC AGE,
by J. R. SEELEY, M.A., Regius Professor of Modern History in the University of Cambridge, with Portraits and Maps. 3 Vols. Demy 8vo. 48s.

"If we could conceive anything similar to a protective system in the intellectual department, we might perhaps look forward to a time when our historians would raise the cry of protection for native industry. Of the unquestionably greatest German men of modern history—I speak of Frederick the Great, Goethe and Stein—the first two found long since in Carlyle and Lewes biographers who have undoubtedly driven their German competitors out of the field. And now in the year just past Professor Seeley of Cambridge has presented us with a biography of Stein which, though it modestly declines competition with German works and disowns the presumption of teaching us Germans our own history, yet casts into the shade by its brilliant superiority all that we have ourselves hitherto written about Stein.... In five long chapters Seeley expounds the legislative and administrative reforms, the emancipation of free administration and free trade, in short the foundation of modern Prussia, with more exhaustive thoroughness, with more penetrating insight, than any one had done before."—*Deutsche Rundschau*.

"Dr Busch's volume has made people think and talk even more than usual of Prince Bismarck, and Professor Seeley's very learned work on Stein will turn attention to an earlier and an almost equally eminent German statesman...... It is soothing to the national self-respect to find a few Englishmen, such as the late Mr Lewes and Professor Seeley, doing for German as well as English readers what many German scholars have done for us."—*Times*.

"In a notice of this kind scant justice can be done to a work like the one before us; no short résumé can give even the most meagre notion of the contents of these volumes, which contain no page that is superfluous, and none that is uninteresting..... To understand the Germany of to-day one must study the Germany of many yesterdays, and now that study has been made easy by this work, to which no one can hesitate to assign a very high place among those recent histories which have aimed at original research."—*Athenæum*.

"The book before us fills an important gap in English—nay, European—historical literature, and bridges over the history of Prussia from the time of Frederick the Great to the days of Kaiser Wilhelm. It thus gives the reader standing ground whence he may regard contemporary events in Germany in their proper historic light..... We congratulate Cambridge and her Professor of History on the appearance of such a noteworthy production. And we may add that it is something upon which we may congratulate England that on the especial field of the Germans, history, on the history of their own country, by the use of their own literary weapons, an Englishman has produced a history of Germany in the Napoleonic age far superior to any that exists in German."—*Examiner*.

THE UNIVERSITY OF CAMBRIDGE FROM THE EARLIEST TIMES TO THE ROYAL INJUNCTIONS OF 1535,
by JAMES BASS MULLINGER, M.A. Demy 8vo. cloth (734 pp.), 12s.

"We trust Mr Mullinger will yet continue his history and bring it down to our own day."—*Academy*.

"He has brought together a mass of instructive details respecting the rise and progress, not only of his own University, but of all the principal Universities of the Middle Ages...... We hope some day that he may continue his labours, and give us a history of the University during the troublous times of the Reformation and the Civil War."—*Athenæum*.

"Mr Mullinger's work is one of great learning and research, which can hardly fail to become a standard book of reference on the subject.... We can most strongly recommend this book to our readers."—*Spectator*.

VOL. II. *In the Press.*

London: Cambridge Warehouse, 17 Paternoster Row.

CHRONOLOGICAL TABLES OF GREEK HISTORY.

Accompanied by a short narrative of events, with references to the sources of information and extracts from the ancient authorities, by CARL PETER. Translated from the German by G. CHAWNER, M.A., Fellow and Lecturer of King's College, Cambridge. Demy 4to. 10s.

HISTORY OF THE COLLEGE OF ST JOHN THE EVANGELIST,

by THOMAS BAKER, B.D., Ejected Fellow. Edited by JOHN E. B. MAYOR, M.A., Fellow of St John's. Two Vols. Demy 8vo. 24s.

"To antiquaries the book will be a source of almost inexhaustible amusement, by historians it will be found a work of considerable service on questions respecting our social progress in past times; and the care and thoroughness with which Mr Mayor has discharged his editorial functions are creditable to his learning and industry."—*Athenæum*.

"The work displays very wide reading, and it will be of great use to members of the college and of the university, and, perhaps, of still greater use to students of English history, ecclesiastical, political, social, literary and academical, who have hitherto had to be content with 'Dyer.'"—*Academy*.

HISTORY OF NEPĀL,

translated by MUNSHĪ SHEW SHUNKER SINGH and PANDIT SHRĪ GUNĀNAND; edited with an Introductory Sketch of the Country and People by Dr D. WRIGHT, late Residency Surgeon at Kāthmāndū, and with facsimiles of native drawings, and portraits of Sir JUNG BAHĀDUR, the KING OF NEPĀL, &c. Super-royal 8vo. Price 21s.

"The Cambridge University Press have done well in publishing this work. Such translations are valuable not only to the historian but also to the ethnologist;......Dr Wright's Introduction is based on personal inquiry and observation, is written intelligently and candidly, and adds much to the value of the volume. The coloured litho-graphic plates are interesting."—*Nature*.

"The history has appeared at a very opportune moment...The volume...is beautifully printed, and supplied with portraits of Sir Jung Bahadoor and others, and with excellent coloured sketches illustrating Nepaulese architecture and religion."—*Examiner*.

SCHOLAE ACADEMICAE:

Some Account of the Studies at the English Universities in the Eighteenth Century. By CHRISTOPHER WORDSWORTH, M.A., Fellow of Peterhouse; Author of "Social Life at the English Universities in the Eighteenth Century." Demy 8vo. cloth. 15s.

"The general object of Mr Wordsworth's book is sufficiently apparent from its title. He has collected a great quantity of minute and curious information about the working of Cambridge institutions in the last century, with an occasional comparison of the corresponding state of things at Oxford....To a great extent it is purely a book of reference, and as such it will be of permanent value for the historical knowledge of English education and learning."—*Saturday Review*.

"Only those who have engaged in like labours will be able fully to appreciate the sustained industry and conscientious accuracy discernible in every page.... Of the whole volume it may be said that it is a genuine service rendered to the study of University history, and that the habits of thought of any writer educated at either seat of learning in the last century will, in many cases, be far better understood after a consideration of the materials here collected."—*Academy*.

THE ARCHITECTURAL HISTORY OF THE UNIVERSITY AND COLLEGES OF CAMBRIDGE,

By the late Professor WILLIS, M.A. With numerous Maps, Plans, and Illustrations. Continued to the present time, and edited by JOHN WILLIS CLARK, M.A., formerly Fellow of Trinity College, Cambridge. [*In the Press.*

London: Cambridge Warehouse, 17 *Paternoster Row.*

MISCELLANEOUS.

LECTURES ON TEACHING,

Delivered in the University of Cambridge in the Lent Term, 1880. By J. G. FITCH, M.A., Her Majesty's Inspector of Schools. Crown 8vo. cloth. New Edition. 6s.

"The lectures will be found most interesting, and deserve to be carefully studied, not only by persons directly concerned with instruction, but by parents who wish to be able to exercise an intelligent judgment in the choice of schools and teachers for their children. For ourselves, we could almost wish to be of school age again, to learn history and geography from some one who could teach them after the pattern set by Mr Fitch to his audience...... But perhaps Mr Fitch's observations on the general conditions of school-work are even more important than what he says on this or that branch of study."—*Saturday Review.*

"It comprises fifteen lectures, dealing with such subjects as organisation, discipline, examining, language, fact knowledge, science, and methods of instruction; and though the lectures make no pretension to systematic or exhaustive treatment, they yet leave very little of the ground uncovered; and they combine in an admirable way the exposition of sound principles with practical suggestions and illustrations which are evidently derived from wide and varied experience, both in teaching and in examining. While Mr Fitch addresses himself specially to secondary school-masters, he does not by any means disregard or ignore the needs of the primary school."—*Scotsman.*

"It would be difficult to find a lecturer better qualified to discourse upon the practical aspects of the teacher's work than Mr Fitch. He has had very wide and varied experience as a teacher, a training college officer, an Inspector of schools, and as Assistant Commissioner to the late Endowed Schools Commission. While it is difficult for anyone to make many original remarks on this subject Mr Fitch is able to speak with authority upon various controverted points, and to give us the results of many years' study, corrected by the observation of the various schemes and methods pursued in schools of all grades and characters."—*The Schoolmaster.*

"All who are interested in the management of schools, and all who have made the profession of a teacher the work of their lives, will do well to study with care these results of a large experience and of wide observation. It is not, we are told, a manual of method; rather, we should say, it is that and much more. As a manual of method it is far superior to anything we have seen. Its suggestions of practical means and methods are very valuable; but it has an element which a mere text-book of rules for imparting knowledge does not contain. Its tone is lofty; its spirit religious; its ideal of the teacher's aim and life pure and good... The volume is one of great practical value. It should be in the hands of every teacher, and of every one preparing for the office of a teacher. There are many besides these who will find much in it to interest and instruct them, more especially parents who have children whom they can afford to keep at school till their eighteenth or nineteenth year."—*The Nonconformist and Independent.*

"As principal of a training college and as a Government inspector of schools, Mr Fitch has got at his fingers' ends the working of primary education, while as assistant commissioner to the late Endowed Schools Commission he has seen something of the machinery of our higher schools... Mr Fitch's book covers so wide a field and touches on so many burning questions that we must be content to recommend it as the best existing *vade mecum* for the teacher.... He is always sensible, always judicious, never wanting in tact.... Mr Fitch is a scholar; he pretends to no knowledge that he does not possess; he brings to his work the ripe experience of a well-stored mind, and he possesses in a remarkable degree the art of exposition."—*Pall Mall Gazette.*

"In its acquaintance with all descriptions of schools, their successes and their shortcomings, Mr Fitch has great advantages both in knowledge and experience; and if his work receives the attention it deserves, it will tend materially to improve and equalize the methods of teaching in our schools, to whatever class they may belong."—*St James's Gazette.*

"In no other work in the English language, so far as we know, are the principles and methods which most conduce to successful teaching laid down and illustrated with such precision and fulness of detail as they are here."—*Leeds Mercury.*

"The book is replete with practical sagacity, and contains on almost all points of interest to the teaching profession suggestive remarks resting evidently on a wide and thoughtful experience of school methods. There are few teachers who will not find aids to reflection in the careful analysis of the qualities required for success in teaching, in the admirable exposition of the value of orderly, methodical arrangement both for instruction and discipline, and in the painstaking discussion of school punishments, contained in the earlier section of the volume.... We recommend it in all confidence to those who are interested in the problems with which the teaching profession has to deal."—*Galignani's Messenger.*

London: Cambridge Warehouse, 17 Paternoster Row.

A CATALOGUE OF ANCIENT MARBLES IN GREAT BRITAIN, by Prof. ADOLPH MICHAELIS. Translated by C. A. M. FENNELL, M.A., late Fellow of Jesus College. Royal 8vo. £2. 2s.

A GRAMMAR OF THE IRISH LANGUAGE. By Prof. WINDISCH. Translated by Dr NORMAN MOORE. Crown 8vo. 7s. 6d.

STATUTA ACADEMIÆ CANTABRIGIENSIS. Demy 8vo. 2s. sewed.

ORDINATIONES ACADEMIÆ CANTABRIGIENSIS. Demy 8vo. cloth. 3s. 6d.

TRUSTS, STATUTES AND DIRECTIONS affecting (1) The Professorships of the University. (2) The Scholarships and Prizes. (3) Other Gifts and Endowments. Demy 8vo. 5s.

COMPENDIUM OF UNIVERSITY REGULATIONS, for the use of persons in Statu Pupillari. Demy 8vo. 6d.

CATALOGUE OF THE HEBREW MANUSCRIPTS preserved in the University Library, Cambridge. By Dr S. M. SCHILLER-SZINESSY. Volume I. containing Section 1. *The Holy Scriptures;* Section 11. *Commentaries on the Bible.* Demy 8vo. 9s.

A CATALOGUE OF THE MANUSCRIPTS preserved in the Library of the University of Cambridge. Demy 8vo. 5 Vols. 10s. each.

INDEX TO THE CATALOGUE. Demy 8vo. 10s.

A CATALOGUE OF ADVERSARIA and printed books containing MS. notes, preserved in the Library of the University of Cambridge. 3s. 6d.

THE ILLUMINATED MANUSCRIPTS IN THE LIBRARY OF THE FITZWILLIAM MUSEUM, Catalogued with Descriptions, and an Introduction, by WILLIAM GEORGE SEARLE, M.A., late Fellow of Queens' College, and Vicar of Hockington, Cambridgeshire. Demy 8vo. 7s. 6d.

A CHRONOLOGICAL LIST OF THE GRACES, Documents, and other Papers in the University Registry which concern the University Library. Demy 8vo. 2s. 6d.

CATALOGUS BIBLIOTHECÆ BURCKHARDTIANÆ. Demy 4to. 5s.

London: Cambridge Warehouse, 17 Paternoster Row.

The Cambridge Bible for Schools.

GENERAL EDITOR: J. J. S. PEROWNE, D.D., DEAN OF PETERBOROUGH.

THE want of an Annotated Edition of the BIBLE, in handy portions, suitable for School use, has long been felt.

In order to provide Text-books for School and Examination purposes, the CAMBRIDGE UNIVERSITY PRESS has arranged to publish the several books of the BIBLE in separate portions at a moderate price, with introductions and explanatory notes.

The Very Reverend J. J. S. PEROWNE, D.D., Dean of Peterborough, has undertaken the general editorial supervision of the work, and will be assisted by a staff of eminent coadjutors. Some of the books have already been undertaken by the following gentlemen:

Rev. A. CARR, M.A., *Assistant Master at Wellington College*.
Rev. T. K. CHEYNE, M.A., *Fellow of Balliol College, Oxford*.
Rev. S. COX, *Nottingham*.
Rev. A. B. DAVIDSON, D.D., *Professor of Hebrew, Edinburgh*.
Rev. F. W. FARRAR, D.D., *Canon of Westminster*.
Rev. A. E. HUMPHREYS, M.A., *Fellow of Trinity College, Cambridge*.
Rev. A. F. KIRKPATRICK, M.A., *Fellow of Trinity College, Regius Professor of Hebrew*.
Rev. J. J. LIAS, M.A., *late Professor at St David's College, Lampeter*.
Rev. J. R. LUMBY, D.D., *Norrisian Professor of Divinity*.
Rev. G. F. MACLEAR, D.D., *Warden of St Augustine's Coll., Canterbury*.
Rev. H. C. G. MOULE, M.A., *Fellow of Trinity College, Principal of Ridley Hall, Cambridge*.
Rev. W. F. MOULTON, D.D., *Head Master of the Leys School, Cambridge*.
Rev. E. H. PEROWNE, D.D., *Master of Corpus Christi College, Cambridge, Examining Chaplain to the Bishop of St Asaph*.
The Ven. T. T. PEROWNE, M.A., *Archdeacon of Norwich*.
Rev. A. PLUMMER, M.A., *Master of University College, Durham*.
The Very Rev. E. H. PLUMPTRE, D.D., *Dean of Wells*.
Rev. W. SANDAY, M.A., *Principal of Bishop Hatfield Hall, Durham*.
Rev. W. SIMCOX, M.A., *Rector of Weyhill, Hants*.
Rev. W. ROBERTSON SMITH, M.A., *Edinburgh*.
Rev. A. W. STREANE, M.A., *Fellow of Corpus Christi Coll., Cambridge*.
The Ven. H. W. WATKINS, M.A., *Archdeacon of Northumberland*.
Rev. G. H. WHITAKER, M.A., *Fellow of St John's College, Cambridge*.
Rev. C. WORDSWORTH, M.A., *Rector of Glaston, Rutland*.

London: Cambridge Warehouse, 17 *Paternoster Row.*

PUBLICATIONS OF

THE CAMBRIDGE BIBLE FOR SCHOOLS.—*Continued.*
Now Ready. Cloth, Extra Fcap. 8vo.
THE BOOK OF JOSHUA. Edited by Rev. G. F.
MACLEAR, D.D. With 2 Maps. 2s. 6d.
THE BOOK OF JUDGES. By the Rev. J. J. LIAS, M.A.
With Map. 3s. 6d.
THE FIRST BOOK OF SAMUEL. By the Rev.
Professor KIRKPATRICK, M.A. With Map. 3s. 6d.
THE SECOND BOOK OF SAMUEL. By the Rev.
Professor KIRKPATRICK, M.A. With 2 Maps. 3s. 6d.
THE BOOK OF ECCLESIASTES. By the Very Rev.
E. H. PLUMPTRE, D.D., Dean of Wells. 5s.
THE BOOK OF JEREMIAH. By the Rev. A. W
STREANE, M.A. 4s. 6d.
THE BOOK OF JONAH. By Archdn. PEROWNE. 1s. 6d.
THE BOOK OF MICAH. By the Rev. T. K. CHEYNE,
M.A. 1s. 6d.
THE GOSPEL ACCORDING TO ST MATTHEW
Edited by the Rev. A. CARR, M.A. With 2 Maps. 2s. 6d.
THE GOSPEL ACCORDING TO ST MARK. Edited
by the Rev. G. F. MACLEAR, D.D. With 2 Maps. 2s. 6d.
THE GOSPEL ACCORDING TO ST LUKE. By
the Rev. F. W. FARRAR, D.D. With 4 Maps. 4s. 6d.
THE GOSPEL ACCORDING TO ST JOHN. By
the Rev. A. PLUMMER, M.A. With Four Maps. 4s. 6d.
THE ACTS OF THE APOSTLES. By the Rev.
Professor LUMBY, D.D. Part I. Chaps. I—XIV. With 2 Maps.
2s. 6d.
PART II. Chaps. XV. to end. *Nearly ready.*
THE EPISTLE TO THE ROMANS. By the Rev.
H. C. G. MOULE, M.A. 3s. 6d.
THE FIRST EPISTLE TO THE CORINTHIANS.
By the Rev. J. J. LIAS, M.A. With a Map and Plan. 2s.
THE SECOND EPISTLE TO THE CORINTHIANS.
By the Rev. J. J. LIAS, M.A. 2s.
THE GENERAL EPISTLE OF ST JAMES. By the
Very Rev. E. H. PLUMPTRE, D.D., Dean of Wells. 1s. 6d.
THE EPISTLES OF ST PETER AND ST JUDE.
By the same Editor. 2s. 6d.

London: Cambridge Warehouse, 17 *Paternoster Row.*

THE CAMBRIDGE BIBLE FOR SCHOOLS.—*Continued.*

Preparing.

THE BOOKS OF HAGGAI AND ZECHARIAH. By Archdeacon PEROWNE.

THE EPISTLE TO THE HEBREWS. By the Rev. F. W. FARRAR, D.D.

THE CAMBRIDGE GREEK TESTAMENT,

FOR SCHOOLS AND COLLEGES,

with a Revised Text, based on the most recent critical authorities, and English Notes, prepared under the direction of the General Editor,

THE VERY REVEREND J. J. S. PEROWNE, D.D.,
DEAN OF PETERBOROUGH.

Now Ready.

THE GOSPEL ACCORDING TO ST MATTHEW. By the Rev. A. CARR, M.A. With 4 Maps. 4s. 6d.

"With the 'Notes,' in the volume before us, we are much pleased; so far as we have searched, they are scholarly and sound. The quotations from the Classics are apt; and the references to modern Greek form a pleasing feature."—*The Churchman.*

"Mr Carr, whose 'Notes on St Luke's Gospel' must have thoroughly approved themselves to all who have used them, has followed the same line in this volume of St Matthew. In both works a chief object has been 'to connect more closely the study of the Classics with the reading of the New Testament.'.... Copious illustrations, gathered from a great variety of sources, make his notes a very valuable aid to the student. They are indeed remarkably interesting, while all explanations on meanings, applications, and the like are distinguished by their lucidity and good sense."—*Pall Mall Gazette.*

THE GOSPEL ACCORDING TO ST LUKE. By the Rev. F. W. FARRAR, D.D. [*Preparing.*

THE GOSPEL ACCORDING TO ST JOHN. By the Rev. A. PLUMMER, M.A. [*Nearly ready.*

The books will be published separately, as in the "Cambridge Bible for Schools."

London: *Cambridge Warehouse,* 17 *Paternoster Row.*

PUBLICATIONS OF

THE PITT PRESS SERIES.

I. GREEK.

THE ANABASIS OF XENOPHON, BOOK IV. With a Map and English Notes by ALFRED PRETOR, M.A., Fellow of St Catharine's College, Cambridge; Editor of *Persius* and *Cicero ad Atticum* Book I. *Price* 2s.

"In Mr Pretor's edition of the Anabasis the text of Kühner has been followed in the main, while the exhaustive and admirable notes of the great German editor have been largely utilised. These notes deal with the minutest as well as the most important difficulties in construction, and all questions of history, antiquity, and geography are briefly but very effectually elucidated."—*The Examiner.*

"We welcome this addition to the other books of the *Anabasis* so ably edited by Mr Pretor. Although originally intended for the use of candidates at the university local examinations, yet this edition will be found adapted not only to meet the wants of the junior student, but even advanced scholars will find much in this work that will repay its perusal."—*The Schoolmaster.*

"Mr Pretor's 'Anabasis of Xenophon, Book IV.' displays a union of accurate Cambridge scholarship, with experience of what is required by learners gained in examining middle-class schools. The text is large and clearly printed, and the notes explain all difficulties.'... Mr Pretor's notes seem to be all that could be wished as regards grammar, geography, and other matters."—*The Academy.*

BOOKS I. III. & V. By the same Editor. 2s. each.

BOOKS II. VI. and VII. By the same Editor. 2s. 6d. each.

"Another Greek text, designed it would seem for students preparing for the local examinations, is 'Xenophon's Anabasis,' Book II., with English Notes, by Alfred Pretor, M.A. The editor has exercised his usual discrimination in utilising the text and notes of Kuhner, with the occasional assistance of the best hints of Schneider, Vollbrecht and Macmichael on critical matters, and of Mr R. W. Taylor on points of history and geography.... When Mr Pretor commits himself to Commentator's work, he is eminently helpful.... Had we to introduce a young Greek scholar to Xenophon, we should esteem ourselves fortunate in having Pretor's text-book as our chart and guide."—*Contemporary Review.*

THE ANABASIS OF XENOPHON, by A. PRETOR, M.A., Text and Notes, complete in two Volumes. Price 7s. 6d.

AGESILAUS OF XENOPHON. The Text revised with Critical and Explanatory Notes, Introduction, Analysis, and Indices. By H. HAILSTONE, M.A., late Scholar of Peterhouse, Cambridge, Editor of Xenophon's Hellenics, etc. 2s. 6d.

ARISTOPHANES—RANAE. With English Notes and Introduction by W. C. GREEN, M.A., Assistant Master at Rugby School. 3s. 6d.

ARISTOPHANES—AVES. By the same Editor. *New Edition.* 3s. 6d.

"The notes to both plays are excellent. Much has been done in these two volumes to render the study of Aristophanes a real treat to a boy instead of a drudgery, by helping him to understand the fun and to express it in his mother tongue."—*The Examiner.*

ARISTOPHANES—PLUTUS. By the same Editor. 3s. 6d.

EURIPIDES. HERCULES FURENS. With Introductions, Notes and Analysis. By J. T. HUTCHINSON, M.A., Christ's College, and A. GRAY, M.A., Fellow of Jesus College. 2s.

"Messrs Hutchinson and Gray have produced a careful and useful edition."—*Saturday Review.*

THE HERACLEIDÆ OF EURIPIDES, with Introduction and Critical Notes by E. A. BECK, M.A., Fellow of Trinity Hall. 3s. 6d.

London: Cambridge Warehouse, 17 *Paternoster Row.*

LUCIANI SOMNIUM CHARON PISCATOR ET DE LUCTU, with English Notes by W. E. HEITLAND, M.A., Fellow of St John's College, Cambridge. New Edition, with Appendix. 3s. 6d.

II. LATIN.

M. T. CICERONIS DE AMICITIA. Edited by J. S. REID, M.L., Fellow and Assistant Tutor of Gonville and Caius College, Cambridge. *Price 3s.*

"Mr Reid has decidedly attained his aim, namely, 'a thorough examination of the Latinity of the dialogue.'..... The revision of the text is most valuable, and comprehends sundry acute corrections.... This volume, like Mr Reid's other editions, is a solid gain to the scholarship of the country."—*Athenæum.*

"A more distinct gain to scholarship is Mr Reid's able and thorough edition of the *De Amicitia* of Cicero, a work of which, whether we regard the exhaustive introduction or the instructive and most suggestive commentary, it would be difficult to speak too highly.... When we come to the commentary, we are only amazed by its fulness in proportion to its bulk. Nothing is overlooked which can tend to enlarge the learner's general knowledge of Ciceronian Latin or to elucidate the text."—*Saturday Review.*

M. T. CICERONIS CATO MAJOR DE SENECTUTE. Edited by J. S. REID, M.L. *Price 3s. 6d.*

"The notes are excellent and scholarlike, adapted for the upper forms of public schools, and likely to be useful even to more advanced students."—*Guardian.*

M. T. CICERONIS ORATIO PRO ARCHIA POETA. Edited by J. S. REID, M.L. *Price 1s. 6d.*

"It is an admirable specimen of careful editing. An Introduction tells us everything we could wish to know about Archias, about Cicero's connexion with him, about the merits of the trial, and the genuineness of the speech. The text is well and carefully printed. The notes are clear and scholar-like.... No boy can master this little volume without feeling that he has advanced a long step in scholarship."—*The Academy.*

M. T. CICERONIS PRO L. CORNELIO BALBO ORATIO. Edited by J. S. REID, M.L. Fellow of Caius College, Camb. *Price 1s. 6d.*

"We are bound to recognize the pains devoted in the annotation of these two orations to the minute and thorough study of their Latinity, both in the ordinary notes and in the textual appendices."—*Saturday Review.*

M. T. CICERONIS PRO P. CORNELIO SULLA ORATIO. Edited by J. S. REID, M.L. [*In the Press.*

M. T. CICERONIS PRO CN. PLANCIO ORATIO. Edited by H. A. HOLDEN, LL.D., Head Master of Ipswich School. *Price 4s. 6d.*

"As a book for students this edition can have few rivals. It is enriched by an excellent introduction and a chronological table of the principal events of the life of Cicero; while in its appendix, and in the notes on the text which are added, there is much of the greatest value. The volume is neatly got up, and is in every way commendable."—*The Scotsman.*

"Dr Holden's own edition is all that could be expected from his elegant and practised scholarship.... Dr Holden has evidently made up his mind as to the character of the commentary most likely to be generally useful; and he has carried out his views with admirable thoroughness."—*Academy.*

"Dr Holden has given us here an excellent edition. The commentary is even unusually full and complete; and after going through it carefully, we find little or nothing to criticise. There is an excellent introduction, lucidly explaining the circumstances under which the speech was delivered, a table of events in the life of Cicero and a useful index." *Spectator,* Oct. 29, 1881.

M. T. CICERONIS IN Q. CAECILIUM DIVINATIO ET IN C. VERREM ACTIO PRIMA. With Introduction and Notes by W. E. HEITLAND, M.A., and HERBERT COWIE, M.A., Fellows of St John's College, Cambridge. *Price 3s.*

London: Cambridge Warehouse, 17 Paternoster Row.

PUBLICATIONS OF

M. T. CICERONIS ORATIO PRO L. MURENA, with English Introduction and Notes. By W. E. HEITLAND, M.A., Fellow and Classical Lecturer of St John's College, Cambridge. **Second Edition**, carefully revised. *Price* 3s.

"Those students are to be deemed fortunate who have to read Cicero's lively and brilliant oration for L. Murena with Mr Heitland's handy edition, which may be pronounced 'four-square' in point of equipment, and which has, not without good reason, attained the honours of a second edition."—*Saturday Review.*

M. T. CICERONIS IN GAIUM VERREM ACTIO PRIMA. With Introduction and Notes. By H. COWIE, M.A., Fellow of St John's College, Cambridge. *Price* 1s. 6d.

M. T. CICERONIS ORATIO PRO T. A. MILONE, with a Translation of Asconius' Introduction, Marginal Analysis and English Notes. Edited by the Rev. JOHN SMYTH PURTON, B.D., late President and Tutor of St Catharine's College. *Price* 2s. 6d.

"The editorial work is excellently done."—*The Academy.*

P. OVIDII NASONIS FASTORUM LIBER VI. With a Plan of Rome and Notes by A. SIDGWICK, M.A. Tutor of Corpus Christi College, Oxford. *Price* 1s. 6d.

"Mr Sidgwick's editing of the Sixth Book of Ovid's *Fasti* furnishes a careful and serviceable volume for average students. It eschews 'construes' which supersede the use of the dictionary, but gives full explanation of grammatical usages and historical and mythical allusions, besides illustrating peculiarities of style, true and false derivations, and the more remarkable variations of the text."—*Saturday Review.*

"It is eminently good and useful. . . . The Introduction is singularly clear on the astronomy of Ovid, which is properly shown to be ignorant and confused; there is an excellent little map of Rome, giving just the places mentioned in the text and no more; the notes are evidently written by a practical schoolmaster."—*The Academy.*

GAI IULI CAESARIS DE BELLO GALLICO COMMENT. I. II. With English Notes and Map by A. G. PESKETT, M.A., Fellow of Magdalene College, Cambridge, Editor of Caesar De Bello Gallico, VII. *Price* 2s. 6d.

GAI IULI CAESARIS DE BELLO GALLICO COMMENT. III. With Map and Notes by A. G. PESKETT, M.A., Fellow of Magdalene College, Cambridge. *Price* 1s. 6d.

"In an unusually succinct introduction he gives all the preliminary and collateral information that is likely to be useful to a young student; and, wherever we have examined his notes, we have found them eminently practical and satisfying. . . . The book may well be recommended for careful study in school or college."—*Saturday Review.*

"The notes are scholarly, short, and a real help to the most elementary beginners in Latin prose."—*The Examiner.*

BOOKS IV. AND V. AND BOOK VII. by the same Editor. *Price* 2s. each.

BOOK VI. by the same Editor. *Price* 1s. 6d.

London: Cambridge Warehouse, 17 *Paternoster Row.*

P. VERGILI MARONIS AENEIDOS LIBER II. Edited with Notes by A. SIDGWICK, M.A. Tutor of Corpus Christi College, Oxford. 1s. 6d.

BOOKS IV., V., VI., VII., VIII., X., XI., XII. by the same Editor. 1s. 6d. each.

"Mr Arthur Sidgwick's 'Vergil, Aeneid, Book XII.' is worthy of his reputation, and is distinguished by the same acuteness and accuracy of knowledge, appreciation of a boy's difficulties and ingenuity and resource in meeting them, which we have on other occasions had reason to praise in these pages."—*The Academy.*

"As masterly in its clearly divided preface and appendices as in the sound and independent character of its annotations.... There is a great deal more in the notes than mere compilation and suggestion.... No difficulty is left unnoticed or unhandled."—*Saturday Review.*

"This edition is admirably adapted for the use of junior students, who will find in it the result of much reading in a condensed form, and clearly expressed."—*Cambridge Independent Press.*

BOOKS VII. VIII. in one volume. *Price 3s.*

BOOKS X., XI., XII. in one volume. *Price 3s. 6d.*

QUINTUS CURTIUS. A Portion of the History. (ALEXANDER IN INDIA.) By W. E. HEITLAND, M.A., Fellow and Lecturer of St John's College, Cambridge, and T. E. RAVEN, B.A., Assistant Master in Sherborne School. *Price 3s. 6d.*

"Equally commendable as a genuine addition to the existing stock of school-books is *Alexander in India*, a compilation from the eighth and ninth books of Q. Curtius, edited for the Pitt Press by Messrs Heitland and Raven.... The work of Curtius has merits of its own, which, in former generations, made it a favourite with English scholars, and which still make it a popular text-book in Continental schools..... The reputation of Mr Heitland is a sufficient guarantee for the scholarship of the notes, which are ample without being excessive, and the book is well furnished with all that is needful in the nature of maps, indexes, and appendices."—*Academy.*

M. ANNAEI LUCANI PHARSALIAE LIBER PRIMUS, edited with English Introduction and Notes by W. E. HEITLAND, M.A. and C. E. HASKINS, M.A., Fellows and Lecturers of St John's College, Cambridge. *Price 1s. 6d.*

"A careful and scholarlike production."—*Times.*

"In nice parallels of Lucan from Latin poets and from Shakspeare, Mr Haskins and Mr Heitland deserve praise."—*Saturday Review.*

BEDA'S ECCLESIASTICAL HISTORY, BOOKS III., IV., the Text from the very ancient MS. in the Cambridge University Library, collated with six other MSS. Edited, with a life from the German of EBERT, and with Notes, &c. by J. E. B. MAYOR, M.A., Professor of Latin, and J. R. LUMBY, D.D., Norrisian Professor of Divinity. Revised edition. *Price 7s. 6d.*

"To young students of English History the illustrative notes will be of great service, while the study of the texts will be a good introduction to Mediæval Latin."—*The Nonconformist.*

"In Bede's works Englishmen can go back to *origines* of their history, unequalled for form and matter by any modern European nation. Prof. Mayor has done good service in rendering a part of Bede's greatest work accessible to those who can read Latin with ease. He has adorned this edition of the third and fourth books of the "Ecclesiastical History" with that amazing erudition for which he is unrivalled among Englishmen and rarely equalled by Germans. And however interesting and valuable the text may be, we can certainly apply to his notes the expression, *La sauce vaut mieux que le poisson*. They are literally crammed with interesting information about early English life. For though ecclesiastical in name, Bede's history treats of all parts of the national life, since the Church had points of contact with all."—*Examiner.*

BOOKS I. and II. *In the Press.*

London: Cambridge Warehouse, 17 Paternoster Row.

III. FRENCH.

LAZARE HOCHE—PAR ÉMILE DE BONNECHOSE.
With Three Maps, Introduction and Commentary, by C. COLBECK, M.A., late Fellow of Trinity College, Cambridge; Assistant Master at Harrow School. *Price* 2s.

HISTOIRE DU SIÈCLE DE LOUIS XIV PAR
VOLTAIRE. Part I. Chaps. I.—XIII. Edited with Notes Philological and Historical, Biographical and Geographical Indices, etc. by GUSTAVE MASSON, B.A. Univ. Gallic., Officier d'Académie, Assistant Master of Harrow School, and G. W. PROTHERO, M.A., Fellow and Tutor of King's College, Cambridge. 2s. 6d.

"Messrs Masson and Prothero have, to judge from the first part of their work, performed with much discretion and care the task of editing Voltaire's *Siècle de Louis XIV* for the 'Pitt Press Series.' Besides the usual kind of notes, the editors have in this case, influenced by Voltaire's 'summary way of treating much of the history,' given a good deal of historical information, in which they have, we think, done well. At the beginning of the book will be found excellent and succinct accounts of the constitution of the French army and Parliament at the period treated of."—*Saturday Review.*

HISTOIRE DU SIÈCLE DE LOUIS XIV PAR
VOLTAIRE. Part II. Chaps. XIV.—XXIV. With Three Maps of the Period, Notes Philological and Historical, Biographical and Geographical Indices, by G. MASSON, B.A. Univ. Gallic., Assistant Master of Harrow School, and G. W. PROTHERO, M.A., Fellow and Tutor of King's College, Cambridge. *Price* 2s. 6d.

Part III. Chap. XXV. to the end. By the same Editors. Price 2s. 6d.

LE VERRE D'EAU. A Comedy, by SCRIBE. With a Biographical Memoir, and Grammatical, Literary and Historical Notes. By C. COLBECK, M.A., late Fellow of Trinity College, Cambridge; Assistant Master at Harrow School. *Price* 2s.

"It may be national prejudice, but we consider this edition far superior to any of the series which hitherto have been edited exclusively by foreigners. Mr Colbeck seems better to understand the wants and difficulties of an English boy. The etymological notes especially are admirable.... The historical notes and introduction are a piece of thorough honest work."—*Journal of Education.*

M. DARU, par M. C. A. SAINTE-BEUVE, (Causeries du Lundi, Vol. IX.). With Biographical Sketch of the Author, and Notes Philological and Historical. By GUSTAVE MASSON. 2s.

LA SUITE DU MENTEUR. A Comedy in Five Acts, by P. CORNEILLE. Edited with Fontenelle's Memoir of the Author, Voltaire's Critical Remarks, and Notes Philological and Historical. By GUSTAVE MASSON. *Price* 2s.

LA JEUNE SIBÉRIENNE. LE LÉPREUX DE LA
CITÉ D'AOSTE. Tales by COUNT XAVIER DE MAISTRE. With Biographical Notice, Critical Appreciations, and Notes. By GUSTAVE MASSON. *Price* 2s.

London: Cambridge Warehouse, 17 Paternoster Row.

LE DIRECTOIRE. (Considérations sur la Révolution Française. Troisième et quatrième parties.) Par MADAME LA BARONNE DE STAËL-HOLSTEIN. With a Critical Notice of the Author, a Chronological Table, and Notes Historical and Philological, by G. MASSON, B.A., and G. W. PROTHERO, M.A. Revised and enlarged Edition. *Price* 2s.

"Prussia under Frederick the Great, and France under the Directory, bring us face to face respectively with periods of history which it is right should be known thoroughly, and which are well treated in the Pitt Press volumes. The latter in particular, an extract from the world-known work of Madame de Staël on the French Revolution, is beyond all praise for the excellence both of its style and of its matter."—*Times.*

DIX ANNÉES D'ÉXIL. LIVRE II. CHAPITRES 1—8. Par MADAME LA BARONNE DE STAËL-HOLSTEIN. With a Biographical Sketch of the Author, a Selection of Poetical Fragments by Madame de Staël's Contemporaries, and Notes Historical and Philological. By GUSTAVE MASSON. *Price* 2s.

"The choice made by M. Masson of the second book of the *Memoirs* of Madame de Staël appears specially felicitous. . . . This is likely to be one of the most favoured of M. Masson's editions, and deservedly so."—*Academy.*

FRÉDÉGONDE ET BRUNEHAUT. A Tragedy in Five Acts, by N. LEMERCIER. Edited with Notes, Genealogical and Chronological Tables, a Critical Introduction and a Biographical Notice. By GUSTAVE MASSON. *Price* 2s.

LE VIEUX CÉLIBATAIRE. A Comedy, by COLLIN D'HARLEVILLE. With a Biographical Memoir, and Grammatical, Literary and Historical Notes. By the same Editor. *Price* 2s.

"M. Masson is doing good work in introducing learners to some of the less-known French play-writers. The arguments are admirably clear, and the notes are not too abundant."—*Academy.*

LA MÉTROMANIE, A Comedy, by PIRON, with a Biographical Memoir, and Grammatical, Literary and Historical Notes. By the same Editor. *Price* 2s.

LASCARIS, OU LES GRECS DU XVE. SIÈCLE, Nouvelle Historique, par A. F. VILLEMAIN, with a Biographical Sketch of the Author, a Selection of Poems on Greece, and Notes Historical and Philological. By the same Editor. *Price* 2s.

IV. GERMAN.

ERNST, HERZOG VON SCHWABEN. UHLAND. With Introduction and Notes. By H. J. WOLSTENHOLME, B.A. (Lond.), Lecturer in German at Newnham College, Cambridge. *Price* 3s. 6d.

ZOPF UND SCHWERT. Lustspiel in fünf Aufzügen von KARL GUTZKOW. With a Biographical and Historical Introduction, English Notes, and an Index. By the same Editor. *Price* 3s. 6d.

"We are glad to be able to notice a careful edition of K. Gutzkow's amusing comedy 'Zopf und Schwert' by Mr H. J. Wolstenholme. . . . These notes are abundant and contain references to standard grammatical works."—*Academy.*

London: Cambridge Warehouse, 17 *Paternoster Row.*

PUBLICATIONS OF

Goethe's Knabenjahre. (1749—1759.) GOETHE'S BOY-HOOD: being the First Three Books of his Autobiography. Arranged and Annotated by WILHELM WAGNER, Ph. D., late Professor at the Johanneum, Hamburg. *Price 2s.*

HAUFF. DAS WIRTHSHAUS IM SPESSART. Edited by A. SCHLOTTMANN, Ph.D., Assistant Master at Uppingham School. *Price 3s. 6d.*

DER OBERHOF. A Tale of Westphalian Life, by KARL IMMERMANN. With a Life of Immermann and English Notes, by WILHELM WAGNER, Ph.D., late Professor at the Johanneum, Hamburg. *Price 3s.*

A BOOK OF GERMAN DACTYLIC POETRY. Arranged and Annotated by the same Editor. *Price 3s.*

Der erste Kreuzzug (THE FIRST CRUSADE), by FRIEDRICH VON RAUMER. Condensed from the Author's 'History of the Hohenstaufen', with a life of RAUMER, two Plans and English Notes. By the same Editor. *Price 2s.*

"Certainly no more interesting book could be made the subject of examination. The story of the First Crusade has an undying interest. The notes are, on the whole, good."—*Educational Times.*

A BOOK OF BALLADS ON GERMAN HISTORY. Arranged and Annotated by the same Editor. *Price 2s.*

"It carries the reader rapidly through some of the most important incidents connected with the German race and name, from the invasion of Italy by the Visigoths under their King Alaric, down to the Franco-German War and the installation of the present Emperor. The notes supply very well the connecting links between the successive periods, and exhibit in its various phases of growth and progress, or the reverse, the vast unwieldy mass which constitutes modern Germany."—*Times.*

DER STAAT FRIEDRICHS DES GROSSEN. By G. FREYTAG. With Notes. By the same Editor. *Price 2s.*

"Prussia under Frederick the Great, and France under the Directory, bring us face to face respectively with periods of history which it is right should be known thoroughly, and which are well treated in the Pitt Press volumes."—*Times.*

GOETHE'S HERMANN AND DOROTHEA. With an Introduction and Notes. By the same Editor. *Price 3s.*

"The notes are among the best that we know, with the reservation that they are often too abundant."—*Academy.*

Das Jahr 1813 (THE YEAR 1813), by F. KOHLRAUSCH. With English Notes. By the same Editor. *Price 2s.*

V. ENGLISH.

LOCKE ON EDUCATION. With Introduction and Notes by the Rev. R. H. QUICK, M.A. *Price 3s. 6d.*

"The work before us leaves nothing to be desired. It is of convenient form and reasonable price, accurately printed, and accompanied by notes which are admirable. There is no teacher too young to find this book interesting: there is no teacher too old to find it profitable."—*The School Bulletin, New York.*

THE TWO NOBLE KINSMEN, edited with Introduction and Notes by the Rev. Professor SKEAT, M.A., formerly Fellow of Christ's College, Cambridge. *Price 3s. 6d.*

"This edition of a play that is well worth study, for more reasons than one, by so careful a scholar as Mr Skeat, deserves a hearty welcome."—*Athenæum.*
"Mr Skeat is a conscientious editor, and has left no difficulty unexplained."—*Times.*

London: Cambridge Warehouse, 17 Paternoster Row.

THE CAMBRIDGE UNIVERSITY PRESS. 31

BACON'S HISTORY OF THE REIGN OF KING HENRY VII. With Notes by the Rev. J. RAWSON LUMBY, D.D., Norrisian Professor of Divinity; late Fellow of St Catharine's College. *Price 3s.*

SIR THOMAS MORE'S UTOPIA. With Notes by the Rev. J. RAWSON LUMBY, D.D., Norrisian Professor of Divinity; late Fellow of St Catharine's College, Cambridge. *Price 3s. 6d.*

"To enthusiasts in history matters, who are not content with mere facts, but like to pursue their investigations behind the scenes, as it were, Professor Rawson Lumby has in the work now before us produced a most acceptable contribution to the now constantly increasing store of illustrative reading."—*The Cambridge Review.*

"To Dr Lumby we must give praise unqualified and unstinted. He has done his work admirably..... Every student of history, every politician, every social reformer, every one interested in literary curiosities, every lover of English should buy and carefully read Dr Lumby's edition of the 'Utopia.' We are afraid to say more lest we should be thought extravagant, and our recommendation accordingly lose part of its force."—*The Teacher.*

"It was originally written in Latin and does not find a place on ordinary bookshelves. A very great boon has therefore been conferred on the general English reader by the managers of the *Pitt Press Series*, in the issue of a convenient little volume of *More's Utopia* not in the original Latin, but in the quaint *English Translation thereof made by Raphe Robynson*, which adds a linguistic interest to the intrinsic merit of the work. . . . All this has been edited in a most complete and scholarly fashion by Dr J. R. Lumby, the Norrisian Professor of Divinity, whose name alone is a sufficient warrant for its accuracy. It is a real addition to the modern stock of classical English literature."—*Guardian.*

SIR THOMAS MORE'S LIFE OF RICHARD III. With Notes, &c., by Professor LUMBY. [*Nearly ready.*

A SKETCH OF ANCIENT PHILOSOPHY FROM THALES TO CICERO, by JOSEPH B. MAYOR, M.A., Professor of Moral Philosophy at King's College, London. *Price 3s. 6d.*

"It may safely be affirmed that Mr Mayor has successfully accomplished all that he here sets out. His arrangement is admirably methodical, his style is simple but nervous, his knowledge of his subject full and accurate, and his analytical expositions lucid and vivid....It is therefore a manual which will prove of great utility to University undergraduates, for whom it was particularly prepared, and also for all who study Plato, Aristotle, or other philosophers, in the original. Educated readers, generally, will find 'it an admirable introduction, or epitome, of ancient speculative thought, and 'a key to our present ways of thinking and judging in regard to matters of the highest importance.'"—*The British Mail.*

"In writing this scholarly and attractive sketch, Professor Mayor has had chiefly in view 'undergraduates at the University or others who are commencing the study of the philosophical works of Cicero or Plato or Aristotle in the original language,' but also hopes that it 'may be found interesting and useful by educated readers generally, not merely as an introduction to the formal history of philosophy, but as supplying a key to our present ways of thinking and judging in regard to matters of the highest importance.'"—*Mind.*

"Professor Mayor contributes to the Pitt Press Series *A Sketch of Ancient Philosophy* in which he has endeavoured to give a general view of the philosophical systems illustrated by the genius of the masters of metaphysical and ethical science from Thales to Cicero. In the course of his sketch he takes occasion to give concise analyses of Plato's Republic, and of the Ethics and Politics of Aristotle; and these abstracts will be to some readers not the least useful portions of the book. It may be objected against his design in general that ancient philosophy is too vast and too deep a subject to be dismissed in a 'sketch'—that it should be left to those who will make it a serious study. But that objection takes no account of the large class of persons who desire to know, in relation to present discussions, what famous men in the ancient and in the whole world thought and wrote on these topics. They have not the scholarship which would be necessary for original examination of authorities; but they have an intelligent interest in the relations between ancient and modern philosophy, and need just such information as Professor Mayor's sketch will give them."—*The Guardian.*

[*Other Volumes are in preparation.*]

London: Cambridge Warehouse, 17 Paternoster Row.

University of Cambridge.

LOCAL EXAMINATIONS.

Examination Papers, for various years, with the *Regulations for the Examination*. Demy 8vo. 2s. each, or by Post, 2s. 2d.

Class Lists, for various years, Boys 1s., Girls 6d.

Annual Reports of the Syndicate, with Supplementary Tables showing the success and failure of the Candidates. 2s. each, by Post 2s. 2d.

HIGHER LOCAL EXAMINATIONS.

Examination Papers for 1881, *to which are added the Regulations for 1882*. Demy 8vo. 2s. each, by Post 2s. 2d.

Reports of the Syndicate. Demy 8vo. 1s., by Post 1s. 1d.

LOCAL LECTURES SYNDICATE.

Calendar for the years 1875—9. Fcap. 8vo. *cloth.* 2s.
"   "   1875—80.   "   "   2s.
"   "   1880—81.   "   "   1s.

TEACHERS' TRAINING SYNDICATE.

Examination Papers for 1880 and 1881, *to which are added the Regulations for the Examination*. Demy 8vo. 6d., by Post 7d.

CAMBRIDGE UNIVERSITY REPORTER.

Published by Authority.

Containing all the Official Notices of the University, Reports of Discussions in the Schools, and Proceedings of the Cambridge Philosophical, Antiquarian, and Philological Societies. 3d. weekly.

CAMBRIDGE UNIVERSITY EXAMINATION PAPERS.

These Papers are published in occasional numbers every Term, and in volumes for the Academical year.

VOL. IX. Parts 105 to 119. PAPERS for the Year 1879—80, 12s. *cloth.*
VOL. X.   "   120 to 138.   "   "   1880—81, 15s. *cloth.*

Oxford and Cambridge Schools Examinations.

Papers set in the Examination for Certificates, July, 1879. *Price* 1s. 6d.

List of Candidates who obtained Certificates at the Examinations held in 1879 and 1880; and Supplementary Tables. *Price* 6d.

Regulations of the Board for 1882. *Price* 6d.

Report of the Board for the year ending Oct. 31, 1881. *Price* 1s.

London: C. J. CLAY, M.A. AND SON.
CAMBRIDGE UNIVERSITY PRESS WAREHOUSE,
17 PATERNOSTER ROW.

www.ingramcontent.com/pod-product-compliance
Lightning Source LLC
Chambersburg PA
CBHW032147160426
43197CB00008B/803